GERMAN POLITICAL TRAGEDY
THE MACHIAVELLIAN PLOT AND THE NECESSARY CRIME

LEGENDA

LEGENDA is the Modern Humanities Research Association's book imprint for new research in the Humanities. Founded in 1995 by Malcolm Bowie and others within the University of Oxford, Legenda has always been a collaborative publishing enterprise, directly governed by scholars. The Modern Humanities Research Association (MHRA) joined this collaboration in 1998, became half-owner in 2004, in partnership with Maney Publishing and then Routledge, and has since 2016 been sole owner. Titles range from medieval texts to contemporary cinema and form a widely comparative view of the modern humanities, including works on Arabic, Catalan, English, French, German, Greek, Italian, Portuguese, Russian, Spanish, and Yiddish literature. Editorial boards and committees of more than 60 leading academic specialists work in collaboration with bodies such as the Society for French Studies, the British Comparative Literature Association and the Association of Hispanists of Great Britain & Ireland.

The MHRA encourages and promotes advanced study and research in the field of the modern humanities, especially modern European languages and literature, including English, and also cinema. It aims to break down the barriers between scholars working in different disciplines and to maintain the unity of humanistic scholarship. The Association fulfils this purpose through the publication of journals, bibliographies, monographs, critical editions, and the MHRA Style Guide, and by making grants in support of research. Membership is open to all who work in the Humanities, whether independent or in a University post, and the participation of younger colleagues entering the field is especially welcomed.

ALSO PUBLISHED BY THE ASSOCIATION

Critical Texts
Tudor and Stuart Translations • *New Translations* • *European Translations*
MHRA Library of Medieval Welsh Literature

MHRA Bibliographies
Publications of the Modern Humanities Research Association

The Annual Bibliography of English Language & Literature
Austrian Studies
Modern Language Review
Portuguese Studies
The Slavonic and East European Review
Working Papers in the Humanities
The Yearbook of English Studies

www.mhra.org.uk
www.legendabooks.com

GERMANIC LITERATURES

Germanic Literatures includes monographs and essay collections on literature originally written not only in German, but also in Dutch and the Scandinavian languages. Within the German-speaking area, it seeks also to publish studies of other national literatures such as those of Austria and Switzerland. The chronological scope of the series extends from the early Middle Ages down to the present day.

Managing Editor
Dr Graham Nelson, 41 Wellington Square, Oxford OX1 2JF, UK
www.legendabooks.com

German Political Tragedy

The Machiavellian Plot and the Necessary Crime

RITCHIE ROBERTSON

LEGENDA
Germanic Literatures 32
Modern Humanities Research Association
2024

Published by Legenda
an imprint of the Modern Humanities Research Association
Salisbury House, Station Road, Cambridge CB1 2LA

ISBN 978-1-83954-325-8

First published 2024

Copy-Editor: Dr Nigel Hope

CONTENTS

ACKNOWLEDGEMENTS

I thank Kevin Hilliard, Graham Nelson, and Joachim Whaley for reading my manuscript in full and making valuable suggestions.

All translations are mine unless otherwise stated.

Some sections of this book are adapted from the following publications:

'Goethe and Machiavelli', in *The Present Word. Culture, Society and the Site of Literature: Essays in Honour of Nicholas Boyle*, ed. by John Walker (Cambridge: Legenda, 2013), pp. 126–37

'The Rediscovery of Machiavelli in Napoleon's Germany: Heinrich von Kleist and his Contemporaries', *Ethics and Politics*, 17.3 (2015), 58–77

'Berlin, Machiavelli and the Enlightenment', in *Isaiah Berlin and the Enlightenment*, ed. by Laurence Brockliss and Ritchie Robertson (Oxford: Oxford University Press, 2016), pp. 137–50

'Machiavelli in Germany, 1678–1810', in *Machiavelli's 'Prince': Traditions, Texts and Translations*, ed. by Nicola Gardini and Martin McLaughlin (Rome: Viella, 2017), pp. 215–37

'"Verdammte Staats-Klugheit / die Treu und Bund heist brechen!" Reason of State in Lohenstein's *Cleopatra*', *Journal of European Studies*, 50 (2020), 77–90

'Goethe's *Faust II*: The Redemption of an Enlightened Despot', *Publications of the English Goethe Society*, 91.1 (2022), 43–57

'Imperial Machiavel: The Morality of Octavio in Schiller's *Wallenstein*', *Germanistik in Ireland*, 17 (2022), 63–74

'Lohenstein's *Sophonisbe*: A Vindication of the Heroine', *Nordic Journal of Renaissance Studies*, 20 (2023), 165–79

R.R., Oxford, July 2024

INTRODUCTION

German literature differs sharply from its neighbours in having a vital tradition of tragedy. In the English and French literatures of the eighteenth and nineteenth centuries, such works as George Lillo's *The London Merchant*, John Home's *Douglas*, or the many plays of Voltaire were acclaimed in their day, but are now read only by literary historians. In Germany, on the other hand, Lessing's *Emilia Galotti* (1772) begins a series of tragic dramas which are recognized as essential items of the literary canon. A roll call of authors would include Goethe, Schiller, Kleist, Hölderlin (on the strength of his unfinished *Der Tod des Empedokles*, 1797–1800), and continue with Büchner, Grillparzer, Hebbel, and Hauptmann, down to Heiner Müller in the late twentieth century. One could extend the list in several directions: Wagner's music-dramas are tragedies, although they culminate in various kinds of redemption. Brecht did not intend to write tragedies, but his masterpiece, *Mutter Courage*, has repeatedly been received by audiences as a tragedy, despite his efforts to make his heroine repulsive. Thomas Mann wrote a tragic novel, *Doktor Faustus* (1947), which was also an ambitious (though questionable) interpretation of German history. And if we extend 'German' to other Germanic literatures, we have in Ibsen the most influential dramatist of the nineteenth century, who is also, with Strindberg, the founder of modern tragedies of marriage.[1]

The scope of this book is much more limited than this rapid survey might suggest. I deal only with political tragedy, and illustrate it from a relatively small number of classic authors and texts, beginning with the great Baroque dramatist Daniel Casper von Lohenstein and ending with Rolf Hochhuth's controversial play *Der Stellvertreter* (*The Representative*, 1963). But the term 'political tragedy' may itself arouse surprise. There is still some lingering belief in the stereotype of the 'unpolitical Germans' who passively suffered their lives to be directed first by absolutist and later by authoritarian rulers. This image goes together with the now threadbare historical thesis that Germany's development followed a special path or *Sonderweg*. It has been claimed that Germany failed to achieve a liberal democratic order because, unlike England and France, it did not experience a 'bourgeois revolution'. The abortive revolutions of 1848 were followed by a compromise in which the bourgeoisie submitted to the rule of traditional elites and became obedient subjects of an authoritarian state. Instead of seeking active involvement in politics, they retreated into private life, economic activity, and aesthetic and/or spiritual 'inwardness' (*Innerlichkeit*). Many Germans subscribed to this thesis, even

---

1   See Franco Moretti, 'The Moment of Truth', in his *Signs Taken for Wonders*, rev. edn, trans. by Susan Fischer, David Forgacs and David Miller (London: Verso, 1988), pp. 249–61.

asserting, as Thomas Mann did in *Betrachtungen eines Unpolitischen* (1918), that the unpolitical German who did his duty and lost himself in music was far preferable to French citizens inhabiting a corrupt culture of political demagogy and shallow journalism. Conversely, after 1945 the *Sonderweg* was seen as a fateful deviation from the proper path towards democracy, and the Germans were considered in desperate need of political re-education.

The *Sonderweg* thesis has never recovered from the battering administered in the 1980s by David Blackbourn and Geoff Eley.[2] They pointed out that neither the English Civil War nor the French Revolution could accurately be described as 'bourgeois revolutions', and that historians, apart from a very few Marxist hold-outs, had already discarded the concept. However, they did not trace the alleged *Sonderweg* back before the nineteenth century. It would seem, at first blush, even more obvious that eighteenth-century Germans were unpolitical. They lived in states which (putting aside the controversies surrounding the term) could be called absolutist in that the prince's powers were not limited by constitutional restrictions and subjects were denied political representation or participation. Surely we find here the origins of German *Innerlichkeit*?

Yet the eighteenth-century 'unpolitical German' has been exposed as a myth, especially by the Göttingen historian Hans Erich Bödeker. In a large number of articles, Bödeker has shown in detail that the many university-trained administrators and officials of the numerous German states formed a politically conscious network.[3] While the *Sonderweg* thesis maintained that officials (who in Germany include university professors) were too embedded in the state to question any aspect of its activities, it now appears that their very involvement obliged them to think constantly about political questions. They discussed the need for reform in the law, education, and economic life. Such discussions took place face to face in the many reading groups and 'patriotic societies' fostered by the Enlightenment. Since the educated class in Germany was scattered over a wide area, they also communicated by correspondence. The solitude sometimes imposed on them by geography gave them scope for reflection, but they then shared their reflections with often distant correspondents. They also published their thoughts in periodicals and newspapers. These might be explicitly political: the most famous examples were the widely circulated journals founded and edited by August Wilhelm Schlözer, professor of history at Göttingen, *Briefwechsel meist historischen und politischen Inhalts* (1778–82) and *Staatsanzeigen* (1782–93). Schlözer called out abuses of political power, notably the trial of Anna Göldi in Switzerland for alleged witchcraft; his articles on the Göldi case introduced the term *Justizmord* (judicial murder) into the language.[4]

---

2   David Blackbourn and Geoff Eley, *The Peculiarities of German History: Bourgeois Society and Politics in Nineteenth-Century Germany* (Oxford: Oxford University Press, 1984).

3   See especially Hans Erich Bödeker, 'Prozesse und Strukturen politischer Bewußtseinsbildung der deutschen Aufklärung', in *Aufklärung als Politisierung — Politisierung der Aufklärung*, ed. by Hans Erich Bödeker and Ulrich Herrmann (Hamburg: Felix Meiner, 1987), pp. 10–31, and 'Aufklärung als Kommunikationsprozeß', *Aufklärung*, 2 (1987), 89–111.

4   On the Göldi case and Schlözer's intervention, see Susanne Kord, *Murderesses in German Writing, 1720–1860: Heroines of Horror* (Cambridge: Cambridge University Press, 2009), pp. 24–33.

These intellectuals did not form an opposition to the ruling powers: they supported the established governments and sought gradual and piecemeal reform.

Against this background it is not at all surprising that the dramatists of the time should deal with political themes. Neoclassical drama admittedly was governed by the *Ständeklausel* which dictated that tragedy should feature characters of high social rank. In Germany as elsewhere, tragedians presented affairs of state in order to teach political lessons. Thus the literary dictator Johann Christoph Gottsched said that tragedy should inculcate 'the true greatness of princes, the nullity of worldly rank, and the abominable nature of tyranny'.[5] Later in the eighteenth century, political themes emerged even when the focus of a play was on domestic life and family relationships. Thus we encounter the abuse of princely power in *Emilia Galotti*; judicial murder in the Gretchen tragedy which forms the core of Goethe's *Faust I*; and Robin Hood-like efforts to avenge injustice and oppression made by Karl Moor in Schiller's *Die Räuber* (1781). The conversations about political and legal issues conducted by Enlightenment thinkers inevitably spilled over into drama. To avoid traversing too much familiar ground, however, I have chosen to focus on one set of issues: the relation between morality and politics, summed up by the concepts of Machiavellianism, reason of state (*Staatsräson, raison d'état*), and *Realpolitik*.

Accordingly, the first part of this book is an essay in the history of political ideas. I have tried to give a fair account of Machiavelli's thought in order to counteract the 'black legend' which automatically associates his name with unscrupulous chicanery.[6] Machiavelli separates moral considerations from the pragmatic analysis of the political options available to a prince. His approach, to borrow a term coined by Nietzsche, is *moralinfrei*, 'free of moralic acid'.[7] Much of the time it is refreshing. It offers many practical lessons from which present-day politicians can benefit, as Jonathan Powell, who served as Chief of Staff in the British government under Tony Blair from 1997 to 2007, has argued in his recollections.[8] Unlike Nietzsche, however, Machiavelli does not reject morality, or maintain that moral considerations have no place in politics. He maintains rather that moral considerations must sometimes be set aside in favour of a pragmatic policy that will actually work.

Machiavelli's pragmatism is perhaps hardest to digest in a passage from the *Discourses on Livy* which explains what a prince needs to do in order to establish his

5   Quoted in Wolfgang Martens, 'Die deutsche Schaubühne im 18. Jahrhundert — moralische Anstalt mit politischer Relevanz?', in Bödeker and Herrmann, *Aufklärung als Politisierung*, pp. 90–107 (p. 95). See Robert R. Heitner, *German Tragedy in the Age of Enlightenment: A Study in the Development of Original Tragedies,1724–1768* (Berkeley and Los Angeles: University of California Press, 1963).
6   In the body of this book I have been obliged to use 'Machiavellian' in the common sense of 'unscrupulous', as in many of the sources quoted. Departing from common usage would have meant disfiguring my text with innumerable scare quotes. The reader is asked, however, to remember that Machiavelli, properly understood, was not a 'Machiavellian'.
7   *Der Antichrist*, §2, in Friedrich Nietzsche, *Kritische Studienausgabe*, ed. by Giorgio Colli and Mazzino Montinari, 15 vols (Munich: dtv; Berlin: De Gruyter, 1988), VI, 170 (henceforth cited as KSA); Friedrich Nietzsche, *Twilight of the Idols and The Anti-Christ*, trans. by R. J. Hollingdale (London: Penguin, 2003), p. 128.
8   Jonathan Powell, *The New Machiavelli: How to Wield Power in the Modern World* (London: Bodley Head, 2010).

power in a newly conquered territory. The prince should create everything anew: he should dispossess the rich and enrich the poor, destroy existing cities and build new ones, and transfer populations, so that in the end everyone will be dependent for their wealth and rank on the new prince. Machiavelli cites as a partial precedent David in the Old Testament, as a fuller one Philip of Macedon, father of Alexander the Great. He deplores such methods:

> These are extremely cruel methods and inimical to every way of life, not only Christian but human, and every man should avoid them and prefer to live as a private citizen rather than as a king with so much damage to other men.[9]

So he is not advocating or justifying such drastic measures. He is saying that if you want to be a prince securely in power, these are the methods you must adopt, because they work. That is a hard truth to accept.

The important point about Machiavelli, for my argument, is that while giving pragmatic advice, he remains aware of the difference between right and wrong. On his showing, a prince must often do wrong, and, however necessary, it is still wrong. For the theorists of reason of state, however, the difference between right and wrong is annulled by the demands of government. Beginning with Giovanni Botero in the late sixteenth century, they maintain that whatever serves the prince's purposes is thereby justified.[10]

The conflict between morality and reason of state is acted out in the dramas that I have chosen to analyse. Many of them turn on the conflict that I have labelled the 'necessary crime'. The tragic potential of this conflict depends on keeping morality and necessity distinct. The 'reason of state' theorists sidestep it by saying in effect that if an action is necessary, it is no longer a crime. It is tragic dramatists who keep the conflict painfully visible.

The political tragedies discussed here are distinctive not only in their subject matter but in their intellectual approach. Most involve explicit debate about the best course of action for rulers to take. When Schiller's Elisabeth consults her advisers on how to handle the problem of Maria Stuart, or when Büchner's Danton argues with himself about the justification for the September Massacres, political issues are formulated with a clarity that is no doubt rarely possible in real life. This makes political tragedies strikingly different from tragedies turning on individual passions and personal relationships. If we look for explicit political debate in Shakespeare's tragedies, we find it above all in *Julius Caesar*, where the morality of assassinating a potential tyrant is debated between Brutus and Cassius, and in the council scene of *Troilus and Cressida* (II, ii), where the Trojan leaders discuss the pros and cons of continuing the war over Helen. Even in *Antony and Cleopatra*, where the fate of an

---

9   Machiavelli, *Discourses on Livy*, trans. by Julia Conaway Bondanella and Peter Bondanella, Oxford World's Classics (Oxford: Oxford University Press, 1997), p. 81. Machiavelli quotes the Bible: David 'filled the hungry with good things, and sent the rich away empty' (p. 80); but his quotation actually has nothing to do with David and comes from Luke 1:53, suggesting that his knowledge of the Bible was not very sound.

10   This contrast is drawn by David Wootton, *Power, Pleasure and Profit: Insatiable Appetites from Machiavelli to Madison* (Cambridge, MA: Harvard University Press, 2018), p. 48.

empire is at stake, the emphasis falls on the relationship between the titular lovers. Strictly political issues are more prominent in the history plays, particularly in the tetralogy running from *Richard II* to *Henry V*, which will be cited several times in the historical survey that forms the first part of this book.

Of the four dramatists discussed at length in part two of this study, Lohenstein, a diplomat in the service of the Habsburg Empire, is a clear exponent, though occasionally an uneasy one, of reason of state. The dramatists of the late Enlightenment discussed here — Goethe, Schiller, and to a certain extent Kleist — are suspicious of the propensity of rulers to excuse their actions by appealing to reason of state.[11] The crucial instance is Schiller's *Maria Stuart* (1801) where full weight is given to the pragmatic arguments for the judicial murder of Maria, yet the deed, once committed, has devastating consequences for the moral stature and self-respect of those responsible.

Schiller inaugurates a lasting concern with the 'necessary crime'. To explore it, I have concentrated in the remaining chapters on texts by seven writers from Georg Büchner in the 1830s to Rolf Hochhuth in the 1960s. Often explicitly citing the concept of reason of state, they address such questions as whether an admittedly unjust death sentence can nevertheless be justified. Supposing the welfare of the whole state, the whole population, depends on it? What does the death of one person matter if it prevents the suffering of millions? But if you continue this argument, you find yourself facing the sorites paradox. How many grains of sand make a heap? How many political murders constitute a massacre? This is the issue in *Danton's Tod*, where the main source Büchner consulted led him to think that the September Massacres for which his Danton assumes responsibility meant the deaths of several thousand people.

The alleged necessity of political crime is of course an inescapable subject in twentieth-century history. What W. H. Auden called '[t]he conscious acceptance of guilt in the necessary murder'[12] is the theme especially of Brecht's *Die Maßnahme* (*The Measures Taken*), discussed here. The cardinal crime defended by its perpetrators as necessary is the Shoah, which enters, albeit peripherally, into the last chapter of this book. That chapter deals with Hochhuth's *Der Stellvertreter*, which arraigns not the perpetrators of the Shoah but rather a bystander, Pope Pius XII, who in this version of history invokes reason of state to justify his refusal to denounce Nazi crimes against the Jews, and thereby makes himself a passive accomplice. Political drama gives the spectator a detached position not available either to the historical actors or to the dramatic characters, and encourages us to treat claims for necessity with some degree of scepticism.

The tragedies discussed here are not to be understood as representing human beings helplessly entangled in metaphysical nets or driven by a cosmic destiny. They are serious and responsible reflections, cast in dramatic form, on the possibilities

11   For the assignment of German classical writers to the Enlightenment, see T. J. Reed, *Light in Germany: Scenes from an Unknown Enlightenment* (Chicago: University of Chicago Press, 2015).
12   W. H. Auden, *Poems*, ed. by Edward Mendelson, 2 vols (Princeton: Princeton University Press, 2022), I: *1927–1939*, p. 772. Auden later toned down this phrase to 'the fact of murder' (ibid., p. 372).

of political action and on the claims of morality versus pragmatism in producing political outcomes. That they are also deeply engrossing human stories testifies to the combination of intellectual reflection and humanity in modern German literature.

PART I

Machiavelli, Machiavellianism, Reason of State, *Realpolitik*

— 1 —
Advice for Princes

Early modern rulers were not short of advice. In the Middle Ages and later, clerics and scholars composed manuals on governing, known as 'mirrors for princes' (*specula principum*, *Fürstenspiegel*), which instructed them in their duties. The king had to have personal virtues, sometimes amounting to sanctity; he had to rule justly, exercising power, goodness, and, above all, wisdom, which increasingly came to mean practical wisdom or prudence. Political thinkers insisted on the importance of justice. This meant, first, obedience to the law of God. Second, it meant observance of natural law, which governs all human relationships and is 'the entire body of all the principles dictated by reason to the human conscience'.[1] Lastly, the king must ensure the proper administration of positive law, the man-made ordinances which may change with time and circumstances. In doing so, the king must serve the common good (*bonum commune*). According to Thomas Aquinas, 'The first duty of a ruler is to govern his subjects according to the rules of law and justice with a view to the common good of the whole community.'[2] The common good is best served by preserving peace and promoting prosperity.

Renaissance humanists continued this tradition, often addressing their advice to individual rulers as an act of homage (which might also be an application for employment).[3] Beginning with Petrarch in the fourteenth century, the humanists turned not to scholastics but to classical writers. The physical and cultural devastation of Europe by the Black Death seemed to demand a programme of moral rearmament, which might rediscover the political virtues preached and sometimes practised in Greek and Roman times. New texts from the ancient world were being discovered in monastic libraries or brought to Western Europe by fugitives from Constantinople after it fell to the Turks in 1453. From Aristotle, Seneca, and above all Cicero, the humanists put together a programme for training rulers in virtue. As James Hankins has powerfully argued, the humanists were far more than the quarrelsome pedants represented disparagingly in Jacob Burckhardt's classic study of the Renaissance.[4] Classical texts provided them with precepts and examples of

1   Bernard Guénée, *States and Rulers in Later Medieval Europe*, trans. by Juliet Vale (Oxford: Blackwell, 1985), p. 41. See also Jeroen Duindam, *Dynasties: A Global History of Power, 1300–1800* (Cambridge: Cambridge University Press, 2016), pp. 21–26.
2   Guénée, *States*, p. 42.
3   Quentin Skinner, *The Foundations of Modern Political Thought*, 2 vols. (Cambridge: Cambridge University Press, 1978), I, 116–38.
4   James Hankins, *Virtue Politics: Soulcraft and Statecraft in Renaissance Italy* (Cambridge, MA: Harvard University Press, 2019). See Jacob Burckhardt, *The Civilization of the Renaissance in Italy*,

virtue, and means of making virtue attractive through eloquent oratory: hence the importance that the humanists attached to rhetoric, the art of persuasion. They urged rulers to practise all the Christian virtues, and also to treat their subjects generously, to display magnificence, and to exercise clemency towards wrongdoers.[5]

It was more difficult, however, to move from generalizations about virtue, justice, peace, and fidelity to show how these principles could be adapted to actual situations. Thus Erasmus in *Institutio principis christiani* (*The Education of a Christian Prince*, 1516), dedicated to Charles, King of Spain (who in 1519 would become the Holy Roman Emperor Charles V), gives unexceptionable advice on civil government, promoting the common good, administering justice, avoiding luxury and ostentation, keeping taxes low and encouraging service to the state. He focuses on 'the arts of peace', because the prince 'must strive to his utmost for this end: that the devices of war may never be needed'.[6] Hence he has little to say about the conduct of war, and nothing about dealing with rebellion or civil disorder. His advice would be excellent when everything was going smoothly, but it would not help with the fire-fighting that often absorbed much of a ruler's time.

The discrepancy between humanist ideals and the actual demands of politics is clear from Shakespeare's *Henry IV* plays. When the dying Henry IV gives advice to his son, he says nothing about the common good or about justice. He is entirely concerned with consolidating and preserving power. He himself was a usurper, who overthrew Richard II, and, like a Machiavellian prince, could not rely on a traditional feeling of loyalty but had constantly to defend himself against enemies who thought that his right to the throne was no better than theirs. Even now, his 'friends' are potential enemies:

> And all my friends, which thou must make thy friends,
> Have but their stings and teeth newly ta'en out;
> By whose fell working I was first advanc'd,
> And by whose power I well might lodge a fear
> To be again displac'd; which to avoid,
> I cut them off; [...] (IV. 5. 205–10)[7]

As the King knows, a rebellion led by Mowbray, Hastings, and the Archbishop of York has just been quelled by means which would conventionally be called 'Machiavellian'. The rebels meet the royal forces in Gaultree Forest (Galtres in Yorkshire). The King's representative, his second son Prince John of Lancaster, promises to redress their grievances and induces them to dismiss their forces, whereupon he arrests the rebel leaders and sends them off to be executed for treason. After all, he points out, he said nothing about sparing their lives. This behaviour is doubtless shocking; Samuel Johnson called it 'this horrible violation

trans. by S. C. G. Middlemore (Oxford: Phaidon, 1944), pp. 162–65.

5   Skinner, *Foundations*, I, 127.

6   Erasmus, *The Education of a Christian Prince*, trans. by Neil M. Cheshire and Michael J. Heath, ed. by Lisa Jardine, Cambridge Texts in the History of Political Thought (Cambridge: Cambridge University Press, 1997), p. 65.

7   All Shakespeare quotations are from William Shakespeare, *The Complete Works*, ed. by Peter Alexander (London and Glasgow: Collins, 1951).

of faith'.[8] Yet it can be defended pragmatically. Mowbray has already warned his fellow rebels that even if they are pardoned, their slightest action will place them under renewed suspicion (IV. I. 189–96). Better, it may be said, to dispose of them promptly than to live with untrustworthy subjects.[9]

Prince Hal, the future Henry V, hardly needs lessons in practical politics. Early in *1 Henry IV*, after Falstaff and his low companions have left him alone on stage, he confides to the audience that his debauchery has an ulterior purpose. As soon as he becomes king, he will step forward as a reformed character, and the contrast with his previous 'loose behaviour' will cause his new-found virtue to be all the more admired. His soliloquy to the audience recalls another in an earlier play, *3 Henry VI*, in which the Duke of Gloucester, later to become Richard III, tells the audience about his plans, parodying humanism by adducing classical models for deceit:

> I'll play the orator as well as Nestor,
> Deceive more slily than Ulysses could,
> And, like a Sinon, take another Troy.
> I can add colours to the chameleon,
> Change shapes with Protheus for advantages,
> And set the murderous Machiavel to school. (III. 2. 188–93)

The presence here of Machiavelli — the only modern author, I believe, mentioned by name in any play by Shakespeare — shows how far his name, some sixty years since the publication of *Il principe* (*The Prince*) in 1532, had become shorthand for unscrupulous, deceitful, and savage methods in the pursuit of power.[10] The machiavel was by now a familiar stage type, especially in blood-boltered dramas set among intriguers and assassins in Italy (the Jacobean equivalent of the American gangland in modern cinema). However, Machiavelli was not a machiavel — his own career was only patchily successful — but a writer who retains the power to shock, not by advocating evil, but by putting forward uncomfortable and sometimes irrefutable arguments about the need to make prudent use of evil in political life. With *The Prince*, he exposed a truth that was unacceptable in his day and remains unpalatable now: to be politically effective, a ruler must often disregard the high-minded moral advice given in mirrors for princes and deliberately behave in an immoral way.[11]

---

8   *Johnson on Shakespeare*, ed. Arthur Sherbo, I (New Haven: Yale University Press, 1968), p. 512.
9   Curiously, this incident is ignored in John Roe, *Shakespeare and Machiavelli* (Cambridge: Brewer, 2002). On Shakespeare and Machiavelli, see John F. Danby, *Shakespeare's Doctrine of Nature: A Study of 'King Lear'* (London: Faber, 1948); Theodor Schieder, 'Shakespeare und Machiavelli', in his *Begegnungen mit der Geschichte* (Göttingen: Vandenhoeck & Ruprecht, 1962), pp. 9–55.
10   Also mentioned in *1 Henry VI*: 'Alençon, that notorious Machiavel' (V. 4. 74). The common usage is illustrated in *The Merry Wives of Windsor*: 'Am I politic? am I subtle? am I a Machiavel?' (III. 1. 92).
11   Duindam, *Dynasties*, p. 55.

Machiavelli's Political Life

A sketch of Machiavelli's career will indicate how he acquired political insights that went into *The Prince*. Niccolò Machiavelli, born on 3 May 1469, was the son of a Florentine lawyer, and received a sound humanist education centring on Latin composition and literature. He entered the bureaucracy of the Florentine republic in 1498, when he was appointed Second Chancellor. This was a surprisingly responsible position for someone so young, for the two chanceries between them were in charge of all domestic, foreign and military affairs, and were at that time the only element of continuity in Florence's constitution.[1]

Machiavelli's life was dominated by what another Florentine, the historian Francesco Guicciardini, called 'the calamities of Italy'.[2] In 1494 Charles VIII of France invaded Italy in pursuit of his claim to the kingdom of Naples. Naples and Florence were allies. As Charles's troops drew closer, the Florentines, terrified that he would sack the city, expelled the ruling Medici family. Charles occupied Florence peacefully, agreed an alliance, and proceeded down the peninsula like 'a flame and a plague'.[3] As they went, his troops spread the new and terrifying disease later known as syphilis. His invasion overthrew the precarious balance which had existed, despite frequent conflicts, among the five major Italian states (Florence, Venice, Milan, Naples, and the Papacy). 'Sudden and violent wars broke out, ending with the conquest of a state in less time than it used to take to occupy a villa', wrote Guicciardini.[4] This new instability was the context in which Machiavelli in *The Prince* would later advise a ruler on seizing and retaining power.

After the expulsion of the Medici, Florence became a broadly based republic, in which, to prevent the emergence of another oligarchy, the *gonfaloniere* of justice, the nominal head of the republic, held office only for two months. The republican cause was first strengthened, then weakened, by the support of the charismatic preacher Girolamo Savonarola, whose moral crusade against luxury and corruption produced a backlash in which Savonarola was charged with heresy and burned alive in 1498. Savonarola's short but dramatic career taught Machiavelli that an 'unarmed prophet', when he loses popular support, has no effectual power to

---

1   See Roberto Ridolfi, *The Life of Niccolò Machiavelli*, trans. by Cecil Grayson (London: Routledge & Kegan Paul, 1963), p. 20.

2   Guicciardini, *The History of Italy*, in his *History of Italy* and *History of Florence* (excerpts), ed. by J. R. Hale, trans. by Cecil Grayson (New York: New English Library, 1966), p. 85.

3   Guicciardini, *The History of Florence*, ibid., p. 19.

4   Ibid., p. 20.

fall back on.[5] Within a few years of Savonarola's death, it became apparent that Florentine government was passing through the hands of too many inexperienced, irresponsible, and venal politicians. In 1502, to provide continuity and stability, the Florentines created a position, modelled on the dogeship of Venice, in which the *gonfaloniere* held office for his lifetime. The first permanent *gonfaloniere* was Piero Soderini, with whom Machiavelli was closely associated.

As Second Chancellor and secretary to the Ten of War (*Dieci di Balia*), the body in charge of foreign relations, Machiavelli was sent on numerous diplomatic missions, without the full powers of an ambassador but as an envoy (*mandatario*) whose duty was to report on the situation or to prepare the way for ambassadorial negotiations.[6] The most memorable of his missions was to Cesare Borgia. Cesare, the son of Rodrigo Borgia who in 1492 became Pope as Alexander VI, was brilliantly successful, first in establishing his father's power over the Papal State, and then in unifying scattered principalities into the Duchy of Romagna. When Cesare threatened to absorb some outlying Florentine territories, Machiavelli was part of a mission that met him at Urbino for negotiations. Later, in the winter of 1502–03, Machiavelli spent three months as an envoy with Cesare, trying to size up his character, policy, and likely intentions for the benefit of the Florentine government. He had a number of conversations with Cesare, and was extremely impressed by Cesare's abilities and by his ruthlessness.

In 1505–06 Machiavelli's responsibilities were extended to include the organization of a militia recruited from the population. His plan was not to create a citizen army, nor to put the whole nation under arms. The militia was to include a maximum of 'one man per household' and many non-citizens recruited from the peasants of the *contado* (the surrounding countryside).[7] Machiavelli had long been convinced that mercenary soldiers were unreliable, and that auxiliary forces borrowed from friendly powers were little better. In his 'Discourse on Florentine Military Preparations', written in 1506, he assured his employers: 'You will see in your own day the difference between having your fellow citizens soldiers by choice, not by corruption, as they are at present.'[8] Machiavelli's militia achieved a striking success in 1509 by recapturing the city of Pisa (previously a Florentine possession, which had taken advantage of Charles's invasion to regain independence). However, such a militia had many drawbacks — for example, its men, especially peasants, could not always be spared from their occupations — and no other city followed Florence's example.[9] Nevertheless, the need for citizens to double as soldiers would later be an essential and influential feature of Machiavelli's political thought.

5   Machiavelli, *The Prince*, ed. by Quentin Skinner and Russell Price, trans. by Russell Price, Cambridge Texts in the History of Political Thought (Cambridge: Cambridge University Press, 1988), ch. VI, p. 21. Future references to *The Prince* will be given in the text as *P* followed by chapter and page number.
6   For a lively, circumstantial and well-documented account of Machiavelli's career, see Niccolò Capponi, *An Unlikely Prince: The Life and Times of Machiavelli* (New York: Capo Press, 2010).
7   Ibid., p. 126; Hankins, *Virtue Politics*, p. 439 and note.
8   Quoted in J. R. Hale, *Machiavelli and Renaissance Italy* (Harmondsworth: Penguin, 1972), p. 72.
9   Hankins, *Virtue Politics*, p. 442.

The Medici were restored to Florence in September 1512. The *gonfaloniere* Piero Soderini fled into exile, with help from Machiavelli. Machiavelli was dismissed from his post as Second Chancellor in November 1512. In February 1513 he was charged with involvement in a plot against the Medici, and was interrogated and tortured by the strappado: with his hands tied behind his back, he was hung by his wrists from a beam and periodically allowed to drop a few feet, which caused agonizing pain and could even dislocate one's shoulders. Though Machiavelli, by his own account, suffered the drop six times, he admitted nothing, and he was released with a heavy fine.[10] The charge against him was probably unfounded, but it shows how closely he was thought to be linked with the exiled Soderini: he had even been called Soderini's 'mannerino' (lackey or puppet).[11] Thus reduced to poverty, he retired to his house in the country at Sant' Andrea in Percussino, seven miles south of Florence, with only occasional visits to the city.

During this self-imposed exile Machiavelli corresponded with his friend and fellow-diplomat Francesco Vettori about Italian politics. *The Prince* was an outgrowth of this correspondence. It was largely based on his own experience: for instance, he advises against the use of mercenary troops and also against friendly or auxiliary troops, recalling how Florence was threatened by the French troops it borrowed to use against Pisa.[12] The book's political advice is aimed specifically, though implicitly, at the situation of the restored Medici. It dwells on the particular difficulties of a ruler who seeks to impose his authority on what has previously been a republic, and it advises that a ruler must go and live in his new territories — something which Lorenzo de' Medici was slow to do. A questionable story says that when Machiavelli presented the book to Lorenzo, the latter was more interested in a pair of greyhounds given to him at the same time.[13] As this story suggests, the first readers of *The Prince* were not scandalized by it. Vettori said he liked it 'immeasurably', but, to Machiavelli's disappointment, was clearly not much interested.[14] At all events, it fell flat.

Machiavelli never again held public office, but lived as a man of letters. In 1516–17 he spent considerable time with the informal discussion group that met in the Rucellai Gardens (Orti Oricellari) in Florence. The gardens had been laid out by Bernardo Rucellai, a close friend of the Medici, and the meetings were presided over by Bernardo's son Cosimo Rucellai. Discussions there stimulated Machiavelli to work on his commentary on Livy which became the *Discourses*. The manuscript was dedicated to two of his interlocutors in the gardens, Zanobi Buondelmonte and Cosimo Rucellai.[15] He also produced *The Art of War*, completed in 1520, and a somewhat unreliable biography of an early fourteenth-century lord of Lucca,

---

10   See the poem quoted and discussed in Robert Black, *Machiavelli* (Abingdon: Routledge, 2013), p. 77.
11   J. R. Hale, *Florence and the Medici* (London: Thames & Hudson, 1977), p. 92; Capponi, *An Unlikely Prince*, p. 85.
12   Hale, *Machiavelli and Renaissance Italy*, p. 116.
13   Ibid., p. 128.
14   Ibid., p. 113; Black, *Machiavelli*, pp. 119–20.
15   Capponi, *An Unlikely Prince*, p. 234.

Castruccio Castracani. In 1520, as a sign of his restoration to favour, the Medici commissioned him to write a history of Florence, which he completed in 1525, ending with the death of Lorenzo the Magnificent in 1492. However, they did not give him any state office. In 1527 the Medici were again driven out of Florence and republican government restored. Machiavelli was now too closely associated with the Medici to be given employment. He died, probably of a stomach ulcer, on 21 June 1527.

— 3 —
The Prince

Machiavelli's reputation as an advocate of calculated wickedness is based on superficial readings of *The Prince*, which certainly runs counter to the high-minded humanist advice-books. The treatise was written late in 1513, when Machiavelli was living in exile on his farm, but published only posthumously in 1532. Although it offers many political maxims of general validity, it is not an abstract treatise on politics, but an attempt to intervene in a specific situation. It is addressed to a prince, Lorenzo de' Medici, duke of Urbino and grandson of the famous Lorenzo known as 'the Magnificent'. At the time of writing, the return of the Medici seemed to open up exciting prospects for Florence and even for Italy as a whole. The third Medici brother, Giovanni, became Pope in March 1513, the first Florentine ever to hold that office. It was not unreasonable to hope that Florence might be strengthened by an alliance between the Papacy and its new rulers; after all, Pope Alexander VI had helped the political career of his son Cesare Borgia.[1] The Pope placed the twenty-one-year-old Lorenzo in charge of Florence in 1513. Despite his inexperience, Lorenzo seemed promising: as captain-general of the Florentine forces he conquered the duchy of Urbino, and the Venetian ambassador described him as 'of a bold temperament, shrewd, fitted for great deeds, and if not equal to Valentinois [Cesare Borgia], very little behind him'.[2] Hence *The Prince* ends with an 'exhortation to liberate Italy from the barbarian yoke', urging the Medici to come forward as national liberators, as Moses had done for the Jews, Cyrus for the Persians, and Theseus for the Greeks, and drive the French out of the peninsula (*P* XVII. 87–91). These hopes were of course disappointed: Giuliano (son of Lorenzo the Magnificent) and Lorenzo died early (in 1516 and 1519 respectively), and Pope Leo was a mild and gentle pontiff, wholly unlike his ferocious predecessors Alexander and Julius. But in 1513 hopes were high.

Since this is Machiavelli's agenda, he concentrates on how princes in general, and the Medici in particular, need to act in order to consolidate their power in Florence before advancing to further goals. Accordingly, the striking feature of *The Prince*, which gained it a reputation for immorality, is its pragmatic approach. '[B]ecause I want to write what will be useful to anyone who understands,' says Machiavelli, 'it seems to me better to concentrate on what really happens rather than on theories or

---

1   See J. H. Whitfield, 'Machiavelli and the Problem of the *Prince*', in his *Discourses on Machiavelli* (Cambridge: Heffer, 1969), pp. 17–35 (p. 24).
2   Quoted in Hale, *Machiavelli and Renaissance Italy*, p. 128. Further testimony quoted in Whitfield, *Discourses*, p. 68. On Lorenzo's brief rule, see John M. Najemy, *A History of Florence 1200–1575* (Oxford: Blackwell, 2006), pp. 427–33.

speculations' (*P* xv. 54). There is no point, he continues, in describing how to live in imaginary states (i.e. where virtue is the rule); the real world is not virtuous, and 'a ruler who does not do what is generally done, but persists in doing what ought to be done, will undermine his power rather than maintain it' (*P* xv. 54).[3]

Contrary to legend, *The Prince* is not a manual of political wickedness, nor a handbook for tyrants. It forms a sharp, but not a total contrast with the tradition of 'mirrors for princes'.[4] A medieval king might owe his position to divine right, but he was supposed to put his subjects' interest before his own and to rule on behalf of the entire commonweal, promoting the common good. Machiavelli ignores divine right. The state for him is not a divine creation but a human construction, a work of art.[5] Nor does Machiavelli, in *The Prince* at least, talk about the common good; he entirely adopts the viewpoint of the prince who wants to retain power for his own sake, not for that of his subjects. The prince's aim is to acquire glory — meaning 'very great fame or honour that is generally recognized, acquired through extraordinary merits or talents, through valorous deeds or great enterprises' — for himself and his state.[6] Such a prince should not oppress his subjects. He needs their support. His subjects are not a homogeneous mass: they are divided between the people (*populo*), who form the majority, and the minority of nobles (*grandi*). The people form a better power-base, because the nobles consider the prince to be one of themselves and will constantly plot his overthrow.[7] The quality he needs most is not piety, magnanimity, or any of the other staples of 'mirrors for princes', but prudence (*prudenzia*). Machiavelli explains this concept: given that every policy involves risks, 'prudence consists in knowing how to assess the dangers, and to choose the least bad course of action as being the right one to follow' (*P* xxi. 79).

When a prince's power is securely established, the mode of government that Machiavelli recommends sounds unexceptionable. A prince should rule in a way that allows his subjects to go about their business peaceably without any fear of being robbed or despoiled. Gifted men and outstanding craftsmen should be suitably rewarded, as should anyone who manages to increase the prosperity of the state. At suitable times of the year the prince should entertain the people with shows and festivities. He should have wise and trustworthy counsellors who are concerned wholly with the prince's interests. He should avoid flatterers (an important theme in mirrors for princes).[8] But he should not encourage his counsellors to criticize him freely, for fear of losing respect; instead, he should allow only trusted counsellors to speak the truth to him, and then only when asked, but he should also question them thoroughly and then make up his mind for himself.

3   In this sentence, Machiavelli does not speak explicitly only of rulers, but of people in general: 'un uomo ...'.
4   Quentin Skinner, *Machiavelli* (Oxford: Oxford University Press, 1981), p. 41; 'Introduction', *The Prince*, ed. Skinner and Price, pp. xv–xxiii.
5   Cf. the famous opening chapter, 'The State as a Work of Art', in Burckhardt, *The Civilization of the Renaissance in Italy*. Burckhardt's *Die Kultur der Renaissance in Italien* first appeared in 1860.
6   Black, *Machiavelli*, p. 102. Definition quoted from Russell Price, 'The Theme of *gloria* in Machiavelli', *Renaissance Quarterly*, 30 (1977), 588–631 (p. 621).
7   As Shakespeare's (and history's) Henry IV found: see above.
8   E.g. Erasmus, *Education*, pp. 54–60.

All this amounts to a recipe for excellent government. So it may seem strange that Machiavelli has been execrated. In giving his advice, however, he does not say that it will promote good government for its own sake, or the happiness of the people for their own sake, but that it will keep the prince securely in power. That may seem the wrong way round. Surely government should be for the sake of the people, not for the benefit of the ruler? But if the same outcome is achieved — peace, security, order, prosperity — what do the motives matter?

In establishing his power, however, a new ruler faces many challenges. Machiavelli distinguishes between principalities which are hereditary and those which have been wholly or partially acquired by a new ruler. Hereditary states pose few difficulties: the prince needs only to pay attention to the institutions established by his ancestors. It is when a prince acquires a new principality, or adds new territories to his previous dominions, that he faces interesting challenges. Machiavelli is entirely pragmatic. You should live in your new state in person, so that you can detect any trouble in time to nip it in the bud, you can prevent your officials from plundering the new territory and thus robbing you, your subjects will be pleased to have access to you, and potential invaders will be frightened off. Alternatively, and even better, you should establish settlements in your new state; nobody will be displeased except the few whom you have dispossessed in order to accommodate the settlers, but you need not worry about those few, and you thus save the expense and danger of imposing a military occupation which will be resented by all the inhabitants.

Gaining secure control of a new state is an even tougher task. Machiavelli begins by referring to leaders from ancient and biblical history who succeeded in doing so: 'Moses, Cyrus, Romulus, Theseus and others of their stamp' (P VI. 20). All these had both the opportunity and the personal qualities that enabled them to seize it. Moses found an enslaved people ready for him to lead them; Cyrus found the Persians ready to rebel against the Medes, who themselves had been rendered 'soft and weak because of the long peace' (P VI. 20). These men seized and held power thanks to their own prowess (virtù) and their military strength. Machiavelli affects to apologize for placing Moses alongside secular figures, but adds ironically that in their methods these differed little from Moses, 'who had such a great master' (P VI. 20).

These distinguished examples form a prelude to a detailed account of the methods used by Machiavelli's hero Cesare Borgia to establish his power in Romagna. Cesare, finding Romagna in a state of virtual anarchy, appointed as governor Remirro de Orco (who as a Spaniard would presumably have had more difficulty in establishing his own power-base there), and this Remirro, described as 'a cruel and energetic man' (P VII. 26), soon pacified Romagna, evidently by terror. Since this harsh regime would be untenable in the long run and was already making Cesare himself unpopular, Cesare established a civil tribunal in the province and then, by a drastic method, deflected hostility from himself to his minister. 'One morning the Duke had Remirro placed in two pieces in the square at Cesena, with a block of wood and a blood-stained sword at his side. This terrible spectacle left the people both satisfied and amazed' (*P* VI. 26). Machiavelli was on the spot and able to report this event on the day it happened.[9]

Machiavelli then tells us how Cesare outwitted some disloyal captains who had just captured the town of Senegallia. Having arranged to meet them, Cesare took them to his quarters and had them taken prisoner, while outside in the town their troops were attacked and disarmed. The two most prominent captains, Vitellozzo and Oliverotto, were strangled that same night. (Machiavelli was in Senegallia that night and must have learnt about the events immediately.)[10] Machiavelli concludes that a prince must not shrink either from deceit or from salutary violence; but if he uses terror, he should be able to blame it on a subordinate and to sacrifice the subordinate for the sake of his own reputation. If the prince uses violence to consolidate his power, he should do it once and for all, for repeated doses of violence will ensure the continued hatred of his subjects, whereas a brief phase of terror will soon be forgotten: 'injuries should be done all together so that, because they are tasted less, they will cause less resentment; benefits should be given out one by one, so that they will be savoured more' (*P* VIII. 33–34). Short and surgical violence is more merciful than prolonged oppression. A ruler should not be gratuitously cruel; he should avoid paranoia ('should not be afraid of his own shadow'), and should apply harsh measures 'with due prudence and humanity' (*P* XVII. 58–59).[11] This advice may sound chilling; but granted that such violence may be necessary, a calculated minimum is surely better than a frenzy of killing — assuming, of course, that violence once unleashed can be brought back under control.

Once he has secured his power, the prince must decide his policy, again on pragmatic rather than moral grounds. For example, he has to decide whether to be generous or parsimonious. Generosity, shown in ostentatious displays, is a fine thing, but to sustain it a prince must impose severe taxes which will make his subjects hate him, so parsimony, though less glorious, is the better policy in the long run. Then the prince must decide between cruelty and compassion. A brief burst of cruelty, such as Cesare exercised through his governor on taking control of Romagna, may cause less suffering than the compassion which tolerates disorder, murder, and robbery. An army can only be disciplined through cruelty. Hannibal kept his multinational troops under control through savage discipline, but historians have failed to recognize that his cruelty was essential to his achievements: 'Thoughtless writers admire this achievement of his, yet condemn the main reason for it' (*P* XVII. 60). The great Roman general Scipio, on the other hand, was so lenient that his troops were insubordinate; it was only

9   Machiavelli's dispatch is quoted in Hale, *Machiavelli and Renaissance Italy*, p. 54. Remirro (in Spanish, Ramiro de Lorqua) was actually executed because he was found to be conspiring with Borgia's enemies (Capponi, *An Unlikely Prince*, p. 91). Machiavelli may still have been right, however, in suggesting that Cesare found him a convenient scapegoat.
10   Capponi, *An Unlikely Prince*, p. 92.
11   Machiavelli also uses the word *umanità* in *P* XXI, where Price translates it as 'affability'; this is no doubt appropriate to the context, where Machiavelli says a prince, meeting guilds or family groups, should 'dare di sé esempli di umanità e di munificenzia' ('display his own affability and munificence', *P* XXI, 79), but it obscures a connection between two distant passages of *P* and their implication that a prince should at all times retain his humanity.

because he acted under orders from the Senate that this characteristic did not spoil his reputation.

Once established in power, a prince may be either loved or feared. That a ruler should be loved was a commonplace. 'The tyrant strives to be feared, the king to be loved', says Erasmus.[12] It might seem obvious that it is preferable to be loved. Machiavelli thinks it desirable to be both loved and feared, but argues that if you have to choose, it is safer to be feared. Since people are ungrateful and fickle, their love is no guarantee of their loyalty, whereas their loyalty can be secured if they are afraid of punishment. However, a prince should not be hated. His subjects can fear him without hating him. And he can easily avoid incurring their hatred if he respects their property — 'because men forget sooner the killing of a father than the loss of their patrimony' (P XVII, 59). If he has to carry out an execution, he should make sure there is clear justification for it. He should be so well respected that nobody dares try to deceive him. If he avoids being hated, he secures himself against internal conspiracies. But a ruler can be hated for good deeds as well as bad ones: Machiavelli instances the Roman emperor Pertinax, who, succeeding the licentious Commodus, tried to impose decent behaviour on the soldiers who despised his lack of military prowess and resented his rule. Machiavelli concludes:

> a ruler who wants to maintain his power is often forced to act immorally [*non essere buono*]. For if a group (whether it is the people or the soldiers or the nobles) whose support you consider necessary for maintaining your power is corrupt, you are forced to indulge its proclivities in order to satisfy it. In such circumstances, good deeds are inimical to you. (P XIX. 68)

The prince must have *virtù*, a term often translated as 'prowess' or 'efficiency', and defined as 'the manly and martial qualities needed to achieve success and above all glory'.[13] It emphatically does not mean the Christian virtues and the associated qualities celebrated by the humanists. Among other things, the prince must be a skilful and intelligent leader in war. The art of war should be his overriding concern. Accordingly Machiavelli offers a great deal of advice on how to employ soldiers. He advises strongly against mercenary troops, because they are disloyal and undisciplined, and anxious to escape defeat by avoiding battle. He gives many examples of polities which have been damaged by mercenary troops. The commercial state of Carthage relied on mercenary troops and was nearly subjugated by them.[14] When the French invaded Italy in 1494, the mercenary troops employed by the Italian states proved entirely useless. Machiavelli here shows his preference for citizen militias: 'For many centuries both Rome and Sparta were armed and independent. Today the Swiss are very well armed and completely independent' (P xii, 44). Auxiliary troops — those borrowed from another prince — are just as bad as mercenaries. It might seem a blot on the reputation of Machiavelli's hero Cesare Borgia that in his conquest of Romagna he first used auxiliary troops, then

12   Erasmus, *Education*, p. 28.
13   Black, *Machiavelli*, p. 103.
14   This refers to the Mercenaries' Revolt, recounted by Polybius, which provides the subject of Flaubert's novel *Salammbô* (1862).

mercenaries, but Machiavelli saves Cesare's name by showing that he finally had the wisdom to raise his own army: 'he was never more esteemed than when everyone saw that he was the complete master of his own forces' (*P* XIII. 49).

As well as a lion, the prince must also be a fox. Machiavelli does not justify deceit, but he points out that deceit works:

> Everyone knows how praiseworthy it is for a ruler to keep his promises, and to live uprightly and not by trickery. Nevertheless, experience shows that in our times the rulers who have done great things are those who have set little store by keeping their word, being skilful rather in cunningly deceiving men; they have got the better of those who have relied on being trustworthy. (*P* XVIII. 61)

Thus Cesare Borgia was a master of deceit: we learn of him that his powers of dissimulation were so great that he managed to keep the Orsini clan on side even after they had become deeply and rightly suspicious of his intentions. Their leader, Signor Paulo, succumbed to his blandishments, accepted his expensive gifts, and as a result saw his clan defeated at the battle of Senegallia. Pope Alexander VI was an even more skilful deceiver: 'No man ever affirmed anything more forcefully or with stronger oaths but kept his word less. Nevertheless, his deceptions were always effective, because he well understood the naivety of men' (*P* XVIII. 62).[15]

This defence of promise-breaking is hard to swallow. It blatantly contradicts the precepts stated in mirrors for princes, for example by Erasmus, who laments that the principles of virtue are so seldom followed in practice:

> The good faith of princes in fulfilling their agreements must be such that a simple promise from them will be more sacred than any oath sworn by other men. How shameful it is, then, to fail to fulfil the conditions of a solemn treaty, one sworn by those things which Christians hold most sacred! Yet every day we can see this becoming the custom.[16]

One may suspect that Machiavelli is deliberately putting forward a paradoxical argument, especially if this passage is contrasted with one in the *Discourses* where it is said, evidently with commendation, that republics are more likely to keep their word than princes are, even when treachery would be advantageous.[17] But if we take this passage at face value, Machiavelli is pushing his pragmatism to its limit. Experience shows that deceit works; and we may add that if keeping one's word always led to good results, there would be no need to recommend it at all, let alone

---

15 Machiavelli advised against trusting Cesare Borgia in a memorandum entitled 'Parole dette sopra la provvisione del denaio', quoted in Capponi, *An Unlikely Prince*, p. 94; though if, as is now thought, this document was composed later (Black, *Machiavelli*, pp. 58–59), Machiavelli would have been writing with hindsight.

16 Erasmus, *Education*, p. 94.

17 Machiavelli, *Discourses on Livy*, trans. by Julia Conaway Bondanella and Peter Bondanella, Oxford World's Classics (Oxford: Oxford University Press, 1997), pp. 146–47. I have used this translation in preference to the widely circulated version by Leslie J. Walker, in view of the serious flaws in the latter, both in translation and in commentary, which have been pointed out in Whitfield, *Discourses*, pp. 231–37. Machiavelli's *Discourses* will henceforth be cited in the text as *D* with book and chapter numbers and page references to the Bondanella version, e.g. in the present instance (*D* I. 59. 146–47).

so emphatically as Erasmus does. Moreover, contrary to the claims by his later detractors, Machiavelli is not advocating that one should in general deceive one's fellows.[18] He is writing specifically about the behaviour of rulers.

All the same, a prince must appear virtuous. He need not have good qualities, but he must appear to have them. He ought 'to seem merciful, trustworthy, humane, upright and devout, and also to be so. But if it becomes necessary to refrain, you must be prepared to act in the opposite way, and be capable of doing it' (*P* XVIII. 62). '[He should] not deviate from right conduct if possible, but be capable of entering on the path of wrongdoing when this becomes necessary' (*P* XVIII. 62). '[T]o those who see and hear him, he should seem to be exceptionally merciful, trustworthy, upright, humane and devout' (*P* XVIII. 62). The last quality, the appearance of religion, is particularly desirable. Machiavelli is not saying that these good qualities are unreal or worthless. They are really good. But they do not always work in practice, least of all for a ruler. So a ruler must be able to discard them when necessary. This seems obvious. Yet this is where innumerable readers of Machiavelli have accused him of cynicism or of advocating hypocrisy or of putting forward a single, coherent doctrine of naked self-interest.

In advising how to bring about a well-governed state, *The Prince* does not simply negate or invert the genre of mirrors for princes. It recommends good government as being in the best interest of the prince, rather than of the people. In requiring the prince not necessarily to have, but certainly to present, a range of virtues, it develops further certain instabilities which can already be found in some mirrors for princes. The king had to rule with wisdom, which increasingly came to mean practical wisdom or prudence. But this meant that the prince had to be successful in worldly affairs, and so moral demands had to be relaxed. The prince cannot always behave virtuously, but he must at least *seem* virtuous. Thus John of Viterbo says in the fifteenth century: 'Si caste non vivere potes, caute tamen agas' ('If you cannot live chastely, at least act prudently').[19]

Machiavelli is not advocating crime. He gives two examples, one ancient and one modern, of people who rose to power by crime and whom he does not admire. The ancient example is Agathocles, who from humble origins became king of Syracuse in 317 BCE, and who gained power by assembling the senate and the leading citizens and having them massacred by his soldiers. Agathocles was courageous, bold, a skilful military leader who twice defended his city against the Carthaginians and counter-attacked with considerable success. But his abilities, according to Machiavelli, do not amount to *virtù*: 'it cannot be called virtue to kill one's fellow-citizens, to betray one's friends, to be treacherous, merciless and irreligious; power may be gained by acting in such ways, but not glory' (*P* VIII. 31). Agathocles was simply too wicked to be admired: 'his appallingly cruel and inhumane conduct, and countless wicked deeds, preclude his being numbered among the finest men' (*P* VIII. 31). The other successful criminal, Oliverotto of Fermo, gained power by inviting all the leading citizens of Fermo to dinner, including the uncle who had

18   Deceit can bring success, but not glory: cf. *D* III. 40.
19   Quoted in Guénée, *States*, p. 73.

brought him up, and inducing them to enter a room with hidden recesses from which soldiers emerged and killed them. Oliverotto then established new civil and military institutions and would have proved a successful ruler if he had not allowed himself to be tricked, trapped, and killed by Cesare Borgia at Senegallia.

One might still wonder why Agathocles is placed not only below Cesare Borgia, but even at the opposite extreme, and why Oliverotto deserves so little credit.[20] The answer is that both Agathocles and Oliverotto performed breath-taking acts of treachery and mass slaughter, and in both cases the victims were their fellow-citizens (and in one case, the uncle to whom Oliverotto owed immense gratitude). Their actions were wantonly savage and outraged the ties which ought to bind blood relatives and members of the same city. They destroyed the solidarity of citizens which Machiavelli — briefly in *The Prince*, at full length in the *Discourses* — thinks the essential foundation for a republic. Machiavelli is here being pragmatic, not immoral.

Machiavelli is being equally pragmatic when he says that even crimes can be committed well or badly, 'if one may use the word "well" of that which is evil' (*P* VIII, 33). Agathocles committed his evil deeds well, that is, effectively: he committed them all at once in a burst of terror, after which he was able to relax his severity and rule for his subjects' benefit. He would have acted badly, that is, ineptly, if he had begun with relatively mild coercion and then, to maintain his power, proceeded to ever harsher measures, thus making himself increasingly unpopular and provoking his people to revolt.

More difficult is the case of the emperor Severus, whom Machiavelli singles out as being both a lion and a fox to a pre-eminent degree. Severus came to power with the help of his troops and had to retain their support at all costs. He possessed so much ability that he was able to keep the soldiers friendly, and rule successfully to the end, even though he oppressed the people. For his outstanding qualities made him so remarkable in the eyes of the soldiers and the people that the latter were astonished and awestruck, while the former were respectful and satisfied. (*P* XIX. 68)[21] The words 'astonished and awestruck' (*attoniti e stupidi*) are close to those describing the impression made on the populace of Romagna by the execution of Remirro de Orco: they were 'satisfied and stupefied' (*satisfatti e stupidi*), so that the prowess of Severus is linked to that of the exemplary Cesare Borgia. Severus was also a fox, in that, faced with two rivals for power, Niger in the East and Albinus in the West, he defeated Niger and strung Albinus along until he could march also against the latter, on a false pretext, and destroy him. Given that Severus plundered the people, and was only kept in power by the support of his armies, it is hard to see what makes him better than Agathocles, except that he somehow managed to retain his subjects' 'respect'.

20   Machiavelli may also disapprove of Agathocles' lowly origins, as he says that he rose 'from the lowest, most abject origins', being 'the son of a potter' (*P* viii, 30); in fact Agathocles' father was not an artisan but a Syracusan citizen who owned a large pottery manufactory (*Oxford Classical Dictionary*).
21   Here the words 'ability' and 'outstanding qualities' both translate *virtù*.

Even the most skilful prince, the most endowed with *virtù*, is still subject to fortune. Machiavelli's hero Cesare Borgia was brought low only by the illness which prevented him from influencing the papal election of 1503 and thus averting the accession of his arch-enemy Giuliano della Rovere as Julius II. This was the one contingency he could not foresee. Machiavelli has this directly from Cesare:

> he told me himself, on the day Julius II was elected, that he had thought about what might happen when his father died, and had provided against everything, except that he had never thought that, when his father was dying, he too would be at death's door. (P VII. 28)

However, Machiavelli has to admit that Cesare was not just a victim of ill fortune; he also made a bad choice over the Papal election. Despite his illness, he was still able to influence it, and though he did not welcome the election of Julius II, he failed to use his influence to promote the election either of another Spaniard like himself, or at least of a cardinal who did not bear him a grudge for an injury. Julius, who reigned as Pope from 1503 till his death in 1513, was a dynamic leader who himself led his forces on arduous military campaigns and acquired the nickname *il terribile*, 'an untranslatable word that suggests a force of nature rather than a personality'.[22]

Fortune, in the sense of luck, often plays an unforeseeable part in events. The warlike Julius II provides an example: he was unwise enough to borrow foreign troops in his campaign against Ferrara and was duly defeated; in the nick of time, however, Swiss troops arrived and drove the victors off, so that Julius avoided either being taken prisoner or falling into the power of the troops he had borrowed (P XIII. 48). However, Machiavelli does not think that human affairs are wholly governed by fortune, though he admits that at times he has been tempted by such fatalism. Human affairs are half under people's control, half under the dominion of fortune. Fortune is like a river which, in flood, can cause widespread destruction, but whose force can be brought under some control by building embankments and dykes. The way to control fortune is to adapt one's methods to the changing times. This, however, is a counsel of perfection. People cannot change their characters with changing circumstances. Somebody who is circumspect by nature is unlikely to act impetuously when the situation demands a different mode of conduct. In troubled times, an impetuous character is more likely to meet with success: Machiavelli again cites Julius II, who in launching his military campaigns behaved with the forcefulness that the times required, but if he had lived longer, into a time when circumspection was the better policy, would have been unable to change his behaviour and would have come to grief. So it would seem that although in theory one can master fortune, in practice one cannot. Inspired by the example of Pope Julius, however, Machiavelli concludes that the impetuous person is more likely to be favoured by fortune, and gives a reason which has often been found distasteful: 'because fortune is a woman, and if you want to control her, it is necessary to treat her roughly' (P XXV. 87).

---

22   Eamon Duffy, *Saints and Sinners: A History of the Popes* (New Haven: Yale University Press, 1997), p. 147.

Perhaps the most indigestible of Machiavelli's beliefs is his unsparingly low estimate of human nature. 'For this may be said of men generally: they are ungrateful, fickle, feigners and dissemblers, avoiders of danger, eager for gain' (*P* XVII. 59). They are hypocritical and cynical, offering every sacrifice when danger is remote, but vanishing when it approaches. Their self-interest is paramount: 'men forget sooner the killing of a father than the loss of their patrimony' (ibid.). Such an epigram anticipates by two centuries the aphorisms of La Rochefoucauld (1613–80), which were to gain him a reputation for intolerable cynicism. La Rochefoucauld maintains that the basis of human nature is self-love (*amour-propre*), which impels self-interest as the strongest motive to action: 'The virtues lose themselves in interest as the rivers are lost in the sea.'[23] But although one may resist such generalizations, it is widely agreed that in politics, even if one does not presuppose people to be wicked, one cannot rely on their virtue. In revolutionary America, Alexander Hamilton warned the other Founding Fathers not to 'forget that men are ambitious, vindictive, and rapacious'.[24] Their solution was to devise a constitution which would restrain egotism and encourage virtue. Kant said that in a well-designed state obedience to the laws would obviously be in everybody's interest, even for a nation of devils (provided they were intelligent).[25] In *The Prince*, however, Machiavelli does not consider how the depravity of human nature might be counterbalanced by political institutions. For him, everything depends on the personal qualities of the prince.

23   Maxim 171 in La Rochefoucauld, *Œuvres complètes*, ed. by L. Martin-Chauffier, Bibliothèque de la Pléiade (Paris: Gallimard, 1964), p. 268.
24   Hamilton, *The Federalist*, no. 6, in Hamilton, James Madison and John Jay, *The Federalist Papers*, ed. by Lawrence Goldman, Oxford World's Classics (Oxford: Oxford University Press, 2008), p. 29.
25   Immanuel Kant, *Zum ewigen Frieden* (1795), in his *Werke*, ed. Wilhelm Weischedel, 6 vols (Darmstadt: Wissenschaftliche Buchgesellschaft, 1956–64), VI, 224; *Kant: Political Writings*, ed. Hans Reiss, trans. by H. B. Nisbet, Cambridge Texts in the History of Political Thought, 2nd edn (Cambridge: Cambridge University Press, 1991), p. 112.

4

The *Discourses*

The *Discorsi sopra la prima deca di Tito Livio* (*Discourses on Livy*), composed probably between 1515 and 1518, arose from discussions of history hosted by Cosimo Rucellai in the Rucellai Gardens. His interlocutors urged Machiavelli to put down on paper his thoughts stimulated by the reading of Livy.[1] The historian Livy (Titus Livius, 59 BCE–17 CE) wrote a history of Rome from the founding of the city in 753 BCE to his own lifetime. The greater part of the History is lost, but the surviving portion includes Books 1–10, dealing with the early history of Rome, and Machiavelli uses them as a framework for his reflections on politics and government. The *Discourses* often feel rather miscellaneous, but each of their three Books covers a different area: the internal government of Rome is dealt with in Book I, Rome's military expansion in Book II, and in Book III the leadership provided by the great men of Rome.[2]

The *Discourses* have sometimes been thought hard to reconcile with *The Prince*. While the latter work describes how a prince should obtain and consolidate power, the *Discourses*, treating ancient Rome as an exemplary republic, show how a republic can maintain popular liberty while strengthening itself at the expense of its neighbours, and they insist that republics are much better for the populace than principalities; Machiavelli not only speaks repeatedly of 'the common good', a concept absent from *The Prince*, but insists that 'this common good is pursued only in a republic', whereas a prince attends to his own good even when (as usual) it harms his subjects (*D* II. 2. 157).[3] He gives as examples Romulus, Moses, Lycurgus and Solon, all legislators 'who were able to create laws for the common good, because they had assumed for themselves sole authority' (*D* I. 9. 46).

The apparent contradiction disappears, however, when we remember that the two works were written in response to different situations. When Machiavelli wrote *The Prince*, it seemed possible that the new rulers of Florence would prove strong enough (especially if they heeded his advice) to expel the foreigners from Italy. By the time he wrote the *Discourses*, it was clear that the Medici were a broken reed. There remained the possibility, however, that at some future time a republic might be restored in Florence. After all, Machiavelli says, not every region is suitable for a republic — Milan and Naples are too used to tyranny — but Tuscany, he implies, is a place where a republic can flourish (*D* I. 17. 66). He emphasizes that

---

1   See the testimony of Filippo de Nerli, quoted in Black, *Machiavelli*, pp. 132–33.
2   Black, *Machiavelli*, p. 135.
3   On the various terms besides *comune bene* used for 'the common good' in *D*, see Black, *Machiavelli*, p. 172.

the most glorious achievements are to found a republic or a kingdom, as Romulus did, and to restore a republic after a crisis. Both require a single strong individual, who however must not be a tyrant. No such individual was on the horizon when Machiavelli was writing, and the Medici would soon decline into grand dukes, but it was a worthwhile aspiration.

Since a republic is sustained by good laws, Machiavelli here, in contrast to *The Prince*, pays close attention to institutions. These must provide both security and liberty: 'experience demonstrates that cities have never enlarged their dominion or increased their wealth unless they have lived in liberty' (*D* II. 2. 156). The Roman republic had strong leaders in the person of two consuls who were elected annually and therefore had not time to become tyrants. Its constitution was neither aristocratic, placing power in the hands of a few, nor democratic, giving all power to the people, but mixed. To mediate between the plebeians and the senate (which represented the nobles), the Romans created the office of tribune of the people. They thus avoided two perils: tyranny resulting from aristocratic rule and anarchy resulting from popular rule. In a national crisis, they appointed a dictator who had unlimited powers for a short and specified period. On one occasion the Romans did make a major political mistake: in order to reform their laws, they entrusted ten citizens (the *decemviri*) with temporary unlimited powers, sidelining the consuls and the tribune. The people wanted by this means to curb the power of the nobles, the nobles that of the people, and the result was that one of the decemvirs, Appius Claudius, became a tyrant. Fortunately for Rome, he abused his position so grossly that he could be overthrown and the consuls and tribunes restored to office. Machiavelli concludes that the power of magistrates must be subject to safeguards: 'the people must [...], in establishing magistrates, appoint them in such a way that they will hesitate before acting wickedly' (*D* I. 40. 111–12).

The surest safeguard against tyranny is popular indignation expressed in disturbances and riots (*tumulti*). Under the Roman republic these disturbances were often alarming but very seldom ended in bloodshed: 'The desires of free peoples are rarely harmful to liberty, because they arise either from oppression or from the suspicion that they will be oppressed' (*D* I. 4. 30). They generally led to the passing of new and better laws, and thus strengthened the republic. The people are sometimes unwise, but they are prepared to listen to a wise man whom they trust: thus in Machiavelli's day the bishop of Volterra was able to calm a mob in Florence (*D* I. 54. 133).[4] The Romans could also defuse tensions by allowing the people to bring a public indictment against a citizen of whose conduct they disapproved, as in the case of the would-be authoritarian Coriolanus (*D* I. 7. 38). An indictment could be dealt with swiftly by legal means, so that neither of the parties could call in foreign aid or set up a faction.

---

4   An example not used by Machiavelli is Menenius Agrippa, who, according to Livy, in 494 BCE persuaded the plebeians to end their secession by telling them the fable of the belly and the members. This event is familiar from Shakespeare's *Coriolanus*. Shakespeare's portrayal of the people, with their credulous acceptance of Menenius' specious reasoning, suggests he held a lower opinion of them than did Machiavelli.

Machiavelli distinguishes sharply between tumults and factions. Tumults are generally short-lived; factional feuds can go on for generations. Factional conflicts, the most famous being the feud between the Colonna and Orsini families, kept Rome in an almost continuous state of war for some 500 years, during which, as Gibbon says, 'the factions of Italy alternately exercised a blind and thoughtless vengeance on their adversaries, whose houses and castles they razed to the ground'.[5] Factions are destructive (*D* I. 7. 39), but tumults are beneficial as a stimulus to liberty. Machiavelli's view here was original, and was condemned by his contemporaries, all of whom considered tumults and factions as equally damaging to a well-run polity.[6]

Institutions, however, must be based on *virtù* — not just that of outstanding individuals, but of the republic as a whole. The general *virtù* is sustained by a high degree of equality: 'those republics, where an uncorrupted body politic has been maintained, do not tolerate any of their citizens acting or living like noblemen; on the contrary, they maintain among themselves a clear equality' (*D* I. 55. 135–36). By noblemen, Machiavelli explains, he means people who live in luxury from their revenues and contribute nothing to the well-being of the state. Citizens should contribute to the state by public methods, i.e. advising and acting on behalf of the common good (*D* III. 28. 322), but they should not be allowed to acquire reputations by using their private funds to do favours for individual citizens and thus gaining the ability to 'corrupt the republic' (*D* III. 28. 323). Late in its history, the Roman republic was corrupted by appointing consuls on the basis of 'charm (*grazia*) rather than ability', 'raising to that rank those men who knew best how to please others rather than those who knew best how to conquer their enemies' (*D* I. 18. 69). In a republic, poverty should be no bar to honour: Machiavelli cites the well-known case of the farmer Cincinnatus, who in a national emergency was appointed dictator, went out and routed the enemy, then returned to his farm (*D* III. 25. 317). Machiavelli opposes the familiar saying that 'wealth is the sinew of warfare' (*D* II. 10. 178). Money is certainly necessary, but it can never make up for the lack of good soldiers, and the best soldiers are those who fight for their own glory and that of their city (*D* I. 43. 113–14).

The *Discourses* therefore devote considerable space to the Romans' conduct of war and to military matters generally. Rome's many wars were concluded quickly, since consuls, being obliged to spend half their period of office at home, had to defeat the enemy within six months (*D* II. 6. 170). The booty was placed in the public treasury, so that Rome was enriched, not impoverished, by wars. Commanders in the field had full discretionary powers and were encouraged to take risks by knowing that they would not be punished if unsuccessful (*D* I. 31. 88–90). In expanding its domains, Rome formed alliances in which it always retained the upper hand, so that, after the conclusion of a war, the allied nation found that it had fallen under Rome's dominion unawares (*D* II. 4. 165).

5   Edward Gibbon, *The History of the Decline and Fall of the Roman Empire*, ed. by David Womersley, 3 vols (London: Penguin, 1994), III, 1075.
6   Skinner, *Foundations*, I, 181–82.

All these reflections make the *Discourses* an important text in the history of republican thought. Its contribution to the black legend of Machiavelli comes from two further main themes: its treatment of religion, and its defence of political ruthlessness.

Personally, Machiavelli was probably at best a nominal Christian.[7] When he was a student, his professor required him to copy out the recently discovered text of Lucretius's *De rerum natura* (*On the Nature of Things*), a famous work of atheism and materialism, though we cannot tell whether the poem persuaded him.[8] In the *Discourses* he was prepared to entertain the ancient philosophical thesis that the world had existed from eternity (*D* II. 5. 167–68). On the other hand, he says that 'our religion has shown us truth and the true path' (*D* II. 2. 158), and expresses indignation at the notorious corruption into which religion had fallen in his day (*D* I. 12. 54–55). He admits that the saints Dominic and Francis have restored respect for religion, but suggests that all they have thus achieved is to discourage criticism of the Church without amending its faults, so that priests are secure from richly deserved censure: 'Thus, the clergy do the worst they can, because they do not fear that punishment they do not see and in which they do not believe' (*D* III. 1. 249).

A republic, however, needs to be solidly founded on religion. Numa Pompilius, the second of the legendary kings of Rome described by Livy, 'turned to religion as something absolutely necessary for maintaining a civilized society' (*D* I. 11. 50). Machiavelli concludes 'that the religion introduced by Numa was among the principal reasons for the happiness of that city'.

Just as the observance of divine worship is the cause of the greatness of republics, so the disregard of divine worship is the cause of their ruin, because where the fear of God is lacking, that kingdom must either come to ruin or be sustained through fear of a prince who makes up for the shortcomings in its religion (*D* I. 11. 52).

Although this may sound very pious, we should remember that Numa Pompilius, who claimed that his religion had been communicated to him by a nymph, was one of the standard examples supporting the theory that religion was an imposture staged by priests.[9] Machiavelli is not concerned about the truth of religion, but about its instrumental value. Christianity is true, but it is not nearly as useful as the false religion of the Romans. Christianity glorifies the contemplative life, downgrades the manly and military virtues, and urges us to place our hopes in the next world. It does permit us to 'exalt and defend our native land' (*D* II. 2. 159), and if the clergy had maintained this aspect of Christianity 'Christian states and Christian republics would be more united and more happy than they are now' (*D* I. 12. 54), but the pagan religion, founded on patriotism and manly strength, is still far better. Moreover, ancient religious ceremonies encouraged a salutary ferocity:

> In their rites neither pomp nor magnificence was lacking in the ceremonies, but there was, in addition, the act of sacrifice full of blood and cruelty, and

7   Black, *Machiavelli*, p. 170.
8   Ibid., p. 19.
9   See for example Thomas Hobbes, *Leviathan*, ed. by J. C. A. Gaskin, Oxford World's Classics (Oxford: Oxford University Press, 1996), p. 77 (chapter XII, §20).

the slaughter of a great number of animals, a spectacle which inspired awe and rendered the men who witnessed it equally awesome. (D II. 2. 159)

Machiavelli recounts with evident relish how the Romans manipulated religion by inventing favourable oracles (D I. 13. 56) and reinterpreting unfavourable auguries (D I. 14. 58–59). Even if the rulers of a republic know better, they must uphold religious belief, and if they do, 'they will find it an easy matter for them to maintain a devout republic and, as a consequence, one that is good and united' (D I. 12. 54).

Nearly as shocking was Machiavelli's defence of ruthlessness, here as in *The Prince*. The founders of kingdoms and republics need to use force. Romulus killed his brother Remus and his companion Titus Tatius, but he did so 'for the common good and not for private ambition', so deserved to be excused (D I. 9. 45). It is important that Machiavelli says 'excused', not 'justified': Romulus' actions were necessary, but that did not make them morally right. Machiavelli's statecraft is not amoral, nor does he set up a new code of morality; he says that it is sometimes necessary to do wrong. Thus he manages to juxtapose two codes of value. Morality and Christianity are true, but sometimes they are inapplicable.[10] What applies to Romulus applies also — a more daring example — to Moses: 'Anyone who reads the Bible intelligently will see that, in order to advance his laws and his institutions, Moses was forced to kill countless men, who were moved to oppose his plans by nothing more than envy' (D III. 30. 326).[11]

The key example of necessary ruthlessness is known by the shorthand term 'killing the sons of Brutus'. Junius Brutus, the founder of the Roman republic, who drove out the last king, Tarquinius Superbus, had to consolidate his rule by firm measures. Two of his sons conspired with the exiled royalists to restore Tarquinius to the throne. Brutus condemned his sons to death and presided at their execution (D I. 16. 63; III. 3. 252). In such a situation, Machiavelli asserts, lenience is self-destructive: 'anyone who creates a free government and does not kill the sons of Brutus, will not sustain himself for long' (D III. 3. 252). In the hands of later writers, as we shall see, 'killing the sons of Brutus' would reveal its ambiguity. It might be presented as an act of impersonal, inflexible justice, or (as here) as the ruthlessness necessary to establish one's power; but justice might be a mask for power–hunger, and might be carried out by a tyrant as well as someone intent on restoring freedom. With Machiavelli, it is a memorable example of the hard-headed pragmatism which would shock so many people down the centuries.

---

10   This feature of Machiavelli's thinking is captured by Isaiah Berlin, 'The Originality of Machiavelli', in his *Against the Current: Essays in the History of Ideas*, ed. by Henry Hardy (Oxford: Clarendon Press, 1989), pp. 25–79.

11   After discovering the worship of the golden calf, Moses gathers 'the sons of Levi': 'And he said unto them, 'Thus saith the Lord, the God of Israel, Put ye every man his sword upon his thigh, and go to and fro from gate to gate throughout the camp, and slay every man his brother, and every man his companion, and every man his neighbour. And the sons of Levi did according to the word of Moses: and there fell of the people that day about three thousand men' (Ex. 32:27–28).

5

Reception

Machiavelli had a twofold reception. It is easy to imagine that Machiavelli was known simply as the demonic embodiment of amoral power politics who was first denounced by the English cardinal Reginald Pole in his *Apologia ad Carolum Quintum* (1539). This hate-figure appears, for example, in the prologue to Marlowe's *Jew of Malta* (1590). As a political thinker, however, Machiavelli was required reading for writers from Francis Bacon down to Kant and Fichte.

How easily could they read him? Many educated people outside Italy could read Italian, but for those who could not, Latin and French translations were available soon after the publication of *The Prince* in 1532. Even before that, the Neapolitan philosopher Agostino Nifo included numerous excerpts from the still unpublished *Prince*, along with the expected references to Aristotle, Cicero, and other ancient and modern sources, in his 'mirror for princes', *De regnandi peritia* (1523).[1] A full Latin translation by Silvestro Tegli (alias Sylvester Telius), a humanist who belonged to the group of Italian refugees in Basel, appeared in 1560, but was of course accessible only to the highly educated. However, two French translations had appeared, both in 1553, in Paris and Poitiers respectively. At least three manuscript versions by unknown authors circulated in Elizabethan England, while in Scotland a translation was made, though not published, by William Fowler, a diplomat, spy, and well-known translator from the Italian.[2] The first full English translation was published by Edward Dacres in 1640. Translations into German were slow to appear: the earliest, made in 1692 by the Silesian nobleman Christian Albrecht von Lenz, relied heavily on the recent French translation by Nicolas Amelot de la Houssaie (1683), and remained unpublished; another, anonymous, German translation appeared at Cologne in 1714.[3] However, translations into German were hardly needed, because most potential readers could have used the French, Latin, or indeed Italian versions.

Moreover, knowledge of Machiavelli's ideas was disseminated by his antagonists. The black legend of Machiavelli was formulated at the greatest length by Innocent

---

1   Caterina Mordeglia, 'The First Latin Translation', in *The First Translations of Machiavelli's 'Prince' from the Sixteenth to the First Half of the Nineteenth Century*, ed. by Roberto de Pol (Amsterdam and New York: Rodopi, 2010), pp. 59–82 (pp. 59–60). A chronological list of early translations is given on pp. 307–08.

2   Alessandra Petrina, 'A Florentine Prince in Queen Elizabeth's Court', in *The First Translations*, ed. by De Pol, pp. 83–115 (pp. 97–100); see also her 'The Travels of Ideology: Niccolò Machiavelli at the Court of James VI', *Modern Language Review*, 102 (2007), 947–59.

3   Serena Spazzarini, 'The First German Translation', in *The First Translations*, ed. by De Pol, pp. 207–46.

Gentillet, a Huguenot lawyer who fled from Toulouse to Geneva to escape the St Bartholomew's Day Massacre. This massacre of French Protestants began in Paris on Sunday 24 August 1572 and lasted three days, during which some 2,000 people were killed, and often horribly mutilated as well; it then spread to cities throughout France and raged for six weeks, with some three thousand further victims. Historians now think that the Massacre was not planned by the court but was an outbreak of popular anti-Protestant fury.[4] To Gentillet, however, it was damning evidence of the pernicious influence of Italians, particularly the Italian Queen Mother, Catherine de' Medici, and the writings of Machiavelli, which had corrupted the French ruling class. 'For are they not Machiavelists, Italian or Italianized, which doe handle and deal with the seales of the kindgome [sic] of France?'[5] Gentillet's method is to select thirty-seven maxims, not quoted but paraphrased from Machiavelli's writings; to enlarge upon them; and to confute them by citing vast numbers of counter-examples from ancient and modern history. The first maxim, that a prince should rely not on counsellors but on his own wisdom, is discussed over twenty-eight pages. The result is hardly a nuanced, but certainly a memorable account of Machiavelli, which made his supposed doctrines accessible and represented them in the most sinister light, as befitted an 'Atheist'.[6] Whether Catherine had read Machiavelli is uncertain, but even if she did not instigate the Massacre, she certainly approved of it, and she was in any case convinced that a ruler was entitled to kill even large numbers of subjects in cases of extreme necessity.[7] Gentillet's treatise was popular: 'between 1576 and 1655, there were twenty-four editions of the Contre-Machiavel in French, Latin, German, Dutch, and English'.[8] But since Simon Patericke's English translation, though completed in 1577, was not published till 1602, Gentillet cannot be blamed for the popularity of the 'Machiavel' figure on stage.[9]

Early readers of Machiavelli seem to have had particular difficulty with his secular approach to politics. For Machiavelli, religion is simply one element in political life. Authority is no longer underwritten by God, nor is it seen as part of a cosmic order. Hence he was denounced as an atheist by the English cardinal Reginald Pole, who associated his doctrines with the opposition to Rome by Henry VIII and Thomas

---

4   Mack P. Holt, *The French Wars of Religion, 1562–1629*, 2nd edn (Cambridge: Cambridge University Press, 2005), p. 90.
5   Innocent Gentillet, *A discourse vpon the meanes of vvel governing and maintaining in good peace, a kingdome, or other principalitie. Divided into three parts, namely the counsell, the religion, and the policie, vvhich a prince ought to hold and follow. Against Nicholas Machiavell the Florentine. Translated into English by Simon Patericke* (London: Adam Islip, 1602), preface to Part One (unpaginated). Originally published in 1576 as *Discours sur les moyens de bien gouverner et maintenir en bonne paix un Royeaume ou autre principauté. Divisez en trois p[arties: assavoir, du Conseil, de la Religion, & Police, que doit tenir un Prince. Contre Nicolas Machiavel Florentin.* Examined in detail by Sydney Anglo, *Machiavelli: The First Century* (Oxford: Oxford University Press, 2005), pp. 271–324.
6   Gentillet, *A discourse*, p. 92.
7   Holt, *French Wars*, pp. 84–85; Friedrich Meinecke, *Die Idee der Staatsräson in der neueren Geschichte*, ed. by Walther Hofer (Munich: Oldenbourg, 1957), pp. 60–61.
8   Anglo, *Machiavelli*, p. 324.
9   Felix Raab, *The English Face of Machiavelli: A Changing Interpretation, 1500–1700* (London: Routledge & Kegan Paul, 1964), p. 56.

Cromwell, and considered him a 'son of Satan'.[10] More judicious readers, such as Richard Morison, Henry VIII's ambassador at the court of the Emperor Charles V, and the Italophile humanist William Thomas, admired Machiavelli as an astute analyst of politics, but balked at the secular world-view that his writings implied.[11]

This conflict between the traditional social order and a secular, individualist view that regards politics as manipulable is embodied in the most memorable machiavels to appear on the Elizabethan and Jacobean stage. Often, especially in plays set in Italy, the machiavel is an unscrupulous villain controlling a sensational plot, like Malevole in John Marston's *The Malcontent* (1604), Bosola in John Webster's *The Duchess of Malfi* (1613), Iago in *Othello*, and Iachimo in *Cymbeline*. Shakespeare, however, also presents English machiavels, notably Richard III, later followed by Edmund in *King Lear*.[12] Both are self-aware individuals, alienated from traditional society by deformity and bastardy respectively. Richard says 'I am myself alone' (*3 Henry VI*, v. 6. 84); Edmund dismisses astrology, and with it the traditional cosmic framework, by saying: 'I should have been that I am, had the maidenliest star in the firmament twinkled on my bastardizing' (*King Lear*, I. 2. 126). Both confront an old order which reveals its decrepitude — especially in the person of Edmund's father Gloucester, with his 'smutty fatuity and doddering superstitiousness'[13] — and overcome it, at least for a while, by their intelligence and lack of scruple. They are terrifying in their absence of virtue and their abundance of *virtù*.

Political thinkers, without approving of Machiavelli, took his analyses seriously. Francis Bacon in his *Essays* (1597) and *The Advancement of Learning* (1605) repeatedly quotes even the most notorious of Machiavelli's maxims — his advice, for example, that the prince must be both a lion and a fox — and commends him for describing how the world really works: 'we are much beholden to Machiavelli and other writers of that class, who openly and unfeignedly declare or describe what men do, and not what they ought to do'.[14] He does not endorse Machiavelli's advice on dissimulation, or his advocacy of ruling by fear rather than love, but he does think that to do good one must understand evil, and here Machiavelli is an invaluable guide. Sir William Drake (1606–69), a Buckinghamshire country gentleman and MP, left behind a large collection of commonplace books which have made it possible to reconstruct his reading habits and his intellectual world in exceptional detail. His favourite author was Machiavelli, followed by Tacitus and Guicciardini, and from them he worked out a surprisingly amoral view of political activity. Bad men might make good kings; rulers sought power as a means to greatness, often using deception and force; if they secured the consent of their subjects, then it was out of expediency; they made promises simply in order to string their subjects along.[15]

10   On Pole, see Anglo, *Machiavelli*, pp. 115–42 (quotation from p. 126).
11   Raab, *English Face*, pp. 34–48.
12   See Danby, *Shakespeare's Doctrine of Nature*, pp. 61–65.
13   Ibid., p. 64.
14   'Of the Dignity and Advancement of Learning', Book VII, ch. 2, in *Collected Works of Francis Bacon*, ed. by James Spedding, Robert Leslie Ellis and Douglas Denon Heath (1879; repr. London: Routledge/Thoemmes, 1996), v. 17. See Raab, *English Face*, p. 74.
15   Kevin Sharpe, *Reading Revolution: The Politics of Reading in Early Modern England* (New Haven: Yale University Press, 2000), pp. 75, 114, 188.

Machiavelli's cool, hard look at the real operations of the political world not only suited the empirical approach to research which Bacon was foremost in developing, but also came as a relief in an age of religious wars. Jean Bodin in 1566 includes Machiavelli among writers on the 'arcana of princes', praising him as the first modern writer to write well about government.[16] In England in the 1650s, Oliver Cromwell seemed like a new Machiavellian prince; John Milton, Andrew Marvell, Lord Clarendon and many others turned to Machiavelli in order to understand how he had seized power, and Marvell's portrayal of Cromwell in his 'Horatian Ode' represents him as a Machiavellian ruler whose *virtù* enabled him to 'cast the kingdom old | Into another mould'.[17] Machiavelli was read attentively by the proponents of an English republic, including James Harrington, who in the preface to his utopian treatise *Oceana* (1656) cites the ideas about government held by 'the ancients and their learned disciple Machiavel, the only politician of later ages'.[18] However, Harrington's ideal republic differs markedly from the Roman republic idealized by Machiavelli. While the Roman republic, according to Machiavelli, was actually strengthened by internal dissensions, and was constantly expanding outwards and thus reuniting its citizens in war against a common enemy, Harrington's Utopia, like many Utopias, is intended to promote unanimity and restrict change. For this purpose its institutions are hemmed in by elaborate rules and orders, like the Venetian republic of his time.[19]

Machiavelli's bad reputation overlapped with that of the Jesuits, with whom he was often associated. Founded by a Papal bull in 1540, the Society of Jesus, initially led by Ignatius of Loyola, was dedicated to propagating the Catholic faith through education and missionary work. In the 1560s it assumed the additional task of combating Protestantism. The religious hatred generated by the Reformation made the Society the object of many terrifying rumours. Organized on quasi-military lines, famous for their missionary activity extending to China and Canada, and not distinguished by any special clothing, the Jesuits were widely thought to be dedicated to maintaining and spreading the Catholic faith by every possible means. After the dissolution of their society by Pope Clement XIV in 1773, they were feared even more because they were now invisible. They were blamed for the assassination of several monarchs (including William the Silent in the Netherlands

16   Quoted in Peter S. Donaldson, *Machiavelli and Mystery of State* (Cambridge: Cambridge University Press, 1988), p. 114.
17   *The Poems of Andrew Marvell*, ed. by Nigel Smith (London: Longman Pearson, 2003), pp. 273–79; Nigel Smith, *Andrew Marvell: The Chameleon* (New Haven: Yale University Press, 2010), pp. 82–83.
18   James Harrington, *The Commonwealth of Oceana* and *A System of Politics*, ed. by J. G. A. Pocock (Cambridge: Cambridge University Press, 1992), p. 10. See Blair Worden, 'English Republicanism', in *The Cambridge History of Political Thought, 1450–1700*, ed. by J. H. Burns (Cambridge: Cambridge University Press, 1991), pp. 443–75.
19   This casts doubt on Pocock's claim that Harrington's treatise is crucial in the transmission of Machiavelli's thought, marking the 'moment of paradigmatic breakthrough, a major revision of English political theory and history in the light of concepts drawn from civic humanism and Machiavellian republicanism' (J. G. A. Pocock, *The Machiavellian Moment: Florentine Political Thought and the Atlantic Republican Tradition* (Princeton: Princeton University Press, 1975), p. 384).

and Henry III and Henry IV in France) and even of two refractory Popes.[20] They often became confessors to monarchs — the emperor Ferdinand II, for example, had as his confessor the Jesuit Wilhelm Lamormaini, mentioned ominously in Schiller's *Wallenstein* — and were thought thereby to exert malign backstairs influence on European politics. They were also credited with encouraging tyrannicide. The Jesuit Juan de Mariana in *De Rege et regis institutione* (1599) argued not only that it was justified to assassinate a usurper or an invader, but that a legitimate ruler who persistently abused his power could be killed by an individual. This was a highly unpopular doctrine in the age of absolutism, when divinity was thought to hedge a king, and the Parlement of Paris had Mariana's book burned by the public hangman in 1610. Machiavelli and the Jesuits were coupled, for example, in John Donne's anti-Jesuit satire *Ignatius his Conclave* (1611), in which Ignatius and 'Machiavel', both teachers of dissimulation and sedition, contend for an honoured place in hell. Donne appears to have been the first writer to credit the Jesuits with the maxim that the end justifies the means, making Ignatius say: 'hee which graunts the end, is by our *Rules of law* presumed to have graunted all meanes necessary to that end'.[21] Machiavelli, however, says something very similar, referring to the founder of a republic: 'It is truly appropriate that while the act accuses him, the result excuses him, and when the result is good, like that of Romulus, it will always excuse him' (*D* I ix 45). Both words, 'Jesuit' and 'Machiavelli', conveyed thrilling suggestions of ruthless calculation and utter wickedness.

20   All these charges are made in the article by Jean d'Alembert, 'Jésuites', in the *Encyclopédie ou Dictionnaire raisonné des sciences, des arts et des métiers*, ed. by Denis Diderot and others, 17 vols (Neuchâtel: Faulche, 1765), VIII, 512–16. These and other accusations were systematically examined and rejected in Bernhard Duhr, SJ, *Jesuiten-Fabeln: Ein Beitrag zur Culturgeschichte* (Freiburg i.Br.: Herder, 1891). On anti-Jesuitism as a conspiracy theory: Peter Burke, 'The Black Legend of the Jesuits: An Essay in the History of Social Stereotypes', in his *Secret History and Historical Consciousness* (Brighton: E. E. Root, 2016), pp. 215–40; on their alleged monarchomachy: Harro Höpfl, *Jesuit Political Thought: The Society of Jesus and the State, c. 1540–1630* (Cambridge: Cambridge University Press, 2004), pp. 318–21.
21   John Donne, *Ignatius his Conclave*, ed. T. S. Healy, SJ (Oxford: Clarendon Press, 1969), p. 23. The maxim is commonly attributed to Hermann Busenbaum's *Medulla theologiae moralis* (1650). Pascal influentially ascribed it to the Jesuits in his *Lettres provinciales* (1656–57), where a Jesuit is made to say: 'nous corrigeons le vice du moyen par la pureté de la fin': Blaise Pascal, *Œuvres complètes*, ed. by Jacques Chevalier (Paris: Gallimard, 1954), p. 729.

6

'Machiavellianism' at Court

The 'Machiavellian' arts of intrigue, dissimulation and deceit were thought to flourish especially in the hothouse atmosphere of a princely court. Hence Gentillet says *The Prince* should be called 'the French Courtiers *Alcoran*'.[1] The tradition of critical writing about courts (*Hofkritik*), stretching back to the Middle Ages, constantly recycles a number of charges. Courtiers are ambitious and unscrupulous: they curry favour with their prince by flattery, and corrupt his morals in the process. They are given to envy, slander, and intrigue, concealed behind skilful dissimulation. They spend their time and the prince's money in drinking, gormandizing, gambling, and lechery. Such topoi are already present in an early English example, John Skelton's *The Bowge of Court* (printed 1499; 'bowge' means 'rations, allowance of food'), in which Drede, a timid newcomer at court, encounters such allegorical figures as Favell (Flattery), Disdayne, Ryott (debauchery), Dyssymulation, and Disceyte, who flatter, threaten, and intimidate him, while others seem to be whispering about him behind his back.[2]

These topoi should not be dismissed as mere literary conventions. Many of the authors of *Hofkritik* had personal experience of princely courts, including the Spanish moralist Antonio de Guevara (court preacher to the Emperor Charles V), whose writings include a much-quoted catalogue of courtly vices, and who is at pains to tell the reader that his knowledge comes not from books but from his own observation.[3] The exemplary court, where the ceremonial and also the intrigue surrounding the monarch were most fully developed, was that of Louis XIV in France. Louis's courtiers engaged in a continual competition for power, as expressed in one's rank within systems of etiquette.[4] In the 1680s the rules of this competition were formulated in a famous passage by Jean de la Bruyère:

> A Man who frequents the Court, is master of his Gestures, his Looks and Complexion; he is profound and inpenetrable. He dissembles when he does ill Offices, smiles on his Enemies, puts a constraint on his Natural Disposition, disguises his Passions, acts against his Inclinations, speaks against his Opinion:

1   Gentillet, *A discourse*, preface to Book 1, unpaginated.
2   John Skelton, *Poems*, ed. by Robert S. Kinsman, Clarendon Medieval and Tudor Series (Oxford: Clarendon Press, 1969), pp. 11–28.
3   'dises alles red ich nit auß den Büchern | sonder weil ichs mit meinen leiblichen Augen gesehen | vnnd selbst erfahren habe': Guevara, *Der wolgezierte Hoffmann/ oder Hoffschul*, trans. from Spanish by Aegidius Albertinus (Frankfurt a.M., 1644), quoted in Helmuth Kiesel, *'Bei Hof, bei Höll': Untersuchungen zur literarischen Hofkritik von Sebastian Brant bis Friedrich Schiller* (Tübingen: Niemeyer, 1979), p. 89.
4   Norbert Elias, *The Court Society*, trans. by Edmund Jephcott (Oxford: Blackwell, 1983), p. 91.

And after all, this great Refinedness is nothing more than the Vice we call
Falshood, which is sometimes as unprofitable even for a Courtier, as Openness,
Sincerity and Vertue.[5]

These arts were thought to be applied with particular expertise by princely
favourites, a type of courtier that became especially visible in the early modern
period. Some favourites, such as Cardinal Richelieu in France or the Count-
Duke of Olivares in Spain, were highly competent administrators who were
indispensable to rulers faced with the bewildering complexity of the early modern
state.[6] Minister-favourites could easily become too powerful, as Richelieu was felt
to be; but monarchs who preferred to rule without such a minister, like Philip II
of Spain or Joseph II of Austria, were liable to wear themselves out in trying to
micro-manage their huge and heterogeneous domains.[7]

Favourites might also serve a more personal need. A ruler surrounded by
flattering and insincere courtiers did not know whom to trust. Bacon says in his
essay 'Of Friendship' that rulers, being remote from their subjects, need people,
called 'favourites, or privadoes', in whom they can confide, 'and we see plainly that
this hath been done, not by weak and passionate princes only, but by the wisest
and most politic that ever reigned'.[8] A favourite was vulnerable to the envy of
less successful courtiers, to his own excessive ambition, and to the whims of the
monarch he served, and his fall would be greeted with malicious pleasure and scant
sympathy.[9] The rise and fall of a favourite was an inviting topic for dramatists:
familiar examples include Gaveston in Marlowe's *Edward II* (1594), Tiberius'
favourite Sejanus in Ben Jonson's *Sejanus His Fall* (1603), and the spectacular
dismissal of Falstaff in *2 Henry IV*.[10] In the last instance, it is Prince Hal who is the
'Machiavellian' dissembler, for he has already made it clear to the audience that
he intends to discard Falstaff and his other disreputable companions as soon as his
accession to the throne requires him to improve his image; by contrast, Falstaff is
almost innocent in his open rapacity ('Rob me the exchequer the first thing thou
doest, and do it with unwash'd hands too', *1 Henry IV*, III. 5. 181).

In the atmosphere of intrigue inseparable from a court, friendship between

5   *The characters, or, The manners of the age* by Monsieur de la Bruyere ... made English by several
hands (London: printed for John Bullord, 1699), p. 164. For the original, see La Bruyère, *Les
Caractères*, ed. by Georges Mongrédien (Paris: Garnier, 1954), p. 194.

6   See Jean Bérenger, 'Pour une enquête européenne: le problème du ministériat au XVIIe siècle',
Annales, 29 (1974), 166–92; J. H. Elliott, *Richelieu and Olivares* (Cambridge: Cambridge University
Press, 1984); *The World of the Favourite*, ed. by J. H. Elliott and L. W. B. Brockliss (New Haven: Yale
University Press, 1999).

7   Geoffrey Parker, *Imprudent King: A New Life of Philip II* (New Haven: Yale University Press,
2014), pp. 61–79; T. C. W. Blanning, *Joseph II* (London: Longmans, 1994), pp. 60–67.

8   'Of Friendship', in Bacon, *Collected Works*, VI/2, 437–43 (p. 438).

9   See the reflections on the fall of Lord Clarendon in Bishop Burnet, *History of His Own Times*,
Everyman's Library (London: Dent, 1906), p. 94.

10   Falstaff is strangely absent (perhaps because the word 'favourite' is not used of him) from Blair
Worden, 'Favourites on the English stage', in Elliott and Brockliss, *The World of the Favourite*, pp.
159–83.

a prince and his favourite was 'innately dysfunctional'.[11] A literary illustration can be found in Lessing's play *Emilia Galotti* (1772), where the tropes of courtly deceit and dissimulation are enthusiastically developed. It is set in the small Italian principality of Guastalla, ruled by Prince Hettore Gonzaga who is in turn governed by his favourite, the suave courtier Marinelli (a name evoking Machiavelli). The Prince, an irresponsible ruler and a womanizer inclined to sentimental self-pity, is enamoured of Emilia Galotti, the daughter of a prominent citizen. Odoardo Galotti, having fallen out with the court, lives mostly on his country estate, but has unwisely allowed his socially ambitious wife to remain in town, thus enabling the Prince to meet Emilia at a party. Emilia is about to marry Count Appiani, who shares her father's taste for rural virtue. The Prince gives Marinelli permission to thwart the marriage by any means and bring Emilia to his country house. Marinelli contrives for Emilia to be kidnapped and Appiani (who had previously insulted him) to be killed. The rape of Emilia is forestalled by the arrival of her parents and of the Prince's cast-off mistress Countess Orsina, and finally by Emilia herself. The Prince and Marinelli manage to handle Odoardo, a gruff soldier, who is out of his depth in a court setting and confused by their smooth manners. Seemingly trapped, Emilia persuades her father, when both are beside themselves with hysteria, to stab her. Discovering the corpse, the Prince puts all the blame on Marinelli, ordering him into perpetual exile.

Although there are no constitutional restraints on the Prince, his power is conditional and limited. He depends on Marinelli to do his dirty work, and while Marinelli depends for his position on the Prince, he is capable of dropping his mask of suavity in letting the Prince know who is really in command. The partnership between the Prince and Marinelli is threatened when Marinelli learns that instead of following his master-plan, the Prince has acted independently by accosting Emilia in church, thereby providing evidence that he is ultimately responsible for the murder of Appiani. At the high point of their confrontation, Marinelli reveals his contempt for the Prince by dropping the polite pronoun 'Sie', not for the intimate 'du' (used between parents and children), but for the crude 'er', a form of address used to servants and other inferiors, which cannot be rendered in English:

DER PRINZ   Rede will ich!

MARINELLI   Nun dann! Was läge an meinen Anstalten? daß den Prinzen bei diesem Unfalle ein so sichtbarer Verdacht trifft? — An dem Meisterstreiche liegt das, den er selbst meinen Anstalten mit einzumengen die Gnade hatte.

DER PRINZ   Ich?

MARINELLI   Er erlaube mir, ihm zu sagen, daß der Schritt, den er heute morgen in der Kirche getan — mit so vielem Anstande er ihn auch getan — so unvermeidlich er ihn auch tun mußte — , daß dieser Schritt dennoch nicht in den Tanz gehörte.[12]

11   James M. Boyden, '"Fortune has stripped you of your splendour": Favourites and their Fates in Fifteenth- and Sixteenth-Century Spain', in Elliott and Brockliss, *The World of the Favourite*, pp. 26–37 (p. 33).

12   *Emilia Galotti*, IV. 1, in Gotthold Ephraim Lessing, *Werke und Briefe*, ed. by Wilfried Barner and others, 12 vols (Frankfurt a.M.: Deutscher Klassiker Verlag, 1987–98), VII, 342.

PRINCE   Speak, I say!

MARINELLI   Very well then! What part of my plan was it that will cause such obvious suspicion to fall on the Prince in this matter? I will tell you: it was the master-stroke with which he himself was graciously pleased to interfere in my arrangements.

PRINCE   I?

MARINELLI   May I be permitted to tell you that the step you took this morning in the church — with whatever circumspection it was taken — however irresistibly you were driven to take it — that that step was nevertheless no part of this particular dance.[13]

Although the Prince is a bit slow on the uptake, it gradually sinks in that he has made a fatal blunder. Guastalla may have no constitution, and he may be above the law, but he still needs to worry about his reputation and public opinion. After this blunt, uncourtly exchange, Marinelli reverts to polite language, but in a transparently hollow manner. The machinery of court intrigue has broken down, and its unsightly inner workings have become visible. At the end, the Prince banishes Marinelli but leaves himself helpless.

The cluster of mostly negative associations surrounding Machiavelli's name, which I am calling 'Machiavellianism', was connected with changes in the vocabulary of political discussion. In the sixteenth century a significant cluster of words appears in English and French, and in the following century in German, broadly denoting politics. These words hover between a neutral, descriptive meaning and a pejorative one. Insofar as they tend to the latter, they are readily associated with Machiavelli and his real or supposed doctrines.

In the Middle Ages the adjective *politicus* was associated with republican as opposed to monarchical government. Hence Machiavelli still calls republican government 'il vero vivere politico' ('the true political way of life', D 1. 6).[14] In the later sixteenth century, however, its derivatives *policy*, *politic*, and *politique* acquired derogatory implications. They suggested expediency, cunning, deceit, and lack of scruple. Thus Shakespeare's Host of the Garter Inn asks: 'Am I politic? Am I subtle? Am I a Machiavel?' (*The Merry Wives of Windsor*, III. 1. 92), and an anonymous character in *Timon of Athens*, deploring the ingratitude shown to Timon by his beneficiaries, concludes:

> But I perceive
> Men must learn now with pity to dispense,
> For policy sits above conscience. (III. 2. 86–88)

In Jonson's *Sejanus*, the devious emperor Tiberius is described as 'a politic tyrant'.[15] The noun *politician* is generally pejorative. Bacon writes of 'worldlings and depraved

13   *Five German Tragedies*, trans. by F. J. Lamport (Harmondsworth: Penguin, 1969), p. 77.

14   Nicolai Rubinstein, 'The History of the Word *politicus* in Early Modern Europe', in *The Languages of Political Theory in Early Modern Europe*, ed. by Anthony Pagden (Cambridge: Cambridge University Press, 1987), pp. 41–56.

15   Act IV, line 474, in *The Complete Plays of Ben Jonson*, ed. by G. A. Wilkes, 4 vols (Oxford: Clarendon Press, 1981–82), II, 315.

politics [*sic*, anglicizing the noun *politique*], who are apt to contemn holy things'.[16] In Shakespeare, *politician* is always derogatory, for example, 'this vile politician, Bolingbroke' (*1 Henry IV*, I. 3. 241); 'a scurvy politician' (*King Lear*, IV. 6. 171).[17] Nathaniel Lee, who in 1679 brought 'Machiavel' on the stage as assistant to Cesare Borgia, has his master, displeased with the result of Machiavel's scheming, abuse him as a 'Pollititian'.[18]

In France, *la politique* was at first simply the study of government.[19] During the Wars of Religion, however, it became the label of those who advocated moderation, compromise, and reconciliation. The Holy Catholic League, directed by the Guise family, used *politique* as a term of particular detestation, accusing the *politiques* of contempt for religion. The lawyer and *politique* Étienne Pasquier (1529–1615) complained that opponents of the League were called 'sometimes politiques, sometimes Machiavellians, that is to say, completely without religion'.[20] In Corneille's *Othon* (1664), the consul Vinius insists that a 'saine Politique' ('sound policy', l. 241) is the only way he, his daughter Plautine, and her fiancé Othon can save their lives: the emperor Galba is weak, unscrupulous rivals concerned with their own affairs instead of the national interest ('raison d'État', l. 26) are converging on Rome, and to avoid their enmity, Othon must break with Plautine, woo Galba's niece Camille, and thus become Galba's appointed successor.[21] Here 'sound policy' means placing self-preservation ahead of either emotional loyalty or the public good.

Among German equivalents, *politisch* is sometimes neutral, sometimes tending towards the pejorative. Grimm's Dictionary gives an illustrative quotation from the satirist Aegidius Albertinus (1560–1620): 'an der jetzwehrenden politischen falschheit ist fürnehmlich jener ertzbub Machiavellus schuldig' ('present-day politic[al] falsehood is mainly the fault of that arch-villain Machiavelli').[22] Herder speaks neutrally of 'the politic spirit' ('der politische Geist') of Roman historians.[23] But the word unequivocally means 'crafty' when Goethe's Werther, having descended into paranoia, responds to Lotte's remonstrances with 'Politisch! sehr politisch!'[24]

16   'Of Unity in Religion', in Bacon, *Collected Works*, VI/2, 381–84 (p. 382),

17   Cf. also *Twelfth Night*, III. 2. 29: 'policy I hate; I had as lief be a Brownist [an extreme Puritan] as a politician'; *Hamlet*, V. 1. 80: 'the pate of a politician [...], one that would circumvent God'.

18   See *Caesar Borgia* in *The Works of Nathaniel Lee*, ed. by Thomas B. Stroup and Arthur L. Cooke, 2 vols (New Brunswick, NJ: The Scarecrow Press, 1954–55), II, 134.

19   See the quotations in Albert Cherel, *La pensée de Machiavel en France* (Paris: L'Artisan du Livre, 1935), p. 50.

20   Quoted in Holt, *French Wars*, p. 128.

21   Pierre Corneille, *Œuvres complètes*, ed. by Georges Couton, 3 vols, Bibliothèque de la Pléiade (Paris: Gallimard, 1980–87), III, 463–70.

22   Grimm gives no more specific reference, but the quotation may come from Albertinus's satire on court life, *Lucifers Königreich und Seelengejäidt* (1616): cf. Kiesel, *'Bei Hof, bei Höll'*, p. 148.

23   Johann Gottfried Herder, *Ideen zur Philosophie der Geschichte der Menschheit* (1784–91), in his *Werke*, ed. by Günter Arnold and others, 10 vols (Frankfurt a.M.: Deutscher Klassiker Verlag, 1985–2000), VI (1989), ed. by Martin Bollacher, p. 584. This edition is henceforth cited as Herder, *Werke*.

24   Johann Wolfgang Goethe, *Sämtliche Werke: Briefe, Tagebücher und Gespräche*, ed. by Friedmar Apel and others, 40 vols (Frankfurt a.M.: Deutscher Klassiker Verlag, 1986–2000), VIII: *Die Leiden des jungen Werthers, Die Wahlverwandtschaften, Kleine Prosa, Epen*, ed. by Waltraud Wiethölter (1994), pp. 220 and 221. This edition is henceforth cited as Goethe, *SW*.

A more neutral term for politics is *Staatskunst*, first recorded by Grimm in the writings of Kaspar Stieler (1632–1707). Schiller often uses it in a neutral sense, equivalent to 'Politik' or 'politics' in modern usage, as when he speaks in the *Geschichte des Abfalls der Niederlande* (*History of the Revolt of the Netherlands*, 1788) of 'die vernünftigste Staatskunst' (the most rational *Staatskunst*') and reproaches Cardinal Granvella because 'er fehlte gegen die Staatskunst' ('he made a mistake in *Staatskunst*').[25] Similarly, Christoph Martin Wieland, asserting that it is better to be the beloved ruler of a small country than the dreaded tyrant of a vast desert, describes this 'great truth' as the 'Grundpfeiler aller wahren Staatskunst' ('foundation of all true *Staatskunst*').[26] It acquires a negative tinge, however, when a bad ruler practises 'tyrannische Staatskunst'.[27] And it is emphatically negative when Friedrich Gottlob Klopstock (1724–1803), in his Biblical epic *Der Messias* (1748–73), makes a priest accuse Caiaphas of lying and add: 'so zeigst du dich deiner römischen Staatskunst | Und des erhandelten Priestertums würdig' ('Thus you show yourself worthy of your Roman statecraft and your venal priesthood').[28] Like the English 'statecraft', it easily becomes judgemental. So, even more readily, does *Staatsklugheit*, defined in Adelung's dictionary as 'prudentia politica'. Prudence easily moves towards cynical calculation, as when Herder says it is generally assumed that the Romans attached such importance to their religion out of *Staatsklugheit*.[29] Kant mostly uses the term with heavy irony, as when he speaks about 'aufgeklärten Begriffen der Staatsklugheit' ('enlightened conceptions of *Staatsklugheit*') and 'staatskluge Männer'.[30]

25 Schiller's works are quoted whenever possible from *Werke und Briefe*, Bibliothek deutscher Klassiker, ed. by Klaus Harro Hilzinger, later by Otto Dann and others, 12 vols (Frankfurt a.M.: Deutscher Klassiker Verlag, 1992–2005). This edition is henceforth cited as Schiller, *WB*. Here: *WB* VI: Historische Schriften I, ed. by Otto Dann (2000), pp. 128, 148. Letters are normally quoted from *Schillers Werke: Nationalausgabe*, ed. by Julius Petersen and others, 42 vols (Weimar: Hermann Böhlaus Nachfolger, 1943–2010), henceforth cited as *NA*.
26 Wieland, *Der goldne Spiegel* (1772), in *Wielands Gesammelte Schriften*, ed. by the Deutsche Kommission der Königlich Preußischen Akademie der Wissenschaften. 1. Abteilung: Werke, 23 vols (Berlin: Weidmannsche Buchhandlung, later Berlin: Akademie-Verlag, 1909–69), IX: *Der goldne Spiegel*, Singspiele und kleine Dichtungen 1772–1775, ed. by Wilhelm Kurrelmeyer (1931), p. 181.
27 Ibid., p. 192.
28 Friedrich Gottlieb Klopstock, *Ausgewählte Werke*, ed. by Karl August Schleiden, 2 vols (Munich: Hanser, 1981), I, 270 (4. Gesang, lines 117–18).
29 Herder, *Ideen*, in *Werke*, VI, 590.
30 Kant, *Zum ewigen Frieden*, in *Werke*, VI, 196, 233. H. B. Nisbet translates 'Staatsklugheit' as 'expediency': see *Kant: Political Writings*, p. 122 and *passim*.

7

Reason of State

In the later sixteenth century, the methods that Machiavelli recommended to his Prince came to be described as the principles of government suitable for absolutism. Absolutism is a heavily contested term. While Louis XIV, often regarded as the supreme and exemplary absolutist, was declared by his court preacher Bossuet to be God's anointed, this sacred conception of kingship was not found in the princely territories of the Holy Roman Empire, where the subject's duty of obedience was founded on the more general principle, formulated by St Paul, that 'the powers that be are ordained of God' (Romans 13:1). Nevertheless, Western and Central European rulers in the early modern period, and especially after the Thirty Years War, managed to achieve a monopoly of judicial, military, and tax-raising power, dominating the nobility either by formal negotiation with representative bodies (estates or *Landstände*) or by informal bargaining.[1] Thus their rule could be effectively absolute.

Absolute rulers, having dominion over large territories and obliged both to control rebellious nobles and to maintain relations with foreign powers, seldom found themselves in such a critical position as Florence at the beginning of the sixteenth century. The expedients that Machiavelli had recommended for an unstable situation or an emergency were now adopted as the inevitable art and craft of government. The term 'reason of state' came into common use. The intellectual historian Friedrich Meinecke finds a casual use in Machiavelli's friend and fellow-historian Guicciardini.[2] It occurs as a set phrase, apparently denoting a distinct concept, used by the papal nuncio Giovanni della Casa, who in 1547 deplores the current expression *ragion di stato* as a pretext for injustice and robbery.[3] The idea was most influentially formulated by the Jesuit Giovanni Botero (1540–1617) in his treatise *Della ragion di stato* (1589), which was rapidly translated into German, French, Spanish, and Latin. The term *ragion di stato*, however, is modelled on the earlier expression *ragion di guerra*, which acknowledged that war could license deceptions that were inadmissible in civil life. The word *ratio* or *ragione* could also mean 'enterprise' or 'business', as David Wootton has recently explained:

> So *ragion di stato* can sometimes mean the law of the state, as compared and contrasted to the laws of nature, of war, of the political community. But it can

1   On debates about absolutism, see Peter H. Wilson, *Absolutism in Central Europe* (London: Routledge, 2000); Duindam, *Dynasties*, pp. 17–18.

2   Friedrich Meinecke, *Machiavellism: The Doctrine of raison d'état and its Place in Modern History*, trans. by M. Douglas Scott (London: Routledge & Kegan Paul, 1957), p. 46; Meinecke, *Staatsräson*, p. 54.

3   Meinecke, *Machiavellism*, p. 47; *Staatsräson*, pp. 55–56.

also mean the business of politics: in Renaissance Italian the word *ragione* refers to a business enterprise, and to the embodiment of that enterprise in an account book. Thus the term *ragion di stato* would have had contemporaries thinking of politics as a business, just like the banking business in which the Medici had made their money. It is this last meaning which eventually gave rise in authors like Botero to an idea of *ragion di stato* as the rational choice made by politicians to maximize their power.[4]

Hence the term 'reason of state' tended to demystify politics, making it seem no longer based on divine ordinances but on human contrivance.

Although Machiavelli does not use the term 'reason of state', Meinecke calls him 'the first person to discover the real nature of *raison d'état*'.[5] Reason of state meant a conception of government as a self-contained and autonomous technique, an art of management, which could be studied and perfected. In this sense, 'reason of state' is a neutral term, like our word 'politics'. Its theorists were anxious to distance themselves from Machiavelli. They wanted to close the gap that Machiavelli had opened up between morality and pragmatism. They could not admit that a Christian prince might experience a conflict between the demands of the good and of the useful. If there appeared to be such a conflict, Christian moral values always had priority but always coincided with the best interests of the ruler.[6] The art of government might require rulers to override legal and even moral restraints, but advocates of reason of state insisted that this was itself a moral action in order to secure the well-being of the state.

The people entitled to practise reason of state were experts in government, qualified to handle the mysteries of statecraft. Such people were entitled to follow a double standard of morality. The virtues of private individuals were different from those permitted to rulers, as Augustus's consort Livia explains in Corneille's political play *Cinna* (1641). Whatever crimes Octavius committed during his ascent to power have been cancelled out since he became Augustus:

> Tous ces crimes d'Etat qu'on fait pour la couronne,
> Le ciel nous en absout alors qu'il nous la donne,
> Et dans le sacré rang où sa faveur l'a mis,
> Le passé devient juste, et l'avenir permis.[7]

> Heaven itself absolves us of the deeds
> Committed for the crown by crowning us,
> And in his sacred rank the past becomes
> Just, and the future is legitimate.[8]

4   Wootton, *Power, Pleasure and Profit*, p. 47.
5   Meinecke, *Machiavellism*, p. 41; *Staatsräson*, p. 49.
6   Wootton, *Power, Pleasure and Proft*, p. 48.
7   Corneille, *Cinna*, ll. 1609–12, in his *Œuvres complètes*, I, 964. For a formulation of this double standard, see Amelot de La Houssaie, quoted in Étienne Thuau, *Raison d'état et pensée politique à l'époque de Richelieu* (Paris: Armand Colin, 1966), p. 43.
8   Pierre Corneille, *The Cid, Cinna, The Theatrical Illusion*, trans. by John Cairncross (Harmondsworth: Penguin, 1975), p. 186. For Machiavellianism in Racine, especially in *Britannicus*, *Bajazet* and *Mithridate*, see Philip Butler, *Classicisme et baroque dans l'œuvre de Racine* (Paris: Nizet, 1959), pp. 176–202.

Such experts were quite different from the amoral, self-seeking prince described by Machiavelli. Their rule was sanctioned by heredity, tradition, and perhaps also by divine right, whereas Machiavelli's typical prince is a self-made man. In practice, however, the expert in government could look very like a 'Machiavellian' ruler.[9]

Botero defines *ragion di stato* innocuously: 'Reason of state is knowledge of the means suitable to found, conserve, and expand dominion.'[10] He reassures his readers that the use of force and fraud, and the political manipulation of religion, though wrong for ordinary mortals and in everyday life, are permissible for kings and ministers laden with the responsibility of government, and in this context perfectly in harmony with the teachings of the Church. Like the authors of mirrors for princes, he says that a prince must have *virtù*, consisting especially in justice, liberality, prudence, and valour.[11] The people should be kept content by abundant supplies and also distracted from rebellion by entertainments, such as the Greeks' Olympic and other games; the Roman gladiatorial spectacles were less effective because the spectators were passive and because the combats were excessively bloody.[12] In unwitting agreement with Shakespeare's Henry IV, Botero points out that a good way of diverting the people is by foreign wars: thus Spain, in contrast to France, is quiet, because its people are partly occupied in campaigns in America and the Low Countries.[13] In dealing with enemies, if they are heretics or infidels, all means are justified. For example, one should stir up factions and dissensions in enemy countries. This means adopting the methods used by one's enemies, but for a Christian purpose, which makes it all right. After all, Botero says: 'the pretended queen of England used this method — which we should use with enemies of the faith — with the Catholic king in Flanders and with the Most Christian King in France'.[14]

For the political theorists following in Botero's wake, 'reason of state' denotes a principle known only to the few people qualified to exercise power in an absolutist state. Divine and natural law remain sacrosanct. But policies pleasing to God always turn out to be those in the best interests of the ruler.[15] A Christian prince, as part of his duty to God, is entitled at times to override positive law, which is merely the law of man, and, when constrained by necessity, to perform actions which he may intensely dislike but which are unavoidable for the good of the state. Cicero's injunction '*salus populi suprema lex esto*', 'let the safety of the people be the supreme law', is often quoted.[16] Similarly, a ruler might need to practise deceit (*fraus*), which the Dutch political theorist Justus Lipsius (1547–1606) defined as 'an artful design departing from the way of virtue and the laws for the good of the king or

9   Meinecke, *Machiavellism*, pp. 135–38; *Staatsräson*, pp. 161–64.
10   Giovanni Botero, *The Reason of State*, ed. and trans. by Robert Bireley, Cambridge Texts in the History of Political Thought (Cambridge: Cambridge University Press, 2017), p. 4.
11   Ibid., pp. 18, 30, 34, 51.
12   Ibid., pp. 72–73.
13   Ibid., p. 75.
14   Ibid., p. 115.
15   Wootton, *Power, Pleasure, and Profit*, p. 48.
16   Cicero, *De legibus*, Book III, part 3, para. 3, in *De re publica, De legibus*, trans. by Clinton Walker Keyes, Loeb Classical Library (Cambridge, MA: Harvard University Press, 1928), p. 467.

the kingdom'.[17] Lipsius thought it justified, for example, for a ruler to persuade rebels to lay down their arms by making promises he did not intend to keep — the conduct, it will be remembered, of Prince John in the Gaultree Forest episode of *2 Henry IV*.[18] A ruler might be obliged by necessity to undertake political murders, as with the many attempts to infiltrate England in order to kill Elizabeth I, and, most appallingly, the massacre of St Bartholomew's Day in 1572.[19] He might even be obliged to kill his own son, as Philip II of Spain was said to have ordered the murder of his wayward son Don Carlos.[20] When undertaken for the public good, such an action was no longer wrong, but sanctioned by God.

Botero and his successors thus lose an essential component of Machiavelli's thought. Despite his posthumous reputation, Machiavelli, as argued earlier, is not an amoral writer. He does not deny or redefine the Christian virtues. As Isaiah Berlin points out:

> He transposes nothing: the things men call good are indeed good. Words like *buono, cattivo, onesto, inumano* etc. are used by him as they were in the common speech of his time, and indeed of our own. He merely says that the practice of those virtues makes it impossible to build a society which, once it is contemplated, in the pages of history or by the political imagination, will surely awaken in us — in any man — a great longing.[21]

'Reason of state' writers, following Botero, hold that actions performed for the public good may be difficult and unpleasing, but they can never be contrary to the will of God. Hence actions that are normally wrong can in exceptional circumstances become right. Thus Botero, in being prepared to annul the difference between right and wrong at the supposed command of God or the monarch, actually shows the amorality with which Machiavelli was so often charged.

Nevertheless, 'reason of state' formalizes the distinction between public and private morality introduced by Machiavelli. Machiavelli's most notorious chapter, 'How rulers should keep their promises', points out, drawing on copious experience, that the most successful rulers in recent times have repeatedly broken their word and deceived others. 'One could give countless modern examples [to] show how many peace treaties and promises have been rendered null and void by the faithlessness of rulers; and those best able to imitate the fox have succeeded best' (*P* XVIII. 62). Machiavelli does not claim that deception is ever right: he is explicit that this is 'the path of wrongdoing' but that the requirements of government often make it necessary. He is talking specifically about princes. A moment's reflection shows that civil life would break down if deception were frequent; no business agreement, for example, could ever be concluded. But public life, where the stakes are very high, often demands a different standard of conduct.

17 Quoted in Robert Bireley, SJ, *The Counter-Reformation Prince: Anti-Machiavellianism or Catholic Statecraft in Early Modern Europe* (Chapel Hill, NC: University of North Carolina Press, 1990), p. 85.
18 Ibid., p. 86.
19 These and other examples are discussed in Walter Platzhoff, *Die Theorie von der Mordbefugnis der Obrigkeit im XVI. Jahrhundert* (Berlin: Ebering, 1906), a study often cited by Meinecke.
20 Meinecke, *Staatsräson*, p. 97; details in J. H. Elliott, *Imperial Spain 1469–1716* (London: Arnold, 1963), pp. 245–46.
21 Berlin, 'The Originality of Machiavelli', pp. 48–49.

The literature of 'reason of state' flourished in Italy between the 1590s and the 1630s. Thereafter it was taken up by German writers. In the German-speaking world, a striking example of 'reason of state' in practice was the assassination of Albrecht von Wallenstein, the general commanding the imperial forces in the middle portion of the Thirty Years War. Wallenstein was a talented and independent-minded general who raised a private army at his own expense and placed it at the disposal of the Habsburgs. Because of his insubordination, he was dismissed from his command in 1630, but the invasion of Germany by a Swedish force under Gustavus Adolphus obliged the emperor and his advisers to recall him. After a narrow defeat by the Swedes in the battle of Lützen (1632) where Gustavus Adolphus was killed, Wallenstein aroused his employers' mistrust by failing to renew his offensive. Instead, he was suspected, with considerable reason, of negotiating with the Swedes in order to place the Habsburgs under pressure and extort a kingdom for himself in Bohemia. In February 1634 he was assassinated at the instigation of the emperor and with the support of the latter's confessor, the Jesuit Wilhelm Lamormaini.[22] These events will concern us again in a later chapter which examines their treatment by Schiller in his *Wallenstein* trilogy. Their importance at present is that Wallenstein's murder provided a conspicuous and much-discussed instance of reason of state in action, in which higher necessity overrode moral constraints.[23]

In the seventeenth century the case for reason of state was made by theorists in Germany, though they added little to the ideas of their Italian and French predecessors. The earliest, Arnold Clapmar (1574–1604), a prodigy who was appointed professor of politics and history at the University of Altdorf at the age of 26, wrote *De arcanis rerum publicarum*, published posthumously in 1605. It associates political knowledge with sacred mysteries and thus suits theorists of absolutism and kingship by divine right.[24] As the Italian theorists had distinguished good reason of state, concerned for the public well-being, from bad and selfish Machiavellianism, so Clapmar, adopting legal terms, explained reason of state as a law of domination (*jus dominationis*) which overrode the law of the land. Clapmar defines *arcana* as 'the private or hidden procedures or counsels of those who would obtain power in a state, sometimes for the purpose of maintaining its tranquillity, sometimes for conserving the present form of its government, for the public good'.[25] Good reason of state may require the ruler to transgress ordinary law and morality; acts that would be condemned as fraud in a private individual may be permissible for the public good. The ruler may even manipulate the appearance of the supernatural in order to control the people. A later theorist, Johann Elias Kessler (1644–1726), developed the argument that a good prince must sometimes do what in a private individual would be accounted evil, and explains that a prince must choose the lesser of two evils. It may seem evil, for example, to enslave a conquered population, and it is certainly

22   See Geoff Mortimer, *Wallenstein: The Enigma of the Thirty Years War* (Basingstoke: Palgrave, 2010).

23   Meinecke, *Machiavellism*, p. 129; *Staatsräson*, p. 153.

24   Donaldson, *Machiavelli*, pp. 122–23; Meinecke, *Machiavellism*, pp. 130–34; *Staatsräson*, pp. 155–58.

25   Quoted in Donaldson, *Machiavelli*, p. 124.

in conflict with natural law; but compared with the genocide frequently practised by the Romans, it is relatively humane.[26]

In the age of absolutism, some political thinkers, beginning with Botero, coupled Machiavelli with the Roman historian Tacitus (c. 56–128 CE) as analysts of the workings of power.[27] Especially in his *Annals*, dealing with the early Roman emperors from Tiberius to Nero, Tacitus offered striking analogies to the present age, in which the Italian republics (except for Venice) had been replaced by despotic princely rule. The Florentine scholar Thomas Sertinus wrote in 1541: 'no historian is superior to Tacitus, either in terms of the resemblance to our own times or in the gravity of his reflections and his skillful analysis of courtly ways'.[28] Comparing him favourably to the moralist Seneca, Montaigne wrote: 'Tacitus can more properly serve a sickly troubled nation such as our own is at present: you could often believe that we were the subject of his narrating and berating.'[29] And the anticlerical humanist Guy Patin (1601–72) wrote of Richelieu, Louis XIII's all-powerful minister: 'Cardinal Richelieu read and practised Tacitus a great deal. That is why he was such a terrible man.'[30]

Along with the author of *The Prince*, Tacitus was considered the best guide to what he called the *arcana imperii*, the secrets of rule.[31] He showed not how rulers should behave but how they actually did behave, especially at their worst with the emperors Tiberius and Nero. Tacitus described how Augustus established his empire, leaving the names of republican institutions such as the Senate intact but draining them of real power and maintaining only the illusion of power (the *simulacra imperii*).[32] He described Augustus's adoptive son and successor Tiberius as a master of dissimulation, who could invite someone to dinner while planning to make him the victim of a show trial.[33] Those around Tiberius treated him with such sycophancy that Tiberius himself despised them, and was heard to exclaim in

---

26   Meinecke, *Machiavellism*, p. 137; *Staatsräson*, p. 163.

27   Botero, *Reason of State*, pp. 1–2; Bireley, *The Counter-Reformation Prince*, p. 50.

28   Quoted in [Anthony Grafton], 'Tacitus and Tacitism', in *The Classical Tradition*, ed. by Anthony Grafton, Glenn W. Most, and Salvatore Settis (Cambridge, MA: Harvard University Press, 2010), p. 921.

29   'On the Art of Conversation', in Michel de Montaigne, *The Complete Essays*, trans. by M. A. Screech (London: Penguin, 2003), p. 1066 (translation modified).

30   Quoted in Thuau, *Raison d'état*, p. 44, and in Elliott, *Richelieu and Olivares*, p. 24. The translation of Tacitus' *Annals* by Perrot d'Ablancourt, published in 1640, was dedicated to Richelieu (Thuau, pp. 40–41).

31   *Annals*, II. 36, in Tacitus, *The Histories*, Books IV–V, trans. by Clifford H. Moore; *The Annals*, Books I–III, trans. by John Jackson (Cambridge, MA: Harvard University Press, 1959), p. 436; translated as 'the arcana of sovereignty', ibid., pp. 437, and as 'the whole unspoken premises of autocracy' in Tacitus, *The Annals of Imperial Rome*, trans. by Michael Grant, rev. edn (London: Penguin, 1996), p. 94. See Donaldson, *Machiavelli*, p. viii; Alexandra Gajda, 'Tacitus and Political Thought in Early Modern Europe, c. 1530–c. 1640', in *The Cambridge Companion to Tacitus*, ed. by A. J. Woodman (Cambridge: Cambridge University Press, 2010), pp. 253–68 (p. 258).

32   Donaldson, *Machiavelli*, pp. 136–37. Cf. the analysis of Augustus's procedure in Gibbon, *Decline and Fall*, I, 187.

33   Tacitus, *Annals*, trans. by Grant, p. 90; cf. pp. 125, 140.

Greek, on leaving the Senate, 'Men fit to be slaves!'[34] The only way to survive in such a state was to practise dissimulation oneself, and here Tacitus's *Annals* could be read as a survival manual. Tacitus's Tiberius was frequently compared to a more recent dissembler, the notoriously wily Louis XI of France, who was often quoted as saying: 'qui nescit dissimulare, nescit regnare', 'he who does not know how to dissimulate does not know how to reign'.[35]

Writing a century after the reign of Tiberius, Tacitus does not condone his cruelty, but neither does he waste time in moralizing about it. In addition, Tacitus offered many instances of rigorous reason of state at work. Thus, when a master has been murdered by a slave, the senator Gaius Cassius Longinus overrides his colleagues' humane hesitancy by advising them to follow the ancient custom of killing all the slaves living under the same roof: 'Exemplary punishment always contains an element of injustice. But individual wrongs are outweighed by the advantage of the community.'[36] The early seventeenth century saw a whole genre of commentaries on Tacitus which used his works as handbooks of reason of state.[37] They had available an important edition of Tacitus's writings, published in 1574 and made, appropriately, by the 'reason of state' theorist Lipsius.[38]

How much did the 'reason of state' theorists affect the actual conduct of politics? Did they provide guidance for rulers to follow, or did they simply justify rulers' actions retrospectively? It is well attested that those with the responsibility for government studied history, as Richelieu did Tacitus, and thus learnt from primary sources.[39] But it is less likely that anyone prepared for a stroke of policy by examining Lipsius's distinction among degrees of deceit and deciding how far to go. Dissimulation and deception, after all, are inevitable in politics. 'Reason of state' might also have sounded unappealingly cynical as an explicit justification of one's policy. When Richelieu justified his actions, he referred to 'necessity'.[40] This too harks back to Machiavelli, who says in *The Prince*: 'a ruler who wishes to maintain his power must be prepared to act immorally when this becomes necessary' (*P* xv, 55).

34   Ibid., p. 150.
35   Quoted e.g. in Botero, *Reason of State*, p. 101; see Bireley, *The Counter-Reformation Prince*, p. 86.
36   Tacitus, *Annals*, trans. Grant, p. 334.
37   See Gajda, 'Tacitus and Political Thought'; Peter Burke, 'Tacitism', in *Tacitus*, ed. by T. A. Dorey (London: Routledge & Kegan Paul, 1969), pp. 149–71; Malcolm Smuts, 'Court-Centred Politics and the Uses of Roman Historians c. 1590–1630', in *Culture and Politics in Early Stuart England*, ed. by Kevin Sharpe and Peter Lake (Basingstoke: Macmillan, 1994), pp. 21–43.
38   Gajda, 'Tacitus and Political Thought', pp. 259–61.
39   See Thuau, *Raison d'état*, pp. 34–35.
40   Elliott, *Richelieu and Olivares*, p. 121.

8

Machiavelli Obsolete?

The Thirty Years War was ended by the Treaty of Westphalia, which strengthened the power of the territorial princes within the Empire, as opposed to the free cities. Hermann Conring (1606–81), professor of politics at the University of Helmstedt, applied Machiavelli to this situation. In his commentary on his Latin translation of *The Prince* (1661), which treated Machiavelli's text simply as political analysis without showing any concern about its irreligion, Conring argued that Machiavelli exaggerated the value of liberty, which made cities unstable, and also, by overstating the severity required of a prince, assimilated the prince to the tyrant. But tyranny, as the example of Cromwell had recently shown, was also unstable.[1] *The Prince* was therefore a stimulating but misguided political text, belonging to its time and ill adapted to the new world of responsible absolute government.

With Conring, we can see the beginning of a change in the reception of Machiavelli. Henceforth he was increasingly seen as a man of his time. The *Discourses* were still a major political work, but the lessons of *The Prince* were no longer relevant and no longer shocking. It could be read as a factual description of how princes behaved, or as a satire warning readers against them. It would still call forth angry attempts at refutation, the best known being the *Anti-Machiavel* of Frederick the Great of Prussia. But on the whole Machiavelli did not have very much to say to the Enlightenment.

Conring's students at Helmstedt included Christian Weise (1642–1708), who for many years was headmaster of the *Gymnasium* (grammar-school) at Zittau in Saxony, and became well known as a political writer and dramatist. As a political writer, Weise released the obligatory broadside against Machiavelli (occasioned not by *The Prince* but by Machiavelli's biography of Castruccio Castracani).[2] As a headmaster, he wrote comedies for the schoolboys to perform, thereby continuing the Silesian tradition of school drama which originated as a riposte to the Jesuit practice of writing plays on sacred subjects to be acted by schoolboys. Weise's comedies include *Bäurischer Machiavellus* (*Peasant Machiavelli*, 1679). In the prologue, a heavenly court, with Apollo presiding, arraigns 'Machiavellus' for corrupting the world by teaching deception. The prosecution is led by 'Gentilletus', who asserts that the massacre of St Bartholomew would not have happened if the statesmen of that time had not read Machiavelli more attentively than they did the Bible. Machiavelli retorts that many

1   Noah Dauber, 'Anti-Machiavellism as Constitutionalism: Hermann Conring's Commentary on Machiavelli's *The Prince*', *History of European Ideas*, 37 (2011), 102–12 (p. 109).
2   Christian Weise, *Der Nothwendigen Gedancken Andrer Theil*, in his *Sämtliche Werke*, ed. by John D. Lindberg, 21 vols (Berlin: De Gruyter, 1971–78), XXI, 517.

murders and massacres took place before his book appeared, instancing the Sicilian Vespers (the massacre of 3,000 French men and women at Easter 1282 which began the Sicilian rebellion against French rule). He claims that *The Prince* was a satire, and regrets not making it obvious that he disagreed with the doctrines presented:

> For although I wanted to expose the customary tyranny of the Italian princes to the whole world through a work of satire, I would have done better not to appear so serious in my book, as though I were presenting a definite opinion.[3]

The main action of the play consists of intrigues surrounding the appointment of a village official, showing that cunning and malice are deeply rooted in human nature, and thus partially exonerating Machiavelli. Having received a mild punishment, he asks the public to regard him as a warning example of 'someone who in his life did not scruple to make a scandalous misuse of the finest intellectual powers'.[4]

Readers of Machiavelli in the eighteenth century generally agreed that *The Prince* was irrelevant to present-day politics. Thus David Hume, in his essay 'Of Civil Liberty', argued that Machiavelli's maxims no longer apply in an age of civilized monarchy, when stability is guaranteed by the laws alone and the personal abilities of the sovereign are of minor importance. Hence 'there is scarcely any maxim in his *Prince* which subsequent experience has not entirely refuted'.[5] Montesquieu agreed, on the grounds that the modern rule of law made it unnecessary to practise Machiavellian duplicity: 'One has begun to be cured of Machiavellianism, and one will continue to be cured of it.'[6] Similarly, Tacitus was reinterpreted. Instead of an apologist for tyranny, or even a neutral analyst of it, he became an enemy of tyrants and a lover of liberty: that was how he was presented by the Scottish republican and Whig publicist Thomas Gordon (*c.* 1691–1750), whose translation of Tacitus became standard in later eighteenth-century Britain.[7]

Machiavelli was still admired as a political thinker, but mainly on the strength of the *Discourses*. The German traveller and writer Johann Kaspar Riesbeck (1754–86) thought that to conduct politics in accordance with *The Prince* was 'wretched folly, first practised by some Italian politicians because they had misunderstood Machiavelli's *Prince*, which that great writer himself thoroughly and clearly refuted in his *Discourses on Livy*'.[8] Diderot, Rousseau and Schiller likewise read *The*

---

3   Christian Weise, *Bäurischer Machiavellus*, ed. by Werner Schubert (Berlin: De Gruyter, 1966), p. 19.

4   Ibid., p. 100.

5   David Hume, 'Of Civil Liberty', in his *Essays Moral, Political and Literary*, ed. by Eugene F. Miller (Indianapolis: Liberty Fund, 1987), pp. 87–96 (p. 88). See further Duncan Forbes, *Hume's Philosophical Politics* (Cambridge: Cambridge University Press, 1975), p. 160.

6   Montesquieu, *The Spirit of the Laws*, ed. and trans. by Anne M. Cohler, Basia C. Miller, and Harold S. Stone, Cambridge Texts in the History of Political Thought (Cambridge: Cambridge University Press, 1989), Book 21, ch. 20, p. 389.

7   See Thuau, *Raison d'état*, p. 51. Gordon's essays on Tacitus were published in French translation at Amsterdam in 1742.

8   Johann Kaspar Riesbeck, *Briefe eines reisenden Franzosen über Deutschland* (Zurich, 1783; repr. Stuttgart: Steingrüben, 1967), pp. 51–52.

Prince as a satire.[9] Rousseau thought that Machiavelli only pretended to praise his 'detestable hero' Cesare Borgia in order to show satirically how bad despotism was and thus indirectly to praise republican liberty, so that *The Prince* was 'the book of Republicans'.[10]

The best-known opponent of 'Machiavellianism' was Frederick the Great, thanks to his *Anti-Machiavel*. Originally written in 1739 as *Réfutation du prince de Machiavel*, revised with help from Voltaire and published as the *Anti-Machiavel* in 1740, it is a chapter-by-chapter rejoinder to Machiavelli, in which the French translation of *The Prince* by Amelot de la Houssaie is printed side by side with Frederick's text. Frederick contrasts the unscrupulous prince described by Machiavelli with the upright and responsible monarch evoked in Fénelon's fictionalized manual for princes, *Télémaque* (1699), and with Frederick's own ideal of the prince as the first servant of his people. In attacking Machiavelli, however, Frederick bears witness to the latter's popularity. His preface begins by denouncing Machiavelli for corrupting politics as Spinoza corrupted religion; but while theologians have (in Frederick's view) seen off Spinoza, moralists have failed to reduce Machiavelli's authority: 'in spite of them and his pernicious morality, [he] has maintained his reputation in political science up until our own times'.[11]

Frederick's high moral tone has often distracted readers from noticing how far his political recommendations are in fact based on interest, and hence pragmatic. Rather than preaching an impractical idealism, like so many 'mirrors for princes', Frederick tries 'to define an enlightened form of reason of state'.[12] He rejects the arguments of *The Prince* not only because they are wicked, but also because they are obsolete. Machiavelli was writing about an Italy divided into small, competing principalities where power was constantly changing hands; modern Europe, by contrast, consists of a number of large and relatively stable states. Since the Peace of Utrecht in 1713, which ended the War of the Spanish Succession and therewith the threat of a French universal monarchy, no state has been strong enough to dominate the others. Machiavelli gave all his attention to military matters, none to commerce, but a modern ruler needs to build up a commercial state, since commerce is the essential foundation not only for prosperity but also for the arts and sciences.

9   Diderot, 'Machiavélisme', in *Encyclopédie*, IX, 793; Jean-Jacques Rousseau, *The Social Contract and the Discourses*, trans. by G. D. H. Cole, rev. by J. H. Brumfitt and John C. Hall, Everyman's Library (London: David Campbell, 1973), p. 242; Schiller, letter to F. W. J. Schelling, 12 May 1801, *WB* XII, 569.

10   Rousseau, *The Social Contract*, p. 242.

11   'Anti-Machiavel, or a Study of Machiavelli's *The Prince*', in *Frederick the Great's Political Writings*, ed. by Avi Lifschitz, trans. by Angela Scholar (Princeton: Princeton University Press, 2021), p. 13. For the original, see *L'Anti-Machiavel, par Frédéric II, roi de Prusse, édition critique avec les remaniements de Voltaire par les deux versions*, ed. by Charles Fleischauer (= Studies in Voltaire and the Eighteenth Century, 5; Geneva: Institut et Musée Voltaire, 1958), p. 169.

12   Isaac Nakhimovsky, 'The Enlightened Prince and the Future of Europe: Voltaire and Frederick the Great's Anti-Machiavel of 1740', in *Commerce and Peace in the Enlightenment*, ed. by Béla Kapossy, Isaac Nakhimovsky, and Richard Whatmore (Cambridge: Cambridge University Press, 2017), pp. 44–77 (p. 46).

Frederick strengthens his argument by pointing out that pragmatism, as well as virtue, requires a prince to gain the affection of his subjects. The wise prince will make his people happy, because a contented populace will not rebel. Responding to Machiavelli's chapter on whether it is better to be loved or feared, Frederick maintains that a prince should not rule by fear. Admittedly, an army needs severity, because soldiers, who are often scoundrels and debauchees, need to be restrained by fear of punishments. But a king who rules by fear will turn his people into slaves, from whom nothing but mediocre achievements can be expected, whereas a king who is loved by his people will thereby bring out the best in them:

> I would suggest that every king whose policies have no purpose other than that of inspiring fear will only reign over cowards and slaves; that he will not be able to expect great acts from his subjects, because everything that is inspired by fear and timidity has always had this outcome.[13]

Frederick denounces Machiavelli's comparison of the prince to a lion and a fox, maintaining that even from the standpoint of interest, princes should keep their word, because one act of deception will deny them the confidence of the other princes. Deceit is bad policy, because people will soon stop trusting you. A prince may have to break treaties, but only in extreme circumstances, if 'the safety of his people, and overwhelming necessity, oblige him to do so'.[14]

In Frederick's view, a prince owes his position not to divine right, but to a kind of utilitarian social contract. The sovereign must put aside every other interest and devote himself to the well-being and happiness of the people he governs. He is less their master than their servant: 'the sovereign, far from being the absolute master of the people who are under his domination, is himself only their first servant' (*le premier domestique*).[15] Voltaire changed 'domestique' to 'le premier magistrat', perhaps because the original formulation seemed too humble; but the replacement of 'servant' by 'magistrate' still made the king, as conceived by Frederick, a functionary in the service of his people as opposed to a divinely appointed ruler.

Although the *Anti-Machiavel* envisages a peaceful and prosperous reign, Frederick necessarily devotes some space to the conduct of war. He actually agrees with Machiavelli that a prince should lead his troops himself; this was becoming unusual in the eighteenth century (another exception being George II of Britain, who led his troops at Dettingen in 1743), but Frederick's military prowess, especially in the Seven Years War, would prove essential to his contemporary reputation. He deplores the conduct of earlier princes (not only Machiavelli's princelings, but above all Louis XIV) who waged war only for their own glory. 'War, in general, is such a fertile source of misfortune, its issue so uncertain, and its consequences so ruinous for a country, that a prince could not reflect long enough before engaging in warfare.'[16] This passage must have rung particularly hollow for readers who noticed how quickly and decisively, after the death of the Holy Roman Emperor

13   'Anti-Machiavel', p. 49; *L'Anti-Machiavel*, p. 276.
14   'Anti-Machiavel', p. 53; *L'Anti-Machiavel*, p. 283.
15   'Anti-Machiavel', p. 15; *L'Anti-Machiavel*, p. 175.
16   'Anti-Machiavel', p. 81; *L'Anti-Machiavel*, p. 352.

Charles VI in 1740, Frederick moved to seize Silesia from his daughter Maria Theresia, who succeeded him on the imperial throne.

Nevertheless, Frederick continues, some wars are justified: not only those fought in self-defence, but also offensive wars which are intended to forestall a greater evil. They may be undertaken to prevent a leading state from becoming all-powerful (Louis XIV's geopolitical aspirations were still remembered), and Frederick seems to regret that the nations eventually conquered by the Romans did not first unite to prevent the growth of the Roman Empire. These preventive wars need to be undertaken at an opportune time, not when one is facing a threat from an overwhelming enemy. In justifying them, Frederick adopts a characteristically sanctimonious tone: 'Wars, therefore, which have no other aims than to repulse usurpers, to maintain legitimate rights, to guarantee universal freedom, and to avoid the oppression and violence of ambitious men will, all of them, be just wars.'[17] The moralistic rhetoric thinly disguises the actual pragmatism of Frederick's programme.[18] He has thus reserved the option of going to war without provocation whenever he believes it to be in his country's interest. And arguably his invasion of Silesia, though it involved a breach of faith, was in the national interest. Brandenburg-Prussia was still a second-rate power. If Frederick had remained inactive, the rich resources of Silesia, and the feeble condition of the Habsburg armies, might well have tempted another state to move in, most likely Saxony, which, being under the same ruler as Poland, would have almost encircled Frederick's domains.[19]

Frederick's contemporaries felt that the programme for benevolent rule, set out with such rhetorical force in the *Anti-Machiavel*, was difficult to reconcile with the succession of wars that dominated his reign from 1740 to 1763. Later, Frederick's military career found many admirers, notably Johann Wilhelm Ludwig Gleim with his bellicose *Kriegslieder* (1757), but also criticism, restrained by prudence. Referring to Frederick's invasion of Saxony which began the Seven Years War, Lessing suggested, in Aesopian language, that Frederick was a tiger who had attacked the flock of the unsuspecting shepherd (i.e. the ruler of Saxony).[20] Herder too, in 1769, found that Frederick's principles contradicted his practice: 'That he follows Machiavelli, although he has refuted him.'[21]

Now that *The Prince* seemed too dated to be shocking, it was possible to appreciate Machiavelli for his merits as a writer. Adam Smith in 1790 praises Machiavelli for 'that pure, elegant and simple language which distinguishes all his writings'.[22] The

17 'Anti-Machiavel', p. 80; *L'Anti-Machiavel*, p. 349.
18 See Theodor Schieder, *Frederick the Great*, ed. and trans. by Sabina Berkeley and H. M. Scott (London: Longman, 2000), p. 79. Schieder reads the *Anti-Machiavel* as a political manifesto for Frederick's reign (pp. 75–83). Contrast Nakhimovsky, 'The Enlightened Prince', p. 44.
19 See Christopher Clark, *Iron Kingdom: The Rise and Downfall of Prussia 1600–1947* (London: Allen Lane, 2006), pp. 192–93; Tim Blanning, *Frederick the Great, King of Prussia* (London: Allen Lane, 2015), pp. 75–77; Nakhimovsky, 'The Enlightened Prince', p. 46.
20 H. B. Nisbet, *Gotthold Ephraim Lessing, His Life, Works, and Thought* (Oxford: Oxford University Press, 2013), p. 234.
21 Herder, *Werke*, IX/2: *Journal meiner Reise im Jahr 1769; Pädagogische Schriften*, ed. by Rainer Wisbert (1997), p. 71.
22 Adam Smith, *The Theory of Moral Sentiments* (revised edition of 1790), ed. by D. D. Raphael and

Berlin Enlightener Friedrich Nicolai tells in his account of his travels in southern Germany and Austria how his friend Johann Nicolaus Meinhard, on arriving in Vienna in 1763, had his copy of the works of Machiavelli confiscated.[23] He applied to Gerard van Swieten, chair of the commission on censorship, hoping at least that the books would be kept till he left Vienna, but van Swieten told him that they had already been burnt, and reproached him for reading Machiavelli. Later, in Klagenfurt, Meinhard found another edition of Machiavelli, which he took to Rome. There his books were again confiscated, but were returned to him next day by a papal secretary, a Dominican, who declared that Machiavelli was 'one of our best authors'; he told Meinhard that as a scholar he could be trusted to be discreet in reading Machiavelli, and recommended a better edition.[24]

The Enlightenment attitude to Machiavelli is summed up in a sympathetic appreciation given in the 1790s by Herder. He defends Machiavelli against his detractors by locating him firmly in his own time:

> How much has been said about Machiavelli's *Prince*, and yet I doubt if it has reached any clear result, some people considering the book a satire, others a pernicious manual, others a foolish, indecisive mixture of both. And Machiavelli was certainly no fool; he was experienced in the study of history and in the ways of the world, and also an honest man, a sharp observer, and a warm friend to his fatherland. His *Decades on Livy* show that he knew the merits and the form of many different kinds of state, and every one of his other works, as well as the life he led till his old age, proves that he had no desire to be a traitor to humanity. What then accounts for the misunderstanding of this particular text by an author who wrote so clearly, elegantly and beautifully? [...] I suspect the entire misunderstanding results from failure to notice the precise relation in that age between politics and morality.[25]

Herder goes on to explain that in Machiavelli's day, and for a long time afterwards, politics and morality were wholly separate, while religion was regarded as a political instrument, and politics was dominated by reason of state. In *The Prince*, therefore, Machiavelli was telling people that if they must practise reason of state, then they should do it effectively:

> 'If this is your trade,' he says in effect, 'then learn it properly, so that you don't remain such wretched bunglers as I can show you to be now and in the past. All you can think of is *power* and *reputation*; very well, then at least employ the *prudence* that can lead you to secure power and Italy ultimately to peace. I didn't give you your job, but if you do it, do it properly.' Every impartial observer will feel that this is the attitude throughout Machiavelli's book.[26]

A. L. Macfie (Oxford: Clarendon Press, 1976), p. 217.

23   Meinhard (1727–67) was then travelling as tutor to a nobleman, Graf Moltke. He made his name by publishing *Versuch über den Charakter und die Werke der besten italiänischen Dichter* (1763), which was praised by Lessing in the *Literaturbriefe*: see Lessing, *Werke und Briefe*, IV, 771–77.

24   Friedrich Nicolai, *Beschreibung einer Reise durch Deutschland und die Schweiz im Jahre 1781. Nebst Bemerkungen über Gelehrsamkeit, Industrie, Religion und Sitten*, 8 vols (Berlin and Stettin: no pub., 1783–87), IV, 854–55.

25   Herder, *Briefe zu Beförderung der Humanität*, in *Werke*, VII, ed. by Hans Dietrich Irmscher (1991), p. 340.

26   Ibid., p. 341.

According to Herder, Machiavelli observes princes and their behaviour with the neutral eye of a zoologist describing members of a particular species, just as coolly as he analyses various forms of government in the *Discourses*. *The Prince* is therefore neither a satire nor a textbook of morals, but 'a *purely political masterpiece for Italian princes of that time, written according to their taste and their principles, with the purpose of freeing Italy from the barbarians*'.[27] And anyway, Herder assures us, very similar things were said by no less than St Thomas Aquinas.[28]

27   Ibid. (author's italics).
28   This mischievous hint is worth following up. Herder knew the Aquinas passage from finding it quoted by the learned libertine writer Gabriel Naudé (1600–53) in the opening chapter of his *Considérations politiques sur les coups d'estat* (1639). Here Naudé excuses himself for writing a book on *coups d'état* on the grounds that one must know about political wickedness in order to prevent it. Hence Aristotle in the *Politics* sets out the precepts on which not only good but also bad forms of government (tyranny, oligarchy, ochlocracy) are founded; and Aquinas, in his commentary on Aristotle, having denounced tyranny, presents in detail the rules which a tyrant must follow in order to establish his power. Thus the tyrant must kill all the powerful, rich, and intelligent people among his subjects, and stir up conflict among the rest. Aquinas also says — here sounding very 'Machiavellian' — that a tyrant must practise hypocrisy and appear to have virtues even if he does not possess them: 'Si non habeat virtutes secundum veritatem, faciat ut opinentur ipsum habere eas.' Remarking that these are strange sentiments coming from a saint, Naudé surmises that Aquinas wrote them in order to forewarn potential victims of tyranny, and perhaps also to tell tyrants how to avoid indiscriminate bloodshed.

9

Machiavelli as Exemplary Patriot:
From Hegel to Bollmann

Machiavelli's ideas assumed new relevance in the wake of the wars between France and the Central European powers which were suspended by a series of peace treaties in the 1790s. Though formally parts of the Holy Roman Empire, a number of states made separate peace treaties with France, thereby indicating that the Empire no longer acted as a unified body. It was agreed that the fate of the Empire should be decided at the Congress of Rastatt (1797–99) where representatives of France and the Empire would negotiate. During the Congress, war again broke out between France and the Empire. In response, an imperial deputation produced a 'final report', the *Reichsdeputationshauptschluss*, which proposed a reorganization of the Empire. It was signed into law by the emperor on 27 April 1803. It abolished a large number of the small and medium-sized territories of the Empire, including all but six of the imperial free cities and all but three of the ecclesiastical territories. On 12 July 1806 Napoleon set up the Confederation of the Rhine (*Rheinbund*), consisting of sixteen states (later joined by twenty-three more) which were to form a buffer zone separating France from Austria and Russia. Under pressure from Napoleon, Francis II agreed to abdicate as Holy Roman Emperor. The Empire was formally dissolved on 6 August 1806.[1] Two years earlier, in response to Napoleon's coronation as French Emperor, Francis had declared himself emperor of the Habsburgs' German-speaking lands, Hungary, and Galicia. He thus brought into being the Austrian Empire, which, known after 1867 as Austria-Hungary, would last until 1918 with the aid of a carefully cultivated 'Habsburg myth'.

The fragmentation of German-speaking countries suggested an analogy with Italy in Machiavelli's time. Then, as later, a politically fragmented region of Europe had been vulnerable to French invasion. Napoleon was now playing the part assumed by Charles VIII in 1494. Some commentators thought the Empire could still survive, perhaps as a federation of states or as a revival of the medieval empire. One observer, however, the young philosopher Hegel, drew from Machiavelli the lesson that nothing could save the German territories except unification under a strong leader. In an essay on the imperial constitution, written in 1799–1800 but published only after his death, Hegel argued that Germany's condition was even

---

[1]   On these events, see James J. Sheehan, *German History 1770–1866* (Oxford: Oxford University Press, 1989), pp. 235, 248–49; Joachim Whaley, *Germany and the Holy Roman Empire*, 2 vols (Oxford: Oxford University Press, 2012), II, 636–44; Peter H. Wilson, *The Holy Roman Empire: A Thousand Years of Europe's History* (London: Allen Lane, 2016), pp. 649–54.

worse than that of Machiavelli's Italy. There the small independent states were swallowed up by larger ones, but this process did not lead to the unification of Italy and left it exposed as a battleground for foreign powers. In this situation Machiavelli alone was far-sighted enough to see that Italy could only be saved by being unified, and that this unification could only be accomplished by a man who was prepared to use the necessary force.

Hegel acknowledges that 'the name of Machiavelli carries with it the seal of disapproval in public opinion, and Machiavellian principles have been made synonymous with detestable ones'.[2] He therefore undertakes a defence of Machiavelli against 'moralizing', such as that of Frederick the Great in his *Anti-Machiavel*. He also repudiates the favoured Enlightenment reading of *The Prince* as a satire. Machiavelli was a patriot; he wrote 'with genuine sincerity', and 'had neither baseness of heart nor frivolity of mind'. He saw that only the most drastic means could save Italy. 'A situation in which poison and assassination are common weapons demands remedies of no gentle kind. When life is on the brink of decay it can be reorganized only by a procedure involving the maximum of force.' Violence is justified as a means of opposing anarchy:

> Those who assail the state directly, and not indirectly as other criminals do, are the greatest criminals, and the state has no higher duty than to maintain itself and crush the power of those criminals in the surest way it can.

Forcible measures to maintain the state are not reprehensible, but can be seen as just punishment. And Machiavelli's conception of the unification of Italy, by whatever means are necessary, is 'an extremely great and true conception produced by a genuinely political head endowed with an intellect of the highest and noblest kind'. Germany needs a conqueror who will impose his will by force, but he will also have to institute some form of organization that gives the people a voice in government. Like Theseus, the legendary hero whose life Plutarch had written, this great man will be both a conqueror and a lawgiver.

In this early essay Friedrich Meinecke sees the germ of Hegel's later philosophy of politics and history. Hegel begins by asserting that Germany is no longer a state.[3] It needs to become a state, but of a distinctively modern kind, different both from Oriental despotism and from Greek republicanism. Republican states such as ancient Athens, in which all free adult males fully participated, are no longer feasible: the modern states which have emerged from medieval feudalism are too large and complex, and depend on representation. Even so, the state should not be merely a functional machine, as envisaged by philosophers of the Enlightenment. It needs to rely on the free, independent, and heartfelt participation of its citizens:

> the free devotion, the self-respect, and the individual effort of the people — on an all-powerful invincible spirit which the hierarchical system has renounced

2   *The German Constitution*, in *Hegel's Political Writings*, trans. by T. M. Knox with an introduction by Z. A. Pelczynski (Oxford: Clarendon Press, 1964), pp. 220–21. For the original, see 'Die Verfassung Deutschlands' in G. W. F. Hegel, *Frühe Schriften*, in his *Werke*, ed. by Eva Moldenhauer and Karl Markus Michel, 20 vols (Frankfurt a.M.: Suhrkamp, 1986), I, 551–58.
3   *Hegel's Political Writings*, p. 143; *Werke*, I, 461.

and which has its life only where the supreme public authority leaves as much as possible to the personal charge of the citizens.[4]

The modern state is national, embodying and expressing the character of its people. But, as a product of history, it is also rational, for history, as Hegel maintained in his *Lectures on the Philosophy of World History* (1830), is a rational process. Hence it is in the national state that the individual can fully realize himself, emotionally and also rationally: 'Only in the state does man have a rational existence.'[5] The state reconciles the objective rationality which is the essence of history with the subjective desires of the individual. Hence the state can reconcile morality — that which should be — with reality — that which is. Each state is itself an individual and guided by morality, but its morality, being rational, is higher than the morality of the human individual, as Meinecke explains:

> Hegel now conceived of the State in general as an 'individual totality', which developed in a quite concrete manner in accordance with its own special and peculiar vital laws, and which was thereby both permitted and obliged to set aside ruthlessly even the universal moral commands. By doing so, it did not (as his words show) behave immorally, but rather according to the spirit of a higher morality which was superior to the universal and customary morality.[6]

As an example of the need to set aside ordinary human morality, Hegel in his *Philosophy of History* again invokes Machiavelli. He notes that although *The Prince* has often been rejected as detestable, it expresses the higher necessity by which states must be formed. It is indeed repugnant for modern readers to see 'Macchiavelli' (as Hegel now spells his name) advocating the most ruthless violence to suppress independent principalities, but that was the only means by which, in a corrupt age, the foundations of a modern state could be laid: 'we must nevertheless confess that the feudal nobility, whose power was to be subdued, were assailable in no other way, since an indomitable contempt for principle, and an utter depravity of morals, were thoroughly ingrained in them'.[7]

Summarizing Hegel's philosophy of history, Meinecke seems a little uneasy. He describes it as an optimistic 'theodicy'.[8] Theodicy, best represented in modern times by Leibniz, seeks to interpret the apparent evils of life as necessary components of a divine plan which we cannot hope to comprehend fully, and in which, in Pope's words, 'all partial Evil' is really 'universal Good'.[9] Hegel's historical theodicy similarly interprets the sufferings undergone by historical actors as brought about

4   *Hegel's Political Writings*, p. 163; *Werke*, I, 484.
5   Hegel, *Lectures on the Philosophy of World History: Introduction*, trans. by H. B. Nisbet (Cambridge: Cambridge University Press, 1975), p. 94.
6   Meinecke, *Machiavellism*, p. 361; *Staatsräson*, p. 423.
7   Hegel, *The Philosophy of History*, trans. by J. Sibree (New York: Dover, 1956), p. 403; *Vorlesungen über die Philosophie der Geschichte*, in *Werke*, XII, 483. The incorrect spelling 'Macchiavelli' is common in nineteenth-century German texts.
8   Meinecke, *Machiavellism*, p. 368; *Staatsräson*, p. 432.
9   *An Essay on Man*, Book I, l. 292, in *The Poems of Alexander Pope*, ed. by John Butt (London: Methuen, 1963), p. 515. See G. W. Leibniz, *Theodicy: Essays on the Goodness of God, the Freedom of Man and the Origin of Evil*, trans. by E. M. Huggard (London: Routledge & Kegan Paul, 1951).

by 'the cunning of reason' in order to further the ultimate self-realization of the spirit, which is the goal of history.[10] This is a rational process, and 'reason cannot stop to consider the injuries sustained by single individuals, for particular ends are submerged in the universal end'.[11] (Callous as this sounds, any conception of history as progress which sees past suffering as necessary for a better future must be similarly callous.) In the shorter term, Meinecke notes in this theodicy 'the danger that moral feeling would become blunted and the excesses of power politics would be taken too lightly'.[12] If the statesmen, above all Bismarck, who brought about the unification of Germany in 1871, did read Hegel — and Meinecke admits that the extent of Hegel's influence 'cannot be measured with certainty'[13] — they would not be encouraged to pursue humanitarian policies.

Hegel's conception of history was deeply influenced by Napoleon, to whose power not only Austria but also Prussia succumbed. After defeating the combined Austrian and Russian forces at Austerlitz on 2 December 1805, setting up the Confederation of the Rhine, and bringing about the dissolution of the Empire, Napoleon turned his attention to Prussia. Prussia was not nearly so formidable an antagonist as in the time of Frederick the Great. Its army lacked capable leaders and had an incoherent command structure. On 14 October 1806 his forces defeated the Prussian army in the battles of Jena and Auerstedt. Prussia collapsed as a military power. Napoleon entered Berlin as a conqueror on 27 October; the Prussian King and Queen fled to Königsberg, far away on the Baltic, while Prussia remained under French occupation, with its army reduced to 42,000 men, and its population was heavily taxed for the benefit of their French occupiers. Patriots placed their hopes in Austrian resistance, but Napoleon decisively defeated Austria at the battle of Wagram on 6 July 1809 and concluded the Peace of Schönbrunn on 14 October.

The collapse of Prussia gave a huge stimulus to German nationalism. One of its main spokesmen was the philosopher Johann Gottlieb Fichte, not only in his famous or notorious *Reden an die deutsche Nation* (*Addresses to the German Nation*, 1808) but in an essay giving a positive revaluation of Machiavelli. A heady patriotic discourse, emphasizing self-sacrifice for the fatherland, had already emerged during the Seven Years War, focused on Prussia.[14] Fichte and his contemporaries transferred the focus to Germany as a whole.

In June 1807 Fichte published in the journal *Vesta*, based in Königsberg, an essay entitled 'Ueber Machiavell, als Schriftsteller, und Stellen aus seinen Schriften' ('On Machiavelli as a writer, and extracts from his writings'). The extracts from Machiavelli that follow the essay begin with a passage from the last chapter of *The*

---

10   For 'the cunning of reason' ('die List der Vernunft'), see Hegel, *Vorlesungen über die Philosophie der Geschichte*, in *Werke*, XII, 49.

11   Hegel, *Lectures*, p. 43.

12   Meinecke, *Machiavellism*, p. 368; *Staatsräson*, p. 433.

13   Meinecke, *Machiavellism*, p. 359; *Staatsräson*, p. 422.

14   See Thomas Abbt, *Vom Tode fürs Vaterland* (1761), in his *Vermischte Werke*, 6 vols (Berlin and Stettin: Nicolai, 1768–80); Ritchie Robertson, 'Cosmopolitanism, Patriotism and Nationalism in the German-Speaking Enlightenment', in his *Enlightenment and Religion in German and Austrian Literature* (Cambridge: Legenda, 2017), pp. 144–62.

Prince, calling on Lorenzo II de' Medici to liberate Italy from the barbarians who have been ravaging it since 1494. They also include an extract from chapter 14, on the duty of a prince to concentrate on warfare.

Fichte finds Machiavelli not only a timely writer, but also a congenial one. The great quality he emphasizes is Machiavelli's realism. Machiavelli is anchored in real life ('ruht ganz auf dem wirklichen Leben').[15] He is an honest and truthful writer, whose moral character inspires love and respect. He is concerned to see and describe matters as they are and to follow his arguments through to their conclusions. He does not advocate wickedness. Far from praising Cesare Borgia's cruelty, he commends Borgia only for establishing order quickly in a disorderly province. Even the paganism that Fichte imputes to him is to his credit, since it is based on a rejection of the monkish, other-worldly Christianity of his time; it resembles the outlook of modern pagans who find inspiration in classical literature (presumably an allusion to Goethe).

Machiavelli does not get everything right. Fichte disapproves of his nostalgia for small independent republics, because such petty states merely retard the progress of humanity. Fortunately, Machiavelli seems eventually to have realized that Italy needed to be united under a single strong leader, such as he demands at the end of *The Prince*. Fichte quotes his testimony that 'no land is ever united or happy unless it comes completely under the obedience of a single republic or a single prince' (D I. 12. 55).[16]

However, Machiavelli has many lessons for the present day. He shows admirable realism in saying: 'it is necessary for anyone who organizes a republic and establishes laws in it to take for granted that all men are evil and that they will always act according to the wickedness of their nature whenever they have the opportunity' (D I iii, p. 28).[17] For the state is not a voluntary association but a coercive one ('eine Zwangsanstalt') which restrains people's natural condition of mutual enmity, the war of all against all, by compelling them to preserve at least the semblance of peace.[18] The prince is entitled to maintain law and order by force, as when he suppresses a rebellion, though Fichte thinks that nowadays, in contrast to Machiavelli's time, uprisings against one's ruler are a rare event, except in Britain (he is no doubt thinking of the Glorious Revolution of 1688 and the rebellions of 1715 and 1745).

Fichte's main concern in the Machiavelli essay is with foreign policy. Here, constant suspicion is essential, because nations really are in a condition of perpetual enmity. Thanks to a drive implanted by God, every nation seeks to increase its influence at the expense of others, and to enlarge itself at others' expense; a state that ceases to expand is liable to be attacked and to diminish. 'Whoever does not

15   Fichte, 'Ueber Machiavell, als Schriftsteller, und Stellen aus seinen Schriften', in *Gesamtausgabe*, ed. by Reinhard Lauth and others (Stuttgart and Bad Cannstatt: Frommann-Holzboog, 1962–2012), IX: *Werke 1806–1807*, ed. by Reinhard Lauth and Hans Gliwitzky (1995), pp. 223–75 (p. 224).
16   Ibid., p. 230.
17   Ibid., p. 239.
18   Ibid.

grow will shrink when others grow.'[19] A private individual may be content with what he has, but a state must always seek to enlarge its possessions, for fear of having them reduced. So you must always assume that other nations are trying to benefit at your expense, and you must be prepared to respond to their aggression. Perpetual enmity, however, does not mean perpetual war, for readiness for war is the best guarantee of peace. To maintain this readiness, Fichte recommends that in peacetime young Europeans should be sent to fight with barbarians, of whom there are some in Europe and many more in other continents.[20]

In dealing with other nations, there is no room for morality. A ruler should observe morality in his private life; in dealing with his subjects, he should strictly observe the law; but towards other nations the only law is that of the stronger:

> in his relation to other states there is neither law nor right, except the right of the stronger, and this relation is placed in the prince's hands, and in his responsibility, by the divine laws of fate and the governance of the universe [*Weltregierung*], raising him above the commands of individual morality to a higher moral order whose material content is expressed in the words: *Salus et decus populi suprema lex esto* (Let the safety and glory of the people be the supreme law).[21]

Unfortunately, Fichte continues, too many people are now misled by liberal doctrines, which, as a veiled allusion shows, he especially associates with Kant.

> In the second half of the past century, this briefly fashionable philosophy had already grown flat, sickly, and impoverished, offering as its highest good a certain humanity, and liberality, and popularity,[22] pleading with people to be good and to leave well alone, constantly recommending the golden mean, that is, the fusion of all antitheses into a dull chaos, the enemy of all seriousness, all consistency, all enthusiasm, of any great idea and decision, and of any phenomenon that stood out a little above the long and broad surface, but especially enamoured of perpetual peace.[23]

Kant's advocacy of peace is thus decisively rejected. Fichte offers instead a vision of a warlike state, ruled by a strong leader but based on law and on popular participation; its young men will engage in military exercises and fight against colonized peoples (who will presumably be in constant rebellion, otherwise fighting would soon cease to be necessary); its people will not seek prosperity and comfort, but military glory, and the natural urge of nations to enlarge their territory ensures that war will break out from time to time. This vision strikingly resembles the expansionist republic, based on Rome, that Machiavelli envisaged in the *Discourses*. It uneasily combines an appeal to hard-headed realism with what now looks like boyish romanticism about warfare.

---

19   Ibid., p. 242. On Machiavelli's imperialism, see especially Mark Hulliung, *Citizen Machiavelli* (Princeton: Princeton University Press, 1983).
20   Fichte, 'Ueber Machiavell', p. 244.
21   Ibid., pp. 244–45.
22   'eine gewisse Humanität, und Liberalität, und Popularität', ibid., p. 245. In using foreign words, he intends further to discredit this philosophy by portraying it as un-German.
23   Ibid., alluding to Kant's essay *Zum ewigen Frieden* (*On Perpetual Peace*, 1795).

Machiavelli's call for a strong leader also appealed to a prominent liberal historian and politician, Georg Gottfried Gervinus (1805–71). Gervinus, best known as author of a pioneering history of German literature (1835–42), previously wrote (among much else) a substantial study of Machiavelli. His courageous liberalism was demonstrated in 1837 when he was one of the seven professors (known as the Göttingen Seven) who resigned their posts in protests against the attempt by the Elector of Hanover to override the constitution by requiring professors to declare their loyalty to his own person. In 1848 Gervinus was briefly a member of the Frankfurt Parliament.

German liberals in the 1830s confronted a situation in which the thirty-nine states comprising the German Confederation accepted to varying degrees the repressive measures which the Austrian Chancellor Prince Metternich had instituted as part of the post-Napoleonic settlement and reinforced by the Carlsbad Decrees (1819). Constitutions were abrogated or had never existed in the first place. Representative assemblies, where they existed, were pressured into subservience to their rulers. Discussion of public affairs was prohibited as far as possible. Censorship and an intrusive bureaucracy constantly hampered people's lives.[24]

Gervinus's essay on Machiavelli occupies about half of the history of Florentine historiography which he published in 1833. Machiavelli is for him the modern successor to his favourite writers on politics, Thucydides and Aristotle. Thucydides was strictly realistic in his history of the Peloponnesian War, while Aristotle was detached and systematic in his study of politics. Their realism is shared by Machiavelli, who is '*one of the very few with worthy conceptions of history*' and 'the father of the modern treatment of history'.[25] Gervinus, like his English contemporary Macaulay, sees no conflict between the precepts of *The Prince* and the *Discourses*.[26] The advice in *The Prince* is intended only for someone establishing his power for the first time, not as a manual for all rulers (as 'reason of state' thinkers assumed), and in any case the general good, as Machiavelli affirms, is best served in republics. Machiavelli is not, as his detractors have claimed, an apologist for despotism, but a defender of the freedom that he found exemplified in the ancient republics. However, Gervinus feels that his own time, like Machiavelli's, requires drastic measures from a strong leader. Machiavelli should not be blamed for seeing such an ideal in Cesare Borgia; Gervinus's contemporaries have recently seen such an ideal in Napoleon:

> [Machiavelli] condemned the feeble politics of his courts and the immense depravity and indifference to principle shown by the people of his age, which was like the present day, when we cling expectantly to every semblance of power, and if in our time and under not dissimilar circumstances we admired

---

24   Sheehan, *German History*, pp. 613–15.
25   G. G. Gervinus, *Geschichte der florentinischen Historiographie bis zum sechzehnten Jahrhundert, nebst einer Charakteristik des Machiavell* (Frankfurt a.M.: Franz Varrentrapp, 1833), pp. 216, 217. Emphasis in original.
26   Cf. 'Machiavelli' (1827) in Lord Macaulay, *Critical and Historical Essays*, 2 vols (London: Longmans, Green, and Co., 1868), I, 28–51.

Napoleon, why should not Machiavelli look with similar yearning at every individual who revealed any ability to fulfil his ideal.[27]

A strong leader is required not only to make Germany into a unitary state, but to ward off the danger that Gervinus, like many contemporaries, foresees from the pauperized and resentful working classes. He is particularly interested in the account that Machiavelli, in his *Florentine Histories*, gives of the revolt by the Ciompi, the impoverished wool-workers, in Florence in 1378. One of the rebels delivered an incendiary speech, quoted by Machiavelli (who, like the ancient historians, put made-up speeches into his characters' mouths) and repeated by Gervinus, who by calling the speaker 'an impertinent Jacobin' suggests an analogy with the French Revolution.[28] Now that they have taken up arms, the speaker says, the wool-workers' best course is to proceed to extremes:

> It is to our advantage, therefore, as it appears to me, if we wish that our old errors be forgiven us, to make new ones, redoubling the evils, multiplying the arson and robbery — and to contrive to have many companions in this, because when many err, no one is punished, and though small faults are punished, great and grave ones are rewarded.[29]

This speech, says Gervinus, shows 'the horrifying and savage features of an insurrectionary crowd and their ruthless and bloody manner of behaving'.[30]

Faced with such dangers, the strong leader will need to behave like Machiavelli's prince. He will not be a dictator; he will act within constitutional limits. But like the prince, he will be a 'harsh, armed legislator, but can never be a really bad man; he does not need, however, to be morally scrupulous; he has no use for timorous clinging to everyday morality'.[31] Here we have the familiar distinction between public and private morality, though Gervinus invokes public morality only in an imagined emergency. At the same time, Gervinus is somewhat ambivalent about great men: they are liable to get carried away by their power and forget about their human limitations, just as it never occurred to Cesare Borgia that he might fall ill at a crucial moment.

The liberalism that Gervinus displays here will strike some readers as distinctly illiberal. He seems to be advocating the violent suppression of popular protests in order to keep the propertied classes secure. He may even seem to anticipate those voters in the Weimar Republic who thought Hitler preferable to communism. But it is important to avoid hindsight. Gervinus and his contemporaries were vividly aware of the horrors of the French Revolution and of how a mob disposed to violence could be manipulated by demagogues. To stop mob violence, they were ready to support drastic measures like those famously taken by Napoleon when, as a young general, he was charged on 14 October 1795 with combating a revolt

27 Gervinus, *Geschichte*, p. 146.
28 Ibid., p. 194. On the Ciompi revolt, see Najemy, *History of Florence*, pp. 161–66.
29 Machiavelli, *Florentine Histories*, trans. by Laura F. Banfield and Harvey C. Mansfield, Jr (Princeton: Princeton University Press, 1988), p. 122.
30 Gervinus, *Geschichte*, p. 194.
31 Ibid., p. 154.

(known as the Vendémiaire) by some 7,000 Royalists. At least according to legend, Napoleon declared that 'a whiff of grapeshot' would dispose of them, and fired two cannons, leaving a hundred or so insurrectionaries dead.[32] In the early nineteenth century, it was widely feared that the urban poor, if they found leaders, could stage a violent insurrection leading at best to death and destruction, at worst to a replay of the French Revolution.[33] It was against this background that Gervinus longed for a strong and not too scrupulous leader.

A quarter of a century later, Machiavelli's Italian patriotism inspired another book, the almost-forgotten *Vertheidigung des Machiavellismus* (*Defence of Machiavellianism*) by Karl Bollmann (1830–63). Bollmann is a shadowy, perhaps shady figure. He was briefly employed as cabinet secretary to the Duke of Sachsen-Gotha, but fell out with his employer, got into debt, fled to Denmark and may have committed suicide.[34] In his book he expresses admiration for Machiavelli as a fervent patriot looking for the man strong enough to unify Italy and expel the invaders. Cesare Borgia would have been that man, but for his premature death. For the politician Machiavelli, good and evil are defined exclusively by the needs of the state:

> In politics, one thing alone must always be placed first, and that is the common good. In this regard there is neither right nor wrong, neither mildness nor cruelty, neither honour nor shame, all that matters is the concept of the appropriate means and the decisiveness that never for a moment doubts what must be decided, and the prince is not worthy to be a prince if he cannot sacrifice his own self with his likes and dislikes to the well-being of the great whole over which he has the honour to preside.[35]

The present-day counterpart to Cesare Borgia is Louis Napoleon, who in December 1851 staged a *coup d'état* that made him Emperor of France as Napoleon III. This Napoleon is concerned not for personal gain or glory, but for the good of France. He has benefited France by suppressing the dangerous popular forces that broke loose in the upheavals of 1848. He has behaved like an exemplary prince. For, as Bollmann maintains with lavish quotations from *The Prince*, politics demands a different morality from that of ordinary life. A prince must know when to be tough. '*Well applied harshness* is better than ill-timed mildness.'[36] He must conciliate the people by making them prosperous and by changing as little as possible in the institutions that are dear to them. He must display good qualities, even if he does

---

32   Compare Michael Broers, *Napoleon: Soldier of Destiny, 1769–1805* (London: Faber, 2014), pp. 100–01, with the more sceptical account in Philip Dwyer, *Napoleon: The Path to Power, 1769–1799* (London: Bloomsbury, 2007), pp. 173–77; Thomas Carlyle, *The French Revolution*, Book 7, ch. vii, entitled 'The Whiff of Grapeshot', in his *Works*, Centenary Edition, 30 vols (London: Chapman & Hall, 1896), IV, 314–20.

33   See Louis Chevalier, *Labouring Classes and Dangerous Classes during the First Half of the Nineteenth Century*, trans. by Frank Jellinek (London: Routledge & Kegan Paul, 1973).

34   See Thomas Nicklas, *Das Haus Sachsen-Coburg: Europas späte Dynastie* (Stuttgart: Kohlhammer, 2003). I thank Kevin Hilliard for directing me to this source. There is a summary of *Vertheidigung* in Markus J. Prutsch, *Caesarism in the Post-Revolutionary Age* (London: Bloomsbury, 2020), pp. 122–23, where the author is mistakenly identified with the politician Carl Bollmann (1833–91).

35   Karl Bollmann, *Vertheidigung des Machiavellismus* (Quedlinburg: H. C. Huch, 1858), p. 31.

36   Ibid., p. 61.

not really possess them. And he must manipulate the press on his own behalf. This last touch looks distinctively modern, but Bollmann quotes another Machiavellian writer, Gabriel Naudé, who in his *Considérations politiques sur les coups d'état* (1639) advises a ruler to employ able writers to support his policies. Bollmann has no time for political moralizing. He mentions with particular disgust the moralism of the English clergy, who nevertheless, he says, would never advise Queen Victoria to give up Bengal just because Robert Clive acquired it by treacherously breaking his word.

The real enemy for Bollmann is popular insurgency. The 1848 revolutions were a wake-up call. He warns: 'it is easy to ignore the demonic force dormant in the spirit of the people. Once it has been aroused, it rushes onwards like a foaming mountain torrent, smashing every dam and spreading fear and horror on all sides'.[37] Hence the need for a new Caesar like Napoleon III.

Such a ruler needs also to do away with liberalism. Liberalism is abstract and mechanical, devoid of feeling. The bourgeoisie rely selfishly on the financial power of the banks. The kind of popular representation conferred by voting rights is merely formal. Instead, society needs to be reorganized, such that each profession will form a corporation, held together by warmer and more immediate social bonds than the mere rights of the citizen. Once restructured along corporatist lines, Germany will again be powerful. This cannot be achieved by revolution from below. It needs a strong leader, a new version of Cesare Borgia and Napoleon III. Bollmann ends his book with the appeal: 'When will you appear, king of the future?'[38]

In his somewhat anachronistic reading of Machiavelli, Bollmann evokes a cluster of widely shared nineteenth-century preoccupations. Many well-known contemporaries deplored the dominance of capital, the reduction of the worker's labour to a marketable commodity instead of an expression of self-respect, and the indifference of free-market liberalism to the immiseration of the masses. By advocating corporatism, Bollmann builds a bridge from Machiavelli to the fascist states of the twentieth century, while his yearning for a strong leader expresses his disillusion — again widely shared — with the emancipatory promises of democracy.

---

37   Ibid., p. 53.
38   Ibid., p. 102.

10

Realpolitik

In the late nineteenth century, and subsequently, the term 'Machiavellianism' was often used interchangeably with *Realpolitik* to imply a morally unscrupulous conduct of politics focused exclusively on the supposed interest of one's own nation. The statesman Otto von Bismarck (1815–98), prime minister and foreign secretary of Prussia from 1862 and chancellor of a united Germany from 1871 to his dismissal in 1890, was regarded as the chief exponent of both. Thus Nietzsche writes in 1886 of 'Bismarck's Machiavellianism with a good conscience, the so-called "Realpolitik"'.[1]

When originally used, however, *Realpolitik* denoted a serious, intellectually respectable, and neither amoral nor immoral political theory, formulated in 1853 by August Wilhelm von Rochau (1810–73). Posterity has sometimes, though unjustly, dismissed Rochau as a thinker who discarded his liberal ideals and became a political reactionary. It is true that Rochau started out on the extreme wing of student radicalism. He was among the students who made a futile attack on the guard post of the military garrison at Frankfurt on 3 April 1833. Sentenced to life imprisonment, he escaped and fled to France, where he made his living as a journalist. Having been enabled by an amnesty to return to Germany, he took part in the revolutionary events of 1848. He was one of the 574 members of the *Vorparlament* which met in Frankfurt on 31 March 1848 in order to set up a parliament representing the whole of Germany, though he failed to be elected to the Parliament itself. The Parliament, meeting in the Paulskirche in the centre of Frankfurt, aimed to transform Germany into a united constitutional monarchy. After debates on whether the solution should be *grossdeutsch* (including Austria, with its many non-German nationalities) or *kleindeutsch* (composed only of German lands, but including the worryingly disproportionate power of Prussia), the *kleindeutsch* group won, and the Parliament resolved on a constitutional state headed by a hereditary emperor. In April 1849 they offered the crown to King Frederick William IV of Prussia, but he refused it, privately dismissing it as a 'dog-collar'.[2] Thus denied support by the only political authority that could have helped them to put their plans into action, the Frankfurt assembly disintegrated.

Rochau deplored the liberals' efforts to draw up a constitutional state without the power to turn it into reality. 'After receiving the negative answer', he wrote, 'they drifted away silently from the Paulskirche like guests leaving a wine-bar late in the

---

1   *Die fröhliche Wissenschaft*, Book v, §356, in Nietzsche, KSA III, 598.
2   Sheehan, *German History*, p. 691.

evening.'[3] His *Realpolitik*, however, is not a rejection of liberalism, but a revision, which tries to salvage liberalism by showing how it can be allied with power.[4] He first set it out in a treatise published in 1853 and reissued, with a new preface but the same text, in 1859, and followed by a second volume in 1868.

The principle Rochau starts from is that 'the law of strength governs politics, just as the law of gravity governs the physical world'.[5] By this he emphatically does not mean that might is right. Right is in principle independent of power, but in practice it needs power in order to achieve anything. Political utopias that ignore this insight, such as Plato's republic or Rousseau's social contract, are mere castles in the air. Ideas do matter, but they have no independent power: 'Ideas only ever have as much power as is bestowed on them by the people who hold them.'[6]

Realpolitik, or realistic politics, must take account of the actual forces (*Kräfte*) present in society. An effective government needs to incorporate new social forces. Rochau gives as examples 'bourgeois self-awareness, the concept of freedom, the sense of nationhood, the idea of human equality, political party spirit, the press', which in many present-day states are 'new factors in social life'.[7] Similarly, politics must acknowledge the force of public opinion. Even if public opinion is stupid or mistaken, politics, while not following it blindly, must yield to it as far as is necessary in order not to antagonize the public. An autocratic government which tries to suppress or even check new social forces will in the long run be weakened or even overthrown. Government needs representative institutions, but the form they take will depend on circumstances in different countries: the US Congress is suitable for American democracy, while the British House of Lords, though outwardly an anachronism, is appropriate for the more traditional British society. There is no one size that fits all, no single political model that can be imposed on all states.

Rochau thus argues for a flexible politics that is realistic in that it responds to what is really happening. National unity is all-important. A sense of nationhood, 'the last and most precious guarantor of the natural social order', can maintain a balance among contending forces. Hence a polity is precarious if it contains several different national (or, as we might say nowadays, ethnic) groups (Rochau is probably thinking of Austria), though even here it is possible for a sense of shared nationhood to transcend such differences. Rochau is emphatically not talking about Jews as aliens: he denounces antisemitism as morally unjustified and as illogical, since the Jewish talents manifested in business and the professions are among the forces that the state needs to incorporate.[8] Nor does Rochau advocate either immorality or

3   [August Ludwig von Rochau], *Grundsätze der Realpolitik, angewendet auf die staatlichen Zustände Deutschlands*, 2nd edn (Stuttgart: Göpel, 1859), pp. 145–46.
4   See Duncan Kelly, 'August Ludwig von Rochau and *Realpolitik* as Historical Political Theory', *Global Intellectual History*, 3 (2018), 301–30. An invaluable study of Rochau is provided in John Bew, *Realpolitik: A History* (New York: Oxford University Press, 2016), pp. 31–64.
5   Rochau, *Grundsätze der Realpolitik*, p. 25.
6   Ibid., p. 28.
7   Ibid., p. 11.
8   Bew, *Realpolitik*, p. 64.

amorality. 'Politics is not freed from ethical duty, but there is a borderline at which the actual fulfilment of this duty ceases to be possible': he instances the compromises that may be necessary in order to end a rebellion or a mutiny.[9]

Rochau's *Realpolitik* was developed, and distorted, by the historian Heinrich von Treitschke (1834–96). Originally a liberal, Treitschke became an ardent supporter of a unified Germany under Prussian hegemony. His zeal for this cause inspired him, even before unification, to leave his professorial chair at Freiburg in south-western Germany and move to Prussia, where he became professor of history at Berlin and editor of the prominent nationalist journal *Preussische Jahrbücher*. He read Rochau's book in 1853 and called it 'brilliant' (*genial*).[10] But he went further than Rochau, and approached Hegel, in magnifying the importance of the state. He attributed this doctrine to Machiavelli, who he said was one of his favourite writers.[11] Treitschke says that for Machiavelli, the state is sheer power, but that Machiavelli ignores the purpose of power: 'He shows no trace of the idea that power, once acquired, must justify itself by being used for humanity's highest ethical goods.' Yet Treitschke also asserts that 'the supreme imperative for the state is always to maintain itself and its power', and here, as has often been pointed out, he is arguing in a circle.[12] It is moral to accumulate power, but power is only justified by a moral purpose. So Treitschke is really advocating *Machtpolitik*, a politics based on power; the impulse underlying such a policy is ethical, but ethical considerations need not play a part in any specific case. Because the state is fundamentally ethical, whatever the state may do has an ethical sanction.

In the decades before the First World War, *Realpolitik* lost its analytic value and, for foreigners, became a boo-word. It was something only Germans did. *Realpolitik*, like 'Machiavellianism', came to imply an amoral, cynical, unscrupulous conduct of politics that readily employed violence and deceit. British commentators on German policies used it as a convenient term of abuse, as when in 1911 the Prime Minister, Herbert Asquith, described Germany's dispatch of a gunboat to Agadir in Morocco in order to deter French territorial claims as 'an interesting illustration of *Realpolitik*'.[13]

---

9   Rochau, *Grundsätze der Realpolitik*, pp. 9–10. On Rochau's possible debt to Machiavelli, whom he does not mention, see Federico Trocini, 'Machiavellismus, Realpolitik und Machtpolitik', in *Machiavellismus in Deutschland*, ed. by Cornel Zwierlein and Annette Meyer, Beiheft zu *Historische Zeitschrift*, 51 (2010), 215–32.

10   Treitschke, letter to Salomon Hirzel, 28 Nov. 1865, quoted in Kelly, 'Rochau and *Realpolitik*', p. 305.

11   Trocini, 'Machiavellismus', p. 221.

12   Erwin Faul, *Der moderne Machiavellismus* (Cologne: Kiepenheuer & Witsch, 1961), p. 158. Quotations from Treitschke come from his *Vorlesungen über Politik*, 5th edn (1922), but as this book was not available to me, I take them at second hand from Gerhard Ritter, *Machtstaat und Utopie: Vom Streit um die Dämonie der Macht seit Machiavelli und Morus* (Munich and Berlin: Oldenbourg, 1943), p. 138. This book, which Ritter, a distinguished historian, produced in Nazi Germany, takes Machiavelli to typify political realism and Thomas More as exemplifying the canting moralism that was often considered typically English. It deserves detailed attention, but that would unfortunately go beyond the limits of this study.

13   Quoted in Bew, *Realpolitik*, p. 96.

Conversely, German commentators accused the British of equally unscrupulous behaviour, made worse because, instead of being frank about it, they dressed it up in high-minded moralistic language, for which the English word 'cant' was borrowed. The liberal imperialism of the later nineteenth century seemed merely a pretext for brutal conquest and exploitation. A conspicuous example was the activities of Cecil Rhodes, who organized a military conquest of what later became Rhodesia, seizing land and cattle and quelling resistance 'with great severity';[14] he destroyed indigenous society, and compelled Africans to work on farms and in mines. The South African War or Boer War, in which Britain deployed over 400,000 troops against the two small Boer republics in which huge quantities of gold and diamonds had been discovered, was another example. Initially expecting a short and easy campaign, the British were humiliated by a succession of Boer victories in the autumn of 1899, and even after they had recaptured the lost towns, they faced a prolonged and resourceful guerrilla campaign. The British deliberately burned and devastated Boer farms and collected women and children in concentration camps, one-quarter of whose inmates perished. There was not so very much to choose between British behaviour in South Africa and the notorious maltreatment of rebellious Africans in the neighbouring German colony of South-West Africa (now Namibia).[15] A relatively detached observer, the economist J. A. Hobson, remarked in his study of imperialism that all the great powers practised such unscrupulous policies under different names, engaging in 'a calculated, greedy type of Macchiavellianism [*sic*], entitled "real-politik" in Germany, where it was made, which has remodelled the whole art of diplomacy and has erected national aggrandisement without pity or scruple as the conscious motive of foreign policy'.[16]

To foreign observers, the supreme practitioner of calculating power-politics was Bismarck. Bismarck does not use the word *Realpolitik*, and refers only rarely to reason of state (*Staatsräson*).[17] Nevertheless, his use of war to further the cause of German unity seemed the epitome of unscrupulous statecraft. The war with Denmark in 1864, prompted by a dispute over the succession to the Danish throne, ended with a rapid victory; the notoriously intractable question of ownership of the mixed-population duchies of Schleswig and Holstein was resolved, at least temporarily, by having them jointly occupied by Prussia and Austria.[18] Two years later, Bismarck managed to manoeuvre Austria into a war which Prussia won after six weeks at the battle of Königgrätz (3 July 1866), so that Prussia became the unchallenged leader of the German states. Finally the Franco-Prussian War, occasioned because France and Prussia were supporting different candidates for the throne of Spain, and

14 Christopher Saunders and Iain R. Smith, 'Southern Africa, 1795–1910', in *The Oxford History of the British Empire*, III: *The Nineteenth Century*, ed. by Andrew Porter (Oxford: Oxford University Press, 1999), pp. 597–625 (p. 611).

15 For a brief but nuanced comparison between British and German activities in southern Africa, see Isabel V. Hull, *Absolute Destruction: Military Culture and the Practices of War in Imperial Germany* (Ithaca, NY: Cornell University Press, 2005), pp. 182–96. More generally: Thomas Pakenham, *The Scramble for Africa 1876–1912* (London: Weidenfeld & Nicolson, 1991).

16 J. A. Hobson, *Imperialism: A Study* (London: James Nisbet & Co., 1902), p. 11.

17 Bew, *Realpolitik*, p. 47; Meinecke, *Staatsräson*, p. 481n.; *Machiavellism*, p. 409n.

18 The issues behind the war are well explained in Clark, *Iron Kingdom*, pp. 524–28.

provoked in part by Bismarck's doctoring of a telegram from the King of Prussia to Napoleon III to make it seem a discourteous rebuff, led to yet another decisive victory at Sedan on 1–2 September 1870. The German army marched on Paris; the advice from Bismarck and the Minister of War, Count Roon, to bombard the city was rejected, partly because it would have harmed civilians; an attempt to starve the city into submission took so long that in January 1871 Bismarck's advice was heeded and the city was shelled, whereupon it soon surrendered. While armistice talks were still in progress, the Hall of Mirrors at Versailles became the setting for the proclamation of a united German Empire ruled by William I, previously King of Prussia, in which Bismarck became Chancellor.[19] How far Bismarck was favoured by luck, and how much nervous strain he endured, were not apparent to the outside world, which saw in him a formidable and ruthless 'Machiavellian'.[20]

Bismarck gives his own view in his self-justifying *Gedanken und Erinnerungen* (*Thoughts and Recollections*), written in the 1890s after his dismissal by the new emperor William II. He tells how, for pressing political reasons, he needed a swift victory before neutral powers could intervene and deprive Germany of the fruits of victory. That required the conquest of Paris. Bismarck wanted to bombard Paris, but many people wanted to reduce it by a siege. Bismarck is sarcastic at the expense of this supposedly humane solution. He objects especially to the idea that Paris was sacrosanct because it was the centre of civilization.

> The notion that Paris, although it was fortified and was our opponents' strongest bulwark, could not be attacked like any other fortress, had reached our camp from England via Berlin, with the lofty phrase about 'the Mecca of civilization' and other expressions of humanitarian feeling that were customary and effective in the *cant* of English public opinion. England expects all other powers to act on such feelings, but does not always allow its own opponents to benefit from them. Our most influential circles upheld the idea, coming from London, that the surrender of Paris could not be brought about by artillery, but only by starvation. One may argue about whether the latter course was the more humane, and also whether the horrors of the Commune would have broken out if the period of starvation had not paved the way for the release of anarchist savagery. I will refrain from deciding whether the English intervention on behalf of humanely starving the Parisians out was based only on sensibility, or whether political calculation also played a part.[21]

Although Bismarck's sarcasm may be repellent, his viewpoint is defensible. The four-month siege, which reduced the Parisians to eating dogs and cats, was not necessarily more humane than the eventual bombardment. After the Prussian Military Council changed its mind at the end of 1870 and launched an attack on 4 January 1871, Paris surrendered quickly. Peace negotiations began on 23 January and the capitulation was signed on 28 January. Moreover, the law of unintended consequences ensured that, as Bismarck indicates, the months of starvation led to

19   On these events, see Jonathan Steinberg, *Bismarck: A Life* (New York: Oxford University Press, 2011), pp. 293–311.
20   On Bismarck's limited control of events, see Clark, *Iron Kingdom*, p. 549.
21   Bismarck, *Gedanken und Erinnerungen* (Stuttgart: Cotta, 1972), pp. 362–63.

the revolutionary uprising known as the Paris Commune. One of the first acts of the new Third French Republic was to suppress the Commune by executing 30,000 revolutionaries. A short, sharp bombardment might after all have been more humane.

Bismarck conspicuously avoids moral language. That does not mean that his political conduct was amoral or immoral. Treitschke, after meeting Bismarck in 1870, reported: 'Of the *moral powers* in the world he has *not the slightest notion!*'[22] Bismarck evidently was not sympathetic to Treitschke's view that the moral impetus behind the German state automatically excused all acts that might be thought immoral. But, in A. J. P. Taylor's judgement, 'Bismarck did not lack morality; what he lacked was uplift. He could not make his voice quiver with unselfish zeal, as Gladstone's voice quivered when he occupied Egypt.'[23] In the passage quoted above, Bismarck is pragmatic. He does not pretend that the attack on Paris was a matter of indifference or that it was excused by a higher purpose. It was the lesser of two evils, but still an evil. It was a crime, but a necessary crime.

A conflict between two courses of action, both unwelcome and perhaps both deplorable, is the stuff of drama, and forms the centre of the plays that will be discussed in the remainder of this book. It also takes a literary form in a novel contemporaneous with Bismarck's memoirs, Theodor Fontane's *Der Stechlin* (1898). Fontane described this novel — often considered his masterpiece, and certainly his fullest fictional engagement with the society and government of imperial Germany — as a 'political novel' centring on a 'contrast between the nobility as it *ought* to be among us, and as it *is*'.[24] The central figure is an elderly Prussian nobleman, Dubslav von Stechlin (the novel's title is the name of a lake on Dubslav's estate), who shares Fontane's dislike of hidebound snobbish fellow-aristocrats and of money-grubbing bourgeois and businessmen. One of Dubslav's intimates, likewise a sympathetic character, is a clergyman, Pastor Lorenzen, who is a Christian Socialist. In chapter 38, Lorenzen visits Dubslav, who feels his death approaching and asks to be told a story, preferably a heroic narrative from Prussian history. After all, he mentions, Lorenzen has always been an admirer of Frederick the Great ('Fridericus-Rex-Mann'). The story Lorenzen tells has no obvious connection with Frederick the Great. It is introduced by a conversation about the nature of heroism. Lorenzen maintains that heroism consists not in actions but in the spirit (*Gesinnung*) in which they are performed. A spy is normally a despicable person, but in Fenimore Cooper's novel *The Spy*, the title character plays a heroic role. To illustrate his claim further, he tells a true story.

The story concerns an American expedition to the Arctic, commanded by one Lieutenant Greeley. He and four other men were trekking across the snow, with just enough supplies to last until they came to a supply depot. They discovered,

22   Quoted in Erich Eyck, *Bismarck and the German Empire*, 3rd edn (London: Unwin University Books, 1968), p. 122.

23   A. J. P. Taylor, 'The Morality of Bismarck', in his *Europe: Grandeur and Decline* (Harmondsworth: Penguin, 1967), pp. 91–95 (p. 94).

24   Fontane, letter to C. R. Lessing, 8 June 1896, in his *Briefe*, 4 vols (Munich: Hanser, 1982), IV, ed. by Otto Drude and Helmuth Nürnberger, p. 562.

however, that one of their number was stealing food, and unless he were stopped, there would not be enough to last out. So Greeley said to the other three, 'We must shoot him from behind', and personally shot the thief in the back. Their supplies then lasted until they reached safety.

This narrative goes back ultimately to a report in the *New York Times* for 14 August 1885.[25] An expedition to Ellesmere Island, near the North Pole, in 1881, led by Lieutenant Greely (*sic*), got stranded and was rescued only in 1884. Out of twenty-five men, nineteen died of starvation or hypothermia. On finding that one of the six survivors, Private Henry, was stealing food, Greely issued written orders that Henry should be shot for disobedience. Three men were detailed to carry out the order. Greely stated that he would have shot Henry himself if he had not been too exhausted, but in fact he did not witness the execution.

Fontane has made two main changes. First, the party know that they have just enough food to reach the depot and safety, so that the need to kill the thief is as conclusive as a mathematical calculation. Second, Greeley not only decides on the execution but performs it himself, shooting Henry in the back (which his historical counterpart did not do). To Dubslav's surprise, Lorenzen, though a clergyman, justifies Greeley's conduct:

> 'I am filled with admiration. Instead of doing what he did, Greeley could have said to his companions: "Our example is wrong, and we are perishing because of one person's guilt; so let us all die." For his own person he could have spoken and acted like this. But it was not just about him, he was the leader and commander, and also had the judicial responsibility, and had to protect the majority of three against a minority of one. What this one person did was trivial in itself, but under those circumstances it was an abominable crime. And so, against the grave action that had been perpetrated, he [Greeley] took upon himself the grave counter-action. To feel rightly in such a moment, and in the conviction of one's rightness firmly and unwaveringly to do something terrible, something that, taken out of its context, runs completely counter to divine commandments, law and honour, *that* impresses me enormously and is in my eyes real, genuine courage.'[26]

Lorenzen thus invokes the much-discussed difference between private and public morality. If there had been only two men on the expedition, Greeley would not have been justified in killing the thief. But he was the leader, he had a political responsibility, and was obliged to perform an immoral action on behalf of his companions. The action is necessary, but that does not make it morally right; it was pragmatically correct. There is even a suggestion that Greeley's guilt is in some measure diminished by his moral courage in taking it upon himself; this would not apply if, like his historical original, he had delegated the killing to a subordinate.

25   See Konrad Feilchenfeldt, 'Leutnant Greeley — ein amerikanisches Vorbild für Europa? Zu Fontanes *Der Stechlin* (Achtunddreißigstes Kapitel)', in *Fontane und die Fremde, Fontane und Europa*, ed. by Konrad Ehlich (Würzburg: Königshausen & Neumann, 2002), pp. 229–47.

26   Fontane, *Der Stechlin*, in his *Sämtliche Romane, Erzählungen, Gedichte, Nachgelassenes*, 2nd edn, ed. by Walter Keitel and Helmut Nürnberger, 7 vols (Munich: Hanser, 1970–84), v (1980), p. 344.

Since the Greeley story feels like a foreign body in Fontane's novel, one looks for some connection with Frederick the Great, mentioned earlier in the same chapter. Presumably we are to see an analogy between Greeley and Frederick. Greeley's responsibility as expedition leader obliged him to violate ordinary morality. Frederick, as ruler of Prussia, was in a similar position: the good of his country obliged him to violate a treaty by invading Silesia in 1740. So we have in Greeley's story an implicit link to Prussian history and also an example of the literary motif of the necessary crime, a motif which the rest of this book will explore.

PART II

❖

Tragedies 1661–1963

1

Lohenstein:
Reason of State Triumphant

Is Daniel Casper von Lohenstein a canonical author? It has been said of him, rightly in my view: 'Both the power of his language and the sweep of his characterisation make Lohenstein the best dramatist in German before Schiller.'[1] And yet who has heard of him outside Germany? Even in Germany, he is probably read only by specialists in seventeenth-century literature. I hope this chapter will introduce him to a wider range of potential readers.

The predicate 'von Lohenstein' was acquired in 1670 by Johann Casper and bequeathed to his son, the dramatist Daniel Casper (1635–83). Daniel Casper — henceforth to be called Lohenstein — was not only the leading figure, alongside Andreas Gryphius (1616–64), in the Silesian school of tragedy, but also a scholar and a man of affairs. Born in Breslau (now Wrocław), he studied law at Leipzig and Tübingen, then travelled, probably as companion to a nobleman, through Germany to Switzerland and the Netherlands. As a citizen of the Habsburg Empire, he also travelled in Austria and Hungary as far as the Ottoman frontier. Having seen the world, Lohenstein married and settled down as a lawyer in Breslau, where he wrote most of his tragedies in the 1660s. After holding several prominent administrative positions in Breslau, he went to Vienna in 1675 to represent his city in negotiations with the imperial court over taxation. Here he made such a good impression that the Emperor, Leopold I, bestowed on him the title of Imperial Councillor. The last years of his life were spent composing an enormous novel, *Arminius*, which runs to 3,000 pages and is much admired by its few readers.[2]

Lohenstein's tragedies are, fortunately, more accessible. The grammar school he attended at Breslau had, like some other German schools, a tradition, borrowed from the Jesuit education system, of having plays performed by the boys. Acting provided the boys with training in memorization, elocution, and graceful action, while inculcating moral, political, and religious lessons. The precocious Lohenstein wrote his first play, *Ibrahim Bassa*, while still at school, and most of his other plays were written for performance by schoolboys. They fall into three groups: the Turkish plays, *Ibrahim Bassa* (performed in 1650 or 1651, published in 1653) and *Ibrahim Sultan* (published in 1673), set at the Ottoman court; the Roman plays,

---

1   Helen Watanabe-O'Kelly, 'The Early Modern Period (1450–1720)', in *The Cambridge History of German Literature*, ed. by Watanabe-O'Kelly (Cambridge: Cambridge University Press, 1997), pp. 92–146 (p. 134).
2   Besides the standard reference works, see the biographical sketch in G. E. P. Gillespie, *Daniel Casper von Lohenstein's Historical Tragedies* (Athens, OH: Ohio State University Press, 1965), pp. 3–5.

Agrippina and *Epicharis* (both published in 1665); and the African plays, the first of which, *Cleopatra*, was first published in 1661 and in a revised version in 1680, while *Sophonisbe* was performed in 1669 and published, probably with little revision, in 1680.[3] *Ibrahim Sultan* stands out in having been commissioned for the wedding of the Emperor Leopold I and Claudia Felicitas, daughter of the Archduke of Tyrol, in 1673, and in dealing with a near-contemporary subject, the reign of the Ottoman Emperor Ibrahim, who was deposed and killed by his Janissaries in 1648. The Ottoman Empire, whose conquests extended to Hungary, was a major threat to the Holy Roman Empire, and would lay siege to Vienna, almost successfully, only ten years after the play's performance.[4]

Baroque drama, and especially that of Lohenstein, shows us a world that now seems strange and remote. That is partly because the dramatic conventions are unfamiliar. The dialogue is stylized and non-naturalistic. Like contemporary French tragedy, it is in alexandrines; the blank verse familiar in English entered German drama only with Wieland's *Lady Johanna Gray* (1758; appropriately on an English subject).[5] There are long stretches of stichomythia, that is, the exchange of single lines: one such exchange in *Cleopatra* covers over 100 lines (III. 416–522 in the 1661 version, III. 698–806 in that of 1680).[6] The language is extravagantly inventive, with imagery taken from natural history and the classics; the effect is sometimes dizzying. In *Sophonisbe*, Masanissa denounces the cruelty of the Roman general Scipio, who has told him he must end his relationship with the Carthaginian queen Sophonisbe, as follows:

> Steinharter Scipio! den ein Hircanisch Tyger /
> Ein Arimaspisch Wolf / ein Basilißk' am Niger
> Mit Gift und Blutt gesäugt! der Zembl- und Caspisch Eiß
> Im kalten Hertzen nehrt [...] (IV. 369–72)

Stony-hearted Scipio! whom a Hyrcanian tiger, an Arimaspian wolf, a basilisk from the Niger, suckled on poison and blood! whose cold heart contains the ice of Novaya Zemlya and the Caspian Sea [...].

---

3   The now standard edition, used here, is: Daniel Casper von Lohenstein, *Sämtliche Werke*, ed. by Lothar Mundt, Wolfgang Neuber and Thomas Rahn (Berlin: De Gruyter, 2005–). Abteilung II: *Dramen*, I: *Ibrahim Bassa, Cleopatra*, ed. by Lothar Mundt (2008); II: *Agrippina, Epicharis*, ed. by Lothar Mundt (2005); III: *Ibrahim Sultan, Sophonisbe*, ed. by Lothar Mundt (2013). In my text, *Cleopatra* is abbreviated where necessary as C, *Sophonisbe* as S.

4   See John Stoye, *The Siege of Vienna* (London: Collins, 1964).

5   Apart from the verse-form, no two dramatists could seem more different than the restrained Racine and Lohenstein with his violent action and extravagant language, yet a closer look suggests important similarities. There is plenty of violence in Racine, but either off stage (e.g. the killing of Hippolyte by the sea-monster in *Phèdre*) or embodied in terrifying tyrants (Thésée, Mithridate, Néron, Agamemnon). See Achim Geisenhanslüke, *Trauer-Spiele: Walter Benjamin und das europäische Barockdrama* (Munich: Fink, 2016), esp. pp. 134–36. It would be worth making an extended comparison.

6   Narrowly beaten by the stichomythic exchange in which the procuress Sekierpera tries to talk the fourteen-year-old Ambre into yielding to Ibrahim's lust: *Ibrahim Sultan*, II. 387–505. Cf. the long exchange between Cromwell and the Scottish ambassador in Gryphius's *Carolus Stuardus* (1657), III. 665–777: Andreas Gryphius, *Dramen*, ed. by Eberhard Mannack (Frankfurt a.M.: Deutscher Klassiker Verlag, 1991), pp. 510–15.

This far-fetched imagery, often thought typically Baroque, immediately recalls Shakespeare (whose plays Lohenstein did not know):

> Approach thou like the rugged Russian bear,
> The arm'd rhinoceros, or the Hyrcan tiger,
> Take any shape but that, and my firm nerves
> Shall never tremble.[7]

Such language evidently thrilled Lohenstein's contemporaries but helped to cause the eclipse of his reputation in the early eighteenth century, when he was disparaged for his bombast ('Schwulst'). By then, public taste was moving away from heroic rhetoric and towards the lifelike expression of emotions to which middle-class audiences could relate. The German stage witnessed 'the transformation of a theatre of cruelty into a theatre of sympathy'.[8] Lohenstein's reputation would not recover till the revival of interest in Baroque literature in the early twentieth century, and then only among a small academic constituency.[9]

This extract from *Sophonisbe* also illustrates the astonishing erudition that Lohenstein displays in detailed notes appended to his published texts. They show how thoroughly the action of his Roman plays was based on Tacitus and other historians, how deeply he delved into comparative ethnography for *Sophonisbe*, and how he studied all the accounts of the Ottoman Empire available in Western languages from historians and travellers.[10]

Alongside his Baroque language and learning, Lohenstein's plays express values

---

7   *Macbeth*, III. 4. 100–03. The tiger goes back to Dido's reproach to Aeneas in Virgil, *Aeneid*, IV. 367: 'Hyrcanaeque admorunt ubera tigres', 'Hyrcanian tigresses gave thee suck' (trans. by H. Rushton Fairclough, Loeb Classical Library, Cambridge, MA: Harvard University Press, 1935). In Jean Mairet's *La Sophonisbe* (1634) cruelty is figured by 'vn Tygre d'Hircanie' (l. 719), which, according to the editor, was a 'cliché tragique': Jean Mairet, *La Sophonisbe*, ed. by Charles Dédéyan, 2nd edn (Paris: Nizet, 1969), p. 56. The Arimaspians were a legendary Siberian people: see Herodotus, *The Histories*, trans. by Aubrey de Sélincourt, rev. by A. R. Burn (Harmondsworth: Penguin, 1972), p. 250. Some of the attention English critics have given to Shakespeare's imagery could rewardingly be devoted to Lohenstein's. Stimulating but unsystematic comments on imagery are scattered throughout Gillespie, *Lohenstein's Historical Tragedies*.

8   Simon Richter, 'German Classical Tragedy: Lessing, Goethe, Schiller, Kleist, and Büchner', in *A Companion to Tragedy*, ed. by Rebecca Bushnell (Oxford: Blackwell, 2005), pp. 435–51 (p. 442). Even in the eighteenth century, however, there are distinct elements of cruelty in Lessing's plays: in *Miß Sara Sampson* (1755) the jilted Marwood compares herself to Seneca's heroine Medea and threatens to torture her and Mellefont's child to death; and in *Emilia Galotti* (1772) the Countess Orsina, likewise jilted by the Prince, fantasizes about assembling all his ex-lovers and tearing him to pieces. See Wilfried Barner, *Produktive Rezeption: Lessing und die Tragödien Senecas* (Munich: Beck, 1973).

9   On Lohenstein's reception, see briefly Gillespie, *Lohenstein's Historical Tragedies*, pp. 14–25, and Reinhart Meyer-Kalkus, *Wollust und Grausamkeit: Affektenlehre und Affektdarstellung in Lohensteins Dramatik am Beispiel 'Agrippina'* (Göttingen: Vandenhoeck & Ruprecht, 1986), pp. 21–25, who notes that in the nineteenth century the frequency of torture and eroticism in his plays led readers to attribute to him a pathological disposition; much more detail in Alberto Martino, *Daniel Casper von Lohenstein: Storia della sua ricezione*, I (1661–1800) (Pisa: Libreria Editrice Athenaeum, 1975).

10   A thorough study of Lohenstein's erudition is needed. Jane O. Newman has made a start in *The Intervention of Philology: Gender, Learning, and Power in Lohenstein's Roman Plays* (Chapel Hill and London: University of North Carolina Press, 2000), e.g. pp. 58–69.

that sound even more alien. By present-day standards, these plays hardly seem suitable to be performed by teenage boys in the presence of their proud parents. The on-stage violence rivals Quentin Tarantino. Yet we know that *Agrippina* and *Epicharis*, one centring on incest, the other on torture, were performed alternately over a period of twelve days in May 1666. Admittedly, there is evidence that the most rawly erotic passages, in which Agrippina nearly seduces her son Nero and later is stabbed while naked in bed, were toned down in these performances, though possibly just because schoolboys could not have acted them convincingly.[11] The performances of *Agrippina* and *Epicharis* did cause some concern among the Breslau authorities, because they distracted the schoolboys from their studies and led to unspecified 'excesses'.[12] The plays were in any case a Protestant counterpart to Jesuit school drama, which often centred on the tortures suffered by Christian martyrs. The adults in the audience, who had lived through the later stages of the Thirty Years War, would have been only too familiar with violence. They were also aware of judicial torture: since the introduction of Roman law in the late Middle Ages, the investigation of a capital crime, where only partial proof was forthcoming, included torture to obtain a confession. And although by the later seventeenth century the most savage punishments prescribed in the *Carolina* (1532) had largely fallen out of use, theft was still normally punished by hanging, and more severe crimes, such as adultery and murder, by public decapitation, after which the body was left to rot on a gibbet as a dreadful warning to all passers-by.[13]

The atmosphere of the dramas is made more un-Christian by their formal and intellectual indebtedness to Lucius Annaeus Seneca (*c.* 1 BCE–65 CE).[14] Lohenstein's contemporaries proudly called him 'our German Seneca'.[15] Seneca was both a philosopher and a dramatist. As a philosopher, he supported the Stoic doctrine of emotional self-control; yet his plays are full of verbal and physical violence, so that in the Renaissance it was assumed that the philosopher and the dramatist must have been different people. Seneca's dramatic characters give way to overpowering passions, vent their feelings in hyperbolic tirades, and commit some of the most shocking actions recorded in mythology. Hercules, driven mad by Juno, slaughters his children; Medea, furious at being abandoned by her husband Jason, kills hers; the Trojan women are killed by the Greek conquerors; Oedipus, learning that he has unwittingly committed parricide and incest, tears out his eyes. Whether these actions were actually presented on stage is not clear: in the nineteenth and much of the twentieth century it was assumed that Seneca's plays were intended only for recitation or reading, but now it is often thought that they were performed in some manner.[16] Even reading the plays in translation, one reels from their impact.

---

11   See Meyer-Kalkus, *Wollust und Grausamkeit*, pp. 15–18.
12   Newman, *Intervention*, pp. 79–80.
13   See Richard J. Evans, *Rituals of Retribution: Capital Punishment in Germany, 1600–1987* (Oxford: Oxford University Press, 1996), pp. 27–50.
14   See Paul Stachel, *Seneca und das deutsche Renaissancedrama* (Berlin: Mayer & Müller, 1907).
15   Sigmund von Birken, quoted in Martino, *Daniel Casper von Lohenstein*, p. 198.
16   Contrast *The Oxford Classical Dictionary*, ed. by Simon Hornblower and Antony Spawforth, 3rd edn (Oxford: Oxford University Press, 1996), p. 97, with the 'Introduction' to Seneca, *Six Tragedies*, trans. by Emily Wilson, Oxford World's Classics (Oxford: Oxford University Press, 2010), p. xxiv. Helen Slaney, in her indispensable history of Seneca's theatrical afterlife, attributes the view that his

It is not surprising, therefore, that in the Renaissance, when Latin was far more commonly known than Greek, Seneca's plays were the most important model for tragic drama. Renaissance dramatists owed to them not only the five-act structure but many conventions which English readers will know best from Elizabethan revenge plays such as Thomas Kyd's *Spanish Tragedy* (1592). Instead of a Christian afterlife, the next world is represented only by vengeful ghosts. Many ghosts appear in Lohenstein. Far from expressing Christian forgiveness, they gloat over the punishments that they think their murderers deserve; in *Cleopatra*, the ghost of Jamblichus, who was killed on Antonius's orders, troubles his killer's dreams with a long list of tortures that he wants Antonius to suffer, from having his limbs scraped with iron combs to being sewn up in a sack and thrown to dogs. One cannot imagine Lohenstein writing anything corresponding to Shakespeare's 'Good night, sweet Prince, | And flights of angels sing thee to thy rest', or to the promise of a peaceful and joyous afterlife held out to the martyred Charles I by the sympathetic virgins in Gryphius's *Carolus Stuardus* (1657).[17]

The Senecan model often produces what Helen Slaney calls 'hypertragedy'.[18] Obsessed characters in the grip of fate vent their raging emotions in powerful, rhetorically elaborate speeches which in seventeenth-century England were called 'rants'. The great English practitioner of hypertragedy was Nathaniel Lee, known as 'Ranting Nat', whose subject matter often overlaps with Lohenstein's, as in his *Nero* (1674) and *Sophonisbe* (1675).[19] Lohenstein's plays likewise deserve the designation 'hypertragedy'. They belong with the 'literature of the extreme' represented in the nineteenth century by Heinrich von Kleist's *Penthesilea* (1807) and in the twentieth by the ultra-violent plays of Hans Henny Jahnn such as *Pastor Ephraim Magnus* (1919), awarded the Kleist Prize, and *Medea* (1926).[20]

Lohenstein's tragedies admit us to a world of harsh political realism. Here 'Staats-Klugheit' is the supreme virtue. As to Lohenstein's understanding of this term, we have some evidence from his translation of *El político*, a eulogy of Ferdinand II of Aragon (1452–1516), who by marrying Isabella of Castile laid the foundations for the kingdom of Spain, and, by conquering the kingdom of Granada, drove the Arabs out of the peninsula. The original author, Baltasar Gracián (1601–58), represents Ferdinand as an almost flawless monarch, especially by virtue of his political intelligence. The word 'staats-klug', corresponding to *político*, appears in Lohenstein's title and is elucidated in the text. Many people, according to Gracián, complain that 'Staats-Klugheit' means cunning and deceit, and that the best rulers, by this criterion, are those who are best at lying, deception, and dissimulation.

plays were unstageable to August Wilhelm Schlegel: see Slaney, *The Senecan Aesthetic: A Performance History* (Oxford: Oxford University Press, 2016), pp. 200–02.

17   Andreas Gryphius, *Ermordete Majestät oder Carolus Stuardus, König von Groß Britanien*, v. 433–36.
18   Slaney, *The Senecan Aesthetic*, pp. 166–88. Slaney borrows the term from Jost Hermand, 'Kleists *Penthesilea* im Kreuzfeuer geschlechtsspezifischer Diskurse', *Monatshefte*, 87 (1995), 34–47; cf. the English version, 'Kleist's *Penthesilea*: Battleground of Gendered Discourses', in *A Companion to the Works of Heinrich von Kleist*, ed. by Bernd Fischer (Rochester, NY: Camden House, 2003), pp. 43–60.
19   See Peter Skrine, 'Blood, Bombast and Deaf Gods: The Tragedies of Lee and Lohenstein', *German Life and Letters*, 24 (1970), 14–30.
20   See Uwe Schütte, *Die Poetik des Extremen: Ausschreitungen einer Sprache des Radikalen* (Göttingen: Vandenhoeck & Ruprecht, 2006).

However, people who practise such deviousness end up being caught in their own snares: Gracián gives the examples of Tiberius and Louis XI, who he thinks have been overpraised by their respective historians, Tacitus and Commines.[21] Ferdinand's 'Staats-Klugheit' consisted in astute political judgement, in knowing how to adjust his behaviour to circumstances, and in pursuing a consistent policy. This is very much the official version of 'reason of state'. It sidesteps the possibility that the prudent monarch may find himself obliged to practise deceit. However, the conflict between morality and 'Staats-Klugheit', in which the latter always wins, is central to Lohenstein's plays.

At the same time, the political realism of the plays may seem difficult to reconcile with Lohenstein's position in a culture dominated by Christianity. As his plays were performed at the grammar schools in Breslau, we should expect them to have an acceptable moral and religious message. The message is indicated mainly in the allegorical 'Reyen', a kind of didactic mini-opera, which ends each Act. All the plays have non-Christian or pre-Christian settings (modern Constantinople, ancient Rome), and the characters say very little that sounds at all Christian. Nor do they show much interest in the pagan gods. The gods are repeatedly reproached either for indifference ('Ihr leichten Götter ihr!' (C III. 539), 'You uncaring gods!') or for their enmity ('Ihr grimmen Götter ihr!' (C III. 613, IV. 396, V. 219), 'You cruel gods!'). Only a handful of Lohenstein's positive characters use any Christian language. Scipio in *Sophonisbe* sounds for a moment incongruously Christian when he admonishes the concupiscent Masanissa, 'Gott ist ein keuscher Geist | liebt Andacht keuscher Hertzen' ('God is a chaste spirit [and] loves the piety of chaste hearts', S IV. 245).[22] Seneca, whose death is shown in Act V of *Epicharis*, talks of how life's end is inevitable and unforeseeable:

> Wir flih'n den Schluß vergebens/
> Den das Gebuhrts-Licht uns in's Himmels-Buch schreib't ein/
> Mit Ziffern/ welche selbst Chaldeern frembde seyn/
> Die GOtt nur lesen kan / und Weise nur verstehen. (V. 260–63)

> It is in vain for us to flee the end which the light of our birth inscribes for us in the book of heaven, in letters which are unknown even to Chaldeans, which only God can read and only sages understand.

Since Christianity is inconspicuous in Lohenstein's plays, they are remote from the 'martyr drama' which was a hugely popular Baroque genre (e.g. Calderón's *El principe constante* (1636), Corneille's *Polyeucte* (1643)). It was especially favoured by Gryphius: the Christian martyr Catharina of Georgia remains steadfast when tortured to death by the Persian king Chach Abbas (*Catharina von Georgien*); Charles I displays the utmost constancy and piety when preparing for his execution

---

21   *Lorentz Gratians Staats-kluger Catholischer Ferdinand. Aus dem Spanischen übersetzet von Daniel Caspern von Lohenstein* (Budißin and Leipzig: Bey Heinrich Simon Hübnern, 1721), pp. 92–93. See Knut Forssmann, 'Spuren Graciáns im Werk Lohensteins', *Daphnis*, 12 (1983), 481–505.
22   Other examples of apparently Christian language in the play, not all of them convincing, are quoted by Judith Popovich Aikin, *The Mission of Rome in the Dramas of Daniel Casper von Lohenstein: Historical Tragedy as Prophecy and Polemic* (Stuttgart: Heinz, 1976), pp. 232–33.

(*Carolus Stuardus*); the upright lawyer Papinian prefers to die rather than condone the immorality of the emperor Bassianus Caracalla (*Sterbender Papinianus*). Attempts have been made to assimilate *Epicharis*, whose heroine remains steadfast under extreme torture, to the 'martyr drama'.[23] However, as I will argue below, Epicharis's undoubted heroism has some dubious aspects. Moreover, the play offers no hint of the transcendence which is supposed to make the martyr's sufferings worthwhile.[24]

Lohenstein's theatre of cruelty had a moral and political purpose. Even the sensational violence and eroticism was meant to provide political lessons by displaying the wickedness of tyrants — Nero and Ibrahim Bassa — and showing that such figures come to a bad end. I will concentrate on the most obviously political dramas, *Epicharis*, *Cleopatra*, and *Sophonisbe*. However, since Lohenstein's plays have a strong didactic component, commentators have often been tempted to reduce them to their didactic message, which is spelt out in the allegorical 'Reyen' which end each Act. The fourth 'Reyen' of *Sophonisbe*, for example, enacts the choice of Hercules between pleasure and virtue, an allegorical counterpart to Masanissa's dilemma between the allure of Sophonisbe and his allegiance to Rome. Hence the play has been interpreted as turning on the conflict between passion and reason, with Sophonisbe representing the former and Scipio the latter.[25] The characters have been simplified even further by the claim that Masanissa 'finds himself between a guardian spirit and a temptress'.[26]

The difficulty is not that such characterizations are wrong, but that they are impossibly one-dimensional. They imply a simple scheme, lacking in ambiguity, whereby Sophonisbe displays continual inconstancy and wickedness, Masanissa is briefly tempted by her but returns to the path of virtue under the guidance of Scipio, and Rome represents peace and benevolence. They take the simplicity of the allegorical choruses and try to impose it on the politically and psychologically complex action of the dramas. In reading and watching Shakespeare, we are used to subtlety and ambivalence. *Macbeth* is not *only* a denunciation of regicide, *Othello* not *only* a warning against jealousy. The human entanglements of Lohenstein's plays, as opposed to the 'Reyen' which proclaim an acceptably simple official message, equally deserve to be appreciated for their subtlety.

23   Pierre Béhar, *Silesia Tragica: Épanouissement et fin de l'école dramatique silésienne dans l'œuvre tragique de Daniel Casper von Lohenstein (1635–1683)* (Wiesbaden: Harrassowitz, 1988), p. 118; more tentatively, Sarah Colvin, *The Rhetorical Feminine: Gender and Orient on the German Stage, 1647–1742* (Oxford: Clarendon Press, 1999), pp. 76–77. Contrast Meyer-Kalkus, *Wollust und Grausamkeit*, p. 223.
24   Considerable attention has been given to the theme of fate in Lohenstein: e.g. Gillespie, *Lohenstein's Historical Tragedies*; Wilhelm Vosskamp, *Untersuchungen zur Zeit- und Geschichtsauffassung im 17. Jahrhundert bei Gryphius und Lohenstein* (Bonn: Bouvier, 1967); Gerhard Spellerberg, *Verhängnis und Geschichte: Untersuchungen zu den Trauerspielen und dem 'Arminius'-Roman Daniel Caspers von Lohenstein* (Bad Homburg v.d.H.: Gehlen, 1970). However, this approach runs the dual risk of treating the 'Reyen' as complete interpretations of the plays, and of elevating the characters' utterances, which can only express their understanding of their situation at a given moment, into a metaphysical doctrine, thereby making them all seem philosophers: thus Gillespie attributes to Masanissa 'an understanding of historical inevitability' (p. 114).
25   Rolf Tarot, 'Zu Lohensteins Sophonisbe', *Euphorion*, 59 (1965), 72–96 (esp. p. 95).
26   Aikin, *Mission of Rome*, p. 229.

It is, finally, remarkable that four of Lohenstein's great plays centre on strong female characters whose centrality is acknowledged by the titles: *Cleopatra*, *Agrippina*, *Epicharis*, and *Sophonisbe*. As long ago as 1907 it was said of him that, as Euripides did for Greek drama, Lohenstein 'discovered woman for German drama'.[27] In each case, the woman leads active resistance to political power. Epicharis inspires a revolt against the clearly inexcusable tyranny of Nero. Agrippina, whose son Nero has already tried to murder her by causing the ceiling of her room to collapse, and later tries to have her drowned, makes a seduction attempt not out of mere wantonness but in order to ensure her own survival. Cleopatra and Sophonisbe are trying to defend their kingdoms against Roman conquest, and to avoid the humiliation of being displayed in a Roman triumph.[28] That invites the audience's sympathy and deters one from experiencing these plays either as exercises in misogyny or as glorifications of Roman power. We know these heroines are doomed, and that they are flawed characters, but we are invited to judge even their unscrupulous actions leniently, as resulting from desperation, and to sympathize with their struggles against fate.

27   Stachel, *Seneca*, p. 292.
28   See the defence of these characters by Cornelia Plume, *Heroinen in der Geschlechterforschung: Weiblichkeitsprojektionen bei Daniel Casper von Lohenstein und die 'Querelle des Femmes'* (Stuttgart and Weimar: Metzler, 1996), pp. 221–42.

2

Lohenstein:
Epicharis (1665) and Stoicism

The philosophy of Lohenstein's plays also goes back to Seneca. It is essentially neo-Stoicism, though in *Epicharis* the Stoicism voiced by Seneca, a character in the play, is also qualified and challenged. The moral outlook of Seneca and Cicero was adapted for modern times in the hugely popular treatise by Justus Lipsius, *De constantia* (1584), which advocated an ethic of steadfastness. The Stoic could not prevent the misfortunes arising from an ultimately uncontrollable fate, or from Machiavelli's *fortuna*, but he could at least withstand them with the aid of his reason, his self-control, and his firmness of character. The constancy he should cultivate was defined (by Lipsius's English translator) as 'a right and immovable strength of the mind, neither lifted up nor pressed down with external or casual accidents'.[1] Many of Shakespeare's heroes are Stoics, but always with an ironic qualification. Julius Caesar, who boasts 'I am constant as the northern star', is nevertheless foolish enough to ignore many prophetic warnings and go to the Capitol where he is assassinated; Horatio, who says 'I am more an antique Roman than a Dane' and is commended by Hamlet for not being 'passion's slave', is only an onlooker at events and is not really tested; while Othello, besides being vulnerable to Iago's insinuations, displays a steadfastness which has been criticized for being too obviously a display and illustrating the theatricality which often accompanies Stoicism.[2] The Stoic should also combine reason and courage to ensure that he acts with prudence and exploits the 'tide in the affairs of men | Which, taken at the flood, leads on to fortune' (*Julius Caesar*, IV. 3. 216–17). Thus Augustus in *Cleopatra*, after shedding a statutory tear for Antonius's death, says that he must not be distracted by sorrow from taking advantage of time and fortune: 'Jedoch der Schmertz muß nicht verspilen Glück und Zeit' (*C* IV. 55).

Stoicism held a cognitive conception of virtue. To do what was right, one first had to know what was right. Hence displays of wrongdoing were useful as an incitement to virtue. The passions by which many of Lohenstein's characters are carried away were lessons to the audience, conveying the necessity of moderating

---

1   Justus Lipsius, *On Constancy*, trans. by Sir John Stradling, ed. by John Sellars (Exeter: The Exeter Press, 2006), p. 37.
2   See T. S. Eliot, 'Shakespeare and the Stoicism of Seneca', in his *Selected Essays* (London: Faber, 1932), pp. 26–40; Geoffrey Miles, *Shakespeare and the Constant Romans* (Oxford: Clarendon Press, 1996); A. D. Nuttall, *Shakespeare the Thinker* (New Haven and London: Yale University Press, 2007), esp. p. 177.

one's own feelings. Hence this kind of tragedy differs from the type theorized by Aristotle in the *Poetics*. According to Aristotle, tragedy takes us on an emotional journey. It stirs up our feelings, especially the feelings of pity and terror, in order to effect a catharsis which purges us of these emotions. For, as Nietzsche would later observe, Aristotle thought that pity, as well as fear, was a feeling one was better without.[3] In the neo-Stoic theory of tragedy, we can of course feel pity for suffering characters, but our journey is primarily an intellectual one, and it ends by strengthening the constancy that steels us against misfortune. The Baroque theorist of tragedy, Martin Opitz, spelt this out in the preface to his translation of Seneca's *The Trojan Women* (1625):

> Such constancy is implanted in us by contemplating the frailty of human life, especially in tragedy: for by often beholding and contemplating the utter downfall of great people, entire cities and countries, we do, as is proper, feel pity for them, and can scarcely hold back our tears of sorrow; but in addition we learn from the frequent observation of other people's suffering and misfortune to fear less and endure better the misfortunes that may happen to us.[4]

The constancy recommended by neo-Stoicism was felt to be particularly necessary in the seventeenth century. It was a period racked by wars, the most devastating being the Thirty Years War, which killed one-third of the population of Germany. People surrounded by catastrophes were receptive to the doctrine that the wise man should steel himself by subordinating his emotions to the supremacy of reason. *Ratio* (reason) was superior to *opinio* (passions, impulses). Such a severely rational person was also well equipped to serve the absolutist state. 'The ideal individual in the political world, as portrayed by Lipsius, is the citizen who acts according to reason, is answerable to himself, controls his emotions, and is ready to fight.'[5]

Lohenstein's Stoicism is most on display in *Epicharis*, a play which is also indebted to Tacitus. In Book 15 of his *Annals*, Tacitus recounts the conspiracy formed against Nero by a group of discontented aristocrats in 65 CE. Although it was named the Pisonian conspiracy after the popular Calpurnius Piso, whom the conspirators intended to place on the throne once they had disposed of Nero, Piso himself, in both Tacitus and Lohenstein, appears languid and ineffectual. The driving force behind the conspiracy is a freedwoman named Epicharis, of whom Tacitus seems to think poorly, saying that 'she had never before interested herself in anything good'.[6] The remaining conspirators, as Lohenstein presents them, come across as windbags, boasting wildly about what they will do to Nero. Since Nero has not only murdered his own mother and brother and burnt down a large part of Rome, but also degraded the imperial office by singing in the theatre, the conspirators resolve to attack him during a stage performance; Epicharis will take part, disguised

---

3   *Der Antichrist*, §7, in Nietzsche, KSA VI, 174.
4   Quoted in John Alexander, 'Early Modern German Drama, 1400–1700', in *The Camden House History of German Literature*, vol. 4: *Early Modern German Literature 1350–1700*, ed. by Max Reinhart (Rochester, NY: Camden House, 2007), pp. 357–94 (p. 367).
5   Gerhard Oestreich, *Neostoicism and the Early Modern State* (Cambridge: Cambridge University Press, 1982), p. 30.
6   Tacitus, *Annals*, trans. by Grant, p. 369.

as a male soldier. But nothing happens, and meanwhile the plot is discovered. Epicharis is betrayed by a rebuffed suitor; another conspirator, Scevinus, by making his will, having an old dagger sharpened, and generally appearing anxious, arouses the suspicions of two servants, who (ungratefully, since Scevinus freed them from slavery) report this to Nero. Scevinus and his friend Natalis are pulled in for questioning. Interrogated separately, they tell different stories. A witch-hunt for their associates begins, terrified people denounce one another, and eventually all are arrested.[7] Meanwhile Epicharis herself is tortured by Nero and his henchman Tigillinus, in a scene whose high point is this:

NERO	Wer nicht bekennen wil/ gehör't auf scharffe Fragen.
EPICHARIS	Ich wil bekennen.
NERO	Wol! Loß!
EPICHARIS	sag's/ was ich sol sagen?
NERO	Setz't der Verzweifelten entflammte Zangen an.
EPICHARIS	Was sol die offenbar'n/ die kaum mehr athmen kan.
NERO	Laß't der Halb-todten Luft: Daß sie noch einmal sterbe.
EPICHARIS	Es thut dem Geiste wol/ schmeckt's gleich dem Cörper herbe.
NERO	Bring't her ein glüend Pferd/ zieht bis sie berst entzwey.
EPICHARIS	Halt Hencker! ich gestehs: Daß ich dein Todfeind sey. (III. 560–66)

NERO	Anyone who won't confess must be interrogated under torture.
EPICHARIS	I will confess.
NERO	Good! Out with it!
EPICHARIS	Tell me what I'm to say.
NERO	Pinch the despairing woman with red-hot pincers.
EPICHARIS	What can someone reveal who can hardly breathe any longer?
NERO	She's half dead, give her air so that she can die a second time.
EPICHARIS	This refreshes the spirit, even if the body finds it bitter.
NERO	Fetch a red-hot horse, rack her till she splits in two.
EPICHARIS	Stop, hangman! I confess — that I am your deadly enemy.

Epicharis then challenges Nero to inflict a further and more fantastic range of tortures on her: to wind her intestines round a red-hot stake, to bury her alive in an ants' nest, to chain her to a rock on which the Furies pour boiling oil, to squeeze the marrow from her bones; all this, she says, will simply make her laugh.

In the remainder of the play, the conspirators are interrogated and dispatched. Most behave abjectly. Some are ordered to commit suicide: Piso opens his veins on stage. Others are executed before the spectators' eyes. Epicharis herself, after a further spell on the rack, manages (as in Tacitus) to strangle herself.

If Stoicism meant simply fortitude in suffering pain, Epicharis would be an exemplary Stoic. But she not only suffers pain: she seems to seek it out, as though driven by algolagnia. She tells Nero that torture gives her pleasure. She herself acknowledges an erotic element in her desire for torture:

> Ich selber rechne mir mein Leid für ein Geschencke
> Der Götter/ ja wenn ich die blutt'gen Glieder schrencke

---

7   On the conspirators' contemptible behaviour, see Erik Lunding, *Das schlesische Kunstdrama* (Copenhagen: Haase, 1940), pp. 122–23.

> Umb Pfal und Folterbanck/ empfind' ich größer Lust
> Als Acte/ die gleich ruht dem Kayser auf der Brust. (IV. 83–86)

> I myself regard my suffering as a gift from the gods, indeed when I wrap my bleeding limbs round the stake and the rack, I feel greater pleasure than Acte [Nero's mistress] when she rests on the emperor's breast.

Moreover, as Natalis points out, her steadfastness under torture will accomplish nothing. The conspiracy has already been revealed. Nero, morbidly suspicious like all tyrants, is never going to believe that, as Epicharis claims, Natalis and Scevinus have been coerced into inventing a story. Although *Epicharis* does not belong to the genre of martyr dramas, its heroine shares the tendency of dramatic martyrs to welcome their torments.[8] Lessing, looking back from the Enlightenment, would complain that Corneille's Polyeucte did not inspire sympathy because he was so keen to be martyred.[9]

Politically, too, Epicharis's conduct demands only qualified admiration. She has admittedly a larger vision than the other conspirators. All they want is a palace revolution in which Nero would be replaced by another emperor. Epicharis, on the other hand, calls for freedom, which she identifies with rule by the people. When Piso makes the standard objection that government must be in the hands of a single person, Epicharis replies: 'Viel Armen können mehr als eine Faust bestreiten' (I. 456: 'Many arms can achieve more than a single fist') — a neat repartee, but not enough to dispel the assumption, standard under absolutism and later, that anything resembling ancient democracy would lead to anarchy and that in turn to tyranny.

Epicharis's methods too are unattractive. To bind the conspirators together, she makes them all take an oath confirmed by drinking wine mixed with blood. In his notes, Lohenstein cites examples of conspirators who took such an oath, the best known being Catiline in his conspiracy against the Roman republic. According to the historian Sallust, before revealing his plot to his fellow-conspirators, Catiline compelled them to take an oath of secrecy and to drink from bowls of human blood mixed with wine.[10] Catiline has served for two millennia as the most terrible example of an irresponsible and crazed enemy of established society. So the implied association with him is not to Epicharis's credit.

The genuine Stoic in the play is Seneca. Historically, Nero, his former pupil, suspected him of complicity in the plot and ordered him to commit suicide, which Seneca did by opening his veins in a warm bath. In Lohenstein's play, the conspirators think Seneca would make a better emperor than Piso and invite him to take part in the plot. Seneca refuses with a number of arguments, of which the most telling is that tyranny, like natural calamities, must simply be endured: 'Man

---

8   Cf. also the Catholic Isabella in *Measure for Measure*, who describes with eroticized enthusiasm how she would rather be tortured than yield her virginity to Angelo: 'Th' impression of keen whips I'd wear as rubies, | And strip myself to death as to a bed | That longing have been sick for, ere I'd yield | My body up to shame' (II. 4. 101–04).

9   Lessing, *Werke und Briefe*, III, 696.

10   Sallust, *The War with Catiline*, trans. by J. C. Rolfe, Loeb Classical Library (Cambridge, MA: Harvard University Press, 1931), section 22, p. 39.

muß die Tyranney wie Hagel/ Mißwachs dulden' (I. 530: 'One must put up with tyranny, as with hail or crop failure'). This, as Lohenstein explains in a note, is a quotation from Tacitus, though it is not presented as Tacitus's own view, but as that of a historical character.[11]

Seneca's quietism may be thought craven.[12] It is certainly rejected by his friend Manlius Festus, who has a long argument with Seneca in Act V of *Epicharis*. Manlius appeals to patriotism:

> Gewiß: Wer's Vaterland nicht rettet wenn er kan/
> Steckt Furien ein Licht/ Tyrannen Weyrauch an;
> Stürtzt Völcker in Verterb/ hilft Freinden auf die Baare
> Und bau't mehr als Busir den Göttern Mord-Altare. (V. 105–08)

> Certainly, anyone who fails to save the fatherland when he can do so provides Furies with light and tyrants with incense; plunges nations into ruin, helps friends to their graves, and outdoes Busiris [a legendary Egyptian tyrant] in building murderous altars to the gods.

Manlius and Seneca talk past each other. Seneca's attitude is not really political at all. He expresses the Stoic view that since the emotions can be controlled by reason, the wise, self-controlled man can therefore be happy no matter what his external circumstances. 'Ein Weiser bleib't auch frey in Feßeln des Tyrannen' (V. 15: 'A wise man remains free even in the tyrant's fetters'). He even cites the most extreme example of Stoics' alleged triumph over pain, the legend of the brazen bull which Phalaris, the tyrant of Agrigentum in Sicily, had made for his enemies: they were put inside the bull which was then heated so that they were roasted alive:

> [...] ein Weiser kan die minsten Schmerzen fühlen/
> Schleust ihn schon Phalaris in glimmen Ochzen ein. (V. 8–9)

> A wise man can hardly feel pain, even if Phalaris shuts him up in a glowing ox.

This example was commonly ridiculed in the seventeenth century: Sir Thomas Browne observes that 'the Stoicks that condemne passion, and command a man to laugh in *Phalaris* his Bull, could not endure without a groane a fit of the stone or collick'.[13] So Seneca's version of Stoicism is to be taken with at least a pinch of

---

11   'You endure barren years, excessive rains, and all other natural evils; in like manner, endure the extravagance or greed of your ruler' (advice by a Roman officer to two Germanic tribes), in Tacitus, *The Histories*, p. 147 (Book IV, section 74). Lohenstein cites another passage from Tacitus with a similar purport, from *Histories*, IV. 8: 'he prayed for good emperors, but endured any sort' (p. 17). The latter passage is paraphrased by Machiavelli: 'Truly golden is that maxim of Tacitus, which declares that men must honour past affairs and endure present ones, and that they should desire good princes, but regardless of what they are like, should tolerate them' (D III. 6. 256).

12   Stachel calls him a hypocrite ('heuchlerischen Tugendbold') and an old pedant and philistine (*Seneca*, pp. 303, 304).

13   Sir Thomas Browne, *Religio Medici* (1642) in *Selected Writings*, ed. by Sir Geoffrey Keynes (London: Faber, 1968), p. 61. For the eighteenth century, cf. Christoph Martin Wieland: 'Vielleicht erinnern sich einige hiebei an den Weisen der Stoiker von welchem man ehmals versicherte, daß er in dem glühenden Ochsen des Phalaris zum wenigsten so glücklich sei, als ein Morgenländischer Bassa in den weichen Armen einer jungen Circasserin' (Wieland, *Werke*, ed. by Fritz Martini and Hans Werner Seiffert, 5 vols (Munich: Hanser, 1964–68), I, 383–84).

salt, and Manlius's defence of tyrannicide is not to be dismissed out of hand. In Lohenstein's play, moreover, Seneca's assertion recalls Epicharis's claim (quoted above) to be enjoying erotic bliss when being tortured; except that Seneca only says that the tortured Stoic will not feel pain, whereas Epicharis professes also to feel pleasure.

In the age of absolutism, when a monarch's person was often held to be sacred because he was the Lord's anointed, regicide was of course an abominable crime. The bodies of the English 'regicides' who had condemned Charles I to death were disinterred at the Restoration and displayed in Westminster Hall.[14] The Jesuits were constantly reviled for asserting that king-killing or monarchomachy was permissible, though with reference only to usurpers, invaders, or tyrants.[15] Here the concept of regicide merged with that of tyrannicide, which had a venerable history. In the ancient world, Harmodius and Aristogeiton were celebrated for killing the tyrant Hipparchus in 514 BCE; Lucius Junius Brutus was admired for killing the tyrannical king Tarquinius and thus founding the Roman Republic; and the second Brutus, who assassinated Julius Caesar, was often praised as a supporter of freedom. But it was not always clear whether a particular case represented wicked regicide or admirable tyrannicide: supposing a legitimate ruler turned into a tyrant? And if he did, who decided at what point he became a tyrant and hence a legitimate target for assassination? Besides, political assassinations often had consequences even worse than the previous state of affairs. Julius Caesar's nephew Octavius, who as Augustus became the first Roman Emperor, managed to extinguish Roman freedom while pretending to preserve the authority of the Senate. These are some of the considerations behind the debate staged by Lohenstein between the activism of Manlius and the quietism of Seneca.

---

14   Samuel Pepys saw them there on 5 February 1661: *Diary*, ed. by Robert Latham and William Matthews, 11 vols (London: Bell, 1970–83), II, 31. The increasingly shrivelled heads remained on display until the 1680s. Of the fifty-nine men who had signed Charles I's death warrant, the eleven who could be apprehended in 1660 (the others having died or fled abroad) were condemned to immediate and painful execution: Anna Keay, *The Restless Republic: Britain without a Crown* (London: Collins, 2022), pp. 350–51.

15   Höpfl, *Jesuit Political Thought*, pp. 316–21.

— 3 —
Lohenstein:
Cleopatra (1661, 1680) —
The Drama of Intrigue

Cleopatra offers perhaps the clearest example of Machiavellian plotting and counter-plotting. It has been called the first drama of intrigue in German.[1] As such, it would have plenty of successors, above all, as we shall see, in the plays of Schiller. Its view of politics is based on 'reason of state', a version of Machiavellianism adapted to the requirements of absolutist government.[2] From various *sententiae* uttered by the characters, especially by minor characters, we can put together the collective world-view which is accepted by everyone in the play (how far it is Lohenstein's view is another, unanswerable question). The goods most worth striving for are power and fame ('Ruhm'). Princes are enviable: 'Fürsten sind ja Götter dieser Welt' (I. 977: 'Princes are the gods of this world'). A prince must be able to dissimulate, like a Machiavellian fox: 'Wer sich nicht anstelln kan / der taug zum herrschen nicht' (IV. 84: 'Anyone who cannot dissimulate is unfit to rule').[3] He must also be a lion and eliminate those who helped him to attain power: 'Ja der zur Herrschafft hilft / muß abgeschlachtet sein' (I. 261: 'He who helps you to power must be slaughtered'). He must sacrifice anything else to the good of his kingdom, which overrides all other laws: 'Das oberste Gesätz' ist eines Reiches Heil' (II. 491: 'The good of a kingdom is the supreme law', adapting Cicero's 'salus populi suprema lex esto').

Like Machiavelli, the characters hold a low view of human nature. People are ungrateful: a small service wins friends, but a greater service arouses resentment because the recipient cannot return it (I. 259–60). Prudence, based on reason, is all-important, but it is not sufficient: one must also be able to command fortune. 'Die Klugheit / die nicht's Glück auf ihren Flügeln träget / Kommt freylich auf den Grund' (III. 498–99: 'Unless it carries fortune on its wings, prudence leads to ruin'). And this is difficult, because we are at the mercy of forces beyond our control. Fortune is blind, and her wheel is constantly turning (V. 1). Behind or above fortune there is the force of destiny ('Verhängnüs'). Our destiny is determined from our birth: 'Auch ist nicht zu vermeiden / Was die Geburts-Gestirn' und Götter uns bescheiden' (V. 171–72: 'There is no avoiding what is decreed for us by the stars

---

1   Stachel, *Seneca*, p. 287.

2   Vosskamp splits hairs by denying that 'reason of state' in Lohenstein is Machiavellian: see his *Untersuchungen zur Zeit- und Geschichtsauffassung*, p. 204.

3   This is a version of the saying commonly attributed to Louis XI of France: 'qui nescit dissimulare, nescit regnare', 'he who does not know how to dissimulate does not know how to reign'.

presiding at our birth and by the gods'). Destiny can mean the inevitable course of history. Lohenstein frames both *Cleopatra* and *Sophonisbe* in the biblical model of history as a succession of empires, derived from Daniel 7–12, with the Roman Empire destined to overcome Egypt, but with the Habsburg Empire as the modern heir to Rome.[4] The closing 'Reyen' of both plays acclaim the Emperor Leopold I (1640–1705) as the future universal ruler whose empire already includes America (*C* v. 840–45) and newly discovered southern islands, presumably the Philippines (*S* v. 692–94).

This world-view owes much to Machiavelli and much also to Stoicism. Lohenstein presents Augustus as a Machiavellian with a large dose of Stoicism, and Scipio in *Sophonisbe* as a Stoic with a large streak of Machiavellianism. Both combine, in various proportions, the Stoic virtues of *constantia* and *prudentia*. Neither is a likeable figure, but they have the stature appropriate to a ruler and a general, and they survive and succeed in the world of Lohenstein's dramas.

Lohenstein's Stoic rulers have no time for love. Love reduces one to being 'passion's slave', as Antonius is erotically enslaved to Cleopatra, and Masanissa to Sophonisbe. It is readily equated with 'Brunst' (erotic passion). Augustus, learning that Antonius has committed suicide because of Cleopatra, deplores the effects of love:

> Uns tauret / daß der Mann durch ein solch Weib sol fallen!
> Der Liebe Gift ist doch das giftigst' unter allen. (IV. 41–42)

[We regret that the man should have fallen because of such a woman! The poison of love is the most poisonous of all.]

His counterpart in *Sophonisbe*, the Roman general Scipio (known in history as Africanus because of his success in the Second Punic War against Carthage), acknowledges no difference between love, lust, and lechery, and prides himself on being superior to them all:

> Von allen grossen Gaben
> Weiß ich mich sonsten arm / in der rühm' ich mich reich:
> Daß meinem Herzen ist der Liebe Trieb zu weich /
> Die Wollust ist mir Gift/ und Geilheit schmeckt mir herbe. (*S* IV. 275–77)

[Although I know I am poor in other ways, I can boast of being rich in this: that the impulse of love is too soft for my heart; sensual pleasure is poison to me, and lechery tastes bitter.]

Female characters are capable of love, but are not mastered by it. Sophonisbe loves her husband Syphax enough to save his life on two occasions, but he is still only one factor, and not the overriding one, in her struggle to defend Carthage. Cleopatra's love for Antonius is apparent after his death, when she praises him as the ideal hero and has his body embalmed, but while he is still alive she plots ruthlessly against him in the hope of saving herself. It is not women who are irrational in Lohenstein's dramatic world, but the men — Antonius and Masanissa — who succumb to their charms.

---

4   On the 'four monarchies' conception, see Aikin, *The Mission of Rome*, pp. 45–61.

Both Lohenstein's African plays show the same constellation of characters. The titular heroine, Cleopatra or Sophonisbe, is plotting desperately to save her country from defeat by Rome, or, failing that, to save herself from being taken to Rome and displayed humiliatingly in an imperial triumph. Her ultimate antagonist, the Roman conqueror, Augustus or Scipio, may have his moments of humanity, but is a Stoic in whom reason firmly dominates passion and a Machiavellian ruler who is ruthless and unscrupulous in pursuing his goals. Between them is the lover, Antonius or Masanissa, who is helplessly under the sway of the beloved woman and sharply conscious of her physical attraction (always described in luscious detail), and whose sensuality either leads to his death (in Antonius's case) or submits finally to the control of manly reason (in Masanissa's).

Cleopatra begins after the battle of Actium and deals with the events which occupy Act v of Shakespeare's play. Antonius and Cleopatra have been defeated at sea by Augustus's fleet, and are now holed up in Alexandria, while Augustus and his troops have begun occupying Egypt. In Act i (rendered too long and undramatic by over-detailed exposition) Antonius and his associates debate what to do. Some recommend coming to terms with Augustus, but Antonius more realistically declares that Augustus is inflexible and insatiable. An imperial negotiator makes clear that although Augustus is prepared to offer Antonius many other eastern territories, he insists on having Egypt, because the fertility caused by the flooding of the Nile makes it the richest country and the most lucrative prize. Augustus also insists that Antonius must give up Cleopatra and return to his wife Octavia (Augustus's sister). This leaves Antonius with a stark choice: 'Eh' oder Thron', marriage or a throne (I 888). Either he retains his relationship with Cleopatra (and what will happen to them then?) or he accepts a throne that he does not particularly want. To his advisers, this is no choice at all. Beauty, even Cleopatra's, is short-lived, but a throne is a solid good. When Antonius worries about what will happen to Cleopatra, they suggest that he should send her poison, as Masanissa did to Sophonisbe, so that she can end her life in the way that Sophonisbe is praised for having done. Antonius is not averse to this idea, but cannot face the prospect of life without Cleopatra and with Octavia. Meanwhile his options keep shrinking. The brief prospect of fleeing to Spain and leading an uprising there vanishes when one of his associates goes over to Augustus with his entire fleet, while another turncoat surrenders the strategically important island of Pharos. So Antonius is obliged to be wholly inactive.

Cleopatra, all this time, is plotting vigorously. What makes her such a fascinating character is that, even in soliloquy and talking to her closest female intimate, she is always acting a part. During Antonius's conversation with his advisers, she was listening at the door, so she knows that Antonius has not told her the full truth of their situation, and reproaches him for it. Apologizing abjectly, he admits that Augustus has demanded the whole of Egypt, plus the surrender of their captive, the Armenian king Artabazes, but affirms that he is prepared only to hand over two pieces of land. Seeing this as the first step on a slippery slope leading to total submission, Cleopatra uses all her powers of persuasion and emotional blackmail, including the staging of pathetic appeals by their three children, to change his mind. This works: Antonius promises to reject Augustus's terms and gives orders to have Artabazes executed forthwith. Thus Cleopatra deliberately makes the breach between him and Augustus irreparable.

Antonius has no idea, however, of the depth of Cleopatra's intrigues. Even before this, she has had a secret conversation with a Roman emissary who assures her that Augustus loves her and wishes to put aside his wife Livia in order to marry her, on condition that she disposes of Antonius. Although Cleopatra does not demur at this condition, she expresses scepticism about Augustus's sincerity, but changes her tune when the envoy shows her a letter in Augustus's own hand. She promises to marry Augustus, to surrender Egypt to him, and to kill Antonius. In the very next scene, she continues her intrigue by plotting Antonius's death; she tells Caesarion (her son by Julius Caesar) and her chief minister Archibius that Antonius is really in league with Augustus and is plotting to kill the three of them, and easily convinces them of this flagrant lie, helped by Augustus's letter in which he asks her to eliminate Antonius. So her associates resolve to kill Antonius before he kills them, and the following scene, in which Cleopatra pathetically implores Antonius not to surrender Egypt, has to be read or watched in the knowledge that she has already arranged to surrender Egypt herself and to have Antonius killed.

Cleopatra now has a soliloquy, the only one in the play. Her soliloquy does not show her working out an inner conflict, like Masanissa's two soliloquies in *Sophonisbe*; instead, she reviews her situation and lets the bewildered reader or spectator know what she is actually up to. Her guides are prudence (she counts herself among the 'klugen Frauen' who are too smart for mere 'Männer-Witz', II. 430–31) and reason. The sun of reason is now dispelling the mist ('Dunst', a recurrent image for deception) that has hitherto obscured it. Using the sustained metaphor of a sea voyage, she asserts that love (that is, Antonius's love for her) is useless as an anchor, because the wind of slander (her insinuations) has driven his ship onto quicksands. Where she is to direct her voyage, however, is less clear. She has lulled Antonius into security, but he is still too unreliable to be trusted; inclination, love, and friendship are too fragile:

> Gunst / Liebe / Freundschafft gleicht sich zarten Berg-Kristallen
> Die keine Kunst ergäntzt / sind einmal sie zerfallen. (II. 453–54)
>
> [Inclination, love and friendship resemble fragile icicles, which no art can restore once they have collapsed.]

In any case, her crown is more important to her than anything else. To keep it, she must steer her ship into the harbour offered by Augustus, relying on his letter. Antonius's death will ensure her safety with Augustus: 'Anton / durch deinen Tod fahrn wir in Hafen ein!' (II. 464: 'Antonius, through your death we will enter the harbour!'). The next question is how to get rid of Antonius. To have him poisoned or stabbed would be dangerous, and might blacken Cleopatra's reputation. Instead, she will take advantage of the extreme to which his erotic passion ('der blinden Brunst', II 470) has brought him, and will pretend to kill herself so as to drive him to despair and suicide. After that, she anticipates no difficulty in bringing Augustus to heel by means of her feminine charms, which, after all, worked on Julius Caesar.

She concludes happily that fortune is now on her side.

Are we to understand Cleopatra simply as a heartless schemer? If so, she would resemble the Sultaness Roxelane in Lohenstein's first play, *Ibrahim Bassa*, who intrigues with furious determination to overcome the hesitancy of the Sultan and bring about Ibrahim's death. Cleopatra is more complex. When the dying Antonius is brought to her, she is clearly distressed; on his death, she faints. Earlier, when she thinks that Antonius is about to betray her, she falls into a fury ('Wir rasen!', II 145), anticipating the raging female figures who appear in eighteenth-century tragedy (e.g. Marwood in Lessing's *Miß Sara Sampson*, Orsina in his *Emilia Galotti*).[5] Commentators often call her demonic, but she is really volatile, and thus she forms a contrast both to the concupiscence of Antonius and the steadfastness and prudence of Augustus.

Cleopatra's plan works admirably. She feigns an elaborate suicide, callously distressing all her devoted female attendants, except for Charmium, who is in the secret. After terrible dreams, and news of further betrayals, Antonius is devastated to hear of Cleopatra's supposed death. He falls on his sword, but fails to kill himself outright. In this state he learns that Cleopatra is alive after all, and is brought to her in the royal vault. She expresses the most intense grief at the death which she has herself contrived, and affirms that she would rather die than kneel before Augustus (which she fully intends to do, and later does do). Unaware of her duplicity, Antonius dies a romantic death with a final kiss from Cleopatra on his lips.

Only now, in Act IV, do we meet Augustus. The act opens with Augustus in his tent, receiving the news of Antonius's death from the slave, Dercetaeus, who has brought the very dagger with which Antonius stabbed himself. Augustus shows his suspicious nature by surmising that the messenger himself committed the crime:

> DERCETAEUS.   Ich habe selbst den Dolch ihm aus der Brust gezogen.
> AUGUSTUS.   Den du gewiß zuvor ihm hast hinein gesteckt. (IV. 6–7)

> [DERCETAEUS.   I myself drew from his breast this dagger.
> AUGUSTUS.   Which I've no doubt you had previously plunged into it.]

Not satisfied by Dercetaeus's denials, Augustus orders him to be kept under guard, and meanwhile expresses regret that Antonius has killed himself merely because of a woman, and also that Antonius's death has deprived him, Augustus, of the chance to show his magnanimity. He shares the news with his lieutenants Agrippa and Maecenas (Lohenstein spells the name 'Mecaenas'). These figures were not in the earlier (1661) version of the play. The introduction of Agrippa serves to place Augustus in a favourable light by showing that he exercises severity only reluctantly. Agrippa, a harsh and brutal character, responds to the news of Antonius's death with 'Glück zu!' (IV. 76, 'Hurrah!') and urges Augustus to treat the defeated Egypt with the utmost severity, while the more reflective Maecenas points out that mild treatment is likely to win the Egyptians to accept Roman rule. Next comes a delegation from Cleopatra, consisting of her and Antonius's three children, accompanied

---

5   Emil Staiger, 'Rasende Weiber in deutschen Tragödien des achtzehnten Jahrhunderts', in his *Stilwandel: Studien zur Vorgeschichte der Goethezeit* (Zurich: Atlantis, 1963), pp. 25–74.

by Archibius. Since the children's emotional appeal earlier worked on Antonius, Cleopatra evidently wants to try the same effect again. Besides pleading for mercy, her envoys promise Augustus the wealth not only of Egypt but of southern African territories, including the Mountains of the Moon and even Madagascar. Augustus responds graciously; although he could have kept the children as hostages, he sends them back and promises mercy to Cleopatra.

In a crucial scene, after the withdrawal of the envoys, Agrippa criticizes Augustus severely for this magnanimity. Instead of treating Cleopatra with such dignity, he ought to bring her to Rome and display her in his triumphal procession, symbolizing the subjection of Egypt to Roman dominion. The Romans deserve this spectacle as a recompense for the war which Antonius has inflicted on them, and for which she bears even more responsibility. When Augustus questions whether a woman can bear so much guilt, Agrippa replies with inflexible misogyny that most misfortune comes from women ('Von Weibern rührt meist alles Unglück her', iv. 228). That she has contrived Antonius's death at Augustus's request should not count in her favour: in Agrippa's view, Augustus was right to order such a measure, but Cleopatra was wrong to carry it out and deserves to be punished. This may seem a super-subtle argument, but, combined with the others, particularly the need to display her in his triumph, it sways Augustus. His last line of defence is that he ought to keep his word, but here Agrippa is at his most Machiavellian, appealing to the general good, and Augustus reluctantly submits to the demands of reason of state:

> AGRIPPA   Das allgemeine Heil zernichtet solch Versprechen.
> AUGUSTUS Verdammte Staats-Klugheit / die Treu und Bund heist brechen!
>
> (IV. 237–38)

> AGRIPPA   The general good annuls such a promise.
> AUGUSTUS Accursed statecraft that compels one to break faith and union!

This is the decisive turning point. All that remains is to work out how best to persuade Cleopatra to come to Rome. Augustus will promise to devote an altar in Rome to Isis, where homage will also be paid to Cleopatra, and, above all, he will pretend to be in love with her. Although he makes a last effort to resist this proposal, Augustus acquiesces, on condition that it is so managed as not to diminish his glory ('Ruhm', iv. 306).

Cleopatra meanwhile realizes that the game is up. The Romans are plundering the city and looting the temples. She and her entourage are virtual prisoners in the citadel (Augustus, even when addressing her delegation most graciously, prudently ordered the citadel to be guarded, ostensibly for fear of a mob attack). The Romans are searching for Cleopatra's son Caesarion, for naturally reason of state makes it advisable to dispose of him as a potential claimant to Egypt and a focus for resistance and rebellion. Cleopatra disguises Caesarion as an African, colouring his face and hands brown and giving him a wig and the appropriate costume.[6] She overcomes Caesarion's initial resistance by saying that everyone now wears a disguise ('Die

---

6   The question of Cleopatra's skin colour and racial identity is explored exhaustively by Newman, *Intervention*, pp. 128–58.

gantze Welt geht itzt vermummt', IV. 344), a statement with resonance far beyond this scene. After Caesarion has escaped, Cleopatra faces a diplomatic battle, first with Augustus's representative, then with Augustus himself. The crucial issue is whether she has to go to Rome or can stay in Egypt. To win Augustus round, she exercises all her sexual charms, acknowledging that she is getting on in years, but claiming that his love will restore her earlier beauty, and urging him not to delay. The sensuality conjured up in this scene bears comparison with such a Renaissance evocation of the senses as the description, in Tasso's *Gerusalemme liberata* (1581), of the beautiful sorceress Armida and her enchanted garden, where a bird urges lovers to pluck the rose before it is too late.[7] But although Augustus professes to be devoted to Cleopatra, he is steely in his insistence that she must come to Rome. She affects to agree, but buys some time by gaining permission to bury Antonius after the Egyptian fashion.

Having seen through Augustus's intentions, Cleopatra intends not only to bury Antonius but to kill herself — this time for real. So Act V opens with Cleopatra giving her attendants remarkably detailed technical instructions on preparing and embalming Antonius's corpse; she even hands Iras an iron hook with which to extract Antonius's brains via his nose. This done, she assures her still hopeful attendants that Augustus is determined to humiliate her by showing her in his triumph. Such humiliation is intolerable, both for her personally and for her as a representative of the empire of the Ptolemies, which, she claims with some exaggeration, once extended from Central Asia to the Pillars of Hercules and the southern tip of Africa. So she has the asp fetched, and receives its fatal bite on her breast in a way that once more underlines her powerful sexuality, addressing the creature:

> Nun stich! Und sauge Gift / wo mancher Rosen-Mund
> Vor Milch und Honig soog. [...] (v. 301–02)

Now bite! and suck poison where many rosy lips formerly sucked milk and honey.

Arriving on the scene just too late, Augustus is distressed both by Cleopatra's death and (still more) by the fact that it will spoil his triumph. 'How could you do this to me?' he asks in effect:

> Welch Grimm / Cleopatra/ welch wütten kam dich an?
> Daß du so mördrisch dir / uns hast so weh gethan?
> Solln itzt die Leichen uns nur unser Sigs-Fest zieren? (v. 505–07)

[What rage, Cleopatra, what fury overcame you, to make you kill yourself and inflict pain on us? Is our victory parade now to be adorned only by corpses?]

His feelings, however, do not swamp his Machiavellianism. Learning that Caesarion has gone into hiding, Augustus orders him to be found and killed for the sake of the empire's security. He does however show magnanimity towards Cleopatra's

---

7   *Gerusalemme liberata*, canto 16, stanzas 13–15. See Torquato Tasso, *The Liberation of Jerusalem*, trans. by Max Wickert, Oxford World's Classics (Oxford: Oxford University Press, 2009), pp. 288–89.

younger children, promising quite convincingly to take care of them and to make them all kings and queens of North African petty states. Since he cannot display Cleopatra in his triumph, he will compensate by showing the Romans such exotic African fauna as the hippopotamus and the rhinoceros. Finally, having given orders for Cleopatra and Antonius to be buried together, he visits the tomb of Alexander the Great, who founded Alexandria, and whom he regards as an exemplar for himself:

> Hier liegt der grosse Held / von dem August muß lernen:
> Der Leib vergeh' in Asch / der Geist steig' an die Sternen /
> Fur dessen todtem Bild (O edle Tugends-Art!)
> Des Caesars Geist beseelt; das Antlitz schamroth ward /
> Die Seele Seufzer ließ. [...] (v. 747–51)

[Here lies the great hero from whom Augustus must learn that if the body perishes in ash, the spirit can ascend to the stars; before whose dead likeness (O noble and virtuous nature!) Caesar's spirit was inspired, his face blushed for shame and his soul emitted sighs.]

In what sense is Augustus using the word 'Tugend' (virtue)? A few decades after Lohenstein, in the early eighteenth century, the ideal of 'Tugend', as Wolfgang Martens has shown in detail, would be propagated by the moral weeklies and the popular philosophers.[8] Such 'Tugend' was shown above all in action: in looking after one's family, in doing one's work honestly and efficiently, and in helping the unfortunate. It included moderation and self-restraint, especially in sexual matters. But it would be hard to think of anyone less moderate, less restrained, and for that matter less of a family man, than Alexander. The virtue he displayed was rather what Machiavelli meant by *virtù*, 'that quality which enables a prince to withstand the blows of Fortune, to attract the goddess's favour, and to rise in consequence to the heights of princely fame, winning honour and glory for himself and security for his government'.[9] So Augustus emerges as a largely positive figure, certainly a Machiavellian, but in a different league from the small-minded, vindictive Agrippa. He is not likeable, but then he has no need to be, for he is not a politician who courts public popularity. He has assumed the task of ruling, defending, and enlarging the Roman Empire, and to do that well he must practise dissimulation, punish enemies severely, and sometimes break his word.

---

8   Wolfgang Martens, *Die Botschaft der Tugend: Die Aufklärung im Spiegel der deutschen moralischen Wochenschriften* (Stuttgart: Metzler, 1968), esp. pp. 231–46.
9   Skinner, *Machiavelli*, p. 40.

Lohenstein:
Sophonisbe (1680)

Lohenstein's other 'African' tragedy, *Sophonisbe*, at least when viewed from a distance, shows a triangular constellation of characters similar to that of *Cleopatra*. Corresponding to Cleopatra, Augustus, and Antonius, we have the female intriguer, Sophonisbe, a Carthaginian queen, wife of the Numidian king Syphax, faced with the Roman advance into North Africa; the Roman general, Scipio, who appears only in Act IV and establishes himself as a figure of authority and exemplar of Stoic self-mastery; and between them another Numidian king, Masanissa (or Masinissa: Lohenstein spells his name both ways), who falls uncontrollably in love with Sophonisbe, even marries her, but is compelled by Scipio to abandon her and return to his allegiance to Rome.[1]

Sophonisbe has another striking feature (absent from the many other plays about this fascinating heroine): exoticism.[2] In set-piece scenes and speeches which provide relief from the headlong dramatic action, Lohenstein explores in rich antiquarian detail the distinctive character of Carthaginian culture. Masanissa describes its history and achievements to the Roman officer Laelius:

> Wir sind Phœnicier; Tsor unser Vaterland/
> Vom grossen Chna gezeugt; durch Sud und Ost bekant.
> Wie weit der Schatten reicht/ der Erdkreiß Sternen schauet/
> Hat unser Mast gefahrn/ und unsre Hand gebauet.
> Wir gaben die Gesetz' und Bau-Kunst aller Welt.
> Wir haben euch gelehrt/ wie man das Kriegs-Volk stellt/
> Wie man die Hand zur Zung/ und's Auge macht zu Ohren/
> Durch die erfundne Schrifft; die Weißheit ist gebohren

---

1   While the erudite Lohenstein drew on all available sources, he is faithful to the concise narrative in Livy's history of Rome: see Livy, *The War with Hannibal*, trans. by Aubrey de Sélincourt (Harmondsworth: Penguin, 1972), pp. 631–38.

2   Nathaniel Lee's *Sophonisba* (1675) has a scene set in 'Bellona's Temple', including a human sacrifice, conjuration of spirits, and a character called Cumana, suggesting the Cumaean Sibyl, who falls into prophetic fury, but there is no attempt at ethnographic authenticity. We do not learn how a temple to Bellona, the Roman goddess of war, comes to be on Carthaginian territory. See *The Works of Nathaniel Lee*, I, 119–22. Emanuel Geibel's *Sophonisbe* (1868) transfers Sophonisbe's exotic ceremonial role to her friend the priestess Thamar, who finally sets fire to the temple at Cirta and plunges into the flames; the central action is a typically nineteenth-century love-triangle of Sophonisbe, the weak Massanissa, and the awe-inspiring and magnanimous Scipio; local colour is provided by many references to the North African landscape (the Atlas mountains, the simoom or desert wind) and fauna (Sophonisbe hunts ostriches and kills a panther).

> Bey uns/ und nach Athen und Memphis überbracht.
> Die ersten Schiffe sind von unser Axt gemacht/
> Die Rechen-Kunst entsprang aus unserem Gehirne/
> Wir segelten zu erst nach Leitung der Gestirne/
> Die Seulen Hercules/ wo er geruhet hat/
> War'n in der Erde Ring ins grosse Meer ein Pfad
> Bis in das rothe Meer umb Africa zu schiffen
> Bis in der Sonnen Bett' in eine neue Welt/
> Die Kaccabe noch itzt für ein Geheimnis hält. (III. 173–90)

We are Phoenicians; our fatherland is Tyre; we were born of the great Chna and are known throughout the South and East. Our ships have sailed and our hands have built as far as the shadow stretches and the earth beholds the stars. We gave laws and architecture to the whole world. We taught you how to deploy an army and how the invention of writing makes the hand into a tongue and the eye into ears; wisdom was born among us and taken thence to Athens and Memphis. The first ships were made by our axes. Mathematics sprang from our brains. We were the first to navigate by the stars. Within the circle of the earth, the Pillars of Hercules, where he rested, were a path into the great ocean, so that we sailed all round Africa as far as the Red Sea and followed the declining sun into a new world which Kaccabe [Carthage] still keeps secret.[3]

The exploration of Carthage's history and customs is not just a gratuitous addition to the story of Sophonisbe, resulting from Lohenstein's antiquarian curiosity. It provides a context which helps us make sense of Sophonisbe's first patriotic act — a human sacrifice. According to the historian Diodorus Siculus (first century BCE), followed by many other authorities whom Lohenstein cites in his extensive notes, the Carthaginians, in times of national emergency, were in the habit of sacrificing their children to the god Moloch. Lohenstein has Sophonisbe invoking the goddess Baaltis. We are to imagine a statue of the goddess with outstretched arms; the victim is to roll down one of the arms into a fiery pit hidden in the statue's belly.[4] Shocking though this doubtless is, Lohenstein does take some steps, not to condone this act of sacrifice, but at least to make it intelligible. Most writers who evoke these Carthaginian ceremonies imagine infants being torn from their mothers' arms by priests, as in Christian Dietrich Grabbe's play *Hannibal* (1835). Here, however, Sophonisbe's two children are not infants, but boys old enough to understand what they are doing and to be willing instead of passive victims. When Sophonisbe tells

---

3   'Chna' is a shortened form of 'Chanaan' (Canaan), the son of Ham (Gen. 9:18), as Lohenstein explains in one of his many notes (*Sämtliche Werke*, III, 664). In the play, Carthage is also called by its Greek names Kaccabe, Carchedon, and Chaedreanech.

4   Lohenstein, *Sämtliche Werke*, III, 592. Lohenstein draws on many ancient sources, the less accessible of which he finds in modern mythographic compilations such as John Selden's *De diis Syris* (1668), Athanasius Kircher's *Oedipus Aegyptiacus* (1652–54), and Samuel Bochart's *Geographia sacra* (1646–51). Much can be learned about the intellectual world Lohenstein inhabited from R. J. W. Evans, *The Making of the Habsburg Monarchy, 1550–1700* (Oxford: Clarendon Press, 1979), esp. pp. 435–40 (on Kircher). On the (strong) evidence for child sacrifice, see Richard Miles, *Carthage must be Destroyed: The Rise and Fall of an Ancient Civilization* (London: Allen Lane, 2010), pp. 68–73; Francesca Stavrakopoulou, 'Child Sacrifice in the Ancient World: Blessings for the Beloved', in *Childhood and Violence in the Western Tradition*, ed. by Laurence Brockliss and Heather Montgomery (Oxford: Oxbow, 2010), pp. 22–27.

them to draw lots to see which of them will be sacrificed, they both clamour for the honour. Adherbal says that as the elder he ought to die for his country, and expresses a sentiment which in many other contexts would be considered admirable: 'Wie seelig | der für's Heil des Vaterland's verschmachtet!' (I. 400: 'How happy is he who dies for the deliverance of his fatherland!'). With a writer so familiar with the classics as Lohenstein, the echo of Horace — '*Dulce et decorum est pro patria mori*'[5] — cannot be accidental. The lot falls to the younger boy, Hierba, who is delighted at the prospect of performing this heroic deed, exclaiming 'Glück zu!' ('Hurrah!', I. 412). Sophonisbe is not ruthless or indifferent to her son's fate; she regrets having to perform the sacrifice herself (I. 414) and feels upset, but agrees that the good of their country comes first:

> Nimm diesen Kuß noch hin. Erschrecklich Hertzens-Stos!
> Jedoch nur fort! Das Heil des Reiches geht für Kinder. (I. 430–31)

Take this last kiss. What a dreadful blow to my heart! But carry on! The salvation of our kingdom is more important than children.

Besides humanizing the sacrifice in this way, Lohenstein introduces into both the text and the notes detailed reminders of the frequency of human sacrifice in the ancient world. Sophonisbe cites examples from Phoenicia, Egypt, the Druids, Crete, and Sparta (I. 393–99). Lohenstein's notes recall how Abraham very nearly sacrificed his son Isaac, how Jephthah sacrificed his daughter in fulfilment of a rash vow, and mention also the sacrifice of Iphigenia by her father.[6] They also go into some detail about the human sacrifices performed by the Aztecs in honour of their gods, for Lohenstein knew the theory of the contemporary historian Georg Horn that America had first been peopled by Carthaginian refugees, who of course brought their religious customs with them.[7] The horror of the ceremony (which is anyway interrupted before it can be completed) is counterbalanced by the philological and ethnographic interest of this information, and human sacrifice, especially with its biblical and classical precedents, ceases to be a uniquely Carthaginian practice and is shown as a widespread custom throughout the pre-Christian world.

5   'The glorious and the decent way of dying | Is for one's country': Odes, III. 2, in *The Odes of Horace*, trans. by James Michie (Harmondsworth: Penguin, 1967), p. 145. The boys' eagerness for the patriotic sacrifice is overlooked by commentators who condemn Sophonisbe's conduct: e.g. Helen Watanabe-O'Kelly, despite acknowledging her 'undoubted courage and determination', thinks that her wearing men's clothes and being prepared to sacrifice her children shows that 'this woman is so unnatural that she is not human at all' (*Beauty or Beast? The Woman Warrior in the German Imagination from the Renaissance to the Present* (Oxford: Oxford University Press, 2010), pp. 195, 198).
6   This shows Lohenstein's independence from Christian orthodoxy. The Old Testament tries to obscure the Israelite practice of human sacrifice, which would later be exposed by Voltaire: see *La Bible enfin expliquée*, in *Œuvres complètes de Voltaire / The Complete Works of Voltaire*, ed. by Nicholas Cronk and others, 205 vols (Geneva: Institut et Musée Voltaire; Toronto: University of Toronto Press; later Oxford: Voltaire Foundation, 1968–2022), vol. 79A, p. 305. Gillespie notes how the Carthaginian priest Bogudes accepts martyrdom, using the Christian image of the cross (*S* III 317), thereby suggesting that Lohenstein's 'cold examination of belief and action as *historical facts*' (*Lohenstein's Historical Tragedies*, p. 123) implies a position above and beyond any particular religion.
7   See the reference to 'Hornius', *De originibus Americanis* (1669), in Lohenstein, *Sämtliche Werke*, III, 670; Béhar, *Silesia Tragica*, p. 174.

Near the end of the play, in order to learn what her chances of survival are, Sophonisbe summons up the ghost of Dido (also known as Elissa), the legendary founder of Carthage. The necessary ritual is described in considerable detail; Lohenstein's notes cite a great variety of sources and mention also the incident in the Old Testament when Saul summoned up the ghost of the prophet Samuel (see I Samuel 28). Lohenstein takes care to distance this Dido from the unfortunate queen who, in Virgil's *Aeneid*, burns herself on a pyre when her lover Aeneas abandons her. In the notes, as Jane O. Newman has pointed out, Lohenstein dismisses Virgil's narrative as a fiction, claiming on the authority of both ancient and modern historians that Dido really immolated herself in order to avoid an unwelcome marriage to her neighbour King Hiarbas.[8] Instead of the *Aeneid*, Lohenstein draws on a number of less-known sources, specified in his notes, which represent Dido as a strong leader calling for resistance to Roman conquest.[9] Even as a ghost, she retains her manly heart ('Ihr männlich Hertz', v. 82). She foretells that although Rome will triumph over Carthage, in the long term Rome will become corrupt and its empire will be overwhelmed by Germanic tribes, while the Arabs will overrun North Africa and Spain; Ferdinand (king of Aragon, who in 1469 married Isabella of Castile and united the kingdoms), however, will ultimately expel the Arabs from Granada, their last stronghold, and Charles V will conquer parts of North Africa, preparing the way for future conquests to be undertaken by Leopold I, the Habsburg Emperor at the time when Lohenstein was writing. By the seventeenth century, the Habsburgs will rule an empire on which the sun never sets.[10] She is, then, an honourable ancestor for Sophonisbe, whose courage (gendered as a male quality) is symbolized by her twice dressing as a soldier (II. 78, 322).

Sophonisbe's actions certainly take one aback. Not only is she prepared to sacrifice one of her children in order to gain the support of the Carthaginian gods (though she is prevented from going through with this act), but her marriage to Masanissa is bigamous since she is already married to the rival king Syphax. Dedicating the play to a nobleman, the Freiherr von Nesselrode, Lohenstein described the misadventures of Sophonisbe and Masanissa as illustrating the dangers of love and ambition. He mentioned particularly Sophonisbe's willingness to sacrifice one of her children in a ceremony in which she dresses as a man and another son puts on women's clothing.[11] In his notes, Lohenstein documents the practice of cross-dressing from a variety of classical and Hebrew sources, making it seem fascinating as well as reprehensible.

In any case, the play's official message, spelt out in the dedication and the 'Reyen', is not the same thing as its total impact on the spectator or reader. Condemning infanticide and bigamy, moreover, does not explain why Sophonisbe does these

8   Newman, *Intervention*, pp. 66–67.
9   Lohenstein, *Sämtliche Werke*, III, 728–34; Newman, *Intervention*, pp. 60–67.
10   This familiar expression appears to originate with the Spanish diplomat and political writer Diego Saavedra Fajardo, *Corona Gothica, Castellana y Austriaca* (1646), quoted in Lohenstein, *Sämtliche Werke*, III, 778. Schiller makes King Philip II of Spain say: 'Die Sonne geht in meinem Staat nicht unter' (*Don Karlos*, I. 5. 860).
11   Lohenstein, *Sämtliche Werke*, III, 398.

things. Some commentators have seen her as illustrating Walter Benjamin's remark about 'a constantly shifting emotional storm in which the figures of Lohenstein sway about like torn and flapping banners'.[12] Others have interpreted her as a single-minded Machiavellian intriguer, 'the female embodiment of reason of state'.[13]

One can make sense of Sophonisbe's conduct in dramatic (as opposed to allegorical) terms by seeing her as motivated throughout by patriotism, which requires her to become, like Cleopatra, a past mistress in dissimulation.[14] She not only wants to save Carthage from Roman conquest but, again like Cleopatra, to save herself from being taken to Rome and displayed in a triumph. Like the great Hannibal, she belongs to the Barca family, who have fought most bitterly against the Romans. Her husband Syphax was previously allied to the Romans, but at Sophonisbe's urging he has broken off this alliance. We hear at the very beginning of the play that her father Hasdrubal Barca and Syphax have been defeated by another Numidian king, Masanissa, who has remained loyal to Rome and who is on the point of capturing Syphax's city of Cyrtha. The play begins with Masanissa reproaching his captive Syphax for being led into disloyalty by his wife. Sophonisbe's role in provoking the rebellion against Rome is confirmed in Act IV, when Syphax, confronting the Roman general Scipio, blames his wife for constantly urging him to break with Rome, and says it was insane folly of him to marry a woman from the Barca family.

When we first meet Sophonisbe, she is in her apartment, surrounded by her intimates, and has no reason to dissimulate. So we can believe her when she says she would rather suffer any torture than become subject to the Romans. From a succession of messengers, she learns, first, that her husband Syphax has been defeated by Masanissa; second, that Masanissa has given her three hours in which to surrender the city, and if she refuses, Syphax will be beheaded. This choice plunges Sophonisbe into indecision. At one moment she says that even if her adversary has Syphax flayed, such atrocities will never cause the city to surrender; at the next, she says she will surrender to Rome and be shown in triumph so long as her husband is safe. Her companions remonstrate with her for not showing the spirit of her father Hasdrubal, and eventually the reflection that Syphax has not asked for his life to be saved carries the day. Sophonisbe assumes warlike resolution, putting on armour and a helmet, and is hailed as Africa's counterpart to the Amazon queen Penthesilea (I. 365).

Sophonisbe's conduct in the next few Acts would seem wildly inconsistent unless we remember that behind it lies her determination to save her people and herself from subjection to Rome at any cost. Thanks to treachery, the city of Cyrtha falls to Masanissa. Sophonisbe throws herself at Masanissa's feet, begging for mercy for herself and her sons. This has the desired effect on Masanissa. Having initially failed

12   Walter Benjamin, *The Origin of German Tragic Drama*, trans. by John Osborne, with an introduction by George Steiner (London: New Left Books, 1977), p. 71.

13   Richard Newald, *Die deutsche Literatur vom Späthumanismus zur Empfindsamkeit* (Munich: Beck, 1951), p. 328.

14   Lunding, *Das schlesische Kunstdrama*, esp. pp. 102–03. Lunding exaggerates Sophonisbe's single-mindedness: the play shows her as quick-witted and opportunistic, but also on several occasions as (understandably) flustered and indecisive (e.g. I. 291–300).

to recognize her in her male attire, he is astonished and moved, addressing her with the utmost respect and ordering that she and her sons be carefully looked after. Left alone, he declares himself helplessly in love with her combination of beauty and courage, and resolves to kill his prisoner Syphax so that he can take the latter's place. Sophonisbe meanwhile enters Syphax's prison, still wearing male clothes, and tells him to change clothes with her and escape, leaving her in his place. Alone, she indicates that her plan is to exploit Masanissa's love for her; she regrets the injustice she will do to Syphax by abandoning him for Masanissa, but she has no choice: 'Jedoch | was widerstehn wir leitenden Gestirnen?' (II. 299: 'But how can we resist the guidance of the stars?'). The plan works: Masanissa enters the prison intending to kill Syphax, is surprised to find Sophonisbe there instead, declares his love for her, and insists that they shall be married forthwith. Sophonisba, at the cost of bigamy, will thus be able to turn Masanissa against Rome.

Act III, which begins with Masanissa's associates remonstrating against the impending marriage, shows that her scheme is working, for Masanissa strongly implies that he is considering breaking his alliance with Rome and supporting the still powerful Carthage. The wedding then takes place, but is interrupted by the arrival of a Roman officer, Laelius, who declares that Masanissa's marriage to Sophonisbe, a member of the Barca family, itself signals a breach with Rome. Eventually Laelius agrees to wait and accept the judgement of the great Roman general Scipio, who is soon to arrive, but he is further incensed on learning that Sophonisbe, prevented by Syphax from sacrificing her son, has instead sacrificed two Roman captives. Laelius insists that in retaliation three Carthaginian captives, who are conveniently to hand, must be sacrificed (thereby annulling any ethical superiority the Romans might have claimed). The priest who has just married Sophonisbe and Masanissa steadfastly refuses to sacrifice his fellow-countrymen, preferring martyrdom to sacrilege (showing that it is not only Christians who can accept martyrdom). In this impasse, Sophonisbe offers to perform the sacrifice herself, in order to confirm that she and Masanissa want to remain on friendly terms with Rome — an act of dissimulation necessitated by the circumstances.

However, Sophonisbe's determination is thwarted by her humanity. She recoils on discovering that one of the prisoners is her husband Syphax in disguise. Sophonisbe is not in fact capable of anything. Reproached for her duplicity, she tells Syphax that she still loves him but was compelled by an emergency ('Noth') to marry Masanissa for the sake of her deliverance ('Heil') (III. 373–75). Since an out-and-out Machiavellian could have sacrificed Syphax to gain favour with the Romans, we must assume that she is sincere.[15] She urges Syphax to see reason ('Vernunft', III. 390), since a conflict between Syphax and Masanissa would achieve nothing, and by voluntarily handing her over to Masanissa he, Syphax, will be able to restore the good relations with Rome that he lost by changing sides. Her plan would seem to be this: previously she persuaded Syphax to switch sides, but he was defeated by the more powerful and effective Masanissa; she has used her sexuality to attract Masanissa, and intends him to be outwardly loyal to Rome (and he must

15   Gillespie, *Lohenstein's Historical Tragedies*, p. 125.

of course seem so when a Roman officer is present), but Sophonisbe will persuade him in turn to break with Rome and support Carthage. But her plan fails, because Syphax understandably refuses to be replaced by Masanissa. Her plan could only have worked if she had the hardihood to kill Syphax, who would then have caused no more trouble. Had she been the monster that some commentators consider her, she would have disposed of Syphax when she got the chance. But her human emotions, which have already made it difficult (though not impossible) for her to sacrifice her son, also prevent her from cold-bloodedly murdering her husband, and thus her humanity frustrates her Machiavellianism and seals her downfall.

Act IV is dominated by the long-awaited figure of Scipio. Since Syphax not only rejected Sophonisbe's persuasions, but demanded that she should stab him, Laelius has intervened by deferring the matter till Scipio's arrival. Scipio shrewdly interrogates Syphax and Masanissa separately; he has no contact with Sophonisbe at all. First, Laelius reports to him how Masanissa defeated Syphax and captured Cyrtha, not mentioning that the victory was actually due to treachery. Scipio rebukes Syphax for breaking faith with the Romans, whereupon Syphax puts all the blame on Sophonisbe, abusing her in her absence as a destructive force like fire and plague, a worm, a viper, a scorpion, and an evil woman comparable to Medea and Circe. He claims that he was bewitched ('behext', IV. 140). These denunciations say little about Sophonisbe herself, but a great deal about Syphax's wounded feelings and about his wish to exonerate himself in the sight of the Romans. He gets scant sympathy from Scipio, who judges that his emotions have carried him away ('Ich glaube Syphax schwermt von Unmuth/ Angst und Schmertzen', IV. 110) and asserts that a man who marries such a pestilential woman has only himself to blame. Syphax is sent off to confinement.

Then Masanissa appears. Masanissa has so far revealed several conflicting aspects of his character. At the beginning of the play, he showed the utmost ferocity in threatening to demolish the city of Cyrtha and not spare even the child in its mother's womb. He took a high moral line in denouncing Syphax's treachery towards Rome, but from his summary of the military situation, in which the Carthaginians have been expelled from Spain and Sicily and even the great Hannibal is in difficulties, it is clear that Masanissa is prudently allying himself with the winning side. There is a remarkable contrast between this ruthless politician and the Masanissa who in Act II is overcome by Sophonisbe's charms. In his soliloquy, the longest in the play, Masanissa utters a series of oxymora: ostensibly the victor, he is in fact defeated; his prisoner Sophonisbe has herself enslaved him. He tries for a while to resist his passion by projecting its unacceptable character onto Sophonisbe, condemning her (as Syphax will do later) as a viper, a Medea, a basilisk, and so forth; but he presently admits that what has enchanted him is Sophonisbe's combination of beauty and spirit, the heart of Hercules in a woman's breast. Even then, however, he was worried about what Scipio would say, but in his passion he has finally resolved to submit entirely to Sophonisbe's wishes, even at the cost of breaking with Rome.

Now, when he confronts Scipio in Act IV, Masanissa is at a disadvantage. Scipio begins by congratulating him at length on his conquest of Cyrtha and promising to work on his behalf in Rome so that he will acquire additional kingdoms. The grateful Masanissa calls down blessings on Rome and Scipio. But Scipio has already found out from Syphax about Masanissa's infatuation with Sophonisbe. So, as Masanissa is about to leave the room, relieved to have got through his interview so well, Scipio — using a trick known to every police inspector — casually calls him back:

> Jedoch halt! Masaniß'. Es fällt uns noch was ein. (IV. 203)

> Wait a minute, Masanissa, there was something else I wanted to say to you.

He asks about Sophonisbe, indicating that she is required in Rome as a trophy in his triumph. Masanissa soon crumbles, confessing his helpless devotion to Sophonisbe. In the course of a long stichomythic exchange, Scipio tells him that marriage to Sophonisbe is incompatible with his duty towards Rome.

This scene requires a somewhat critical look at Scipio. He is presented as the play's figure of authority. Everyone waits for his judgement. And, as he is a successful general, and the representative of Rome which is steadily enlarging its power over the known world, his authority is strengthened by sheer military success. In the previous scene, however, we have had a glimpse of the basis on which his successes rest. When Syphax denounced Sophonisbe as a viper, Scipio replied that *no* woman could be trusted:

> Ein kluger Herrscher pfleget
> Für Weibern seinen Rath und Ohr zu schlüssen ein
> Wie Schlangen | die umbkreißt von dem Beschwerer sein. (IV. 86–88)

> A sensible ruler keeps his counsel and his ear from women, who are like
> snakes circling round their conjurer.

His blanket rejection of love, lust and sensuality helps to make Scipio a perfect neo-Stoic, as imagined by Justus Lipsius. He is not the unfeeling monster of Stoic virtue that Johann Christoph Gottsched would present in the next century in *Der sterbende Cato* (1732). He tells Masanissa that he feels sorry for his emotional pain, and we have no reason to suspect Scipio here of insincerity.[16] But Scipio is a man for whom the highest virtue is reason ('Vernunft') made manifest as prudence ('Klugheit'). He tells Masanissa to consult his own intelligence ('Verstand', IV. 343) and his self-interested prudence: 'Du bist dir selber klug' (IV. 344: 'You are prudent enough to consult your own interest'). When Masanissa objects that, as an African, he cannot help being a slave to his sensual passion, Scipio pooh-poohs this excuse by pointing to Hannibal, who is cold when drinking wine and icy when offered love: Hannibal is prudent ('klug', IV 317). What Scipio preaches is therefore virtue only in the Stoic sense of prudence, an ideal to which the senses are to be subordinated. It has been aptly said of him that 'Scipio may appear to be moral, but in fact he is only puritanical for the sake of more effective involvement in history.'[17] Scipio is,

16   Cf. Machiavelli's evocation of Scipio's 'sexual restraint, affability, humanity and generosity' (*P* XIV. 54).
17   Gillespie, *Lohenstein's Historical Tragedies*, p. 128.

both in his actual dealings with people and in his general principles, a Machiavellian for whom amoral calculation is the high road to power. With regard to the allegory that frames the play, in which Scipio is leading Masanissa back to virtue, his methods may not matter, but with regard to the dramatic action we can see that Scipio is exercising a skilful combination of flattery and coercion which will ensure Masanissa's future obedience to Rome. 'Machiavellian Scipio', as Gerald Gillespie calls him, is thus the counterpart to Sophonisbe, another Machiavellian, who will stop at almost nothing — as we have seen, she does draw the line at slaughtering her husband — in order to secure the state, Carthage, to which she is attached.[18] Masanissa falls between the two, an all-too-human figure who alternates between firm resolution and subjugation to what Scipio (and sometimes Masanissa himself) dismissively calls 'Brunst' (erotic passion).

Of all the characters in the play, it is Masanissa whose inner life is displayed most fully. He has two long soliloquies in which he wrestles with himself, whereas we never see Scipio alone, and Sophonisbe's ten-line monologue expressing her difficulty in choosing between her country and her husband is delivered in the presence of her associates (I. 291–300) so does not count as a soliloquy. Masanissa's second soliloquy comes after Scipio has dismissed him with advice to be reasonable. First, Masanissa expresses horror at the thought of Sophonisbe becoming a prisoner of the Romans. He denounces the Romans for their cynical policy in stirring up antagonisms among the North African states in order to weaken them. He accuses Rome of spewing gall and venom on all other nations in order to attain the mastery of the world. He surmises that the Romans are really afraid, not of Sophonisbe, but of Hannibal, and that they think that by capturing Sophonisbe and bringing Masanissa to heel they will be able to master the notorious uncertainty of fortune: they will clip her wings, stop her wheel from rolling, and prevent her from deserting Rome. He resents this treatment all the more since Carthage has already been brought low. He continues by dwelling on Sophonisbe's beauty. By comparison, kingship is mere glorious slavery. Rome is welcome to Numidia, so long as he, Masanissa, can possess Sophonisbe.

Here, however, Masanissa has a sudden change of heart. The pleasure of sex is short-lived, especially with a deceitful woman who has betrayed her previous husband. Instead of being led astray by sensual desire, he should see with the eye of reason ('Das Auge der Vernunfft', IV. 409). He should reflect that he has serious responsibilities, that his real spouse is his kingdom. Above all, a mere woman (Sophonisbe is now downgraded from an individual to 'ein Weib', interchangeable with others) can hardly be more important than his own well-being: 'Beherzig': ob ein Weib mehr als dein Wolstand gilt' (IV. 412: 'Consider whether a woman counts for more than your own well-being'). Instead of the blindness of passion, or the will-o'-the-wisp of sensual temptation, he now wants to follow the light of reason, which Scipio has lit for him, and — in another significant image — to allow reason its proper place in the clockwork mechanism of behaviour: 'Im Uhrwerck unsers Thuns muß die Vernunfft's Gewichte | Das Auge Weiser sein' (IV. 413–14).

18 Ibid., p. 114.

Reason, in this analogy, is a weight which keeps the clock moving at the right pace, while the eye is the pointer indicating the right time. Given the political context, it is also reason of state. So reason and self-interest together dictate that Sophonisbe must meet her doom. Masanissa finds it hard to reach this harsh decision, but despite his scruples, he concludes that in order to attain lasting fame, he must shun the temptations of his senses. His last act, therefore, is to send Sophonisbe a vial of poison to ensure that she will not fall into the hands of the Romans. Drastic as this sounds, it will in fact save her from the fate she most dreads, and confirms Masanissa's humanity. It also confirms, however, that under pressure from Scipio he has been successfully converted to Machiavellianism.

As for Sophonisbe, her Machiavellian policy has failed, and she courageously accepts the consequences. They are confirmed when the ghost of Dido foretells the impending destruction of Carthage. Seeing no hope, Sophonisbe and her sons are prepared to follow Dido's example of self-immolation by setting fire to the temple and citadel and perishing in the flames, but then Masanissa's messenger arrives with poison. The boys, who were so eager to sacrifice themselves in Act I, are just as keen to follow their mother's example by committing suicide, an act that Sophonisbe commends as the final triumph over one's enemies and over the inconstancy of fortune:

> Recht so! wer hertzhaft stirbt | lacht Feinde | Glück und Zeit;
> Verwechselt Ruh und Ruhm mit Angst und Eitelkeit. (v. 479–80)

Quite right! Someone who dies bravely can laugh at enemies, fortune, and time, and exchanges fear and vanity for rest and fame.

That the final act shows Sophonisbe in a heroic light is confirmed by a reference to her death in Lohenstein's earlier play *Cleopatra*. Since Antonius is worried about what Cleopatra may suffer if Augustus gains Egypt, his companions suggest that he repeat Masanissa's praiseworthy deed by sending Cleopatra poison, and commend Sophonisbe's action:

> Wo Sophonißbe nicht sol ihren Ruhm beschämen
> Die in der Sterne Gold ihr Grabmahl eingeetz't
> Als sie den Gifft-Kelch hat so freudig angesetz't
> Umb ihres Liebsten Ruhm | und Zepter zu erhalten. (*C* I. 1008–11)

Sophonisbe did not disgrace her reputation, but inscribed her monument in the gold of the stars, when she joyfully drank from the poisoned goblet in order to save the reputation and the sceptre of the man she loved.

Her male companions, Himilco and Micipsa, fall on their swords, leaving only Sophonisbe's female attendants to show Masanissa what has happened when he arrives in the vain hope of saving Sophonisbe's life. Scipio's influence seems to have been short-lived, for on seeing Sophonisbe's corpse Masanissa falls into an agony of grief and self-reproach. Scipio himself appears, however, and rebukes Masanissa severely for yielding to erotic passion ('Brunst', v 553); points out that it was Sophonisbe's own choice to take the poison, so Masanissa should not blame himself; and adds that Masanissa is mad to regret the loss of a lustful woman.

Despite this brutal speech, Scipio consents to Masanissa's request that Sophonisbe should receive a decent burial instead of having her body displayed in Rome. He repeats that Carthage will be destroyed. Syphax is sent to Rome as a prisoner, and his kingdom is handed over to Masanissa, in fulfilment of the promise Scipio made to Masanissa in Act IV. Masanissa, having promised to overcome his emotions, is now rewarded for his renewed loyalty to Rome. He has not heard what the ghost of Dido prophesied about him:

> Denn Masanissa | den die Stadt
> Carchedon auferzogen hat /
> Wird Kronen zwar | doch in den Fesseln tragen.
> Rom | das die Dienstbarkeit der Welt
> Fur himmlisches Verhängnüs hält /
> Wird seinen Stamm selbst in die Eisen schlagen.
> Ich sehe 's Joch schon seinen Enckel zihn. (v. 131–37)

> For Masanissa, brought up in the city of Carthage, will indeed wear crowns, but in fetters. Rome, which considers the subjugation of the world to be its heavenly destiny, will place his whole tribe in chains. I can already see his grandson carrying the yoke.

In terms of its allegorical framework, the play sets Masanissa firmly back on the path of virtue. In terms of the political realities that it stages, however, it leaves Masanissa in an uncomfortable half-way house between the unsuccessful Machiavellianism of Sophonisbe and the successful Machiavellianism of Scipio. Sophonisbe at least met her fate with fortitude and voluntarily accepted a heroic death. Masanissa has been disloyal to Sophonisbe, has silently acquiesced in Scipio's dismissal of her as worthless, and has been rewarded with a crown which merely disguises his servitude to the ruthless power of Rome.

If one can sum up the ethos underlying Lohenstein's most clearly political plays, it is reason of state, or Machiavellian pragmatism. The general good demands harsh measures which can be painful even for the people executing them. For politics cannot be operated like a machine. Human emotions enter into it. Epicharis's algolagnia, Cleopatra's tempestuously conflicting emotions, and Sophonisbe's struggles of love with patriotism are all political factors. Augustus and Scipio are successful, but not ideal figures. Lohenstein's view of politics is complex, chilling, and grown-up.

In the eighteenth century, when Lohenstein's plays were rejected as old-fashioned and tasteless, their lessons about reason of state were also dismissed as obsolete. As we have seen, the Enlightenment in general considered the political doctrines of *The Prince* to have lost their relevance in the modern world. The dominant political model was now a monarchy under a clearly legitimate ruler who did not have to worry about would-be usurpers and who needed only to use his virtually unrestricted power to make his subjects happy. This is the assumption behind the political novels (*Staatsromane*), which appeared in large numbers throughout the century, and which revive the genre of 'mirrors for princes' in fictional form.[19]

19   Exhaustively surveyed in Wolfgang Biesterfeld, *Der Fürstenspiegel als Roman: Narrative Texte*

Their model is Fénelon's *Télémaque* (1699), in which Telemachus, the son of Odysseus, under the guidance of Mentor (who is really Athena, the goddess of wisdom in disguise), tours the Mediterranean to observe how various types of polity function or fail to function. In a self-contained episode, Mentor takes charge of the declining kingdom of Salente (based on Louis XIV's France) and institutes a large number of reforms. Subsequent political novels similarly set out reform programmes which are put into practice either by a counsellor of unshakable integrity, such as Count Rivera in Johann Michael von Loen's *Der redliche Mann am Hofe* (The Honest Man at Court, 1740), or by a talented prince who has been educated far from the corrupt life of normal courts, such as the eponymous regenerator of Persia in Albrecht von Haller's *Usong* (1771) or Tifan in Wieland's *Der goldne Spiegel* (The Golden Mirror, 1772).[20] Whenever possible, the new enlightened ruler makes a fresh start, because established rulers are likely to be too set in their ways to act on good advice. Wieland's urbane and amusing novel acknowledges this by making the good-natured but indolent Schach-Gebal, ruler of India, often respond to the advice of his court philosopher Danischmend by making good resolutions, which he completely forgets about the next day.[21]

The lessons are predictable: the good monarch should rule justly, consult wise counsellors and avoid flatterers, discourage luxury, have a modest life-style, promote trades, manufactures, and agriculture, and take care not to burden his subjects with heavy taxes. In return they will love him so warmly that any malcontents will be unable to find support. Hence really difficult issues, which still existed in the eighteenth century, are ignored in fiction. How do you pacify and conciliate a newly conquered territory (such as Frederick the Great's Silesia)? How do you control over-mighty subjects? How do you cope with rebellions (such as those of 1715 and 1745 in Britain, or Pugachev's uprising in Russia)? How do you handle cultural and religious diversity? To most of these questions Machiavelli at least has answers, however unpalatable they may be. But the political novel, which keeps conflict to the margins, is of limited value as a guide to actual politics.

Conflict is essential to drama, and the political dramas of Goethe, Schiller, and Kleist address many of the thorny issues which the *Staatsroman* tries to screen out. Unlike Lohenstein, however, they rarely invoke reason of state. This generation of playwrights balked at the inhumanity required by reason of state and wished to give not only emotions but personal morality a larger place in political behaviour. Goethe, Schiller, and Kleist were all shaped by the Enlightenment, which exalted feeling alongside reason. It emphasized what Adam Smith called 'moral sentiments', a union of morality and sensibility. Hence the very concept of statecraft came to be presented critically.

---

zur Ethik und Pragmatik von Herrschaft im 18. Jahrhundert (Baltmannsweiler: Schneider Verlag Hohengehren, 2014), and Christopher Meid, *Der politische Roman im 18. Jahrhundert: Systementwurf und Aufklärungserzählung* (Berlin: De Gruyter, 2021).

20   The ancestors of these narratives also include Xenophon's *Cyropaedia*, a fictitious biography of Cyrus the Great of Persia, commended by Machiavelli (*P* XIV. 53–54).

21   Wieland, *Der goldne Spiegel*, p. 110.

— 5 —
Goethe:
Machiavell and Machiavels in
Egmont (1787)

Although Goethe makes no comment on Machiavelli's writings, and perhaps never read them, he lived at a time when Machiavelli was no longer found shocking. This tolerance is apparent in the work of Goethe's great-uncle, Johann Michael von Loen (1694–1776), a copious writer on political matters, who wrote an essay on Machiavelli's statecraft. Loen was also the author of the political novel entitled *Der redliche Mann am Hofe* (The Honest Man at Court, 1740), of which his great-nephew wrote much later: 'Dieses Werk wurde gut aufgenommen, weil es auch von den Höfen, wo sonst nur Klugheit zu Hause ist, Sittlichkeit verlangte; und so brachte ihm seine Arbeit Beifall und Ansehen' ('This work was well received, because it demanded that courts, where normally only prudence dwells, should also obey morality, and so his labours brought him approval and respect').[1]

Loen detested the spirit of intrigue and dissimulation that he found prevailing at princely courts. In his essay on Machiavelli he read *The Prince* as a satire, obliquely warning against misgovernment. He explained that Machiavelli did not intend to support tyranny, but to warn readers against it. A highly intelligent writer, living in an age when misgovernment could not be openly denounced, he had attacked it obliquely by means of irony:

> He talks about princes as Mandeville does about the bees. He describes what great people generally do in order to attain the heights of unrestricted power. But he does not approve of this unrestricted power, any more than an ingenious mathematician who writes an elegant work on the art of making bombs and reducing cities to ash thereby approves of such violence.[2]

The comparison with Bernard Mandeville's *Fable of the Bees* (1714), another work reviled by the *bien-pensants*, shows how open Loen was towards unconventional views.

1   Goethe, *Sämtliche Werke* [henceforth *SW*], XIV: *Dichtung und Wahrheit*, ed. by Klaus-Detlef Müller (1986), p. 84. On Loen and his novel, see Ritchie Robertson, 'Difficulties of a Statesman: Johann Michael von Loen and *Der redliche Mann am Hofe*', in *Edinburgh German Yearbook 12: Repopulating the Eighteenth Century: Second-Tier Writing in the German Enlightenment*, ed. by Michael Wood and Johannes Birgfeld (Rochester, NY: Camden House, 2018), pp. 71–89.
2   Johann Michael von Loen, 'Von der Staats-Kunst des Machiavels', in *Des Herrn von Loen gesammlete kleine Schriften*, 4 vols (Frankfurt a.M. and Leipzig: Philipp Heinrich Hutter, 1750), IV, 270–81 (p. 279).

Hence Loen was able to praise Frederick the Great's *Anti-Machiavel* in the most flattering terms, because he thought that Frederick and Machiavelli, despite appearances, were on the same side. Frederick's treatise gave him hope that sovereigns might acquire a love of virtue and learning, and concern for the well-being of the people whom Providence had entrusted to their care. After all, Loen maintained, people were naturally linked by bonds of love and sympathy. If only princes would act accordingly, the age of the Antonines would return, and politics ('Staats-Kunst') would consist in reproducing on earth the order which the Creator had designed for the universe, and enabling all his creatures to enjoy the goods which he had provided for their benefit. The king would be the earthly counterpart of God. Loen thus accepts the view, associated especially with Shaftesbury, that 'natural affection [is] implanted in our natures'.[3] And since Loen would become the great-uncle of Goethe, his response tells us something about the intellectual atmosphere in which Goethe grew up.

Goethe seldom mentions the historical figure of Machiavelli. He does so in a letter to the Swiss theologian J. K. Pfenninger of 26 April 1774, saying that he regards all human utterances as the word of God, however heretical — 'Apostel, Spinoza oder Machiavell'. Here Machiavelli features as a proponent of scandalous doctrines, but his juxtaposition with the apostles and with Spinoza, whose pantheism strongly appealed to Goethe, implies a sympathetic view of him.[4]

Machiavellianism, however, is prominent throughout Goethe's dramatic work, from *Götz von Berlichingen* (1773) to *Faust II* (1832). The politics of intrigue, double-dealing, and unscrupulous power-play, which Machiavelli was now supposed to have satirized, are repeatedly contrasted with a kind of heroic innocence, or guile-lessness, embodied in the hero, or with a courageous sanctity represented by the heroine.

The prose tragedy *Egmont*, which Goethe worked on intermittently from 1775 onwards and completed in 1787, not only has an eminently political subject, the beginnings of the Dutch revolt in the 1560s against Spanish rule, but also a character named Machiavell. This person is confidential secretary to Margaret of Parma, the Regent of the Netherlands, and advises her how to handle the civil disorders that reached their peak in the iconoclastic riots of 1566. Machiavell is a historically attested figure as one of the Regent's attendants who carried messages between the Netherlands and Spain. He is mentioned also by Schiller in his history of the Dutch revolt.[5] But it is not enough to say, as Dieter Borchmeyer does in his edition of *Egmont*, that the similarity of the name to that of Niccolò Machiavelli is fortuitous.[6] In a well-composed poetic work, nothing is fortuitous. The name cannot fail to

3   Anthony Ashley Cooper, third Earl of Shaftesbury, *Characteristics of Men, Manners, Opinions, Times*, ed. by Lawrence E. Klein (Cambridge: Cambridge University Press, 1999), p. 216.
4   Goethe, *SW* XXVIII: *Von Frankfurt nach Weimar. Briefe, Tagebücher und Gespräche vom 23. Mai 1764 bis 30. Oktober 1775*, ed. by Wilhelm Grosse (1997), p. 359. For further commentary on this letter, see *SW* I: *Gedichte 1756–1799*, ed. by Karl Eibl (1987), pp. 815–17. On Goethe's possible knowledge of Machiavelli's writings, see Heinrich Clairmont, 'Die Figur des Machiavell in Goethes *Egmont*', *Poetica*, 15 (1983), 289–313 (p. 296).
5   Schiller, *WB* VI: *Historische Schriften I*, ed. by Otto Dann (2000), p. 369.
6   Goethe, *SW* V: *Dramen 1776–1790*, ed. by Dieter Borchmeyer (1988), p. 1270.

attract attention, signalling that we are entering the world of modern court-based politics, about which Goethe had mixed feelings: 'the author of *Il Principe* stands for the modern notion of the state, theorized by lawyers and put into practice by a new breed of courtiers, diplomats and civil servants'.[7] I suggest that Goethe seized on the name, and even drew attention to Machiavell's prudent and far-sighted character, in order to announce that his play was concerned with various ways of conducting politics, including some of those conventionally referred to as Machiavellianism.

The name Machiavell immediately and inevitably calls to mind an ongoing debate about politics. Is politics an autonomous area where the rules of morality do not apply, where pragmatic solutions are the only solutions, and where future contingencies can be anticipated by rational calculation? Or should politics also accommodate the qualities — not just the moral virtues, but attributes like courage, honesty, openness — that appear in social life and that strengthen relations between individuals? For this argument, it does not matter whether Goethe knew Machiavelli at first or second hand; what Machiavelli stood for (or was thought to stand for) was already common knowledge.

To begin exploring these questions, let us look at the use Goethe has made of the source in which he found the character Machiavell. This was the *De Bello Belgico decades duae* (1632, 1647) by Famianus or Famiano Strada (1572–1649), a Jesuit scholar, historian, and teacher of rhetoric. Strada wrote his history around 1602 with the help of Alexander Farnese, who was governor of the Netherlands from 1578 to 1592 and was also the son of the Regent Margaret of Parma, who figures in Goethe's play. It provided not only an indispensable account of the Dutch revolt against Spanish rule but was also timely for an English readership during the Civil War between the forces of Charles I and those of Parliament. Strada is particularly good at drawing character portraits; among his most searching are those of William of Orange and of Cardinal Antonio Granvella, a figure who plays a large part in Schiller's history of the revolt but is omitted from Goethe's play. As one would expect, Strada clearly favours the Spanish side. He was opposed to Tacitism and Machiavellianism. Believing that the behaviour of divinely appointed rulers should not be questioned by mere mortals, he did not approve of the analyses of autocracy that took their inspiration from Tacitus's account of Tiberius, and any association with Machiavelli and political calculation serves in his narrative to incriminate a character.

In Strada's history, the character named Machiavell makes a very brief appearance as a messenger sent by Margaret of Parma to Spain with a request to Philip II to relieve her of her regency because of her poor health. Machiavell returns from Spain with a reply from the king consenting to her request and also with a commission placing the government of the Netherlands in the hands of the Duke of Alva.[8] That is all we hear about him.

7   K. F. Hilliard, *Freethinkers, Libertines and 'Schwärmer': Heterodoxy in German Literature, 1750–1800* (London: Institute of Germanic and Romance Studies, 2011), p. 140.
8   Famianus Strada, *De bello Belgico: The history of the Low-Countrey warres*, written in Latine by Famianus Strada; in English by Sr. Rob. Stapylton (London: Humphrey Modseley, 1650), Book VI, p. 35.

Goethe, however, allows Machiavell to hold an important conversation with the Regent and to offer her political advice. The occasion is the outbreak of iconoclasm by crowds of Calvinists in the summer and autumn of 1566. It was not just religious images that were destroyed: churches and abbeys were attacked and pillaged, vestments, art treasures and libraries were burnt, as Machiavell describes in shocking detail.[9] The Regent is understandably distressed by this sacrilegious violence and at a loss how to bring it under control. Machiavell puts forward his own ideas with due modesty, describing them as little more than whims ('Grillen').[10] In his view, the progress of the new faith cannot be stopped. The only way to control it is a pragmatic policy of toleration which should drive a wedge between the moderate Protestants and the extremists. The moderates, instead of listening to incendiary sermons by hedge-preachers, should be allowed their own churches and thus enclosed within the order of civil society. This will put an end to violence. Any other policy will lead to civil war, because the new faith is not confined to the social fringes but has made headway among the broad mass of the people and the soldiers, and has penetrated as high as the nobility and the mercantile class; therefore an attempt to suppress the new faith will unite the whole nation in opposition.

The view expressed here by Machiavell seems entirely practical, especially since the iconoclasts were known at the time not to be a mass movement but to be led, according to the historian Geoffrey Parker, by 'a hard core [...], between fifty and a hundred strong'.[11] Machiavell's advice was also borne out by events, at least in the sense that the brutal intolerance soon afterwards imposed by Alva ('Alba' in Goethe's play) did indeed unite the nation and lead to the ultimately successful revolt of the Netherlands led by William of Orange, who appears in the play as Oranien. So the political doctrine associated with Machiavelli here is toleration, based admittedly on pragmatic grounds rather than on the principle of freedom of conscience, but nevertheless a policy which seems eminently sensible and commendable. Such a policy was in fact advocated by several of Philip II's advisers, including his minister and favourite Antonio Pérez, who drew their ideas from Machiavelli.[12] Machiavelli in the *Discourses* warns that it is dangerous for princes 'to break the laws and to disregard the ancient traditions and customs under which men have long lived'.[13]

This pragmatism, however, finds no favour with the Regent, who tells Machiavell never to say such things again. To her, it means applying a rigid, amoral calculation, which may be an unfortunate necessity in worldly affairs, to the sphere of religion,

9   See Geoffrey Parker, *The Dutch Revolt* (London: Allen Lane, 1977), pp. 75–80; Jonathan I. Israel, *The Dutch Republic: Its Rise, Greatness, and Fall, 1477–1806* (Oxford: Clarendon Press, 1995), pp. 148–52.

10   Goethe, *SW* v, 469.

11   Parker, *The Dutch Revolt*, p. 78.

12   See Aline Goosens, 'Machiavélisme, antimachiavélisme, tolérance et répression religieuses dans les Pays-Bas méridionaux (seconde moitié du XVIe siècle)', in *L'Antimachiavélisme de la Renaissance aux Lumières*, ed. by Alain Dierkens (Brussels: Editions de l'Université de Bruxelles, 1997), pp. 71–85 (pp. 80–81).

13   *D* III v. 255; pointed out by Clairmont, 'Die Figur des Machiavell', p. 310.

which ought to be governed by heartfelt loyalty to tradition and where pragmatic calculation has no place:

> Ich weiß wohl, daß Politik selten Treu und Glauben halten kann, daß sie Offenheit, Gutherzigkeit, Nachgiebigkeit aus unsern Herzen ausschließt. In weltlichen Geschäften ist das leider nur zu wahr; sollen wir aber auch mit Gott spielen, wie untereinander? Sollen wir gleichgültig gegen unsere bewährte Lehre sein, für die so viele ihr Leben aufgeopfert haben?[14]

> I know that in affairs of state we can rarely keep faith, that our hearts learn to forget frankness, kindness and generosity. I fear in worldly matters that is all too true; but should we play God the tricks we play on one another? Should we be so indifferent to the fate of our established faith, for which so many have offered up their lives in sacrifice?[15]

She thus reinterprets Machiavell's policy, transforming it from pragmatism into cynicism. The translation 'affairs of state' obscures her echo of the French term 'politique', which in the later sixteenth century was applied to moderate opponents of the Catholic League during the French wars of religion. While the Catholic League, led by the Guise family, wanted heretics to be exterminated, the 'politiques', on pragmatic grounds, wanted to reach some accommodation with the Huguenots rather than allow their country to be devastated. They often drew inspiration from the pragmatism of Machiavelli. Commentators on *Egmont* frequently treat the Regent as a clearly positive character.[16] Yet, however attractive her personality may be, in her policy towards the Protestants she is, in principle, as hard-line as Alba, though in practice she abhors his brutal methods. By contrast, Goethe himself was a lifelong advocate of religious toleration.[17]

It is a commonplace of critical discussion that *Egmont* presents an intricate pattern of similarities and differences among the main characters and their approaches to life. Thus the Regent and Egmont are both well disposed towards the Netherlands, but they differ widely in their characters and conduct. Margaret wears herself out with worry about the unrest, cancelling a hunting trip because she is consumed with futile cares, whereas Egmont famously or notoriously refuses to worry about what merely *might* happen. There are also some resemblances between Egmont and Machiavell. Both advocate a policy of toleration towards the Dutch Protestants, Machiavell because of his pragmatic realism, Egmont because of another kind of realism — one based on thorough knowledge of the Dutch people. He knows how to manage them, how to win their confidence and cope with their obstinacy. He compares them to a pedigree horse that one must know intimately and treat with respect, in contrast to a flock of sheep or a plodding ox. He proves his ability in action when he rapidly quells the unrest in Act II.

---

14   Goethe, *SW* v, 470.
15   *Egmont*, in *Five German Tragedies*, trans. Lamport, p. 116.
16   E.g. W. Daniel Wilson, 'Goethe and the Political World', in *The Cambridge Companion to Goethe*, ed. by Lesley Sharpe (Cambridge: Cambridge University Press, 2002), pp. 207–18 (p. 216).
17   See Paul Kerry, *Enlightenment Thought in the Writings of Goethe: A Contribution to the History of Ideas* (Rochester, NY: Camden House, 2001).

It may be going too far, however, to say that 'there is virtually nothing to choose between the enlightened arguments put forward by Machiavell in Act One [...] and those of Egmont in the play as a whole'.[18] Egmont is actually less permissive than Machiavell, for he adjures people to resist Calvinist doctrines — 'Steht fest gegen die fremde Lehre', 'Stand firm in the true faith'[19] — though in the scene with Alba he recommends a general amnesty. At times his views are quite close to Alba's. When he calms the crowd in Brussels by telling them that 'Ein ordentlicher Bürger, der sich ehrlich und fleißig nährt, hat überall so viel Freiheit als er braucht' ('A good citizen earning his living by honest work will always enjoy all the liberty he needs'),[20] he anticipates Alba's famous words: 'Was ist des freisten Freiheit? — Recht zu tun! — und daran wird sie der König nicht hindern' ('What is the freest man free to do? What is right! And the King will hinder no man from doing that').[21] Both Alba and Egmont here seem broadly to agree with the sentiments expressed by Goethe in a letter of 15 March 1783 in which he reviews sceptically his experience of the secret societies that started up in Weimar: 'Und aufrichtig, wenn man vernünftig und wohlthätig seyn will und weiter nichts; so kann das ieder für sich und am hellen Tage in seinem Hauskleide' ('And honestly, if all one wants is to be rational and do good, everyone can do that for himself in broad daylight wearing his dressing-gown').[22] Goethe's innate conservatism made him look suspiciously on members of the lower orders who sought to intervene in the conduct of politics. Hence the oddity that Vansen, who reminds the Netherlanders of their ancient rights, is portrayed unfavourably and described as a bad lot who has been dismissed from many posts for his roguery, yet represents much the same standpoint as Egmont.[23]

Although Egmont looks backward and Machiavell forward, Egmont's general policy broadly converges with that advocated by Machiavell. Both disapprove of the Spanish policy of repression. In the second scene between the Regent and Machiavell, the latter, though suitably discreet, clearly agrees with her expectation that the Spanish intervention will only do harm. Egmont, speaking with Oranien, has already dismissed the idea of a Spanish invasion as both unjust and foolish. In this respect his political judgement is entirely right. The Spanish policy of repression was damaging, futile, and self-defeating; it led to the loss of the Netherlands and the

18   John R. Williams, *The Life of Goethe* (Oxford: Blackwell, 1998), p. 154.
19   Goethe, *SW* v, 487; *Five German Tragedies*, p. 132.
20   Goethe, *SW* v, 486–87; *Five German Tragedies*, p. 131.
21   Goethe, *SW* v, 525; *Five German Tragedies*, p. 166. F. J. Lamport notes that Alba's and Egmont's messages are 'very little different': see '"Entfernten Weltgetöses Widerhall": Politics in Goethe's Plays', *Publications of the English Goethe Society*, 44 (1973–74), 41–62 (p. 44). W. Daniel Wilson even finds in Egmont's words 'the credo of authoritarianism': see 'Hunger/Artist: Goethe's Revolutionary Agitators in *Götz, Satyros, Egmont* and *Der Bürgergeneral*', *Monatshefte*, 86 (1994), 80–94 (p. 85).
22   Goethe, SW xxix: *Das erste Weimarer Jahrzehnt: Briefe, Tagebücher und Gespräche vom 7. November 1775 bis 2. September 1786*, ed. by Hartmut Reinhardt (1997), p. 473.
23   See Wilson, 'Hunger/Artist', p. 85. Cf. Goethe's disapproval of the figure of the 'Kannegiesser' or alehouse politician who puts forward ignorant opinions about politics, such as Breme in *Die Aufgeregten* (1793). Breme claims to be descended from the original 'Kannegiesser', the hero of Ludvig Holberg's comedy *Den politiske Kandestøber* (*The Political Tinsmith*, 1722).

triumph of Calvinism after a destructive war. As John Ellis writes in his vindication of Egmont's political judgement, Egmont in this scene 'grasps political reality better than anyone [...] and errs only in underestimating Alba's total lack of political understanding'.[24] One could go further. We learn that by the time Alba arrives the tumults have already died down.[25] Alba's policy of violent repression therefore represents not the rational use of force, but the irrational savagery of the tyrant.

There is also a certain resemblance in personal style between Machiavell and Egmont. Machiavell is efficient, providing the Regent with an executive summary of the available options. Egmont likewise goes straight to the point. Like the Prince in Lessing's *Emilia Galotti*, he dislikes paperwork, but unlike the Prince he administers justice briskly, fairly, and leniently.[26]

Moving from the dramatic character Machiavell to the thinker Machiavelli, yet more affinities with Egmont can be found. Machiavelli was not only the advocate of political pragmatism, but one of the major theorists of republicanism. Egmont himself is no republican: he advocates loyalty to the King, along with the retention or restoration of the Netherlanders' ancient rights. Yet by his martyr-like death he helps to found the Dutch republic through providing a lasting symbol of freedom which will come to be understood as republican liberty. By an irony of history, the conservative defence of the Netherlanders' traditional rights developed into the republican claim that the States governing the various provinces were in fact sovereign, rather than the King, and that citizens had a civic duty to defend their liberty; these arguments were not, unless very indirectly, derived from Machiavelli, but they ran parallel to Machiavellian republicanism.[27]

Egmont can also be seen as embodying Machiavelli's concept of *virtù*, the quality which enables a prince to master Fortune and to gain fame, honour, and glory. Goethe's hero displays *virtù* in this positive sense. Instead of the middle-aged, careworn husband and father known from history, he appears as youthful, debonair, attractive, successful in war, irresistible in love, and also (despite his complaints about paperwork) a competent and responsible governor.

Egmont's *virtù* finds expression in his famous image of the 'Sonnenpferde der Zeit', 'time's horses of the sun', which may also convey Machiavelli's concept of *fortuna*.[28] Machiavelli is very conscious of the instability of fortune. Thus Cesare Borgia owed his success more to fortune than to his own *virtù*, outstanding though that was, and lost his power again because of bad fortune — the fact that when Pope Alexander VI died, Cesare was too ill to be able to prevent the election of his

24   John M. Ellis, 'The Vexed Question of Egmont's Political Judgment', in *Tradition and Creation: Essays in Honour of Elizabeth Mary Wilkinson*, ed. by C. P. Magill, Brian A. Rowley, and Christopher J. Smith (Leeds: Maney, 1978), pp. 116–30 (p. 122).

25   See the conversation between Silva and Gomez, in Goethe, *SW* v, 516.

26   The contrast with Lessing's Prince makes it difficult to agree with Hilliard (*Freethinkers, Libertines and 'Schwärmer'*, p. 135) in classifying Egmont as a libertine, unless of a very domesticated sort. We do not, for example, learn of previous mistresses before Clärchen.

27   See Martin van Gelderen, 'The Machiavellian Moment and the Dutch Revolt: The Rise of Neostoicism and Dutch Republicanism', in *Machiavelli and Republicanism*, ed. by Gisela Bock, Quentin Skinner, and Maurizio Viroli (Cambridge: Cambridge University Press, 1990), pp. 205–23.

28   Clairmont, 'Die Figur des Machiavell', p. 307.

arch-enemy Julius II (*P* VII. 28–29). In Machiavelli's view, fortune is not in complete control of human affairs. He would not have agreed with the Regent when she says despairingly: 'O was sind wir Große auf der Woge der Menschheit? wir glauben sie zu beherrschen und sie treibt uns auf und nieder, hin und her' ('Oh, what are we, we great ones, on the waves of mankind? We think we can command them, and they toss us up and down, they drive us to and fro').[29] Rather, Machiavelli opines, 'I am disposed to hold that fortune is the arbiter of half our actions, but that it lets us control roughly the other half' (*P* XXV, 85). He goes on to compare fortune to a violent river, which floods the plains and tears down trees and buildings when it is in spate, but, when it is quiet, can be controlled by building dykes and embankments. The prince who has *virtù* will be able, at least in some measure, to master fortune, for, Machiavelli says in a notorious passage, she is a woman who likes young, courageous men and submits to them more willingly than to cold and prudent characters.

The 'Sonnenpferde der Zeit' symbolize Egmont's precarious mastery of fortune. The horses are not out of control, but under the partial control of the charioteer. He is not Apollo, guiding the horses on their regular course, for they have bolted; but neither is he Phaethon, who came to grief through being utterly unable to manage his team:

> Wie von unsichtbaren Geistern gepeitscht gehen die Sonnenpferde der Zeit mit unsers Schicksals leichtem Wagen durch, und uns bleibt nichts als mutig gefaßt die Zügel zu erhalten, und bald rechts, bald links vom Steine hier, vom Sturze da die Räder weg zu lenken.[30]

> Our destiny is like the sun; invisible spirits whip up time's swift horses, away with its light chariot they run, and all we can do is take courage, hold the reins in a firm grip, and keep the wheels clear of the rocks on one hand, the precipice on the other.[31]

Unlike the adaptation of this image by Büchner in *Danton's Tod*, where Danton dreams of sitting astride the globe and desperately clinging on, this does not imply helplessness, but control within narrow limits. Egmont is not a fatalist, but neither does he overestimate the degree to which events can be managed.[32]

In the person of Machiavell, then, and to some extent also in Egmont, we have a version of Machiavellianism centring on what I have called pragmatic tolerance. And, as I have mentioned, this was one of the consequences that in the sixteenth century were actually drawn from Machiavelli's writings. We can also see Egmont as embodying the best aspects of princely *virtù*, including a limited control over fortune. But of course Machiavelli was most often associated with a cynical, amoral,

---

29   Goethe, *SW* V, 468; *Five German Tragedies*, p. 114.
30   Goethe, *SW* V, 493.
31   Ibid.; *Five German Tragedies*, p. 13. Cf. Goethe's poem about a frantic journey in a post-chaise, 'An Schwager Kronos' (1774), *SW* I, 201, 324.
32   On possible allusions to Apollo and Phaethon, see L. A. Willoughby, 'The Image of the Horse and Charioteer in Goethe's Poetry', *Publications of the English Goethe Society*, n.s. 15 (1946), 47–70 (pp. 60, 62). Cf. Sander L. Gilman, 'The Uncontrollable Steed: A Study in the Metamorphosis of a Literary Image', *Euphorion*, 66 (1972), 32–54.

and calculating attitude to politics, and this kind of Machiavellianism also finds a place in the play. One version is represented by Alba and his henchmen, another by Oranien.

Alba believes in planning and calculating his actions down to the last detail. He has instructed his agent Silva to make all necessary preparations to take Egmont and Oranien prisoner when they call on him. Silva replies confidently: 'Vertrau auf uns, ihr Schicksal wird sie, wie eine wohlberechnete Sonnenfinsternis pünktlich und schröcklich treffen' ('You may rely on us. Their fate will be upon them like an eclipse of the sun, terrible and punctual to the minute').[33] The simile is revealingly inappropriate. One can calculate the timing of an eclipse of the sun, and remain calm when the ignorant are alarmed, but one cannot make it happen, as Silva implies. And indeed Alba's plans for the arrest of Egmont and Oranien are partially frustrated by Oranien's failure to show up. Even before this becomes apparent, Silva, in a short soliloquy, shows that he is not really so confident as he seemed when reporting to his employer: he speaks nervously of the 'Eigensinn des Schicksals' ('the wilfulness of fate') which may make events turn out in an unpredictable manner. And when Oranien fails to appear, Alba swings from his former assurance into complete pessimism, surmising that whatever one does is simply a gamble on an unknowable and uncontrollable future: 'wie in einen Lostopf greifst du in die dunkle Zukunft, was du fassest ist noch zugerollt dir unbewußt sei's Treffer oder Fehler!' ('The future is a dark lottery. Whatever you draw, it is still folded tight and sealed; it may be a prize or a blank').[34] This shows how fragile Alba's trust in his own calculations really was. When his calculations prove partially mistaken, he runs to the other extreme and claims that it is futile ever to plan for the future at all. He falls into the fatalism which is briefly espoused by the protagonist of *Wilhelm Meisters Lehrjahre* and which there earns the rebuke: 'Mit diesen Gesinnungen könnte kein Mädchen ihre Tugend, niemand sein Geld im Beutel behalten' ('With sentiments like these, no girl could retain her virtue, nobody could keep his money in his wallet').[35]

The scene between Alba and Egmont swerves away to other important themes, notably the contrast between Egmont's conservative defence of the Netherlanders' traditional rights and Alba's ruthless insistence on homogenizing and modernizing their government. Alba claims to be coercing them for their own good:

> Des Königs Absicht ist: sie selbst zu ihrem eignen Besten einzuschränken, ihr eigen Heil, wenns sein muß ihnen aufzudringen, die schädlichen Bürger auf-zuopfern damit die übrigen Ruhe finden, des Glücks einer weisen Regierung genießen können.

> The King's intention is to constrain them for their own good, to force salvation on them if it must be so, to sacrifice the troublesome citizens so that the others may enjoy peace and the good fortune that wise government brings.[36]

33   Goethe, *SW* v, 517; *Five German Tragedies*, p. 159.
34   Goethe, *SW* v, 521; *Five German Tragedies*, p. 163.
35   Goethe, *SW* IX: *Wilhelm Meisters theatralische Sendung, Wilhelm Meisters Lehrjahre, Unterhaltungen deutscher Ausgewanderten*, ed. by Wilhelm Vosskamp and Herbert Jaumann (1992), p. 424.
36   Goethe, *SW* v, 527; *Five German Tragedies*, p. 168.

Goethe, like some late-Enlightenment contemporaries, is here criticizing the paternalism which was part of enlightened absolutism.[37] He himself noted the parallel between the riots in his play and the resistance in the 1780s to the legal and constitutional reforms which the enlightened Joseph II, committed to homogenizing the diverse provinces of his patchwork Habsburg Empire, was trying to impose on the Austrian Netherlands — the very territory where the events of *Egmont* take place.[38] This disregard for the Netherlanders' sentiments, however, helps to explain why Alba's calculations are so vulnerable. He forgets that other people have wills of their own; they are not a flock of sheep to be helplessly driven about, nor are they automata who will wait passively for him to capture them.

An image of calculation that contrasts revealingly with Alba's is that of the chessboard, used by Oranien when he tells Egmont: 'ich stehe immer wie über einem Schachspiele und halte keinen Zug des Gegners für unbedeutend' ('for many years I have watched carefully over our affairs like a game of chess, where I have to look for some significance in every move my opponent makes').[39] With this image he acknowledges, unlike Alba, that his opponents have wills of their own. In Oranien we come much closer to the conventional conception of Machiavellianism. First, he believes that political behaviour can be calculated and predicted. Second, unlike Egmont, he does not overvalue traditional and emotional loyalties. Egmont refuses to believe that King Philip will do anything so base as to break his word to the Netherlands and authorize a Spanish invasion. He gives as a reason that Philip is the son of the noble Emperor Charles V and therefore incapable of baseness. Although this may sound naïve, it shows that Egmont shares the feudal assumptions of an earlier generation, whereas Oranien has a much more neutral, value-free, perhaps cynical attitude to politics. In an excellent discussion of the scene between Egmont and Oranien, Irmgard Hobson contrasts their positions as follows:

> Oranien's view of the feudal code of ethics, in which loyalty is an essential value, is that of the skeptical pragmatist, a Machiavellian outlook: there are no absolute values for his rulers. Like Machiavelli, his position is outside of his time, ahead of it. For Egmont, the feudal order is a living reality; he is part of it; he represents that code and that era.[40]

Egmont is betrayed not only by his personal qualities of trustfulness and openness, but by the dying epoch with which he identifies, whereas Oranien is a man of the future.

His historical original, William of Orange, as he appears in Goethe's source Strada, is explicitly represented as a Machiavellian figure. The Jesuit Strada is not

37   Cf. Diderot, 'Essai sur la vie de Sénèque le philosophe, sur ses écrits, et sur les règnes de Claude et de Néron' (1779), in *Œuvres complètes*, ed. by Roger Lewinter, 15 vols (Paris: Le Club Français du Livre, 1969–73), XII, 509–744 (p. 524); Kant, 'On the Common Saying: "This may be true in Theory, but it does not Apply in Practice" ', in *Kant: Political Writings*, pp. 61–92 (p. 74).
38   See Goethe, *SW* v, 1260–61, and Derek Beales, *Joseph II*, 2 vols (Cambridge: Cambridge University Press, 1987, 2009), II: *Against the World, 1780–1790*, pp. 502–25.
39   Goethe, *SW* v, 495–96; *Five German Tragedies*, p. 140.
40   Irmgard Hobson, 'Oranien and Alba: The Two Political Dialogues in *Egmont*', *Germanic Review*, 50 (1975), 260–74 (p. 264).

well disposed towards the Protestant leader, and charges him with changing his religion out of mere opportunism.

> [...] it is most probable, his Religion was but pretended, which he could put on like a Cloke, to serve him for such a time; and put it off again, when it was out of fashion. Truly, that Religion was not much to be regarded, when Authority was to be acquired, or established; are the words of his own letter to *Alençon,* Brother to the *French King;* part whereof in its due place, I shall insert. This, it was thought, he learned in the villanous school of *Machiavel,* whose Books he seriously studied; as *Granvel* affirms in his Letter from *Spain,* directed to *Alexander* Prince of *Parma.*[41]

This opportunism, according to Strada, was part of William's character, which excelled in dissimulation:

> Indeed for altering of a Government, I know not if any man ever lived, fitter then the Prince of *Orange.* He had a present wit, not slow to catch at opportunities, but subtill; concealing himself, not to be sounded, even by those that were thought privy to his secrets. Then he had a rare way to ingratiate himself with any that but came to speak with him: so unaffectedly he conformed to strangers' manners, and served himself of others ends; not that he stooped to the poor forms of complement [sic], and common professions of imaginary services, wherewith at this day men do honourably mock one another. But shewing himself, neither sparing nor prodigall of his Courtship, he so cunningly contrived his *words,* that you could not but think, that he reserved farre more for *action.* Which begat a greater opinion of his discretion: and gave more credit to his pretensions.[42]

A modern historian confirms this characterization by saying of William of Orange: 'his later sobriquet "the Silent" referred not to any taciturn inclination — he was in fact loquacious — but to his not saying what he thought'.[43]

Goethe thus had before him a distinct type of early modern politician — a cynically pragmatic Machiavellian, a practitioner of 'Staatskunst' as a demanding art. Turning William into the dramatic character Oranien, Goethe avoided making him a villain, but his portrayal is still highly, even unfairly, critical. It is easy to be biased in Oranien's favour by historical hindsight. After all, his historical prototype did eventually lead a successful rebellion against the Spaniards. In the play, however, neither Oranien nor Egmont knows what is going to happen. Oranien puts forward a series of hypotheses; Egmont dismisses them on the grounds that the King can be trusted. They talk past each other because each is speaking from a different mentality, Oranien from that of 'Staatskunst', politics as calculation and manipulation, Egmont from that of feudal loyalty. It has been remarked that in contrast to Egmont, who speaks eloquently about freedom and about traditional rights, Oranien never puts forward his own conception of politics, though he might have done so during this discussion as a means of persuading Egmont to flee with

41   Strada, *De bello Belgico*, trans. Stapylton, Book 1, p. 46.
42   Ibid., p. 45.
43   Israel, *The Dutch Republic*, p. 139.

him.[44] Alternatively, he might have proposed, as Strada says his original did, that he and Egmont should raise a popular army, meet Alba's troops, and fight a single battle instead of a long and bloody war.[45] Instead, he seems to be speaking only of self-preservation. Egmont warns him that if he refuses a summons from Alba, he will be giving a signal for rebellion; that rebellion will provoke the repression which at present Oranien fears only as a possibility; and that repression will undoubtedly mean bloodshed and devastation on an enormous scale. Oranien's reply is public-spirited: 'Wir sind nicht einzelne Menschen Egmont. Ziemt es sich uns für tausende hinzugeben: so ziemt es sich auch uns für tausende zu schonen' ('Egmont, our lives are not simply our own. If it is our duty to sacrifice ourselves for thousands, then it is our duty to spare ourselves for thousands').[46] However, it can hardly be expected to cut any ice with Egmont, who, far from sparing himself, risked his life at the battle of Gravelines. Having fought there at the head of his troops, men whom he knows well, he will scarcely be prepared to direct a rebellion from a safely distant headquarters. He makes Oranien's proposed flight sound shabby by replying: 'Wer sich schont muß sich selbst verdächtig werden' (He who spares himself must suspect himself).[47] Although this reply may sound heroic, it reveals that Egmont does not understand the distinction Oranien assumes between private and public morality. To Egmont, courage means standing your ground and confronting an enemy face to face; to escape from the enemy, even for public-spirited reasons, is cowardice. To Oranien, public morality permits him, indeed requires him, to escape from immediate danger in order to carry on the campaign of resistance from abroad.

About the Machiavellian Oranien we can say that, like other courtiers in the plays, he represents the new world dominated by politics in the sense of *politique*: rational calculation. Machiavell, arguing with the devout Regent, advocates putting aside one's personal attachment to a particular religion and instituting toleration for the sake of civil peace. Oranien puts aside the ethos of personal courage in order to conduct a long-term political campaign. And Oranien's campaign will succeed, in leading to a formal declaration of Dutch independence in 1581. Goethe's play obscures Oranien's success and puts all the emotional weight on Egmont's heroic martyrdom, even sending him in his prison cell an allegorical dream about freedom. Granted, a struggle for liberty requires both inspiring heroes and astute politicians. Goethe, however, exalts the former and elides the latter, suggesting how uneasy he was in the new world of politics inaugurated by Machiavelli.

---

44   See Peter Michelsen, 'Egmonts Freiheit', *Euphorion*, 65 (1971), 274–97 (esp. pp. 286–87).
45   See Hobson, 'Oranien and Alba', p. 265.
46   Goethe, *SW* v. 498; *Five German Tragedies*, p. 142. This statement must qualify the view that Oranien shows concern *only* for his personal safety: cf. Michelsen, 'Egmonts Freiheit', p. 287; Ellis, 'The Vexed Question', p. 121.
47   Goethe, *SW* v, 498; *Five German Tragedies*, p. 142.

6

Goethe:
Other Goethean Machiavels

To see how lastingly Goethe was worried about the Machiavellian conception of politics, we need to look at some Machiavellian figures from other dramas.

Weislingen in Goethe's early play *Götz von Berlichingen* (1773) is a complex character, not only ambitious, but also emotionally volatile, and sometimes sentimental and self-pitying. Despite his efforts, he never escapes from the shadow of his childhood playmate Götz, who has grown into an eminent warrior, a Robin Hood figure who rights the people's wrongs, but — like Egmont — devoid of political prudence. Götz and Weislingen are living at a historical conjuncture when the feudal and military values of the Middle Ages, which so appeal also to Egmont, are giving way to a more orderly society in which commerce, bureaucracy, and humanistic learning are prominent. Small territorial sovereigns like Götz, who owes allegiance directly to the emperor, are being elbowed aside or swallowed up by powerful princes and prelates, represented here by the Bishop of Bamberg, to whose court Weislingen attaches himself. Estranged from his former friend Götz, Weislingen intrigues against him by advising the emperor Maximilian to deal harshly with Götz and similar imperial knights whose activities, he says, are spreading discontent among the people. Eventually, Weislingen's chance to annihilate Götz comes when the latter, partly out of public spirit and partly out of boredom, breaks his house arrest and intervenes in the Peasant War of 1525, hoping to mediate between the peasants and the nobles whose mansions they are burning down. Weislingen is appointed as commissioner responsible for quelling the revolt. We are told that a peasant leader has been burned alive and hundreds of others beheaded, impaled, quartered, or broken on the wheel.[1] An appeal to Weislingen's sentimental side saves Götz's life. Before that, however, Goethe has given us in Weislingen a complex picture of a tyrant who resorts to senseless cruelty, like Alba in *Egmont*, as an escape from his own inner instability.

Weislingen is a Machiavellian in practice; Goethe's next play, *Clavigo* (1774), introduces a character who is also a Machiavellian in theory. The play's action is based on real-life events reported in the memoirs of Pierre Augustin de Beaumarchais, later famous as the author of *Le Mariage de Figaro* (1784). Beaumarchais comes to Madrid to reconcile his sister Marie with her unfaithful lover Clavigo. He succeeds,

---

[1]   Goethe, *SW* IV: *Dramen 1765–1775*, ed. by Dieter Borchmeyer (1985), p. 381. For a seventeenth-century description of breaking on the wheel, see Evans, *Rituals of Retribution*, pp. 27–30.

in the play as in real life, but Goethe then alters events by introducing a friend of Clavigo, called Carlos, who brings about a tragic ending. Warning Clavigo that marriage to a middle-class girl would hamper his career as royal archivist, Carlos advises him, as a 'klugen Gedanken' (prudent idea), to abandon her. Carlos further induces the indecisive and feebly ambitious Clavigo to agree to a plan in which Beaumarchais will be accused of extorting by force a promise from Clavigo to marry Marie, and after a spell of imprisonment, will return to France. On hearing of the charge against Beaumarchais, however, Marie dies of shock. Meeting at her funeral procession, Clavigo and Beaumarchais fight a duel and Clavigo is fatally stabbed. He describes Marie and himself to Carlos as 'die Opfer deiner Klugheit' ('victims of your prudence').[2]

Together, Clavigo and Carlos form a dyad in which the qualities combined in Weislingen, irresolution and unscrupulousness, are split among two characters who thus complement each other. Clavigo and Carlos thus anticipate the dyad in *Faust* formed by the emotional, irresolute Faust and the cynical, calculating Mephisto. Carlos unfolds a doctrine that morality is only for little people, and exceptional people are entitled to override it:

> Möge deine Seele sich erweitern, und die Gewißheit des großen Gefühls über dich kommen, daß außerordentliche Menschen eben auch darin außerordentliche Menschen sind, weil ihre Pflichten von den Pflichten des gemeinen Menschen abgehen; daß der, dessen Werk es ist, ein großes Ganzes zu übersehen, zu regieren, zu erhalten, sich keinen Vorwurf zu machen braucht, geringe Verhältnisse vernachlässiget, Kleinigkeiten dem Wohl des Ganzen aufgeopfert zu haben.[3]

> May your soul be enlarged, and may you be possessed by the great feeling of certainty that exceptional people are exceptional people also because their duties differ from the duties of ordinary people; that he whose work it is to oversee, to rule, to maintain a great whole, has no need to reproach himself for having ignored petty circumstances and sacrificed trifles to the good of the whole.

In his insistence that public duties require one to ignore private obligations, Carlos is like a malign parody of Oranien. He has been described as appealing to 'the Machiavellian doctrine of "Staatsräson"'.[4] His Machiavellian calculation is shown to be self-defeating, because one cannot foresee every contingency: he did not foresee the duel between Clavigo and Beaumarchais, any more than Alba foresaw the flight of Oranien.

Goethe's polemic against cynical Machiavellianism continues in *Iphigenie auf Tauris* (begun in 1779, completed during Goethe's stay in Italy and published in 1787). The character of Pylades may not spring to mind immediately as a candidate for Machiavellian status. He is the reliable friend of Orest, accompanying the latter to the remote land of Tauris (modern Crimea); Orest, having avenged the death of

---

2   Goethe, *SW* IV, 492.
3   Goethe, *SW* IV, 480.
4   Eudo C. Mason, 'Goethe's Sense of Evil', *Publications of the English Goethe Society*, 34 (1964), 1–53 (p. 23).

his father Agamemnon by killing his mother Clytemnestra, is under a curse which, according to the Delphic oracle, can only be expiated by bringing back 'the sister' from Tauris to Greece. Orest assumes that 'the sister' refers to the statue of Apollo's sister Artemis (or Diana) kept at Tauris, since he has no way of knowing that the priestess of Diana is his own sister Iphigenie, whom the goddess saved from being sacrificed by her father at Aulis.

On his first appearance, Pylades reveals two qualities which may seem incongruous. On the one hand, he is an unfailingly cheery, never-say-die character who, as Orest admits, has been 'ein immer munterer Geselle' ('an always cheerful companion', 647) ever since their childhood.[5] Even in what seems a desperate situation, captured by Taurians, confined in the sacred grove, and expecting soon to be sacrificed, Pylades describes himself as 'immer noch voll Mut und Lust' ('still full of courage and good spirits', 664). He urges Orest not to think about his murder of his mother but instead to dwell on pleasant memories, though this bouncy cheerfulness makes no impression on his depressed companion. Meanwhile he is confident that his ingenuity can find a way out of their present fix. 'Ich denke nicht den Tod; ich sinn' und horche [...]' ('I'm not thinking about death; I'm pondering and keeping my ears open', 601). From his view of the gods, he clearly upholds what William James called the religion of healthy-mindedness,[6] being convinced that 'Die Götter rächen | Der Väter Missetat nicht an dem Sohn' ('The gods do not take revenge on the son for the fathers' misdeeds', 713–14), despite all the evidence to the contrary in the Tantalids' family history, and that 'Der Götter Worte sind nicht doppelsinnig' ('The gods' words are not ambiguous', 613), though they undoubtedly are: the resolution of the plot depends on revealing the ambiguity of the divine command to remove 'the sister' from Tauris. With this positive outlook, he is convinced that the gods will support his 'Klugheit' (prudence, 742: the quality which Carlos in *Clavigo* so badly overestimated). Orest ironically compares him to Ulysses, famous for his cunning, and Pylades hardly seems a natural plotter, but he defends his combination of 'List und Klugheit' (cunning and prudence, 766) and in fact he has made a start by questioning the guards and learning about the character of the priestess, who he thinks will, as a woman, be both less bloodthirsty and more reliable than a man.

On meeting Iphigenie in the next scene, Pylades starts putting his ingenuity into practice by telling her a highly circumstantial fabrication to the effect that he and Orest are two brothers and that Orest has killed the third brother in a dispute over their inheritance and is therefore being pursued by the Furies. He also brings her up to date with the outcome of the Trojan War and the fates of Agamemnon and Clytemnestra, to which Iphigenie listens with visible though restrained emotion. She abruptly leaves, with the words 'Es ist genug. Du wirst mich wiedersehn' ('That's enough. You'll see me again', 918). Although, since Pylades believes Iphigenie to have died at Aulis, he could not possibly realize that he has just been unwittingly giving her distressing news about her closest relatives, his words on her departure

5   Goethe, *SW* v, 573. Quotations are identified by line number.
6   See William James, *The Varieties of Religious Experience* (London: Longmans, Green & Co., 1902), Lectures IV and V.

— 'Von dem Geschick des Königs-Hauses scheint | Sie tief gerührt' ('The fate of the royal house seems to move her deeply', 919–20) — do cast a somewhat ironic light on the 'Klugheit' to which he has laid claim. It would be quite easy to play the role of Pylades for laughs.

In Act III, which centres on the healing of Orest, Pylades plays only a small part. He appears towards the end, urging Orest and Iphigenie to lose no time in deciding how to escape. In Act IV Iphigenie appears very impressed by Pylades, asserting that his soul is peaceful — 'Denn seine Seel' ist stille' (1386) — which has not been obvious from his demeanour, and ascribing to him various other good qualities of which she can have no knowledge. It emerges that Pylades has concocted a plan which requires Iphigenie to claim that the strangers have rendered the temple impure so that before performing the ceremony she and her maidens must take the statue down to the seashore to wash it. This stratagem conflicts not only with her truthfulness but with the undoubted prospect, as the messenger Arkas assures her, that if she displeases her captor King Thoas by seeming ungrateful he will restore Tauris to the barbarous condition from which she has slowly raised it. As Iphigenie hesitates, Pylades appears, tells her that the ship is ready for their escape, and reproaches her for delaying. He now tells Iphigenie to make a further excuse for delaying the sacrifice by saying that one of the strangers is insane; meanwhile, he wants to carry off the statue on his own shoulders.[7] Iphigenie at last explains her scruples about deceiving the King, who has been a second father to her, and now Pylades reveals himself as a Machiavellian, for whom necessity excuses any deception and absolves her from ingratitude: 'Das ist nicht Undank, was die Not gebeut' ('It isn't ingratitude if an emergency dictates it', 1645). For Pylades, a wrong action ceases to be wrong if necessity commands it, whereas for Iphigenie it may be required by necessity, but is still wrong: she replies: 'Es bleibt wohl Undank, nur die Not entschuldigt's' ('It is still ingratitude, only an emergency excuses it', 1646). The difference between Iphigenie and Pylades replicates the difference between Machiavelli and the reason of state theorists led by Botero. Machiavelli is clear that bad actions remain bad, although in politics they often cannot be avoided; Botero and his ilk think that if reason of state requires bad actions, they thereby cease to be bad.

The play's further action proves Pylades wrong. Iphigenie musters all her courage and tells Thoas the truth about the two strangers. Her gamble succeeds, partly because it was not entirely a gamble. She treats Thoas as a fellow-human being susceptible to argument and emotion, not as an object to be manipulated. Similarly, Egmont, in contrast to Alba, treats the Netherlanders with empathy and good nature, even when admonishing them, and, unlike Oranien, he does not regard politics as a game of chess. The situation is in fact resolved, however, not through Iphigenie's truth-telling, but through Orest's sudden and unexplained realization that the oracle referred not to Apollo's sister but his own.[8]

---

7   No explanation is given for the contradiction between this scheme and the earlier plan of taking the statue to the seashore on a pretext: see Wolfdietrich Rasch, Goethes 'Iphigenie auf Tauris' als Drama der Autonomie (Munich: Beck, 1979), p. 131.

8   For this interpretation, see ibid., pp. 177–78.

For an indirect and only slightly anachronistic commentary on Pylades' conduct, we can turn briefly to another political thinker who is in many ways the antithesis to Machiavelli, namely Kant. In the decade after *Iphigenie*, Kant published a treatise on politics, *Zum ewigen Frieden* (1795), which has often been dismissed as utopian, but which has been shown to be thoroughly realistic in its awareness of political facts and human nature.[9] Just after the passage quoted earlier, in which Kant denounces the twists and turns of an immoral 'Klugheitslehre' (doctrine of prudence), he directs his fire against the political moralist who adjusts morality to suit his own purposes, subordinates principles to serve his immediate ends, and thus puts the cart before the horse.[10] The cap fits Pylades, whose morality Wolfdietrich Rasch rightly describes as relativistic and pragmatic.[11] Iphigenie, on the other hand, corresponds to the antithetical type, the moral politician, and her conduct in revealing the truth to Thoas finds a retrospective justification a few pages later in Kant's treatise, when he talks about the need for 'Publizität', or what we might call transparency, in public affairs. A secret conspiracy or rebellion, such as Pylades tries to organize, goes against this principle and is therefore impossible and self-defeating.[12]

Machiavellian intrigue of the worst sort appears nakedly a few years later in Goethe's strange play *Die natürliche Tochter* (1803). Goethe intended it as the first part of a trilogy in which he hoped to give poetic form to his understanding of the French Revolution. What he achieved in this, the only part of the trilogy he did write, was to shroud in mythical and theological imagery a harsh picture of political life under the *ancien régime*. The core of the action concerns the title figure, Eugenie, the 'natural daughter' of a Duke. Her father has had her brought up in a secluded part of the countryside. He now wants to have her legitimized, and the King agrees, but the Duke's scapegrace son, unwilling to lose part of his inheritance, arranges for Eugenie to be kidnapped and shipped off to the West Indies where it is hoped she will die of fever. She avoids this fate by renouncing her noble status and agreeing to marry a lawyer, the Gerichtsrat, who represents 'des Bürgers hohen Sicherstand' ('the citizens' assured estate', 2205).[13]

This is not the place for a detailed account of the play; I want simply to indicate two contrasting political values it contains. Brought up in seclusion, Eugenie has retained her childlike devotion to her King and her country. On regaining consciousness after her riding accident, she insists on kneeling before the King. To his remonstrance she replies:

> Doch was, in Augenblicken der Entzückung,
> Die Kniee beugt, ist auch ein süß Gefühl.
> Und was wir unserm König, Vater, Gott,

9   Reed, *Light in Germany*, p. 74.
10   Kant, *Werke*, VI, 239.
11   Rasch, *Goethes 'Iphigenie auf Tauris'*, pp. 141–42.
12   Kant, *Werke*, VI, 244–46.
13   Goethe, *SW* VI: *Dramen 1791–1832*, ed. by Dieter Borchmeyer and Peter Huber (1993). Quotations are identified by line number. Translations are mostly taken from Goethe, *The Natural Daughter* (with Schiller, *The Bride of Messina*), trans. by F. J. Lamport (Cambridge: Modern Humanities Research Association, 2018), here p. 67.

> Von Wonnedank, von ungemeßner Liebe,
> Zum reinsten Opfer bringen möchten, drückt
> In dieser Stellung sich am besten aus. (350–55)

> The feeling that compels us to our knees,
> In rapturous moments, is delightful too.
> This is the posture that can best express
> The purest sacrifice we long to make
> Unto our king, our father, and our God,
> In blissful gratitude and boundless love.[14]

This beautiful profession of feudal loyalty belongs in a pre-modern world, like the one inhabited by Egmont. Eugenie can only make it because her secluded upbringing has kept her unaware of modern political realities. The King is a weak figure who later betrays her by signing the *lettre de cachet* providing for her expulsion. Her father the Duke is discontented with the King and disposed to plot against him. Her governess turns out to be in league with the Secretary who arranges her kidnapping and who is a shameless Machiavellian. He pays lip service to the idea of a supreme moral authority, 'ein Herrschendes' (a power above, 853),[15] but says that nobody takes its laws and rules seriously. Living not in heaven but down on earth, we have to survive by the unscrupulous use of our reason, and acknowledge no law except self-interest:

> Verstand empfingen wir, uns, mündig, selbst,
> Im ird'schen Element, zurecht zu finden,
> Und was uns nützt, ist unser höchstes Recht. (859–61)

> We have been given wits to find our way
> As best we can in this material world,
> And what is our advantage is our right.[16]

The word 'mündig' deserves some comment, especially as the translation obscures its significance. It means 'of age', that is, having the capacities, responsibilities, and rights of an adult. It was famously used by Kant in his essay on the meaning of 'enlightenment':

> *Aufklärung ist der Ausgang des Menschen aus seiner selbst verschuldeten Unmündigkeit. Unmündigkeit ist das Unvermögen, sich seines Verstandes ohne Leitung eines anderen zu bedienen.* [...] *Sapere aude! Habe Mut, dich deines eigenen Verstandes zu bedienen! ist also der Wahlspruch der Aufklärung.*[17]

> *Enlightenment is man's emergence from his self-incurred immaturity. Immaturity* is the inability to use one's own understanding without the guidance of another. [...] The motto of enlightenment is therefore: *Sapere aude!* Have the courage to use your *own* understanding![18]

---

14   Goethe, *SW* vi, 314. My translation, used in Ritchie Robertson, *Goethe: A Very Short Introduction* (Oxford: Oxford University Press, 2016), p. 77.
15   Goethe, *SW* vi, 328; *The Natural Daughter*, p. 31.
16   Goethe, *SW* vi, 329; *The Natural Daughter*, p. 31.
17   'Beantwortung der Frage: Was ist Aufklärung?' (1783) in Kant, *Werke*, vi, 53–61 (p. 53). The phrase 'Sapere aude', 'Dare to be wise', comes from Horace, *Epodes*, i. 2. 40.
18   'An Answer to the Question: What is Enlightenment?' in *Kant: Political Writings*, pp. 54–60 (p. 54).

'Mündig' was a key word in the political and cultural debates of Goethe's time. Sympathizers with the French Revolution held that it had made the French people mature.[19] Friedrich Schlegel described Greek art as culturally 'mündig', the product not of nature but of human freedom.[20] Schiller, on the other hand, uses the word more cautiously. When asked to choose between his loyalty to Wallenstein and his duty to the Emperor, Max Piccolomini responds uneasily: 'Mein General! Du machst mich heute mündig.'[21] And Queen Elisabeth, herself shown in *Maria Stuart* as a cynical manipulator, seems to equate maturity with deceit in saying approvingly to the double agent Mortimer:

> Wer schon so früh der Täuschung schwere Kunst
> Ausübte, der ist mündig vor der Zeit.

> One who can practise in such tender years
> The taxing art of self-disguise is ripe
> Before his time, and wins the test of manhood.[22]

Goethe in *Die natürliche Tochter* goes much further in implicitly contradicting Kant. It seems that maturity admits us to a world of cynical manipulation suited to people like the Secretary. It is far inferior to the feudal world, in which one stood in a relation of childlike submissiveness to the authority above one. That authority, moreover, was a person whom one could meet — one's father, one's king — or at least imagine — one's God — whereas in the modern world relationships are abstract and God is a mere force that one can know nothing about.

As his henchman, the Secretary has recruited a priest who is his pupil ('Schüler', 1195) in following these principles. Although the Secretary and the Priest are not seen after Act III, there are some hopeful signs that they may be falling out: the Priest complains of being used as a mere tool and demands to take part in making decisions. So the Secretary may, like Alba, be making a fatal mistake in treating people as puppets to be manipulated. However, the play suggests that this unscrupulous amorality is the political norm. The Gerichtsrat, who observes the great world from his quiet retreat in a provincial port, thinks that all rulers, even if not driven by self-interest, are obliged to place expediency above principle:

> Ich schelte nicht das Werkzeug, rechte kaum
> Mit jenen Mächten, die sich solche Handlung
> Erlauben können. Leider, sind auch sie
> Gebunden und gedrängt. Sie wirken selten
> Aus freier Überzeugung. Sorge, Furcht
> Vor größerm Übel nötiget Regenten
> Die nützlich ungerechten Taten ab. (1794–1800)

---

19   W. Daniel Wilson, *Das Goethe-Tabu: Protest und Menschenrechte im klassischen Weimar* (Munich: dtv, 1999), p. 184.

20   Friedrich Schlegel, *Über das Studium der griechischen Poesie* (written 1795, published 1797), in his *Kritische Schriften*, ed. by Wolfdietrich Rasch (Munich: Hanser, 1970), pp. 113–230 (p. 173).

21   *WB* IV: *Wallenstein*, ed. by Frithjof Stock (2000), p. 179. The nuance of 'mündig' is not quite conveyed by Lamport's translation: 'My general! Today you make me free' (Schiller, *The Robbers* and *Wallenstein*, trans. by F. J. Lamport (Harmondsworth: Penguin, 1979), p. 348).

22   Schiller, *Maria Stuart*, 1574–75, in *Werke und Briefe*, IV, 60; *Five German Tragedies*, p. 238.

> I do not scold the instrument, nor scarcely
> Dare to dispute the powers that permit
> Themselves a deed like this. For sadly they
> Themselves are bound and forced. They rarely act
> Out of conviction. Fear and anxious dread
> Of greater evils can compel our rulers
> To deeds unjust, though they be expeditious.[23]

Through the Gerichtsrat, the play seems to advocate steering clear of the great world of politics and living in quiet obscurity. Initially, fearing that Eugenie and her governess will get him into trouble, he tells the latter:

> Vollbringe was du mußt, entferne dich
> Aus meiner Enge reingezognem Kreis. (1801–02)

> Do what you have to do, but go and leave
> My life in pure and narrow-bounded circle.[24]

Later, by asking Eugenie to marry him, he invites her into this circle and thus brings the play to a cautiously happy ending. Its message is clearly that high politics are unscrupulous, amoral, and pernicious, and that decency is much more likely to be found, as in *Herrmann und Dorothea* (1797), among the unambitious middle classes. If so, it is hardly surprising that Goethe got no further with his trilogy about the French Revolution.

---

23   Goethe, *SW* VI, 358; *The Natural Daughter*, pp. 56–57. 'Expeditious' presumably means 'expedient'.
24   Goethe, *SW* VI, 358; *The Natural Daughter*, p. 57.

7

Goethe:
Faust (1808, 1832) —
Beyond Good and Evil

The conception of the 'great man' appealed to Goethe throughout his life. In the lecture on Shakespeare that he delivered on 14 October 1771, he declared that Shakespeare created human beings 'in *kolossalischer Größe*' (on a colossal scale).[1] In *Götz von Berlichingen*, the monk Brother Martin (obviously suggesting Luther) treats Götz with reverence, saying: 'Es ist eine Wollust, einen großen Mann zu sehn' ('It is a delight to see a great man').[2] Some early dramatic fragments present heroic figures such as Prometheus and 'Mahomet' (Muhammad) who transgress accepted norms, Prometheus by defying the gods, Mahomet by proclaiming a new (Spinozan) god who is omnipresent in nature.[3] In *Clavigo*, as we have seen, Carlos asserts that a great man is entitled to override ordinary morality. His claim stands out from its context because it goes far beyond what is needed to tempt Clavigo to betray Marie. It combines two elements: the ruthless Machiavellian ambition of the courtier, familiar from such earlier dramatic characters as Marinelli in Lessing's *Emilia Galotti*; and the cult of genius upheld by young writers of the Sturm und Drang period. The genius was entitled to transgress the rules of literary composition laid down by neoclassicism and to produce stirringly emotional odes in free verse and loosely structured dramas allegedly modelled on Shakespeare. Analogously, Carlos dismisses the rules of morality as inapplicable to him or Clavigo.[4]

Egmont belongs only partly in this series. He is certainly a great man, never criticized in the play but held in high esteem even by his antagonists; he has been aptly described as a charismatic figure.[5] But he does not claim to be in any way a genius. He has no ambition to transgress the norms of his day by seeking excessive power or forbidden knowledge. He is, rather, a conservative figure who fails to

---

1   'Zum Shakespears Tag' in Goethe, *SW* XVIII: *Ästhetische Schriften 1771–1805*, ed. by Friedmar Apel (1998), pp. 9–12 (p. 12).
2   Goethe, *SW* IV, 289.
3   Goethe, *SW* IV, 250.
4   Jochen Schmidt, *Die Geschichte des Genie-Gedankens in der deutschen Literatur, Philosophie und Politik 1750–1945*, 2 vols, 3rd, rev. edn (Heidelberg: Winter, 2004), I, 131.
5   See F. J. Lamport, 'The Charismatic Hero: Goethe, Schiller, and the Tragedy of Character', *Publications of the English Goethe Society*, 58 (1988), 62–83; Matthew Bell, '"This was a man!": Goethe's *Egmont* and Shakespeare's *Julius Caesar*', *Modern Language Review*, 111 (2016), 141–61.

grasp the magnitude of the Protestant Reformation that is going on around him, or the new style of politics introduced by Philip II and his courtiers.

The idea that great and exceptional people are not bound by ordinary moral laws recalls Machiavelli's adulation of Cesare Borgia in *The Prince*. Peter von Matt has drawn attention also to the chapter in the *Discourses* entitled 'Men very rarely know how to be entirely good or entirely bad'.[6] Here Machiavelli tells of one Giovampagolo Baglioni, tyrant of Perugia, who missed an opportunity for a spectacularly wicked action which would have gained him immortal fame. Pope Julius II, having resolved to depose Giovampogolo, entered Perugia with some cardinals and a small guard, yet faced down Giovampagolo and his numerous troops, deposed him, took him away, and left a more suitable governor in his place. According to Machiavelli, an eyewitness, everyone was amazed not only at the Pope's rashness but also at Giovampagolo's cowardice in failing to capture the Pope, the cardinals, and the goods they had brought with them. This anecdote serves to illustrate Machiavelli's concept of fame:

> Thus, Giovampagolo, who felt no concern about being guilty of incest or public parricide, did not know how, or to put it better, did not dare — having the perfect opportunity for doing so — to perform a feat for which everyone would have admired his courage and which would have secured him eternal renown as being the first man to have shown these priests how little there is to value in those who live and rule as they do, and he would have performed a deed the greatness of which would have surpassed all the infamy and all the danger that could possibly have come from it. (*D* I. 27. 82)

Machiavelli is clearly not saying that Giovampagolo was an exceptional person who was entitled to override morality. Giovampagolo comes across as a small-time villain who was easily overawed by the formidable Julius II. But he is saying that an exceptional action, such as the capture of the Pope and cardinals, can bring its perpetrator immortal fame, even if it rests on violence and treachery.

Faust, the protagonist of the largest of Goethe's early fragments, considers himself an exceptional person. His story would be given to the public only partially in *Faust. Ein Fragment* (1790) and *Faust. Der Tragödie erster Teil* (1808); the complete text of Parts One and Two would appear only on Goethe's death in 1832. From the outset — as is well known — Faust is disillusioned with the academic study to which he has dedicated his life hitherto. Having gone through every subject taught in the medieval university, he feels that he still really knows nothing. He wants to escape from dry book-learning and grasp the secrets of nature with an intimacy that is almost erotic.

Here, however, Goethe introduces the conflict that will structure the whole play. Faust is indeed an exceptional person, but he is not superhuman. Inhabiting a mortal body, he is always subject to the constraints that Goethe evokes in the poem 'Grenzen der Menschheit' ('Human Limitations').[7] He fantasizes about becoming

6   Peter von Matt, *Die Intrige: Theorie und Praxis der Hinterlist* (Munich: Deutscher Taschenbuch Verlag, 2008), pp. 364–65.
7   Goethe, *SW* I, 332–33.

a pure spirit, even a god (439).[8] He imagines himself the equal of the Earth Spirit, who embodies the raging energies of the natural world, but is rejected, the Spirit mocking him as a pathetic would-be 'Übermensch' (490). The Spirit (at least according to some textual indications, contradicted by others) sends him as an appropriate companion the devil Mephisto, whose function is to bring Faust down to earth, in two senses. Mephisto ironizes Faust's high-flown rhetoric (1734–35), reminds him of his human limitations (1806), and points out the sexual urge that underlies Faust's bombast (3291–92). But he also reintroduces Faust, whose life has hitherto been lived among abstractions, to ordinary human experience, including lust, love, and guilt. In the course of his love-affair with Gretchen, Faust kills her brother and connives at the death of her mother. Pregnant by Faust, abandoned by him, and finding no mercy in a rigidly inhuman Christianity, Gretchen drowns their child and is sentenced to execution. Entering her prison cell with Mephisto's help, Faust finds that grief and ill-treatment have driven her mad so that for a while she does not recognize him. The encounter makes him wish he had never been born (4596). Implicitly refuting his belief that every problem can be solved, that there is always another chance, Gretchen heroically refuses to flee with him and consigns herself to God's judgement. This is a moment of the most searing tragedy. By a questionable aesthetic decision, Goethe, in keeping with the aversion he proclaimed to tragedy, has blunted its impact by making an unidentified Voice from Above declare that Gretchen will be saved.[9] Even so, the tragedy brings Faust up against the effects of his action and shows that they cannot be put right — a further, painful reminder of his human limitations.

The Faust of Part 1 does not get beyond provincial Germany. He inhabits the private world of personal morality, not yet the political world where the rules of Machiavellianism may apply. When Mephisto announces, on their setting out together, 'Wir sehn die kleine, dann die große Welt' ('We'll see the little world, then the great'), he is recalling the traditional Faust legend, in which Faust goes to the emperor's court and conjures up Helen of Troy, the most beautiful woman who ever lived. These things happen (with much else that is not in the Faust legend) in Part Two, but before that Faust himself is transformed. Since the Helen he conjures for the emperor is only a phantom, he resolves with Mephisto's help to descend to the underworld and bring back the real Helen. When she reappears, Faust woos her in the guise of a medieval knight, and they have a son, Euphorion, who tries to fly but falls to earth like Icarus — a parallel with Faust's misguided aspirations in Part 1. Helen having vanished, Faust, with the help of Mephisto's magic, enables the emperor to defeat a rival. As a reward he is given a tract of land along the coast. He sets in motion great engineering works to reclaim more land from the sea. But his wealth cannot protect him from the allegorical figure of Care, who blinds him.

8   Goethe, *SW* VII/1, *Faust*, ed. by Albrecht Schöne (1994), p. 35. Quotations will be identified henceforth by line numbers.
9   For Goethe's aversion to tragedy, see his letter to Schiller, 9 Dec. 1797, in *SW* XXXI: *Mit Schiller, I. Briefe, Tagebücher und Gespräche vom 24. Juni 1794 bis zum 31. Dezember 1799*, ed. by Volker C. Dörr and Norbert Oellers (1998), p. 461; Nicholas Boyle, 'Goethe's Theory of Tragedy', *Modern Language Review*, 105 (2010), 1072–86.

When he thinks he hears Mephisto's workmen digging a canal, they are actually digging his grave.

The Faust of Part II, who is a universal figure rather than a personality, still poses, though in a new way, the moral problem raised in Part I. The Prologue in Heaven (written around 1800 and included in the 1808 publication) shows us the Lord (he is never called 'God') attended by archangels and also by Mephisto, who, like Satan in the Book of Job, is among the Lord's servants. Mephisto deplores humanity's misery. He refuses to accept the Lord's implication that Faust is an exceptional human being. Faust certainly has exceptional aspirations, Mephisto admits, but he undertakes to prove to the Lord that such aspirations are entirely futile. The Lord, who is very much an optimistic, Enlightenment deity, accepts this challenge with the reassuring words:

> Ein guter Mensch in seinem dunklen Drange
> Ist sich des rechten Weges wohl bewußt. (328–29)

> A good man, in his dark, bewildered stress,
> Well knows the path from which he should not stray.[10]

Yet to see Faust as a good man is notoriously difficult. The charge sheet against him is long and serious. It is extended in the last Act of Part Two, when Faust reinvents himself as the director of a vast land reclamation project. His motives appear to be self-aggrandizement: he hopes for dominion and property — 'Herrschaft gewinn' ich, Eigentum!' (10187). This project, also carried out apparently by magical means, takes a heavy toll in human lives:

> Menschenopfer mußten bluten,
> Nachts erscholl des Jammers Qual,
> Meerab flossen Feuersgluten;
> Morgens war es ein Kanal. (11127–30)

> They used human sacrifice:
> Fire ran down, like rivers burning,
> All night long we heard the cries —
> A canal was built by morning.[11]

The wrongdoing involved in Faust's great engineering works is focused on the episode of Philemon and Baucis. In Ovid's *Metamorphoses*, these are the names of an old couple who give hospitality to the gods and are rewarded by being transformed after their deaths into an intertwined pair of trees. In *Faust*, they are the occupants of a cottage which, to Faust's annoyance, is not part of his possessions. He has no reason for wanting it except greed; the story in 1 Kings, chapter 21, of how King Ahab coveted Naboth's vineyard, is recalled (11287). Faust wishes to evict the old couple and has set aside a small estate for them elsewhere. Impatient with their refusal to move, he tells his agent Mephisto: 'So geht und schafft sie mir zur Seite!'

10   Goethe, *Faust Part One*, trans. by David Luke, Oxford World's Classics (Oxford: Oxford University Press, 1987), p. 12.
11   Goethe, *Faust Part Two*, trans. by David Luke, Oxford World's Classics (Oxford: Oxford University Press, 1994), p. 209.

(11275) ('Well, do it! Clear them from my path').[12] Mephisto, obeying the letter rather than the spirit of Faust's order to get rid of them, burns down the cottage with the old couple and a visitor in it. And so, just as Ahab was denounced for his crime by Elijah, Faust has been denounced by a long series of Goethe commentators.

Even apart from this incident, however, Faust's scheme of reclaiming land from the sea and draining a swamp may be dubious. A long tradition of interpretation, which has given the adjective 'Faustian' a bad name, saw Faust as an exemplary figure of indomitable, restless energy, a model for Western and particularly German humanity.[13] The mirror-image of this interpretation is the Marxist one, represented by Georg Lukács, in which Faust's destructive activities are justified as necessary aspects of the historical process and the individual tragedies along the way are objectively necessary: 'for Goethe [...], the increasing progress of the human species results from a chain of individual tragedies'.[14] More recently, the pendulum has swung the other way. In the last few decades Faust has been seen as a large-scale capitalist, industrial magnate, or developer, destroying large numbers of little people in his insatiable drive for wealth and progress. An influential interpretation of *Faust II* sees it as a proleptic allegory of nineteenth-century capitalism, virtually a companion piece to the work of Karl Marx.[15] Another commentator has compared Faust to the developer Robert Moses who had many New York neighbourhoods razed to the ground to make way for the freeway system, and finds here

> the modern romance of construction at its best — the romance celebrated by Goethe's Faust, by Carlyle and Marx, by the constructivists of the 1920s, by the Soviet construction films of the Five-Year Plan period, and the TVA and FSA documentaries and WPA murals of the later 1930s.[16]

However, there is another side to Faust and his enterprises. He destroys, but he also aims to construct. In his final speech he has a vision of a future free society:

> Ein Sumpf zieht am Gebirge hin,
> Verpestet alles schon Errungene:
> Den faulen Pfuhl auch abzuziehn
> Das Letzte wär das Höchsterrungene.
> Eröffn' ich Räume vielen Millionen,
> Nicht sicher zwar, doch tätig-frei zu wohnen.
> Grün das Gefilde, fruchtbar; Mensch und Herde
> Sogleich behaglich auf der neusten Erde,
> Gleich angesiedelt an des Hügels Kraft,

---

12   Ibid., p. 214.

13   Hans Schwerte, *Faust und das Faustische: Ein Kapitel deutscher Ideologie* (Stuttgart: Klett, 1962). The author of this still valuable book was, ironically, a former high-ranking SS officer who assumed a new identity in 1945 and became a professor of German literature and Rector of the University of Aachen: see Hans Reiss, 'The Case of Hans Schwerte: The German Response to a Murky Tale', *Oxford German Studies*, 29 (2000), 181–216.

14   Georg Lukács, *Goethe and his Age*, trans. by Robert Anchor (London: Merlin Press, 1968), p. 181.

15   Heinz Schlaffer, *Faust Zweiter Teil: Die Allegorie des neunzehnten Jahrhunderts* (Stuttgart: Metzler, 1981).

16   Marshall Berman, *All that is Solid Melts into Air: The Experience of Modernity* (London: Verso, 1983), p. 300.

Den aufgewälzt kühn-emsige Völkerschaft.
Im Innern hier ein paradiesisch Land,
Da rase draußen Flut bis auf zum Rand,
Und wie sie nascht gewaltsam einzuschließen,
Gemeindrang eilt die Lücke zu verschließen. (11559–72)

A swamp surrounds the mountains' base,
It poisons all I have achieved till now.
I'll drain it too; that rotten place
Shall be my last great project. I see how
To give those millions a new living space:
They'll not be safe, but active, free at least.
I see green fields, so fertile: man and beast
At once shall settle that new pleasant earth,
Bastioned by great embankments that will rise
About them, by bold labour brought to birth.
Here there shall be an inland paradise:
Outside, the sea, as high as it can reach,
May rage and gnaw, and yet a common will,
Should it intrude, will act to close the breach.[17]

This reads like a wonderful vision of the future, in which Faust will 'stand | With a free people on free land'. Eudo Mason argues that Faust has undergone a decisive change of heart since he enthused about 'Herrschaft' and 'Eigentum'. He is now concerned, not only with himself, but with the well-being of the future generations who will live on the land obtained by draining a pestilential swamp and by building flood defences: 'Faust's dying vision, humanly and ethically considered, embodies a magnanimous, altruistic programme motivated by high ideals and a sense of the brotherhood of man'.[18] The historian Simon Schama quotes Faust's vision at the culmination of his account of Dutch defence against the sea, calling it 'a redemptive vision that precisely rehearses the moral geography of Netherlandish freedom'.[19] Many other commentators condemn it. Some have thought it trivial. The American philosopher George Santayana said: 'After Greece, Faust has a vision of Holland', implying that this was a sad comedown.[20] Erich Heller in 1952 (perhaps provoked by disapproval of the 1945–51 Labour government?) found Faust's vision 'totally unconvincing in its meagre guilt-burdened town-and-country planning bliss'.[21] Critics writing since the fall of communism have disapproved much more vehemently, seeing Faust's free society as a 'hideous vision of millions like himself, alienated from nature', criticizing it as an unrealizable utopia, or complaining that even if it could be realized it would be horrible: the population of Faust's

17   *Faust Part Two*, p. 223.
18   Eudo C. Mason, *Goethe's 'Faust': Its Genesis and Purport* (Berkeley: University of California Press, 1967), p. 343. Similarly John R. Williams, *The Life of Goethe* (Oxford: Blackwell, 1998), p. 209.
19   Simon Schama, *The Embarrassment of Riches: An Interpretation of Dutch Culture in the Golden Age* (New York: Knopf, 1987), pp. 49–50.
20   George Santayana, *Three Philosophical Poets: Lucretius, Dante, and Goethe* (Cambridge, MA: Harvard University Press, 1933), p. 182.
21   Erich Heller, *The Disinherited Mind* (first published 1952; Harmondsworth: Penguin, 1961), p. 51.

colony, enclosed by earthworks on one side and mountains on the other, would be compelled to toil ceaselessly for bare survival.[22] They see Faust as embodying Goethe's fears about industrialization and revolution. Faust is now a technocrat who fails to perceive reality and instead subordinates it to his abstract planning. Acts IV and V are thus a bitter prophetic satire on modernity. And since Faust employs Mephisto in his enterprises, it would follow that modernity is the work of the Devil.

These negative interpretations do not correspond to Goethe's numerous statements about his intentions. Unless one believes in the 'intentional fallacy' (which, as commonly understood, is itself a fallacy), Goethe's statements cannot be set aside. Goethe told Eckermann in 1831 that Faust would owe his salvation in part to 'a higher and purer endeavour that persists to the end'.[23] That certainly seems a euphemistic description of Faust's engineering works. But nowhere does Goethe say that his hero would fall ever further into tyranny and self-delusion.

Moreover, Goethe was not uniformly negative about technology. On 21 February 1827 he talked enthusiastically to Eckermann about possible engineering projects: about building canals through the isthmuses of Panama and Suez, and linking the rivers Rhine and Danube by a canal. He concluded: 'I should love to live long enough to see these three great projects completed, and it would probably be worth the effort of hanging on for another fifty years, just to be able to do so.'[24] In practice he would have needed more than fifty years: the Panama Canal was opened only in 1914, the present Rhine–Main–Danube Canal only in 1992. The image of Goethe the grouchy technophobe is the product of highly selective quotation.

If, instead of interpreting *Faust II* with reference to future capitalists, we think about figures from the past who presented possible models for Faust, one who comes immediately to mind is Napoleon. Nietzsche was probably right in saying: 'the event on account of which he *rethought* his *Faust*, indeed the whole problem of "man", was the appearance of Napoleon'.[25] Goethe's admiration for Napoleon is well known. It began with Napoleon's spectacular victories over Prussia at the battles of Jena and Auerstedt in October 1806. His audience with Napoleon in Erfurt on 2 October 1808 was one of the great moments of his life. On 11 March 1828 Goethe described Napoleon to Eckermann as a superhuman figure: 'Sein Leben war das Schreiten eines Halbgottes von Schlacht zu Schlacht und von Sieg zu Sieg' ('He lived life as a demigod who strode from battle to battle, and from victory to victory').[26] Admittedly, we might wonder if we can trust Eckermann here. This is the conversation, covering some ten pages, which he wrote up fourteen years

22 Boyle, 'Goethe's Theory of Tragedy', p. 1083; other criticisms by Jochen Schmidt, *Goethes 'Faust', Erster und Zweiter Teil: Grundlagen — Werk — Wirkung* (Munich: Beck, 1999); Michael Jaeger, *Fausts Kolonie: Goethes kritische Phänomenologie der Moderne* (Würzburg: Königshausen & Neumann, 2004).
23 Goethe, *SW* XXXIX: Eckermann, *Gespräche mit Goethe* (1999), pp. 488–89; conversation of 6 June 1831. Johann Peter Eckermann, *Conversations with Goethe in the Last Years of his Life*, trans. by Allan Blunden, ed. by Ritchie Robertson (London: Penguin, 2022), p. 423.
24 Goethe, *SW* XXXIX, 581; Eckermann, *Conversations*, p. 503.
25 Friedrich Nietzsche, *Beyond Good and Evil*, trans. by R. J. Hollingdale (Harmondsworth: Penguin, 1973), p. 156 (section 244); KSA V, 185.
26 Goethe, *SW* XXXIX, 651; Eckermann, *Conversations*, p. 562.

later, on the basis of only four words he had noted down at the time: 'productivity, genius, Napoleon, Prussia'.[27] But it is supported by other utterances such as this on 3 February 1807, recorded by Friedrich Wilhelm Riemer: 'Außerordentliche Menschen, wie Napoleon, treten aus der Moralität heraus. Sie wirken zuletzt wie physische Ursachen wie Feuer und Wasser' ('Exceptional people, like Napoleon, are outside morality. They operate, in the last analysis, as physical causes, like fire and water').[28] Goethe seems untroubled by Napoleon's huge sacrifice of human lives in his battles, by his reversal of much progressive legislation, or by his crowning himself Emperor. An exceptional person, we infer, can get away with such things. Indeed Napoleon appears less as an individual than as an elemental force of nature. Here, therefore, the distinction between moral and physical evil breaks down: Napoleon's actions are to be equated, not with moral or immoral actions, but with the creative and destructive energies of storms and floods.

Napoleon could be seen as the last of the enlightened despots. Goethe was a man of the Enlightenment also in this respect, that he expected political reforms to be handed down from above, not won by popular let alone revolutionary action. The Enlightenment had no interest in anything resembling what we call democracy. Hence Voltaire's fascination with Frederick the Great, and that of Diderot with Catherine the Great. Enlightened rulers, seeking to benefit their subjects, sometimes carried out great programmes of land reclamation. In a pioneering work of ecological history, David Blackbourn has recounted how successive rulers of Prussia, beginning with the Great Elector, drained the Oderbruch and other wetlands, thereby creating new agricultural land.[29] Peter the Great drained a huge area of marshland on the shore of the Gulf of Finland to create a site for his new capital St Petersburg. Voltaire, in his history of Peter's antagonist Charles XII of Sweden, estimates that the building of St Petersburg cost 200,000 lives.[30] In the long conversation on 11 March 1828 reconstructed by Eckermann, Goethe gave three examples of political genius: Frederick the Great, Napoleon, and Peter the Great.[31]

If we are to take Faust seriously as the founder of a free society, what are we to think about Philemon and Baucis? A Marxist like Lukács might claim their deaths are objectively necessary, but the play makes clear that their deaths are not necessary, and invites us to see them as deplorable. The destruction is carried out by Faust's unruly assistants, not by Faust himself, but that scarcely exonerates him. There is a parallel with Pushkin's almost contemporary poem *The Bronze Horseman* (1833). Pushkin begins by celebrating the modern city brought into being by the will of Tsar Peter. Then, by telling the sad story of a young man's fate after the river Neva

---

27   Goethe, *SW* XXXIX, 918–19; quoted in 'Introduction' to Eckermann, *Conversations*, p. xliv.

28   Extract from Riemer, *Mittheilungen über Goethe* (Berlin, 1841), in Goethe, *SW* XXXIII: *Napoleonische Zeit I: (Briefe, Tagebücher und Gespräche, von Schillers Tod bis 1811*, ed. by Rose Unterberger (1993), p. 167.

29   David Blackbourn, *The Conquest of Nature: Water, Landscape and the Making of Modern Germany* (London: Cape, 2006); Ritchie Robertson, *The Enlightenment: The Pursuit of Happiness, 1680–1790* (London: Allen Lane, 2020), p. 425.

30   *Histoire de Charles XII, roi de Suède*, in Voltaire, *Œuvres historiques*, ed. by René Pomeau, Bibliothèque de la Pléiade (Paris: Gallimard, 1957), pp. 125–26.

31   Goethe, *SW* XXXIX, 653; Eckermann, *Conversations*, p. 563.

has flooded, he alludes indirectly to the loss of life that Peter's project involved. Edmund Wilson says of it: 'The poem deals with the tragic contrast between the right to peace and happiness of the ordinary man and the right to constructive domination of the state.'[32] That might apply also to the fate of Philemon and Baucis, the old couple whose cottage is burnt down by Mephisto in an over-enthusiastic interpretation of Faust's orders. It does not mean that either St Petersburg or Faust's future utopia is less than worthwhile. But in both cases we are given a reminder of the human cost. The deaths of Philemon, Baucis, and their guest may fairly be described as tragic.

In his presentation of politics, Goethe has, over an unusually long literary career, come full circle. Initially he rejected the idea, essential to reason of state and stemming from Machiavelli, that the moral demands of politics were different from the moral standards required between individuals. To Götz von Berlichingen, the high politics involved in modernizing Germany by introducing Roman law and curbing the activities of predatory knights simply presaged an age of deceit. He prophesies on his death-bed: 'Es kommen die Zeiten des Betrugs, es ist ihm Freiheit gegeben. Die Nichtswürdigen werden regieren mit List, und der Edle wird in ihre Netze fallen' ('The times are coming when deceit will rule freely. Scoundrels will govern by cunning, and the noble man will fall into their snares').[33] Egmont fails to understand the requirements of a far-sighted politics which make Oranien's flight prudent rather than cowardly. The view put forward by Carlos in *Clavigo* that exceptional people are entitled to override morality was at least cast in doubt by the play's tragic ending.

By contrast, the Faust of Part Two (apart from his interlude with Helen of Troy) lives entirely in the world of great politics. He deals with the emperor and plans a new society. And he takes for granted that the morality of great politics is dictated by reason of state, not by relationships between individuals. Goethe himself expressed a similar opinion when, a few months before his death, he told one of his Weimar friends, the Chancellor von Müller, that Prussia was right to take a share of the spoils during the partition of Poland: 'Poor layfolk like us are obliged to act in the opposite way, but that does not apply to the powerful on earth.'[34] A poem from the *West-östlicher Divan* (1819) goes further by celebrating the powerful:

> Uebermacht, Ihr könnt es spüren,
> Ist nicht aus der Welt zu bannen;
> Mir gefällt zu conversiren
> Mit Gescheiten, mit Tyrannen.[35]

Superiority, you can sense it, cannot be banned from the world; I like to converse with the clever and with despots.[36]

32 Edmund Wilson, 'In Honour of Pushkin', in his *The Triple Thinkers* (Harmondsworth: Penguin, 1962), pp. 40–71 (p. 58).

33 Goethe, *SW* IV, 388.

34 Goethe, *SW* XXXVIII: *Die letzten Jahre. Briefe, Tagebücher und Gespräche von 1823 bis zu Goethes Tod. Teil II: Vom Dornburger Aufenthalt 1828 bis zum Tode*, ed. by Horst Fleig (1993), p. 501.

35 Goethe, *SW* III: *West-Östlicher Divan*, ed. by Hendrik Birus (1994), p. 54.

36 Johann Wolfgang von Goethe, *West-Eastern Divan*, trans. by Eric Ormsby (London: Ginkgo,

If Faust follows the morality of great politics and exceptional people, that still does not excuse all his actions, as the case of Philemon and Baucis shows. But it means that the deaths of many workmen, like the huge loss of life in the building of St Petersburg and in Napoleon's battles, are not to be counted against the long-term benefit to humanity that is expected to result. Here Goethe seems close to Hegel, who in 1806 wrote about Napoleon in similarly adulatory terms:

> I saw the Emperor, this soul of the world [*Weltseele*], riding through the town to reconnoitre; it is indeed a wonderful feeling to see such an individual, who, concentrated on a single point, mounted on a horse, reaches across the world and dominates it.[37]

Hegel's historical theodicy similarly interprets the sufferings undergone by historical actors as brought about by 'the cunning of reason' in order to further the ultimate self-realization of the spirit, which is the goal of history.[38] This is a rational process, and 'reason cannot stop to consider the injuries sustained by single individuals, for particular ends are submerged in the universal end'.[39] Callous as this sounds, any conception of progress which sees past suffering as necessary for a better future must be similarly callous.

Insofar as Faust, like Napoleon, is a force of nature, he is beyond good and evil. Goethe consistently imagined nature as a simultaneously creative and destructive force, comprehending good and evil and thus transcending both. In 1772, reviewing a book that in his opinion presented a too sunny and one-sided view of nature, he wrote:

> Was wir von Natur sehn, ist Kraft, die Kraft verschlingt[,] nichts gegenwärtig alles vorübergehend, tausend Keime zertreten[,] jeden Augenblick tausend geboren, groß und bedeutend, mannigfaltig ins Unendliche; schön und häßlich, gut und bös, alles mit gleichem Recht nebeneinander existierend.[40]

> What we see of nature is force consuming force; nothing is established, everything is transitory; in every moment a thousand germs are crushed and a thousand born; great and meaningful, infinitely diverse; beautiful and ugly, good and evil, everything existing side by side with an equal right.

Nature, thus conceived as amoral energy, is embodied in the Earth Spirit, to whom Faust absurdly claims to be equal:

> In Lebensfluten, im Tatensturm
> Wall' ich auf und ab,
> Wehe hin und her!
> Geburt und Grab,

2019), p. 127. The translation softens 'Uebermacht', which implies superior or supreme *power*.

37   Hegel, letter to Friedrich Immanuel Niethammer, 13 Oct. 1806, in *Briefe von und an Hegel*, ed. by Johannes Hoffmeister, 4 vols (Hamburg: Meiner, 1952–81), I, 120.

38   For 'the cunning of reason' ('die List der Vernunft'), see Hegel, *Vorlesungen über die Philosophie der Geschichte*, in *Werke*, XII, 49.

39   Hegel, *Lectures*, p. 43.

40   Goethe, review of Sulzer's *Die schönen Künste in ihrem Ursprung [...] betrachtet*, in *Frankfurter gelehrte Anzeigen*, 1772, *SW* XVIII, 99.

> Ein wechselnd Weben,
> Ein glühend Leben [...][41]

> In life like a flood, in deeds like a storm
> I surge to and fro,
> Up and down I flow!
> Birth and the grave
> An eternal wave,
> Turning, returning,
> A life ever burning [...][42]

And in a conversation of 8 September 1815 with the art historian Sulpiz Boisserée, Goethe described nature as 'eine Orgel, auf der unser Herr-Gott spielt, und der Teufel tritt die Bälge dazu' ('an organ on which our Lord God plays while the Devil treads the bellows').[43]

Faust's death and posthumous existence are similarly natural processes. Unlike in most versions of the Faust story, Goethe's protagonist does not go to hell but ascends to heaven. Although Goethe adapts much Christian imagery, it is no orthodox heaven. The female figure who dominates heaven is not quite the Virgin Mary, just as the Lord in the Prologue was not quite the Christian God. She is called the Mater Gloriosa, but also a goddess ('Göttin', 12103). The obvious question how Faust, with all his wrongdoing, can deserve to go to heaven, is beside the point. Admission to this heaven does not have to be earned. We are not in the Christian domain of moral effort, but in that of natural processes. Goethe believed in continued existence after death, but thought there was little point in speculating about the form it would take. On one of the rare occasions when he did indulge in such speculations, emotionally stirred by the funeral of Christoph Martin Wieland, he surmised that the soul, for which he was equally happy to use Leibniz's term 'monad', would undergo transformation. There would be a hierarchy among souls:

> Nun sind einige von diesen Monaden oder Anfangspunkten, wie uns die Erfahrung zeigt, so klein, so geringfügig, daß sie sich höchstens nur zu einem untergeordneten Dienst und Dasein eignen. Andere dagegen sind gar stark und gewaltig.[44]

> Now some of these monads or starting-points, as experience teaches us, are so small, so slight, that they are suitable at best for subordinate service and existence, whereas others are very strong and powerful.

Faust is clearly such a powerful soul. His own nature ensures his survival. But he is still described as being 'im Puppenstand' (11982), a chrysalis. His transformation is conceived along the lines of the natural morphology which Goethe had studied intensively. He will develop into a new being, as yet unknowable. Thus Goethe's heaven, as envisaged in *Faust II*, is in motion. The striving which qualified Faust to

---

41   Goethe, *SW* VII/1, 37.
42   *Faust Part One*, p. 19.
43   Goethe, *SW* XXXIV: *Napoleonische Zeit II: Briefe, Tagebücher und Gespräche von 1812 bis zu Christianens Tod*, ed. by Rose Unterberger (1994), 306.
44   Goethe, *SW* XXXIV, 171.

enter it — not moral effort in the Christian sense, but something more akin to vital energy — continues there. By contrast, heaven was traditionally conceived of as static. It was imagined that the blessed would spend eternity rapt in contemplation of the Beatific Vision.[45] In the eighteenth century, however, it came to be thought that an eternity of contemplation would be boring, and alternatives were imagined in which the dead would pursue a great variety of activities, continue the personal relationships they had established during life, and monitor the behaviour of those they had left behind on earth.[46]

Striving in Goethe's heaven is particularly directed towards purification. Hence one of the versions of eternal life which has been suggested as a source for Goethe is the mind-boggling conception presented by the early theologian Origen (*c*. 185–*c*. 254).[47] Origen was a universalist. He put forward the doctrine of 'apocatastasis', or the restitution of all things, whereby ultimately all beings who proceed from God will, after innumerable aeons, be again gathered into God. This conception implies that in the very long run everyone will be saved, even the Devil — a daring idea that leads a subterranean life throughout the Christian centuries.[48]

Goethe would have known Origen through the account of him in a book whose importance for him is attested in *Dichtung und Wahrheit*: Gottfried Arnold's *Kirchen- und Ketzergeschichte* (1699–1700).[49] Arnold encouraged a tolerance of diverse religious views which Goethe found deeply congenial. However, neither Goethe's text nor his recorded utterances make it likely that the Faustian heaven is intended for everyone. 'Wir sind nicht auf gleiche Weise unsterblich' ('We are not all immortal in the same way'), Goethe once said to Eckermann.[50]

What Goethe does seem to take from Origen, via Arnold, is the idea of purification. Origen emphasizes that all beings, even the angels, still need to be purified:

> that after time is over, hence only after earthly life, we shall encounter true purification. I think that even after our resurrection we shall require a mystery that will purify and cleanse us, for nobody will rise again without stains, and there can hardly be any soul that is immediately freed from all faults.[51]

---

45   See Bernhard Lang and Colleen McDannell, *Heaven: A History* (New Haven: Yale University Press, 1988).

46   See the fantasies of Emanuel Swedenborg, described by Lang and McDannell, *Heaven*, pp. 181–227; Eudo C. Mason, '"Wir sehen uns wieder!": Zu einem Leitmotiv des Dichtens und Denkens im 18. Jahrhundert', *Literaturwissenschaftliches Jahrbuch der Görres-Gesellschaft*, n.s. 5 (1964), 79–109; Roger Paulin, '"Wir werden uns wieder sehn!": On a Theme in *Werther*', *Publications of the English Goethe Society*, 50 (1980), 55–78; Lieselotte Kurth-Voigt, *Continued Existence, Reincarnation, and the Power of Sympathy in Classical Weimar* (Rochester, NY: Camden House, 1999).

47   See Goethe, *SW* VII/2, ed. by Albrecht Schöne (1994), pp. 788–92. Schöne's interpretation is convincingly questioned in Dieter Bremer, '"Wenn starke Geisteskraft [...]" Traditionsvermittlungen in der Schlußszene von Goethes *Faust*', *Goethe-Jahrbuch*, 112 (1995), 287–307. Bremer points out that the divine love celebrated in 'Bergschluchten' is markedly Neoplatonic.

48   See C. A. Patrides, 'The Salvation of Satan', *Journal of the History of Ideas*, 28 (1967), 467–78.

49   Goethe, *SW* XIV: *Dichtung und Wahrheit*, ed. by Klaus-Detlef Müller (1986), p. 382.

50   Goethe, *SW* XXXIX, 361 (1 September 1829).

51   *Gottfrid Arnolds Unparteyische Kirchen- und Ketzer-Historie / von Anfang des Neuen Testaments biß auff das Jahr Christi 1688*, 2 vols (Frankfurt: Thomas Fritsch, 1699 and 1700), II, 359, quoted in Schöne's commentary, Goethe, *SW* VII/2, 790.

Accordingly, the angels say:

> Uns bleibt ein Erdenrest
> Zu tragen peinlich,
> Und wär' er von Asbest,
> Er ist nicht reinlich. (11954–57)

> An earthbound, immature
> And fragmentary,
> Fireproof yet still impure
> Burden we carry.[52]

This is one of the many internal echoes that unify the poetic texture of *Faust*, binding together what often seems a loose baggy monster.[53] Early in Part I, rebuffed by the Earth Spirit, Faust claimed that he had already practically 'abgestreift den Erdensohn' (617) ('stripped away the son of Earth'). What was then a hubristic fantasy is now within sight of coming true: his impure earthly nature will be stripped away. And that has one final implication that confirms the bold heterodoxy of Goethe's imagination. The heaven in which Faust is purified and thus redeemed is also Purgatory.

The idea of purgation after death, absent from the Gospels, is found in St Augustine, who says that some people after death will suffer pains and 'receive forgiveness in the world to come for what is not forgiven in this [...] that they may not be punished with the eternal chastisement of the world to come'.[54] It was hugely elaborated during the Middle Ages, and rejected by the Protestant reformers. Although Purgatory was not Hell, its pains were generally thought to be equally severe. Hamlet's father, visiting from Purgatory, tells his son that he must return to 'sulph'rous and tormenting flames', and that 'the secrets of my prison-house' are too dreadful for a mortal to endure hearing about (*Hamlet*, I. 5. 3, 14). Dante makes the doctrine more tolerable by removing Purgatory from Hell and imagining it as a mountain in the Southern Ocean, diametrically opposite to Jerusalem.[55] The souls suffering in his Purgatory do so joyfully because they know they are on the way to salvation. And the mountain which the souls ascend anticipates the motif of ascent in the Faustian heaven.

An important difference, however, is that in *Faust* there is no suggestion that purgation is painful. As they gradually shed their earthly remains, the souls here are encouraged not only by the distant prospect of salvation, as in Dante, but by actually beholding the Mater Gloriosa, the 'Ewig-Weibliche' (12110), 'Eternal Womanhood', which 'draws us on high'.[56] This feminine deity may suggest the Virgin Mary, but the Virgin is not a goddess. Given Goethe's sympathetic interest in Indian literature and religion, the 'Ewig-Weibliche' seems to be a syncretic figure, indebted partly to

---

52   *Faust Part Two*, p. 235.
53   See Charlotte Lee, *The Very Late Goethe: Self-Consciousness and the Art of Ageing* (Cambridge: Legenda, 2014), pp. 124–29.
54   St Augustine, *Concerning the City of God against the Pagans*, trans. by Henry Bettenson (London: Penguin, 1984), pp. 990–91 (Book XXI, ch. 13).
55   See Willi Hirdt, 'Goethe und Dante', *Deutsches Dante-Jahrbuch*, 68/69 (1993/94), 31–80.
56   *Faust Part Two*, p. 239.

the Hindu goddess Shakti who is the feminine driving force behind creation, thus complementing the masculine energy represented by Faust's continual striving.[57] She is not enthroned above a crowd of worshippers, like the Lord in the Prologue; rather, she is the asymptotic point which attracts desire towards a goal that can never finally be reached.

57   Jeremy Adler, *Goethe: Die Erfindung der Moderne* (Munich: Beck, 2022), pp. 528–29.

8

Schiller:
History as Progress

It has been said of Schiller that even if he had not read Machiavelli, most of his major characters appear to have done so.[1] His knowledge of Machiavelli, at least at second hand, is attested by a reference in a letter to Schelling of 12 May 1801.[2] There were many sources from which he could have learned about Machiavelli's ideas, such as Helvétius's *De l'homme*, which he studied at school, and the sympathetic short account given by Herder in *Briefe zur Beförderung der Humanität*.[3]

In his depiction of politics, however, Schiller differs from Machiavelli in being historically minded. Machiavelli is interested in what is unchanging in human nature: 'Anyone who studies current and ancient affairs will easily recognize that the same desires and humours exist and have always existed in all cities and among all peoples' (*D* I. 39. 105). He shares the confidence of Renaissance humanists that, thanks to the constancy of human nature, history provides a fund of models and examples to guide political action in the present. Humanists loved to quote Cicero's definition of history:

> Historia vero testis temporum, lux veritatis, vita memoriae, magistra viae, nuntia vetustatis, qua voce alia nisi oratoris immortalitati commendatur.

And as History, which bears witness to the passing of the ages, sheds light upon reality, gives life to recollection and guidance to human existence, and brings tidings of ancient days, whose voice, but the orator's, can entrust her to immortality?[4]

Even then, however, there were dissenting views. In his 'mirror for princes', *Institutio principis christiani* (1516), Erasmus warns that exemplars from pagan antiquity must not be exactly imitated: 'for a Christian prince to want to copy them completely would be utter insanity'.[5] Machiavelli's fellow-historian Guicciardini

1   Kurt Wölfel, 'Machiavellische Spuren in Schillers Dramatik', in *Schiller und die höfische Welt*, ed. by Achim Aurnhammer, Klaus Manger and Friedrich Strack (Tübingen: Niemeyer, 1990), pp. 318–40 (p. 318).

2   Schiller's works are quoted whenever possible from *Werke und Briefe* (see note to p. 41 above), abbreviated as *WB*. Letters, if not given in this edition, are quoted from Schiller, *NA*.

3   Herder, *Werke*, VII, 340–42. See Peter-André Alt, *Schiller: Leben — Werk — Zeit*, 2 vols (Munich: Beck, 2000), I, 342–44; Walter Müller-Seidel, *Friedrich Schiller und die Politik* (Munich: Beck, 2009), p. 91.

4   Cicero, *De oratore*, I–II, trans. by E. W. Sutton and Harris Rackham, Loeb Classical Library (Cambridge, MA: Harvard University Press, 1942), pp. 224, 225.

5   See Timothy Hampton, *Writing from History: The Rhetoric of Exemplarity in Renaissance Literature*

cautioned that past examples might be deceptive, since changing circumstances might mean that they were no longer appropriate for imitation.[6] And in Schiller's first play, *Die Räuber*, Karl Moor reads Plutarch's biographies of great men with admiration, but comes to grief when he tries to perform great deeds himself.

Schiller was not only a historical dramatist but also a historian. From 1789 to 1791 he held a professorship at the University of Jena, earned by his best-selling *Geschichte des Abfalls der Niederlande*. His inaugural lecture, delivered to over 500 enthusiastic hearers on 26 and 27 May 1789, developed the conception of 'universal history' formulated especially by the eminent Göttingen historian August Ludwig von Schlözer. Schlözer, however, was criticized in his time for presenting only a compilation of facts. While Schiller accepted that part of the historian's duty was to ascertain and assemble the verifiable facts of history, he also went further: the 'universal' part was to interpret them as constituting a meaningful narrative. Schiller's narrative ran from barbarous beginnings through the gradual ascent of civilization to the largely peaceful commercial society of modern Europe. It was a history of progress, centring on the growth of human autonomy and freedom. It drew on Lessing's *Die Erziehung des Menschengeschlechts* (*The Education of the Human Race*, 1780), which rewrote Christian history as a series of divine revelations suited to humankind's developing intellectual capacity, so that Moses provided his followers with a kind of child's primer and Christ later replaced it with a more advanced textbook in the form of the Gospels. Schiller was also deeply impressed by Kant's essay 'Idee zu einer allgemeinen Geschichte in weltbürgerlicher Absicht' ('Idea for a Universal History with a Cosmopolitan Purpose'), which argues that, since nature must intend humanity's capacities to be fully developed, history is the gradual and unsteady progress towards the form of society most conducive to human flourishing, a cosmopolitan republic, 'the matrix in which all the original capacities of the human race may develop'.[7]

This view of history as progress features also in Schiller's historical dramas when the characters appear conscious of their own historicity. In *Don Karlos*, set in Counter-Reformation Spain where the Inquisition flourishes, the enlightened Marquis Posa urges the King to introduce freedom of thought, acknowledging that he is ahead of his time:

> Das Jahrhundert
> Ist meinem Ideal nicht reif. Ich lebe
> Ein Bürger derer, welche kommen werden.[8]

(Ithaca: Cornell University Press, 1990), pp. 53–54. Similarly, Erasmus says that a pagan writer cannot completely express the ideal of a Christian prince (*Education*, p. 60).

6   François Rigolot, 'The Renaissance Crisis of Exemplarity', *Journal of the History of Ideas*, 59 (1998), 557–63 (p. 560).

7   Immanuel Kant, 'Idea for a Universal History with a Cosmopolitan Purpose', in *Kant: Political Writings*, pp. 41–53 (p. 51). Schiller praises this essay in a letter to his friend Christian Gottfried Körner, August 1787, NA xxiv. 143.

8   *WB* III: *Don Carlos*, ed. by Gerhard Kluge (1989), p. 311, lines 3670–72. In verse plays, quotations will be identified by line numbers in the text.

>   This century
>   Is far from ripe for my designs. I live
>   Among the citizens that are to come.[9]

He is a kind of emissary from the future. When Elisabeth and her councillors in *Maria Stuart* are discussing what to do with the imprisoned Mary Queen of Scots, Talbot advises the Queen to think about how her actions will be judged by posterity:

> Dies heutge England ist das künftge nicht,
> Wie's das vergangne nicht mehr ist — Wie sich
> Die Neigung anders wendet, also steigt
> Und fällt des *Urteils* wandelbare Woge. (1326–29)[10]

> England today is not what she will be
> In future years, nor what she has been — Just
> As inclinations change, so do the scales
> Of justice and of judgement rise and fall.[11]

In *Die Jungfrau von Orleans*, Johanna reveals a prophetic gift which enables her to foretell to the King and his nobles the future of their families. Her prophecies include the discovery of America (2117–18) and the French Revolution (2099–2101). And in Schiller's last completed play, *Wilhelm Tell*, the Swiss liberate themselves from Austrian tyranny by a democratically planned rebellion which implicitly shows how the French Revolution *ought* to have been conducted and symbolically coincides with the abolition of serfdom.

In going out of his way to remind his audiences of change and progress in history, Schiller aligns himself with Kant, and particularly with the appendix to *Zum ewigen Frieden* (1795), which shows Kant's acquaintance with Machiavelli.[12] Here Kant distinguishes the 'moral politician', who approaches politics in the light of principles of justice, from the 'political moralist', who subordinates morality to politics and the means to the end. The latter is a Machiavellian, and in sketching him and his maxims, Kant provides a virtual mini-parody of *The Prince*. The political moralist prides himself on his knowledge of how the world works and on how people actually behave. His understanding of humanity is based on how people act now, not on a wider, anthropological understanding of human nature and of people's potential for acting differently. Relying on his empirical viewpoint, he regards morality as mere empty words, and derives from his experience various practical maxims which express prudence ('Klugheit') but not wisdom. He is like a lawyer who acts as an advocate for his employer, makes up arguments in order to win his case, and never considers the principles of justice. Convinced that human beings can never rise to the moral standards prescribed by reason, he actually prevents

---

9   Friedrich Schiller, *Don Carlos* and *Mary Stuart*, trans. by Hilary Collier Sy-quia and Peter Oswald, Oxford World's Classics (Oxford: Oxford University Press, 1996), p. 112.
10   *WB* v: *Maria Stuart, Die Jungfrau von Orleans, Die Braut von Messina, Wilhelm Tell*, ed. by Matthias Luserke (1996), p. 52.
11   *Five German Tragedies*, trans. by Lamport, p. 230.
12   In what follows, I paraphrase Kant, *Werke*, vi, 228–40. See *Kant: Political Writings*, pp. 116–25.

them from becoming any better than they are. His basic maxims are (1) act first and explain or apologize afterwards; (2) deny responsibility — for example, if you drive your subjects into rebellion, blame their own refractory character, or the irremediable faults of human nature; (3) divide and rule.

The moral politician, on the other hand, is aware not only of what people do now but of what they may do in the future when their potential is more fully realized. In politics, he will not rest content with the *status quo*, but, when he sees that reforms are needed, he will try to introduce or at least encourage them. He will not bring in reforms so precipitately as to create disorder — here political prudence harmonizes with morality — and if his reforms are too hasty, he can at least learn from experience to practise his principles more sensibly, whereas his antithesis, the political moralist, has nothing but experience and never rises to the level of principle. While the political moralist decides on his purpose and then finds the most effective means, the moral politician will choose his means in the light of the principle 'do as you as you would be done by' or the categorical imperative, here formulated as: 'Act in such a way that you can wish your maxim to become a universal law (irrespective of what the end in view may be).'[13] For the moral politician there is no conflict between politics and morality.

Schiller's historical awareness also governs his views about political change. He had little respect for royalty and aristocracy, and considerable sympathy for republicanism. Karl Moor talks of founding a 'Republik'. However, despite his upbringing under the well-intentioned tyranny of the Duke of Württemberg, Schiller was at no time a revolutionary.[14] Nor did he admire democracy, since, as usual in the eighteenth century, he understood by it the direct democracy which had existed in ancient Athens. In his lecture *Die Gesetzgebung des Lykurgus und Solon*, although the contrast between Sparta and Athens was favourable to the latter, he admitted that the Athenians' thirst for fame and love of novelty kept them in continual disorder,[15] and in his last, unfinished play *Demetrius* he presented a debate in the Polish diet which rapidly degenerated into chaos. By contrast, the democratic debates staged in *Wilhelm Tell* are conducted (anachronistically) by delegates in a representative democracy.[16]

Schiller sympathized with the American War of Independence and with its goals of establishing humanity's rights to life, liberty, and the pursuit of happiness.[17] He even contemplated emigrating to the United States himself if the revolution there proved successful.[18] But, from Schiller's point of view, the American Revolution

13   *Kant: Political Writings*, p. 122; Kant, *Werke*, VI, 239.
14   See Jeffrey L. High, *Schillers Rebellionskonzept und die Französische Revolution* (Lewiston, ME: Mellen, 2004).
15   *WB* VI: *Historische Schriften I*, ed. by Otto Dann (2000), p. 508.
16   In 'Lykurgus und Solon' Schiller uses 'Demokratie' five times disapprovingly to mean direct democracy, once approvingly to mean representative democracy: Yvonne Nilges, 'Schiller und die Demokratie', in *Who is this Schiller Now? Essays on his Reception and Significance*, ed. by Jeffrey L. High, Nicholas Martin, and Norbert Oellers (Rochester, NY: Camden House, 2011), pp. 205–16 (p. 210).
17   See Jeffrey L. High, 'Introduction: Why is this Schiller [still] in the United States?', in *Who is this Schiller Now?*, ed. by High, Martin, and Oellers, pp. 1–21 (pp. 4–5).
18   'Wenn Nordamerika frei wird, so ist es ausgemacht, daß ich hingehe': letter to Henriette von Wolzogen, 8 January 1783, *NA* XXIII, 60.

succeeded because the populace that carried it out was already politically mature. In this it differed from most revolutions, including the French Revolution, which, as Schiller argues in the *Letters on the Aesthetic Education of Man* (1795), degenerated into rule by terror because the people were not prepared for their historic opportunity — 'der freigebige Augenblick findet ein unempfängliches Geschlecht' ('[A] moment so prodigal of opportunity finds a generation unprepared to receive it').[19] It was Schiller's consistent view that only a politically mature people could carry through a successful revolution, and that political maturity presupposed a harmonious balance within each individual. Hence the *Aesthetic Letters* have a strongly political purpose: to describe the psychological constitution that is desirable in citizens of a republic.[20]

In the ages before democratic suffrage, political change might be achieved through open insurrection or secret conspiracy. In the 1780s there was a widespread panic about conspiracies. The Freemasons were under suspicion, but more severe anxiety focused on their offshoot, the Illuminati, a body founded in Bavaria in 1776 by the jurist Adam Weishaupt in order to infiltrate Masonic lodges and spread radical republicanism. Weishaupt had been educated by Jesuits and was deeply influenced by Jesuit organization and discipline.[21] In 1785, rumours about the activities of the Illuminati led the Elector of Bavaria to ban Freemasonry and Illuminism in his territories. Their premises were raided, and letters were found showing that the Illuminati spied on their own members and planned political assassinations. Several of Schiller's close friends were Freemasons. He was invited to join, but never did. In 1787 the Weimar-based journalist Johann Joachim Bode tried to recruit Schiller to the Illuminati, but again Schiller refused, and in the letters on *Don Karlos* that he published in the journal *Teutscher Merkur* in 1788 he thought it necessary to declare: 'Ich bin weder I– noch M–' ('I am neither an Illuminist nor a Mason'; the abbreviations were transparent).[22] He made clear his disapproval of secret societies, however noble their aims might be, for their methods were liable to frustrate and degrade their ideals:

> Nennen Sie mir, lieber Freund [...] den Ordensstifter oder auch die Ordensverbrüderung selbst, die sich — bei den reinsten Zwecken und bei den edelsten Trieben — von Willkürlichkeit in der Anwendung, von *Gewalttätigkeit* gegen fremde Freiheit, von dem Geiste der *Heimlichkeit* und der *Herrschsucht* immer rein erhalten hätte?[23]

> Name me, dear friend, [...] any founder of a [secret] society, or indeed the society itself, that, with the purest aims and the noblest impulses, has always managed to avoid applying them tyrannically, violating other people's freedom, and being corrupted by the spirit of secrecy and power-hunger.

19   *Über die ästhetische Erziehung des Menschen in einer Reihe von Briefen*, 5. Brief, in *WB* VIII, 568; Schiller, *On the Aesthetic Education of Man in a Series of Letters*, ed. and trans. by Elizabeth M. Wilkinson and L. A. Willoughby (Oxford: Clarendon Press, 1967), p. 25.
20   See Frederick Beiser, *Schiller as Philosopher: A Re-examination* (Oxford: Clarendon Press, 2005), pp. 123–26.
21   J. M. Roberts, *The Mythology of the Secret Societies* (London: Secker & Warburg, 1972), p. 119.
22   *WB* III, 461.
23   *WB* III, 465. See Hans-Jürgen Schings, *Die Brüder des Marquis Posa: Schiller und der Geheimbund der Illuminaten* (Tübingen: Niemeyer, 1996).

Yet conspiracies, although deplorable in life, were fascinating as historical and dramatic subjects. One of the projects by which Schiller sought to earn his living in the 1780s was a collection of narratives about famous conspiracies in history.[24] Several volumes were planned, but only one appeared, recounting Cola di Rienzo's attempt to restore the Roman Republic in 1347; the Pazzi conspiracy against the Medici in 1478; and the conspiracy by the Marquis of Bedamar against the Venetian Republic in 1618.[25] Schiller intended to contribute an account of the revolt of the Netherlands against Spanish rule, but the subject proved so rich that he made it into a book, the *Geschichte des Abfalls der Niederlande*. Almost all his plays turn on conspiracies, mostly those attested by history. As a result, however, the historical dramas can say little about history as a gradual progression towards freedom. We mainly see the enormous obstacles to freedom — various forms of tyranny and the political manipulations, usually in the name of 'reason of state', that sustain them.

Why conspiratorial intrigues are fascinating is a question that Schiller addressed as a philosopher. He argued that villains like Iago, Richard III, and Lovelace can give us pleasure so long as our minds are averted from their evil purposes and we can concentrate on the ingenuity of their machinations: 'Die höchste Konsequenz eines Bösewichts in Anordnung seiner Maschinen ergötzt uns offenbar, obgleich Anstalten und Zweck unserm moralischen Gefühl widerstreiten' ('The extreme consistency of a villain in operating his machinery clearly gives us pleasure, although his plotting and his aims run counter to our moral feelings').[26] Conspiracy as a mechanism, with all its moving parts duly falling into place, can be a source of aesthetic enjoyment. But the moral and political purpose of a conspiracy cannot be banished from our minds for long. Schiller's intriguers soon develop into political moralists — politicians who subordinate morality to politics and justify the means by reference to the end.

---

24   *Geschichte der merkwürdigsten Rebellionen und Verschwörungen aus den mittleren und neuern Zeiten* (1788); analysed by Torsten Hahn, *Das schwarze Unternehmen: Zur Funktion der Verschwörung bei Friedrich Schiller und Heinrich von Kleist* (Heidelberg: Winter, 2008).
25   The Bedamar plot was also the subject of Thomas Otway's *Venice Preserv'd, or A Plot Discover'd* (1682).
26   'Über den Grund des Vergnügens an tragischen Gegenständen', *WB* VIII, 247.

9

Schiller:
Political Moralists from
Die Räuber (1781) to *Don Karlos* (1805)

Among Schiller's early plays, *Die Räuber* (1781) and *Kabale und Liebe* (1784) both feature unscrupulous intriguers, albeit in the restricted settings of a noble household in one case, a petty principality (based on Schiller's Württemberg) in the other. Of the two Moor brothers in *Die Räuber*, the elder, Karl, is warm-hearted and courageous, but dissolute, while the younger, Franz, is a heartless intriguer and an expert in the psychological manipulation of other people. Having managed to get his elder brother disinherited, Franz now wishes to obtain the family estate by bringing his elderly father's life to an end by some safer and subtler means than outright murder. Schiller credits him with the psychological and physiological knowledge that Schiller himself had acquired as a student of medicine, when he wrote a dissertation on the relation between the body and the soul. Franz is moreover a thorough-going materialist and atheist, following the radical French Enlightenment doctrines of Helvétius and La Mettrie. Armed with up-to-date psychology and untroubled by any moral scruples, Franz considers which emotions he should encourage in his father as being most damaging, and finally settles on grief, penitence, and self-reproach as being most likely to destroy his father psychologically.[1]

In *Kabale und Liebe*, it is Wurm, the middle-class secretary to the chief minister, who manipulates the Miller family. To end the love-affair between the aristocratic Ferdinand and the middle-class Luise Miller, Wurm, acting on behalf of his employer, Ferdinand's father, induces Luise to write a false letter which will make her seem unfaithful to Ferdinand and will therefore cause him to reject her; by threatening to have her parents imprisoned, Wurm persuades her both to write the letter and to swear to keep his intervention a secret. He exploits her piety by making her swear on the sacrament, thus revealing that his own depravity borders on the devilish; Luise even calls him 'Satan'.[2] Being himself familiar with middle-

---

1   On Franz and materialism, see Alt, *Schiller*, I, 122–23; Wolfgang Riedel, 'Die Aufklärung und das Unbewußte. Die Inversionen des Franz Moor', *Jahrbuch der Deutschen Schiller-Gesellschaft*, 37 (1993), 198–220. Schiller made his disapproval of materialism clear in 'Philosophie der Physiologie', *WB* VIII, 39–40.

2   *WB* II, 628 (Act III, scene 6); Peter-André Alt, 'Dramaturgie des Störfalls: Zur Typologie des Intriganten im Trauerspiel des 18. Jahrhunderts', *Internationales Archiv für Sozialgeschichte der deutschen*

class moral constraints though emancipated from them, Wurm knows that he can rely both on Luise's filial loyalty and on the bourgeois rectitude and piety that will ensure she keeps her word — qualities which are shown to be long since extinct among the corrupt aristocracy.

These experts on individual and social psychology may be Machiavellian in the sense of being unscrupulous, but they do not act on a political stage where Machiavelli's teaching can be applied in a thorough-going way. A much more Machiavellian figure is the protagonist of Schiller's second play, *Die Verschwörung des Fiesko zu Genua* (1783), who inhabits the world of Italian principalities and power struggles that Machiavelli wrote about. The play deals with the unsuccessful revolt by Giovanni Luigi de'Fieschi, count of Lavagna, against the Doria dynasty in Genoa in 1547. The aged Andrea Doria is an effective and imposing ruler, but people are apprehensive about his heir, the vicious libertine Gianettino, and so a number of citizens with republican sympathies, or with hopes of benefiting materially from a change of government, form a conspiracy which they persuade Fiesko to lead. Fiesko, whose playboy lifestyle keeps him from political suspicion, is contrasted with Verrina, a staunch republican who further hates Gianettino for raping his daughter. Fiesko is moreover a dashing young man of twenty-three, a womanizer, a charismatic speaker, with enough nerve and quick enough reactions to deflect an assassin's dagger and take the would-be assassin into his service: he has considerable *virtù* (though little virtue), and he pursues his conspiracy with gusto, in contrast to the gloomy doggedness of Verrina. He is an amoral technician of power who describes his plots as machinery: 'Alle Maschinen des großen Wagestücks sind im Gang' ('All the machines of the great venture are at work').[3] He immediately adds an aesthetic analogy by saying that all his instruments are tuned for a concert. By this aestheticization of politics Fiesko anticipates the figure of the amoral Renaissance despot who would be popularized in the next century by Burckhardt's *Die Kultur der Renaissance in Italien* (1860).[4]

Although Fiesko is a figure of unusual stature, he is, like Karl Moor, a would-be great man who comes to grief. He suffers from vanity. He is concerned not so much with his political goals as with his personal greatness.[5] After telling the assembled populace a political fable about how the animals chose the lion as their king, Fiesko comes down among his audience, as the stage direction tells us, 'mit Hoheit' (with majesty).[6] Like Machiavelli, and Shakespeare's Henry V, he knows the importance of performing rule as well as exercising it. The trouble is that he also performs for his own benefit, and becomes enraptured by his own performance. In a soliloquy, he considers making himself the autocratic ruler of Genoa, and finally rejects the

Literatur, 29 (2004), 1–28 (p. 24).

3   *WB* II, 372 (Act II, scene 16).
4   See Martin Ruehl, 'Ruthless Renaissance: Burckhardt, Nietzsche, and the Violent Birth of the Modern Self', in his *The Italian Renaissance in the German Historical Imagination, 1860–1930* (Cambridge: Cambridge University Press, 2015), pp. 58–104.
5   See Peter Michelsen, 'Schillers Fiesko: Freiheitsheld und Tyrann', in *Schiller und die höfische Welt*, ed. by Aurnhammer, Manger, and Strack, pp. 341–58 (pp. 343–45).
6   *WB* II, 362 (Act II, scene 8).

idea, preferring to become a citizen of a Genoese republic. He is motivated not by principle but by the desire to make a grand gesture: 'Ein Diadem erkämpfen ist *groß*. Es wegwerfen ist *göttlich*' ('To fight one's way to a diadem is *great*. To throw it away is *divine*').[7] However, he does not stick to this resolution, and when the Dorias are (temporarily) overthrown and Fiesko is about to be proclaimed Duke, the republican Verrina murders him in order to prevent him from becoming a tyrant. Verrina pushes him into the sea (the historical Fieschi fell off a gang-plank and drowned in his heavy armour, but this contingent fact was of little use to the dramatist).

Although the play bears the subtitle 'A republican tragedy', it hardly makes a strong case for republicanism. Neither Fiesko nor his fellow-conspirators display the virtue which Montesquieu described as the ruling force in democracy.[8] The only character who could be said to embody republican virtue is Verrina, but he is a repellently harsh and rigid character. On learning that his daughter has been raped by the Doge's dissolute son, he confines her in a cellar until the conspiracy shall have succeeded: 'Ich verwahre sie zum Geisel des Tyrannenmords'[9] ('I shall keep her as a hostage to tyrannicide'). The ideal of inflexible republican virtue, represented by such famous Romans as Cato, was no longer attractive in the age of sensibility.[10] Nor was conspiracy a method to be recommended. Fiesko does seem to be following Machiavelli's advice that one should give one's fellow-conspirators no time to change their minds (D III. 6. 263). But Machiavelli begins his long chapter on conspiracies by warning that 'private citizens cannot enter into a more dangerous or more foolhardy enterprise than this one, because it is difficult and extremely dangerous at every one of its stages, which results in the fact that many conspiracies are attempted but very few reach their desired goal' (D III. 6. 256). Reminiscences of the infamous Catiline have been detected both in Fiesko's character and in that of his associate Sacco, who, like Catiline, wants to overthrow the government in order to avoid paying his debts.[11] Their antagonist, the Doge Andrea Doria, is a dignified and resolute figure, not a hateful tyrant. In short, *Fiesko* is not a republican manifesto, but a study of how a person ostensibly dedicated to liberty can be led astray by his power-hunger and his vanity.[12]

The enormous drama *Don Karlos* takes Machiavellian intrigue to extremes, being held together by a plot which is notoriously difficult to follow. To complicate matters further, the play exists in several versions. Schiller published an early version of Acts I–III in *Thalia*, a literary journal he edited, which appeared intermittently

7   WB II, 378 (Act II, scene 19).

8   Montesquieu, *De l'esprit des lois*, ed. by Victor Goldschmidt, 2 vols (Paris: Garnier-Flammarion, 1979), I, 144–46.

9   WB II, 345 (Act I, scene 12).

10   Cf. Lessing's *Emilia Galotti*, where the hapless Odoardo has to be manipulated by his daughter into behaving like a Roman father; and Goethe's rejection of Josef von Sonnenfels's *Ueber die Liebe des Vaterlandes* as too abstract: 'Römerpatriotismus! Davor bewahr uns Gott, wie vor einer Riesengestalt!' (*Sämtliche Werke*, III, 27).

11   Reginald H. Phelps, 'Schiller's *Fiesko* — a Republican Tragedy?', *PMLA* 89 (1974), 442–53 (pp. 445, 449–50).

12   High, *Schillers Rebellionskonzept*, p. 46.

from 1785 to 1793.[13] The first publication in book form (1787) ran to 6,283 lines. Both these versions were entitled *Dom Karlos*.[14] Schiller shortened it, and the version now usually read, published in 1805 as *Don Karlos*, has 5,370 lines. We also have to take into account the series of letters about the play which Schiller, in response to a critical review, published in four issues of the *Thalia*, from March 1785 to January 1787, partly in order to clarify the plot — though it is disputed how far Schiller's account of the play actually matches the text. Here, the version mainly used will be that of 1805, and the 1787 text will be identified in footnotes.

The play takes us to Madrid, to the court of Philip II of Spain (1527–98), in 1567. The Netherlands are in full revolt (as shown by Goethe in *Egmont*), and the Duke of Alva (here, as in Goethe, called Alba) is about to be sent there to crush the rebels. For some time, however, politics remain in the background, and the focus is on Karlos and his relations with his father Philip and his stepmother Elisabeth de Valois. Schiller described the play, in a footnote to the *Thalia* version, as 'a family portrait from a royal house', no doubt hoping to exploit the vogue for family dramas inspired by Diderot's *Le père de famille* (1758).[15]

This required a very free use of historical materials. The Carlos of history (1545–68) was an unpromising subject. A modern historian says of him:

> Don Carlos, the child of Philip's first wife, Maria of Portugal, had grown up to be an abnormally vicious creature of uncontrollable passions, totally unfit for the government of an empire. Added to this was a deep hatred for his father, and an unmeasured ambition which may have led him into making sympathetic overtures to the Dutch rebels.[16]

On the night of 18 January 1568 Carlos was imprisoned in his chamber by his father, who announced that he would treat the young man as a subject, not as a son; four days later he was arrested. He died on 24 July after ruining his health by hunger-strikes. It was widely believed that the King had poisoned his son.

Although Schiller conscientiously consulted historians, he found a more usable version of Carlos in a work of historical fiction, *Don Carlos: Nouvelle historique* (1672) by the abbé de Saint-Réal (1639–92). The historical Elisabeth (1545–68) was only fourteen when Philip married her, but since dynastic marriages were generally arranged while the prospective spouses were still children, she had previously been betrothed to the child Carlos; political circumstances made it expedient to dissolve the engagement and marry her to Philip when the latter was widowed by the death of his second wife, Mary of England. Saint-Réal uses poetic licence to blur the dates and to suggest that Elisabeth and Carlos had been and still were in love. Courtiers

13   It was initially entitled the *Rheinische Thalia*, because Schiller was then living at Mannheim on the Rhine. When he moved away, he changed the title to *Thalia*, and in 1792 it became the *Neue Thalia*.
14   Schiller always spelt the name 'Karlos'. Other Spanish names in the play are spelt with a k: Mondekar, Merkado, Alkala. The spelling 'Carlos' became usual in the 1830s and is of course familiar also from Verdi's opera (1867).
15   *WB* III, 137. Schiller uses a similar expression in a letter to the Mannheim theatre director Dalberg, 7 June 1784 (ibid., p. 1021). For a list of family dramas, see ibid., p. 1022.
16   Elliott, *Imperial Spain*, p. 245. For a fuller account, see Parker, *Imprudent King*, pp. 175–91.

suspect them of a clandestine relationship, and use their suspicions as a political weapon. Schiller takes over the emotional triangle and many other plot details.

Saint-Réal has much to say about the power of the Spanish Inquisition. Schiller's animus against Christianity, above all against Catholicism, was already apparent in *Die Räuber*, which contains two clergymen: the ranting Catholic 'Pater' and the upright Protestant Pastor Moser, who speaks truth to power when confronting Franz Moor. When first thinking about *Don Karlos*, Schiller wrote to Wilhelm Reinwald (a friend who would in 1786 become his brother-in-law): 'Außerdem will ich es mir in diesem Schauspiel zur Pflicht machen, in Darstellung der Inquisition die prostituirte Menschheit zu rächen und ihre Schandflecken fürchterlich an den Pranger zu stellen' ('Besides, I want to make it my duty in this play, when portraying the Inquisition, to avenge the debasement of humanity and to give a terrible denunciation of its [the Inquisition's] shameful blemishes').[17]

The *Thalia* version of *Don Karlos* opens with the King's confessor (and formerly an Inquisitor), Father Domingo, observing Karlos from a distance, while Karlos chafes under the scrutiny of this 'Erzspion' (arch-spy).[18] The King invites the entire court to attend an auto-da-fé (899–900); in the *Thalia* text there are to be a hundred victims, and the King coerces Elisabeth into watching.[19] Schiller evidently believed that heretics were burnt in public, whereas in fact, having been dressed in robes called sanbenitos and high hats, they were paraded and displayed before a large public, and later burnt at night before a much smaller audience.[20] The King is such a fanatic that in the *Thalia* fragment Schiller alludes to a story in Saint-Réal about how he suspected his own father, Charles V, of heresy, and burnt the latter's will.[21] All this material supports the widespread view (sometimes dismissed by Spaniards as a 'black legend') of a backward and priest-ridden Spain, which Schiller also found luridly depicted in the historians he consulted.[22] The Marquis Posa denounces all Christianity, at least prior to the Reformation, as 'den gift'gen Schierlingstrank | des Pfaffentums' ('the poisoned hemlock draught of priestcraft').[23] He himself may well be a Protestant: when the King puts the question to him, he gives an evasive answer (3065–66). Towards the end of the play the terrifying extent of the Inquisition's power is revealed: it has been keeping Posa under surveillance; on the insistence of the Grand Inquisitor, who controls the King, Karlos, unlike his historical original, is handed over to the Inquisition.

Saint-Réal also helped Schiller to widen the family drama into a political play.

17   Letter of 14 April 1783, *WB* III, 1074.
18   *WB* III, 22.
19   *WB* III, 62–63.
20   Henry Kamen, *The Spanish Inquisition: A Historical Revision*, 4th edn (New Haven: Yale University Press, 2014), pp. 250–59.
21   *WB* III, 82; Abbé de Saint-Réal, *Don Carlos: Nouvelle historique, 1672, par Saint-Réal*, ed. by André Lebois (Avignon: Edouard Aubanel, 1964), pp. 171–79.
22   Especially Robert Watson, *History of the Reign of Philip the Second King of Spain*, 2 vols (London: Cadell, 1778), which Schiller read in French translation (*WB* III, 1053). See Barbara Becker-Cantarino, 'Die schwarze Legende: Ideal und Ideologie in Schillers *Don Carlos*', *Jahrbuch des Freien Deutschen Hochstifts* 1975, pp. 153–73.
23   *WB* III, 34, 183; this strong expression is absent from the 1805 text.

The fictional Carlos hears about the oppressed state of the Flemish nobility, and feeling ashamed to have done nothing to earn glory, asks his father to send him to Flanders to sort matters out, claiming that the Protestants have promised to obey him. The King sends Alba instead, but Carlos is about to leave for Flanders illicitly when he is arrested and soon afterwards killed. In Schiller, Karlos's interest in the Netherlands is aroused by Posa. This is in Saint-Réal the name of a minor character, a favourite of Carlos, whom the King, suspecting him of having designs on Elisabeth, causes to be murdered.

Schiller builds Posa up into a major character and a well-intentioned arch-Machiavellian. Posa and Karlos were fellow-students at the University of Alcalá. Since then, Posa has been travelling around Europe. His travels have included the Spanish Netherlands, where he has found evidence of the atrocities practised against Protestants by the Spanish occupiers (even before the arrival of Alba). He hopes to use Karlos, the heir to the Spanish possessions, to obtain religious liberty for the Netherlanders. To his dismay, he finds Karlos obsessed almost to the point of insanity by his love for Elisabeth; Karlos makes it sound even worse by announcing dramatically: 'Ich liebe meine Mutter' ('I am in love with my mother'). (She is of course only his stepmother, so there is no question of incest.)

However, in order to further his unquestionably noble ideals, Posa presently devises another plan. It depends on the distinction made by reason of state between public and private morality. Since the plot of the play now becomes, as an early reviewer complained, 'intolerably complicated', it may be helpful to explain Posa's plan at length.[24] The 'wild, bold, happy thought' (2452), which he avoids explaining to Karlos, but does partly explain to the Queen later, is this. He will encourage and exploit Karlos's love for the Queen by getting her to send Karlos to the Netherlands, against his father's will and thus illegally, so that he can place himself at the head of the rebels, thereby strengthening their cause. Threatened by Karlos's power, the King will give way, and father and son will be reconciled:

> Die gute Sache
> Wird stark durch einen Königssohn. Er mache
> Den Span'schen Thron durch seine Waffen zittern.
> Was in Madrid der Vater ihm verweigert,
> Wird er in Brüssel ihm bewilligen. (5473–77)

> The good cause will become strong thanks to the Prince. Let him shake the throne of Spain with his weapons. What his father refused him in Madrid, he will grant him in Brussels.

In the 1787 text, Posa also says that other European states will intervene and mediate between Philip and Karlos.[25] Evidently he has used his travels to establish diplomatic contacts and ensure that all the Northern powers will support the Netherlands (4989–93). He does not tell anybody, however, that he has also been in

---

24   Review ascribed to Johann Friedrich Jünger in the Jena *Literatur-Zeitung*, partially reproduced in *WB* III, 1116–21 (p. 1118). The *Briefe über Don Karlos* are a reply to this and another review (repr. ibid., III, 1122–31), partly explaining the intricacies of the plot.
25   Schiller, *WB* III, 329 (lines 4171–72).

touch with the Ottoman Empire and arranged for a Turkish fleet to attack Spain (4984–88). This would not only be an enormous act of treason, but would put many lives at risk. In 1480 the Turks captured Otranto, in the heel of Italy, massacred 12,000 of the inhabitants, and enslaved 5,000. It was almost a year before Neapolitan troops managed to recapture the city. Is Posa really prepared to expose his fellow-Spaniards to a similar fate?

Posa's plan involves exploiting private individuals and their emotions for the public good. Most obviously, he is using Karlos's passion for Elisabeth and her affection for him. He is also exploiting the King. In a famous scene, the King has summoned Posa to his presence because he is curious about a nobleman who has not asked him for favours. Posa declares, with a manly independence and dignity which impress the king, that he cannot be the servant of a prince, but must be independent. He tells the King about the repression going on in the Netherlands, and urges him to permit freedom of thought. The King, feeling that in a court riddled by intrigue he has at last found a person he can trust, gives him the task of ascertaining the true feelings of the Queen and Karlos. So Posa, despite his declaration, does become the servant of a prince, and he abuses the King's trust by planning acts of treason which, he claims, serve the King's true interests (3415). The Queen reasonably asks whether the good end really justifies the bad means: 'kann | Die gute Sache schlimme Mittel adeln?' (3408–09). But Posa clearly has no doubt that the deception of trustful individuals is justified by his enlightened aim of freeing the Netherlands. He also deceives Karlos, who is naturally curious about Posa's long interview with the King. Posa says vaguely that he was offered a job, and when Karlos says 'Which you refused?', Posa replies 'Of course' (3577–78).

Although Posa is supposed to have insight into human nature, and is certainly more perceptive than the naïve Karlos, he shows a fatal lack of judgement in choosing Karlos for his instrument. Karlos has no military experience. In a campaign in the Netherlands, especially if up against troops commanded by the formidable Alba, he could only be a figurehead. His character is turbulent, erratic, and inconstant. After Elisabeth has treated him with proper reserve, he receives a letter inviting him to a rendezvous, signed 'E', and absurdly imagines that Elisabeth has suddenly changed her attitude. In fact the letter is from the lovelorn Princess Eboli; Karlos goes to her room, hears how she loves him but is being forced to marry a courtier, and is so carried away that he embraces her. He then has the embarrassing task of explaining that he is not really in love with her. This situation, reminiscent of a farce, nevertheless leads to the tragic outcome. Eboli, realizing that Karlos actually loves Elisabeth, resolves on revenge. The King has been making advances to her; she now yields to him, and, having broken open Elisabeth's jewel case, gives him the love letters that Karlos wrote to Elisabeth before her marriage.[26]

26 Eboli confesses everything, including her adultery, to Elisabeth in IV. 19. The magnanimous Elisabeth is prepared to forgive the theft of the letters, but not the adultery: it appears that Eboli is to be banished to a convent (4198–4200). On the uses made of letters throughout the play, see Oskar Seidlin, 'Schillers "trügerische Zeichen": Die Funktion der Briefe in seinen frühen Dramen', in his *Von Goethe zu Thomas Mann: Zwölf Versuche* (Göttingen: Vandenhoeck & Ruprecht, 1963), pp. 94–119 (pp. 111–18); Steffan Davies, ' "Du wagst es, meine Worte zu *deuten*?": Unreliable Evidence

Since the letters are apparently undated, the King presumes them to be recent and thinks they confirm his fears that Karlos and Elisabeth still have a liaison. This rules out any prospect of a reconciliation between father and son, which was a crucial component of Posa's great plan.[27] However, to protect Karlos temporarily from his father's wrath, Posa uses the powers the King has given him to have Karlos arrested — without telling him why. At least Eboli has not betrayed the plan to send Karlos to Flanders, and Posa has arranged for a coach to take him to Cadiz in the dead of night and for a ship to take him thence to Flushing. In order to distract the King and divert attention from Karlos's flight, Posa has written a letter, which he knows will be intercepted, claiming that *he* is the Queen's lover. On reading this letter, the King, to the horrified astonishment of his courtiers, breaks down in tears (4465–66). Posa intended to kill himself and bequeath his task of liberation to Karlos, but this perhaps heroic self-sacrifice never happens, because, on the King's orders, Posa is shot by a hidden assassin.

So what, finally, are we to think of Posa? Schiller explains his conduct in the *Briefe über Don Karlos* by maintaining that a noble purpose, such as Posa undoubtedly has, can fatally mislead one if it depends too much on abstract ideals. 'The most selfless, purest and noblest person, through enthusiastic devotion to *his conception* of virtue and the prospect of creating happiness, can manipulate individuals as arbitrarily as the most selfish despot.'[28] An abstract ideal, existing in one's own mind, can cut one off from the reality of other people. And when one is thus isolated, one's devotion really becomes directed to one's own self. This is compatible with the judgement that Elisabeth, who is mostly (not invariably) the moral centre of the play, passes on Posa: 'Sie haben | Nur um Bewunderung gebuhlt' ('You have only courted admiration', 4387–88), probably referring to Posa's admiration of his own heroic self-image.[29] Here Posa is a successor to Karl Moor, whom his fellow-robbers charge with megalomania and the desire for admiration at any cost, and to Fiesko, whose vanity we have already seen.[30] Like Karl Moor, he has spent too much time reading Plutarch and filling his head with images of great men:

> Who does not discover in the entire fabric of his life, as he lives it before our eyes in the play, that his whole imagination is filled and saturated with images of romantic greatness, that the heroes of Plutarch are alive in his soul, and therefore, faced with two alternatives, he must always, first and last, choose the *heroic* one?[31]

His suicide plan is a sign of vanity, and also, in the effect it is intended to have on

on Schiller's Stage', *Modern Language Review*, 106 (2011), 518–35 (p. 524).

27   This motive, which it is not easy to reconstruct from the text, is explained by the editor in *WB* III, 1319–20.

28   *WB* III, 463. Emphasis in original.

29   It is a pity to draw attention to the flaws in such an attractive heroine, but she should surely have had more prudence than to support, admittedly in a generous spirit, Posa's harebrained and also treasonable plan of sending Karlos to lead a rebellion in Flanders (Act IV, scene 3).

30   'RÄUBER. Laßt ihn hinfahren. Es ist die Groß-Mann-Sucht. Er will sein Leben an eitle Bewunderung setzen', *WB* II, 160.

31   *WB* III, 470.

Karlos, an act of moral blackmail. That he never completely confides in anybody suggests that he takes a solitary, narcissistic pleasure in pulling everyone else's strings. Some degree of isolation from other people may also help to explain his overestimation of Karlos and his investment in a far-fetched but adventurous plan. The scheme to bundle Karlos into a coach at 2 a.m. and hurry him to Cadiz and thence to the Netherlands feels like a pre-echo of the romantic adventurous spirit in the early poetry of W. H. Auden — 'Leave for Cape Wrath tonight'.[32]

Much commentary on *Don Karlos* dwells on the corruption whereby an idealist becomes a despot. Posa has even been compared to the chilling figure of Robespierre whom we meet in Büchner's *Danton's Tod*.[33] It may well be, however, that Schiller himself exaggerated Posa's despotic aspect.[34] I would see Posa more as illustrating the self-centred and self-aggrandizing fantasies of the type of person that the late eighteenth century called a 'Schwärmer', someone emotionally carried away by speculative ideas who needs to be grounded in the human world.[35]

32   *The English Auden: Poems, Essays and Dramatic Writings, 1927–1939*, ed. by Edward Mendelson (London: Faber & Faber, 1977), p. 28.
33   Ulrich Karthaus, 'Schiller und die französische Revolution', *Jahrbuch der Deutschen Schiller-Gesellschaft*, 33 (1989), 210–39 (p. 220).
34   Karl S. Guthke, *Schillers Dramen: Idealismus und Skepsis* (Tübingen: Francke, 1994), p. 137.
35   See Hilliard, *Freethinkers, Libertines and 'Schwärmer'*, pp. 185–218. The King calls Posa 'Sonderbarer Schwärmer' (3216), and Schiller uses the word in the *Briefe über Don Karlos: WB* III, 447.

10

Schiller:
Wallenstein (1799):
The Machiavellian Realist

Historical optimism, a valid ideal despite the flawed methods of its spokesman Posa, seems to be in abeyance in the *Wallenstein* trilogy, which Schiller wrote between 1797 and 1799 after a long period in which he had concentrated largely on philosophy. During the same period the French Revolution had run its course from initial euphoria via radicalism and the Reign of Terror to its suppression by the Directory and the advent of Napoleon. Having at first welcomed the Revolution, though with more reserve than many other German intellectuals, Schiller was shocked by the execution of Louis XVI on 21 January 1793.[1] His essay *Über das Erhabene* (On the Sublime), written at an uncertain date in the mid to late 1790s and published in 1801, denies that real moral progress can be found in history:

> If one approaches history with great expectations of illumination and insight, how bitterly one finds oneself disappointed! All philosophy's well-meaning attempts to match the *demands* of the moral world with the *achievements* of the real world are refuted by the voices of experience.[2]

Hence the *Wallenstein* trilogy shows Germany being devastated by the Thirty Years War (which at this point, February 1634, is only half-way through) with no signs of future hope. In his history of the war Schiller struck a hopeful note by telling how the war was concluded by the Treaty of Westphalia, which established a largely peaceful international order.[3] The world of the play, however, is unrelievedly bleak. Two of its protagonists, Wallenstein and his secret enemy Octavio, are Machiavellian intriguers who get caught in their own snares. This admittedly is not Schiller's last word. His next play, *Maria Stuart*, as we shall see, suggests a more hopeful perspective; in *Die Jungfrau von Orleans* a proleptic allusion to the

---

1   See his letter to Körner, 8 February 1793, expressing his loathing for 'diese elenden Schindersknechte', 'these wretched butchers' (*NA* XXVI, 183).

2   *WB* VIII: Theoretische Schriften, ed. by Rolf-Peter Janz (1992), p. 835. See Wolfgang Riedel, '"Weltgeschichte ein erhabenes Object": Zur Modernität von Schillers Geschichtsdenken', in *Prägnanter Moment: Studien zur deutschen Literatur der Aufklärung und Klassik: Festschrift für Hans-Jürgen Schings*, ed. by Peter-André Alt and others (Würzburg: Königshausen & Neumann, 2002), pp. 193–214. But cf. the argument for the continuity of Schiller's historical thinking in High, *Schillers Rebellionskonzept*, esp. p. 3.

3   *WB* VII, 447–48. On the underlying historical scheme, see Alt, *Schiller*, 1, 669.

SCHILLER: *WALLENSTEIN*, THE MACHIAVELLIAN REALIST

French Revolution implies that it represents the deserved popular revenge for prolonged misgovernment (2098–2101); and *Wilhelm Tell* shows a popular revolution succeeding with minimal bloodshed. These last two plays will not be discussed in any detail here, because they move away from history towards legend and offer little scope for an analysis of Machiavellianism.

Posa's tendency to lose himself in fantasies reappears in Wallenstein, who dominates the trilogy named after him even though he makes major appearances only in the last part, *Wallensteins Tod*. As the leader of a mercenary army in the Thirty Years War, Wallenstein inhabits a setting similar to the unstable political landscape in which Machiavelli imagined his prince operating. A charismatic general, Wallenstein is as obsessed as Fiesko with his own image. Serving the imperial court in Vienna, but discontented with its treatment of him, he is contemplating going over to the Protestant side, and is negotiating with the Swedes about transferring to them his private army of 60,000 men.[4] He will use the resulting position of power perhaps to make himself King of Bohemia, perhaps to impose a peace on war-torn Europe. Although the historical record is clouded by uncertainty, Schiller constructs a clear dramatic plot by showing Wallenstein negotiating with his Swedish counterpart. At the same time, however, Wallenstein's motives and intentions remain obscure, especially to himself: concern for the good of Europe plays a very small part compared to resentment at his previous shabby treatment by the Habsburg court, personal ambition, and a confused belief in his own greatness — a confusion characteristic of Schiller's charismatic heroes.

To his enemies, Wallenstein appears to be an unscrupulous political calculator. Buttler, who plots Wallenstein's death after being told that Wallenstein prevented him from receiving the title of Count, says bitterly:

> Ein großer Rechenkünstler war der Fürst
> Von jeher, alles wußt er zu berechnen,
> Die Menschen wußt er, gleich des Brettspiels Steinen,
> Nach seinem Zweck zu setzen und zu schieben.[5]

> The Prince was always skilled in reckoning;
> All things were subject to his calculations.
> Men too, like pieces in a game of chess,
> He placed and moved according to his purpose.[6]

If we look at Wallenstein's actual behaviour in the play, however, we may doubt if he really is this kind of Machiavellian. His dealings with the Swedes, as he admits in soliloquy, arise less from calculation than from a self-aggrandizing fantasy which he is now compelled to turn into reality. Rather than calculation, he relies on fortune and fate. He is widely supposed, like a Machiavellian prince, to control *fortuna*.

---

4   On the historical circumstances, see Geoffrey Parker, *The Thirty Years' War* (London: Routledge & Kegan Paul, 1984), pp. 132–40; Peter H. Wilson, *Europe's Tragedy: A History of the Thirty Years War* (London: Allen Lane, 2009), pp. 527–29; Mortimer, *Wallenstein*, pp. 182–98.
5   *WB* IV: *Wallenstein*, ed. by Frithjof Stock (2000), p. 255 (lines 2853–56). Quotations from the trilogy will henceforth be identified by line number and the following abbreviations: L = *Wallensteins Lager*, P = *Die Piccolomini*, WT = *Wallensteins Tod*.
6   Schiller, *The Robbers* and *Wallenstein*, trans. by Lamport, p. 431.

The soldiers speak of '[s]eine Fortuna' ('his Fortuna', *L* 715) and believe that he has fortune at his command (*L* 349). Wallenstein, privately, is not quite so sure. He tells himself that his proposed defection to the Protestant side is no worse than Julius Caesar's action in leading Roman legions against Rome, and wishes for Caesar's good fortune (*WT* 843). To the soldiers whom he is trying to win over, he presents a brave face, claiming to be a man of destiny (*WT* 1989), but his associates are aware of the instability of fortune's wheel (*WT* 2789). Alongside 'Glück' (fortune), the play is dominated by the concepts of fate and destiny, and at times Wallenstein pays gloomy homage to the classical notion of Nemesis, as when he reflects on the antagonism between himself and the emperor:

> Es ist sein böser Geist und meiner. *Ihn*
> Straft er durch mich, das Werkzeug seiner Herrschsucht,
> Und ich erwarte, daß der Rache Stahl
> Auch schon für *meine* Brust geschliffen ist. (WT 645–48)[7]

> It is his evil genius, and mine,
> Punishing him through me, the tool of his ambition,
> And I expect that vengeance is already
> Whetting its blade to pierce my breast as well.[8]

At his side Wallenstein has an arch-Machiavellian, his sister, who is married to his lieutenant Terzky. Countess Terzky has been described as a political moralist (in Kant's disparaging sense) and called 'Frau Machiavelli'.[9] She judges actions only by their success, and is convinced that Wallenstein's proposed treachery, if it succeeds, will be admired and forgiven. She assures Wallenstein that he owes no loyalty to the emperor:

> Gestehe denn, daß zwischen dir und ihm
> Die Rede nicht sein kann von Pflicht und Recht,
> Nur von der Macht und der *Gelegenheit*! (*WT* 624–26)

> Admit then, that between yourself and him
> There never can be talk of right and duty,
> Only of power, and opportunity![10]

Her world is a bare, amoral space in which natural forces contend for power, driven on by the Machiavellian force of *necessità*, which she calls 'Die ungestüme Presserin, die *Not*' (*WT* 576), 'Necessity, that tarries for no man'.[11] Ideals have no place among these harsh realities. At times Wallenstein likewise presents himself to others as a realist, who knows that the world is a bad place in which you have to ally yourself with evil forces. Thus, when Max Piccolomini, a young officer who hero-

---

7   See 'Wallenstein: Man of Destiny?', in my *Enlightenment and Religion in German and Austrian Literature* (Cambridge: Legenda, 2017), pp. 60–74.
8   Schiller, *The Robbers* and *Wallenstein*, p. 345.
9   Dieter Borchmeyer, *Macht und Melancholie: Schillers 'Wallenstein'* (Frankfurt a.M.: Athenäum, 1988), p. 120.
10   Schiller, *The Robbers* and *Wallenstein*, pp. 344–45.
11   Ibid., p. 343. 'Not', strictly, is not 'necessity' but conveys the impetuous, violent pressure exerted by exceptional circumstances.

worships Wallenstein, expresses shock at Wallenstein's plan to desert to the Swedes, Wallenstein scorns him as a head-in-the-clouds idealist and depicts himself as in touch with reality. High-minded young people, he says, are quick to pass moral judgements, but the only standard of judgement lies in things themselves (another version of his sister's amorality). Many incompatible thoughts can sit side by side in the mind, but out there in the real world there are hard choices to be made:

> Wer nicht vertrieben sein will, muß vertreiben,
> Da herrscht der Streit, und nur der Starke siegt. (*WT* 791–92)

> [...] who would not be driven out, must drive;
> Strife is the rule, and strength alone will conquer.[12]

If one has no desires, Wallenstein continues, it is easy to remain pure. But he is not such a person; he has desires, and he knows he must get his hands dirty in order to realize them:

> Mich schuf aus gröberm Stoffe die Natur,
> Und zu der Erde zieht mich die Begierde.
> Dem bösen Geist gehört die Erde, nicht
> Dem Guten. Was die Göttlichen uns senden
> Von oben, sind nur allgemeine Güter,
> Ihr Licht erfreut, doch macht es keinen reich,
> In ihrem Staat erringt sich kein Besitz.
> Den Edelstein, das allgeschätzte Gold
> Muß man den falschen Mächten abgewinnen,
> Die unterm Tage schlimmgeartet hausen.
> Nicht ohne Opfer macht man sie geneigt,
> Und keiner lebet, der aus ihrem Dienst
> Die Seele hätte rein zurückgezogen. (*WT* 797–809)

> But nature made me of a coarser stuff,
> And my desires will hold me fast to earth.
> The evil spirit rules this earth, and not
> The good. The gifts that heaven sends down to us
> Are only common goods, that all may share;
> Their brightness gladdens, but makes no man rich,
> And in their realm are no possessions won.
> The precious stone, the gold that all men prize,
> They must be wrested from the fickle powers
> That hold their evil sway beneath the light.
> Not without sacrifice their grace is won,
> And there is no man living on this earth
> Who served them yet, and kept his soul unspotted.[13]

This is an arch-realist talking, and realism, in a particular sense, was an essential part of Wallenstein's character as Schiller conceived it. His great essay of 1795, *Über naive und sentimentalische Dichtung*, ends with the antithesis between two perennial human types, the realist and the idealist. The realist attends to nature, namely the

12   Ibid., p. 350.
13   Ibid., p. 351.

way the world is, whereas the idealist is sharply aware of how the world *ought* to be. The realist accepts necessity (which is not the same as blind submission to fate), the idealist defies it. The realist asks what something is good *for*, the idealist asks whether something is good in itself. The realist thinks about consequences, the idealist ignores them. The realist is consistent in his behaviour and will never do anything very good or very bad; the idealist is capable of noble but also of base actions. Writing to Wilhelm von Humboldt, Schiller explained that this description of the realist applied perfectly to the historical Wallenstein:

> There is nothing noble about him, no action in his life makes him appear great, he has little dignity and the like, but all the same I hope by using realistic means to present him as a dramatically great character who has in him a genuine living principle.[14]

Clearly Wallenstein as a dramatic protagonist could not remain the petty manipulator that Schiller's account of the realist implies. Nor could he be simply the gloomy tyrant depicted in Schiller's *Geschichte des Dreißigjährigen Krieges* (*History of the Thirty Years War*). The dramatic Wallenstein, however, has considered himself an exceptional person from his youth, 'ein begünstigt und befreites Wesen' (*WT* 2568); 'He felt that now | He bore a favour and a charm of freedom'.[15] That this is not just self-delusion is shown by his military successes, which have made him indispensable to the imperial cause, and by his charismatic power over his troops and indeed — until the disillusioning revelation of his treachery — over Max. But there is self-delusion too, shown by Wallenstein's irresolution in private, his resorting to astrology to prop up his self-belief, and his assertions that his governing planet is the lordly Jupiter, whereas his tendency to melancholy and lethargy much more suggests the planetary influence of Saturn.[16]

In other ways, Wallenstein's professions of realism undermine themselves. In paraphrasing Wallenstein's philosophy of life a few pages back, I deliberately introduced clichés ('out there in the real world'), because his philosophy is itself a bargain-basement Machiavellianism masquerading as hard-won practical wisdom. This philosophy has a strong appeal, however, just because of its clichéd nature, and also because such realism flatters both the person who utters it and the person who accepts it; they are able to congratulate themselves on their courage in facing unpleasant truths and their straightforward avoidance of moral fussiness. Thus Wallenstein's tough talk is part of the persona that he cultivates to impress not only others but also himself.

For the reader or spectator, Wallenstein's professed realism is also undermined by its context. Although Wallenstein speaks here with great forcefulness, we have already heard the soliloquy in which he dithers hopelessly about whether to join the Swedes, and we have seen him pushed over the edge by the assured amoralism of his sister. And, like other Machiavellians in Schiller, Wallenstein reveals the limited extent to which one can in practice control one's destiny. At the beginning

---

14   Letter to Humboldt, 21 March 1796, quoted in *WB* IV, 590.
15   Schiller, *The Robbers* and *Wallenstein*, p. 420.
16   This is the argument of Borchmeyer, *Macht und Melancholie*.

of *Wallensteins Tod*, when he is about to enter on the fateful negotiation with the Swedes, he learns that the messenger he sent to them, with incriminating letters to the leading Swedish politicians, has been captured by imperial troops, so that all Wallenstein's plans are already known to the emperor. When browbeating Max, he may sound like the master of his fate and the captain of his soul, but in fact his freedom of choice, his ability to manipulate fortune, has been taken away from him. He now confronts *necessità*: 'Ernst ist der Anblick der Notwendigkeit' (*WT* 183); 'A grim and deadly earnest is this moment'.[17]

At the same time, the speech quoted above has deeper resonances. In his dark talk of subterranean powers to which one must make a sacrifice, Wallenstein evokes the Faustian pact with the devil, a motif which pervades German literature and turns up not only in the many versions of the Faust legend but in the most unexpected places.[18] We find it, most remarkably, in Max Weber's well-known lecture 'Politik als Beruf' ('Politics as a Vocation', 1919). Towards the end, Weber contrasts the 'ethic of conviction' (*Gesinnungsethik*) with the 'ethic of responsibility' (*Verantwortungsethik*). *Gesinnungsethik* is an ethic that refuses to compromise but insists on remaining faithful to lofty ideals. *Verantwortungsethik*, by contrast, recognizes not only that it is necessary often to use bad means to attain good ends, but, further and more melodramatically, that the world is inhabited by demonic forces and that the exercise of power requires a pact with the Devil:

> Auch die alten Christen wußten sehr genau, daß die Welt von Dämonen regiert sei, und daß, wer mit der Politik, das heißt: mit Macht und Gewaltsamkeit als Mitteln, sich einläßt, mit diabolischen Mächten einen Pakt schließt.[19]

> The early Christians too knew very well that the world was governed by demons, that anyone who gets involved with politics, which is to say with the means of power and violence, is making a pact with diabolical powers.[20]

Wallenstein is hardly a *Verantwortungsethiker*. Such a person makes moral compromises in the hope of achieving something which is good for the state or community at large. Wallenstein is brutally frank about making a pact with the dark powers for the sake of his own personal ambitions. But the contrast between him and Max follows or rather anticipates Weberian lines. Max, the idealist, is also the *Gesinnungsethiker* who warns Wallenstein not to trust the dark powers; Wallenstein, the realist, asserts that the pursuit of his ambitions requires an agreement with those powers.

17   Schiller, *The Robbers and Wallenstein*, p. 330. More literally, 'It is a serious matter to face Necessity'.
18   For example, in E. T. A. Hoffmann's *Der Sandmann* (1816), the narrator's account of spying on his father and the sinister Coppelius strongly implies that the two are joined by a Satanic pact. Jeremias Gotthelf's famous novella *Die schwarze Spinne* (1842) turns on an erotic pact which Christine makes with the devil, disguised as the Green Huntsman, by letting him kiss her on the cheek. The story, intended as a didactic tale about Christian resistance to sin, is full of ambivalences that complicate and undermine its message.
19   Max Weber, 'Politik als Beruf', in his *Gesammelte politische Schriften*, ed. by Johannes Winckelmann (Tübingen: Mohr Siebeck, 1988), pp. 505–60 (p. 554).
20   Max Weber, 'The Profession and Vocation of Politics', in *Weber: Political Writings*, ed. by Peter Lassman and Ronald Speirs, Cambridge Texts in the History of Political Thought (Cambridge: Cambridge University Press, 1994), pp. 309–69 (p. 362).

Wallenstein's speech is thus significant in two ways. First, it is a convenient and quotable expression of the Machiavellian realism which, as we shall see in later chapters, became a widespread attitude in nineteenth-century Germany. Second, with its Faustian and quasi-religious overtones that go far beyond Machiavelli, it adumbrates the notion of the 'necessary crime' which we shall presently find expressed in a variety of literary and historical texts.

Schiller:
Wallenstein (1799):
The Public Servant

Schiller's description of the realist, and Weber's conception of the *Verantwortungsethiker*, apply much better to another character in *Wallenstein*: Max's father Octavio Piccolomini. Octavio is a general on the imperial side, but appears mainly as a diplomat. He is based on the historical figure of Ottavio Piccolomini (1599–1656), a close associate of Wallenstein who turned against him.[1] Since, even before the discovery of Wallenstein's secret correspondence, the emperor and his court have ceased to trust Wallenstein, Octavio has been given the task of countering Wallenstein's intentions. He has been sent to Wallenstein's military camp in northern Bohemia with imperial orders to persuade Wallenstein's generals, who have signed a declaration of personal loyalty to him, to desert him and return to their Imperial allegiance; Octavio is then to assume the command himself.

In addition, Octavio is a spymaster. He tells the imperial envoy Questenberg that he has surrounded Wallenstein with eavesdroppers:

> Überraschen
> Kann er uns nicht, Sie wissen, daß ich ihn
> Mit meinen Horchern rings umgeben habe;
> Vom kleinsten Schritt erhalt ich Wissenschaft
> Sogleich [...] (P 340–44)

> He cannot take
> Us by surprise, for as you know, I have
> Him set about with spies on every hand;
> One step, and straightway I shall be informed
> Of it.[2]

Max, himself one of the commanders around Wallenstein, initially refuses to believe that Wallenstein can intend such treachery. When Octavio assures him that he heard it from Wallenstein's own lips, Max asks why he did not tell Wallenstein what a shocking plan it was, and Octavio's reply — that he expressed misgivings,

---

1   See Thomas M. Barker, 'Ottavio Piccolomini (1599–1656): A Fair Historical Judgment?', in his *Army, Aristocracy, Monarchy: Essays on War, Society and Government in Austria, 1618–1780* (Boulder, CO: Social Science Monographs, 1982), pp. 61–111.
2   Schiller, *The Robbers* and *Wallenstein*, p. 231.

but concealed his profound disapproval — sounds rather lame. Moreover, although Max does not mention this, we know that for several years Wallenstein has regarded Octavio as a special friend, though Octavio does not understand why and does not reciprocate the feeling. Wallenstein's reasons have to do with his superstitious belief in dreams and portents, not with personal liking for Octavio, so Octavio may be excused for his coolness; nevertheless, this does make Octavio seem a more unfeeling character.[3]

Critics readily condemn Octavio's duplicity and call his final reward that of a 'Judas'.[4] The only positive appreciation of Octavio that I know, dating from 1961, notes that his detractors generally base their arguments on what others — especially Wallenstein and Max — say about him. Its author, Wolfgang Wittkowski, sums up the general view of Octavio as follows:

> Wallenstein's antagonist — insofar as he was counted as such — has always been charged with a merely external, self-interested loyalty; further, with conduct at least bordering on the petty, base, contemptible, with mediocrity and lack of straightforwardness, with moral relativism, and especially, of course, with exploiting Wallenstein's confidence in order to destroy him.[5]

Still, Octavio is not a villain, as Schiller made clear in a letter:

> He is even quite a law-abiding man, by worldly standards, and the shameful act he commits can be seen repeated on every stage of the world by people who, like him, have strict notions of justice and duty. He does choose a bad means, but he is pursuing a good purpose.[6]

Octavio virtually admits the necessity for Machiavellianism when he tells the outraged Max that in this wicked world you sometimes have to get your hands dirty — 'In steter Notwehr gegen arge List | Bleibt auch das redliche Gemüt nicht wahr' (P 2450–51): 'In constant battle with despite and malice | Even the upright spirit stays not true'.[7] In his own mind at least, Octavio is a Weberian *Verantwortungsethiker*.

The deeper objections to Octavio's conduct are expressed involuntarily in his self-defence against Max's reproaches. In real life, he explains, one cannot always follow the pure morality enjoined by the inner voice:

> Ich klügle nicht, ich tue meine Pflicht,
> Der Kaiser schreibt mir mein Betragen vor.
> Wohl wär es besser, überall dem Herzen

---

3   For a defence of Octavio on this point, see Borchmeyer, *Macht und Melancholie*, pp. 122–24.
4   'Judaslohn': Herbert Singer, 'Dem *Fürsten* Piccolomini', *Euphorion*, 53 (1959), 281–303 (p. 301).
5   Wolfgang Wittkowski, 'Octavio Piccolomini: Zur Schaffensweise des *Wallenstein*-Dichters', *Jahrbuch der Deutschen Schiller-Gesellschaft*, 5 (1961), 10–57 (p. 28). This still continues: see Nikolaus Immer, *Der inszenierte Held: Schillers dramenpoetische Anthropologie* (Heidelberg: Winter, 2008), pp. 338–41. Wittkowski develops his defence of Octavio in 'Höfische Intrige für die gute Sache: Marquis Posa und Octavio Piccolomini', in *Schiller und die höfische Welt*, ed. by Aurnhammer, Manger, and Strack, pp. 378–97.
6   Letter to Böttiger, 1 March 1799, quoted in *WB* IV, 701. On divergent views of Octavio, see Steffan Davies, *The Wallenstein Figure in German Literature and Historiography 1790–1920* (London: Maney, 2010), pp. 67–68.
7   Schiller, *The Robbers* and *Wallenstein*, p. 310.

> Zu folgen, doch darüber würde man
> Sich manchen guten Zweck versagen müssen.
> Hier gilts, mein Sohn, dem Kaiser wohl zu dienen,
> Das Herz mag dazu sprechen, wie es will. (*P* 2454–60)

> I split no hairs, I only do my duty,
> I carry out my Emperor's commands.
> Better indeed if we could always follow
> The promptings of our heart, but we must then
> Give up all hope in many a worthy purpose.
> Our place, my son, is here to serve the Emperor,
> Our hearts may say about it what they will.[8]

Octavio is neither amoral nor irreligious. He regrets the necessity for betrayal, and he affirms that he is not only serving the emperor, but subject to God: 'Ich stehe in der Allmacht Hand' (*P* 2514), 'The Almighty holds me in his hand'.[9] This simple and dignified declaration is practically the only affirmation of Christianity by any character in the play (unless one counts the comic figure of the ranting priest in *Wallensteins Lager*). The real, unscrupulous Machiavellians are Wallenstein and the Terzkys. Terzky opines: 'Denn nur vom Nutzen ist die Welt regiert' (*WT* 443); 'It is advantage rules the world's affairs',[10] and his wife dismisses morality as mere superstition (*WT* 539–41).[11]

Octavio is a conservative who supports established authority, on the grounds that even if it is faulty, the disorder resulting from its overthrow would be worse. Order is better than 'Willkür', the arbitrary authority which would arise in its place, and indirect and crooked means are justified to sustain it. For Schiller and his contemporaries, this was a highly pertinent argument, for the French Revolution had just overthrown a traditional authority, admittedly a dysfunctional one, and replaced it with tyranny, civil strife, arbitrary executions, and suffering on a massive scale.[12] To Octavio, abrupt political change is destructive, like the straight path of the cannonball; indirect methods correspond to the natural pathways gradually formed by rivers and valleys, which are the appropriate setting for human life:

> Mein Sohn! Laß uns die alten, engen Ordnungen
> Gering nicht achten! Köstlich unschätzbare
> Gewichte sind's, die der bedrängte Mensch
> An seiner Dränger raschen Willen band;
> Denn immer war die Willkür fürchterlich —
> Der Weg der Ordnung, ging er auch durch Krümmen,
> Er ist kein Umweg. (*P* 462–69)

> My son! Let us not look with scorn upon
> These ancient ordinances, narrow though they seem.

---

8   Ibid., p. 310.
9   Ibid., p. 312.
10   Ibid., p. 339.
11   Yvonne Nilges, *Schiller und das Recht* (Göttingen: Wallstein, 2012), pp. 277–80.
12   This suggests a response to the objection that 'Octavio is not dignified by the fact that he serves traditional authority, in fact his treachery undermines its moral claim': Lesley Sharpe, *Friedrich Schiller: Drama, Thought and Politics* (Cambridge: Cambridge University Press, 1991), p. 236.

> For they are precious, priceless: checks and weights
> That man oppressed can bind to hem the will
> And tyrant whim of those who might oppress him;
> For tyrant's will is always to be feared. –
> The paths of order, crooked though they seem,
> Lead surely to their goal.[13]

Schiller is here putting into Octavio's mouth a conservative argument, reminiscent of Edmund Burke, against the attempt to subject reality to an abstract political model — an error with which Posa was charged in the *Briefe über Don Karlos*.[14] Moreover, despite the shortcomings of the imperial leadership, its emissary, Questenberg, supports Octavio's conservative outlook by arguing that even warfare should be carried on according to principles of international law, and the subject should be protected from the depredations of the soldiery, whereas Wallenstein, as is clear from the *Lager*, allows his troops to reduce the rural population to beggary.[15]

Since Octavio's actions are based on principles, as opposed to theories, it is unjust to suggest (as even Max does, *WT* 1210) that he is motivated by hopes of self-advancement and material gain, even if the malicious Illo is right in saying he has long aspired to a princely title (*WT* 2765–66).[16] He is unmoved by Wallenstein's promise to give him the princedoms of Glatz and Sagan (*P* 2378–79: present-day Kładsko and Żagań, both now in Poland). To underline Octavio's integrity, Schiller has made this a better offer than the one the historical Ottavio received: he was only to have Glatz, whereas Galasso (Gallas) was promised Sagan and the duchy of Glogau (present-day Głogów).[17]

Still, Octavio's action remains bad, as he admits, despite his attempts to palliate it. Only it may have been slightly less bad than the alternatives. What, after all, were Octavio's options? He could have dismissed Wallenstein's plans as pipe-dreams, as some historians do.[18] However, these plans, even if they were merely fanciful (as Wallenstein himself suggests: 'In dem Gedanken bloß gefiel ich mir', *WT* 148), were described in Schiller's source as extremely drastic and circumstantial: Wallenstein spoke of exterminating the House of Austria and endowing his followers with territories all over Central Europe.[19] One could hardly ignore or dismiss such talk. Octavio could have tried to dissuade Wallenstein, and he did (*P* 2436–37), but again Schiller knew from his source that Wallenstein was inflexible: 'So ist er doch nichts desto weniger [i.e. despite Piccolomini's remonstrances] auff seinem vorhaben halßstarrig verblieben' ('So nevertheless he persisted stubbornly in

---

13   Schiller, *The Robbers* and *Wallenstein*, p. 235.
14   See the important discussion of this passage in Alt, *Schiller*, II, 449.
15   *P* 130–42, discussed by Nilges, *Schiller und das Recht*, p. 262.
16   See e.g. Dolf Sternberger, 'Macht und Herz oder der politische Held bei Schiller', in *Schiller: Reden im Gedenkjahr 1959*, ed. by Bernhard Zeller (Stuttgart: Klett, 1961), pp. 310–29 (p. 319).
17   *Alberti Fridlandi Perduellionis Chaos*, in *Die Hauptquellen zu Schillers Wallenstein*, ed. by Albert Leitzmann (Halle: Niemeyer, 1915), p. 28.
18   Golo Mann, *Wallenstein: His Life Narrated*, trans. by Charles Kessler (London: Deutsch, 1976), pp. 771–72.
19   See *Alberti Fridlandi Perduellionis Chaos*, in Leitzmann, *Die Hauptquellen*, pp. 26, 28.

his project').[20] Alternatively, Octavio could have done what Max thinks he should, and refused to have anything to do with such detestable plans. But had he done so, he would have had to break with Wallenstein. He would have lost any chance to influence Wallenstein, or (if that was hopeless) influence Wallenstein's followers. Finally, he could have said nothing, and avoided interfering in any way, which would have meant supporting Wallenstein by default. But that was no longer an option. Wallenstein's revelation of his plans merely confirmed the suspicions that Octavio and the imperial court already held.

Octavio's methods deserve a close look. When winning Wallenstein's officers back to their imperial allegiance, Octavio behaves with authority, confidence and shrewdness. His first victim, Isolani, is a fairly soft touch. The elderly colonel Buttler, as Octavio evidently expects, is a much harder case. He brusquely rebuffs all appeals to his loyalty to the emperor. Octavio then plays his winning card, but first he employs a standard trick used by policemen interviewing suspects (and by Lohenstein's Scipio): he lets Buttler leave the room in a confident mood, then calls him back, and asks him about his quest for the title of Count. This touches Buttler to the quick. Octavio plays on his resentment and his sense of inferiority. Then he shows Buttler a letter, purportedly from Wallenstein, which shows that, far from encouraging and supporting Buttler's aspirations, as Buttler has hitherto believed, Wallenstein dismissed them contemptuously. The effect is immediate. Buttler almost collapses, then responds tearfully to Octavio's assurances that the emperor will not only forgive his planned treachery but give him the title that Wallenstein denied him.

This episode is crucial for our judgement of Octavio. Something analogous appears in the historical record, but the victim of Wallenstein's disparagement was Christian Illow ('Illo' in the play).[21] May the alleged letter from Wallenstein be a forgery? How Octavio obtained it is left mysterious; he merely says that he has it 'by chance' (*WT* 1136), and one could be forgiven for finding this an inadequate explanation. After all, Wallenstein says that he never puts things in writing (*P* 854).[22] On the other hand, Wallenstein says this, and Terzky partially repeats it later (*WT* 68), in the context of negotiations with the Swedes, where he is anxious not to provide any written evidence that might incriminate him. Moreover, Wallenstein, showing an uncharacteristically tender conscience, talks later about an injustice he inflicted on Buttler: 'So hab ich diesem würdig braven Mann, | Dem Buttler, stilles Unrecht abzubitten' (*WT* 1448–49). ('And so I must atone for silent wrong | That I have done this brave and worthy Butler [sic]'.[23] This must refer to the letter; otherwise it is a blind motif with no explanation.[24] Wallenstein adds that he wrote

20 Ibid., p. 26.
21 For the sources, see Davies, *The Wallenstein Figure*, p. 39 and note.
22 William F. Mainland, *Schiller and the Changing Past* (London: Heinemann, 1957), p. 38.
23 Schiller, *The Robbers* and *Wallenstein*, p. 375.
24 Florian Krobb, *Die Wallenstein-Trilogie von Friedrich Schiller: Walter Buttler in Geschichte und Drama* (Oldenburg: Igel, 2005), p. 35. Davies, '"Du wagst es [...]"', gives a nuanced survey of written communication in Schiller's plays and argues that in the case of this letter, 'the audience cannot judge conclusively either way' (p. 525). He does not consider the passage about Wallenstein's feeling of guilt

the letter because for some inexplicable reason he always felt uneasy in Buttler's presence, as though he were receiving a supernatural warning (WT 1454–55). This illustrates how much Wallenstein's actions are motivated by superstition, as when he develops a blind confidence in Octavio because of a dream. In both instances he is of course utterly mistaken: Buttler has just come voluntarily to place his regiment at Wallenstein's disposal, but this is really part of the plot Buttler is now hatching to strengthen Wallenstein's trust as a prelude to murdering him. The balance of probability, therefore, exonerates Octavio from the charge of forgery.

However, this argument does not end the matter. When one reads the play at leisure, one can compare passages that are distant from one another in the text. In the theatre, however, one is under the spell of the actors' demeanour at each moment. One may not clearly remember what was said much earlier, and of course one cannot foresee what will be said later. It has been pointed out that in the Elizabethan theatre, where play-texts were not normally available, Shakespeare was able to get away with gross inconsistencies like that whereby Horatio in *Hamlet* is both a stranger to the Danish court, who needs to have affairs explained to him, and a native of Denmark who is better informed than the other characters.[25] This sleight of hand is permitted by the nature not just of Elizabethan drama, but of all drama, which moves too fast to allow the audience much time for reflection, and it enables Schiller as well as Shakespeare to mask inconsistencies and present some insufficiently motivated events.[26] So while a cool analysis of the text may exonerate Octavio, the impression created in the theatre may be different.

What about the charge that Octavio instigated the murder of Wallenstein? Here Schiller has departed significantly from history. The historical Ottavio Piccolomini, along with Galasso (Schiller's Gallas) and their associates, was ordered to fetch Wallenstein to Vienna, dead or alive. Octavio's commission is different: if Wallenstein refrains from treasonable actions, he will be quietly deprived of his command and sent into honourable exile on his estates (P 2526–30). Only if he undertakes unmistakable treason will he be condemned and outlawed ('verurteilt und geächtet', P 2500). The murder of Wallenstein is therefore no part of Octavio's plans.

However, the issue is again not quite clear-cut. By the time Octavio speaks to Buttler, matters have moved on. Wallenstein's messenger has been caught with clear written evidence of his treasonable dealings. So Octavio tells Buttler that Wallenstein has already been outlawed: 'Dies Manifest erklärt ihn in die Acht' (*WT* 1081). Hence when Buttler, shocked by the revelation that Wallenstein frustrated his chances of becoming a Count, exclaims 'O! er soll nicht leben!' (*WT* 1169) ('He

---

towards Buttler.

25   John Dover Wilson, *What Happens in Hamlet* (Cambridge: Cambridge University Press, 1935), pp. 229–37.

26   An example of inconsistency: in *P* II. 2 Wallenstein's wife reports on her recent experiences in Vienna; but we have already learnt that Max has just escorted her and Thekla from Carinthia (*P* I. 1. 31–32). Why should the Duchess travel from Vienna to Pilsen via Carinthia? Inadequate motivation: the excitement of Octavio's unexpected arrival at Eger immediately after Wallenstein's murder distracts us from wondering why he and the imperial troops have suddenly turned up (*WT* 3756).

shall not live!'),[27] Octavio *might* have foreseen that Buttler would act on his words.[28] But to take Buttler's words literally might also have meant over-interpreting an emotional outburst. To that extent Octavio is justified, when he learns of the murder, in saying: 'War das die Meinung, Buttler, als wir schieden?' (*WT* 3783) ('Was this intended, Butler, when we parted?'),[29] and in lamenting that Buttler has been precipitate in putting the emperor's intentions into practice, without waiting in case the emperor changes his mind (*WT* 3795–96). The diplomat, used to slow and indirect conduct, has been caught out by a soldier, a man of action, driven moreover by passion, who goes straight to his goal like the cannonball whose destructive effects Octavio evoked much earlier in conversation with Max (P 470).

Octavio therefore, almost through no fault of his own, is left in an invidious position. Buttler is not justified in his accusation: 'Ihr habt den Pfeil geschickt, | Ich hab ihn abgedrückt' (*WT* 3805–06): 'you forged the bolt, | I fired it'.[30] But appearances are against Octavio. He is a victim of what Wallenstein much earlier called the 'Doppelsinn des Lebens' (*WT* 161), 'life's ambiguity'.[31] He will not only seem complicit in Wallenstein's murder, but people will think that he has instigated it in order to gain the title of Prince, as Gordon implies by his reproachful glance at Octavio when handing him the Imperial letter addressed, as he emphasizes, to 'Dem *Fürsten* Piccolomini' (*WT* 3866), '*Prince* Piccolomini'. The title is devalued because of course he wanted it not just for himself but for his family. By this point in the play, Max, bitterly disillusioned by both his real and symbolic fathers, has sought and found death in battle. Now that Octavio has lost his only son, the title will die with him.

Octavio may therefore be seen as a modern tragic figure. He is not an exceptional person, and his experience does not culminate in any catharsis. As Prince Piccolomini, with no descendants, he will simply live on, unhappy in himself and unfairly maligned by the outside world — and by posterity.

27   Schiller, *The Robbers* and *Wallenstein*, p. 375.
28   Nilges, *Schiller und das Recht*, p. 283.
29   Schiller, *The Robbers* and *Wallenstein*, p. 469.
30   Ibid., p. 470.
31   Ibid., p. 329.

12

Schiller:
Maria Stuart (1801)

The more a ruler is concerned for the public good, the more justification he or she can claim for deploying the techniques of power known in early modern times as reason of state or 'Staatskunst'. Although most writers are too mealy-mouthed to admit it in theory, it is agreed in practice that bad means — means which are known to contravene strict morality — may be used to achieve desirable political ends. Such a policy, however, falls foul of the distinction drawn by Kant between 'Staatsklugheit', or expediency, and 'Staatsweisheit', in which political morality coincides with universal morality.[1] Schiller, in his *Geschichte des Abfalls der Niederlande*, distinguishes similarly between 'sieche gekünstelte Politik' and 'wahre Staatskunst' ('sickly artificial politics' and the 'true art of the state').[2] In the *Geschichte des Dreißigjährigen Kriegs* he calls the Treaty of Westphalia 'dieses mühsame, theure und dauernde Werk der Staatskunst' ('this laborious, precious, and enduring work of statecraft').[3]

In *Maria Stuart*, Schiller shows a modern state based on the rule of law and threatened by international terrorism. Elisabeth, one of the two queens who dominate the play, is a monarch who has actually tried to rule for her subjects' good and who now finds herself forced into an unpalatable decision. So long as Maria, with her claim to the English throne, remains a prisoner in England, security cannot be guaranteed, for emissaries from the Catholic powers on the Continent will try to set her free. In this situation, Schiller explores a range of possible responses. One is violent: to dispose of the inconvenient prisoner, either by having her secretly assassinated, or by a public execution which will please the populace at first but eventually alienate them from the monarch who has ordered this savage penalty. The other is to follow the laws: not only the law of the land, but the law of nations and of human rights. Schiller, with some anachronism, projects these concepts back onto Elizabethan England, and suggests a conception of politics which is forward-looking and takes account of the likely judgement of posterity.

Earlier in his career, Schiller shared the widespread Enlightenment conception of Britain as the land of freedom, and projected this conception back onto Elizabethan and earlier periods. His poem about the defeat of the Spanish Armada, 'Die unüberwindliche Flotte' (1785), alludes to Magna Carta.[4] In 1785 he published

1   'Zum ewigen Frieden', in Kant, *Werke*, vi, 233 and 240.
2   *WB* vi, 91.
3   *NA* xviii, 384.
4   *WB* i: Gedichte, ed. by Georg Kurscheidt (1992), p. 252.

in *Thalia* his own translation and adaptation of Louis-Sébastien Mercier's essay on Philip II of Spain, where Queen Elizabeth, as the 'Urheberin der Freiheit' (originator of freedom), provided a foil to Philip's tyranny.[5] And in *Don Karlos* Posa draws the same contrast when he tells Philip how refugees are flocking from Spain to England:

> Mit offnen Mutterarmen
> Empfängt die Fliehenden Elisabeth,
> Und fruchtbar blüht durch Künste dieses Landes
> Britannien. [...] (3172–75)

> With open mother's arms
> Elizabeth receives your refugees,
> And all the craftsmanship of your domains
> Is building England handsomely.[6]

In *Maria Stuart*, however, we encounter a different Elisabeth, or rather several different Elisabeths who are not easy to reconcile with one another. She is one more in his long succession of self-defeating Machiavellians. In public, she is a skilful dissimulator. In the scene where her counsellors give her conflicting advice about how to handle Maria, she plays one off against the other, rebuking Burleigh for his inhumanity and Shrewsbury for an apparent fondness for Maria which verges on disloyalty. Her Machiavellianism emerges fully in the scene where she is having a private conversation with Mortimer, the nephew of Sir Amias Paulet, who is in turn Maria's jailer. Having failed to suborn the staunch morality of the uncle, Elisabeth turns to the nephew and indicates that she would like her prisoner to be secretly murdered. She laments that if she orders Maria to be executed, all the odium of the deed will fall on her. Mortimer asks why she need worry about a bad appearance when her cause is good; Elisabeth gives a reply that is taken almost verbatim from Machiavelli:

> Ihr kennt die Welt nicht, Ritter. Was man *scheint*,
> Hat jedermann zum Richter, was man *ist*, hat keinen. (1601–02)

> You do not know the world. Appearance, sir,
> Is judged by every man, and truth by none.[7]

Here Schiller is putting into Elisabeth's mouth some of Machiavelli's most notorious words:

> [M]ost men judge more by their eyes than by their hands. For everyone is capable of seeing you, but few can touch you. Everyone can see what you appear to be, whereas few have direct experience of what you really are; and those few will not dare to challenge the popular view, sustained as it is by the majesty of the ruler's position. (P XVIII. 63)[8]

This exchange also illustrates a feature of Schiller's treatment of political Machia-

5   *WB* VI, 20.
6   *Don Carlos*, trans. by Sy-quia and Oswald, p. 115. I have modified the translation because Sy-quia and Oswald misread 'fruchtbar' as 'furchtbar' ('fearfully').
7   *Mary Stuart*, in *Five German Tragedies*, p. 238.
8   The echo of Machiavelli is pointed out by Mainland, *Schiller and the Changing Past*, pp. 69–70.

vellianism. As we have seen with Wallenstein, the schemer is never quite as much in control as he or she thinks. Elisabeth has just complimented Mortimer on the duplicity with which, as she supposes, he has used his time in France to nose out the plots her enemies are contriving against her. Although she thinks she is rebuking Mortimer's naivety, she does not realize that in this world of plot and counter-plot, intrigue and counter-intrigue, Mortimer is one step ahead of her, for he is in fact a double agent, having converted to Catholicism at Rome and conceived a quasi-religious devotion to Maria which is encouraged by Maria's powerful relatives in the Guise family. He is intent on setting Maria free, whatever bloodshed the attempt may cost. So what may have seemed to Elisabeth a masterstroke of intrigue turns out to be a monumental blunder. The secret plotting that in Lohenstein was part of the normal process of rule is presented by Schiller as both morally and pragmatically mistaken, and even given a tinge of farce.

Moreover, the Machiavellian who believes himself or herself to be a coolly rational manipulator is all the more likely to be swayed by unacknowledged emotions. Schiller has invented a plot twist whereby Maria and Elisabeth were formerly both in love with the courtier Leicester. Maria relies on Leicester to get her out of prison by obtaining a personal interview with Elisabeth, but Elisabeth takes the opportunity to humiliate her defeated rival in a way that provokes Maria to fury, and that has even been called devilish.[9] When Elisabeth is hesitating whether to sign Maria's death warrant, she is pushed into a final and fatal decision by the memory of how Maria, turning the tables, humiliated *her* in Leicester's presence. That Elisabeth should condemn Maria to death for such a petty motive may be thought disparaging not just to her, but to all women, or to all women politicians; but most of the male politicians in the play are hardly more cool-headed, and it should be understood as indicating that self-styled Machiavellians deceive themselves more effectively than they deceive others.

Elisabeth is represented not as an absolute ruler who claims divine right, but as a constitutional monarch whose position depends on being seen to uphold the law. When one of Mortimer's companions tries to assassinate her and nearly succeeds, the pressure to have Maria executed becomes irresistible, but Elisabeth knows that an obvious act of judicial murder will satisfy popular demand in the short term but, in the longer term, destroy the public's trust in her. Hence Elisabeth laments in soliloquy:

> Warum hab ich Gerechtigkeit geübt,
> Willkür gehaßt mein Leben lang, daß ich
> Für diese erste unvermeidliche
> Gewalttat selbst die Hände mir gefesselt! (3200–03)

> Why have I heeded all my life the voice
> Of justice, scorned the act of tyranny,
> Only to find that when I can no longer
> Abstain from violence my hands are bound?[10]

---

9   Ludwig Börne, '*Maria Stuart*. Trauerspiel von Schiller' (theatre review, 1818), in his *Sämtliche Schriften*, ed. by Inge and Peter Rippmann, 5 vols (Dreieich: Melzer, 1977), I, 410–14 (p. 413).
10   *Five German Tragedies*, p. 290.

This is hypocritical, since she has tried to have Maria murdered and since, as we shall see, she violated justice in having Maria imprisoned in the first place, but it does underline the limits on her power. She knows that she is dependent on popular support and cannot resort to tyranny like that of her predecessor on the throne, Queen Mary, who had heretics burnt alive. Her rule is a definite improvement on that of Catholic autocrats like Mary or Philip II. But since she is not an autocrat, she has to court the favour of a public whom she despises:

> Die Meinung muß ich ehren, um das Lob
> Der Menge buhlen, einem Pöbel muß ichs
> Recht machen, dem der Gaukler nur gefällt. (3194–96)

> I must conciliate their wishes, seek
> Their praise with flattery, and please a mob
> Only a mountebank will satisfy.[11]

Within these constraints, Elisabeth has to deal with a terrorist threat whose reality is brought home to us when one of Mortimer's lieutenants tries to assassinate her. Moreover, as the play repeatedly reminds us, Mortimer's is only the latest in a succession of plots to free Mary, kill Elisabeth, invade England, and restore the Catholic faith. These are recounted in Schiller's most important source, William Robertson's *History of Scotland*. Two of them involved the Duke of Norfolk, who had hopes of marrying Mary. He fomented a Catholic rising in the North of England in 1569, but when it was revealed to the Queen, she sent Norfolk to the Tower for over nine months, whereupon he promised not to communicate any more with Mary.[12] Norfolk is the clearest historical prototype for the dramatic figure of Leicester who vacillates between the two women. Norfolk broke his promise, and in 1571 entered into the Ridolfi plot for a Catholic uprising with 10,000 troops led by the Duke of Alva; this conspiracy was planned by John Leslie, the Bishop of Ross (also mentioned by Schiller), but it was betrayed, and Norfolk was executed for high treason in 1572. This provided, as Robertson says,

> the clearest evidence that Mary, from resentment of the wrongs she had suffered, and impatience of the captivity in which she was held, would not scruple to engage in the most hostile and desperate enterprises against the established government and religion.[13]

The 1580s saw attempted risings in the West of Ireland, the single-handed attempt on Elizabeth's life by William Parry, and the conspiracy revealed by Francis Throckmorton, who in 1584 confessed under torture that he had secretly corresponded with Mary and that the Duke of Guise was planning to invade England with the

11   Ibid., p. 290.
12   William Robertson, *History of Scotland during the Reigns of Queen Mary and of James VI*, 2 vols (1759; 1794 edition reprinted, London: Routledge/Thoemmes Press, 1996), I, 524. For an excellent survey of Schiller's dealings with his historical sources, see William Witte, 'Schiller's *Maria Stuart* and Mary, Queen of Scots', in *Stoffe, Formen, Strukturen: Studien zur deutschen Literatur, Hans Heinrich Borcherdt zum 75. Geburtstag*, ed. by Albert Fuchs and Helmut Motekat (Munich: Hueber, 1962), pp. 238–50.
13   Robertson, *History of Scotland*, II, 30.

financial support of the Pope and the King of Spain. The previous Pope, Pius V, had excommunicated Elizabeth in 1570. His successor, Gregory XIII, gave Parry a plenary indulgence for his intended assassination of Elizabeth and is reported as declaring that to 'send' the excommunicated Elizabeth 'out of the world' would be a meritorious action, requiring no penance — a view not supported by canon law.[14] This plenary indulgence, reported by Robertson, is expanded by Schiller into the absolution granted in advance to Mortimer and his gang for all murders they may commit in trying to free Maria, while the would-be lone assassin Parry provides the model for the Barnabite monk who in the play tries to murder Elisabeth. All this justifies Burleigh's description of Maria as 'Die *Ate* [goddess of strife] dieses ewgen Kriegs, die mit | Der Liebesfackel dieses Reich entzündet' (1281–82; '[T]he Ate of this endless war, | Who sets this realm on fire with brands of love').[15]

No wonder then that the Babington plot, emphasized by Schiller, should be seen as the latest in a series of conspiracies in which Maria is involved.[16] Historically, it was in part a sting mounted by Francis Walsingham, Elizabeth's spymaster. He succeeded in turning round a Catholic emissary, Gilbert Gifford, who henceforth provided him with all Mary's correspondence. Before long another plot arose. A priest at Rheims persuaded the Spanish ambassador in Paris to arrange an invasion of England, and for this purpose engaged Anthony Babington, with eleven other associates, to murder Elizabeth and rescue Mary. Walsingham, using not only Gifford but another mole whom he had introduced among the plotters, allowed the plot to develop, then informed Elizabeth and had the conspirators arrested and executed. Mary was put on trial for complicity, the evidence against her being her correspondence with Babington. Robertson takes her side, asking why the originals of the letters were never produced and why she was not confronted with the witnesses against her, her secretaries Curle and Nau. The first question invites the answer that since the letters had been turned into cipher, it was not likely that anyone would preserve the originals. The second question is answered by David Hume in his *History of England*, another intertext used by Schiller (the relevant volume first appeared in 1759, the same year as Robertson's *History of Scotland*), in which he points out that in the sixteenth century it was not legally required, and unusual in practice, for a defendant to meet his or her accusers.[17] Modern historians think Mary's complicity in the Babington plot beyond doubt.[18] Schiller, however, enlarging on Robertson's defence, has the letters revealed as forgeries, and allows

14 Arnold Oskar Meyer, *England and the Catholic Church under Queen Elizabeth*, trans. by J. R. McKee, reissued with introduction by John Bossy (London: Routledge & Kegan Paul, 1967), p. 271.
15 *Five German Tragedies*, p. 229.
16 The conspirators Norfolk, Parry, Tichborn, and Babington are all mentioned in the play (the last-named eleven times): see Nikolaus Immer, 'Die schuldig-unschuldigen Königinnen: Zur kontrastiven Gestaltung von Maria und Elisabeth in Schillers *Maria Stuart*', *Euphorion*, 99 (2005), 129–52 (p. 136).
17 David Hume, *The History of England from the Invasion of Julius Caesar to the Revolution in 1688*, 6 vols (London: Cadell, 1778; repr. Indianapolis: Liberty Classics, 1984), IV, 235.
18 See Jenny Wormald, *Mary Queen of Scots: A Study in Failure* (London: George Philip, 1988), p. 186; John Guy, *My Heart is my Own: The Life of Mary Queen of Scots* (London: HarperCollins, 2004), pp. 482–84.

Maria to repeat under the seal of the confessional that although she has asked foreign princes to rescue her she has never sought Elisabeth's death.

Although Schiller has palliated the situation by detaching Maria from the Babington conspiracy, he shows that Elisabeth's position, and that of her country, is still highly precarious, and will remain so as long as Maria is in captivity. As an alternative to Machiavellian intrigue, Schiller proposes the rule of law. In the same spirit, Herder, after his account of Machiavelli, says that the politics of intrigue, whether advocated by Machiavelli or by the Jesuits, are now obsolete, and gives a eulogy of the founder of international law, Hugo Grotius: 'You failed to unite the religions, as you wished; but you united the principles of humanity, and one day nations will subscribe to them.'[19] Elisabeth is flanked by two advisers, Burleigh and Shrewsbury, whose contrasting counsels somewhat resemble those of the less fully developed figures Agrippa and Maecenas in Lohenstein's *Cleopatra*. Both Burleigh and Shrewsbury appeal to the law, and thus differ from Elisabeth's third adviser, Leicester, who is an advocate of reason of state. When speaking in a public assembly, Leicester says, one may support the law, but in private conversation the only consideration is political advantage ('Vorteil', 2441).

Burleigh and Shrewsbury appeal to the law in very different ways. Burleigh argues with furious vehemence that Maria must be executed in order to end the threat of constant conspiracies. To drive home his message, he presents Elisabeth with a stark choice between black and white: 'Ihr Leben ist dein Tod! Ihr Tod dein Leben!' (1294). He can appeal to the fact that Parliament has found Maria guilty of involvement in the Babington conspiracy, so that the execution would be an act of justice and not of tyranny. Shrewsbury's counter-arguments do not engage with Burleigh's; he argues rather that the execution of Maria, since she is Elisabeth's equal, not her subject, would be an illegal act, even though Parliament has sanctioned it. Where Burleigh argues from the present emergency, Shrewsbury appeals to the future:

> England ist nicht die Welt, dein Parlament
> Nicht der Verein der menschlichen Geschlechter,
> Dies heutge England ist das künftge nicht,
> Wie's das vergangne nicht mehr ist [...] (1524–27)

> England is not the world, your Parliament
> Not the assembly of humanity,
> England today is not what she will be
> In future years [...][20]

The cosmopolitan outlook that Schiller reveals here is linked to his reading of international law. While working on his history of the Dutch Revolt he had read the work of Grotius, including *De jure belli et pacis* (1625), which from then on assumed an importance in his work that Yvonne Nilges has recently explored. Often, as Nilges shows, international law is present only by its absence. In the *Geschichte des Dreißigjährigen Krieges* the Swedish troops under Gustav Adolf conduct war in

19   Herder, *Werke*, VII, 343.
20   *Five German Tragedies*, p. 230.

an orderly fashion without oppressing civilians, but the imperial troops rage as savagely as did the troops which the Duke of Alva led into the Netherlands.[21] In *Maria Stuart*, Maria's attendant Hanna Kennedy complains that Maria's treatment is 'wider Völkerrecht und Königswürde' (90);[22] Maria accuses Elisabeth of ignoring 'des Gastrechts heilige Gesetze, | Der Völker heilig Recht' (2299–300).[23] As a refugee, she was entitled to asylum, and as a queen, she was entitled to dignified treatment. Grotius had laid down the principle that 'personae regis parcendum [est]', the monarch's person must be spared.[24] Not only is Maria imprisoned, but her room is searched and her few remaining possessions are taken from her. These privations are considerably worse than those suffered by the historical Mary, who was allowed to have 'five cartloads and four horse-loads of clothes and personal effects' sent from Scotland, and who, during the fifteen years she spent in Shrewsbury's custody, was allowed many luxuries and occasional visits to the spa at Buxton.[25] The treatment of Maria in the play was suggested by a much more recent event, the imprisonment of Marie Antoinette, and Maria's trial before forty-two commissioners reflects that of Louis XVI.[26]

Maria complains not only that the court was not entitled to try her, but also that its procedures were faulty at every point: she had no advocate, she was not shown the originals of the documents that were supposed to incriminate her, Babington was executed before she could challenge him on his testimony, and she was not confronted with the still living witnesses Kurl and Nau. She adds that a law has been passed specially in order to condemn her: this is the 'Act for the Security of the Queen's Royal Person', which provides that disorders intended to support any person's claim to the throne shall make that person liable to the death penalty.[27] Here law is a mere mask for arbitrary victimization. Her complaints receive no proper answer. It is clear that the law, which could and should be a means of obtaining justice, has been bent on grounds of reason of state.

However, although international law is violated, and the law of the land is manipulated for political ends, Schiller's references to them remind us that international and civil law can also be upheld, and that ultimately they offer a better safeguard against terrorist threats than the underhand intriguing to which Elisabeth resorts or the kangaroo court which is set up to try Maria. Here Schiller's technique of controlled anachronism reveals its purpose. The international law to which Maria appeals did not yet exist in the sixteenth century; Grotius would write only some decades later. Shrewsbury similarly refers to the future, indicating that what seemed legal in the sixteenth century will come to be condemned by future generations who have a better and fairer understanding of legal procedures. It is essential to Schiller's

---

21 Nilges, *Schiller und das Recht*, pp. 102, 146–47.
22 'Against the laws of nations and against | The dignity of kings' (*Five German Tragedies*, p. 195).
23 'the sacred laws | of hospitality and [...] the rights of nations' (*Five German Tragedies*, p. 260).
24 Nilges, *Schiller und das Recht*, p. 295.
25 Guy, *My Heart is my Own*, pp. 437–49 (quotation from p. 439).
26 Peter-André Alt, *Klassische Endspiele: Das Theater Goethes und Schillers* (Munich: Beck, 2008), pp. 143–44; Nilges, *Schiller und das Recht*, pp. 306–07.
27 Nilges, *Schiller und das Recht*, p. 301.

conception of the law that it should be capable of development and self-correction. In his lecture *Die Gesetzgebung des Lykurgus und Solon* (*The Legislation of Lycurgus and Solon*) (1790) Schiller contrasted the legal and political constitutions which the two legislators, according to Plutarch, drew up for Sparta and Athens respectively. The basic contrast is that Lycurgus's constitution confined the Spartans' activities within narrow limits for all future time with no possibility of development or innovation, whereas Solon, though his legislation was not flawless, went on the principle that the laws should allow the citizens to advance and improve in unpredictable ways; from which it follows that the laws themselves cannot be immutable but must be changed according to the changing needs of the citizens. Schiller returns here to the word 'Staatskunst' and commends Solon for initiating the best kind of politics:

> Bewundernswert bleibt mir immer der Geist, der den Solon bei seiner Gesetzgebung beseelte, der Geist der *gesunden* und *echten* Staatskunst, die das Grundprinzipium, worauf alle Staaten ruhen müssen, nie aus den Augen verlor: sich selbst die Gesetze zu geben, denen man gehorchen soll, und die Pflichten des Bürgers aus Einsicht und aus Liebe zum Vaterland, nicht aus sklavischer Furcht vor der Strafe, nicht aus blinder und schlaffer Ergebung in den Willen eines Obern zu erfüllen.[28]

> I still find admirable the spirit that animated Solon in his legislation, the spirit of *sound* and *genuine* politics, which never lost sight of the basic principle on which all states must rest: to give oneself the laws that one must obey, and to fulfil the citizen's duties out of understanding and patriotism, not out of servile fear of punishment, not out of blind and sluggish submission to the will of a superior.

The 'Staatskunst' of a far-sighted legislator is therefore quite different from the 'Staatskunst' practised by Octavio Piccolomini and denounced by Max. Octavio regarded Wallenstein as a known quantity, somebody who could not be reasoned with, but rather an enemy who must be manipulated and sidelined. The point of Solon's legislation is that people are not known quantities but capable of change, development, and improvement in ways that cannot be foreseen, so that 'Staatskunst' must allow not only for their present condition but also for their future potential. Similarly, the 'moral politician' envisaged by Kant considers not only what people are now but what they may become.

Elisabeth, whatever may be said in mitigation, remains a political moralist, and her moral dilemma centres on the issue of the necessary crime. The judicial murder of Maria appears necessary, because her presence in England does attract terrorists who, judging by Mortimer's example, are more dangerous than can easily be foreseen, and whose existence serves to demonstrate the truth of Burleigh's arguments for having Maria executed. The truth, but not the whole truth: Shrewsbury's standpoint is humane, future-oriented, and also pragmatic. He points out that the political necessity to which Burleigh appeals serves Elisabeth as an excuse for failing to use her free will. The morally right course is to exercise

28 *WB* VI, 505–06.

humanity by sparing Maria's life. Though he does not draw the conclusion in so many words, he implies that this solution is also the best pragmatically, because it will strengthen the affection of Elisabeth's subjects, whereas having Maria executed will look tyrannical and make her less unpopular (and therefore even more exposed to terrorist attacks). The execution of Maria is shown to be a crime, and though there are arguments in its favour, it is not truly necessary.

However, Maria is executed, and Elisabeth shabbily tries to push the responsibility onto the unfortunate courtier Davison (as her historical counterpart did). Her inner discomfort is revealed by her treatment of Burleigh. Expecting gratitude for having disposed of Maria, he finds himself rebuked for his haste in using the death warrant Davison gave him, instead of giving Elisabeth time to exercise clemency, and he is banished perpetually from her presence. It is not a bold conjecture that in this monstrous display of hypocrisy she is also getting rid of a powerful politician whose abrasive manner has long grated on her. But she then suffers a shock when, having turned instead to the mild and congenial Shrewsbury, she finds him refusing the dangerous office of her principal counsellor, ostensibly on grounds of age, but really because he does not want to serve a monarch who has entered on a moral decline. 'Ich habe deinen edlern Teil | Nicht retten können' (4027–28; 'I could not save your nobler self').[29] Thus abandoned, Elisabeth sends for her favourite Leicester, hoping for emotional support from him, but learns that he has taken ship for France. This is the consequence of her own action. Suspecting him of an intrigue with Maria, she compelled him to oversee and witness Maria's execution, in an extraordinary act of emotional sadism.[30] Leicester is now a broken man and has gone into voluntary exile, leaving her obliged to exercise self-control over her own hollowness. Several nineteenth-century dramatists will explore the situation where a political crime seems necessary, and they will sometimes come to a conclusion different from the one strongly suggested by Schiller.

It may be asked whether Schiller's last completed drama, *Wilhelm Tell* (1804), centres on a 'necessary crime'. The 'crime' in question would be Tell's assassination of the tyrannical Swiss governor Gessler, who previously commanded Tell to endanger his son's life by shooting an arrow off the boy's head. Afterwards, the nephew of the Emperor, Johannes, who has earned the sobriquet Parricida by assassinating his uncle, seeks refuge with Tell and claims that their deeds are similar. Tell indignantly denies any similarity:

> Unglücklicher!
> Darfst du der Ehrsucht blutge Schuld vermengen
> Mit der gerechten Notwehr eines Vaters?[31]
>
> [Wretch, you confound your selfish, bloody deed
> With a just father's act of self-defence?][32]

---

29   *Five German Tragedies*, p. 318.

30   On the emotional cruelty that is surprisingly frequent in Schiller's plays, see Karl S. Guthke, 'Schiller und das Theater der Grausamkeit', *Euphorion*, 99 (2005), 7–50.

31   *Wilhelm Tell*, ll. 3174–76, in *WB* v, 501.

32   *Wilhelm Tell*, trans. by Francis Lamport (London: Libris, 2005), p. 132. I am grateful to the late Nicholas Jacobs for giving me a copy of this book.

It has been argued that Tell is on shaky ground here; that his assassination of Gessler is not an action committed spontaneously in self-defence, but a planned act of revenge; that the severity of his response betrays his insecurity about a deed which, after all, he earlier described as 'murder' (2621, 2654); and that his silence at the end of the play confirms his unease.[33] On the other hand, Schiller told the theatre director August Wilhelm Iffland that the play's tendency was 'unschuldig und rechtlich' (innocent and legal). The Parricida scene showed 'das Notwendige und Rechtliche der Selbsthilfe in einem streng bestimmten Fall', 'the necessity of taking the law into one's own hands in a strictly defined case'.[34] Tell's act was not directly political in motivation; it was prompted by the tyrant's potentially murderous intrusion into his domestic sphere. He does it to protect his children:

> Und doch an *euch* nur denkt er [sc. Tell], lieben Kinder,
> Auch jetzt — Euch zu verteidgen, eure holde Unschuld
> Zu schützen vor der Rache des Tyrannen,
> Will er zum Morde jetzt der Bogen spannen! (2631–34)

> [And yet, dear children, it is you he thinks of,
> You, even now — to shield your innocence,
> That vengeful tyrant never more shall harm,
> For that he will raise up his murderous arm.][35]

But since Gessler's behaviour had implications for the nation as a whole, Tell acknowledges that his act was political. On returning home, he tells his wife that his hand 'Hat euch verteidigt und das Land gerettet' (3143; 'Defended you and saved our country's freedom').[36] His act is therefore a classic case of tyrannicide.[37] Although tyrannicide had famous classical exemplars, it was denounced under early modern European absolutism, which considered the person of a monarch sacred and king-killing or monarchomachy the worst of crimes. Absolutists could appeal to St Paul's assertion that 'the powers that be are ordained of God' (Romans 13. 1). Both Luther and Kant demanded unqualified submission to authority.[38] Tell, however, acts under the most extreme provocation, and initially at least for personal reasons. This distinguishes him from the French revolutionaries whom Schiller detested for their execution of Louis XVI: he described them as 'diese elenden Schindersknechte' (wretched butchers).[39] It also makes his case, as Schiller insisted to Iffland, a very specific one, from which no general conclusions should

---

33   These objections are critically reviewed in F. J. Lamport, 'The Silence of Wilhelm Tell', *Modern Language Review*, 76 (1981), 857–68 (p. 859); a strong but not, I think, convincing case against Tell has since been made by Guthke, *Schillers Dramen*, pp. 279–304.

34   Quoted in Lamport, 'The Silence', p. 866.

35   *Wilhelm Tell*, trans. by Lamport, p. 108.

36   Ibid., p. 131.

37   See Müller-Seidel, *Friedrich Schiller und die Politik*, pp. 192–203; Nilges, *Schiller und das Recht*, pp. 343–45.

38   For Luther, see Skinner, *Foundations*, II, 18–19; Kant, *Die Metaphysik der Sitten* (1797), in *Werke*, ed. by Weischedel, IV (1956), 439, and *Über den Gemeinspruch: Das mag in der Theorie richtig sein, taugt aber nicht für die Praxis*, ibid., VI (1964), 156.

39   Letter to Christian Gottfried Körner, 8 February 1793, *NA* XXVI, 183.

be drawn. Finally, therefore, Tell's assassination of Gessler is not a crime, and thus differs widely from the judicial murder which Maria Stuart suffers on grounds of reason of state.

13

Kleist:
Machiavelli through Rousseau

The erratic, tormented, often impoverished life led by Heinrich von Kleist (1778–1811) can be seen as having two fixed points: Prussia and Napoleon. The Kleist family was an extensive and distinguished branch of the Prussian nobility. It included the once famous poet Ewald von Kleist (1715–59), who died in the Battle of Kunersdorf in the Seven Years War, and would include Ewald von Kleist-Schmerzin (1890–1945), a lawyer executed for his part in the 20 July plot against Hitler, and Field-Marshal Paul Ludwig Ewald von Kleist (1881–1954), who was dismissed for disagreeing with Hitler's military strategy and died in Soviet captivity.

For young nobles like Heinrich von Kleist, entering the Prussian army was a matter of course. He joined as a corporal at the age of fourteen in June 1792 and attained full officer status in March 1797.[1] However, he came to feel that military discipline was a soulless, mechanical tyranny:

> The greatest wonders of military discipline, which were the object of astonishment to all who knew them, became the object of my most heartfelt contempt; I considered the officers as so many drill-sergeants, the soldiers as so many slaves, and when the whole regiment displayed its skills, it seemed to me a living monument of tyranny.[2]

In 1799 Kleist was granted permission to leave the army in order to study. His studies at the university of his birthplace, Frankfurt an der Oder, which included law, mathematics, and physics, lasted only a year and did not help him to find a material basis for pursuing his literary ambitions. His first play, *Die Familie Schroffen-stein*, was published anonymously in 1803. An ambitious tragedy on the charismatic medieval leader Robert Guiscard, perhaps suggested by the figure of Napoleon, proved impossible to complete satisfactorily, and Kleist burned it.[3] In October 1803 we find him at Saint-Omer, on the English Channel, seeking to join the army that

1   Biographical details from Gerhard Schulz, *Kleist: Eine Biographie* (Munich: Beck, 2007).
2   Letter to Christian Ernst Martini (his former tutor), 19 March 1799, in Heinrich von Kleist, *Sämtliche Werke und Briefe*, ed. by Ilse-Maria Barth and others, 4 vols (Frankfurt a.M.: Deutscher Klassiker Verlag, 1989), IV, 27. This edition is henceforth cited as *SWB*.
3   Kleist reconstructed ten scenes and published them in his journal *Phöbus* in 1808. A connection has been suggested between Guiscard, whose troops outside Constantinople are afflicted by plague, and Napoleon, whose army outside Jaffa suffered from plague in March 1799: Dirk Grathoff, 'Heinrich von Kleist und Napoleon Bonaparte', in his *Kleist: Geschichte, Politik, Sprache* (Opladen: Westdeutscher Verlag, 1999), pp. 175–98 (pp. 181–82).

Napoleon had assembled to invade Britain — not, as he assured his sister Ulrike, one of his main confidantes, out of any sympathy for the French cause, but in the despairing search for a soldierly death in battle.[4] However, he was rejected. Back in Berlin, he explained this dubious escapade as an attempt to distract himself from his headaches, and in January 1805 he obtained a civil service post under the intelligent and sympathetic minister Altenstein.[5]

It was not long, however, before Napoleon's attention turned to Prussia. After losing the battles of Jena and Auerstedt in 1806, Prussia collapsed as a military power. Kleist expressed his horror in a letter to his sister on 24 October 1806: 'It would be terrible if this tyrant [Wütherich] established his empire. Only a very small part of mankind realizes how pernicious it is to come under his rule. We are the subjugated nations of the Romans.'[6]

In the plays, stories, and political essays which Kleist completed in the remaining few years of his life, prominent themes include power, resistance, and statecraft. Resistance to foreign rule is a recurrent topic. In *Penthesilea* (written 1807, published 1808) the Amazon state is said to have originated in armed resistance to the foreign tyranny of the Ethiopians, and to illustrate the general truth that tyranny will be overthrown once it becomes intolerable:

> Doch Alles schüttelt, was ihm unerträglich,
> Der Mensch von seinen Schultern sträubend ab;
> Den Druck nur mäß'ger Leiden duldet er. (1934–36)

> But what is not to be endured, we shake
> Its weight with fearful struggle from our shoulders;
> Only a lesser suffering we bear.[7]

The story *Die Verlobung in St. Domingo* (published 1811), though rich in ambivalence, shows considerable sympathy for the Black resistance to French colonial rule in Santo Domingo in 1803. *Die Herrmannsschlacht* (written 1808–09) stages the ancient Germans' resistance to the Romans; and Kleist's last play, *Prinz Friedrich von Homburg*, adapts an episode from Prussian history to explore internal power structures in the context of resistance to invasion by the Swedes. In these resistance struggles, what role is played by Machiavellianism?

Although it is doubtful whether Kleist ever read Machiavelli, in his writings two versions of Machiavelli can be discerned. Given Machiavelli's reputation, one did not need to have read him in order to know that Machiavellianism was shorthand for a strictly pragmatic conduct of politics. The article 'Machiavélisme' in the *Encyclopédie*, written by Diderot, defined it as: 'espece [sic] de politique détestable qu'on peut rendre en deux mots, par l'art de tyranniser, dont Machiavel le florentin a répandu les principes dans ses ouvrages' ('a detestable kind of politics which can be summed up as the art of tyranny, and whose principles were spread by Machiavelli

---

4   Letter to Ulrike von Kleist, 26 October 1803, *SWB* IV, 321.
5   Karl Sigismund Franz Freiherr von Stein zum Altenstein (1770–1840), not to be confused with Heinrich Friedrich Karl Freiherr von und zum Stein (1757–1831) whom we shall meet later as 'Stein'. For the headache story, see letter to Ulrike von Kleist, 24 June 1804, *SWB* IV, 323.
6   *SWB* IV, 364.
7   *Five German Tragedies*, p. 384.

the Florentine in his works').[8] It is a commonplace of Kleist criticism that several of his main characters, including some presented as heroes, are unscrupulous Machiavellians.[9]

The other Machiavelli present in Kleist's writings is the analyst and historian of republicanism. Kleist's reception of the republican Machiavelli was probably indirect, via Rousseau. He read Rousseau at an early age and accepted the critique of society by the standards of nature given in the two Discourses. In *Die Familie Schroffenstein*, two families who once lived in Rousseauesque harmony have become estranged by property, thanks to an agreement about inheritance ('Erbvertrag'); when Eustache appeals to nature, Rupert replies that nature is a mere 'fairy-tale for children' ('Märchen der Kindheit', 40–50); the 'Erbvertrag' is the apple for whose sake they have lost Paradise (184–86). Kleist promised Wilhelmine von Zenge, to whom he was engaged from early 1800 to May 1802, that he would give her Rousseau's complete works and tell her the order in which she should read them.[10] He took his desire for a Rousseauesque simple life so far that he wanted to become literally a farmer, and in 1802 attempted an idyllic solitary existence on the island of Delosea in Lake Thun in Switzerland.[11] In *Das Erdbeben in Chili* (1807), however, the Rousseauesque ideal is balanced pessimistically against the apparently irremediable corruption produced by civilization. As survivors of the earthquake gather in a valley outside the city, all social differences seem annulled, but on returning to the city the characters encounter the evil influence of a preacher whipping up a fanatical mob.

Rousseau wrote of Machiavelli in *The Social Contract*: 'He professed to teach kings; but it was the people he really taught. His *Prince* is the book of Republicans.'[12] Especially in his first Discourse (1750), Rousseau idealized simple, cohesive societies, such as ancient Sparta and modern Switzerland, which were held together by the citizens' shared commitment to self-defence. In portraying a militarized nation, he recalls Machiavelli's conception of a self-reliant citizen body which has no need to employ mercenary troops; Machiavelli even mentions the Swiss as a present-day example of such a body (*P* XII. 44). Rousseau provides other examples which are significant for Kleist:

> Such were the Scythians, of whom wonderful eulogies have come down to us. Such were the Germans, whose simplicity, innocence, and virtue afforded a most delightful contrast to the pen of an historian, weary of describing the baseness and villainies of an enlightened, opulent, and voluptuous nation.[13]

8   *Encyclopédie*, IX, 793.
9   See e.g. William C. Reeve, *In Pursuit of Power: Heinrich von Kleist's Machiavellian Protagonists* (Toronto: University of Toronto Press, 1987); Schulz, *Kleist*, p. 415; Ingo Breuer (ed.), *Kleist-Handbuch* (Stuttgart and Weimar: Metzler, 2009), pp. 242, 262; Peter Philipp Riedl, 'Texturen des Terrors: Politische Gewalt im Werk Heinrich von Kleists', *Publications of the English Goethe Society*, 78 (2009), 32–46 (p. 40).
10   Letter to Wilhelmine von Zenge, 22 March 1801, *SWB* IV, 203. For the end of their engagement, see his final letter to her, 20 May 1802, *SWB* IV, 308–09.
11   For his wish to buy a farm and become 'im eigentlichsten Verstand ein *Bauer*', see his letter to Wilhelmine, October 1801, *SWB* IV, 275.
12   Rousseau, *The Social Contract and the Discourses*, p. 242.
13   Rousseau, 'A Discourse on the Moral Effects of the Arts and Sciences', ibid., pp. 1–29 (pp. 9–10).

The Amazons in *Penthesilea* are Scythians. They come from 'the Scythian forests' (17). Ancient authorities locate the Amazons in Asia and their capital, Themiscyra, on the Black Sea.[14] Kleist's text contains several, mostly inconspicuous references to Central Asia. The first Amazon queen, Tanaïs, bears the name given in ancient times to the river Don; the names of Penthesilea's dogs (1425–26) include Hyrkaon (suggesting Hyrcania, a region corresponding to modern Iran and Turkmenistan) and Oxus (the ancient name of the river now called the Amu Darya). After killing their male oppressors, we are told, the Amazons, in a version of Rousseau's social contract, set up a state of free and autonomous women:

> Ein Staat, ein mündiger, sei aufgestellt,
> Ein Frauenstaat, den fürder keine andre
> Herrschsücht'ge Männerstimme mehr durchtrotzt,
> Der das Gesetz sich würdig selber gebe,
> Sich selbst gehorche, selber auch beschütze:
> Und Tanaïs sei seine Königin. (1957–62)

> Let there be now a nation, fully fledged,
> A state of women, where from this day on
> Imperious voice of man shall not be heard;
> To make its laws itself, as it is fitting,
> Obey itself, and be its own defence;
> And Tanaïs shall be proclaimed its queen.[15]

The translator's 'fully fledged' renders Kleist's *mündig*, a word which points emphatically to the Enlightenment and to Kant. As we have seen, Goethe and Schiller imply some scepticism by the way they make their characters use the word.[16] No such scepticism is audible in this passage from Kleist. The original Amazon state was a Rousseauesque polity. Hans M. Wolff showed in detail many years ago how it corresponds to Rousseau's conception of a state, founded on an original contract, which guarantees the freedom and safety of each of its individual members, so long as all consent to the governing principles.[17] This means that the private life of each individual must be subordinate to the needs of the community as a whole. Private life necessarily centres on established sexual and emotional relationships. The Amazons (officially at least) do without these. As compensation, and to ensure the continuation of the race, they make war on a different nation every year and take their captives home to Themiscyra, where they celebrate the 'Feast of Roses' — evidently an occasion where each Amazon couples with a randomly chosen male partner, who is afterwards sent home. Odd as this sounds, Wolff argues that it

---

He is referring to Tacitus's *Germania*, which uses the supposed virtues of the Germans as a foil to the corruption of Rome.

14   *SWB* II, 806; cf. W. Blake Tyrrell, *Amazons: A Study in Athenian Mythmaking* (Baltimore: Johns Hopkins University Press, 1984), p. 2; for the legend of Penthesilea, see pp. 78–81.

15   *Five German Tragedies*, p. 385.

16   See Chapter 16.

17   Hans M. Wolff, *Heinrich von Kleist als politischer Dichter* (Berkeley and Los Angeles: University of California Press, 1947), pp. 437–51.

represents an ideal state modelled on Enlightenment principles of reason.[18] It is not reprehensible or absurd, as the great majority of Kleist commentators maintain.[19] Although all the Amazons are engaged in military training and warfare, they enjoy equality and dignity, and treat one another with courtesy and even affection, as in the touchingly tender relationship between Penthesilea and Prothoe.[20]

Within this well-functioning polity there would seem to be no place for Machiavellianism or reason of state. We might look for Machiavellianism rather among the Greeks, above all in the person of Odysseus, the proverbial embodiment of reason. However, his rationality is defeated by the incomprehensible behaviour of Penthesilea in siding neither with the Greeks nor with the Trojans (125–38), and later by Achilles' (as it turns out, misguided) decision to yield himself as captive to Penthesilea. Odysseus has only a minor role, and does not appear after scene 21. Reason of state, however, dominates the entire play, inasmuch as it is embodied in the rational law governing the Amazon state. And this is the source of the tragedy, for Penthesilea's powerful feelings cannot be satisfied by the 'Feast of Roses' (an occasion whose purpose she seems, naively, not quite to understand). Her mother, now dead, told her to single out Achilles as her mate, and the combination of respect for her mother's wishes, her own passionate nature, and the (superficial) attraction of the famous warrior Achilles causes Penthesilea's emotions to become increasingly powerful, damaging to her fellow Amazons (several of whom Achilles shoots), and ultimately destructive to both Achilles and herself. When she thinks Achilles has slighted her, Penthesilea's emotions issue in a notorious act of uncontrolled violence, in which she and her dogs attack Achilles, kill him, and devour his flesh.

Kleist is addressing a question which, in less extreme versions, also preoccupied contemporaries. The modern state was a rational construction, requiring, especially in Germany, a large staff of university-trained professional administrators. Such a construction could easily feel cold, mechanical, inhuman. To gain full acceptance from its citizens, it needed also to appeal to their emotions. It had to be ruled by a king, not by the chairman of a committee, and he had to deserve and obtain not just the obedience but the warm-hearted devotion, indeed the love, of his subjects. Thus Novalis, in the aphorisms headed *Glauben und Liebe* (Faith and Love) which

18 'Der Amazonenstaat ist der Idealstaat der Aufklärung', Wolff, *Kleist als politischer Dichter*, p. 450.
19 The still dominant critical view is represented, among many others, by H. M. Brown, *Kleist and the Tragic Ideal* (Bern: Peter Lang, 1977), p. 65; Walter Müller-Seidel, 'Penthesilea im Kontext der deutschen Klassik', in *Kleists Dramen: Neue Interpretationen*, ed. by Walter Hinderer (Stuttgart: Reclam, 1981), pp. 144–71 (pp. 147, 149); Catherine E. Rigby, *Trangressions of the Feminine: Tragedy, Enlightenment and the Figure of Woman in Classical German Drama* (Heidelberg: Winter, 1996), p. 152; and H. M. Brown, *Heinrich von Kleist: The Ambiguity of Art and the Necessity of Form* (Oxford: Clarendon Press, 1998), pp. 311–14, emphatically seconded by Watanabe-O'Kelly, *Beauty or Beast?*, p. 71. I find much more convincing the positive account of the Amazon state given by Ruth K. Angress, 'Kleist's Nation of Amazons', in *Beyond the Eternal Feminine*, ed. by Susan L. Cocalis and Kay Goodman (Stuttgart: Heinz, 1982), pp. 99–134.
20 Insufficiently appreciated by commentators; a welcome exception is Seán Allan, *The Plays of Heinrich von Kleist: Ideals and Illusions* (Cambridge: Cambridge University Press, 1996), pp. 159–61. I have offered a fuller interpretation of *Penthesilea* in 'Women Warriors and the Origin of the State: Werner's *Wanda* and Kleist's *Penthesilea*', in *Enlightenment and Religion in German and Austrian Literature*, pp. 94–114.

he addressed to the new king of Prussia, Frederick William III, in 1798, maintained that law was founded, not on theoretical consent to a rational principle, but on love for an individual ruler: 'Was ist ein Gesetz, wenn es nicht Ausdruck des Willens einer geliebten, achtungswerten Person ist?' ('What is a law if not the expression of the will of a beloved and respected person?').[21] Kleist would pursue this issue, and bring it to a poetic resolution, in his last play, *Prinz Friedrich von Homburg*.

21   Novalis, *Schriften*, ed. by Paul Kluckhohn and Richard Samuel, 5 vols (Stuttgart: Kohlhammer, 1960–88), II, 487.

— 14 —

Kleist:
Die Herrmannsschlacht (1808–09)

First, however, the catastrophic events of the day demanded Kleist's full attention. He had long observed Napoleon's conquests with revulsion. In 1802, when staying at Thun in Switzerland, he condemned the brutality with which the French had invaded Switzerland, suppressed cantonal self-government, and set up the Helvetic Republic as an enforced ally. Calling the French 'apes of reason', he aimed his polemic against the rationalist spirit of the Revolution rather than against Napoleon himself.[1] In 1805 he expressed the wish that someone would dispose of Napoleon, now 'this evil spirit of the world', by shooting him through the head.[2] Napoleon's victories at Jena and Auerstedt, and his occupation of Prussia, provoked Kleist to a new patriotic fury, in which the French seemed a modern counterpart to the Romans, subjugating the modern Germans as Rome had done the Germanic tribes. Moreover, Kleist was personally affected: in February 1807 he and two other Prussian officers were arrested in Berlin by the French on suspicion of espionage and transported to France. Kleist was first imprisoned in Fort Joux in the Jura mountains and then transferred to an internment camp at Châlons-sur-Marne. What Kleist was doing in Berlin, since his bureaucratic post was in Königsberg, and exactly why he was arrested, are still unclear. He was released, after friends and relatives had written petitions on his behalf, and was back in Berlin by 14 August 1807.

Kleist's patriotic activity reached its peak in 1809. His membership of the clandestine networks trying to foment an insurrection is well attested.[3] He was very excited by the Austrian counter-attack on the French, led by Archduke Carl in April 1809. After an initial defeat, Carl's forces retreated to the Danube, leaving the French free to occupy Vienna on 19 May, but two days later Carl managed to defeat the French at the battle of Aspern. Kleist celebrated this victory in a poem and himself visited the battlefield a few days later.[4] Immediately after the battle, Kleist expected King Frederick William III to launch an insurrection which would

1   Letter to Ulrike von Kleist, 18 March 1802, *SWB* IV, 302.
2   Letter to Rühle von Lilienstern, December 1805, *SWB* IV, 352.
3   See his cryptic letter to Ulrike von Kleist from Dresden (August 1808, *SWB* IV, 420–21) and the mention of Kleist in the memoirs of General Johann von Hüser (quoted in *SWB* II, 1171).
4   See 'An den Erzherzog Carl', *SWB* III, 439. For Kleist's visit, see his letter to Joseph von Buol, 25 May 1809, *SWB* IV, 414, and Schulz, *Kleist*, pp. 432–33.

raise the whole of northern Germany against the French.[5] He was aware that the well-known officer Major Ferdinand von Schill (1776–1809) had led his troops out of Berlin, without official permission, in the hope of heading an uprising in the Kingdom of Westphalia (set up by Napoleon in 1807 under his brother Jérôme); Schill was forced to retreat to Stralsund on the Baltic, where he was killed in street fighting on 31 May 1809.[6]

Kleist's patriotism found expression also in poems that are notorious for enjoining the Germans to slaughter the French like hunters pursuing wolves and to dam the Rhine with their corpses, thereby altering the course of the river and extending Germany's frontiers.[7] His reading of the military and political situation was still over-hopeful. Not only did Napoleon reverse the disaster of Aspern by decisively defeating the Austrians at Wagram on 6 July 1809, forcing them to agree to the Peace of Schönbrunn on 14 October 1809; but the Austrians' aim was never, as Kleist fondly imagined, the restoration of the Holy Roman Empire, which had been dissolved at Napoleon's behest in 1806, so that his invocations of 'the Emperor Francis the Second, the old Emperor of the Germans' are wide of the mark.[8] Nor was there any likelihood that the cautious king would support an insurrection: it was not until March 1813, after Napoleon's retreat from Moscow, that Frederick William was persuaded to break his alliance with France and issue a proclamation announcing that his soldiers would 'fight for our independence and the honour of the *Volk*'.[9]

Before turning to essays and poems, Kleist tried to intervene in politics by means of drama. *Die Herrmannsschlacht*, written in 1808, was, like his political essays, published only after his death.[10] It appeared in 1821, together with *Prinz Friedrich von Homburg*, in an edition by Ludwig Tieck. While *Homburg*, however, is a rich and rounded work, *Die Herrmannsschlacht* is a comparatively one-dimensional propaganda piece. As such, it advocates in the person of Herrmann the most unscrupulous Machiavellianism.[11] In the cause of national liberation, any means is justified.

Kleist returns to a long-standing icon of German nationalism. An event which has often been claimed as part of German history is the *clades Variana* or *Varus-*

---

5   Letter to Joseph von Buol, 25 May 1809, *SWB* IV, 434.

6   Writing from Prague on 13 July to Friedrich Schlegel in Vienna, Kleist hopes that Schill may be rescued from Stralsund, having evidently not yet learnt of Schill's death (*SWB* IV, 436). On Schill, see Clark, *Iron Kingdom*, pp. 347–49.

7   'Germania an ihre Kinder', *SWB* III, 430. But even this poem is less gruesome than the one in which Theodor Körner (1791–1813), whose death in battle made him a patriotic icon, relishes the thought of splitting an enemy's head so that the brains stick to the sword (quoted by Schulz, *Kleist*, p. 427).

8   'Katechismus des Deutschen', *SWB* III, 483. Francis II (1768–1835) was 'the Second' as Holy Roman Emperor, but in 1804 he assumed the title of Emperor of Austria and was thenceforth Francis I.

9   Quoted in Sheehan, *German History 1770–1866*, p. 315.

10   The spelling 'Herrmann' is used by Kleist and adopted in *SWB*, the most recent edition.

11   Herrmann's Machiavellianism, a commonplace of criticism, is examined in helpful detail by Reeve, *In Pursuit of Power*, pp. 25–97.

schlacht, the battle in the Teutoburg Forest in 9 CE.[12] Arminius, war-chief of the Cherusci, lured the Roman general Publius Quinctilius Varus and three legions into swamps and massacred them. This was a triumph not only of leadership but of cunning, indeed treachery, for Arminius was a Roman citizen and was thought by the Romans to be an ally. Arminius' triumph was only temporary, for twelve years later he was murdered by opponents within his own tribe who felt he was becoming too powerful.

Our knowledge of these events comes in large part from Books I and II of Tacitus' *Annals*. Books I–VI of the *Annals* exist in a single manuscript which was discovered in 1508 in the monastic library at Corvey in Westphalia and published at Rome in 1515. German readers were pleased to find that Tacitus called Arminius the 'liberator Germaniae'. Very soon the idea emerged that 'Arminius' must really have been named Hermann. The first person to call him Hermann was probably the Bavarian chronicler Johannes Aventinus in 1528. This made him seem even more German. Hence in the eighteenth century Klopstock composed three patriotic dramas on him, beginning with *Hermanns Schlacht* (1769). Klopstock pays homage to Tacitus's inspiring account of the ancient Germans by calling his play a 'Bardiet', adapting the term *bardita* which, according to Tacitus, was the name the Germans gave to their heroic songs. His Hermann appears both as a patriotic warrior and as an affectionate paterfamilias, not unlike Goethe's Götz von Berlichingen.[13]

Tacitus's idealized Germans also figured in the Berlin lectures, *Reden an die deutsche Nation*, delivered by Fichte (whom we have already met as an enthusiast for Machiavelli) in the winter of 1807–08. According to Fichte, a 'Volk' is eternal; it is a continuity extending before the birth and after the death of the individual; this sense of belonging to a larger whole is the foundation of patriotism, of devotion to 'Volk und Vaterland', which can inspire one to die for one's country. As an example, Fichte returns to the ancient Germans: 'In this belief our oldest common forefathers, the ancestral people of the new culture, called Teutons [*Germanier*] by the Romans, bravely opposed the encroaching world dominion of the Romans.'[14] They wanted the freedom to remain Germans without adopting Roman ways. And at this point Fichte's audience must have felt acutely conscious that their country was occupied by a foreign nation claiming cultural superiority and apparently striving for world dominion ('Weltherrschaft').

Contemporaries recognized that to avenge the humiliation of Prussia at the hands of Napoleon, not only a renewal of patriotic fervour, but internal political reforms would be necessary. Kleist sympathized with the Prussian Reform Movement and

---

12   See Hinrich C. Seeba, 'Hermanns Kampf fur Deutschlands Not: Zur Topographie der nationalen Identität', in *Arminius und die Varusschlacht: Geschichte — Mythos — Literatur*, ed. by Rainer Wiegels and Winfried Woesler (Paderborn: Schöningh, 1995), pp. 355–66.

13   On *Die Herrmannsschlacht* in the context of other Arminius dramas, see Gesa von Essen, *Hermannsschlachten: Germanen- und Römerbilder in der Literatur des 18. und 19. Jahrhunderts* (Göttingen: Wallstein, 1998).

14   *Fichte, Addresses to the German Nation*, trans. by Gregory Moore, Cambridge Texts in the History of Political Thought (Cambridge: Cambridge University Press, 2008), p. 108; Johann Gottlieb Fichte, *Reden an die deutsche Nation*, ed. by Reinhard Lauth, Philosophische Bibliothek 204 (Hamburg: Meiner, 1978), p. 135.

particularly with the radical aims of Count Neidthart von Gneisenau (1760–1831), Gerhard von Scharnhorst (1755–1813) and Baron Karl vom Stein (1757–1831). Aiming ultimately at national regeneration, they wanted to reduce class privileges, to replace the influence of the king's cronies with responsible ministerial government, to abolish serfdom, to transform the population from subjects into citizens, and to promote national identity and solidarity. They particularly wanted to reform the army, to get rid of the elderly and incompetent officers who had been responsible for Prussia's defeat, and to create a clear command structure in which officers would be promoted according to their talent, not their family connections. Following the example of the French revolutionary armies, their goal was 'the nation in arms, a citizen army led by the most talented professionals society could produce'.[15] They recommended conscription for all men aged between 20 and 35. Stein asserted that the combination of a standing army with a national militia would produce 'the universality of responsibility for service in war, binding upon every class of civil society'.[16] Instead of the clumsy, slow-moving armies which had been defeated in 1806, such an army should be light, mobile, and flexible, like Napoleon's victorious troops. Its members, unlike the cannon-fodder that populated eighteenth-century armies, should be individuals, each with his own sense of responsibility and patriotic commitment. Humiliating punishments, such as flogging or running the gauntlet, should be abolished. The ideal was a Kantian army of autonomous citizens.

The reformers went even further. The entire nation should mount an insurrection against the French, following the guerrilla tactics employed with conspicuous success by the Spanish population, who in 1808 had forced the French to evacuate Madrid and put Joseph Bonaparte, the king installed by his brother Napoleon, to flight. Kleist too was enthusiastic about Spanish successes; he addressed a poem to General Palafox, who had defended Saragossa against French troops (albeit by regular, not guerrilla methods), and compared him to Arminius, Wilhelm Tell, and the Spartan hero Leonidas.[17] In addition, the reformers urged that the Germans should adopt a scorched-earth policy, transferring their corn reserves along with their women and children to places of safety and laying waste the territory which the invaders were entering.[18] To motivate the population, they proposed negative propaganda to nourish the Germans' resentment against the occupiers, and a positive campaign to strengthen the feeling of German nationhood. For this purpose, not only a sense of a shared fatherland but a degree of democratic self-determination would be necessary, as Gneisenau wrote:

> If the peoples (*Völker*) are to defend a fatherland powerfully, it is at once just and politic (*staatsklug*) to give them a fatherland. This is especially needful for those German-speaking populations which formerly did not live under the

15   Sheehan, *German History*, p. 309.
16   Quoted in Gordon A. Craig, *The Politics of the Prussian Army, 1640–1945* (Oxford: Clarendon Press, 1965), p. 47.
17   'An Palafox', *SWB* III, 436.
18   Memorial presented by Gneisenau, 14 August 1808; quoted in Wolf Kittler, *Die Geburt des Partisanen aus dem Geist der Poesie: Heinrich von Kleist und die Strategie der Befreiungskriege* (Freiburg: Rombach, 1987), p. 223.

Prussian sceptre but would like to join us in order to liberate the common German fatherland.[19]

These are the policies advocated by Herrmann in *Die Herrmannsschlacht*, which is, as Kleist indicated in a letter to Altenstein, a disguised representation of contemporary events.[20] Herrmann stands for Prussia, while his antagonist, the powerful chieftain Marbod, represents Austria, and the chieftains who squabble among themselves and worry about preserving their property represent the remaining German princes, especially perhaps the sixteen states which Napoleon on 12 July 1806 formed into the Confederation of the Rhine as a buffer between France and his eastern enemies, Austria and Prussia. When the play begins, the Germans are close to despair because of the 'murderous battle' ('Mordschlacht', l. 46) recently lost by Ariovist, and corresponding to the battle of Jena. They recognize the cunning 'Staatskunst' (l. 185) by which Herrmann has held the Romans at bay till now, but they are puzzled by his claim that he intends to submit to the Romans as a first step towards defeating them. Herrmann has in fact welcomed the Romans into his territory, Cheruska, and allowed their general Varus to occupy its capital, Teutoburg, as a way of gaining time to plan resistance. He takes his deception further by offering Varus a contingent of German troops who can be turned against the Romans at the right moment. This corresponds to a scheme of Stein's which has been described as 'truly Machiavellian': he offered the French a German auxiliary corps, intending to turn it against the French, and privately justified this deception to the more scrupulous Gneisenau by asking why only Napoleon should be allowed to lie.[21] As part of Herrmann's dissimulation, in the first scene we find the Roman legate Ventidius accompanying him and others on a hunting party, in which Herrmann's wife Thusnelda shoots an 'Ur' (aurochs), a metaphor for the longed-for destruction of the Roman army.[22] Talking with the other German chiefs, Herrmann dismays them by proposing a scorched earth policy in which they destroy their towns and farms. When they protest that their towns and farms are exactly what they want to defend: 'Oh,' replies Herrmann off-handedly, 'I thought it was your freedom'.[23]

Like the Prussian reformers, Herrmann wants to unite all the German peoples in a single nation. He talks, not about his own territory, but about 'Deutschland' or 'Germanien' (762, 1661, 1720), and anachronistically describes the emperor Augustus as the 'Feind des Reichs', the enemy of the as yet non-existent Empire (2134). Hence his severity towards Aristan, the chief of the Ubians, who insists on his freedom to pursue his own policy, and is finally led off to be executed: German

19 Gneisenau, memorial of 14 August 1808, quoted ibid., p. 222. See also Richard Samuel, 'Kleists *Hermannsschlacht* und der Freiherr vom Stein', in *Heinrich von Kleist: Aufsätze und Essays*, ed. by Walter Müller-Seidel (Darmstadt: Wissenschaftliche Buchgesellschaft, 1973), pp. 312–58.

20 Letter to Altenstein, 1 January 1809, *SWB* IV, 426–27. Kleist again stressed the play's contemporaneity in letters to Heinrich von Collin, 22 February and 20 April 1809 (*SWB* IV, 428–29, 431–32).

21 Samuel, 'Kleists *Hermannsschlacht*', pp. 437–38.

22 Kittler, *Die Geburt des Partisanen*, p. 232.

23 'Nun denn, ich glaubte, Eure Freiheit wär's' (388). Quotations from the play are identified by line number.

unity depends on concerted, not individual action, and cannot risk being weakened by rogue politicians.[24] Herrmann's declared aim is equally broad: he plans to exterminate all the Romans in Germany, comparing them to a swarm of insects; they must all be destroyed by 'the sword of revenge' (1684).

Herrmann is a master of black propaganda and what would now be called false flag operations.[25] Having invited the Romans into his territory, he secretly welcomes the pillage and destruction that they practise. When they burn down three towns, he spreads rumours that it was seven. When they cut down a sacred oak, he puts it about that they also compelled the locals to worship Zeus. He sends out his agents disguised as Romans to rouse the population by further acts of destruction. And when a young German woman is gang-raped by Romans, and suffers an honour killing by her father, Herrmann orders her body to be cut into fifteen pieces and a piece sent to each German tribe, in order to maximize hostility and resistance to the invaders.[26] Herrmann is also skilled at manipulating people's emotions, including their religiosity.[27] He is quite happy for the Romans to cut down the sacred oak so long as it inflames the Germans' political passions. These measures succeed, combined with a secret alliance with Marbod. Varus's legions, unfamiliar with the swampy and forested terrain, are led into a trap and annihilated. Herrmann's fellow-Germans proclaim him their king.

Kleist is exploiting a feature of the historical Arminius which might seem to disqualify him as a national hero: Arminius did not overcome the Romans in open battle, but took advantage of their unfamiliarity with German terrain to lure them into swamps. Kleist's Herrmann, accordingly, is less a warrior than an intriguer, a Machiavellian fox rather than a lion. He appears as a technician of power, a hyperrational calculator who not only foresees all his enemies' moves but inflicts suffering on his own people, and manipulates his wife's emotions, in his all-consuming campaign against the Romans.[28] Although he appeals to the Germans' love of their country, his principal method is to stir up their hatred of their enemy. In subordinating everything else to the national cause, he appears as a rational fanatic. He is not a charismatic leader, like Schiller's Wallenstein, because charisma implies an interaction between the leader and his followers. Herrmann's followers,

---

24   This consideration invalidates the plea for Aristan made by Seán Allan, '"Die Rache der Barbaren sei dir fern!"': Myth, Identity, and the Encounter with the Colonial Other in Heinrich von Kleist's *Die Hermannsschlacht*', *Publications of the English Goethe Society*, 78 (2009), 47–59.

25   Cf. Kleist's satirical description of the deceitful methods of French journalism: 'Lehrbuch der französischen Journalistik', *SWB* III, 462–68; von Essen, *Hermannsschlachten*, pp. 179–81.

26   This is modelled on an incident in the Old Testament: see Judges 19. 29, and *SWB* II, 1134. The father who kills his dishonoured daughter appears to be a contrafacture of Odoardo in Lessing's *Emilia Galotti* (1772), who performs a similar action *without* political consequences.

27   On Herrmann's manipulation of religion, see Steven Howe, 'Erziehung zur Nation: Die antinapoleonischen Kampfschriften, *Die Herrmannsschlacht* und *Prinz Friedrich von Homburg*', in *Unverhoffte Wirkungen: Erziehung und Gewalt im Werk Heinrich von Kleists*, ed. by Ricarda Schmidt, Seán Allan and Steven Howe (Würzburg: Königshausen & Neumann, 2014), pp. 129–59 (pp. 140–42); Howe draws a telling contrast with Schiller's Johanna (in *Die Jungfrau von Orleans*) whose religious appeal is genuine, not manipulative.

28   Riedl, 'Texturen des Terrors', p. 39.

just as much as his enemies, are pieces on a chessboard which he moves about with sovereign omniscience.[29] If Penthesilea, rejecting the rational planning of the Amazon state, fell victim to uncontrollable emotions, so Herrmann seems equally one-sided in his Machiavellian control of everyone around him. His affection for Thusnelda does appear to be genuine, judging by the scene where, having managed to alienate her from Ventidius, he falls at her feet.[30] If it were not genuine, his declaration that Ventidius cannot love her as a German could —

> So, was ein Deutscher lieben nennt,
> Mit Ehrfurcht und mit Sehnsucht, wie ich dich — (667–68)

> What a German calls love,
> With yearning reverence, as I do you —

would be a mere lie (and would also run counter to his plan to use her against Ventidius). It is clear also that his patriotism is heartfelt, not just a pretext for the pursuit of power. Having heard the bards intone a patriotic chorus, Herrmann leans against an oak-tree (the symbol of Germany), evidently lost for words and, according to the stage-direction, 'heftig bewegt' (powerfully moved; after line 2243). Here we glimpse a further dimension in his character.

An uneasy response may well be heightened rather than diminished by the element of humour in the play. It has been said that there is more laughter in *Die Herrmannsschlacht* than in any other of Kleist's works, even those explicitly labelled comedies.[31] Herrmann clearly enjoys scheming, just as Shakespeare's Richard III does. Playing the game of intrigue, at which he is expert, by his sheer gusto he does something to put the audience on his side.[32] Black humour reaches its high (or low) point in the relations between Herrmann and Thusnelda, who is courted by the dandified Roman Ventidius. The gullible Thusnelda is flattered by his attentions, but annoyed when he snips a lock of hair from her head, meaning to send it to the Empress Livia. Herrmann takes advantage of this incident, telling Thusnelda that if the Romans conquer them, her blonde hair will be cut off and used to make wigs for Roman ladies. (The Romans are supposed to be devotees of fashion and elegance, like the modern French.) He also tells her that her teeth will be removed and used to make dentures for the Romans. Later, when Thusnelda is pleading for Ventidius's life to be spared, Herrmann gives her a letter, allegedly intercepted by chance, in which Ventidius promises to make Livia a present of Thusnelda's hair and teeth.[33] Thusnelda, with the proverbial fury of a woman scorned, later takes her revenge by luring Ventidius into an enclosure containing a hungry bear.[34]

29 Riedl, ibid.; contrast Howe, 'Erziehung zur Nation', p. 142.
30 See Reeve, *In Pursuit of Power*, p. 75.
31 Schulz, *Kleist*, pp. 417–18; Rolf N. Linn, 'Comical and Humorous Elements in Kleist's *Die Hermannschlacht*', *Germanic Review*, 47 (1972), 159–67.
32 Von Essen describes him as an 'intellektuelle Spielernatur' (*Hermannsschlachten*, p. 146). For a comparison with Shakespeare's machiavels, see Reeve, *In Pursuit of Power*, pp. 178–81.
33 Riedl ('Texturen des Terrors', p. 40) suggests that the letter may be forged — a suspicion also attaching to letters in Schiller's *Wallenstein* (see above, p. 171).
34 A much darker reading of this episode is possible if one understands Ventidius's death as a human sacrifice: Derek Hughes, *Culture and Sacrifice: Ritual Deaths in Literature and Opera* (Cambridge:

While Herrmann can hardly foresee this sadistic action, he understands Thusnelda's emotions enough to induce her to string Ventidius along until the latter can no longer be useful. He makes her, in short, as manipulative as he is himself.

Since even Thusnelda, who is initially shocked by Herrmann's plan to kill all the Romans, is transformed in his image, the play offers no internal criticism of Herrmann. A critique of Herrmann's Machiavellianism could, however, be based on the ambition to conquer Rome that he suddenly reveals at the end:

> Ihr aber kommt, ihr wackern Söhne Teuts,
> Und laßt, im Hain der stillen Eichen,
> Wodan für das Geschenk des Siegs uns danken!
> Uns bleibt der Rhein noch schleunig zu ereilen,
> Damit vorerst der Römer keiner
> Von der Germania heilgem Grund entschlüpfe:
> Und dann — nach Rom selbst mutig aufzubrechen!
> Wir oder unsre Enkel, meine Brüder!
> Denn eh doch, seh ich ein, erschwingt der Kreis der Welt
> Vor dieser Mordbrut keine Ruhe,
> Als bis das Raubnest ganz zerstört,
> Und nichts, als eine schwarze Fahne,
> Von seinem öden Trümmerhaufen weht! (2623–36)

> But come, ye stalwart sons of Teut,
> And in the grove of quiet oak-trees, let us
> Thank Wodan for the gift of victory!
> First we must march onwards to the Rhine,
> And speedily, that not a single Roman
> May slip away from Germania's sacred soil:
> And then — set out courageously for Rome!
> We or our grandchildren, my brothers!
> For I see clearly that this murderous brood
> Will never leave the whole round world in peace
> Until its robbers' nest is all destroyed
> And nought remains except a black flag
> Waving above its desolate ruins!

Not content to rule a united Germany, Herrmann is planning further wars of aggression. This corresponds to Machiavelli's commendation, in the *Discourses*, of the Roman republic for its expansionism. The Romans, he says, constantly waged wars against other states, using both force and fraud to subjugate their enemies. 'Republicanism is predatory, and especially so when untroubled by a Christian conscience — such is Machiavelli's striking claim.'[35] These wars not only increased Rome's greatness, but were a valuable distraction from domestic conflicts. Moreover, it is a commonplace of statecraft that internal solidarity is best ensured by fear of an external enemy. War promotes unity in a republic (*D* II. 25. 227). Shakespeare's Henry IV advises his son to 'busy giddy minds | With foreign quarrels' (*1 Henry IV*, IV. 5. 214–15). Montesquieu points out that a state governed

Cambridge University Press, 2007), p. 141.
35   Hulliung, *Citizen Machiavelli*, p. 26.

by an aristocracy can become too relaxed, and needs an external enemy: 'A republic must dread something.'[36] So the aggression that Herrmann proposes is actually a structural necessity in order to maintain the unity of the nation that he has brought into being. And one might ask what is gained in the long term by simply subjugating or even annihilating one's enemies, when one could convert them into useful trading partners? Machiavelli does not address the question of when conquest becomes self-defeating.[37]

One can well understand the unease with which many post-1945 commentators have regarded Herrmann, especially when one recalls that the play was used in the First World War to animate the patriotism of German troops, and later pressed into service to support the racist nationalism of the Nazis.[38] But all the characters, apart from Herrmann, are such cardboard cut-outs that I find it hard to share the shock some commentators express, for example, at Thusnelda's 'descent into bestiality' in the episode with the bear.[39] Thusnelda is a very different figure from the almost unfathomably complex tragic heroine Penthesilea. The problem with the play seems rather to be that in it Kleist has abandoned literature for propaganda, and has thus fallen between two stools. Like Brecht's *Die Maßnahme*, to be discussed in a later chapter, *Die Herrmannschlacht* fails as literature because it denies what Schiller called 'the republican freedom of the reading public' and imposes a single, unchallengeable interpretation.[40] But, again like *Die Maßnahme*, it also fails as propaganda. It is far too frank about the deception, dirty tricks, false flags, and atrocities — including the slaughter of an enemy who has honestly surrendered (Septimius, 2206–26) — that Kleist thinks a successful campaign requires. No practical politician could openly admit to following such guidelines, even if he did obey them in action, and he would not thank their author for exposing the dirty secrets of power and warfare. In Herrmann, Kleist 'projects as the hero of historical action a man of his own type: intellectual and artist'.[41] The play is thus a frustrated intellectual's fantasy about politics: the author wants to convey, not only the course that Germany ought to take, but how much better it would do so if he were in sole charge.

---

36 Montesquieu, *The Spirit of the Laws*, p. 116 (Book VIII, ch. 5).
37 Hulliung, *Citizen Machiavelli*, pp. 58–59.
38 See *SWB* II, 1089–92.
39 Reeve, *In Pursuit of Power*, p. 87.
40 Schiller, *Verbrecher aus Infamie*, in *NA* XVI, 39. The comparison with Brecht is briefly suggested by Jeffrey L. Sammons, 'Rethinking Kleist's *Hermannsschlacht*', in *Heinrich von Kleist Studien*, ed. by Alexej Ugrinsky (Berlin: Erich Schmidt, 1980), pp. 33–40 (p. 35).
41 Sammons, 'Rethinking Kleist's *Hermannsschlacht*', p. 35. Cf. Riedl, 'Texturen des Terrors', p. 43.

15

Kleist:

Prinz Friedrich von Homburg (1810)

Prinz Friedrich von Homburg, Kleist's last play and the acknowledged masterpiece among his dramas, continues his project of supplying models for present-day politics. Compared to *Die Herrmannsschlacht*, however, its relation to Kleist's present is highly indirect. It purports to be a historical drama, based on a patriotic legend that grew up in the eighteenth century, concerning the battle of Fehrbellin (1675) in which Brandenburg defeated an invading Swedish army.[1] The Great Elector, Frederick William I, had instructed the Prince of Homburg to use his troops for reconnoitring instead of taking part in the fighting. Carried away by enthusiasm, the Prince nevertheless plunged into battle and might have endangered the outcome if the Elector's forces had not come to his support. Since Brandenburg nevertheless won, the Elector pardoned the Prince, telling him that the laws of war strictly demanded the death penalty for his disobedience, but that the glory of the victory, to which he had contributed, should not be clouded by bloodshed.[2] Kleist has altered history, notably by making the Prince, who was forty-two, married, and had an artificial leg (now on display in the palace at Bad Homburg), into an impetuous young man, and by inventing several key characters (Natalie, Kottwitz). The result is an image of an ideal Prussia, but one which continues to pose innumerable problems of interpretation.

In keeping with the original legend, which celebrated the Elector's magnanimity, a long interpretative tradition reads the play as a kind of dramatic Bildungsroman, in which the headstrong young Prince is educated into maturity and responsibility by the wise Elector.[3] Friedrich Hebbel, a great admirer of Kleist's plays, presented in 1850 a summary of *Homburg* based on this assumption.[4] On the night before the

---

1   Brandenburg was the territory ruled from 1417 by the Hohenzollern family. Its ruler was one of the seven princes entitled to elect the Holy Roman Emperor: hence his title was Elector (*Kurfürst*). In 1618 the Hohenzollerns inherited Ducal Prussia (later East Prussia), though their legal sovereignty there was confirmed only in 1660. In 1700 Brandenburg-Prussia was raised to a kingdom by the then emperor, unusually one whose territory lay partly outside the Empire. In *Prinz Friedrich von Homburg* the characters think of their territory as Brandenburg. See Clark, *Iron Kingdom*, pp. xxiii, 5–6, 54.
2   See *SWB* II, 1165–66.
3   See e.g. Georg Lukács, *German Realists in the Nineteenth Century*, trans. by Jeremy Gaines and Paul Keast (London: Libris, 1993), p. 37; *SWB* II, 1228–31; and the survey of previous interpretations in J. M. Ellis, *Kleist's 'Prinz Friedrich von Homburg': A Critical Study* (Berkeley: University of California Press, 1970), pp. 3–10.
4   Friedrich Hebbel, 'Der Prinz von Homburg oder die Schlacht bei Fehrbellin', in *Werke*, ed. by

battle, the officers are receiving their orders. Homburg is distracted by his love for the Princess Natalie, an orphaned niece of the Elector who has found refuge in Brandenburg, and by his dreams of glory. In the battle, his role — hardly a suitable one for a young man of his fiery temperament — is to wait until the Swedish troops are already fleeing and then charge and annihilate them. In the battle, he charges prematurely and performs wonders of valour. Rumour says the Elector has been killed; the Prince consoles the distressed Electress and promises to protect Natalie. When news comes that the Elector is alive and well, the Electress gives her consent to their marriage. The Elector announces that whoever led the premature charge will be court-martialled and condemned to death for breaking the laws of war, and the Prince, to his amazement, is duly arrested. When the sight of his grave already dug at last convinces him that the Elector is serious, the Prince falls into the most abject despair (the notorious *Todesfurchtszene*). Natalie goes to plead with the Elector, who writes the Prince a letter, saying that if he thinks his sentence is unjust, then he will be freed. This is the key moment in the educational process. Having digested the letter, the Prince decides that his sentence is justified and he will accept his death. Natalie loves him all the more for this decision. However, she would still prefer her lover to remain alive, and since she is commander of a regiment, she orders it to leave its quarters and come to the Elector's palace. She and all the officers sign a petition on the Prince's behalf. Under this pressure, and having heard an eloquent and (as he admits) unanswerable speech by the elderly colonel Kottwitz, the Elector announces that the case will be decided by the Prince himself. The latter appears and declares that his death is deserved. When he is seemingly about to be shot, however, he is instead reprieved, and everyone celebrates him as the hero of Fehrbellin.

Anyone who knows the play even superficially will be struck, even in this drastic summary, by Hebbel's omissions. The play begins in a moonlit garden outside the palace at Fehrbellin, where the Prince is sitting under an oak-tree and plaiting a laurel wreath.[5] Alerted by his friend Hohenzollern, the Elector and the rest of the court watch him, find that he is in a somnambulistic state, and surround him inquisitively. The Elector, tempted by curiosity, takes the wreath from him, adds his own chain, and hands both to Natalie, whereupon the Prince rises and follows Natalie, addressing her as his bride, and seizing one of her gloves. The court party retires in dismay. Having gradually regained his senses, the Prince recounts to Hohenzollern what he thinks is a dream, though he cannot remember who the woman was whose glove he seized; and he is baffled to find that the glove of his dream is still in his possession. It is hardly surprising that when the battle orders are given shortly afterwards (in the middle of the night) the Prince should be distracted. Hebbel, however, thought this scene a mere outgrowth of Romanticism which could easily be dispensed with. He was equally dismissive about the final scene, again set in the garden at night, where the Prince again receives the wreath and chain, this time from Natalie, and is hailed as a hero. Yet these scenes are indispensable. They place the Prince in a night-time reality of unconscious desires and dreams, sharply distinguished from the practical, daytime reality of the Elector and his court.[6] In the final scene, the atmosphere of the first is artificially recreated, providing a satisfying symmetry.

It is now generally agreed that the play moves towards some kind of reconciliation between the worlds of the Prince and the Elector. The Elector educates the Prince, but himself goes through a learning experience. The need to reconcile the play's antitheses is formulated by Natalie when she pleads with the Elector for the Prince's life:

> Das Kriegsgesetz, das weiß ich wohl, soll herrschen,
> Jedoch die lieblichen Gefühle auch. (1129–30)[7]
>
> I know the law of warfare should prevail,
> But so should our sweet feelings of affection.

To see how this conflict between law and emotion might be resolved, Kleist appears to have drawn on the writings of Adam Müller (1779–1829), with whom he co-edited the journal *Phöbus* in 1808. His letters show that he repeatedly read Müller's political treatise *Elemente der Staatskunst* (1809).[8] Müller argues that the relation between the state and emotion should be reciprocal. The state should not only invite emotional attachment from its citizens, but should also respond to their feelings. There should be a living emotional interchange between state and citizen, not a mere adherence to abstract principles. Concepts like that of freedom become dangerous when they are taken as absolute and imposed on the fluid and ever-changing nature of reality.[9] Kleist formulated a similar idea in one of his patriotic essays, 'Katechismus des Deutschen' ('The German's Catechism'). Here the Germans are charged with the bad habit ('Unart') of reflecting too much instead of feeling and acting. The son says to his father, who is putting him through a patriotic catechism,

> You have told me that the Germans' intellect has been overstimulated by an ingenious teacher; that they reflect when they should feel or act, that they think they can accomplish everything through their wits, and no longer set store by the old, mysterious power of hearts.[10]

The Elector embodies the worries that Kleist, Müller, and many other contemporaries felt about the rational, bureaucratic state built up by enlightened despots such as

6   See Ellis, *Kleist's 'Prinz Friedrich von Homburg'*, p. 14.
7   Quotations from *Homburg* are identified by line number.
8   See the eulogy of Adam Müller in Kleist's letter to Altenstein, 1 January 1809, *SWB* IV, 427–28; later he regrets having lent the book to someone who has not returned it (letter to Fouqué, 25 April 1811, *SWB* IV, 482–83).
9   See Wolff, *Kleist als politischer Dichter*, pp. 494–95; Marcel Krings, 'Der Typus des Erlösers: Heilsgeschehen in Kleists *Prinz von Homburg*', *Deutsche Vierteljahrsschrift für Literaturwissenschaft und Geistesgeschichte*, 79 (2005), 64–95 (pp. 71–72).
10 *SWB* III, 486; also quoted in this connection by Howe, 'Erziehung zur Nation', p. 157.

Frederick the Great. In 1798 Novalis addressed to the new king of Prussia, Frederick William III, a series of aphorisms headed *Glauben und Liebe oder Der König und die Königin* (*Faith and Love or The King and the Queen*). He complained that in the past sixty or so years Prussia had been governed like a factory:

> No state has been managed like a factory more than Prussia since the death of Frederick William I [in 1740; Novalis really means since the accession of Frederick the Great, but is too tactful to say so]. However necessary such a mechanical administration may be for the physical health, strength, and agility of the state, yet if the state is treated only in this manner, it will essentially perish.[11]

He thought the state should be united by love, as typified by the love-match between Frederick William III and Queen Luise. The King and Queen should be the visible and admirable objects of their citizens' affections. People could feel whole-hearted love for the persons of a king and queen, but they could not love a constitution: 'A true royal couple is for the whole person what a constitution is for the mere intellect.'[12] Adam Müller likewise saw the state as modelled on the family:

> The state is not a mere manufactory, dairy-farm, insurance company, or mercantile society; it is the heartfelt combination of all the physical and spiritual needs, all the physical and spiritual wealth, all the inner and outer life of a nation, forming a great, energetic, infinitely mobile and living whole.[13]

That is, the state is not an artificial construction put together for a merely practical purpose. Rather, Müller saw the state as an extension of the family, in that the basic contrasts within humanity — between age and youth, and between male and female — shape the structure of the family, and must therefore ultimately structure the state: 'All political theory [*Staatslehre*] must begin [...] with the *theory of the family*'.[14]

As ruler of Brandenburg-Prussia, Kleist's Elector is caught in an uncomfortable tension between several roles. The domestic atmosphere of the family cannot really be extended to government, which necessarily involves the operation of an abstract system. On the other hand, the abstract law that he upholds in speaking to Natalie cannot be maintained in the varied and unpredictable circumstances of actual life. The Elector has to be a politician. Further, he practises reason of state at times in a decidedly Machiavellian way. Having failed to impose on the Swedes such a crushing defeat as he would have wished, he negotiates with their envoy Graf Horn. His object is to secure a peace which will be sealed by marrying Natalie to the King of Sweden, Karl Gustav (1028; referred to as Gustav Karl at line 1780).[15]

11   Novalis, *Schriften*, II, 494.
12   Ibid., II, 487.
13   Adam Müller, *Die Elemente der Staatskunst*, 2 vols (Berlin: Sander, 1809), I, 37; discussed in Klaus Peter, 'Für ein anderes Preußen: Romantik und Politik in Kleists *Prinz Friedrich von Homburg*', *Kleist-Jahrbuch* 1992, pp. 95–125.
14   Müller, *Elemente*, I, 100.
15   This figure corresponds to the historical King Charles XI of Sweden (reigned 1660–97), who was not available, since in 1675 he became engaged to Ulrika Eleonora, daughter of the King of Denmark. On the fictional negotiations with Graf Horn, see Peter U. Hohendahl, 'Der Paß des

Knowing this, Hohenzollern suggests to the Prince that the Elector may want him out of the way because his relationship with Natalie risks frustrating the Elector's plans. This cannot be the reason why the Prince was arrested, because when the Elector declared that whoever led the charge should be executed he did not yet know that it was the Prince, but it may be a reason for taking advantage of his guilt to eliminate him. When he accepts his sentence, the Prince urges the Elector to abandon the negotiations, not for Natalie's sake (there is no sign that she knows how she is being used) but because peace would be dishonourable (1779–83). The play tries to repudiate Machiavellianism and calculation in government.

After his arrest, the Prince criticizes the Elector's conduct with the help of a significant classical reference:

> Mein Vetter Friedrich will den Brutus spielen,
> Und sieht, mit Kreid auf Leinewand verzeichnet,
> Sich schon auf dem kurulschen Stuhle sitzen:
> Die schwedschen Fahnen in dem Vordergrund,
> Und auf dem Tisch die märkschen Kriegsartikel.
> Bei Gott, in mir nicht findet er den Sohn,
> Der, unterm Beil des Henkers, ihn bewundre.
> Ein deutsches Herz, von altem Schrot und Korn,
> Bin ich gewohnt an Edelmut und Liebe,
> Und wenn er mir, in diesem Augenblick,
> Wie die Antike starr entgegenkommt,
> Tut er mir leid, und ich muß ihn bedauren! (777–88)

> My cousin Friedrich sees himself, in fancy,
> Sketched on the canvas in the role of Brutus,
> Already seated on the curule chair,
> The Swedish colours waving in the foreground,
> Brandenburg's articles of war before him.
> By God, he will not find in me a son
> To worship him beneath the headsman's axe.
> A German heart, and loyal to tradition,
> I still expect nobility and love,
> And if he comes towards me at this moment
> Stiff with the rigour of antiquity,
> I'm sorry for him, and I pity him!

The Brutus mentioned here is not the assassin of Julius Caesar, but Lucius Junius Brutus, who according to Livy overthrew the last king of Rome and became its first consul. His sons joined in a conspiracy to restore the monarchy, and Brutus condemned them to death on the grounds that justice was impersonal. This was a standard example and a limiting case of political virtue.[16] Kleist was probably inspired by Jacques-Louis David's painting of Brutus condemning his sons; the painting was completed in 1789 and displayed in the Louvre where Kleist must have

Grafen Horn: Ein Aspekt des Politischen in *Prinz Friedrich von Homburg*', German Quarterly, 41 (1968), 167–76.
16   On its implications here, see Steven Howe, *Heinrich von Kleist und Jean-Jacques Rousseau: Violence, Identity, Nation* (Rochester, NY: Camden House, 2012), pp. 181–85.

seen it.[17] Machiavelli refers repeatedly to 'killing the sons of Brutus' as shorthand for the ruthlessness that must be exercised by the founder of a democracy (D 1. 16. 65; III. 3. 252–53). Montesquieu is more reserved, considering Brutus's punishment of his sons excessive: as consul, he was continuing to exercise the arbitrary power previously available to the kings, and should instead have referred the decision to the Senate.[18] Kleist seems close to Montesquieu. His Elector resembles Brutus in going beyond his formal powers. Instead of announcing that whoever led the charge prematurely would be executed, the Elector should have awaited the decision of the court martial. Kleist also implies, by the Prince's word 'spielen', that it is a piece of showmanship in which the Elector represents himself as constrained by impersonal virtue. The Prince himself contrasts such behaviour with the 'nobility and love' which he expects as a German; and though his protest is of course self-righteous and self-serving, it also fits in with the emphasis laid by Natalie, and presently by others, on the need for emotion and the heart to find a place within the machinery of state.

In Acts IV and V, the Elector is obliged to hear remonstrances from three characters, which gradually soften his rigid outlook. A detailed examination of these episodes will reveal the cumulative reduction of the Elector's authority.

Natalie

After witnessing the Prince's moral collapse in the *Todesfurchtsszene*, Natalie hastens to the Elector. She first minimizes the Prince's offence and points out that he did after all show exceptional courage and gain a victory, so that to execute him would seem an act of justice so sublime ('erhaben') as to be inhuman (1109–10). The Elector's reply, that however much he might wish to, he cannot change the decision of the court martial (though he had decided on the outcome before the court was summoned), must be disingenuous, since as sovereign he has the right to pardon. Natalie replies that to pardon the Prince would not in the least endanger the fatherland, as the Elector claims, and having compared Brandenburg to a mighty edifice, she uses a disturbing image:

> Das braucht nicht dieser Bindung, kalt und öd,
> Aus eines Freundes Blut, um Oheims Herbst,
> Den friedlich prächtigen, zu überleben. (1139–41)

> It does not need this cold and wretched mortar,
> Made from a friend's blood, to outlast
> My uncle's peaceable and splendid autumn.

The suggestion that the Prince's blood is being used to strengthen the state has connotations of human sacrifice.

However, this is not yet enough to sway the Elector, so Natalie plays her trump card by telling him about the Prince's abject terror of death. The Elector is astonished and confused. He seems mainly affected, not by concern for the Prince, but by Natalie's tears. He promptly writes a letter which Natalie thinks contains

17   Grathoff, 'Kleist und Napoleon', pp. 191–95; Brown, *Heinrich von Kleist*, p. 369.
18   Montesquieu, *Spirit*, p. 180 (Book XI, ch. 18).

a pardon, though as we know it will condemn the Prince to death even more effectively than the original sentence.

Natalie's role in pleading with the Elector recalls that of Queen Luise of Prussia. On 6 July 1807 the Queen had a one-on-one interview with Napoleon, pleading with him to soften the harsh terms he intended to impose on Prussia.[19] Although the Queen's efforts were unsuccessful, and the Treaty of Tilsit, signed on 9 July, deprived Prussia of almost half its territory and demanded costly reparations, Queen Luise became a patriotic icon, embodying, not only for Kleist, the dream that a new Prussia might reconcile power with love.[20] For Luise's birthday on 10 March 1810, Kleist wrote her a sonnet, which his sister Ulrike handed to her in person.[21] Natalie's crucial contribution implies that the new utopian Prussian state emerging from the reconciliation between the Elector and the Prince will be feminized, though remaining a military power that will firmly resist its enemies.

On learning what the letter actually says, and seeing the Prince determined to accept his death, Natalie takes independent action. Being herself the commander of a regiment of dragoons headed by Colonel Kottwitz, she orders it to leave its quarters and assemble outside the Elector's palace. This is an act of mutiny, and leads to the second remonstrance.

Kottwitz

Admitted to the Elector's presence, Kottwitz presents a petition supported by the entire army, pleading for the Prince. The Elector has previously made it clear that he does not consider 'Hans Kottwitz aus der Priegnitz' a serious adversary (1417), but Kottwitz proves to be a match for him. Asked why he left his quarters, Kottwitz shows the Elector an order signed by Natalie who claims to be acting on the instructions of her uncle. This is surely a serious abuse of the Elector's authority, but Natalie is never called to account for it, and the Elector pretends to Kottwitz that he did give the order (1495–96). Kottwitz defends the Prince for charging prematurely, arguing that the Elector's strategy was flawed because it gave the Swedes time to regroup; the Elector naturally denies this, and also insists that he only values a victory gained according to law, namely his pre-established strategy. Irrespective of the military details, the Elector's fault lies in devising a rigid plan and insisting that everyone must adhere to it despite changing circumstances. Not only is such conduct of warfare liable to be frustrated by unpredictable events, but, as Kottwitz points out, it means treating his soldiers as mere instruments, instead of building on their ardent loyalty to the 'Vaterland':

> Herr, das Gesetz, das höchste, oberste,
> Das wirken soll, in deiner Feldherrn Brust,

---

19   See Daniel Schönpflug, *Luise von Preußen, Königin der Herzen: Eine Biographie* (Munich: Beck, 2010), pp. 231–33.
20   Hermann Kurzke, *Romantik und Konservatismus: Das 'politische' Werk Friedrich von Hardenbergs (Novalis) im Horizont seiner Wirkungsgeschichte* (Munich: Fink, 1983), pp. 174–75.
21   'An die Königin Luise von Preußen zur Feier ihres Geburtstags den 10. März 1810' (*SWB* III, 442–43).

> Das ist der Buchstab deines Willens nicht;
> Das ist das Vaterland, das ist die Krone,
> Das bist du selber, dessen Haupt sie trägt. (1570–74)

> Sir, the law, the highest, the supreme,
> That operates in your commanders' breasts,
> Is far more than the letter of your will;
> It is the fatherland, it is the crown,
> It's you yourself, upon whose head it lies.

Kottwitz accuses the Elector of 'schlechte | Kurzsicht'ge Staatskunst', bad, short-sighted statecraft (1183–84). The word 'Staatskunst' goes beyond military strategy and arraigns the Elector's whole mechanical approach to government. The Elector, admitting that he has no answer to Kottwitz's reproaches, summons the Prince, whose voluntary submission to the law is supposed to prove to everyone that the Elector has behaved rightly. While the Prince is on his way, however, a third remonstrance comes.

Hohenzollern

After the Elector has received (and tried to brush off) petitions and remonstrances from his officers, Hohenzollern appears with a document entitled 'Beweis, daß Kurfürst Friedrich des Prinzen Tat selbst — ' (1623–24). The Elector is too annoyed to finish reading the title, but it is presumably 'Proof that Elector Frederick himself [caused] the Prince's deed'. For, Hohenzollern explains, the Elector's intervention, in giving his chain and the wreath to the sleep-walking Prince, so bewildered the latter that when he was supposed to receive instructions he was completely distracted. The Elector, having listened to Hohenzollern's lengthy exposition, replies that Hohenzollern is as much to blame for summoning him down into the garden in the first place; but this argument — in effect, that a causal chain can be traced back indefinitely, so there is *no* efficient cause – is a feeble rhetorical ploy, however vehemently the Elector states it, and Hohenzollern sees that his arguments have made an impact.[22]

   Hohenzollern's Poirot-like unravelling of the chain of events not only under-mines the Elector's reputation as a wise educator but identifies him as a type of semi-comic figure, the unjust judge who should himself be on trial. Kleist's comedy *Der zerbrochne Krug* (written 1802–07, published 1808) centres on the village judge Adam, who has to find the person responsible for breaking a jug, and tries desperately to conceal the fact that he himself broke it when climbing out of a young woman's bedroom window. He further planned to get his victim's fiancé out of the way by having him sent as a soldier to the East Indies.

   Unjust judges appear in a play that has left considerable traces both in *Der*

---

22   See Ellis, *Kleist's 'Prinz Friedrich von Homburg'*, pp. 91–92. Arguing plausibly that the Elector is jealous of the Prince's military reputation, Ellis underrates the play's political dimension and hence lapses from his usual subtlety by dismissing Kottwitz's speech as 'largely prejudicial and irrelevant appeals to sentiment' (p. 91).

zerbrochne Krug and in *Prinz Friedrich von Homburg*, namely Shakespeare's *Measure for Measure*. We have here the unjust magistrate Angelo, who, trading on his reputation for inflexible virtue, plots to seduce Isabella. But we also have the Duke of Vienna himself, who, having allowed his duchy to slide into a moral breakdown, goes abroad leaving Angelo in charge, but returns in disguise to observe events and eventually to sort things out.[23] The connections between *Homburg* and *Measure for Measure* extend further. Isabella's brother Claudio has been condemned to death for getting a woman pregnant. Terrified by the prospect of death, he makes a famous speech ('Ay, but to die, and go we know not where', etc., III. I. 119), which has long been recognized as a model for Kleist's *Todesfurchtszene* in which the Prince shows abject terror of dying.[24] When Isabella pleads with Angelo for Claudio's life, Angelo counters with serious arguments against weakening the force of the law by making an exception in favour of a single person, thereby (despite his private corrupt motives) anticipating the Elector's moral rigorism. And the part played by the impish Hohenzollern recalls the mischievous figure Lucio who talks about the Duke's weaknesses and may not always be wrong.

The Prince's submission to the law impresses everyone. He has in a sense changed places with the Elector: his 'inflexible resolve' to glorify the 'sacred law of war' by a voluntary death (1749–50) expresses the rigid attitude which Natalie, Kottwitz, and Hohenzollern have successively challenged. The Elector may (and certainly should) be having doubts, the Prince now has none. At the Prince's request, the Elector gives up the plan to marry Natalie off to the King of Sweden (not being present at this point, she presumably never knows anything about it). The Prince returns to prison to await execution; Natalie collapses, wishing only to die; and the Elector springs his surprise. Dismissing the Swedish ambassador, he will resume the campaign, and put the Prince in charge. Kottwitz expresses the general delight, saying that the Prince can now be trusted *not* to use his own initiative: even if the Elector were in imminent danger of death, the Prince would make no move to rescue him without an order (1816–18). This not only undermines Kottwitz's earlier plea that soldiers should not be treated as automata, but undercuts those interpretations of the play, however tempting otherwise, that would see the Elector as coming half-way to meet the Prince's values.

It is hard to tell just when the Elector decides not to proceed with the execution. Of the three remonstrances, it is likely that the third, Hohenzollern's, is the most effective. It sets the Elector thinking (stage direction after line 1692), although his explicit reply consists only of sophisms and angry insults. If so, the scene in which the Prince announces his decision to die, and is congratulated by everyone from the Elector downwards, is a charade, since the Elector now no longer means to go through with the sentence. Its real purpose is to let the Elector score a point by proving that he was right. Since, however, the play is not set in an ethical laboratory but in a pressing political and military context, the Elector could not have carried

23   For a summary of the Duke's dubious actions, see Nuttall, *Shakespeare the Thinker*, p. 266.
24   See Meta Corssen, *Kleist und Shakespeare* (Weimar: Duncker, 1930); Brown, *Heinrich von Kleist*, p. 360n.

out the sentence anyway. After all, the Prince displayed heroism and won the battle, albeit not conclusively. Once the patriotic excitement had worn off, his execution would have been seen as an act of gratuitous cruelty and the loyalty of the army would have been at risk. Another campaign against the Swedes is a good way of recreating solidarity. So despite the febrile emotions he whips up, the Elector never ceases (and in his political role, could not cease) to be a Machiavellian.

It is easier to talk about the Elector's political behaviour than about his character. Characterization in this play is problematic and puzzling. The persons are vivid, their emotions are compelling, but it is hard to put together the various emotions they display in order to give them psychological consistency. In the most searching examination of this problem, Anthony Stephens notes that 'Kleist's interest seems focused on evoking emotional states that are not causally linked in the manner of conventional dramatic exposition'.[25] For example, the Prince is throughout prone to egoistic fantasies, and although many commentators assert that the Elector has educated him out of them, the speech he gives when he thinks he is about to be executed, beginning 'Nun, o Unsterblichkeit, bist Du ganz mein!' ('Now, immortality, you are all mine!', 1830) belies this claim. His moral collapse in the *Todesfurchtsszene* has no apparent explanation. His relationship with Natalie develops with implausible speed and appears unimpeded by the scene in which he renounces her love and advises her to retire to a Protestant convent; Natalie, perhaps thinking he is too distressed to be responsible for his words, herself displays the courage he has lost and addresses him as 'young hero' (1032).[26] Going, as he thinks, to his death, he ignores her distress and does not even bid her farewell (1801–09).

The different aspects displayed by the Elector are also difficult to put together. He is kindly, fatherly, and affectionate towards Natalie. His confidence is evidently shaken by her account of the Prince's misery, as it is later by Hohenzollern's 'proof'. But, in writing the letter that puts the Prince's decision in his own hands, the Elector allows Natalie to think that he is giving him an unconditional pardon, thus setting her up for a bitter disappointment, for if his plan to educate the Prince succeeds, Natalie will be bereft of her lover. In many other ways his behaviour is incongruous for somebody whom commentators have hailed as the embodiment of law and even of Kantian moral rigorism.[27] His intervention in the opening scene shows that the Prince's somnambulism, and the sphere of unconscious desires that it reveals, has an appeal for him as well. His wish to deny this appeal perhaps accounts for the strange hostility with which he leaves the sleepwalking Prince: 'Ins Nichts mit dir zurück, Herr Prinz von Homburg, | Ins Nichts, ins Nichts!' ('Back into nothingness with you, Prince von Homburg, into nothingness, nothingness!', 74–75). In the battle, he chooses to ride a white horse which must make him a

25   Anthony Stephens, *Heinrich von Kleist: The Dramas and Stories* (Oxford: Berg, 1994), p. 176. Stephens argues that critics' many efforts at 'discursive unification' of characters and their motivations are ultimately futile (p. 177).
26   Cf. David Deissner, *Moral und Motivation im Werk Heinrich von Kleists* (Tübingen: Niemeyer, 2009): Natalie's tolerance of his behaviour can only imply 'dass sie ihn in jenem Moment der Todesangst für unzurechnungsfähig hält' (pp. 129–30).
27   Deissner, *Moral und Motivation*, p. 132.

conspicuous target for enemy fire. Kleist works into his play the well-known story of Froben, the loyal Master of the Horse, who, perceiving this risk, persuaded the Elector to change horses with him and was himself killed (hence the rumour of the Elector's death when in fact the victim is Froben).

The Elector's strangest and darkest action is leading the Prince to expect his execution, then releasing him at the last moment. Surprisingly few commentators have been troubled by what Stephens, rightly but too mildly, calls the 'gratuitous cruelty of the mock execution'.[28] To prepare oneself for death, then be released at the last moment, must be a shattering experience. This is done in Lohenstein's youthful tragedy *Ibrahim Bassa*, where the violent but irresolute Sultan Soliman, one of the psychopathic tyrants who dominate the Baroque stage, has his general Ibrahim tied up and prepared for ceremonial strangling, only to release him at the very last moment.[29] The Elector maintains that he is not an Oriental tyrant like the Dey of Tunis (1412), but here he behaves like one. Closer to Kleist's time, a similar trick is employed in Schiller's story *Spiel des Schicksals* (*Play of Fate*), based on the historical commandant of Stuttgart, Philipp Friedrich Rieger. Rieger is gratuitously made to suffer 'alle Qualen der Todesangst' ('all the tortures of the fear of death') before being reprieved.[30] Such practices still existed in Kleist's time and later. The Prussian officer Karl von François (1785–1855), having disobeyed a higher officer, was sentenced to death in 1808 but pardoned, just before his planned execution, by the King of Württemberg at the last moment. He described the experience as horrible: 'I had suffered too much; my soul was already on its way to another world and the summons to return felt to me like a new cruelty, more severe than any that had preceded it.'[31] Perhaps the best-known such incident came a few decades after Kleist's death, when a similar experience was imposed on Dostoevsky and the other young men accused of conspiracy. On 21 December 1849 fifteen of them were taken to Semenovsky Square in St Petersburg, made to mount a scaffold, and unexpectedly confronted with a firing squad. After a minute the firing squad lowered their rifles, and the conspirators were instead sentenced to confinement in Siberia. The experience of that minute, however, sent one of Dostoevsky's companions permanently insane, and changed Dostoevsky's own life by laying the foundation for his religious faith.[32] Does Kleist's Elector really not know what a cruel trick he is playing on the Prince? He comes across as an irrational and powerful man unaware of his own impulses.

These impulses conflict with the movement in the play that would see Prussia recreated, in line with Müller's theories, as a happy family.[33] The Prince regards the Elector and the Electress as surrogate parents. The Prince's mother on her deathbed

---

28   Stephens, *Heinrich von Kleist*, p. 176.
29   See Lohenstein, *Sämtliche Werke*, I, 79.
30   Schiller, *NA*, XVI, 39. For the historical events on which the story is based, see Alt, *Schiller*, I, 478.
31   Quoted in *SWB* II, 1174–75.
32   See Joseph Frank, *Dostoevsky: The Years of Ordeal, 1850–1859* (Princeton: Princeton University Press, 1983), pp. 55–58.
33   See Peter, 'Für ein anderes Preußen': 'Der Staat als Familie: dieser Gegenentwurf Kleists zum Staat als Maschine triumphiert am Schluß des Stückes' (p. 102).

entrusted him to them as a son (1010–15). Once the Prince has accepted his death sentence, the Elector kisses him on the forehead and calls him 'my son' (1784). The elderly Kottwitz has already called him 'my son' (1763). Natalie, the Elector's niece, is addressed as 'my little daughter' (1147). This atmosphere of domestic emotion recalls the sentimental family dramas popular in the late eighteenth century, such as Otto von Gemmingen's *Der teutsche Hausvater* (1780). It would spoil this utopia to recall the murderous tensions which can exist within the family, and which notoriously feature in other works by Kleist.[34] Even here one could easily construct an oedipal rivalry between the Prince and the Elector, noting 'the strange mixture of adulation and aggression in Prince Friedrich's attitudes to the Kurfürst'.[35] It is particularly remarkable that instead of being grieved by the false news of the Elector's death, the Prince is highly excited by the prospect of replacing him as Brandenburg's commander-in-chief and Natalie's protector (581–86).

However, it is not in the conclusion, whose artificiality is acknowledged in Kottwitz's statement that it is 'Ein Traum, was sonst?' ('A dream, what else?', 1856), but in the course of the action, that the play suggests a new kind of political state — one that is indebted to republican thinking. It may seem perverse to argue that *Prinz Friedrich von Homburg* is a republican play, since, with whatever qualifications, it exalts the figure of the Elector and never raises any possibility of replacing him with a president. But around 1800 it was possible to envisage a monarchy which was also republican. Novalis predicts a time when people will say that there can be no king without a republic and no republic without a king.[36] Kant's programme for a perpetual peace has as its first principle that the civil constitution of every state must be republican, that is, the executive power must be separated from the legislative power; provided this happens, the form of government 'accords with the *spirit* of a representative system'.[37] A monarchy, agrees Novalis, could permit 'genuine republicanism, universal participation in the whole state, heartfelt contact and harmony among all its members'.[38]

The tradition of republican thought can be traced back to Machiavelli via Montesquieu and Adam Ferguson, and has been identified as providing the key idea in Schiller's *Letters on the Aesthetic Education of Man*.[39] Montesquieu in *The Spirit of the Laws* makes a famous distinction among monarchies which are governed by honour, republics which are governed by virtue, and despotisms which are governed by fear. Schiller, who read Montesquieu and Ferguson at school, discusses in the *Aesthetic Letters* how an aesthetic education can modify the current imbalance

---

34 For example, in *Die Marquise von O.* the Marquise's father, having expelled his daughter from their home and fired a gun at her, is eventually brought round and caresses her 'pressing long, ardent, avid kisses on to her mouth, just like a lover!' Heinrich von Kleist, *The Marquise of O– and Other Stories*, trans. by David Luke and Nigel Reeves (Harmondsworth: Penguin, 1978), p. 107. On how Kleist exposes and reverses Enlightenment sentimentality, see Ruth Angress, 'Kleists Abkehr von der Aufklärung', *Kleist-Jahrbuch 1987*, pp. 98–114.

35 Stephens, *Heinrich von Kleist*, p. 177.

36 Novalis, *Schriften*, II, 490.

37 *Perpetual Peace*, in *Kant: Political Writings*, p. 101.

38 Novalis, *Schriften*, II, 496.

39 See Beiser, *Schiller as Philosopher*, pp. 123–29.

between the intellect and the senses (seen most starkly in the hyper-rationality and inhumanity of the French revolutionaries) and bring into being people whose inner harmony qualifies them to undertake a change of government without the disastrous consequences seen in France.

Kleist's Brandenburg, though technically a monarchy, is pervaded by the spirit of a republic. Characters are motivated by virtue rather than honour. The Prince goes astray in part by pursuing personal fame (or honour) as though he were living under a monarchy as described by Montesquieu. In the course of the play he comes closer to the ideal of republican and patriotic virtue. The Elector has a corresponding fault: he is in danger of becoming a despot. He insists that he is not a tyrant, contrasting himself with the Dey of Tunis — a stock example of the Oriental despot. The Prince, when angry with him, compares him to a whole series of despots: the Dey of Algiers, the Babylonian king Sardanapalus, and all the tyrannical Roman emperors. The Prince's insubordination, in leading a charge prematurely, puts the Elector to the test. His first response — whoever led the charge must suffer the death penalty — is despotic. Forgetting that the decision must be left to a court martial, he tries to combine the legislative with the executive power. Natalie's intervention persuades him to put the decision in the Prince's own hands. The subsequent remonstrances by Kottwitz and Hohenzollern convince him, first, that he cannot impose his will on an army that is prepared to mutiny, and, secondly, that he himself is fallible and even helped to provoke the Prince's disobedience.

Despite its endless ambiguities, the play vindicates the republican freedom of citizens to contest the decisions of the ruling power. The Elector knows that he is not in danger of being overthrown. In leading a mutiny, Natalie and Kottwitz are not rebels but a loyal opposition. They embody the republican principle whereby, in the words of Adam Ferguson, 'even the safety of the person, and the tenure of property, [...] depend, for their preservation, on the vigour and jealousy of a free people'.[40]

---

40   Adam Ferguson, *An Essay on the History of Civil Society*, ed. by Duncan Forbes (Edinburgh: Edinburgh University Press, 1966), p. 167.

16

Büchner:
Danton's Tod (1835)

One of the most intense scenes in *Danton's Tod*, Georg Büchner's drama of the French Revolution, concerns an allegedly necessary crime. Danton, in March 1794, is haunted by memories of the killings conducted in September 1792.[1] He has just spent some time wandering about and wrestling with his agonizing memories. The climax of the scene deserves close attention:

> [DANTON]   O hilf mir Julie, mein Sinn ist stumpf. War's nicht im September Julie?
> JULIE   Die Könige waren nur noch 40 Stunden von Paris ...
> DANTON   Die Festungen gefallen, die Aristokraten in der Stadt.
> JULIE   Die Republik war verloren.
> DANTON   Ja verloren. Wir konnten den Feind nicht im Rücken lassen, wir wären Narren gewesen, zwei Feinde auf einem Brett, wir oder sie, der Stärkere stößt den Schwächeren hinunter, ist das nicht billig?
> JULIE   Ja, ja.
> DANTON   Wir schlugen sie, das war kein Mord, das war Krieg nach innen.
> JULIE   Du hast das Vaterland gerettet.
> DANTON   Ja das hab' ich. Das war Notwehr, wir mußten. Der Mann am Kreuz hat sich's bequem gemacht: es muß ja Ärgernis kommen, doch wehe dem, durch welchen Ärgernis kommt.
>   Es muß, das war dies Muß. Wer will der Hand fluchen, auf die der Fluch des Muß gefallen? Wer hat das *Muß* gesprochen, wer? Was ist das, was in uns hurt, lügt, stiehlt und mordet?
>   Puppen sind wir von unbekannten Gewalten am Draht gezogen; nichts, nichts wir selbst! Die Schwerter, mit denen Geister kämpfen, man sieht nur die Hände nicht wie in Märchen.
>   Jetzt bin ich ruhig.
> JULIE   Ganz ruhig, lieb Herz?
> DANTON   Ja Julie, komm, zu Bette![2]

> DANTON   Oh help me, Julie, my mind's gone numb. September, Julie: isn't that when it happened?
> JULIE   The foreign kings were only forty hours from Paris.

---

1   The nineteenth-century spelling *Danton's Tod* is used in Georg Büchner, *Sämtliche Werke, Briefe und Dokumente*, ed. by Henri Poschmann, 2 vols (Frankfurt a.M.: Deutscher Klassiker Verlag, 1999). Henceforth cited as *SW*.

2   *Danton's Tod*, II. 5, in Büchner, *SW* I, 49–50.

DANTON   The outposts had fallen, the aristocrats were in the city.
JULIE   The Republic was doomed.
DANTON   Yes, doomed. We couldn't leave an enemy at our backs, we'd have been fools: two enemies on a plank, it's us or them, whichever is the stronger chucks the other off, that's fair, isn't it?
JULIE   Yes, yes!
DANTON   We fought them and won, that wasn't murder, it was war with the enemy within.
JULIE   You saved your country.
DANTON   I did, I did! It was self-defence, we had to do it. The man on the cross, how easily it tripped off his tongue: 'It must needs be that offences come, but woe unto him through whom they come.'
       'It *must* needs be': it's this 'must' that did it, Who'd ever curse the hand on whom the curse of 'must' has fallen? Who spoke the curse, who? What is it in us that whores, lies, steals and murders?
       Puppets, that's all we are, made to dance on strings by unknown forces; ourselves we are nothing, nothing — mere swords in the hands of warring spirits, the hands themselves cannot be seen, that's all, like in some child's fairy-tale.
       That's it. I'm happy now.
JULIE   Truly happy, my darling?
DANTON   Yes, Julie; come on, let's go to bed![3]

The September massacres are represented here as a necessary crime. They prey on Danton's conscience. One has the impression that he is working through the issue, with Julie as therapist (probably not for the first time). Once the therapeutic session is over, Danton and Julie go to bed so that he can find temporary oblivion in sex. What actually happened — according to Büchner's sources, and also according to modern historians? And how far was Danton directly responsible?

In August 1792, the armies of a coalition led by Austria and Prussia, and supported by émigrés who had fled from the Revolution, were marching towards Paris. They captured the frontier fortress of Longwy on 23 August. On 2 September, news reached Paris that the much closer fortress of Verdun had also fallen. A battle for Paris, and possibly its fall, was expected within a few days. The most authoritative source available to Büchner, Adolphe Thiers's *Histoire de la Révolution française*, describes how in the preceding weeks Paris had been overcome by panic. It was thought that the king, although a prisoner, was conspiring to open Paris to the invaders, and that all the great houses of Paris were full of armed royalists ready, on a signal, to break out and deliver Paris to the Coalition forces. From 27 August on, arrests were made of all those connected with the court or known to favour the king, including those whose enemies denounced them; 12,000–15,000 such people were thrown into prison. When news came of the fall of Verdun, panic led crowds to invade the prisons, ostensibly fearing a mass break-out. Tribunals were hastily set up which briefly interrogated each prisoner, released a few, but sent the great majority to be shot or hacked to death. The massacres continued till Wednesday

3   Georg Büchner, *Complete Plays, 'Lenz' and Other Writings*, trans. by John Reddick (London: Penguin, 1993), pp. 38–39.

5 September. Acknowledging how widely estimates of the number of victims differed, Thiers places the total somewhere between 6,000 and 12,000.[4]

What part did Danton play in this? Thiers describes Danton, then minister of justice, as 'the most powerful man in Paris'.[5] He gave the orders for the arrests of suspected royalists beginning on 27 August. Danton inspired his colleagues with a will to resist the enemy through boldness.[6] According to Thiers, Danton shared the general belief in an internal enemy or fifth column. He said there was a secret royal command centre in Paris that was corresponding with the Prussian army. So it was necessary to intimidate the royalists — '*il faut faire peur aux royalistes*'.[7] Danton therefore joined with Marat in a plot which Thiers does not specify, beyond stressing its atrocious character, but which sounds like a plan to instigate the massacres:

> Danton, que toujours on trouva sans haine contre ses ennemis personnels, et souvent accessible à la pitié, prêta son audace aux horribles rêveries de Marat: ils formèrent tous deux un complot dont plusieurs siècles ont donné l'exemple, mais qui, à la fin du XVIIIe, ne peut pas s'expliquer par l'ignorance des temps et la férocité des mœurs.[8]

> [Danton, whom we always find devoid of hatred for his personal enemies, and often accessible to pity, lent his boldness to Marat's horrible reveries: the two of them formed a plot of which there are examples in several previous centuries, but which, at the end of the eighteenth, cannot be explained by the ignorance of the age or the savagery of its manners.]

From Thiers's account, therefore, Büchner could conclude that Danton was principally responsible for the massacres; that there really was an internal enemy which had to be destroyed in case it joined forces with the invaders; and that the massacres were a hideous atrocity on a massive scale.

Recent historians paint a rather different picture. The massacres were not the result of a prior conspiracy, but the spontaneous action of a panic-stricken crowd. It was widely feared that large numbers of aristocrats were hiding in tunnels, with caches of weapons, ready to emerge, and that prisoners were planning to break out and join forces with them and the invaders.[9] If any individual can be assigned responsibility for organizing the massacres, it was Stanislas Maillard, famous for his leading part in the storming of the Bastille and now the captain of a troop of paramilitaries. Thiers says he presided over the tribunals that carried out the massacres; Büchner does not mention him.[10] When Danton was warned that the

4   Adolphe Thiers, *Histoire de la Révolution française*, 13th edn, 10 vols (Paris: Furne, 1847–65), II, 330.

5   Ibid., II, 298.

6   Ibid., II, 302, 309.

7   Ibid., II, 303.

8   Ibid., II, 304.

9   Timothy Tackett, *The Coming of the Terror in the French Revolution* (Cambridge, MA: Harvard University Press, 2015), p. 202; Michel Biard and Marisa Linton, *Terror: The French Revolution and its Demons* (Cambridge: Polity, 2021), p. 123; and on the atmosphere of rumour, made worse by the absence of official information, Côme Simien, 'Rumeurs et Révolution: la saison des massacres de septembre 1792', *Annales Historiques de la Révolution Française*, no. 404 (2020), 3–31.

10   Simon Schama, *Citizens: A Chronicle of the French Revolution* (New York: Viking, 1989), p. 633.

prisoners might be massacred, he is said to have replied 'Je m'en fous des prisonniers' ('I don't give a damn about the prisoners').[11]

The question of Danton's responsibility for the massacres was investigated thoroughly by Pierre Caron in the 1930s. It is clear that he took no direct part. Nor is there any record of his attempting to stop the massacres. Caron concludes that he regarded them with reserve and perhaps with tacit disapproval.[12] Afterwards, addressing the National Convention, he referred to them as 'those terrible acts which make us all groan'.[13] When setting up the Revolutionary Tribunal on 10 March 1793, he asserted, appealing to witnesses, that 'no human power was in a position to arrest the overflowing of national vengeance'.[14] When the executions were in full swing, he is reported to have justified them as a necessary sacrifice 'to appease the people of Paris'.[15] The only time he actually claimed responsibility was in a conversation with the Duc de Chartres (later King Louis-Philippe) which Caron considers insufficiently authenticated. Even if authentic, Danton's words leave the degree and nature of his responsibility obscure.[16] It does not appear that he conspired with Marat; given Marat's notorious bloodthirstiness, Thiers was perhaps assigning Danton guilt by association.

As for the numbers executed, Thiers's enormous estimates have now been reduced to between 1,100 and 1,400: terrible enough, but not the huge killing spree with many thousands of victims that Büchner was led to imagine.[17] By way of comparison, the most notorious massacre in French history, that of Huguenots on St Bartholomew's Day in 1572, killed some 2,000 people in Paris and perhaps a further 3,000 in provincial centres.[18] Moreover, many of the September victims, perhaps most, were not aristocrats. They included some 200 priests; 200 thieves and debtors; 35 women charged with prostitution, who were raped before being killed; and 160 inmates of the Bicêtre reformatory, including 43 teenage boys.[19] The murder of criminals was excused by the fear that the nobles had paid them to break out of prison and attack patriots.

The actions attributed to Büchner's Danton are far from historically accurate, but they reflect the best sources available to Büchner. Danton is represented as responsible for slaughter on a gigantic scale, with no precedent in recent history. The slaughter is presented as necessary in order to save the Revolution from being

11   Ibid. However, this utterance is reported by Madame Roland, a hostile witness.
12   Pierre Caron, *Les Massacres de septembre* (Paris: La Maison du livre français, 1935), pp. 245–46.
13   Quoted in Caron, *Les Massacres de septembre*, p. 244.
14   Quoted ibid., p. 245.
15   Schama, *Citizens*, p. 633. Caron is dubious about this and similar testimonies. However, they almost all agree that Danton blamed the massacres on the enraged populace, so this must have seemed the most plausible explanation at the time.
16   Caron, *Les Massacres de septembre*, pp. 249, 252; cf. Norman Hampson, *Danton* (London: Duckworth, 1978), p. 82.
17   William Doyle, *The Oxford History of the French Revolution*, 2nd edn (Oxford: Oxford University Press, 2002), p. 191; Tackett, *The Coming of the Terror*, p. 202.
18   Holt, *The French Wars of Religion*, p. 95.
19   See the list compiled by Ruth Scurr, *Fatal Purity: Robespierre and the French Revolution* (London: Chatto & Windus, 2006), p. 199.

defeated by internal as well as external enemies. Later in the play, when on trial before the Revolutionary Tribunal, Danton boasts of his responsibility in words that appear to be Büchner's invention: 'Ich habe im September die junge Brut der Revolution mit den zerstückten Leibern der Aristokraten geätzt' ('It was I in September that fed the tender brood of the revolution on the shattered bodies of aristocrats').[20] Here he says nothing about self-defence, but talks, in cannibalistic imagery, as though the death of aristocrats were necessary to feed the new revolutionary generation.[21]

In his dialogue with Julie, Danton suddenly veers away from the question of political necessity into metaphysical and even theological issues. He quotes from a passage in the Gospels, which in the Authorized Version runs:

> Woe unto the world because of occasions of stumbling! for it must needs be that the occasions come; but woe to that man through whom the occasion cometh! (Matt. 18. 7)

In the Gospel it is not altogether clear how this passage is related to its context. Jesus has been talking about how wicked it is to corrupt the minds of children. In the quoted passage, is he saying that children's minds are going to be corrupted, come what may, but that that in no way excuses the corrupter? Or has he moved onto a more general plane, saying that 'occasions of stumbling', offences, or sins are bound to happen, but that the sinner still deserves to be punished? Either way, the passage still casts doubt on divine justice. It anticipates the agonizing and perennial questions that Danton asks a few speeches later. We are made in such a way that we cannot help sinning, sometimes indeed committing horrific crimes. These crimes need not be forced on us by external necessity; they may spring from our own innate wickedness. Yet, in a paradoxical travesty of justice, we are liable to be held responsible, condemned, and even damned for what we could not help doing.

By turning to this theme, Danton has changed the subject. The September massacres have now been pushed into the background. Danton has just claimed that he was forced to instigate the massacres by the pressure of circumstances. Yet the change of subject implies, absurdly, that he ordered the massacres to satisfy his own personal bloodlust. He might no doubt be taken to mean that the perpetrators of the massacres illustrate the inexplicable wickedness of human nature, but he does not say so. Examined closely, his speech is incoherent.

In the famous letter to his fiancée Wilhelmine Jaeglé, which has become known as the 'fatalism letter', Büchner similarly links two issues, historical necessity and the evil intrinsic to human nature, and shows how churned up his feelings are by both:

> Ich studierte die Geschichte der Revolution. Ich finde mich wie zernichtet unter dem gräßlichen Fatalismus der Geschichte. Ich finde in der Menschennatur eine entsetzliche Gleichheit, in den menschlichen Verhältnissen eine unabwendbare Gewalt, Allen und Keinem verliehen. Der Einzelne nur Schaum auf der Welle,

---

20 *Danton's Tod*, III. 4, in Büchner, *SW* I, 62; *Complete Plays*, p. 51.
21 Margarete Kohlenbach, 'Puppen und Helden: Zum Fatalismusglauben in Georg Büchners Revolutionsdrama', *Germanisch-Romanische Monatsschrift*, n.s. 38 (1988), 395–410 (p. 400).

die Größe ein bloßer Zufall, die Herrschaft des Genies ein Puppenspiel, ein lächerliches Ringen gegen ein ehernes Gesetz, es zu erkennen das Höchste, es zu beherrschen unmöglich. [...] Ich gewöhnte mein Auge ans Blut. Aber ich bin kein Guillotinenmesser. Das *muß* ist eins von den Verdammungsworten, womit der Mensch getauft worden. Der Ausspruch: es muß ja Ärgernis kommen, aber wehe dem, durch den es kommt, – ist schauderhaft. Was ist das, was in uns lügt, mordet, stiehlt? Ich mag dem Gedanken nicht weiter nachgehen. Könnte ich aber dies kalte und gemarterte Herz an Deine Brust legen![22]

I've been studying the history of the French Revolution. I felt as though utterly crushed by the hideous fatalism of history. I find in human nature a terrible sameness, in human circumstances an ineluctable violence vouchsafed to all and to none. Individuals but froth on the waves, greatness a mere coincidence, the mastery of geniuses a dance of puppets, a ridiculous struggle against an iron law that can at best be recognized, but never mastered. [...] My eye has grown accustomed to blood. But I'm no guillotine blade. 'Must' is one of those words by which mankind was damned from the very beginning. The saying, 'It must be that offences come, but woe to that man by whom the offence cometh', is horrifying. What is it in man that lies, murders, steals? I can't bear to take the thought any further. But if only I could lay this tortured heart of mine on your breast![23]

Here again Büchner moves from the feeling of helplessness in the face of historical circumstances, via the paradox that one may still be held responsible for actions that were forced upon one, to the dark and inexplicable depths of human nature. Again the development of these thoughts is less than coherent. Compulsion stemming from external circumstances is a different matter from the compulsion arising from within our own natures.

The 'fatalism letter' poses problems not only of interpretation but even of dating. Like the other surviving letters to Wilhelmine Jaeglé, it is undated. It was long thought to date from March 1834, but its conjectural date has now been pushed back to January.[24] That mitigates what otherwise has seemed an enigma. For in March 1834 Büchner helped to found a revolutionary secret society, called the Gesellschaft der Menschenrechte (Society for Human Rights), and in July 1834 to print and distribute the pamphlet *Der hessische Landbote*, which urges the Hessian peasantry to rise and overcome their oppressive rulers (without in any way offering to lead or assist such a rebellion). No uprising happened; instead, it is reported that the peasants handed many copies of the pamphlet in to the authorities.[25] Its discovery obliged Büchner to flee across the French border to Strasbourg.

---

22   Letter to Wilhelmine Jaeglé, in Büchner, *SW* II, 377–78.
23   *Complete Plays*, pp. 195–96.
24   Poschmann dates the letter to the middle or end of January 1834 (*SW* II, 1098–1105). Previous editors dated it to March 1834, because Büchner mentions a journey he intends to take at Easter, and because he says 'Bei uns ist Frühling'. However, besides the fact that he hardly needed to tell his fiancée that March was in the spring, it has been established that in Hessen January 1834 was extraordinarily warm: Jan-Christoph Hauschild, 'Neudatierung und Neubewertung von Georg Büchners "Fatalismusbrief"', *Zeitschrift für deutsche Philologie*, 108 (1989), 511–29 (pp. 515–17). Hauschild suggests that the letter was written between 10 and 20 January (p. 526).
25   Testimony of August Becker, *SW* II, 665.

How are Büchner's highly dangerous actions compatible with the despair of the 'fatalism letter'? One possible answer is that the 'fatalism letter' should not be taken seriously, but instead dismissed as an expression of mood, a 'rhetorical extravaganza' which deflected Büchner only briefly from his political aims.[26] However, the letter seems to express much stronger feelings than a mere passing mood. And since its sentiments lead directly to the scene from *Danton's Tod* written about a year later, 'they must therefore', as J. P. Stern argued in 1964, 'have occupied his mind more or less continuously throughout the period in which he engaged in subversive activities'.[27] If we dismiss the letter, we must downplay also the scene in which Danton unburdens himself (probably not for the first time) to Julie. Yet the scene is so powerful that Friedrich Sengle carries full conviction in saying: 'Anyone who makes light of the September massacres misses the nerve-centre of the drama.'[28]

It would of course be impertinent to criticize Büchner for a failure of logic in a private letter, one moreover clearly written in a state of distress. In any case Büchner's biography is not our concern here. His letters make clear that for the rest of his short life he continued to worry about poverty, denounce the selfishness of the ruling classes, and wish for society to be transformed. One can infer the same feelings behind the exceptional intensity of the scene from *Danton's Tod* just quoted. In the play, however, the material needs to make sense without reference to the author's state of mind. Here the similar change of subject is troubling because it blurs Danton's motivation. Is he upset because political circumstances compelled him to instigate the September massacres, or because of the ineliminable evil latent in human nature?

A further reason for taking Danton's agonies with full seriousness is that the issues that torment him are more than personal concerns. They are among the painful riddles that have worried philosophers, theologians, and many other thinking people down the ages. When we look back over history, most of it seems to be a series of catastrophes — wars, massacres, oppression, famine — inflicted on the powerless. Even the rulers who normally exercise power can easily be shown to have minimal freedom of action. 'History is a nightmare from which I am trying to awake.'[29] Then, when we turn to the individual, we find within ourselves drives and desires which even for the best people are difficult to subdue. Christianity tries to explain our propensity for evil by the myth of the Fall; the rabbis spoke of the 'evil impulse' (*yetser ha-ra*); Kant was driven to postulate 'radical evil' within human nature.[30] Both these sets of insoluble problems powerfully counteract the revolutionary élan which many interpreters have tried to find in *Danton's Tod*.

26   John Reddick, *Georg Büchner: The Shattered Whole* (Oxford: Clarendon Press, 1994), p. 109.

27   J. P. Stern, *Re-interpretations: Seven Studies in Nineteenth-Century German Literature* (London: Thames and Hudson, 1964), p. 96.

28   *Büchner-Handbuch*, ed. by Roland Borgards and Harald Neumeyer (Stuttgart and Weimar: Metzler, 2009), p. 26. Cf. Friedrich Sengle, *Biedermeierzeit*, 3 vols (Stuttgart: Metzler, 1971–80), iii (1980), p. 304.

29   James Joyce, *Ulysses* (Harmondsworth: Penguin, 1969), p. 40.

30   See the classic work by N. P. Williams, *The Ideas of the Fall and of Original Sin* (London: Longmans, Green & Co., 1927), and the section entitled 'Der Mensch ist von Natur böse' in Kant, *Die Religion innerhalb der Grenzen der bloßen Vernunft* (1793), *Werke*, ed. Weischedel, iv. 680–88.

In presenting Danton as under compulsion to commit a monstrous crime, Büchner seems to owe something to Schiller's representation of political action in *Maria Stuart*.[31] It is true that he disparaged Schiller in a letter to his parents, but to do that he had to have read Schiller and could not but have been impressed.[32] In *Maria Stuart*, it will be remembered, Elisabeth finds herself under pressure to commit a crime, the illegal execution of Maria, which is forcefully presented to her as necessary. Her discomfort is obvious in the soliloquy in which she agonizes over his situation, and from the shabby (but historically attested) artifice by which she pins the responsibility on Burleigh and Davison. Büchner's Danton is a considerably more impressive dramatic figure than Schiller's Elisabeth. But his situation, hemmed in by overwhelming political pressures, his discomfort, and his arguably evasive response, are comparable.

Can any light be shed on Danton's position by looking at that of his antagonist Robespierre? In Act I, scene 6, Danton tries to persuade Robespierre that the Reign of Terror is no longer necessary and should cease forthwith. It is, after all, now April 1794, and since the defeat of the Coalition forces at Valmy on 20 September 1792 France has no longer been threatened by external aggression, so that self-defence can no longer be cited as justification. Robespierre, however, replies in a characteristically robotic manner that the Revolution still has to defeat its internal enemies:

> Die soziale Revolution ist noch nicht fertig, wer eine Revolution <nur> zur Hälfte vollendet, gräbt sich selbst sein Grab. Die gute Gesellschaft ist noch nicht tot, die gesunde Volkskraft muß sich an die Stelle dieser nach allen Richtungen abgekitzelten Klasse setzen. Das Laster muß bestraft werden, die Tugend muß durch den Schrecken herrschen.[33]

> The social revolution is not yet finished, and to try to end a revolution in the middle is to dig your own grave. The world of the idle rich is not yet dead, the healthy vigour of the people must replace this utterly effete and played-out class. Vice must be punished, virtue must rule through terror.[34]

Robespierre's political motivation is transparent. To justify staying in power, he needs to claim that the dangers against which he is supposedly defending the Revolution are still in being. So when one enemy has been defeated, he fabricates another. We have already seen him (in Act I, scene 2) flattering the Paris populace and warning them of the dangers that still threaten them, thus distracting them from the fact that they are starving and diverting their indignation from himself onto other political groups.

Instead of pursuing the political argument with Robespierre, however, Danton, as he does in the later scene with Julie, moves the argument onto moral issues. He attacks Robespierre's narrowly puritanical conception of virtue and his insistence on

31   See Sengle, *Biedermeierzeit*, III, 303.
32   See letter of 28 July 1835, *SW* II, 411.
33   Büchner, *SW* I, 32.
34   Büchner, *Complete Plays*, p. 23.

imposing it on others, as 'heaven's policeman' ('der Polizeisoldat des Himmels').[35] But, as commentators have often pointed out, the libertarian and libertine principles professed by the Dantonist group are politically irrelevant: they will not put bread in the people's mouths. They enable Danton to turn his argument with Robespierre into a confrontation of (predominantly sexual) virtue and vice. Yet the vice against which the historical Robespierre campaigned was primarily financial corruption, living in luxury while the people went hungry, and abusing public office to enrich oneself. Dorothy James has most forcefully pointed out that Büchner has transformed the political antagonism between Danton and Robespierre into a moral one. He has made the formidable revolutionary Robespierre into 'a puritanical moralist who is against sex and drinking and getting into debt, and doesn't want anyone to enjoy himself', and 'appears to be persecuting a harmless, pleasure-loving Danton to punish him for his sins'.[36]

This is another example of how this supposedly political drama keeps veering away from politics into moral, philosophical, and existential questions which its protagonists, as historical figures engaged in life-or-death political struggles, are unlikely to have had on their minds. It illustrates the well-known inconsistency in the portrayal of Danton, who is sometimes a cynical libertine, sometimes a loving husband, sometimes a hardened revolutionary and mass murderer who boasts of the September massacres, sometimes conscience-stricken and terrified by the prospect of death.[37] There are many other contradictions in the play, which Büchner, after all, wrote in five weeks, constantly afraid of being arrested for his subversive activities.[38] He crammed into it all the moral and existential questions which were preoccupying his exceptionally well-stocked and fertile mind. So we have the free-standing scene in which Marion reveals the outlook of someone who lives solely by her senses; a rant about the deficiencies of classical theatre (II, 3); and a long speech, put in the mouth of Saint-Just, placing the horrors of the Revolution within the history of the cosmos. All this makes the play extraordinarily rich and powerful. One would not want to lose any of the apparent irrelevancies. But its richness is gained at the expense of coherence. And one aspect of its incoherence is Danton's conflation of different kinds of compulsion in his formulation of the necessary crime.

With Robespierre, there is no question of a *necessary* crime, except as a flimsy self-justification in which he himself does not really believe, nor of acting under compulsion. His wishes are put into practice by his colleague Saint-Just, a highly efficient political fixer and (in the view of Georg Lukács) an exemplary

35   *SW* I, 33.

36   Dorothy James, *Georg Büchner's 'Dantons Tod': A Reappraisal* (London: MHRA, 1982), p. 44. It is regrettable that this excellent book has made so little impact on Büchner studies: it is not mentioned in the *Büchner-Handbuch*, and is casually dismissed by Reddick (*Georg Büchner*, p. 7n.) on the grounds that it treats *Danton's Tod* as the work of an immature dramatist. It is fortunately acknowledged in Jan-Christoph Hauschild, *Georg Büchner: Biographie* (Stuttgart and Weimar: Metzler, 1993), p. 447.

37   See Ronald Peacock, *The Poet in the Theatre* (London: MacGibbon & Kee, 1961), on 'Büchner's private Danton' (p. 184), a line of argument developed by James.

38   See his letter to Gutzkow accompanying the MS of *Danton's Tod*: 21 February 1835, *SW* II, 392–3.

revolutionary.[39] Saint-Just shows immense gusto in arranging a show trial in which the Dantonists will be sandwiched between some forgers and some alleged foreign agents, so that the association will seem to strengthen the charges against them. He has no problem with agency, nor with humanity; he cracks callous jokes at the expense of his intended victims.

All these actions, performed by Danton, Robespierre and Saint-Just, occur of course within a much larger historical framework, that of the whole history of the Revolution. Büchner and his eventual readers knew that Robespierre and Saint-Just were themselves under the shadow of the guillotine. Both would be executed, along with their political associates, on 28 July (less than three months after the events shown in the play), in the revolutionary month of Thermidor, a name which would become shorthand for the reaction against the Terror. Beyond that, Büchner knew that the Revolution had failed. Its course involved bloodshed on a massive scale, civil war and widespread starvation. The reaction against it would bring Napoleon Bonaparte to power as First Consul and eventually as Emperor. The play shows that it did nothing for the poor of Paris, apart from providing a gruesome spectacle with which mothers could distract their hungry children.

One cannot therefore help wondering about the coherence of Büchner's politics. His letters show that he wanted society to be transformed by sweeping away the wealthy upper classes, and that he thought this would be accomplished by a widespread popular revolt. His politics, in theory at least, seem much closer to Robespierre's than to the libertarian individualism he ascribes to the Danton faction.[40] He expresses his conviction that the educated minority will never make a difference. Only the great masses can transform society, and to set them in motion there are only two levers:

> Ich habe mich überzeugt, die gebildete und wohlhabende Minorität, so viel Konzessionen sie auch von der Gewalt für sich begehrt, wird nie ihr spitzes Verhältnis zur großen Klasse aufgeben wollen. Und die große Klasse selbst? Für die gibt es nur zwei Hebel, materielles Elend und *religiöser Fanatismus*. Jede Partei, welche diese Hebel anzusetzen versteht, wird siegen. Unsere Zeit braucht Eisen und Brot — und dann ein *Kreuz* oder sonst so was.[41]

> I have become convinced that the educated and prosperous minority, whilst keen to wrest concessions for itself from those holding power, will never be willing to give up its own barbed relationship to the great mass of the people. And the masses themselves? For them there are only two levers: material poverty and *religious fanaticism*. Any party adept at applying these levers will carry the day. Our age needs weapons and bread — and then a *cross* or some such.[42]

Promoting religious fanaticism, especially for merely instrumental purposes, is a dangerous game. Robespierre seems to be playing it in encouraging the crowd to

39   Lukács, *German Realists in the Nineteenth Century*, p. 83.
40   On the inadequacy and implausibility of the political programme ascribed to the Dantonists, see James, *Georg Büchner's 'Dantons Tod'*, pp. 29–34.
41   Letter to Karl Gutzkow, beginning of June 1836, *SW* II, 440.
42   *Complete Plays*, pp. 204–05.

regard him as a Messiah (I, 2). But the play, with the truthfulness of great literature, exposes what is really happening. Because Robespierre can do nothing for the people's poverty, he falls back on the other lever, stimulating their fanaticism and thus giving them illusory satisfaction.

As for material misery, Büchner's reliance on this motive places him in an awkward position that has been shared by other revolutionaries. If the authorities manage to improve the people's material position, the people will no longer support revolution. 'Mästen Sie die Bauern, und die Revolution bekommt die Apoplexie. Ein *Huhn* im Topf jedes Bauern macht den gallischen *Hahn* verenden',[43] Büchner wrote to Gutzkow: 'Fatten the peasants, and the revolution will die of apoplexy. Put a chicken in the pot of every peasant, and the Gallic cockerel will drop down dead.'[44] It follows logically that revolutionaries must dread even the mildest attempts at reform by the authorities. After the discovery of the *Landbote* plans, August Becker testified that Büchner wanted a mass popular uprising and maintained that if the princes cut back their extravagant courts, armies and administrations and fed the people better,

> *dann ist die Sache der Revolution*, wenn sich der Himmel nicht erbarmt, in *Deutschland* auf immer *verloren*. Seht die *Oestreicher*, sie sind *wohlgenährt* und *zufrieden!* Fürst *Metternich*, der geschickteste unter allen, hat allen revolutionären Geist, der jemals unter ihnen aufkommen könnte, für immer in ihrem eigenen *Fett* erstickt. So sind die eigenen Worte des *Büchner* gewesen.[45]

> Then, unless Heaven has mercy, the revolutionary cause in Germany is lost for ever. Look at the Austrians, they are well-fed and contented! Prince Metternich, the most adroit of all, has smothered in their own fat for ever any revolutionary spirit that could ever arise among them. These are Büchner's own words.

The revolutionary is opposed not to oppression but to reform. Reform threatens his goals, oppression seems to bring them closer, and therefore the revolutionary must wish the people to suffer even more. It was for this reason — to hasten revolutionary changes — that Vladimir Ulyanov, later known as Lenin, refused to help with the efforts at famine relief organized by Tolstoy in the province of Samara in 1891–92. According to a political opponent, 'Vladimir welcomed the famine as a factor in breaking down the peasantry and creating an industrial proletariat'.[46] We shall see in a later chapter how Brecht got into trouble with Communist orthodoxy by ingenuously explaining this aspect of revolutionary praxis in *Die Maßnahme*.

43 Letter to Gutzkow, after 19 March 1835, *SW* II, 400.
44 *Complete Plays*, p. 201.
45 *SW* II, 660–61.
46 Edmund Wilson, *To the Finland Station: A Study in the Writing and Acting of History* ([1940]; Glasgow: Fontana, 1960), p. 371; see also Robert Service, *Lenin: A Biography* (London: Macmillan, 2000), pp. 85–86.

17

Wagner:
Die Walküre (1851–52)

Richard Wagner is not usually included in histories of German drama. Although his works are conventionally called operas, he insisted that they were music–dramas. Opera to him meant the relatively trivial art form, flourishing especially in France, in which music was a superficial adornment to a text. Instead of merely setting a libretto to music, Wagner aimed at an all-inclusive work of art, a *Gesamtkunstwerk*, in which music and drama formed an integrated whole, and were able to address profoundly important issues, including those of politics and religion. In this chapter, lack of musical expertise forces me to concentrate on Wagner's literary text, but I hope to show that it places Wagner firmly in the great tradition of German political tragedy.[1]

Wagner's tetralogy *Der Ring des Nibelungen* was conceived on a cosmic scale. Running from the initial theft of the Rhine treasure in *Das Rheingold* to the destruction of the gods in *Götterdämmerung*, it imitates the grand narrative of the Bible from the Fall to the Apocalypse. In its second part, entitled *Die Walküre* (*The Valkyrie*) and written by Wagner in 1851–52, two necessary crimes are forced on the god Wotan by the intrigues in which he has enmeshed himself. First, he is obliged to permit the death of his beloved son Siegmund, whom he has reared to regain the ring of power and thus secure the gods against the malice of the dwarf Alberich. Then, because his daughter Brünnhilde, his favourite among the Valkyries, disobeys him by trying to protect Siegmund, Wotan, despite his love for her, is obliged to punish her by taking away her semi-divine status and leaving her asleep in a circle of fire from which only a supreme hero can wake her.

While *Die Walküre* obviously cannot be considered in isolation from the *Ring* as a whole, there are grounds for focusing on it as in some measure a self-contained tragedy. It is unified, firstly, by the compulsion Wotan finds himself under to injure the two people dearest to him, his son Siegmund and his daughter Brünnhilde; secondly, by the resistance that beings lower in the scale of creation repeatedly offer to the gods' power — Siegmund and Sieglinde by breaching the incest taboo; Siegmund by refusing Brünnhilde's order to accompany him to Valhalla; and Brünnhilde by her disobedience to Wotan.

---

[1]   For a combination of literary and musical analysis, see the chapter 'From Political Freedom to Self-Denial: Wagner's *Ring* and the Revolutions of 1848', in William J. McGrath, *German Freedom and the Greek Ideal: The Cultural Legacy from Goethe to Mann* (New York: Palgrave Macmillan, 2013), pp. 75–130.

The incestuous union between Siegmund and Sieglinde, which will result in the birth of Siegfried, might be considered a further crime. It is certainly a crime in the eyes of Wotan's wife Fricka, the guardian of marriage ('der Ehe Hüterin'),[2] who describes it as 'Frevel', a word with overtones of sacrilege (*Ring*, p. 353; cf. 'die That | des frech frevelnden Paar's', 'the deed | of that brazenly impious pair', p. 141). Wagner seems originally to have likewise regarded the incest as criminal. In the prose summary which he completed on 4 October 1848 and later published as *Der Nibelungen-Mythus als Entwurf zu einem Drama*, he says that Siegmund must die to atone for this crime ('dem Verbrechen zur Sühne').[3] In the completed text, however, Siegmund dies for a different reason, and the incest, in being opposed to the divinely imposed order, is a liberating act with consequences that could have redeemed the world.

The cosmic order within which these events take place is itself founded on crimes, committed respectively by Alberich and Wotan. Alberich's crime is clear: rebuffed by the Rhinemaidens, he renounces love and is thus enabled to steal their treasure from the bed of the Rhine and make from it the ring of power. He thus violates nature and imposes on the natural order an artificial civilization based on money. There is a disturbing affinity between Alberich and his antagonist Wotan. In the mythology of the *Ring*, Alberich and his kin are 'black elves' ('Schwarzalben'), while Wotan describes the gods, including himself, as 'light elves' and even calls himself 'Licht-Alberich' (*Ring*, p. 211). Both Wotan and Alberich have semi-divine sons. Wotan is the father of Siegmund and the grandfather of Siegfried. Alberich, having seduced a member of the Gibichung family, is the father of the evil Hagen. In a further symmetry, it is Hagen who will treacherously murder the hero Siegfried.

If Alberich ravishes nature by converting the gold into treasure, Wotan performs an analogous act by breaking off a branch from the World Ash, making it into his spear, and carving contracts and treaties (*Verträge*) on it. As a result, so the Norns tell us, the wound inflicted on the World Ash has caused the tree to decay, and the well of wisdom at its base has dried up (*Ring*, p. 281). It has therefore been suggested that Wotan, rather than Alberich, committed the 'primal crime' ('Ur-Frevel') from which all the disasters of the Ring narrative proceed.[4] The text, however, suggests that the two act in parallel. Driven by the desire for power, Alberich converts natural products into money, while Wotan devises a system of laws which are supposed to create stability but in fact permit deception and injustice. This implies yet another 'necessary crime'. Not just any particular political action, but the establishment of civilization itself, was a criminal act. Nature has been abused to

2   Quotations in German and English are from *Wagner's 'Ring of the Nibelung: A Companion*, text trans. by Stewart Spencer, with commentaries by Barry Millington and others (London: Thames & Hudson, 1993), identified as *Ring* and page number; here p. 141.

3   Wagner, *Skizzen und Entwürfe zur Ring-Dichtung, mit der Dichtung 'Der junge Siegfried'*, ed. by Otto Strobel (Munich: Bruckmann, 1930), p. 27.

4   Hartmut Reinhardt, '"Eine Tragödie von der erschütterndsten Wirkung": Richard Wagners *Der Ring des Nibelungen* als Beitrag zur Dramatik des 19. Jahrhunderts', in *Die Tragödie der Moderne: Gattungsgeschichte — Kulturtheorie — Epochendiagnose*, ed. by Daniel Fulda and Thorsten Valk (Berlin: de Gruyter, 2010), pp. 127–59 (p. 154).

serve human interests, while the natural force of love has been subjected to the law of marriage, where it withers away. The union of Siegmund and Sieglinde defies all laws, being also adulterous since Sieglinde is married to Hunding. It thus offers a glimpse of a future realm of restored freedom, a promise, however, that the *Ring* as Wagner completed it does not fulfil.

As a perfectly rounded drama, *Die Walküre* is aesthetically satisfying in a way that the entire *Ring*, magnificent work though it is, does not quite achieve. To see why not, and why the utopian promise suggested in *Die Walküre* is not kept, we need to look at the genesis of the *Ring* text between 1848 and 1852. The prose sketch *Der Nibelungen-Mythus* deals in far the greatest detail with the events that Wagner took from the *Nibelungenlied* and that would later appear in *Götterdämmerung*. The hero Siegfried arrives at the hall of King Gunther on the Rhine; Gunther's sister Gudrun (later 'Gutrune') is already enamoured of him; to secure him, Gunther's evil half-brother Hagen prepares a love-philtre which makes him fall in love with Gudrun and forget all about Brünnhilde, whom he has left on her mountain-top. Hagen has already told Gunther what a desirable woman Brünnhilde is. To win her, Gunther enlists the help of the unsuspecting Siegfried. With the Tarnhelm, a magic device that permits shape-shifting, invisibility, and instantaneous travel, Siegfried, disguised as Gunther, overcomes Brünnhilde's resistance (but avoids sexual contact) and brings her back to the Rhine. Enraged by Siegfried's apparent betrayal, Brünnhilde reveals to Gunther and Hagen that although Siegfried's skin is proof against weapons, his back is vulnerable (because it was assumed that he would never show his back to an enemy), and Hagen duly shoots him. The dying Siegfried recognizes Brünnhilde and begs her to guide him to Valhalla. She joins him on his funeral pyre, having first promised the ring, which she received from him, to the Rhinemaidens, its rightful owners, and addressed 'Wodan' (as he is called here): 'Nur Einer herrsche, Allvater! Herrlicher! Du! Daß ewig deine Macht sei, führ' ich dir diesen zu: empfange ihn wohl, er ist es werth!' ('Let only one rule, father of all! Glorious one! You! That your power may be eternal, I lead this man to you; receive him well, he is worthy of it!').[5] In this version, there is as yet no suggestion that the gods are doomed whatever happens, as in the final *Ring*. Once the ring has been restored to the Rhinemaidens, there is apparently nothing to fear from Alberich and the gods can rule securely for ever.

From *Der Nibelungen-Mythus* Wagner extracted the events that now appear in *Götterdämmerung* and revised the draft as an opera libretto under the title *Siegfrieds Tod*. However, the draft presupposed the back-story set out in *Der Nibelungen-Mythus*, so the potential audience was left with many unanswered questions. How did Brünnhilde come to be on the mountain-top? What were her previous relations with Siegfried? How did Siegfried acquire the ring, and what was its previous history? Some information was provided in the dialogue, thus slowing down the action: Hagen tells Gunther and Gudrun how Siegfried killed the dragon and gained the treasure, and Siegfried then amplifies the story; Brünnhilde is visited by the other Valkyries and tells them how she defied Wotan; Alberich, Hagen's father,

5   *Skizzen*, p. 33.

tells him how the gods stole the ring from him.[6] To start filling in the back-story, Wagner set to work on *Der junge Siegfried*, intended as a light, semi-comic opera. Even here, however, he included a long exposition by Brünnhilde telling Siegfried who the Valkyries are and recounting the history of his own ancestors.[7] Presently he realized that he had to do more: 'I now see that in order to be completely comprehensible from the stage I shall have to dramatize the whole myth.'[8]

In the course of his work, Wagner developed the idea of the doom of the gods and their displacement by human beings. In *Der Nibelungen-Mythus* three Norns (later, in *Das Rheingold*, replaced by Erda) warn Wotan that if the gods keep the ring, they will be doomed.[9] This persuades Wotan to give the ring to the two giants who built Valhalla, and its destructive influence is promptly shown when Fafner kills his brother Fasolt. In the final text of the *Ring*, privately published in 1853, it is not clear whether the gods are doomed by their own corruption, or by a natural process of evolution whereby gods give way to humans. Either way, one expects a humanist myth in which humanity struggles towards autonomy, and to some extent Wagner does provide this, especially, as we shall see, in *Die Walküre*. But the final stage of the myth, set among the human beings living beside the Rhine, does not live up to such expectations. Gunther is an unheroic character who needs Siegfried to win his bride for him; Gutrune is a nonentity; Hagen (admittedly, as the son of Alberich, only half human) is downright evil; and even Siegfried cuts an unimpressive figure. He succumbs so rapidly to the love-philtre which makes him forget Brünnhilde that he comes across as shallow; and it is notorious that the boisterous Siegfried of the preceding drama is a bit of a lout, although it was Wagner's intention to present in him 'the most perfect human being that I can comprehend', for whom 'consciousness is always expressed only in the most immediate living and acting'.[10] Moreover, although Siegfried was supposed to be 'the human being of the future', he has no future, because Wagner's plan always led up to the events taken from the *Nibelungenlied* in which Siegfried is treacherously killed.[11] Better, therefore, to take *Die Walküre* on its own and explore how Wagner's tragic conception is most finely and movingly developed through the characters of Wotan, Siegmund, and Brünnhilde.

The back-story, especially as Wagner developed it in *Die Walküre* and *Das Rheingold*, is imbued with the political beliefs that also led him into revolutionary activity in Dresden in 1849. In his essay *Die Kunst und die Revolution* (1849) Wagner drew a contrast between the place of art in ancient Greece and its position in the modern world. Greek culture centred on the theatre, which embodied the national

6   *Siegfrieds Tod*, in *Skizzen*, pp. 39, 40, 42, 44.

7   *Der junge Siegfried* in *Skizzen*, pp. 186-88.

8   Letter to Theodor Uhlig, 12 November 1851, in Wagner, *Sämtliche Briefe*, ed. by various editors, 27 vols to date (orig. Leipzig: VEB Deutscher Verlag für Musik, now Breitkopf & Härtel, 1967–), IV (1979), 174; quoted in Elizabeth Magee, *Richard Wagner and the Nibelungs* (Oxford: Clarendon Press, 1990), p. 10.

9   *Skizzen*, p. 26. Cf. Erda's warning, *Ring*, p. 112.

10   Letter to August Röckel, 25/26 January 1854, in Wagner, *Sämtliche Briefe*, VI (1986), 69–70.

11   'Siegfried [ist] der von uns gewünschte, gewollte Mensch der Zukunft' (ibid., p. 68).

self-understanding. Nowadays, theatre, like the other arts, is simply a branch of industry. The defect of Greek culture, however, was its reliance on slavery. So we should not aspire to become Greeks again. Instead, we need a revolution which will free us from our enslavement to the machine and make the machine into our slave:

> From its state of civilized barbarism true art can rise to its dignity only on the shoulders of our great social movement: both share a common aim and can only attain it if they realize it together. This aim is *the strong and beautiful human being*: the *revolution* must give him *strength*, and *art beauty!*[12]

In the same essay Wagner delivers a polemic against Christianity for depreciating earthly life and urging people to place all their hopes in a future existence. The effect of Christianity has been 'arrogant hypocrisy, usury, robbery of nature's goods, and egoistic contempt for one's suffering fellow-humans'.[13] Siegfried was to typify 'the strong and beautiful human being', later 'the *fearless* human being who always loves'.[14] In his intensive explorations of mythology, Wagner found that Siegfried had originally been conceived as a sun-god or solar myth. Something of this conception survives in the *Ring* when Brünnhilde, on being woken by Siegfried with a kiss, exclaims: 'Heil dir, Sonne!' ('Hail to you, sun!', *Ring*, p. 267).[15]

For Wagner, political liberation went together with sexual liberation. In the early 1830s he came in contact with the sexual politics of the Young German movement (Junges Deutschland), especially through Heinrich Laube, whom he got to know in Leipzig in 1832. Inspired by the Saint-Simonians, an eccentric French group of early socialists, the Young Germans rejected Christian asceticism and spoke enthusiastically about 'the emancipation of the flesh'. Laube encouraged Wagner to read Wilhelm Heinse's novel *Ardinghello* (1787), in which the hero, a Renaissance painter, establishes on two Greek islands a colony dedicated to free love; this novel had a lasting appeal for Wagner, who re-read it, together with his then lover Cosima, in 1873.[16] Wagner's opera *Das Liebesverbot* (1836), an adaptation of Shakespeare's *Measure for Measure*, pits sexual permissiveness against gloomy puritanism.[17] In the 1840s Wagner read Ludwig Feuerbach, who argued that 'God' embodied the qualities that man had alienated from himself: 'The divine being is nothing else than the human being, or rather, the human nature purified, freed from the limits of the individual man, made objective — i.e. contemplated and revered as another, a distinct being.'[18] By rejecting the concept of God and adopting

---

12   *Die Kunst und die Revolution*, in Wagner, *Sämtliche Schriften und Dichtungen*, Volks-Ausgabe, 12 vols (Leipzig: Breitkopf & Härtel, n.d.), III, 32.
13   Ibid., III, 36.
14   Ibid.; letter to Röckel, 25/26 January 1854, p. 68.
15   See Magee, *Wagner and the Nibelungs*, pp. 143–52.
16   Martin Gregor-Dellin, *Richard Wagner: Sein Leben, sein Werk, sein Jahrhundert* (Munich: Piper, 1980), pp. 92–93. See Cosima's diary, 15 June 1873, quoted ibid., p. 861.
17   Wagner gives a detailed synopsis in *Mein Leben* (Munich: List, 1963), pp. 138–43. See Yvonne Nilges, *Richard Wagners Shakespeare* (Würzburg: Königshausen & Neumann, 2007), pp. 54–89 (esp. pp. 57–59 on Laube and *Ardinghello*).
18   Ludwig Feuerbach, *The Essence of Christianity*, trans. by George Eliot (New York: Harper & Row, 1957), p. 14; *Das Wesen des Christenthums* in Feuerbach, *Sämtliche Werke*, ed. by Wilhelm Bolin and Friedrich Jodl, 10 vols, 2nd edn (Stuttgart: Frommann-Holzboog, 1960), VI, 17. Wagner

atheism, humanity could take back the qualities it had projected onto God and start to realize its potential. In particular, the Christian ideal of celibacy denied sexual difference and pretended that the individual could lead a sexless existence, whereas, according to Feuerbach, 'Man and woman together first constitute the true man [*Menschen*]; man and woman together are the existence of the race, for their union is the source of multiplicity, the source of other men.'[19] So the *Ring* envisages sexual as well as political liberation.

Wagner's revolutionary career was brief but dramatic. 'A dam has to be pierced, and the means is — revolution!' he wrote to the music journalist Ernst Kossak in 1847.[20] On 14 June of the following year he delivered a rousing speech to the Vaterlands-Verein, a republican society, calling for the abolition of the aristocracy and the creation of a citizen militia, and asserting that the dismantling of the money economy would lead to 'the emancipation of the human race'.[21] Early in May 1849, well-founded rumours spread that the King of Saxony would call in Prussian troops to maintain order; barricades went up, several days of street fighting were ended by the military, and Wagner barely managed to escape to Switzerland. His friends the composer and political radical August Röckel and the Russian anarchist Mikhail Bakunin were caught and sentenced to death; their sentences were commuted, but Röckel spent thirteen years in prison, while Bakunin was deported to Russia.[22]

Frustrated in practice, Wagner worked his revolutionary beliefs into the *Ring*. Ever since Bernard Shaw's still stimulating and broadly persuasive political interpretation of the *Ring*, it has been customary to interpret Alberich as a capitalist, though he uses his ring only to accumulate treasure, not to invest it or achieve anything with it.[23] The power from which Siegfried seems briefly to promise liberation, before he becomes enmeshed in the Gibichungs' intrigues, is above all that of Wotan. Wotan's power is not based on divine right, nor on mere physical power, but on contracts or treaties (*Verträge*), through which he gained control of the world. As he confesses to Brünnhilde, his motives and conduct were not pure: 'Unwissend trugvoll, | Untreue übt' ich, | band durch Verträge | was Unheil barg' ('Unwittingly false, | I acted unfairly, | binding by treaties | what boded ill', *Ring*, p. 149). He puts some of the blame on Loge, his companion, whom the other gods all dislike, and who seems to stand in a relation to Wotan similar to that which Goethe's Mephistopheles has to Faust: 'listig verlockte mich Loge', 'cunningly Loge lured me on' (*Ring*, p. 149). Wotan made a contract with the giants to build Valhalla, promising them his sister-in-law, Freia, in exchange, but he did not intend to keep this contract,

dedicated the first edition of *Das Kunstwerk der Zukunft* (1850) to Feuerbach. See Wagner, *Mein Leben*, pp. 500–02; George G. Windell, 'Hegel, Feuerbach, and Wagner's *Ring*', *Central European History*, 9 (1976), 27–57.

19   Feuerbach, *The Essence of Christianity*, p. 167; *Das Wesen des Christenthums*, pp. 202–03.

20   Letter, 23 November 1847, in *Sämtliche Briefe*, II (1970), 578.

21   Quoted in Gregor-Dellin, *Wagner*, p. 239.

22   On Wagner's revolutionary experiences, see Gregor-Dellin, *Wagner*, pp. 234–76.

23   See Shaw, *The Perfect Wagnerite* (first published 1898), in *Major Critical Essays* (London: Constable, 1932); Anthony Arblaster, 'The *Ring* as a Political and Philosophical Drama', in *The Cambridge Companion to Wagner's 'Der Ring des Nibelungen'*, ed. by Mark Berry and Nicholas Vazsonyi (Cambridge: Cambridge University Press, 2020), pp. 185–204.

relying on Loge to find a way out of it. The giant Fasolt warns him: 'Was du bist, | bist du nur durch Verträge' ('What you are | you are through contracts alone', *Ring*, p. 75). So something must be done to satisfy the giants. Wotan persuades them to accept, instead of Freia, the treasure which Alberich has stolen from the Rhinemaidens. He and Loge contrive to steal the treasure from Alberich. Along with the treasure, Wotan, with extreme reluctance, gives the giants the ring of power, which immediately brings about the death of Fasolt, and for many years Fafner, having used the Tarnhelm to turn himself into a dragon, guards the treasure and the ring in his cave.

Wotan is now in a precarious position. Alberich, obsessed with his loss and the desire for revenge, will try to regain the ring and use its power against the gods. Wotan has the idea of filling Valhalla with dead heroes who will guard it against an attack.[24] He also hopes for a hero who will be strong enough to win the ring back from the dragon. To this end he fosters the clan of the Volsungs (*Wälsungen*) and becomes the father of the twins Siegmund and Sieglinde.[25] He plunges into a tree-trunk the sword, Nothung, which only Siegmund will be strong enough to draw out, and with which he is supposed to kill the dragon. But here Wotan has miscalculated, as Nietzsche explained in his essay 'Richard Wagner in Bayreuth':

> He needs a free, fearless human being who, without his assistance or advice, indeed in conflict with the divine order, will of his own volition perform the deed denied to the god: this human being is nowhere to be seen, and it is precisely when a new hope of him dawns that the god is compelled to obey the constraint that binds him: what he loves most he has to destroy, and has to punish an act of the purest pity.[26]

Wotan has to destroy Siegmund by allowing him to be killed in combat, because, as Fricka makes clear to him, Siegmund is not an autonomous actor. Wotan, as his father Wälse, brought him up, prepared him for his mission, and left the sword for him to find. That he has to 'punish an act of the purest pity', Brünnhilde's attempt to save Siegmund and Sieglinde, wounds his emotions yet more deeply. He is trapped, because he cannot get outside his own power. His omnipotence is now a burden, because nobody is really 'other' to him and therefore nobody can perform an action which Wotan has not somehow programmed in advance:

> Wie schüf' ich den Freien, | den nie ich schirmete, | der im eig'nen Trotze | der trauteste mir? | Wie macht' ich den And'ren, | der nicht mehr ich, | und aus sich wirkte | was ich nur will? – | O göttliche Noth! | Gräßliche Schmach! | Zum Ekel find' ich | ewig nur mich | In Allem was ich erwirke!

---

24 This is presumably the plan which he mentions enigmatically to Fricka at the end of *Das Rheingold* (p. 117): cf. Deryck Cooke, *I Saw the World End: A Study of Wagner's 'Ring'* (London: Oxford University Press, 1979), p. 237.

25 We do not learn who their mother was. *Der Nibelungen-Mythus* says that Wotan, finding a barren couple among the Volsungs, made them fertile by one of Freia's apples (which in *Das Rheingold* keep the gods young) so that they produced the twins: *Skizzen*, p. 27.

26 Friedrich Nietzsche, *Untimely Meditations*, trans. by R. J. Hollingdale (Cambridge: Cambridge University Press, 1997), p. 253.

How fashion a free man | whom I never sheltered | and who, in his own defiance, | is yet the dearest of men to me? | How can I make that other man | who's no longer me | and who, of himself, achieves | what I alone desire? — | O godly distress! | O hideous shame! | To my loathing I find | only ever myself | in all that I encompass! (*Ring*, p. 152)

If Wotan here comes to understand his own position, in other respects he is blind. For in Brünnhilde he has another being who is capable of autonomy, yet Wotan regards her as a mere extension of his own will. Hence he feels he can confide in her because he is really only talking to himself (*Ring*, p. 149). But when she defies him by trying to save Siegmund and actually saving Sieglinde, he berates her for having a will of her own (*Ring*, pp. 180–81). He does not realize that thanks to Brünnhilde, Sieglinde will survive long enough to give birth to the hero Siegfried, who, knowing nothing of Wotan, is the autonomous human being who kills the dragon and recovers the ring *without* having been programmed to do so by Wotan. Sieglinde hands him over to the dwarf Mime, along with the remains of Siegmund's sword, Nothung, which was shattered by Wotan's spear. Wotan knows about Siegfried, watches over him, and visits Mime in order to tell him that Nothung can be reforged (and hence the dragon slain) only by someone who does not know fear, that person being Siegfried. Wotan's guise as the Wanderer suggests that he has been reduced from his role of ruler of the world to that of a vagrant, watching events unfold but (fortunately) no longer able to shape them.

We might want to say that Wotan is saved from his tragic entrapment by a providential chain of events: Siegmund refuses to accompany Brünnhilde to Valhalla, Brünnhilde is moved enough to save Sieglinde, and as a result the longed-for hero is born. But the providential force is love. Wotan seems not to have foreseen that Siegmund and Sieglinde would fall in love, nor that Siegmund's love for Sieglinde would so impress Brünnhilde that she would rescue her in defiance of Wotan's orders. Moreover, as Brünnhilde explains, in her rescue attempt she was defying one of Wotan's wishes but obeying another. Aware of the self-division ('Zwiespalt', *Ring*, p. 185) within him, she carried out the wish inspired by Wotan's love for his son, and disobeyed the wish based on Wotan's duty as upholder of treaties.[27] Love is the only force capable of breaking through the net of contracts in which Wotan has sought to bind the world. This brings to a focus the conflict between love and power which, as has often been observed, is central to the *Ring*.

Wotan, like Alberich though less bluntly, is tempted by power at the expense of love. His original contract with the giants stipulates that he will hand over Freia, the goddess of love. By calling her also 'Holda', Wagner associates her with a figure from Germanic legend who easily merged with the goddess Venus, familiar already from *Tannhäuser* (1845).[28] Freia is admittedly a less impressive figure than one might hope — hardly a Nordic Aphrodite — but it may be that, as Deryck Cooke

27   On Brünnhilde's twofold relation to Wotan's will, see Magee, *Wagner and the Nibelungs*, pp. 173–77.
28   On these connections, including Wagner's debt to Heine's writings on Germanic myth, see Dieter Borchmeyer, *Die Götter tanzen Cancan: Richard Wagners Liebesrevolte* (Heidelberg: Manutius, 1992), pp. 91–95.

argues, love has so little place in Wotan's domain that 'it has shrunk into the weak, helpless, hunted figure of Freia'.[29] In the world that Wotan has built up by means of contracts, marriage, policed by Fricka, takes precedence over love. Wotan chafes in his marriage to Fricka, and has had many extramarital affairs (*Ring*, p. 143 — like Zeus in Greek mythology). Fricka wishes to preserve marriages even if they are as unhappy as Sieglinde's marriage to Hunding. In his original plan for the *Ring*, Wagner imagined the gods 'ordering the world [and] binding the elements through wise laws', but added that their order was nevertheless based on 'force and cunning' ('Gewalt u. List').[30] The contracts, inscribed as runes on Wotan's spear, provide stability, but not happiness. When Siegfried encounters Wotan as the Wanderer and breaks his spear with Nothung, he is symbolically destroying the old, corrupt, contractual order of things.

Hence the importance of the taboo-breaking union between Siegmund and Sieglinde. They have been brought up apart, so they meet only as adults, when Siegmund, a hunted fugitive, seeks refuge in Hunding's house and arouses sympathy from Sieglinde. Wagner believed that incest in such circumstances — as opposed to within a settled family — was not reprehensible. In a discussion of the Oedipus story, he pointed out that if the union between Oedipus and Jocasta had been unnatural, it would not have produced children, whereas they had several offspring.[31] In the *Ring*, it is legal marriages — the stale marriage between Fricka and Wotan, the forced marriage of Sieglinde to the brutal Hunding — that are barren and hence unnatural.

Since the incestuous love between Siegmund and Sieglinde defies all laws and conventions, its product, Siegfried, is thereby qualified to found a new order of things independent of the discredited old order of the gods (though in practice he only destroys, and his betrayal and death in *Götterdämmerung* end his mission). Wotan intends to punish Brünnhilde by turning her from a Valkyrie with superhuman powers into an ordinary woman; but in line with the humanist message still discernible in the *Ring*, he is really elevating her into something better than a semi-divine figure, namely a human being. Her development towards humanity, which began with her compassion for Siegmund and Sieglinde, has been summed up by Elizabeth Magee: 'To attain world-redemptive compassionate womanhood Brünnhilde must emancipate herself from Wotan's will; the road from divinity to humanity lies through disobedience.'[32]

Brünnhilde has a classical prototype in Prometheus. Studying Greek drama in the late 1840s, Wagner read the translation of Aeschylus's *Prometheus Bound* by Johann Georg Droysen, who tried to reconstruct the dramatic trilogy of which he assumed *Prometheus Bound* was the second part; the first would have shown Prometheus stealing fire from heaven for the benefit of humankind, the second

29   Cooke, *I Saw the World End*, p. 156.
30   *Skizzen*, p. 27.
31   *Oper und Drama* in Wagner, *Sämtliche Schriften und Dichtungen*, IV, 57; discussed by Cooke, *I Saw the World End*, p. 300.
32   Magee, *Wagner and the Nibelungs*, p. 175.

his punishment, the third his eventual liberation by Heracles.[33] Greek trilogies were in practice tetralogies, since the three main plays were followed by a satyr-play; Wagner's *Ring* is also a tetralogy, with *Das Rheingold* as a prelude to the three main dramas. Wagner called Aeschylus's *Prometheus Bound* 'the profoundest of all tragedies'.[34] Brünnhilde, like Prometheus, disobeys the gods in order to help humanity (in her case, by rescuing Sieglinde). Prometheus is chained on Mount Caucasus; Brünnhilde is placed on a mountain-top and surrounded by flames (in *Götterdämmerung* she actually says she was chained, *Ring*, p. 301). She is rescued by Siegfried, as Prometheus will be by Heracles. Prometheus's mother is the earth-goddess Gaia; Brünnhilde's mother is Erda, whom Shaw called 'the voice of the fruitful earth'.[35] The redemptive role that Wagner initially imagined for Siegfried is in the final text transferred to Brünnhilde.

The primordial crime — the violation of nature by Alberich in stealing the gold and by Wotan in cutting a branch from the World-Ash — lends itself to interpretation in gendered terms. Erda and the Rhinemaidens can be understood, according to Derek Hughes, as 'primordial manifestations of femininity'.[36] Feminine nature even lets us glimpse a realm prior to language: Wagner gives some female figures an 'ur-language of sung vocalizations', represented by 'the chants of the Rhinemaidens and the whoops of the Valkyries'.[37] By drinking the dragon's blood, Siegfried too gains an affinity with nature which enables him to understand the language of birds. Brünnhilde and Siegfried are thus in touch with the primordial realm of nature prior to (Wotan's and Alberich's) civilization.

Under the influence of Feuerbach, Wagner intended Brünnhilde's immolation, when she rides her horse into the flames of Siegfried's funeral pyre, to be an act of self-sacrifice with the power to redeem the world through love.

> Verging wie Hauch | der Götter Geschlecht, | lass' ohne Walter | die Welt ich zurück: | meines heiligsten Wissens Hort | weis' ich der Welt nun zu. — | Nicht Gut, nicht Gold, | noch göttliche Pracht; | nicht Haus, nicht Hof, | noch herrischer Prunk; | nicht trüber Verträge | trügender Bund, | nicht heuchelnder Sitte | hartes Gesetz: | selig in Lust und Leid | läßt — die Liebe nur sein. —

> Though the race of gods | passed away like a breath, | though I leave behind me | a world without rulers, | I now bequeath to that world | my most sacred wisdom's hoard. — | Not wealth, not gold, | nor godly pomp; | not house, not garth, | nor lordly splendour; | not troubled treaties' | treacherous bonds, | not smooth-tongued custom's | stern decree: | blessed in joy and sorrow | love alone can be. (*Ring*, pp. 362–63)

---

33 Detailed comparison in Wolfgang Schadewaldt, 'Richard Wagner und die Griechen: Drei Bayreuther Vorträge', in his *Hellas und Hesperien. Gesammelte Schriften zur Antike und zur neueren Literatur*, 2 vols (Zurich: Artemis, 1970), II, 341–405 (esp. 371–81); see also McGrath, *German Freedom*, pp. 81–86.
34 *Sämtliche Schriften und Dichtungen*, III, 11.
35 Shaw, *Major Critical Essays*, p. 183.
36 Hughes, *Culture and Sacrifice*, p. 186.
37 Ibid.

Here Brünnhilde systematically goes through and rejects the attributes of the gods that we have seen earlier in the cycle. 'House' and 'garth' recall Loge's charge in *Das Rheingold* that Donner and Froh are too fond of domesticity, 'think only of house and home' (*Ring*, p. 77). 'Godly pomp' and 'lordly splendour' allude to Valhalla. 'Troubled treaties' treacherous bonds' are the means by which Wotan has established and consolidated his power. 'Smooth-tongued [literally 'hypocritical'] custom's stern decree' refers to Fricka's pitiless insistence on the sanctity of marriage, however unhappy. In place of all this Brünnhilde proclaims a new order pervaded by love.

Wagner, however, lost faith in this 'Feuerbach ending'.[38] After his immersion in Schopenhauer, whose work he discovered in 1854, Wagner substituted what is called the 'Schopenhauer ending', in which Brünnhilde welcomes the dissolution of the world and concludes: 'enden sah ich die Welt', 'I saw the world end' (*Ring*, p. 363).[39] He then discarded that as well and replaced it with the present ending, in which Brünnhilde follows Siegfried in death by riding into the flames. Just before this, Brünnhilde has finally refused to return the ring to the gods to save them from destruction, and resolved to give it back to the Rhinemaidens. Thus she symbolically brings about the doom of the gods: 'so – werf' ich den Brand | in Walhalls prangende Burg', 'thus do I hurl the torch | into Valhalla's proud-standing stronghold' (*Ring*, p. 350). This is supposed to be a redemptive action, the 'erlösende Weltenthat', 'the deed that redeems the world' (*Ring*, p. 258). But although her deed provides the cycle with a grandiose ending, it is not clear, as Bernard Williams has objected, that it is anything besides 'suttee on horseback'.[40] What is redeemed, and how? Is this the end of the world, or only the end of the gods? In the former case, it is rather like ending a play by killing off all the characters because you cannot think what else to do with them. In the latter case, if the Gibichungs' household and the rest of humanity (almost entirely absent from the cycle so far) are going to survive, how will their world have changed?

Although these questions may be unanswerable, we can at least discern a pattern in which Siegfried, the human being unburdened by the past, destroys the old order by breaking Wotan's spear, while his partner Brünnhilde performs an act of redemption, however obscure. What about Wotan? His tragic fate is that when love gradually gains the upper hand over his power-hunger, he is obliged, as a result of his own contrivances, to punish the very people he loves: Siegmund, by bringing about his death, and Brünnhilde, by confining her within the circle of fire. Beyond *Die Walküre*, a kind of expiation or atonement comes about when Wotan consents to perish. As Wagner explained to Röckel, 'Wodan [*sic*] rises to the tragic height of *willing* his own downfall. That is all we have to learn from the history of humanity: *to will what is necessary* and to accomplish it.'[41] This sounds vaguely Hegelian, and

38   See his letter to August Röckel, 23 Aug. 1856, *Sämtliche Briefe*, VIII (1991), 153.
39   See his letter to Franz Liszt, 16 December 1854, *Sämtliche Briefe*, VI (1986), 298.
40   Bernard Williams, 'Wagner and the Transcendence of Politics', in his *Essays and Reviews 1959–2002* (Princeton: Princeton University Press, 2014), pp. 398–405 (p. 399).
41   Letter to Röckel, 25/26 January 1854, *Sämtliche Briefe*, VI, 68.

we know that Wagner had at least read Hegel on the philosophy of history.[42] Wotan thus expiates the crimes in which he has involved himself; it remains unclear how far we are to understand the end of the *Ring* as an apocalyptic destruction, not just of the gods, but of a civilization based on the primal crime — the rape of Nature.

42   On his reading of Hegel, see Wagner, *Mein Leben*, pp. 501–02; Windell, 'Hegel, Feuerbach, and Wagner's *Ring*'.

18

Hebbel:
Agnes Bernauer (1852)

In 1856, when Friedrich Hebbel had at last earned fame for his series of dramas beginning with *Judith* (1840), a friend suggested that he should write a play about 'Macchiavell'. Hebbel replied: 'You would like a Macchiavell from me? There is one already. That which is justified in Macchiavell lives in my Duke Ernst.'[1] Duke Ernst of Bavaria is one of the three main characters in the play *Agnes Bernauer*, which had its premiere in the Munich Court Theatre on 25 March 1852. As a ruler, he accepts responsibility for what he considers a necessary crime — the execution of the guiltless but politically inconvenient heroine.

The play is based on a historical event. In the early fifteenth century, Albrecht, the heir to the Duchy of Munich-Bavaria, fell in love with Agnes Bernauer, the beautiful daughter of a barber-surgeon in Augsburg. She became his mistress, possibly his wife. However, Albrecht's father, Duke Ernst, disapproved of the liaison. Agnes was accused of witchcraft. Ernst arranged for her to be condemned and drowned in the Danube, probably on 12 October 1435.

Agnes Bernauer stands out among Hebbel's dramas in a number of ways. It focuses, more sharply than any other, on high politics. Even in *Herodes und Mariamne* (1849), where intrigues at the court of Judaea are prominent, the main focus is on the difficult and ultimately disastrous relationship between husband and wife, which looks forward to Strindberg's tragedies of marriage such as *The Father* (1887) and *The Dance of Death* (1901).[2] And while many of Hebbel's plays are, nominally at least, historical dramas, the setting of *Agnes Bernauer* in fifteenth-century Bavaria is much more vivid than the thinly imagined ancient world of *Herodes* or *Gyges und sein Ring* (1856). In his well-known essay 'Mein Wort über das Drama!' (My Opinion on Drama, 1843) Hebbel made a virtue of this colourless representation: 'Die Geschichte ist für den Dichter ein Vehikel zur Verkörperung seiner Anschauungen und Ideen, nicht aber ist umgekehrt der Dichter der Auferstehungsengel der Geschichte' ('History is for the poet a vehicle to embody his views and ideas, but the poet is not history's angel of the resurrection').[3]

1   Letter to Arnold Schloenbach, 3 June 1856, quoted in Friedrich Hebbel, *Werke*, ed. by Gerhard Fricke, Werner Keller, and Karl Pörnbacher, 5 vols (Munich: Hanser, 1963), I, 810.
2   The Strindbergian character of the erotic conflict in *Die Nibelungen* (1862) is noted by Jost Hermand, 'Hebbels *Nibelungen*: Ein deutsches Trauerspiel', in *Hebbel in neuer Sicht*, ed. by Helmut Kreuzer, 2nd edn (Stuttgart: Kohlhammer, 1969), pp. 315–33 (p. 325).
3   'Mein Wort über das Drama!' in *Werke*, III, 545–76 (p. 550).

Among the ideas that particularly interested Hebbel was that of historical transition. Often he tracks a transition from ancient despotism, where only the despot
could be an individual, to the emergence of an individualist society. Thus in *Herodes
und Mariamne*, where Herod treats his wife as a 'thing' rather than a person, the
development of individualism is heralded by the contemporaneous birth of Christ
(conveyed, at the end of the play, by the arrival of the Three Wise Men asking
the way to Bethlehem).[4] *Agnes Bernauer*, however, moves in a different direction,
towards a conception of the modern state as having higher claims than those of the
individual.

The rich local colour, and the way in which, as Friedrich Sengle complains,
Bavarian patriotism is 'laid on with a trowel', may indicate that Hebbel hoped to
be invited to the circle of writers, artists, and academics whom King Maximilian II
(reigned 1848–64) had attracted to Munich.[5] One of the beneficiaries of the King's
patronage, Franz Dingelstedt, the director of the Court Theatre, was anxious to
stage new as well as classic plays and aware of Hebbel's talent; among his first
productions was Hebbel's *Judith*, and discussions with him contributed to the
shaping of *Agnes Bernauer*, which, with its tournament scenes, satisfied Dingelstedt's
liking for visual spectacle.[6]

The audience's response to the premiere of *Agnes Bernauer* testified to the play's
power. The central conflict is between Albrecht and his father. Duke Ernst is
determined to resolve the unstable political situation in Bavaria. Not only has the
duchy recently lost some of its territory, but what remains is divided among three
rival dukes, based in Munich, Landshut, and Ingolstadt. Ernst's plan is to strengthen
his dominions by marrying his son Albrecht to the daughter of the Duke of
Brunswick and eventually incorporating the other two duchies. He is so convinced
that Albrecht will agree to this marriage that he has not bothered to consult him.
It is a shock, therefore, to discover that Albrecht has not just taken a mistress but
has actually married her. At a tournament Ernst publicly disinherits Albrecht, who
appeals to townsfolk and peasants for support: 'Bürger und Bauern, heran!' (p. 732).[7]
At this, the climactic end of Act III, some of the first-night audience, especially
those in the cheap seats, burst into applause, while the well-off spectators in the
boxes hissed, and the resulting tumult made the last two acts almost inaudible.[8]

Between Acts III and IV, three and a half years pass. During that time, the heir
to Ernst's dominions is Adolf, the sickly young son of his cousin Wilhelm. But
Adolf dies, and civil war looks inevitable. However, the prudent Ernst, immediately
after proclaiming Albrecht's disinheritance, procured a warrant for Agnes's death.

---

4   Cf. Hebbel's letter to Robert Zimmermann, 22 May 1850: Mariamne wants Herod to stop
treating her as a 'Ding' and begin seeing her as a person (*Werke*, V, 686).
5   Sengle, *Biedermeierzeit*, III, 394; see Dieter Breuer, 'Der Münchner Dichterkreis und seine
Anthologien', in *Handbuch der Literatur in Bayern*, ed. by Albrecht Weber (Regensburg: Pustet, 1987),
pp. 301–13. Cf. Hebbel's letter to his wife Christine, 3 March 1852, *Werke*, V, 715–19.
6   See Monika Ritzer, *Friedrich Hebbel: Der Individualist und seine Epoche. Eine Biographie* (Göttingen:
Wallstein, 2018), pp. 554–58.
7   *Agnes Bernauer* is quoted from *Werke*, I.
8   Ritzer, *Friedrich Hebbel*, p. 566.

The warrant has been signed by three eminent lawyers and awaits only the ducal signature. Agnes is now abducted and imprisoned. Ernst's right-hand man, the Chancellor Hans von Preising, tries his best to persuade her to divorce Albrecht and enter a convent, but Agnes is steadfast. No alternative remains but for Ernst to sign the death warrant and for Agnes to be hanged. We are told that the hangman proves unable to carry out the sentence, so a serf, in return for being freed, drowns her in the Danube. Albrecht and his father meet on the battlefield. The hot-headed Albrecht even threatens to burn Munich (p. 760). They are reconciled by the highest available authorities: a herald sent by the Holy Roman Emperor, and a legate sent by the Pope. Albrecht knuckles under. In return, Ernst abdicates in his favour, intending to enter a monastery, and orders that Agnes, as his widow, will receive a dignified burial and be commemorated by solemn ceremonies.

Duke Ernst dominates the action from the opening of Act III, when we find him in his private office ('Kabinett'), its walls covered with maps and with portraits of Bavarian princes. Hebbel presents him throughout as a serious and responsible ruler, concerned above all for the long-term good of Bavaria, whereas Albrecht places his private, individual happiness before the political duties that accompany his rank. When Preising tells Albrecht that his exalted position demands the sacrifice of private happiness, Albrecht replies that that is too much to ask: 'Nicht bloß auf mein Glück soll ich Verzicht leisten, ich soll mein Unglück liebkosen, ich solls herzen und küssen, ja ich soll dafür beten, aber nein, nein, in alle Ewigkeit nein!' ('I am supposed not only to renounce my happiness but to caress my unhappiness, to hug and kiss it, even pray for it, but no, no, in all eternity no!', p. 727). Ernst, however, is more than an individual. He speaks for Bavaria, indeed for a larger entity. 'Oder bin ichs, der zu dir redet, ists nicht das ganze Deutsche Reich?' ('Or is it [merely] I who am speaking to you, is it not the entire German Empire?'), he asks his son.

In this conflict between the individual and the state, Hebbel was firmly on the side of the state. 'You are quite right', he told a friend, 'that the author himself is on the side of the old Duke, so decidedly, indeed, that it was only the latter who inspired his enthusiasm for the entire subject'.[9] So we have a tragedy about Agnes Bernauer in which the focus is not really on Agnes but on the Duke who condemns her to death. He, not she, is the main tragic figure, compelled by necessity to commit what he knows is a crime. In this sense Ernst is a very nineteenth-century Machiavellian figure: not an unscrupulous intriguer, like the 'machiavels' of earlier drama, but a practitioner of reason of state. He is not a sacral ruler, but more resembles Frederick the Great, who described himself as the first servant of his people.[10] Although Hebbel is known to have read Hegel's *Philosophy of Right*, he avoids the step taken notoriously by Hegel, who regarded not the monarchy but the state itself as a sacred object. For Hebbel, and for Ernst, the state is a practical arrangement for the security and well-being of the population.[11] Ernst's policy even

---

9   Letter to Friedrich von Uechtritz, 14 December 1854, *Werke*, v, 760.
10   This is suggested by Axel Schmitt, ' "Auctoritas", "Veritas" oder "Divinitas"? Zur Legitimierung der Gewalt in Hebbels *Agnes Bernauer*', in *'Alles Leben ist Raub': Aspekte der Gewalt bei Friedrich Hebbel*, ed. by Günter Häntzschel (Munich: iudicium, 1992), pp. 165–82 (p. 175).
11   See Schmitt, ' "Auctoritas" ', p. 177.

resembles *Realpolitik*. Georg Lukács noted in 1911 that the idea Ernst represents 'contains something of Bismarck's ideal of *Realpolitik*'.[12] In his eyes, politics becomes a matter of calculating actions and consequences. If Agnes remains as Albrecht's wife, Bavaria will be devastated by civil war; many men will be killed, leaving widows and orphans. Humanity too dictates that she must be removed from the equation. Preising, showing Agnes her death sentence, explains that it is no longer an issue of guilt or innocence: it is now a pragmatic, not a moral matter:

> Die Ordnung der Welt gestört, Vater und Sohn entzweit, dem Volk seinen Fürsten entfremdet, einen Zustand herbei geführt, in dem nicht mehr nach Schuld und Unschuld, nur noch nach Ursach und Wirkung gefragt werden kann! (p. 751)

> The order of the world [has been] disturbed, the people alienated from their prince, a condition brought about in which the question is no longer one of guilt and innocence, but only of cause and effect!

Hebbel described his heroine as 'a modern Antigone', thereby comparing the conflict between Ernst and Agnes to that between Creon and Antigone in Sophocles' drama.[13] As he had read Hegel's *Aesthetics*, he knew also Hegel's interpretation of *Antigone*. The brother of Antigone has brought an army of soldiers against his native city in order to unseat its ruler, Creon, and has been killed in the battle. Creon has forbidden anyone to bury the corpse; if they try, they will be killed too. Antigone disobeys the order and buries her brother's body. Creon insists on her punishment, even though she is engaged to his son. She is imprisoned in a rock chamber to starve to death, but commits suicide, followed by her lover. Now for Hegel this is not just a tragedy of clashes between individuals. It is a clash between moral principles, human values, ideas — expressions of the Spirit. The idea for which Antigone dies is loyalty to the family. Creon, in letting her brother's body lie unburied and in punishing her for burying it, upholds the idea of the state, but at the cost of dishonouring the dead man and behaving impiously towards the gods. Each character is wholeheartedly, one-sidedly devoted to his or her cause, for it is characteristic of the tragic hero that he or she cannot compromise. Both are right: Sophocles has written a tragedy in which the heroine is right to insist on burying her brother's corpse and Creon is right to insist on leaving the corpse unburied as punishment for his rebellion.

However, Hebbel's play is an *Antigone* rewritten in favour of Creon. Agnes is not without agency: she voluntarily accepts her fate by refusing to divorce Albrecht, and she shows remarkable self-assurance throughout.[14] Hebbel attributed her fate to a collision between absolute right (the eternal laws of morality) and positive right (the laws of the state currently in force).[15] Unlike Sophocles, who shows a

---

12 Georg Lukács, 'Hebbel und die Grundlegung der modernen Tragödie', in *Friedrich Hebbel*, ed. by Helmut Kreuzer (Darmstadt: Wissenschaftliche Buchgesellschaft, 1989), pp. 46–70. First published in Hungarian, 1911.

13 Letter to Dingelstedt, 9 January 1852, quoted in *Werke*, I, 809.

14 Ritzer, *Friedrich Hebbel*, p. 574.

15 See letter to Dingelstedt, 26 January 1852, *Werke*, V, 708.

direct conflict between Antigone and Creon, Hebbel never brings Agnes face to face with Ernst. Ernst deals with her indirectly through the mediation of Preising, who visits her in her prison, does his best to reason with her, and is later obliged to attend her execution. The confrontation between the demands of the state and what Hebbel considered the excesses of modern individualism is embodied in the dialogue between Ernst and Albrecht, which ends with Albrecht acknowledging his father's viewpoint and eagerly accepting the staff which symbolizes the ducal office.

Hebbel's uncompromising support for state authority may take some present-day readers aback. It needs to be seen in its historical context. Hebbel's political aspirations were characteristic of mid-century German liberals. He wished for a constitutional monarchy, freedom of the press, and some measure of representative government. When revolutions broke out in 1848, first in Paris, then in Berlin and soon afterwards in Vienna, where Hebbel had been living since 1845, he hoped that the upheavals would bring about these reforms. He took an active part, standing as a candidate for the Frankfurt Parliament (unsuccessfully; his Viennese hearers were put off by his North German accent), and in May forming one of a four-man delegation which tried (again unsuccessfully) to persuade the emperor to return to Vienna from his refuge at Innsbruck. He was repelled by the Viennese revolution's rapid shift to the left and by the increase in mob violence. On 6 October a crowd, angered by the official policy of forcibly repressing the rebellion in Hungary, invaded the Ministry of War and lynched the minister. The emperor, having briefly returned to Vienna, again retreated, this time to Olmütz in Moravia, and gave General Windischgrätz, who had put down the uprising in Prague, full powers to restore order in Vienna. Windischgrätz encircled the city on 23 October and gave the Viennese forty-eight hours to surrender. The revolutionaries insisted on trying to resist, supported by the extreme radical Robert Blum who had arrived from Saxony, though food was already running short; the water supply in some areas ran out on 24 October. On the 28th Windischgrätz's forces bombarded and entered the city and fought their way street by street. Their soldiers, especially the notoriously savage Croatian troops, looted houses and killed people in the suburbs. On the 29th representatives of all the military companies in Vienna voted for unconditional surrender, though the extreme radicals still wanted to go down fighting, and despite the terms of the surrender a Citizens' Guard division attacked Windischgrätz's troops so that they had to fight their way right through to the city centre. About 4,000 people were killed, many of them civilians. Hebbel lived through all this, worried by his responsibility for his wife and their small daughter. He remained cool enough to complete *Herodes und Mariamne* while Vienna was being bombarded, but he was fully aware of the constant danger: 'in such moments nobody is in safety; in a city under bombardment there are no more secure places than there are on a foundering ship', he wrote.[16] It is not surprising that in November he expressed his satisfaction that governments were once again in control and waging 'their just and holy struggle against the unbridled rabble [*Pöbel*]'.[17]

16   Letter to Gustav Kühne, 21 November 1848, *Werke*, v, 675. For a detailed account of Hebbel's experiences in 1848, see Ritzer, *Friedrich Hebbel*, pp. 451–79.
17   *Werke*, v, 675.

In making his Duke Ernst warn against the danger of civil war, therefore, Hebbel knew what he was talking about. Ernst's evident sincerity in the last scenes serves, as Helmut Kreuzer says, to dispel any doubts that he is objectively in the right.[18] We are to believe him when he says to Albrecht: 'Ich mußte tun, was ich tat, du wirst es selbst dereinst begreifen' (p. 759: 'I had to do what I did, you will understand it yourself one day'). Admittedly he cannot be seen as a wholly ideal ruler. When he first appears in the play, his conduct of internal politics is unappealing. Told about a pogrom against Jews in Nuremberg, he refuses to get involved, saying only that his Jews should conduct themselves so as not to invite violence (p. 715). At the tournament, he subjects Albrecht to public disgrace — hardly the way to win over a headstrong young man. We have to assume that during the three and a half years' interval between Acts III and IV Ernst has reflected and grown wiser. He does at least seek the support of leading lawyers for the death sentence against Agnes, and he plausibly assures Preising: 'Ich bin kein Tyrann, und denke keiner zu werden' (p. 736: 'I am not a tyrant and do not intend to become one'). Here he recalls the Elector in Kleist's *Prinz Friedrich von Homburg*, a play that, as we have seen, Hebbel greatly admired: the Elector likewise insists that he is not a tyrant, and succeeds in imbuing a self-willed young man with a sense of responsibility. Hebbel's reading of the play does not allow for the unacknowledged and (in a bad sense) Machiavellian motives which may enter into the Elector's calculations. In the case of Duke Ernst, it is also somewhat unappealing that Ernst does not witness the execution of Agnes himself, but has it overseen by the long-suffering Preising, who is shattered by the experience. This might be thought to make Ernst a *Schreibtischtäter* who orders executions from the safety of his desk and remains a long way from where they actually happen.

Hebbel underlines the necessity of Ernst's crime by having it repeatedly described as a sacrifice. The theme of sacrifice echoes throughout the play. We have already seen that Preising asks Albrecht to sacrifice his domestic happiness for the greater good of the state. In a parallel conversation with Agnes, he tells her that she must either sacrifice Albrecht, or be sacrificed herself:

> Wohl mags ein schweres Opfer für Euch sein, doch wenn Ihrs verweigert, so wird man — könnt Ihr noch zweifeln nach allem, was heute geschah? — aus Euch selbst ein Opfer machen! (p. 750)

> It may well be a difficult sacrifice for you, but if you refuse — can you still doubt after everything that has happened today? — you yourself will be made a sacrifice!

Hebbel is here exploiting the ambiguity of the word *Opfer*, which means both 'sacrificial ceremony' and 'sacrificial victim'.[19] Thanks to this ambiguity, when someone is described as a victim, the associated meaning of 'sacrifice' implies that their victimhood is in some way legitimate. Agnes accepts the term, describing

18   Helmut Kreuzer, 'Hebbels *Agnes Bernauer* (und andere Dramen der Staatsraison und des politischen Notstandsmordes)', in *Hebbel in neuer Sicht*, ed. by Kreuzer, pp. 267–93 (p. 271).
19   Noted for example by J. P. Stern, *Hitler: The Führer and the People* (Glasgow: Fontana, 1975), p. 33.

herself as 'Euer Opfer' (p. 754: 'your sacrifice/victim'). At the very end of the play, Ernst speaks of her as 'das reinste Opfer, das der Notwendigkeit im Lauf aller Jahrhunderte gefallen ist' (p. 764: 'the purest sacrifice/victim that in the course of all the centuries has ever been made to necessity'). Agnes, then, is not only the object of a necessary crime; she is also a sacrificial victim, and the word *Opfer* places the event in a religious as well as a political light.

Sacrifice can be defined very broadly: 'Sacrifice is fundamentally the offering to the deity of a gift in the expectation that the transfer of the sacrificed object (*victima*) into the sacred sphere effects a spiritual or moral transformation in the person that brings it.'[20] However, a sacrifice is often made on behalf not of an individual but of a community. And sacrifice is often best understood as a transaction in which something valuable is surrendered in order to obtain something yet more valuable. Human lives may be 'sacrificed' in order to preserve a nation. Humanity gives something to God or the gods, in order to obtain blessings — health, good harvests, prosperity — in return. What you sacrifice must be precious; otherwise the sacrifice has no value. The Carthaginians, as Lohenstein presents them, sacrificed children for the sake of national survival. Agamemnon was prepared to sacrifice his daughter Iphigenia so that the Greek fleet, stranded by contrary winds at Aulis, could sail to Troy.[21]

Duke Ernst himself refers to a precedent for sacrifice: the story in Genesis 22 of how the Lord commanded Abraham to sacrifice his son Isaac, and, just as Abraham was about to plunge the knife into the boy's throat, rescinded his command by allowing Abraham instead to sacrifice a ram caught in a thicket. He says that in making Albrecht accept the death of Agnes, he is treating Albrecht as Abraham treated Isaac: 'geht er in der ersten Verzweiflung unter, und es ist sehr möglich, daß ers tut, so lasse ich ihn begraben, wie sie, tritt er mir im Felde entgegen, so werf ich ihn oder halte ihn auf, bis der Kaiser kommt' (p. 738: 'if he perishes in his first despair, and it is quite possible that he will, I shall have him buried like her; if he confronts me on the battlefield, I shall defeat him or keep him in check until the emperor comes'). This is a very curious adaptation of the Bible story. Abraham did not give Isaac any choice; the boy was supposed to accept his fate passively. It was not Isaac whose obedience was tested, but Abraham's. Implicitly, therefore, Ernst is equating his own position with that of the Lord and testing Albrecht as the Lord tested Abraham. This runs counter to the understanding of the story of Abraham and Isaac that prevailed in the Enlightenment. Voltaire interpreted it as a surviving piece of evidence that the ancient Hebrews practised human sacrifice,

20 'Sacrifice', in *The Oxford Dictionary of the Christian Church*, 4th edn, ed. by Andrew Louth (Oxford: Oxford University Press, 2022), p. 1715. This entry is an abridgement of the valuable article by Johannes Zachhuber, 'Modern Discourse on Sacrifice and its Theological Background', in *Sacrifice and Modern Thought*, ed. by Julia Meszaros and Johannes Zachhuber (Oxford: Oxford University Press, 2013), pp. 12–28.

21 On sacrifice in Greek tragedy, see Hughes, *Culture and Sacrifice*, pp. 19–43. Hughes is sceptical about René Girard's well-known theory that sacrifice deals with society's violence by deflecting communal guilt onto a (literal or metaphorical) scapegoat: see Girard, *Violence and the Sacred*, trans. by Patrick Gregory (Baltimore and London: Johns Hopkins University Press, 1977), and Hughes, pp. 23–24 and elsewhere.

like their neighbours, and therefore could not provide a reputable foundation for Christianity.[22] Kant denounced the story on the grounds that Abraham's innate moral sense should have told him that such a patently immoral command could not have come from God.[23]

Hebbel's interest in sacrifice runs through his dramas.[24] It appears most remarkably in the fragmentary drama *Moloch*, written in 1849–50 and thus contemporaneous with *Agnes Bernauer*, in which two priests, who have fled from Carthage after its conquest by the Romans, arrive in ancient Germany and introduce the inhabitants to the cult of Moloch and the practice of agriculture. The play seems to be an allegorical history of the development of religion, with human sacrifice and agriculture linked as the foundations of civilization.[25] In *Agnes Bernauer*, the sufferings and death of Agnes are associated, by a whole network of allusions, to the Passion and crucifixion of Christ.[26] Beyond the political necessity for her judicial murder, the play seems to be hinting at a further, perhaps anthropological necessity. While Ernst's decision is ostensibly based on the rational calculation appropriate to Machiavellianism and reason of state, the sacrifice of an innocent victim has deeper and darker implications. It is as though the authority of the state needs to rest on a primal, quasi-religious, morally indefensible act of sacrifice.

22   *La Bible enfin expliquée*, in *Les Œuvres complètes de Voltaire*, 9A, p. 305.
23   Kant, *Der Streit der Fakultäten* (1798), in *Werke*, VI, 333n.
24   References are listed in Birgit Fenner, *Friedrich Hebbel zwischen Hegel und Freud* (Stuttgart: Klett-Cotta, 1979), p. 147. See also Hebbel's cryptic diary entry of 1841 concerning Abraham, *Werke*, IV, 435.
25   See the interpretation in Sengle, *Biedermeierzeit*, III, 396–97.
26   The New Testament allusions are listed briefly by Kreuzer, 'Hebbels *Agnes Bernauer*', pp. 280–83, and exhaustively by Mary Garland, *Hebbel's Prose Tragedies: An Investigation of the Aesthetic Aspect of Hebbel's Dramatic Language* (Cambridge: Cambridge University Press, 1973), pp. 273–93.

19

Nietzsche:
Die Geburt der Tragödie (1872)

Although Nietzsche was not a dramatist, he did produce what is probably the second most influential treatise on tragedy ever written (Aristotle's *Poetics* being the first): *The Birth of Tragedy* (1872). In it he formulates the idea of the necessary crime: 'die dem titanisch strebenden Individuum gebotene Nothwendigkeit des Frevels' ('the necessity of sacrilege as it is imposed on the Titanically striving individual').[1] 'Sacrilege' is too limiting a translation for *Frevel*, which implies a particularly heinous and outrageous crime, whether against the gods or against humanity. Thus the aged Faust regrets the blasphemy ('Frevelwort') with which he once comprehensively cursed the world.[2] The Elector in *Prinz Friedrich von Homburg* condemns the Prince's disobedience on the battlefield by calling it a 'Frevel'.[3]

To explain the necessity of crime, Nietzsche, in his account of Greek tragedy, removes Oedipus from the position of archetypal tragic hero, and replaces him with Prometheus. The story of Oedipus, who committed incest and parricide and solved the Sphinx's riddle, contains, according to Nietzsche, the terrifying intimation that to learn the secrets of nature one must violate the taboos which nature has imposed on family life. Nevertheless, Oedipus is an essentially passive figure, subordinate to a fate which he does not understand till too late, and one who, in *Oedipus at Colonos*, Sophocles' sequel to *King Oedipus*, passes through suffering to 'heavenly serenity [*Heiterkeit*] which descends from the divine sphere'.[4] In this respect Sophocles' passive Oedipus contrasts with the active Prometheus whom Aeschylus presents in *Prometheus Bound*. When Aeschylus's play opens, we see Prometheus being led by the allegorical figures of Power and Violence to Mount Caucasus, where Hephaestus, the smith of the gods, fixes him with metal bolts and wedges to the rock. Each day thereafter his liver will be torn out by an eagle and grow again so that it can be torn out the following day. The crime for which Prometheus is being punished is that, out of pity for humankind, he stole fire from heaven, concealing it in a stalk of fennel. Human beings, who had previously had to shelter in underground caves, were now able to build houses and cities on the surface of the earth. Besides giving them fire, Prometheus taught them the arts of culture: how to count and write, how to measure time by the heavenly bodies, how to domesticate animals, as well

1   Nietzsche, *Die Geburt der Tragödie*, §9, KSA 1, 70. Translation from *The Birth of Tragedy*, trans. by Douglas Smith, Oxford World's Classics (Oxford: Oxford University Press, 2000), p. 58.
2   *Faust*, l. 11409, referring back to ll. 1587–1606 in the scene 'Studierzimmer II'.
3   *Homburg*, l. 1626, in Kleist, SWB II, 634,
4   *The Birth of Tragedy*, p. 54; KSA 1, 66.

as navigation, metallurgy, medicine and prophecy.[5] An image of Prometheus finally breaking his chains, with the eagle dead at his feet, appeared on the cover of the first edition of *The Birth of Tragedy*.[6]

Nietzsche, glossing this myth, explains that for early humanity fire was the prerequisite and starting point of all civilization, for which he consistently uses the word *Kultur* (still often spelt *Cultur* in the nineteenth century). Previously, fire was outside human control. Whether as a lightning bolt or as warm sunshine, it was a weapon or a gift from heaven. When man became able to store and manipulate fire, this new ability was felt as a sacrilegious crime, 'as a sacrilege [*Frevel*], as a theft committed against divine nature'.[7] It followed that civilization or culture as such was criminal:

> The best and the highest blessing which humanity can receive is achieved through sacrilege and its consequences must be accepted, namely the whole flood of suffering and troubles with which the insulted gods have no other choice but to afflict humanity as it strives nobly upward.[8]

To underline the nobility of Prometheus's crime, Nietzsche quotes from another version of the myth, Goethe's poem 'Prometheus' (1773). This is a monologue in the spirit of the radical Enlightenment. Prometheus defies Zeus, calling him an impotent deity who can throw thunderbolts against mountain tops and treetops but cannot do any real harm. Zeus is only worshipped by the deluded among humanity, who burn incense for him but have never aroused his pity nor received any benefits from him. Instead of Olympus, Prometheus is content with his hearth and his cottage, and (invoking another version of the Prometheus myth) he is creating a race of human beings in his own image. Nietzsche quotes the last stanza:

> Here I sit, make men
> In my image,
> A race the same as I,
> In order to suffer, to cry,
> To delight and to enjoy,
> And to show you no respect,
> Just the same as I![9]

To the Enlightenment, the supreme symbol of humanity's emancipation from God or the gods was the lightning conductor, invented once Benjamin Franklin had proved experimentally that lightning was a phenomenon of electricity. Kant, whose early publications were on natural science, called Franklin 'the Prometheus of modern times'.[10]

---

5   Aeschylus, *Persians, Seven against Thebes, Suppliants, Prometheus Bound*, ed. and trans. by Alan H. Sommerstein, Loeb Classical Library (Cambridge, MA: Harvard University Press, 2008), pp. 493–99.
6   M. S. Silk and J. P. Stern, *Nietzsche on Tragedy* (Cambridge: Cambridge University Press, 1981), p. 244.
7   *The Birth of Tragedy*, p. 57; KSA I, 69.
8   Ibid.
9   Translation by Douglas Smith. Original in Goethe, *Sämtliche Werke*, II, 298–300. On the enlightened Prometheus, see Jonas Jølle, '"prince poli & savant": Goethe's Prometheus and the Enlightenment', *Modern Language Review*, 99 (2004), 394–415.
10   Kant, 'Continued observations on the earthquakes that have been experienced for some time'

Prometheus is thus the progenitor of the Enlightenment and the original perpetrator of the crime, sacrilege, or transgression on which all civilization and all culture are built. Here civilization is opposed to a merely natural way of living, and culture means not only the arts but a whole spectrum of attitudes and behaviours that gives a society its style. In German, *Kultur* is often contrasted with *Zivilisation*, with the latter meaning the material infrastructure and the 'civilized', non-violent manners that are often thought to mark the progress of society, as in Norbert Elias's sociological classic *The Civilizing Process*.[11] Nietzsche himself draws this contrast in his notebooks: 'Die Höhepunkte der Cultur und der Civilisation liegen auseinander' ('The high points of culture and civilization are remote from each other').[12] Culture is compatible with moral corruption, whereas civilization, essentially a means of domesticating the human animal, encourages mediocrity and suppresses strong and bold characters; Nietzsche's favourite example of a strong character is Machiavelli's hero Cesare Borgia.[13] At the risk of producing unnatural English, *Kultur* will henceforth be translated consistently as 'culture', even though 'civilization' would sometimes be the more obvious English equivalent.

Having established Prometheus, with his theft of fire from heaven, as the founder of human culture, Nietzsche promptly develops this idea in a more specific way. Prometheus, as a heroic criminal, is a particularly Aryan figure. The Aryan myth of stealing fire from heaven has a counterpart in the Semitic myth of the fall of humanity by tasting the forbidden fruit. The two myths are related, Nietzsche tells us, as brother to sister, and are accordingly gendered. The dignity attached to the noble Aryan thief 'stands in strange contrast to the Semitic myth of the Fall, in which curiosity, dissimulation, the readiness to be led astray [*Verführbarkeit*], lasciviousness, in short a series of eminently feminine feelings, are viewed as the origin of evil'.[14] Nietzsche accepts the widespread assumption that a warlike Aryan race, speaking an early version of the languages later classified as 'Aryan' or 'Indo-European', originated perhaps in southern Russia, conquered the Indian subcontinent, and founded the great early civilizations that used the Sanskrit language. He is not contrasting Aryans and Semites as good and evil, in the manner of the influential racial thinker Gobineau, and he would consistently dismiss with scorn the use of the term 'Aryan' in racialist discourse.[15] He maintained that the racial mixture and interbreeding of 'Aryans' and 'Semites' could lead to cultural

(1756), trans. by Olaf Reinhardt, in *Natural Science*, ed. Eric Watkins, The Cambridge Edition of the Works of Immanuel Kant (Cambridge: Cambridge University Press, 2012), pp. 367–73 (p. 373). Franklin had proposed his experiment in 1750 and it had already been carried out by Thomas-François Dalibard at Marly, near Paris, on 10 May 1752.

11   Norbert Elias, *Über den Prozess der Zivilisation*, 2 vols (Basel: Haus der Falken, 1939); *The Civilizing Process*, trans. by Edmund Jephcott, 2 vols (Oxford; Blackwell, 1969, 1982).

12   Nietzsche, 1888 notebook, KSA XIII, 485.

13   See e.g. *Jenseits von Gut und Böse*, §197, in KSA V, 117; *Beyond Good and Evil*, trans. by R. J. Hollingdale (Harmondsworth: Penguin, 1973), p. 100.

14   *The Birth of Tragedy*, p. 57; KSA I, 69.

15   KSA XII, 50; see Nicholas Martin, 'Breeding Greeks: Nietzsche, Gobineau, and Classical Theories of Race', in *Nietzsche and Antiquity: His Reaction and Response to the Classical Tradition*, ed. by Paul Bishop (Rochester, NY: Camden House, 2004), pp. 40–53.

greatness, and recommended (how seriously?) that the German aristocracy should intermarry with Jewish families.[16] Nevertheless, and despite Nietzsche's constant aversion to antisemitism, one can see here the trope of the 'feminine Jew' which would come to play a large part in antisemitic discourse.[17]

Since Nietzsche is concerned in *The Birth of Tragedy* and other early writings with the ancient Greeks, he inevitably explores how far Greek culture is based on what modern people would call crime. Here he takes issue with the tradition of Graecophilia which arose in eighteenth-century Germany and led to the idealization of ancient Greece in well-known works by Goethe (*Iphigenie auf Tauris*), Schiller ('Die Götter Griechenlands'), and Hölderlin ('Der Archipelagus'; 'Brot und Wein').[18] Neohumanist idealization had a lasting influence on nineteenth-century German culture. Appointed minister of education in Prussia in 1809, Wilhelm von Humboldt (brother of the traveller and naturalist Alexander) established the humanistic *Gymnasium* or secondary school, in which the study of antiquity was the essential tool in the shaping of modern citizens. The much-read *Griechische Geschichte* (1857–67) by Ernst Curtius presents a sunny view of the Greeks, never mentioning slavery. Richard Wagner idealizes ancient Greece in *Das Kunstwerk der Zukunft* and *Die Kunst und die Revolution* (1849), seeing it as an integrated society embodying cultural and moral perfection, based on the public performance of tragedy, and thus antithetical to the commercial, fragmented, and in Wagner's view Judaized society of nineteenth-century Europe. We find this idealization of the Greeks even in such a hard-headed individual as Karl Marx. He tries to explain the paradox whereby, though art is shaped by economy and society, the art of such a relatively primitive society as the Greeks has not been surpassed:

> There are ill-bred children and precocious children. Many of the ancient nations belong to the latter class. The Greeks were normal children. The charm their art has for us does not conflict with the primitive character of the social order from which it had sprung. It is rather the product of the latter, and is due rather to the fact that the immature social conditions under which the art arose and under which alone it can appear can never return.[19]

This may be thought not to be an explanation at all, but rather to continue Germany's long-standing idealization of the Greeks.

Nietzsche is far more radical. His Greeks, by contrast, are aware of the horror of life: 'The Greek knew and felt the terrors and horrors of existence.'[20] The beautiful image of Mount Olympus, where the gods eternally feast on ambrosia and nectar, was a fiction necessary for the Greeks to go on living at all. It was only in tragedy

---

16   KSA XII, 45; *Jenseits von Gut und Böse*, §251, KSA V, 192–95; *Beyond Good and Evil*, pp. 162–64.
17   See Ritchie Robertson, *The 'Jewish Question' in German Literature 1749–1939* (Oxford: Oxford University Press, 1999), pp. 296–307.
18   See Joachim Wohlleben, 'Germany 1750–1830', in *Perceptions of the Ancient Greeks*, ed. by K. J. Dover (Oxford: Blackwell, 1992), pp. 170–202.
19   Marx, 'General Introduction to the *Grundrisse*', in *Karl Marx: Selected Writings*, ed. by David McLellan (Oxford: Oxford University Press, 1977), p. 360. On Marx and the Greeks, see S. S. Prawer, *Karl Marx and World Literature* (Oxford: Clarendon Press, 1976), pp. 278–88.
20   *The Birth of Tragedy*, §3, p. 28; KSA I, 35.

that the Greeks could look into the heart of things, and the horror of life was made temporarily bearable by its presentation in art. The Greeks had a profoundly pessimistic outlook on life, akin to what the young Nietzsche eagerly absorbed from reading Schopenhauer.

Nietzsche's disillusioned view of the Greeks had antecedents. Goethe in 1824 deplored the continual internecine wars among the Greek states, which he found 'even harder to stomach' by contrast with the Greeks' glorious resistance to the Persians.[21] The classical historian August Böckh published in 1817 a study of the Athenian economy. At the outset, Böckh pays tribute to the spiritual legacy of the Greeks that has shaped subsequent generations, but argues that the faults which the Greeks shared with the rest of humanity were exacerbated by their vehement passions:

> that in their passionate natures these faults only burst forth in stronger and cruder form, the less their hearts were piously animated by the mildness and humility of a gentler religion, of which they felt no need; that finally these faults, fostered and cherished, undermined and toppled the magnificent edifice of Antiquity itself.[22]

Nietzsche's older colleague at the University of Basel, Jacob Burckhardt, with whom he had many conversations, appealed to Böckh in support of his view that the Greeks were much more unhappy than their latter-day admirers liked to think.[23] In the lectures he was giving at the time, published posthumously as *Griechische Kulturgeschichte*, Burckhardt highlights the Greeks' unbridled appetite for revenge; the ruthlessness with which successful rulers punished and even annihilated their political enemies; and the 'diabolical delight in ruining others' evident from surviving law-court speeches.[24]

While *The Birth of Tragedy* focuses on aesthetic matters, Nietzsche's wider view of Greek civilization appears in two contemporaneous essays, 'Der griechische Staat' (The Greek State) and 'Homers Wettkampf' (Homer's Contest), which he did not publish but presented as a gift to Cosima Wagner at Christmas 1872. Here, following Burckhardt, Nietzsche stresses the omnipresence of the agon, of competition, in all areas of Greek life: in sport, in the arts, in crafts; according to Hesiod, even beggars compete in begging.[25] Hence the Greeks placed the supreme value on genius. The most ruthless competition was justified if it fostered genius. And the ultimate purpose of the state was to promote genius. To this end, the state needed to rest on slavery. This, according to Nietzsche, is true of all states, and to reinforce his point he again invokes the myth of Prometheus:

21   Eckermann, *Conversations with Goethe*, p. 102 (24 November 1824).
22   August Böckh, *Die Staatshaushaltung der Athener* (Berlin: Realschulbuchhandlung, 1817), p. 2.
23   Lionel Gossman, *Basel in the Age of Burckhardt: A Study in Unseasonable Ideas* (Chicago: University of Chicago Press, 2000), p. 302.
24   Jacob Burckhardt, *The Greeks and Greek Civilization*, trans. by Sheila Stern (London: HarperCollins, 1998), pp. 66, 61, 80.
25   Hesiod is quoted at KSA I, 786.

> Accordingly we must accept, and present as a cruel-sounding truth, that *the essence of a culture includes slavery*: a truth, indeed, that leaves no doubt concerning the absolute value of existence. This truth is the eagle that gnaws at the liver of the Promethean exponent of culture. The misery of people who live by toil must even be sharpened in order to enable a small number of Olympian people to produce the world of art.[26]

Here too, Prometheus is being punished for founding human culture. His crime now consists, not in defying the gods, but in creating a system whose achievements inexorably require the vast majority of people to suffer. This unwelcome truth corresponds to the eagle that gnaws his liver, and that must likewise torment everyone who promotes the achievements of culture. For modern culture, as Nietzsche will emphasize later, equally rests on slavery. Indeed modern wage-slaves lead harder, less secure lives than slaves in traditional slave societies.[27] The cult of incessant hard work, which has spread from America to Europe, means that employers are also slaves, obliged constantly to keep their eye on the clock.[28] 'Anyone who does not have two-thirds of a day for himself is a slave, be he who he may: statesman, businessman, civil servant, or academic.'[29] We try to disguise this state of affairs with such hollow slogans as 'human dignity' and 'the dignity of labour'.[30] But the truth is that while slavery can be mitigated, as it was in the relatively humane serfdom of the Middle Ages, it cannot be done away with.[31] Only a privileged elite can produce the high art which alone makes existence worthwhile: 'for only as an *aesthetic spectacle* are existence and the world *justified* to eternity'.[32] All culture, therefore, rests on a necessary crime, and its beneficiaries are necessarily criminals.

One reason why Nietzsche values the Greeks is that, unlike modern humanitarians, they acknowledged and accepted this state of affairs. They admitted that culture requires hierarchy, and that hierarchy needs to be imposed and maintained by the state. The state is the embodiment of power, which, Nietzsche says, is always evil, and operates by channelling the cruelty which is intrinsic to human nature. Thus art, religion, and politics centre on a tragic conflict, which is in turn a reflection of the 'primal pain and primal contradiction' that the spectator of Greek tragedy was able to apprehend in exalted moments of insight.[33] One may well shed tears of sympathy for suffering humanity: 'Culture, that opulent Cleopatra, repeatedly throws the most priceless pearls into her golden goblet: these pearls are tears of compassion for slaves and the slaves' misery.'[34] The Greeks, however, were not

---

26 'Der griechische Staat', KSA I, 767.
27 *Menschliches Allzumenschliches*, I, §457 (KSA II, 296).
28 *Die fröhliche Wissenschaft*, §329 (KSA III, 556–57).
29 *Menschliches Allzumenschliches*, I, §283 (KSA II, 231–32).
30 *The Birth of Tragedy*, §18, p. 98 (= KSA I, 117); also at KSA I, 764.
31 Cf.: 'How elevating it is to contemplate the medieval serf, connected by powerful and delicate legal and moral relationships to his social superior, and with his own existence enclosed in profound peace — how elevating — and what a reproach!' ('Der griechische Staat', KSA I, 769).
32 *The Birth of Tragedy*, §5, p. 38 (= KSA I, 47).
33 'Der griechische Staat', KSA I, 768.
34 Ibid., p. 769. The story of how Cleopatra took luxury to an extreme by dissolving a pearl in

troubled by compassion. Their competitive character and their devotion to their various states made them rather rejoice in violence and cruelty. 'This bloody jealousy of one state for another, of one party for another, the murderous greed of those petty wars, the tiger-like triumphing over the corpse of the defeated enemy', was simply the military aspect of the competitive instinct which caused them, in brief intervals of peace, to bring forth 'the radiant blossom of genius'.[35]

Much more than a historian of culture, Nietzsche is also a prophet, and in his later writings, published and unpublished, he asks insistently whether a society comparable to that of the Greeks can be hoped for in the future. That would be a society which accords supreme value to culture and treats the bulk of humanity as mere material. The 'free spirits' whom Nietzsche is addressing will not wait passively for such a society to emerge, but will do their utmost to promote it. He spells this vision out most challengingly in *Beyond Good and Evil*:

> To teach man the future of man as his *will*, and to prepare for great enterprises and collective experiments in discipline and breeding [*Gesammt-Versuche von Zucht und Züchtung*] so as to make an end of that gruesome dominion of chance and nonsense that has hitherto been called 'history' — the nonsense of the 'greatest number' is only its latest form — : for that a new kind of philosopher and commander will some time be needed, in face of whom whatever has existed on earth of hidden, dreadful and benevolent spirits may well look pale and dwarfed.[36]

Nietzsche foretells that these future leaders will sweep away democracy and take in hand the future of humanity. These leaders, as they reshape humanity, will not know compassion: their consciences will be steely, their hearts transformed into metal. Their task is to save humanity from the danger that currently threatens it, namely the degeneration of the human species into the feeble, cowardly, comfort-loving mediocrities which are the true ideal of modern humanitarianism, 'this animalization of man to the pygmy animal of equal rights and equal pretensions'.[37]

Does Machiavelli, whom Nietzsche admires as a stylist,[38] play any part in Nietzsche's thoughts about the future? Machiavelli makes occasional appearances in Nietzsche's notebooks. His future tyrants will be animated by the will to power, and power is always Machiavellian, albeit unconsciously so — presumably in being amoral.[39] The 'new Enlightenment' that Nietzsche proclaims will be Machiavellian in opposing hypocrisy ('Tartüfferie').[40] Machiavelli licenses amoral and prudent behaviour. Hence Nietzsche opposes John Stuart Mill's principle of doing as you would be done by; Mill presupposes that an action always leads to retaliation, whereas the reader of Machiavelli will know how to forestall retaliation: 'What if

---

vinegar and then swallowing it is told by Pliny the Elder in his *Natural History*.
35   Ibid., p. 772.
36   *Beyond Good and Evil*, § 203, p. 108 (KSA v, 126).
37   Ibid., p. 209 (KSA v, 127).
38   Ibid., §28, p. 42 (KSA v, 47): 'the tempo of Machiavelli, who in his *Principe* lets us breathe the subtle dry air of Florence and cannot help presenting the most serious affairs in a boisterous *allegrissimo*'.
39   Nietzsche notes emphatically: '**unbewußter Macchiavellismus**', KSA xii, 419.
40   KSA xi, 87.

someone with *Il Principe* in his hand were to say "these are exactly the things one *must* do so that others do not anticipate us — so that we make others incapable of doing such things to *us*?"[41] He understood Bismarck's frankly amoral *Realpolitik* as 'Machiavellianism with a good conscience'.[42]

A foreshadowing of the future tyrants can be found in those nineteenth-century figures who override moral boundaries thanks to their genius. Bismarck is mentioned as one such figure; Napoleon is another, but greater. When he seized power, according to Nietzsche, 'an unparalleled sense of well-being went through Europe: genius was to be *master*, the stupid "prince" of the past appeared a caricature'.[43] Napoleon prolonged the spirit of antiquity and the Renaissance (i.e. through his affinity to such personalities as Julius Caesar and Cesare Borgia); he gave Europe a new ideal of masculinity and introduced an era of great wars. It will be thanks to him that 'the *man* in Europe' will overcome the merchant and the Philistine, and even the feminization resulting from Christianity and humanitarianism.[44] His emergence was the most important event of the last thousand years.[45]

Nietzsche's culture heroes are criminals, like Prometheus. Napoleon's amorality, his imperious thirst for success, his indifference to the means he needed to achieve his ends, are all qualities of the criminal.[46] 'Every large-minded person [*Jeder großgesinnte Mensch*] has committed *every* crime'; whether his actions are crimes in the juridical, legal sense depends merely on the laws that happen to be in force.[47] In our modern, civilized [*civilisiert*] world, we know the criminal only as an inferior being, oppressed by feeling the disapproval of society, and lacking the confidence to assert himself against society. For that reason we are reluctant to admit 'that *all great men were criminals*, only in the grand style, not in a contemptible manner, [and] that crime is part of greatness'.[48]

Future tyrants will clearly not hesitate to commit necessary crimes. All culture, after all, originates from violence. If one sees a terrain deeply furrowed by glacial activity, one has difficulty in imagining that one day that land will be covered by woods and meadows. Yet so it is also in human history: where life is now mild and humane, the ground was prepared for it by a furious clash of destructive energies. These energies are necessary. 'The terrible energies — what is called evil — are the Cyclopean architects and road-builders of humanity.'[49] Progress lies not in eradicating these energies, as feeble humanitarians nowadays imagine, but in mastering and channelling them for the promotion of culture. 'To take everything frightful into one's service, singly, gradually, experimentally — that is what the task of culture demands.'[50]

41   KSA XIII, 583.
42   *Die fröhliche Wissenschaft*, §357 (KSA III, 598).
43   KSA XI, 79–80.
44   *Die fröhliche Wissenschaft*, §362 (KSA III, 610).
45   KSA XI, 539.
46   KSA XI, 40.
47   KSA XI, 79.
48   KSA XII, 405–06.
49   *Menschliches Allzumenschliches*, I, §246 (KSA II, 205).
50   KSA XIII, 484.

Progress happens through violence, and its violence includes sacrifice. Nietzsche has several reflections on sacrifice, notably a passage in *Morgenröthe* (*Daybreak*) where he questions the morality of treating one's neighbour as one would oneself. This strikes him as a narrow, petty-bourgeois morality, if indeed it can be called morality at all. Sometimes we should ignore the consequences that our actions will have for our neighbour and pursue more distant goals at the cost of making our neighbour suffer. If we are prepared to sacrifice ourselves, why should we not also sacrifice our neighbour? After all, the state sacrifices its citizens for the general good. Why should we not sacrifice individuals for the future good of humanity? 'Why should not some individuals of the present generation be sacrificed for the sake of generations yet to come? — so that their sorrow, their unease, their despair, their mistakes and fear-driven actions would be judged necessary, because a new ploughshare must break up the soil and make it fertile for everyone?'[51] Sacrifice is thus a means of progress, perhaps the main engine of progress: 'the species survives only through human sacrifices'.[52]

In Nietzsche's late writings, the kind of sacrifice he envisages becomes disturbingly clear. Progress consists in sacrificing inferior human beings to stronger ones. The more inferior people are sacrificed, the greater the progress: 'The extent of an "advance" is even *measured* according to the scale of the sacrifice required; the mass of humanity sacrificed to the flourishing of a single *stronger* species of man — now that *would* be progress.'[53] This was not a thought confined to Nietzsche's notebooks; he gave it to the world in *On the Genealogy of Morals*, and he was equally open with the notorious injunction near the beginning of *Der Antichrist*: 'The weak and ill-constituted [*Missrathnen*] shall perish: first principle of *our* philanthropy. And one shall help them to do so.'[54] He did not intend, however, to publish the following elaboration, written in spring 1884:

> Jene ungeheure *Energie der Größe* zu gewinnen, um, durch Züchtung und andrerseits durch Vernichtung von Millionen Mißrater, den zukünftigen Menschen zu gestalten und *nicht zu Grunde* zu gehn an dem Leid, das man *schafft* und dessengleichen noch nie da war![55]

> To gain that prodigious *energy of greatness*, in order, by breeding and also by annihilating millions of ill-constituted people, to shape the humanity of the future *without perishing* as a result of the unprecedented suffering that one *creates*!

Nietzsche is talking here about the qualities of the great man. The great man enjoys the feeling of power and finds it magnified when he identifies himself with a nation. He wants to communicate himself by reshaping communities in his own image. His love for humanity is divine, in that it includes contempt and the willingness to

---

51   *Morgenröthe*, §146 (KSA III, 138).
52   KSA XIII, 470.
53   *On the Genealogy of Morals*, trans. by Douglas Smith, Oxford World's Classics (Oxford: Oxford University Press, 1996), II, §12, p. 59 (KSA V, 315).
54   *Twilight of the Idols and The Anti-Christ*, trans. by R. J. Hollingdale (London: Penguin, 2003), p. 128; KSA VI, 170.
55   KSA XI, 98.

transform and elevate the object of his love. In doing this he will somehow manage not to perish ('*nicht zu Grunde* zu gehn') despite the prodigious amount of suffering he causes. ('Perishing' presumably means not physical destruction but psychological trauma.) His task may be mitigated by the predisposition of the 'Mißrathenen' to sacrifice themselves, shown for example in the monastic orders that take a vow of chastity (and more generally in the various forms of asceticism analysed in Part III of *On the Genealogy of Morals*).

It would be a relief if one could regard this passage as a momentary lapse. But it is consistent with the assumptions that, from *The Birth of Tragedy* onwards, underlie Nietzsche's cultural criticism and only occasionally break the surface. Although his thinly veiled agenda becomes increasingly explicit in his later writings, the desire to restore a heroic, elitist, hierarchical, militarized society runs through all his works. One can certainly extract a great deal of lasting interest and value from his moral analyses and his critique of nineteenth-century society. But to what extent can one cherry-pick insights from Nietzsche while keeping one's distance from the agenda which his insights presuppose and to which they lead? In particular, can one resist the conclusion that Nietzsche welcomed selective breeding (*Züchtung*) and looked forward to the extermination of large numbers of human beings considered, for whatever reason, 'failures' or unfit?

I have argued elsewhere that Nietzsche, leading an isolated existence and living largely inside his own head, simply did not imagine what his visions might be like in practice, so that his prophecies were frivolous rather than malign.[56] But the passage just quoted makes me wonder. It is disturbingly specific in that it begins to quantify the deaths that will be required ('millions'). Thus it moves one step away from cloudy fantasies and one step towards the extermination programmes put into action by the Nazis. The 'necessary crime' for which it argues was not necessary, but neither was it fantasy.

Moreover, admittedly without Nietzsche's doing, this passage was among the many selected from the notebooks and published, under the direction of Nietzsche's sister Elisabeth Förster-Nietzsche, as *Der Wille zur Macht* (*The Will to Power*).[57] She evidently did not think that it would reflect any discredit on her brother's memory. Along with the many other notebook entries which Nietzsche, during his (sane) lifetime, did *not* think fit to publish, it found thousands of readers in early twentieth-century Germany. With hindsight, it reads like a pre-echo of the address that Heinrich Himmler delivered to an audience of SS officers in occupied Poland on 4 October 1943, and in which he spoke explicitly of the extermination of the Jewish people:

> Today I am going to refer quite frankly to a very grave chapter. We can mention it now among ourselves quite openly and yet we shall never talk about it in public. I'm referring to the evacuation of the Jews, the extermination of

56   Ritchie Robertson, *Friedrich Nietzsche* (London: Reaktion, 2022), p. 195.
57   Friedrich Nietzsche, *Der Wille zur Macht: Versuch einer Umwertung aller Werte*, ed. by Peter Gast with the collaboration of Elisabeth Förster-Nietzsche, Kröners Taschenausgabe (Stuttgart: Kröner, 1959), § 964, p. 643.

the Jewish people. Most of you will know what it is like to see 100 corpses lying side by side or 500 or 1,000 of them. To have coped with this and — except for cases of human weakness — to have remained decent, that has made us tough. This is an unwritten — never to be written — and yet glorious page in our history. For we know how difficult we would have made it for ourselves if, on top of the bombing raids, the burdens and the deprivations of the war, we still had Jews today in every town as secret saboteurs, as agitators and troublemakers.[58]

---

58   Quoted in Peter Longerich, *Heinrich Himmler*, trans. by Jeremy Noakes and Lesley Sharpe (Oxford: Oxford University Press, 2012), p. 689. Longerich says that Himmler was ensuring his hearers' complicity in preparation for the escalation of the extermination programme which was about to include the Jews of Italy (p. 690).

20

Hofmannsthal:
Der Turm (1924–27)

Throughout his life Hugo von Hofmannsthal was fascinated by *La vida es sueño* (*Life is a Dream*, 1635), perhaps the most famous play by the Spanish Golden Age dramatist Pedro Calderón de la Barca (1600–82). The plot of Calderón's play is original: assiduous search through world literature has found no prior models. Basilio, the king of a vaguely imagined Poland, has been warned by his astrological studies that his son Segismundo will grow into a cruel monster and bring ruin on the kingdom. He has therefore confined Segismundo — whose mother's death in childbed is thought to be the first proof of his murderous disposition — in a remote tower on the kingdom's frontier. Segismundo's guardian gives him a rudimentary education. When we first see him, however, Segismundo, because of his alleged savagery, is chained up and clad in wild beast skins. Basilio tries an experiment: Segismundo is drugged and brought to the court, to test whether he is suitable for his kingly office; if the experiment fails, Segismundo can be drugged again, returned to the tower, and told that his brief visit to the court was only a dream. Not surprisingly, the experiment fails. Segismundo proves tyrannical and violent, throwing a courtier out of the window to his death. He is sent back to the tower, but released by a rebellion of populace and soldiers, who bring him to back to the royal palace. There he rebukes Basilio for treating him so foolishly and inhumanely, but the two are reconciled, and the play ends with Segismundo, now showing true kingly virtues, established as sovereign of Poland.

This at least is the strand of the action that appealed to Hofmannsthal. There is a further elaborate plot centring on Rosaura, a lady who has come to Poland in men's clothes to seek her unfaithful lover Astolfo, thereby, as commentators have argued, providing a parallel to Segismundo: if he straddles the boundary between animal and human, Rosaura's cross-dressing makes her neither male nor female. Segismundo finally resolves the Rosaura plot by commanding a series of marriages which make everyone happy (at least for the time being). The Rosaura plot did not much interest Hofmannsthal, however, and appears only fragmentarily in his draft adaptations.[1] There is also a possible question mark over Segismundo's conduct as ruler. Just before the end of the play, a soldier asks to be rewarded for raising

---

[1]   See Hugo von Hofmannsthal, *Sämtliche Werke*, ed. by Rudolf Hirsch and others, 37 vols (Frankfurt a.M.: Fischer, 1975–), xv: *Dramen* 13 (*Das Leben ein Traum; Dame Kobold*), ed. by Christoph Michel and Michael Müller (1989); Christoph König, *Hofmannsthal: Der Dichter unter den Philologen* (Göttingen: Wallstein, 2001), pp. 82–84.

the rebellion that finally freed Segismundo from captivity. Segismundo rewards him with lifelong imprisonment in the tower, on the grounds that 'traitors are of no use once their treachery has passed'.[2] Although the other characters applaud Segismundo's wisdom and prudence, and some commentators have agreed, others find his decision, and particularly the justification he gives, quite as Machiavellian as the unscrupulous conduct of his father.[3]

Machiavellianism, reason of state, and necessary crimes appear bluntly and shockingly in Hofmannsthal's mature tragedy, very loosely based on Calderón, *Der Turm*. Three complete versions exist: the first, published in book form in 1925 (henceforth *T1*); the second, differing from the first only in the shortening of two important scenes, published in a limited de luxe edition in late 1925; and the third, in which the final two acts have been thoroughly reconceived and revised, in 1927 (henceforth *T3*).[4] No version can be regarded as definitive. The second version, with its restricted settings, is certainly much more suitable for the theatre; but the first, despite its highly problematic ending, seems to me to have more poetic and political coherence. In what follows, therefore, I shall focus on the 1925 version, referring to the 1927 revision only to comment on significant differences.

Formally, the 1925 *Turm* is unusual and unclassifiable, even for a period in which the Expressionist playwrights, not to mention the young Brecht, produced many dramatic innovations. On its appearance, Walter Benjamin wrote Hofmannsthal an enthusiastic letter, maintaining that he had, with brilliant success, revived the Baroque genre of the *Trauerspiel* or mourning-play:

> In truth I see in your work a *Trauerspiel* in its purest, canonical form. And at the same time I feel the extraordinary dramatic power of which this form, contrary to conventional opinion, is capable in its highest manifestations. It would not be proper for me to make a comparison with your other works, but perhaps my feeling is right when I regard this latest one as crowning the renewal and rebirth of that German Baroque form and as a work of supreme authority for the stage.[5]

What Benjamin meant by *Trauerspiel* is not altogether easy to reconstruct, even though he had written a whole book on the subject. This was originally presented in 1925 for his *Habilitation* (i.e. it was a postdoctoral thesis, and its acceptance

2   Pedro Calderón de la Barca, *Life's a Dream / La vida es sueño*, trans. and ed. by Michael Kidd (Oxford: Aris & Phillips, 2011), p. 261.
3   Segismundo's action is defended by A. A. Parker, 'Calderón's Rebel Soldier and Poetic Justice', *Bulletin of Hispanic Studies*, 46 (1969), 120–27, on the grounds that 'seventeenth-century Spain considered rebellion against lawfully constituted authority the gravest of all political crimes' (p. 122). It is condemned for example by Stephen Rupp, *Allegories of Kingship: Calderón and the Anti-Machiavellian Tradition* (University Park, PA: Pennsylvania State University Press, 1996), p. 52, and Jeremy Lawrance, '*La vida es sueño*', in *A Companion to Calderón de la Barca*, ed. by Roy Norton and Jonathan Thacker (London: Tamesis, 2021), pp. 72–89: a 'Machiavellian automaton' (p. 87). On Basilio as Machiavellian, see Rupp, *Allegories*, p. 40.
4   Hofmannsthal, *Sämtliche Werke*, XVI.1: *Dramen*; XIV.1: *Der Turm*, Erste Fassung, ed. by Werner Bellmann (Frankfurt a.M.: Fischer, 1990); and XVI.2: *Dramen* XIV.2: *Der Turm*: Zweite und dritte Fassung, ed. by Werner Bellmann and Ingeborg Beyer-Ahlert (Frankfurt a.M.: Fischer, 2000).
5   Benjamin, letter of 11 June 1925, in his *Briefe*, ed. by Gershom Scholem and Theodor W. Adorno, 2 vols (Frankfurt a.M.: Suhrkamp, 1966), I, 384–87; also in *T1* 500–01.

was required to qualify him for a German university post). The thesis was rejected, leaving Benjamin obliged to make his way as a freelance writer, but it was published, thanks partly to Hofmannsthal's good offices, as *Der Ursprung des deutschen Trauerspiels* (The Origin of the German *Trauerspiel*) in 1928.[6] Benjamin's ostensible subject is seventeenth-century German Baroque drama, particularly the plays of Andreas Gryphius (1616–64), but rather than discuss them in detail, he places them in a rich though often bewildering historical context.

The *Trauerspiel*, according to Benjamin, is non-Aristotelian drama. Instead of moving towards a catharsis, it is static, allowing the martyr-hero to display superiority to a historical world from which all traces of divinity have departed and which can only inspire melancholy and mourning: *Hamlet*, whose melancholy hero regards the world as 'an unweeded garden', is also claimed as a *Trauerspiel*. Benjamin minimizes the unquestionable influence of Seneca and seeks, perfunctorily and implausibly, to derive the *Trauerspiel* from medieval mystery plays. *Der Turm* fits this pattern: the action is iterative rather than cumulative (Sigismund goes to and fro between the tower and the court); the world depicted is chaotic and ruinous; the protagonist is mostly passive and suffers a martyr's death. One could go further. Benjamin insists that the figures of tyrant and martyr are complementary, 'the two faces of the monarch'.[7] In the 1925 *Turm* Sigismund appears largely as a martyr, but he shows his potential for tyranny briefly in Act III and again in Act V, when he figures as king and military commander. In this sense his servant Anton (a brilliant comic creation) inadvertently sums up his ambivalence when addressing him, with a Freudian slip, as 'du heiliger verklärter Marterer' (*T1* 66), replacing 'Märtyrer' (martyr) with 'Marterer' (torturer).

Benjamin's letter, while of course coloured by his own preoccupations, shows an immensely sensitive and insightful response to Hofmannsthal's extraordinary drama. It is unlikely that Hofmannsthal took any interest in German Baroque drama, but his ultimate model, Calderón, qualifies for Benjamin as an outstanding author of *Trauerspiele*, albeit differing widely, in their Catholic exuberance, from the Lutheran austerity of the Germans. Indeed Benjamin once said that the *Trauerspiel* book was really about Calderón, its 'virtual subject'.[8]

---

6   See Ute Nicolaus, *Souverän und Märtyrer: Hugo von Hofmannsthals späte Trauerspieldichtung vor dem Hintergrund seiner politischen und ästhetischen Reflexionen* (Würzburg: Königshausen & Neumann, 2004), pp. 132–36.

7   Benjamin, *The Origin of German Tragic Drama*, p. 69; 'Tyrann und Märtyrer sind im Barock die Janushäupter des Gekrönten', in *Der Ursprung des deutschen Trauerspiels* in Benjamin, *Gesammelte Schriften*, ed. by Rolf Tiedemann and Hermann Schweppenhauser, 7 vols (Frankfurt a.M.: Suhrkamp, 1972–89), I/1 (1974), p. 249.

8   See Benjamin's letter to Gershom Scholem, 22 December 1924, in Benjamin, *Gesammelte Briefe*, 6 vols, ed. by Christoph Gödde and Henri Lonitz (Frankfurt a.M.: Suhrkamp, 1995–2000), II: *1919–1924* (1996), p. 508. Cf.: 'Nowhere but in Calderón could the perfect form of the baroque *Trauerspiel* be studied', *The Origin of German Tragic Drama*, p. 81. While writing this chapter I had the good fortune to examine the thesis by Jacobo de Camps Mora, 'In Defence of Aesthetic Attachment: A Response to Walter Benjamin's Critique of Calderón de la Barca' (D.Phil. Oxford, 2022), which is invaluable for understanding Benjamin's relation to Calderón; now forthcoming as *Walter Benjamin's Calderón: Literary Criticism and the Baroque* (Cambridge: Legenda, 2025).

Although *Der Turm* is in every version clearly a political play, its central figure, Sigismund, represents a type which had fascinated Hofmannsthal for many years, independent of politics. Such a person lives remote from the world, perhaps in luxury, perhaps in confinement and even degradation, but enjoys a rich imaginative life which feels as real as, or more real than, the world outside. While he revels in his fantasy world, he also resents his confinement and both desires and fears to break out of it. This, which could be called Hofmannsthal's master narrative, is already perfectly formulated in his early story *Das Märchen der 672. Nacht* (1895), a pseudo-Oriental tale in which a wealthy merchant's son leaves his luxurious solitude to suffer terrors and eventually meet a degrading death in a labyrinthine city. The heroine of *Elektra* (1904), haunting the palace courtyard like a caged animal and obsessed with the need to avenge the death of her father Agamemnon, is a more deeply negative counterpart to Sigismund. Hofmannsthal at the same period wanted to use the figure of Sigismund for psychological exploration: 'in die tiefsten Tiefen des zweifelhaften Höhlenkönigreiches "Ich" hinabzusteigen und dort das Nicht-mehr-Ich oder die Welt zu finden' ('to descend into the deepest depths of the ambiguous cave-kingdom of the Self and there to find the No-longer-Self or the world').[9] These figures are obviously related to Hofmannsthal's solitary, protected childhood and the need he felt in adult life to break through into social and political responsibilities, while often seeming, even to sympathetic observers, somewhat detached and disorientated.[10]

Sigismund in his remote tower is not yet a political actor, but he is the object of political intrigues. He is after all heir to the throne of Poland, a country we are invited to imagine as more legendary than historical (*T1* 6). His confinement is explained by his father as a necessary crime in order to prevent the fulfilment of a prophecy:

> [...] dass die Rebellion ihre Fahne bekommt: das ist ein Bündel klirrender, zerrissener Ketten an einer blutigen Stange, und der, dem sie vorangetragen wird, das ist mein leiblicher Sohn, mein einziges Kind, den ich gewonnen habe in rechtmässiger Ehe — und sein Gesicht ist wie eines Teufels Gesicht wiedergeboren aus dem höllischen Feuer und er ruht nicht bis er mich findet und seinen Fuss auf mein Genick setzt. (*T1* 44)

> [...] rebellion will get its flag: that is a bundle of torn, rattling chains on a bloodstained pole, and he before whom it is borne is my bodily son, my only child, whom I gained in lawful wedlock — and his face is like a devil's face born again from infernal fire and he will not rest until he finds me and puts his foot on my neck.

It was hardly necessary, though, to load Sigismund with chains and keep him in squalor, where he spends his time wielding a horse's bone in a fight against the

9   Letter to Hermann Bahr, 1904, in Hofmannsthal, *Briefe 1900-1909* (Vienna: Bermann-Fischer, 1937), p. 155.

10   For psychological studies of Hofmannsthal, see Wolfram Mauser, *Hugo von Hofmannsthal: Konfliktbewältigung und Werkstruktur* (Munich: Fink, 1977); Stefan Breuer, *Ästhetischer Fundamentalismus: Stefan George und der deutsche Antimodernismus* (Darmstadt: Wissenschaftliche Buchgesellschaft, 1995), pp. 128-48; Ulrich Weinzierl, *Hofmannsthal: Skizzen zu seinem Bild* (Vienna: Zsolnay, 2005).

vermin that inhabit his cell. In this treatment the Physician who visits Sigismund in his captivity finds a crime against God and humanity: 'Hier ist Adam, des obersten Königs erstgeborener Sohn, geschändet' (*T1* 21: 'Here Adam, the supreme King's first-born son, has been abused'), he tells Sigismund's jailer. In Sigismund we are to see something like King Lear's vision of 'unaccommodated man'.

Now that almost twenty-two years have passed since Sigismund's birth, the world outside the tower has changed. Four years of warfare have produced inflation and famine, accompanied by pestilence, and rebellion is widespread. King Basilius has lost control. His long-standing adviser, the ninety-year-old Grand Almoner, has retired to a monastery, and news has just come that his nephew has been killed in a hunting accident. Although he has been a compulsive womanizer, Basilius has (so far as he knows) never produced another son. Perhaps Sigismund will have to serve after all. A nobleman fetches Julian, Sigismund's jailer, who assures the King that his charge is gentle and well-behaved, and proposes an experiment. Sigismund will be drugged and brought to court; if he fails in kingly behaviour, he can be sent back to the tower. Although Basilius briefly worries that Sigismund will arouse popular sympathy as an 'Opfer der Staatsräson' (*T1* 76: 'victim of reason of state'), he has no humane scruples about accepting the proposal.

Much hangs on the outcome, not only for Sigismund, but for his jailer. During the more than twenty years he has spent as guardian of the tower, Julian has been consumed by ambition. Seeing him reanimated by the prospect of returning to court, the Physician, an astute reader of character, quotes Virgil's line 'Flectere si nequeo superos, Acheronta movebo' (*T1* 29): 'if Heaven I cannot bend, then Hell I will arouse!'[11] Having taught Sigismund to read and educated him for future kingship, he considers himself Sigismund's true parent; the father and mother provided the 'clod of earth', but Julian has shaped Sigismund into the instrument of his plans (*T1* 93), and nothing will stand in his way.

The royal court soon reveals itself as a den of intrigue, and Basilius proves to be an extreme Machiavellian. On receiving Sigismund, he says: 'Son, we have forgiven you' (*T1* 80), though it is Sigismund who has much to forgive. After initial difficulty in speaking, Sigismund manages to ask: 'Where does so much power [*Gewalt*] come from?' (*T1* 82) and receives a short lesson on absolutist monarchy.[12] Power comes directly from God the Father, and is confirmed by the holy oil, the crown, and the cloak that the king receives at his coronation. The confused Sigismund makes an incoherent demand for fatherly affection, but is coldly rebuked: 'Enough. I do not like this mask' (*T1* 82).[13] Evidently Basilius cannot imagine sincere communication without a mask.

Projecting his own character onto Sigismund, Basilius supposes him to be ambitious, power-hungry, reserved, and cunning. He gives him a Machiavellian

---

11   *Aeneid*, VII.312, in Virgil, *Aeneid VII–XII; The Minor Poems*, trans. by H. Rushton Fairclough, rev. edn, Loeb Classical Library (Cambridge, MA: Harvard University Press, 1986), p. 25.

12   'Power' here usually translates *Gewalt*. The German words for 'power' do not map neatly onto English equivalents. *Gewalt* can be a constitutional term (*Gewaltentrennung*, 'separation of powers'), but often overlaps with 'violence' or 'force'.

13   Later changed to the feebler 'I do not like such words' (*T3* 178).

lesson in statecraft. Rulers must learn to cope with their evil advisers. Chief among these, at present, is 'the serpent Julian' (*T1* 82). It was he, according to Basilius, who kept Sigismund in chains and sent back false reports about his savagery, simply in order to drive a wedge between father and son and consolidate his own power. The disorder in the country is the result of Julian's evil schemes. Sigismund is to act swiftly, divide the rebels, and crush the rebellion:

> Verhafte diesen Julian und sieh zu, ob der angezettelte Aufruhr nicht dahin fällt wie ein Bündel Reisig. Jeder deiner Schritte sei furchtbar, schnell und entscheidend. Überwältige die Bösgesinnten ehe sie sich vom blassen Schreck zu einer rebellischen Besinnung erholt haben. Treibe Stand gegen Stand, Landschaft gegen Landschaft, die Behausten gegen die Hauslosen, den Bauer gegen den Edelmann. Der Menschen Schwäche und Dummheit sind deine Bundesgenossen, riesengross, unerschöpflich (*T1* 84).

> [Arrest this Julian and watch the rebellion fall apart like a bundle of twigs. Let each of your steps be terrible, swift and decisive. Overpower the malevolent before they have recovered from their terror and come to their rebellious senses. Stir up class against class, region against region, the house-dwellers against the houseless, the peasant against the nobleman. Your allies are people's weakness and stupidity, gigantic, inexhaustible.]

This is Machiavellian advice, recalling the account of how Cesare Borgia restored order in his newly conquered territory of Romagna (*P* vii). It is too much for Sigismund. He strikes Basilius in the face, seizes his sword, dons his robe, and treads on his neck just as the prophecy foretold. He proclaims himself a tyrant: 'Ich will mit euch hausen wie der Sperber im Hühnerhof' (*T1* 85: 'I will deal with you like the sparrowhawk in the hen house'). He is soon overpowered and tranquillized. The King threatens to execute him, but instead he and Julian are sent back to the tower.

The 1927 version keeps Sigismund in the royal palace awaiting his execution, which is to take place on a scaffold sixty steps high. Besides planning this spectacular act of cruelty, Basilius is here shown to be a spymaster, having people arrested for probably innocent private conversations, and a sensualist, who requires an elderly courtier to let him enjoy the latter's two virginal nieces.

In both versions, the next stage is a popular rebellion which seeks to put Sigismund on the throne. Julian stirs up the rebellion, employing as his instrument the ex-student and soldier Olivier, who appeared at the beginning of *T1* as one of the guards at the tower. Olivier heightens the seventeenth-century atmosphere. He is based on a scribe turned soldier in Grimmelshausen's great novel of the Thirty Years War, *Der abenteuerliche Simplicissimus* (1669), and his extravagant language borrows from Gryphius's comedy *Horribilicribrifax* (1663). Like his namesake in Grimmelshausen, this Olivier is an unscrupulous criminal who despises all authority. The purpose of his rebellion is sheer destruction and mass murder. The aristocracy and the educated are to be slaughtered: 'Die Zucht soll verschwinden! Es sollen hinter uns die Geier und Wölfe kommen und sie sollen nicht sagen, dass wir halbe Arbeit getan haben' (*T1* 110: 'The breed shall disappear! After us the kites and wolves shall come, and they shall not say that we have done our work by halves'). This, as Julian admits, is the result of his raising hell (as foretold in the above quotation from Virgil), and now hell is let loose upon the earth (*T1* 99).

From now on the two versions diverge widely. In both, Olivier hopes to use Sigismund as a symbolic figure to attract the destitute to his banner. In *T3*, Olivier, having broken into the palace and confronted Sigismund, finds that Sigismund will not serve his purposes, so he looks for a double to appeal to the masses and contrives to have the real Sigismund assassinated. The Olivier of *T3* talks more rationally than the *miles gloriosus* of *T1*. He professes to embody reality (*T3* 215), calls himself a tool in the hands of political 'fatality' (*T3* 131, 215), and favours the word 'nüchtern' (sober, down-to-earth): 'Es ist ein nüchterner Tag über der Welt angebrochen' (*T3* 217: 'A sober day has dawned upon the world'). Although he may use the figure of Sigismund to exploit popular religiosity, Olivier has nothing idealistic about him: whatever his purposes, he is severely rational in his pursuit of them.[14] He makes one think of the *Sachlichkeit*, matter-of-factness, which was becoming a catchword of the time, as in Hermann Broch's novel *Huguenau oder die Sachlichkeit* (1932).

It would be even more appropriate, however, to associate Olivier with the Bolshevik revolution in Russia.[15] He conceals his name, like Lenin (*T3* 219). He has had Basilius murdered in a cellar, like the Russian imperial family (*T3* 216).[16] And he claims that he and his associates are sacrificing themselves for the good of the people: 'Denn ich und einige, wir haben uns aufgeopfert und nehmen dem Volk die Last des Regimentes ab, damit es nicht schwindlig werde' (*T3* 218: 'For I and some others have sacrificed ourselves and are taking the burden of government from the people, so that they may not become giddy'). Hofmannsthal originally wrote: 'die Last der *Freiheit*' (*T3* 359: 'the burden of *freedom*', his emphasis). This claim to be taking upon oneself the burden of freedom was of course made by Dostoevsky's Grand Inquisitor to justify the servitude imposed by the Catholic Church, and the obvious comparison with the Bolsheviks was indeed made in a book that Hofmannsthal read.[17] This it seems was the view that Hofmannsthal in 1927 took of left-wing revolution: alongside the bloodshed, it expressed a coldly rational outlook on the world, devoid of spirituality or even any respect for humanity, but prepared to use the language of sacrifice as a cynical justification for the assumption of power.

---

14   Perhaps by a fortunate coincidence, his name suggests the usurper Oliver Cromwell. Cromwell appears as a tyrant in Gryphius's *Carolus Stuardus* (1657, revised version 1663) and as the stolid victor over Charles I in Heine's *Französische Maler*, 'brutal as a fact' — Heinrich Heine, *Sämtliche Schriften*, ed. by Klaus Briegleb, 6 vols (Munich: Hanser, 1968–76), III, 67.

15   See Marcus Twellmann, *Das Drama der Souveränität: Hugo von Hofmannsthal und Carl Schmitt* (Munich: Fink, 2004), pp. 139–40; Alexander Mionskowski, *Souveränität als Mythos: Hugo von Hofmannsthals Poetologie des Politischen und die Inszenierung moderner Herrschaftsformen in seinem Trauerspiel 'Der Turm' (1924/25/26)* (Vienna: Böhlau, 2015), pp. 579–626. Mionskowski aptly compares Olivier to the Nameless One in Ernst Toller's *Masse Mensch* (1924): both exploit the altruistic ardour of earlier revolutionaries to consolidate their own ruthless and inhuman power.

16   Mionskowski briefly makes this comparison: *Souveränität als Mythos*, p. 310.

17   René Fülöp-Müller, *Geist und Gesicht des Bolschewismus* (1926). Pertinent quotations are given at *T3* 537.

The Sigismund of *T3*, Act v, is wholly passive. He preserves his inner integrity at the cost of staying aloof from the outside world. It has been claimed that his inaction is not really passivity, but a Buddha-like spiritual superiority.[18] Nevertheless, the saintly Sigismund allows Olivier to have his own way unimpeded. And his inaction cuts short any engaging dramatic conflict between the two, making the conclusion of the play distinctly feeble.

Act v in the 1925 version is entirely different. Ten years have passed since Act iv. Sigismund is now king and military commander. His troops are the poor, those who hailed him as 'Armeleut-König' (Poor Folk's King, *T1* 10), following him under a banner with the symbolic image of broken chains. He is a charismatic leader, as defined by Max Weber: one whose authority depends on his quasi-magical powers which ensure the emotional devotion of his followers.[19] His disciple Indrik says:

> Du hast uns gezeigt: Gewalt, unwiderstehliche, und über der Gewalt ein Höheres, davon wir den Namen nicht wissen, und so bist du unser Herr geworden, der Eine, der Einzige, ein Heiligtum, unzugänglich. (*T1* 132)

> You have shown us power, irresistible, and above power something higher, of which we do not know the name, and so you have become our master, the one, the only one, sacred, inaccessible.

He has allied himself with the King of the Tartars, who has established an Asiatic empire, separated from Sigismund's domain by the river Dniepr (here called by its ancient name, Borysthenes, *T1* 133). This already gives Act v a new atmosphere. The previous action took place in confined settings, either the tower or the royal palace. Now Sigismund is encamped somewhere in the vast spaces where Eastern Europe passes into Asia. His kingdom of Poland should not be identified with any of the modern versions of Poland, but with the area, stretching from the Baltic via much of Ukraine almost to the Black Sea, which in early modern times formed the Polish-Lithuanian Commonwealth. Even this risks being too precise an identification: names of places and peoples only provide momentary orientation within a blurred, dreamlike landscape.

Sigismund has apparently waged war against two enemies. One is the Polish nobility, and, again without being too precise, we may recall how in actual history the *szlachta* or magnates preferred weak monarchs and used their political rights to prevent reforms. The other is Olivier and his anarchic, destructive followers, representing what Hofmannsthal called 'the eternal ochlocratic element' (ochlocracy means 'rule by the mob', the antithesis of aristocracy or 'rule by the best').[20] We learn from Act V that both campaigns have been successful. Olivier is dead, and the nobility have come to offer Sigismund their allegiance. He accepts it,

18   Wolfgang Nehring, *Die Tat bei Hofmannsthal* (Stuttgart: Metzler, 1966), p. 133; Freny Mistry, 'Towards Buddhahood: Some Remarks on the Sigismund Figure in Hofmannsthal's *Turm* Plays', *Modern Language Review*, 69 (1974), 337–47 (esp. p. 344).

19   See Nicolaus, *Souverän und Märtyrer*, pp. 221–22; Max Weber, 'Die drei reinen Typen der legitimen Herrschaft', in *Gesammelte Aufsätze zur Wissenschaftslehre*, ed. by Johannes Winckelmann, 3rd edn (Tübingen: Mohr Siebeck, 1968), pp. 475–88 (esp. pp. 481–82).

20   Letter to an unnamed young man, December 1925, in Hofmannsthal, *Gesammelte Werke in Einzelbänden*, ed. by Bernd Schoeller, 10 vols (Frankfurt a.M.: Fischer, 1979), III, 474.

but makes clear that he does not intend to restore their old feudal power over the peasantry. He has come to create order and to found a new order. 'Ich trage den Sinn des Begründens in mir und nicht den Sinn des Besitzens, und die Ordnung, die ich verstehe, ist gefestigt auf der Hingabe und der Bescheidung' (*T1* 132: 'I am minded to establish, not to possess, and the order I mean is based on devotion and humility'). Here Hofmannsthal has put into Sigismund's mouth words ascribed to Napoleon, 'J'avais le goût de la fondation et non celui de la propriété' (*T1* 548).[21] Sigismund has yet more ambitious plans: with the help of his ally, the Tartar Khan, he means to mingle all the small nations in a great melting-pot, and perhaps to conquer Constantinople while he is at it (*T1* 133).

These plans may remind us of Napoleon's self-destructive invasion of Russia, and of the conquests made by Alexander the Great which disintegrated after his premature death. Sigismund himself names yet more disturbing analogies. 'Wenn das, was ich schaffen werde, nicht dauern kann, so werft mich auf den Schindanger zu Attila und Pyrrhus, den Königen, die nichts begründet haben' (*T1* 133: 'If what I shall create cannot last, then throw me on the rubbish heap along with Attila and Pyrrhus, the kings who founded nothing'). The nobles have already compared him to Attila by describing how his banner with the torn chains was swung over their heads like God's scourge. Attila the Hun, known as *Flagellum Dei* or 'the scourge of God', is of course a byword for destructive conquest. Pyrrhus (319–272 BCE) may be less familiar: he was a cousin of Alexander the Great, based in the Balkans, who led the Greek inhabitants of Italy in an attempt to conquer Rome, which failed despite several costly victories ('Pyrrhic victories'); in the end, according to the biography by Plutarch, he was fatally injured by a tile thrown from a house-top by an old woman.[22] Attila and Pyrrhus have been ominously linked before in German drama. In Schiller's *Wallensteins Tod*, the Swedish envoy compliments Wallenstein on his military prowess by saying:

> Euer Gnaden sind
> Bekannt für einen hohen Kriegesfürsten,
> Für einen zweiten Attila und Pyrrhus.[23]

> Your grace is much renowned,
> A mighty prince of war, as all men know,
> A second Pyrrhus and a new Attila![24]

This echo is doubly ominous, for Wallenstein will be killed a few days after this scene.

Sigismund too dies at the end of the play. Commentators often attribute his downfall to the necessary incompatibility between spiritual purity, such as

---

21   An authentic source in Napoleon's writings has not been found; Hofmannsthal copied these words from a notebook kept by his friend Carl J. Burckhardt.

22   *Plutarch's Lives*, trans. by John Dryden, revised by Arthur Hugh Clough, Everyman's Library, 3 vols (London: Dent, 1910), II, 74. This may be the Plutarchan biography which Sigismund has read on the Physician's recommendation (*T1* 119).

23   Schiller, *Werke und Briefe*, IV, 164 (ll. 285–87).

24   Schiller, *The Robbers* and *Wallenstein*, trans. by Lamport, p. 333.

Sigismund has gained, and the brutal world of power politics.[25] But Sigismund has after all survived in the world for ten years, and the cause of his death is something much more curious. His soldiers bring in a gipsy woman who is known to be Olivier's mistress, pregnant by him, and privy to all his plans. Left alone with Sigismund, she utters magical incantations and creates an atmosphere reminiscent of his original confinement in the tower, with crawling vermin and rattling bones. She summons up apparitions of the dead Julian, a fox symbolizing Basilius, and Olivier with his skull split, final confirmation of his death. This superb, spine-chilling scene is said to have been inspired by Hofmannsthal's reading of Ferdinand Ossendowski's *Beasts, Men and Gods*, an account of experiences in the Central Asian steppes which included witnessing magical ceremonies in a Mongolian yurt.[26] Sigismund is not terrified by these apparitions. However, the gipsy manages to stab him with a tiny poisoned needle, which brings about his death within a few hours.

The gipsy's action forms part of an elusive strand of meaning which assists the coherence of *T1* and is largely absent from *T3*. Sigismund says of her:

> Sie ist jung und eher schön als hässlich, und dennoch schauderts mich. — Aber wir haben nichts anderes, das uns Mutter werden könnte, als dieses Geschlecht, und dies ist der Stoff aus dem die Welt gemacht ist. (*T1* 122)

> She is young, and beautiful rather than ugly, and yet I shudder. — But we have nothing else to provide us with mothers than this sex, and this is the material from which the world is made.

Sigismund assigns the feminine to the material world, himself to the spiritual world. His mother died giving birth to him. He has never had any contact with women except for the kindly peasant woman who looked after him for part of his childhood. During his violent outburst in Act III, he exclaims: 'An mir ist nichts vom Weib!' (*T1* 84: 'There is nothing of the woman about me!'). By contrast, his father Basilius has a powerfully erotic disposition, as he makes clear in a lyrical speech charged with sexuality:

> Heut ist St. Aegydi Tag: da geht der Hirsch in die Brunft. — Ein schöner, heller Abend: die Elstern fliegen paarweise vom Nest ohne Furcht für ihre Jungen, und der Fischer freut sich: sie laichen bald, aber sie sind noch begierig und springen im frühen nebligen Mondschein, ehe es noch Nacht ist. Es bleibt lange noch schusslicht zwischen dem Fluss und dem Wald, und gross und fürstlich tritt der Hirsch aus dem Holz, und löst die Lippen, dass es scheint als ob er lache, und schreit machtvoll, dass die Tiere im Jungholz ihre zitternden Flanken aneinanderdrücken vor Schreck und Verlangen. — Wir waren wie er und haben majestätische Tage genossen, ehe das Wetter umschlug, und den schönen Weibern lösten sich die Knie beim Laut unseres Kommens, und wo wir beliebten einzutreten, da beschien der silberne Leuchter oder der russige Kienspan die Vermählung Jupiters mit der Nymphe. (*T1* 42)

---

25   See e.g. Nehring, *Die Tat bei Hofmannsthal*, p. 130; Mistry, 'Towards Buddhahood', pp. 343–44.
26   See *T1* 172–73; Brian Coghlan, *Hofmannsthal's Festival Dramas* (Cambridge: Cambridge University Press, 1964), pp. 269–70. Hofmannsthal read the German translation, *Götter, Tiere und Menschen* (1923).

Today is St Giles' Day, when the stag goes into rut. — A fine, clear evening: the magpies fly in couples from their nest without fear for their young, and the fisherman is pleased that the fish will soon spawn, but they are still ardent and leap in the early misty moonlight, before it is night. It will long remain light enough for a shot between the river and the forest, and out of the wood the stag steps, great and princely, and opens his lips, as though laughing, and utters such a powerful cry that the animals in the undergrowth rub their quivering flanks against each other out of terror and desire. — We were like him and enjoyed majestic days before the weather changed, and beautiful women became weak at the knees at the sound of our approach, and wherever we were pleased to enter, the silver candelabra and the sooty torch illuminated the coupling of Jupiter with the nymph.

Olivier, with his women, is another such erotic being. Sigismund says of his apparition: 'he stinks of fire and blood like the rutting stag!' (*T1* 124). Sigismund's purity is connected with his detachment from the sexual, sensual side of life. Repellent as Basilius and Olivier are, the lyricism of Basilius's speech just quoted pays an irresistible homage to the senses. Sigismund, on the other hand, stands as far as possible outside the chain of generation. His mother died at his birth; his father feared and maltreated him, and is in turn rejected; Julian, as his teacher, claims to be a substitute parent, but compares Sigismund to a golem — the artificial man made from clay, familiar from Jewish legend: 'you lump of clay, under whose tongue I placed the wrong word' (*T1* 107). Sigismund's fate, stabbed by a pregnant woman, symbolizes the fatal vulnerability of the spirit detached from the senses.

Before his death, Sigismund receives a visit from a new figure, the Kinderkönig (Children's King). He leads a company of children, orphaned during the wars, who now form a new community, practising agriculture and crafts. He is said to be a son of Basilius by 'a beautiful wild woman', but not to know his father's identity, any more than Basilius knew of this son (*T1* 120). He tells Sigismund that his mother saved his life by hiding him in a well (*T1* 138). Thus he has already been reborn from water, an analogue to baptism. He tells Sigismund, his half-brother, how he and his followers are building a new civilization:

> Wir haben Hütten gebaut und halten Feuer auf der Esse und schmieden die Schwerter zu Pflugscharen um. Wir haben neue Gesetze gegeben, denn die Gesetze müssen immer von den Jungen kommen. (*T1* 138)

> We have built huts and keep fire on the forge and turn swords into ploughshares. We have given new laws, for laws must always come from the young.

Sigismund, he explains, was only a 'transitional king' (*Zwischenkönig*), preparing the way for the children to establish a new order, in which Sigismund's grave will help to sanctify the Kinderkönig's dwelling.

The Children's King has been much criticized.[27] Hofmannsthal removed him altogether from *T3*. Critics complain that, with his appearance, the play moves away from imaginable events into a symbolic, utopian dimension. But the play never had any pretensions to realism. Its semi-legendary Poland was always a setting for

---

27   See e.g. Martin Buber's misgivings, in Nicolaus, *Souverän und Märtyrer*, pp. 40–41.

fantastic events that derived their meaning from their internal poetic coherence. And the coherence of *T1* extends further than has been generally recognized. Probably in 1921, Hofmannsthal read a study by Konrad Burdach concerning conceptions of historical renewal and rebirth.[28] Among much else he found the tripartite scheme of history put forward by the medieval mystic Joachim of Fiore (c. 1135–1202). Joachim's first age was that of the Father, in which humanity lived under the Law (corresponding to the Old Testament); the second, inaugurated by Christ, was that of the Son, when humanity lived by grace; and the third, future age would be that of the Holy Spirit when humanity would be able to live in freedom within a spiritual Church.[29] Hofmannsthal noted down various versions of this scheme (*T1* 160–61, 368–69). Applied to the structure of *Der Turm*, it divides the play into three ages: the age of the father, Basilius, a period of monarchy which has reached a point of extreme decay and corruption; then the age of the son, Sigismund, which is really an interregnum, preparing through necessary violence the third age, that of the Kinderkönig (Basilius's other son), who will bring about the purification and renewal that Sigismund could only imagine.

Read in this way, *Der Turm* is revealed as a visionary work of poetic imagination, independent of any actual political project. That is just as well, for in his later years Hofmannsthal's distress at the state of post-1918 Europe led him to envisage, in very woolly fashion, a 'conservative revolution', and to propose such an idea in the speech 'Das Schrifttum als geistiger Raum der Nation' ('Literature as the Nation's Spiritual Space'), delivered at the University of Munich on 10 January 1927.[30] His speech deals with literature as the embodiment of a nation's cultural traditions and unity. It places the future of German culture in the hands of a few unnamed but identifiable 'seekers' ('Suchende'). These are the agents of a 'conservative revolution whose dimensions have no precedent in European history'. Thomas Mann warned Hofmannsthal in conversation that the looming revolution was something much less palatable.[31] The term 'conservative revolution' is now commonly applied retrospectively to thinkers of the radical right such as Oswald Spengler and Ernst Jünger, with whom, however, Hofmannsthal had no connection.[32]

Particular efforts have been made to connect *Der Turm* with the ideas about sovereignty put forward by Carl Schmitt in *Politische Theologie* (1922).[33] Schmitt

---

28   Konrad Burdach, 'Sinn und Ursprung der Worte Renaissance und Reformation', a lecture originally published in 1910, reprinted in Burdach, *Reformation, Renaissance, Humanismus: Zwei Abhandlungen über die Grundlage moderner Bildung und Sprachkunst* (Berlin: Paetel, 1918), pp. 13–96. For Joachim's three ages, see esp. pp. 50–51.

29   See *The Oxford Dictionary of the Christian Church*, 4th edn, ed. by Andrew Louth, 2 vols (Oxford: Oxford University Press, 2022), I, 1013.

30   For a summary, see Nicolaus, *Souverän und Märtyrer*, pp. 60–63; for analysis, Klaus Dethloff, 'Hugo von Hofmannsthal und eine konservative Revolution', *Deutsche Vierteljahrsschrift für Literaturwissenschaft und Geistesgeschichte*, 92 (2018), 531–55.

31   Nicolaus, *Souverän und Märtyrer*, pp. 77–78.

32   See Roger Woods, *The Conservative Revolution in the Weimar Republic* (London: Macmillan, 1996). Nicolaus establishes that Hofmannsthal found the term in a much more obscure writer, Paul Landsberg, author of *Das Mittelalter und wir* (see *Souverän und Märtyrer*, pp. 75–76).

33   See especially Twellmann, *Das Drama der Souveränität*. Twellmann admits (p. 8) that Schmitt's

defines the sovereign as one who intervenes in an emergency or exceptional situation (*Ausnahmezustand*) and establishes power and takes decisions solely on the basis of his personal authority, not of the laws.[34] Hofmannsthal found many references to this book in Benjamin's *Ursprung*, and read it himself with enthusiasm in October 1926.[35] Given the dates, however, it cannot have helped him to shape *T1*, while Schmitt's sovereign does not resemble the passive Sigismund of *T3*. A case could be made for Olivier as a Schmittian sovereign, but he is clearly someone we are not invited to admire or approve. Schmitt himself, as is well known, joined the National Socialist Party on 1 May 1933, obtained the chair of public law at Berlin, and supported Nazi policies though privately he found some of them absurd; despite this time-serving, he fell from favour. Some disapproving commentary on the later Hofmannsthal appears to associate him with Schmitt in order to cast him as a proto-fascist, but his activities and utterances of the 1920s seem not malign but simply clueless.[36]

Why does Sigismund fail? In *T1*, his campaign of conquest evidently increases the devastation that he wants to repair. It is necessary in finally sweeping away the old order. But Sigismund is unable to establish the new order, which he can only vaguely imagine. That task is left to the redemptive figure of the Children's King, and Sigismund proves to have been a merely transitional figure. Moreover — and here the play bends away from politics — Sigismund's strength, but also his fatal weakness, consists in his detachment from ordinary sensual life and especially from femininity. Hence it is symbolically appropriate that he falls victim to the gipsy woman, who, being pregnant, embodies the maternal domain which Sigismund acknowledges only regretfully. In *T3* the omission of the Children's King sharply reduces the play's imaginative coherence. We now have the saintly, passive Sigismund confronting the modern, Lenin-like revolutionary Olivier who registers only brute fact and is, besides, an unscrupulous Machiavellian, worse than Julian and as bad as Basilius. The final version of *Der Turm* is an expression of political despair, but the first version, if we accept it as a symbolic work, contains a vision of redemption.

ideas are unlikely to have had any effect on even the second version of *Der Turm*; his book tries only to draw parallels. Some claims about Hofmannsthal and Schmitt are discussed sceptically by Mionskowski, *Souveränität als Mythos*, pp. 67–73.

34   See Carl Schmitt, *Political Theology: Four Chapters on the Concept of Sovereignty*, trans. by George Schwab, 2nd edn (Chicago: University of Chicago Press, 1985), and the summary in Nicolaus, *Souverän und Märtyrer*, p. 53.

35   Letter to Josef Redlich, 8–9 November 1926, in Hofmannsthal and Redlich, *Briefwechsel*, ed. Helga Fußgänger (Frankfurt a.M.: Fischer, 1971), pp. 77–78. Mionskowski, *Souveränität als Mythos*, pp. 428–35, has tried to argue, admittedly inconclusively, that Hofmannsthal had read *Politische Theologie* earlier, but his letter to Redlich strongly implies that he has just read it for the first time. See Nicolaus, *Souverän und Märtyrer*, pp. 51–55.

36   See Weinzierl, *Hofmannsthal*, pp. 91–102.

21

Brecht:
Die Maßnahme (1930–31)

Die Maßnahme (known in English, rather clunkily, as *The Measures Taken*), one of Brecht's most original, astonishing, disturbing, and controversial plays, centres on an action which is acknowledged to be atrocious but declared to be necessary. Four agitators, who have been working illegally in China to foment revolution, explain to their superiors, the 'Kontrollchor' (Examining Chorus) back in Moscow, why they were obliged to kill a young Chinese activist who was endangering their mission.[1] They regret their deed, saying emphatically: '*Furchtbar ist es, zu töten*' (*BFA* III, 97, 124), 'It is a terrible thing to kill' (*MT* 32).[2]

While the play expresses Brecht's commitment to communism, which would remain constant throughout his life despite his awareness of the terror in the Soviet Union initiated by Lenin and immeasurably extended by Stalin, his communism was never quite in line with the orthodoxy of the KPD (German Communist Party). It was shaped by his friendship with the unorthodox theoretician Karl Korsch, who argued that theory was not a mere reflection of the social movement but a dialectical component of it — thus encouraging Brecht to write plays that aimed to change consciousness, and hence reality, by inducing the audience to reflect on what they were shown.[3] In 1930 Brecht came closer to the KPD by

---

1   As often with Brecht's plays, *Die Maßnahme* exists in several versions. Four different versions were published during Brecht's lifetime. The first appeared in autumn 1930 as the ninth instalment in the series of Brecht's works published under the general title *Versuche* between 1930 and 1933. A considerably revised version appeared as the twelfth instalment of *Versuche*, at the end of 1931. Brecht made some further changes when including *Die Maßnahme* in the second volume of his *Gesammelte Werke*, published in exile by the Malik Verlag in London in 1938. A fourth version, closely based on the 1931 text, appeared in the postwar edition of Brecht's plays issued as *Stücke* by the Suhrkamp Verlag in West Germany and the Aufbau Verlag in East Germany. The most authoritative edition of Brecht's work, the *Große kommentierte Berliner und Frankfurter Ausgabe*, ed. by Werner Hecht and Jan Knopf, 30 vols (Berlin and Weimar: Aufbau; Frankfurt a.M.: Suhrkamp, 1988–2000), includes both the 1930 and 1931 texts in vol. III, and will be cited here as *BFA* III with page number. See *BFA* III, 433–39; *Die Maßnahme*. Kritische Ausgabe mit einer Spielanleitung, ed. by Reiner Steinweg (Frankfurt a.M.: Suhrkamp, 1972), henceforth cited as Steinweg; Erdmut Wizisla, 'Brecht Editions', in *Bertolt Brecht in Context*, ed. by Stephen Brockmann (Cambridge: Cambridge University Press, 2021), pp. 233–41.

2   References in this form are to Brecht, *The Measures Taken*, trans. by Carl R. Mueller (London: Eyre Methuen, 1977).

3   Stephen Parker, *Bertolt Brecht: A Literary Life* (London: Bloomsbury, 2014), pp. 254–55; see Leszek Kołakowski, *Main Currents of Marxism*, trans. by P. S. Falla, 3 vols (Oxford: Clarendon Press,

adopting Leninism.[4] He maintained that revolutionary violence was necessary to establish the dictatorship of the proletariat. The Party as Brecht imagines it in *Die Maßnahme* corresponds to the hierarchical model set out by Lenin in his early pamphlet *What is to be Done?* (1902), in which the leadership of a centralized and disciplined party directs local groups who in turn agitate among the working class.[5]

To communicate the lessons of Marxism, Brecht devised a new type of drama, the *Lehrstück* (didactic play). The *Lehrstück* avoids superficial realism. It stages an abstract model of a situation in order to reveal the forces at work under the surface of society and to provide guidance on how to behave in politically problematic situations. This analysis does not exclude emotion. The figures in the play are intended to be human beings, not machines, and they have to wrestle with their feelings. Besides, *Die Maßnahme* is a musical as well as a theatrical work, on which Brecht collaborated with the composer Hanns Eisler. But the music is not supposed to immerse the audience in a warm bath of feeling. Quite the contrary, it is, as an early reviewer said, 'Aktionsmusik', stimulating the audience's critical faculties and helping them to follow alertly the logically constructed text.[6]

Hence detachment, not identification, is all-important. Explaining to the Examining Chorus why they had to kill the Young Comrade, the agitators take it in turns to play him, as well as playing the other characters who appear in various scenes, such as a coolie hauling a barge and the overseer who keeps the coolies hard at work. They are thus re-enacting events in a manner which advertises its own artificiality. They are also using their imaginations, since the scenes they re-enact include some where none of them was present (e.g. the Young Comrade's dinner with a rich businessman). Hence the disruptive emotions of the Young Comrade are conveyed, but filtered through the words of another character, whose empathy with him is outweighed by disapproval.

Compared to Brecht's previous *Lehrstücke*, this play qualifies its abstractness by being set in a particular place and time. The events it recounts took place in Mukden (now Shenyang) in northern China, and the time, though never specified, must be the present (1930) or the recent past. The four agitators are required to pass as Chinese, with yellow skins and speaking Chinese even in their sleep or when delirious.[7] This hardly seems possible, and is presumably to be understood symbolically, like the masks which they are handed by the director of the last Communist Party house on the Russian side of the frontier. The point is that

1978), III, 308–23 (esp. pp. 311–12); Wolfdietrich Rasch, 'Bertolt Brechts marxistischer Lehrer: Zum ungedruckten Briefwechsel zwischen Brecht und Karl Korsch', in Rasch, *Zur deutschen Literatur seit der Jahrhundertwende* (Stuttgart: Metzler, 1967), pp. 243–73.

4   Parker, *Brecht*, p. 278; Erdmut Wizisla, *Benjamin und Brecht: Die Geschichte einer Freundschaft* (Frankfurt a.M.: Suhrkamp, 2004), pp. 15–16.

5   Service, *Lenin*, p. 142. See Günter Hartung, 'Leninismus und Lehrstück. Brechts *Maßnahme* im politischen und ästhetischen Kontext', in *Brecht 85: Zur Ästhetik Brechts* ([East] Berlin: Henschelverlag, 1986), pp. 126–43 (esp. p. 137).

6   Hans Heinz Stuckenschmidt in *Der Anbruch*, 13 (Berlin, 1931), repr. in Steinweg, pp. 343–50 (here pp. 344–45).

7   Cf. Frank Thomsen, Hans-Harald Müller, and Tom Kindt, *Ungeheuer Brecht: Eine Biographie seines Werks* (Göttingen: Vandenhoeck & Ruprecht, 2006), p. 125.

devotion to revolutionary activity requires one to abandon one's identity. The director instructs the agitators:

> Dann seid ihr nicht mehr ihr selber, du nicht mehr Karl Schmitt aus Berlin, du nicht mehr Anna Kjersk aus Kasan und du nicht mehr Peter Sawitsch aus Moskau, sondern allesamt ohne Namen und Mutter, leere Blätter, auf welche die Revolution ihre Ausweisung schreibt. (*BFA* III, 78, 104)[8]

> Then be no longer yourselves: you no longer Karl Schmidt from Berlin; you no longer Anna Kjersk from Kazan; and you no longer Peter Sawitsch from Moscow. You are nameless and without a past, empty pages on which the revolution may write its instructions. (*MT* 12)[9]

This self-abnegation makes one recall how monks committing themselves to an enclosed life are required to break with their past and assume new names; it is one of several indications that Brecht's adoption of Marxism in the late 1920s resembled a religious conversion.

Working with the agitators to spread the revolutionary spirit in Mukden, the Young Comrade was assigned four tasks, which he performed inadequately and sometimes disastrously. His problem, we gather, was his intense emotional commitment to revolution ('Mein Herz schlägt für die Revolution', *BFA* III, 75, 101; 'I sympathize with the revolution', *MT* 10). He had not learned that pity for the sufferings of the poor must be subjected to the discipline of the Party if it is to achieve long-term goals: not the abolition of this or that injustice, but the destruction of capitalist society and its replacement by a just social order. So when he was ordered to spread propaganda among the coolies who dragged barges laden with rice, he was so upset by seeing them barely able to stagger through the mud that he put down stones to give them a solid footing — but this was not really helpful, since he could not lay down stones all the way to Mukden (*BFA* III, 82). In the 1931 version he more sensibly advised them to demand shoes such as were worn by coolies elsewhere, but he thus got himself identified as a trouble-maker, so that he and the agitators had to go on the run for a week (*BFA* III, 108–09). His next task was to hand out leaflets urging the cotton-spinners to strike; a policeman, seeing a worker with a leaflet, murdered him; the workers did strike, but ineffectually (*BFA* III, 86). In the second version the strike was already in progress; the Young Comrade, in response to police violence, quarrelled with those who were still at work, and the strikers' pickets were driven away.

The Young Comrade's next assignment was demoralizing in a different way. The British, who controlled Mukden (presumably because they had been granted a concession, as the British and French were in many Chinese cities), were at odds with the local businessmen over customs dues. The agitators hoped to divide these two groups and give the workers, whom they had been teaching about street-fighting, a chance to seize power. The Young Comrade was therefore sent to the

---

8   Although the director of the Party house addresses three agitators, the stage directions mention only two. One is playing the director, and presumably the fourth is playing the Young Comrade, who may be present in this scene though he does not speak.

9   The translation seems at fault here: 'seid ihr' is not imperative but indicative ('you are').

richest businessman to ask him to give the coolies weapons with which to fight the British. The businessman invited him to dinner and described the economic contradiction whereby he paid the coolies starvation wages so that they could not buy the rice in which he traded (of course no businessman would say this, but Brecht's purpose is to reveal, by non-naturalistic means, the internal contradictions of capitalism). His cynicism so disgusted the Young Comrade that the latter walked out, and the coolies remained without weapons (which the businessman, who was presumably not a fool, seemed in no hurry to give them).

Here the Young Comrade's mistake was to cling to his self-respect. To advance the revolutionary cause, he ought to have ingratiated himself with the businessman, no matter how loathsome he found the latter. The revolutionary has not only to sacrifice identity, but to abandon shame and self-respect. This message is reinforced by the Examining Chorus to which the agitators are reporting:

> Welche Niedrigkeit begingest du nicht, um
> Die Niedrigkeit auszutilgen?
> Könntest du die Welt endlich verändern, wofür
> Wärest du dir zu gut?
> Versinke in Schmutz
> Umarme den Schlächter, aber
> Ändere die Welt: sie braucht es! (*BFA* III, 89, 116)

> What vileness would you not commit to
> Annihilate vileness?
> If at last you could change the world, what
> Could make you too good to do so?
> Sink in filth
> Embrace the butcher, but
> Change the world: It needs it! (*MT* 25; translation modified)

In its own terms, this argument — in effect, that the end justifies the means — is perfectly logical. It is presumably what an anonymous left-wing reviewer had in mind when he complained that the play's morality was 'not proletarian, but jesuitical'.[10] But, looked at sceptically, the injunction to 'change the world', though repeated *ad nauseam* from Brecht's day to ours, is vacuous. Not all change is for the better. Hitler changed the world by destroying many millions of its inhabitants. Yet 'change the world' has a far more impressive ring than, say, 'try to make the world a better place'. While the latter may suggest small, timid adjustments to the status quo, the demand for 'change' sounds sweeping, even revolutionary, and yet it commits one to nothing in particular.[11]

10   'Florian' in *Die Front* (Vienna), nos. 1–2, repr. in Steinweg, pp. 358–60 (p. 359). David Josef Bach, writing in the Vienna *Arbeiter-Zeitung* (24 Sept. 1932), was more forthright: 'Es [*sc.* the play] lehrt einfach die *Jesuitenmoral*: der Zweck heiligt die Mittel' (repr. in Steinweg, pp. 400–02 (p. 401)).
11   As the philosopher John Searle noted in 1972: 'Publicists seldom speak any more of "reform" or "improvement"; these words have a quaint old-fashioned ring to them, implying as they do a basic continuity of the present and the future. Now one speaks of the desirability of social, political, educational *change*, as if any alteration of the *status quo* were for the better provided it be drastic enough. But most of the possible changes that could occur are for the worse' (*The Campus War* (Harmondsworth: Penguin, 1972), p. 196).

Thanks to the Young Comrade's impetuosity, the agitators were by now in trouble. They were being vigorously pursued and had only one small room as refuge, where they kept their printing-press and their leaflets. So they were surprised when the Young Comrade showed them sacks full of leaflets out on the street, and announced that he would distribute them forthwith to support the general strike which he had just initiated. The agitators pointed out that the resulting insurrection would be easy to suppress, whereas they, guided by the wisdom of the (Marxist-Leninist) classics,[12] were working for a revolutionary transformation, and the Examining Chorus at this point chants the praises of the omniscient Party:

> Denn der einzelne hat zwei Augen
> Die Partei hat tausend Augen.[...]
> Der einzelne kann vernichtet werden
> Aber die Partei kann nicht vernichtet werden
> Denn sie beruht auf der Lehre der Klassiker
> Welche geschöpft ist aus der Kenntnis der Wirklichkeit
> Und bestimmt ist, sie zu verändern, indem sie, die Lehre
> Die Massen ergreift. (*BFA* III, 92–93)[13]

> The individual has only two eyes
> The Party has a thousand eyes. [...]
> The individual can be annihilated
> But the Party cannot be annihilated
> For it is the vanguard of the masses
> And it lays out its battles
> According to the methods of our classics, which are derived from
> The recognition of reality. (*MT* 29)[14]

In response to the agitators' remonstrances, however, the Young Comrade denounced the classics, declared himself for freedom and immediate revolution, and tore off his mask, announcing to anyone within earshot that he and his companions had come from Moscow. As he would not be quiet, the agitators knocked him down and carried him bodily out of the city. They were being pursued, and had five minutes to decide what to do with him. Take him back over the frontier? No: the masses were in the streets, and had to be induced to attend a revolutionary meeting before they dispersed.[15] Hide him? No: he might be found, and then the

12   One reviewer doubted whether the audience would realize that 'the classics' meant Marx and Lenin, not Schiller and Goethe: Paul Friedländer (co-founder of the Austrian Communist Party) in *Die Welt am Abend*, 24 January 1931, repr. in Steinweg, pp. 367–68 (p. 368).

13   The 1931 text changes the last four lines to: 'Denn sie ist der Vortrupp der Massen | Und führt ihren Kampf | Mit den Methoden der Klassiker, welche geschöpft sind | Aus der Kenntnis der Wirklichkeit' (*BFA* III, 120).

14   The translation here follows the slightly different 1931 version, in which the antepenultimate line reads: 'Und führt ihren Kampf' (*BFA* III, 120). Cf. Arthur Koestler's fictional Old Bolshevik: '"The Party can never be mistaken," said Rubashov. "You and I can make a mistake. The Party, comrade, is more than you and I and a thousand others like you and I. The Party is the embodiment of the revolutionary idea in history. History knows no scruples and no hesitations. [...] He who has not absolute faith in History does not belong in the Party's ranks' (Koestler, *Darkness at Noon*, trans. by Daphne Hardy (Harmondsworth: Penguin, 1947), pp. 40–41).

15   The agitators are evidently confident that they can shake off the pursuers, whom they can

agitators' mission (and their lives) would be over. Get rid of him? Yes: terrible though it would be, they decided to shoot him and throw his body into one of the conveniently nearby lime-pits. First, though, they gained his acquiescence in his own execution (though they would have killed him even if he had not acquiesced: BFA III, 124). Just before they shot him, he affirmed his faith:

> Er sagte noch: Im Interesse des Kommunismus
> Einverstanden mit dem Vormarsch der proletarischen Massen
> Aller Länder
> Ja sagend zur Revolutionierung der Welt. (*BFA* III, 97, 125)

> And he said: In the interests of Communism
> In agreement with the progress of the proletarian masses
> Of all lands
> Consenting to the revolutionizing of the world. (*MT* 34)

The Examining Chorus approves this decision and congratulates the agitators on their success in spreading Marxism, class-consciousness, and revolutionary zeal. They bear no guilt for the Young Comrade's death: 'Nicht ihr spracht ihm sein Urteil, sondern | Die Wirklichkeit' (BA III, 124); 'It was not you who sentenced him, but | Reality' (*MT* 33).

The play is clearly intended to teach the correct course of action in extreme and confessedly difficult circumstances. Brecht was revealing the logic of revolutionary activism. Communist commentators, though they praised many aspects of the play, did not thank him for his truthfulness. They objected that the reasons given for shooting the Young Comrade were inadequate; that the Party would never have shot a dissident anyway; that Brecht lacked experience of actual revolutionary work; and that his conception of the Party was idealist and mystical — 'an alien, almost mysterious power, an order of revolutionaries, detached, almost isolated'.[16] Besides, experienced Bolsheviks would never have entrusted someone so unreliable with increasingly demanding tasks; if the agitators had really been following Party discipline, they should have sent the Young Comrade packing after his first failure.[17] Brecht acknowledged this objection in the 1931 text by making the agitators explain that they still needed the Young Comrade because of his large following among youth organizations (*BFA* III, 116), but this argument seems rather lame. The fiercest critique came from Alfred Kurella, who, having seen the premiere in Berlin in 1930, wrote in a Moscow publication that the four agitators were misguided, right-leaning opportunists, while the Young Comrade was correct in attempting an immediate insurrection (he evidently had in mind the Bolsheviks' seizure of power in St Petersburg in October 1917, when the Mensheviks wanted still to co-operate with Kerensky's Provisional Government).[18]

actually see coming after them, and get back into the city to hold a public meeting at very short notice: this does seem a little strange.
16   Otto Biha in *Linkskurve*, January 1931, repr. Steinweg, pp. 352–56 (p. 354).
17   Biha, ibid., and the anonymous reviewer in *Die Rote Fahne*, 24 December 1930, repr. in Steinweg, pp. 341–43 (p. 342); Paul Friedländer (co-founder of the Austrian Communist Party) in *Die Welt am Abend*, 24 January 1931, repr. ibid., pp. 367–68 (p. 367).
18   Alfred Kurella, 'Ein Versuch mit nicht ganz tauglichen Mitteln', *Literatur der Weltrevolution*

A further difficulty, which I have not seen raised by commentators, concerns the play's relation to actual events in China.[19] The specific geographical references to Mukden and Tientsin mean it cannot be understood simply as an abstract model. The Chinese Communist Party, initially very small — its first Congress in 1921 had only twenty attendees, among them Mao Zedong — was directed by the Communist International (Comintern), that is, by Moscow. The Comintern required the CCP to form an alliance with the Chinese Nationalist Party or Guomindang, founded by Sun Yat-sen and led, after Sun's death in 1925, by Chiang Kai-shek. This alliance was uneasy, for the Guomindang's main aim was to unify the country, while the CCP wanted to promote revolution among the increasingly restive peasants. Trotsky thought the CCP should split from the Guomindang, whereas Stalin wanted them to continue the alliance on the Leninist grounds that the first objective should be national unification, for which the Communists had to make common cause with the bourgeoisie; only then would a proletarian revolution be possible. (This may lie behind the Young Comrade's short-lived attempt to curry favour with a rich businessman.[20]) However, Chiang cut the Gordian knot. As soon as his forces had captured Shanghai in March 1927, he launched an attack on the Communists. On 12 April all their leaders in Shanghai were arrested and executed.[21] The Party did not see this disaster coming. Brecht must have known about it; that he followed the news from China is clear from his poem of 1926, 'Dreihundert ermordete Kulis berichten an eine Internationale' ('Three hundred murdered coolies report to an international body').[22] Did he not realize that Chiang's assault on the Communists undermined the message of his play? Was the zeal of the recent convert to Marxism such that he simply could not assimilate information that contradicted his convictions?

Whereas Brecht evokes a super-rational, hierarchical organization run on the principles advocated by Lenin, the historical record suggests an indecisive leadership dominated by the power struggle between Stalin and Trotsky. The *Lehrstück* model, purporting to disclose the abstract pattern underlying historical events, serves to obscure and obfuscate actual history. Brecht's emphatic rhetorical use of the word 'Wirklichkeit' contrasts ironically with his play's remoteness from historical reality.

Brecht not only screens out history; he also screens out politics. This may seem an absurd thing to say about a play which after all concerns revolution. But there

(Moscow, 1931), no. 4, repr. in Steinweg, pp. 378–93 (esp. p. 381). See Service, *Lenin*, p. 310.

19   This paragraph is based mainly on Peter Zarrow, *China in War and Revolution 1895–1949* (London: Routledge, 2005).

20   Kurella notes that the businessman represents the Guomindang's standpoint: 'Ein Versuch', p. 383.

21   These events feature in André Malraux's novel *La Condition humaine*, which won the Prix Goncourt in 1933. At the end, captured Communists are said to be thrown into the boilers of locomotives, but there appears to be no evidence that this was actually done (even if it were technically possible). It may have been a recollection of Malraux that enabled George Orwell to assert: 'In 1927 Chiang Kai-shek boiled hundreds of Communists alive' ('Notes on Nationalism' (1945) in *The Complete Works of George Orwell*, ed. by Peter Davison, 20 vols (London: Secker & Warburg, 1986–98), XVII, 141–55 (p. 148)).

22   *BFA* XIII: *Gedichte 3* (1993), pp. 343–44.

is a great deal of political activity — meetings, oratory, negotiation, compromise, personal conflicts, duplicity — which Brecht does not dramatize. Here and elsewhere, he prefers to present a model of political discussion in which different viewpoints are clearly formulated and a rational conclusion is reached. For example, in *Der kaukasische Kreidekreis* (*The Caucasian Chalk Circle*), he shows us an argument between the farmers who want to continue cultivating their valley in the time-honoured way and those who want to irrigate it and plant orchards and vineyards; the dispute is settled in favour of the latter group by the convincing parable of the chalk circle. Actual political negotiation, with all its dramatic potential, is suppressed, in what could perhaps be defended as a technique of utopian simplification.[23] But one only needs to think of Schiller — for example, the council scene in *Maria Stuart*, where Elisabeth plays off Burleigh against Shrewsbury and manipulates Leicester — to see what real political drama is like.

Such criticisms, however, do not dispose of *Die Maßnahme*. It remains fascinating just because it exceeds Brecht's doctrinaire intentions. The didacticism of the *Lehrstück* genre, for example, would seem to preclude any interpretation of *Die Maßnahme* as tragedy. It offers the hopeful message, quoted verbatim from Lenin, that one can always learn from one's mistakes and amend them:

> Klug ist nicht, der keine Fehler macht, sondern
> Klug ist, der sie schnell zu verbessern versteht. (*BFA* III, 83, 110)[24]

> He who makes no mistakes is not wise; but rather: He who quickly corrects his mistakes is wise. (*MT* 18)

Tragedy, however, centres on a disaster that cannot be put right or compensated for, but that can, at most, be mourned. Often such a disaster arises from an irresoluble conflict of values. There is such a conflict between the Young Comrade's passionate desire to relieve human suffering and the greater good, as the agitators represent it, of exercising temporary restraint in order to end injustice once and for all. The sympathy which the Young Comrade invites gives the play 'a genuinely tragic dimension'.[25] The tragedy comes to a head when the Young Comrade tears off his mask, and the agitators report:

> Und wir sahen hin, und in der Dämmerung
> Sahen wir sein nacktes Gesicht
> Menschlich, offen und arglos. (*BFA* 93, 121)

> And we watched him, and in the twilight

---

23   See Walter H. Sokel, 'Brecht's Split Characters and his Sense of the Tragic', in *Brecht: A Collection of Critical Essays*, ed. by Peter Demetz (Englewood Cliffs, NJ: Prentice-Hall, 1962), pp. 127–37 (p. 137).

24   From Lenin's essay 'Left-Wing Childishness — the Petty-Bourgeois Mentality' (1918)', partially repr. in Steinweg, pp. 311–15 (p. 311).

25   Keith Dickson, *Towards Utopia: A Study of Brecht* (Oxford: Clarendon Press, 1978), p. 54. See Reinhold Grimm, 'Ideologische Tragödie und Tragödie der Ideologie. Versuch über ein Lehrstück von Brecht', *Zeitschrift für deutsche Philologie*, 78 (1959), 394–424 — an essay which some Brechtians condemn: see Klaus-Detlef Müller, *Bertolt Brecht: Epoche — Werk — Wirkung* (Munich: Beck, 1985), p. 136.

> We saw his naked face
> Human, innocent, and without guile. (*MT* 30)

Touchingly, even for the agitators, the Young Comrade reveals the humanity which has to be sacrificed to the cause of revolution (and which may prove impossible for the agitators to regain).

The word 'sacrifice', though not used in the text, draws attention to the religious, cultic atmosphere that commentators have often noted. The scene in which the Young Comrade is killed is headed 'Die Grablegung', irresistibly recalling the entombment of Jesus.[26] In fact the play is all about sacrifice in the sense used in Chapter 18: to obtain something supremely valuable, you have to offer up something which is of great value to yourself. Thus the agitators offer up their names, faces, and identities. In the hope of changing the world, they have to be prepared to sacrifice their self-respect by such despicable actions as flattering an exploitative businessman — the point at which the Young Comrade revolts. He thus fails at the task of what has been called 'redemption through sacrifice'.[27] The Communist's self-annihilation is presented as a means of redeeming the world. Hence the emotionally charged injunction to 'change the world': communism is supposed to bring about not small, incremental changes, but a vast transformation from which a new world will emerge. The Young Comrade, however, by tearing off his mask, regains his individuality and therefore does not contribute to the world's revolutionary redemption. By acquiescing in his fate, he becomes a sacrifice of a different kind, with the implication that his death somehow enhances the legitimacy of the future post-revolutionary order.[28]

---

26   Thus in both the 1930 and 1931 versions. Only in the Malik-Verlag version of 1937 was the scene's title changed to the more clinical 'Die Maßnahme'. Cf. the allusions to Christ's Passion in other early plays: Parker, *Brecht*, pp. 270, 274.

27   Dickson, *Towards Utopia*, p. 54.

28   A reviewer astutely noticed that the sacrifice of individuality was a personal issue for Brecht: Friedländer in Steinweg, p. 368. This has invited much psychological analysis, which will not be pursued here, but see W. A. J. Steer, 'Baal: A Key to Brecht's Communism', *German Life and Letters*, 19.1 (1965), 40–51, and Thomsen, Müller and Kindt, *Ungeheuer Brecht*, p. 93 and *passim*.

22

Hochhuth:
Der Stellvertreter (1963)

In 1963 the play by Rolf Hochhuth, *Der Stellvertreter* (variously translated as 'The Representative' or 'The Deputy'), caused an international controversy by portraying Pope Pius XII as guilty of a crime of omission. During the Second World War the Pope had failed to use his authority in order to condemn publicly the fate of the Jews whom the Germans were transporting to death camps. In the play, moreover, both the Pope and his associates defend his silence by appealing to 'reason of state' ('Staatsräson').

The role of Pius XII (Eugenio Pacelli, 1876–1958) is still controversial. After his death, many prominent Jews, including the President of Israel and the head of the World Jewish Congress, paid tribute to his memory and thanked him for helping Jews in the Second World War. Golda Meir sent a cablegram to the Vatican which read:

> We share the grief of humanity at the passing away of His Holiness Pope Pius XII. In a generation afflicted by wars and discords, he upheld the highest ideals of peace and compassion. When fearful martyrdom came to our people in the decade of Nazi terror, the voice of the Pope was raised for the victims. The life of our times was enriched by a voice speaking out on the great moral truths above the tumult of daily conflict.[1]

But it has also been argued that the Pope's public utterances during the War were bland and ineffectual. Although he deplored the sufferings of innocent civilians, he never specifically mentioned Jews. When the Germans occupied Rome in September 1943, the Jews of Rome were rounded up and sent to Auschwitz. The only one of them to return from Auschwitz, a young woman called Settimia Spizzichino who was found lying among a pile of corpses, said in a BBC interview in 1995:

> I came back from Auschwitz on my own. I lost my mother, two sisters, a niece, and one brother. Pius XII could have warned us about what was going to happen. We might have escaped from Rome and joined the partisans. He played right into the Germans' hands. It all happened right under his nose. But he was an anti-Semitic Pope, a pro-German Pope. He didn't take a single risk.[2]

1   Quoted in Peter Gumpel, 'Pius XII as he really was', *The Tablet*, 13 February 1999, 204–06 (p. 204).

2   Quoted in John Cornwell, *Hitler's Pope: The Secret History of Pius XII* (London: Viking, 1999), pp. 317–18.

The truth about Pius XII is for historians to establish, but the copious published research shows how difficult it is for historians to detach themselves from partisan presuppositions. Of Pius XII it can be said, as Schiller says of Wallenstein in the prologue to his trilogy,

> Von der Parteien Haß und Gunst verwirrt,
> Schwankt sein Charakterbild in der Geschichte.[3]

> Partisan hatreds and affections shroud
> His character, as history portrays it.[4]

The dramatist is not neutral either: certainly Hochhuth was not. But the dramatist has liberty denied to the historian: the freedom, for example, to supplement his story with invented characters, and to devise scenes that never actually occurred in order to explore 'what might have happened *if ...*' What might have happened, for example, if direct, face-to-face appeals on behalf of the Jews had been made to Catholic dignitaries and even to the Pope himself?

Der Stellvertreter turns on two appeals to the Church. In the first Act, Hochhuth dramatizes an incident that *almost* occurred. He presents the historical character of Kurt Gerstein, a Protestant who joined the SS in order to undermine its activities from within, who visited Belzec in 1942 in order to advise on the use of Zyklon B in killing Jews, and who subsequently tried to inform the Papal nuncio in Berlin, Cesare Orsenigo, about the exterminations that were already in progress.[5] In fact, Orsenigo refused to receive Gerstein, whereas in the play Gerstein forces his way into the nuncio's apartments and is rebuffed. Hochhuth then introduces the wholly imaginary character of the young Jesuit Riccardo Fontana, son of a leading lay adviser to the Pope. In Act IV Fontana gains access to the Pope and urges him to protest against the mass murder of Jews and particularly against their deportation from Rome. He finds the Pope, however, preoccupied with the effect of the War on the Vatican's investments and concerned with grandiose geopolitical plans which require a weakened Germany, still led by Hitler, to survive as a buffer between East and West. Driven to desperation, Fontana expresses his identification with the victims by attaching a yellow star to his cassock, whereupon the Pope becomes furious at the insult to clerical garb. Finally Fontana manages to accompany the Roman Jews to Auschwitz, where the play ends in a confrontation with the forces of evil embodied in the devilish figure of 'the Doctor', loosely suggested by Josef Mengele.

Hochhuth's play made an immense sensation. Originally staged at the Freie Volksbühne in Berlin by the veteran director and one-time collaborator with Brecht, Erwin Piscator, it was performed throughout Germany and in London, Stockholm, Basel, Paris, and Vienna. A performance in Rome was declared illegal under the Lateran accords, which obliged the Italian government to avoid any

3   Schiller, *Werke und Briefe*, IV, 16.
4   Schiller, *The Robbers* and *Wallenstein*, trans. by Lamport, p. 168.
5   The extermination camp at Belzec in Poland — the camp with the highest number of victims, after Auschwitz and Treblinka — is not to be confused with the concentration camp known as Bergen-Belsen in Lower Saxony, where Anne Frank met her death.

insult to the sanctity of the Holy See. The Papal nuncio in Germany demanded that the Federal Government should condemn the play, which it also associated with Communist propaganda. A written question was put by CDU members of the Bundestag to the Foreign Minister, who replied by regretting the attacks on Pius XII, without naming the play. The Vatican secretly explored the possibility of prosecuting Hochhuth for the offence of defaming a dead person, which under the West German criminal code could incur either a fine or a prison term of up to two years; since such an action could only be brought by a relative of the deceased, the Pope's one surviving sister, Elisabetta Pacelli (1880–1970), might be asked to do so; but after these plans had been revealed by the indiscretion of a German clerical functionary, they came to nothing.[6]

The controversy helped to make *Der Stellvertreter* a crucial landmark in the long-drawn-out process by which Germany came to terms with its past. Hochhuth was of course far from the first writer to thematize the events known euphemistically as the 'jüngste Vergangenheit' ('recent past').[7] The penultimate chapter of Heinrich Böll's *Wo warst du, Adam?* (1951) is set in an extermination camp, and Günter Grass introduces a survivor of Treblinka, Mariusz Fajngold, into *Die Blechtrommel* (1959). But its unyielding dramatic realism (not naturalism: it is a poetic drama) forced key events vividly onto the audience's attention. When published, moreover, the play was accompanied by a long appendix, 'Historische Streiflichter' ('Historical Sidelights'), relating its events to documented history.[8]

The controversy did have the positive result that the Vatican published some extracts from its otherwise inaccessible archives: eleven volumes of documents under the title *Actes et documents du Saint Siège relatif à la seconde guerre mondiale*, detailing the efforts of officials at the Vatican Secretariat of State to protect Jews and other victims, end the war, and safeguard Rome and other cities from destruction. Other revealing documents have become available, including the diaries of Sir D'Arcy Godolphin Osborne, British Minister at the Holy See from 1936 to 1947.[9] More archival materials are used in John Cornwell's controversial but richly documented study *Hitler's Pope* (1999).[10] In March 2020 Pope Francis gave researchers access to the Vatican archives for Pius XII's papacy, and these have been mined, along with many other far-flung archival sources, in a massive study by David Kertzer.[11]

---

6   'Die "Kleine Anfrage" im Bundestag', *Der Spiegel*, 20/1963, repr. in *Rolf Hochhuth: Dokumente zur politischen Wirkung*, ed. by Reinhart Hoffmeister (Munich: Kindler, 1980), pp. 56–60.

7   Reinhart Hoffmeister, 'Vorbemerkung', in *Hochhuth: Dokumente*, pp. 23–31 (p. 24).

8   In Hochhuth, *Der Stellvertreter: Schauspiel* (Reinbek bei Hamburg: Rowohlt, 1963), the appendix contained no footnote references. That may have created the impression that Hochhuth's research had been scanty (as alleged in Cornwell, *Hitler's Pope*, p. 375). Ample references and some additional materials are supplied in the paperback edition, *Der Stellvertreter: Eine christliche Tragödie* (Reinbek bei Hamburg: Rowohlt, 1967), and in the text in Hochhuth's collected plays, *Alle Dramen*, 2 vols (Reinbek bei Hamburg: Rowohlt, 1991), I, 9–448. The latter is cited here as *S* with page number.

9   These form the core of Owen Chadwick's *Britain and the Vatican during the Second World War* (Cambridge: Cambridge University Press, 1986).

10   See Cornwell's appendix, 'Sources, the "Silence" Debate, and Sainthood', pp. 372–84, for a brief historiographical survey.

11   David I. Kertzer, *The Pope at War: The Secret History of Pius XII, Mussolini, and Hitler* (Oxford:

Hochhuth studied the sources conscientiously. But he was dependent on what was available. And he was a dramatist first and foremost. Dealing with murky areas of history, the historical dramatist can be like a historian in putting forward a hypothetical but plausible version of events. A famous example is Schiller's *Wallenstein*. Wallenstein's negotiations with the Swedes in the period between the battle of Lützen in November 1632 and his assassination in February 1634 are obscure, because dangerous negotiations are by their very nature unlikely to be recorded in documents, and much historical ink has been spilt in trying to reconstruct them. Schiller's version of events, centring on Wallenstein's vague ambitions and indecision, seems as plausible as any other version. Besides, we need to remember that a historical drama is not to be judged simply by its accuracy. The historical dramatist, as Hebbel said, is not the 'Auferstehungsengel der Geschichte' ('history's angel of the resurrection').[12] The dramatist has the licence to imagine scenes that should have happened but didn't, like Gerstein's interview with Orsenigo, and to invent characters such as Riccardo Fontana and his father.

Moreover, the dramatist is transposing historical material into another medium, that of drama, which has its own structural demands. Hochhuth turns against the type of historical drama pioneered by Brecht, which replaces plot with a series of narratively linked scenes and uses two-dimensional characters to represent political and intellectual positions; he returns to the five-act drama, based on a series of confrontations, that is best exemplified by Schiller. In his lengthy afterword to the play, Hochhuth quotes Schiller's demand that one should declare war on naturalism in art (S 354).[13] Instead, the drama should create an illusion only to destroy it. Hence Hochhuth makes his characters speak anti-naturalist dialogue, consisting of short, concentrated, free verse related to iambic pentameter, which proves remarkably supple in allowing distinct, memorable, and relatable characters to emerge.[14]

Hochhuth's debt to Schiller lies not just in his approach to drama but in the character types he favours. Schiller is well known for his distinction between the idealist and the realist, set out with great psychological acumen towards the end of *Über naive und sentimentalische Dichtung* and applied in various of his plays. In Gerstein and Fontana we recognize versions of the idealist who occurs in Schiller. The idealist, Schiller tells us, may well descend to the moral depths in the hope of ascending to the heights. He may do evil in the hope that good will come. Just as Posa in *Don Karlos* engages in intrigue and deception for the ultimate goal of religious liberty, so Gerstein not only joins the SS but advises on techniques of gassing, though he also sabotages the supplies of Zyklon B he takes to Belzec. In his activity as a double agent, he also recalls Mortimer in *Maria Stuart*, though he is not, like Mortimer, presented as a self-deluded fanatic. The suspicion of fanaticism

Oxford University Press, 2022).

12   Hebbel, 'Mein Wort über das Drama!' in *Werke*, III, 545–76 (p. 550).

13   Referring to Schiller's preface to *Die Braut von Messina*, 'Über den Gebrauch des Chors in der Tragödie', *WB* v, 285.

14   See the judicious aesthetic appreciation of the play by Egon Schwarz, 'Rolf Hochhuth's *The Representative*', *Germanic Review*, 39 (1964), 211–30 (pp. 216–17 on language; pp. 219–20 on characterization).

attaches itself rather to Riccardo Fontana, who in his refusal to compromise or defer to authority recalls Max Piccolomini in *Wallenstein*. Max has two antagonists. The first is his father Octavio, a diplomat in the service of the Habsburg Court, who justifies his double-dealing by appealing to the imperfection of the world and the authority of the Emperor. Octavio's counterpart in Hochhuth's play would seem to be the unnamed Cardinal, who puts the case for realism:

> Der Riccardo — Vorsicht, lieber Graf! —
> ist ein Idealist, will sagen,
> ein Fanatiker, nicht wahr. Zuletzt
> vergießt der Idealist immer Blut in dem Wahn,
> Gutes zu stiften — *mehr* Blut als jeder Realist. (S 144–45)

> Our Riccardo — careful, my dear Count —
> is an idealist. One might even say
> a fanatic, mm, what. In the last resort,
> an idealist will always spill blood
> in his mania for doing good — more blood than any realist.[15]

Are we also to see the Pope as a realist in Schiller's sense? Certainly he appeals to reason of state ('Staatsräson') when setting out his geopolitical plans. Reason of state, he tells Riccardo, makes it impossible to attack Hitler, who is Europe's only defender against the threat of Bolshevism and must be maintained in power until he ceases to be useful. But if the Pope were to be seen simply as a realist, he would merely duplicate the dramatic role of the Cardinal. He is more than that. He represents the idealized father. Both Max and Riccardo are estranged from their literal fathers. Max is horrified to learn that Octavio is plotting against Wallenstein; Riccardo cannot accept his father's assurances that the Pope genuinely cares about Hitler's victims. Both young men pin their hopes on a meeting with the ultimate father-figure, respectively Wallenstein and the Pope. Wallenstein becomes Max's second antagonist. Max has to learn that Wallenstein is indeed planning to desert the Emperor; Riccardo has to learn that the Pope has no intention of protesting against the deportation of the Roman Jews. Both Wallenstein and the Pope are invested with tremendous hopes and expectations, and when they disappoint these hopes, the young idealists see no way out but death. However, while Max finds death in battle, Riccardo seeks a redemptive death through martyrdom.

A further feature shared by Hochhuth and Schiller is the presentation on stage of shocking near-contemporary events. Schiller's third play, *Kabale und Liebe* (1784), is set in an unnamed German principality which could easily be recognized as based on Württemberg. Schiller had been brought up there and placed by its authoritarian duke Karl Eugen in the Karlsschule intended to train bright boys for administrative and similar posts; Schiller was to be an army doctor. After *Die Räuber* had been performed in Mannheim, Schiller was officially forbidden to write any more plays, whereupon he fled from Württemberg and sought to establish himself in the theatre at Mannheim. *Kabale und Liebe* not only satirizes foppish courtiers and

---

15   Hochhuth, *The Representative*, trans. by Robert David MacDonald (London: Methuen, 1963), p. 98; cited henceforth as *R* with page number.

state oppression, but includes a famous scene in which the duke's mistress receives a present of jewellery and learns that the duke paid for it by selling 7,000 of his subjects as mercenary soldiers to support the British against the American rebels. There was a brief attempt at resistance:

> Es traten wohl so etliche vorlaute Bursch vor die Front heraus und fragten den Obersten, wie teuer der Fürst das Joch Menschen verkaufe? — aber unser gnädigster Landesherr ließ alle Regimenter auf dem Paradeplatz aufmarschieren und die Maulaffen niederschießen. Wir hörten die Büchsen knallen, sahen ihr Gehirn auf das Pflaster sprützen, und die ganze Armee schrie: *Juchhe nach Amerika!*[16]

> A few uppity lads stepped forward and asked the colonel how much the Prince was getting for a yoke of men? But our gracious sovereign ordered all the regiments to march onto the parade-ground and shoot the loud-mouths down. We heard the crack of the rifles, saw their brains splashing on the pavement, and the whole army cried: 'Hurrah, off to America!'

This narrative, which was omitted in most contemporary performances, was based on fact. Not only did the petty German states sell many subjects as mercenaries, but a short-lived mutiny took place at Ochsenfurt on the river Main on 10 March 1777 and was suppressed as described here.[17] Hochhuth does not just tell us, but shows graphically on stage, how a Catholic family of Jewish origin, the Luccanis, are arrested by a brutal and callous SS officer, robbed of their watches and rings, and carted off, ultimately to Auschwitz. The pathos of this scene makes it even today hard to read. Yet a million such scenes took place in real history.[18] This one occurs on the evening of 16 October 1943 on a house on the Via di Porta Angelica, next to St Peter's Square, just after the Luccanis have been reassuring themselves that although terrible things have happened in Poland, their location will ensure their safety — 'Wir sind hier nicht in Polen. | Unser Nachbar ist der Papst, der läßt | nicht zu, daß man uns einfach wegschleppt' (S 161); 'We are not in Poland. | The Pope is our next-door neighbour; he won't | just let us be carted off' (R 112). No previous German play had shown audiences just what happened to countless ordinary families who were victims of the campaign to exterminate the Jews. Hochhuth's achievement, said the historian Golo Mann, was to present 'die menschliche Wirklichkeit des Judenmordes', the human reality of the mass murder of Jews.[19]

---

16   Schiller, *Kabale und Liebe*, II. 2.

17   Horst Dippel, *Germany and the American Revolution 1770–1800*, trans. by Bernhard A. Uhlendorf (Wiesbaden: Franz Steiner, 1978), pp. 123–24; Alt, *Schiller*, I, 353.

18   On the round-up of 1,259 Roman Jews on 16 October 1943, and the memory of these events in literature and historiography, see now Mara Josi, *Rome, 16 October 1943: History, Memory, Literature* (Cambridge: Legenda, 2023).

19   Golo Mann, 'Die eigentliche Leistung', in *Rolf Hochhuth: Dokumente*, pp. 46–48 (p. 47; orig. in *Basler Nachrichten*, 17 September 1963). There is a problem of terminology here. What Mann calls the 'Judenmord' is commonly called the 'Holocaust', but this term, meaning a sacrificial burnt-offering, risks seeming to legitimize these events by attributing them to the will of God: see Zev Garber and Bruce Zuckerman, 'Why Do We Call the Holocaust "the Holocaust?" An Inquiry into the Psychology of Labels', *Modern Judaism*, 9 (1989), 197–211. The preferable term 'Shoah', meaning

Hochhuth's case against Pius XII is that the Pope had immense moral authority which he did not use. He was particularly well known, and thus potentially influential, in Germany, where he had been the Vatican's nuncio, initially based in Munich, then in Berlin, from 1917 to 1929, when he returned to Rome as Cardinal Secretary of State (responsible for the Vatican's foreign policy). Hence Riccardo asserts:

> Es ist aber ausgerechnet die Person
> *dieses* Papstes, dieses zwölften Pius,
> die Hitler fürchtet: das Ansehen Pacellis
> in Deutschland ist größer als irgendwo sonst.
> Vielleicht hat seit Jahrhunderten kein Papst
> in Deutschland diesen Ruf genossen. (*S* 133)

> But it is precisely the person
> of *this* Pope, of Pius XII,
> that Hitler fears: Pacelli's reputation
> is greater in Germany than anywhere else.
> No Pope for centuries, perhaps, has had
> a standing such as his in Germany. (*R* 88–89)

As Secretary of State Pacelli negotiated the Concordat, which was supposed to secure the position of the Catholic Church in Germany. Hitler's government promised to guarantee freedom of worship and protect Catholic lay institutions; in return, the Church was to avoid any involvement in politics.[20] This meant the immediate dissolution of the Catholic political party, the Centre Party, which had been founded in 1870. Far from being protected, Church institutions were from 1933 on restricted, attacked, and expropriated. By summer 1939, all Catholic schools had been deprived of their denominational status and turned into community schools. Pacelli as Secretary of State sent the German government many detailed complaints about such violations, but with no effect. Hitler considered repudiating the Concordat, but refrained, because he feared the hostility of the Vatican and the protests that would come from other Catholic states.[21]

Might the Vatican have taken the initiative and rejected the Concordat? This is an issue in Hochhuth's play. Riccardo suggests it in Act I to the nuncio in Berlin, Orsenigo, who replies that the Concordat has prevented many anticlerical measures which Hitler's henchmen were contemplating (*S* 30). Hochhuth in the appendix opines plausibly that Orsenigo (even if he had received such pleas, which his historical counterpart did not) could hardly have persuaded the Pope to repudiate the agreement which he had himself negotiated (*S* 364). When Fontana senior suggests to the unnamed Cardinal that the Pope might threaten to revoke the Concordat unless Hitler halts the campaign against the Jews, the latter replies that

simply 'calamity', would be anachronistic in the early 1940s when the full scale of the catastrophe was not yet visible.

20   Richard J. Evans, *The Third Reich in Power* (London: Allen Lane, 2005), p. 235; Cornwell, *Hitler's Pope*, pp. 143–52; detailed account in Guenter Lewy, *The Catholic Church and Nazi Germany* (London: Weidenfeld & Nicolson, 1964), pp. 79–86.

21   Evans, *The Third Reich in Power*, p. 247.

the Concordat protects Catholics, but 'für die Juden | wird sich der Chef nicht exponieren' (*S* 142), 'the Boss will not | put himself in a false position | to help the Jews' (*R* 96).[22] From the Nazi characters we have already heard that the Concordat was invaluable in supporting the Nazis after their seizure of power:

> Pacelli, Baron, des isch a Edelmann, natürlich.
> Daß er's Konkordat g'schlosse hot,
> war unbezahlbar noch d'r Machtergreifung. (*S* 75)

> Of course, Pacelli is an aristocrat, Baron.
> His concluding of the Concordat after
> our rise to power, was of inestimable value. (*R* 41)

Testimonies that have emerged since Hochhuth's play confirm that the Pope's failure to protest against atrocities weakened his moral authority. The occasions on which he did protest effectively make his inaction in Germany look worse. He intervened on behalf of the Hungarian Jews, albeit several months after their deportations had begun, by protesting in an open telegram to Admiral Horthy, the dictator of Hungary, on 25 June 1944.[23] And the Holy See saved thousands of Jews in Budapest by giving them letters of accreditation and encouraging Catholics to conceal them.[24] But one wonders why such protests were not made more often and more vigorously. Again, many Italians, possibly as many as 200,000, were saved by being sheltered by Italian religious and laity in extraterritorial religious institutions, as we see in Act III, scene 2 of *Der Stellvertreter*.[25] They included some Jews. In May and June 1944 there were 160 refugees being sheltered in Vatican City; among them the papal State Secretariat counted about forty Jews, some of whom were baptized.[26] Efforts to shelter Jews, however, were if anything discouraged by the Vatican, and individuals who did so, like the French priest Maria Benedetto (Marie Benoît), were acting independently or in conjunction with Delasem, the Italian Jewish refugee organization.[27]

It is of course possible that protests might have made matters worse — not for the Jews, who were doomed anyway, but for Catholics in Germany and occupied territories.[28] An often-cited example comes from the Netherlands. In 1942 the Catholic and Protestant Churches there combined to protest against Jewish deportations. In reply, the Nazis offered to exempt Christian Jews on condition that the Churches remained silent. The Dutch Reformed Church agreed, but the

---

22   Translation modified: MacDonald renders 'der Chef' colourlessly as 'the Chief'.
23   Michael Feldkamp, *Pius XII. und Deutschland* (Göttingen: Vandenhoeck & Ruprecht, 2000), p. 143.
24   Cornwell, *Hitler's Pope*, p. 326. Cf. *S* 238.
25   Feldkamp, *Pius XII.*, p. 152; cf. Cornwell, *Hitler's Pope*, pp. 309–10.
26   Kertzer, *The Pope at War*, p. 422.
27   Susan Zuccotti, *Under his Very Windows: The Vatican and the Holocaust in Italy* (New Haven and London: Yale University Press, 2000), pp. 181–85. On Benoît's earlier work saving Jews in France, see ibid., pp. 144–46. For the Vatican's reluctance to shelter Jews, see Kertzer, *The Pope at War*, p. 380.
28   On learning that Jews from Bratislava had been gassed and their bodies used to make soap, the State Secretariat advised against an official response for fear that 'harsher' (!) anti-Jewish measures might be introduced: Feldkamp, *Pius XII.*, p. 143.

Catholic archbishop of Utrecht refused and issued a pastoral letter denouncing the deportations, which was to be read aloud in all churches. The Germans thereupon deported a large number of Dutch Catholic Jews, including the philosopher Edith Stein. When Pius XII was being posthumously considered for beatification, his housekeeper, the German nun Pascalina Lehnert, testified that he had told her that he had drafted a protest against the maltreatment of Jews, but intended not to have it published because he had just heard that the archbishop's pastoral letter had led to the murder of 40,000 Dutch Jews. This testimony is far from plausible. The figure of 40,000 has been explained as a mistake for 4,000, but research has found that the number of Catholic Jews deported was 92, and up to September 1942 the total number of Jews deported from the Netherlands was 20,588.[29] It is necessary to give so much detail because this 'evidence' has been used so often to defend Pius XII's silence as a wise and humane policy. Even François Mauriac, no uncritical apologist for Catholicism, wrote in 1951: 'no doubt the silence of the Pope and his cardinals was a most terrible duty, the important thing being to avoid even worse misfortunes'.[30]

Pius XII preferred to work via *Eingabepolitik*, the discreet submission of diplomatic remonstrances.[31] In the judgement even of sympathetic Catholic observers, he thereby achieved nothing save to diminish or even forfeit the moral stature which belonged to him as a non-political religious leader. This was the view of Sir D'Arcy Osborne, the British envoy to the Holy See, who in 1942 wrote in a private letter:

> The fact is that the moral authority of the Holy See, which Pius XI and his predecessors had built up into a world power, is now sadly reduced. I suspect that H[is] H[oliness] hopes to play a great role as peace-maker and that it is partly at least for this reason that he tries to preserve a position of neutrality as between the belligerents. But, as you say, the German crimes have nothing to do with neutrality [...] and the fact is that the Pope's silence is defeating its own purpose because it is destroying his prospects of contributing to peace.[32]

That public protests could achieve something is shown by the example of Bishop Galen of Münster (1878–1946), referred to several times in Hochhuth's play. In July and August 1941 Galen, who had long been an outspoken critic of Nazi anti-religious policies, denounced in sermons the Gestapo's attacks on religious orders and the unacknowledged but unmistakable policy of subjecting the mentally defective to euthanasia. The Nazis were furious, and contemplated having Galen executed, but Goebbels warned that any action against the bishop would alienate the people of Münster and the surrounding province of Westphalia, and the euthanasia programme was quietly halted.[33] In *Der Stellvertreter*, Galen's success is

29   Feldkamp, *Pius XII.*, p. 141; Cornwell, *Hitler's Pope*, p. 287.
30   R xii; S [11]; from Mauriac's preface to Léon Poliakov, *Bréviaire de la haine: Le IIIe Reich et les juifs* (Paris: Calmann-Lévy, 1951), pp. ix–xii (p. x).
31   Feldkamp, *Pius XII.*, p. 142.
32   Letter of 31 July 1942 to Mrs McEwen, quoted in Cornwell, *Hitler's Pope*, p. 284. For similar judgements by Osborne, see Kertzer, *The Pope at War*, pp. 157, 220.
33   Lewy, *Catholic Church*, pp. 264–67; Ian Kershaw, *Hitler 1936–45: Nemesis* (London: Allen Lane, 2000), p. 429. Michael Burleigh points out that the programme was only halted, not abandoned,

mentioned with surprise by the nuncio Orsenigo (S 30) and with apprehension by the Nazis, who express fear that a similar fuss might be made about the Jews (S 57). Riccardo, arguing with his father, voices the inadmissible suspicion that Galen only protested on behalf of Christian victims (S 126).

The previous Pope, Pius XI, risked antagonizing the Nazi regime further by his encyclical, written in German, *Mit brennender Sorge* (With Burning Concern), which was read from the pulpits of all Catholic churches in Germany on Palm Sunday (21 March) 1937, and denounced the deification of the Volk, the state or the race, and the Nazis' continual breaches of the Concordat. The encyclical was drafted in German by Cardinal Faulhaber of Munich and revised by Pacelli, which may help to explain its relative mildness. It contrasts sharply, however, with the entire absence of protest by Pius XII against the much worse atrocities committed during his papacy. In Hochhuth's play we see the Pope dictating a letter of protest against the deportation of the Roman Jews. This is the article that was published in the *Osservatore Romano* on 25–26 October 1943, ten days after the deportations had begun and at a time when most of the deportees were already dead. It includes the sentence (which appears in Hochhuth):

> With the growth of so much evil, the universally paternal charity of the Supreme Pontiff has become, one could say, even more active; it does not pause before boundaries of nationality, religion, or descent.[34]

Here Hochhuth presents the Pope as slightly more outspoken than he was. For he is made to say:

> ... kennt keinerlei Grenzen, Komma, weder der
> Nationalität, Komma, noch der Religion,
> noch der *Rasse*.
> (*Zu den Fontanas:*) Zufrieden, ihr Lieben im Herrn? (S 263–64)

> Knows no frontiers, comma, neither of
> nationality, comma, nor of religion, comma,
> nor of *race*.
> (*to the Fontanas*)
> Satisfied, beloved in Christ? (R 196)

However, the original Italian word, as Zuccotti makes clear, is not *razza*, which would have alluded clearly to racial policies, but the more general word *stirpe* ('descent'). And that word might suggest that the Pope's main concern was not with people of Jewish race but with Catholics of Jewish descent. In the play, the Pope, having explicitly refused to include a specific reference to the Jews because that would be a direct comment on the war, continues:

> Nun sagen Wir: durch die erhöhten ... ja:
> durch die *erhöhten* Leiden

and suggests that a more compelling reason was that experienced murderers were by then needed to conduct the Final Solution in the East: *Death and Deliverance: 'Euthanasia' in Germany c. 1900–1945* (Cambridge: Cambridge University Press, 1994), p. 180.

34   Quoted in Zuccotti, *Under his Very Windows*, p. 163. Cf. S 263; Kertzer, *The Pope at War*, pp. 370–71.

so ... so *vieler* Unglücklicher.
Eminenz, Wir denken, das ist *umfassender*,
als wenn Wir nur die Juden hier erwähnen. (*S* 264–65)[35]

Now let us say: Due to the aggravation ... yes —
due to the aggravation of the sufferings
of so ... so *many* unfortunates.
Eminence, we find that more *comprehensive*
than if we mentioned the Jews alone. (*R* 197)

We do not know if the Pope did in fact consider mentioning Jews. Hochhuth was right to draw attention to this detail, however, for the article was read and sent to Berlin by the German ambassador to the Holy See, Ernst von Weizsäcker, who noted:

> The Pope, although under pressure from all sides, has not permitted himself to be pushed into a demonstrative censure of the deportation of the Jews of Rome. Although he must know that such an attitude will be used against him by our adversaries and will be exploited by Protestant circles in the Anglo-Saxon countries for the purpose of anti-Catholic propaganda, he has nevertheless done everything possible even in this delicate matter in order not to strain relations with the German government and the German authorities in Rome.[36]

It has sometimes been alleged — for example, by Father Robert Leiber, Pius XII's personal secretary – that the Pope was too poorly informed to realize how extensive the murderous campaign against the Jews was.[37] Hochhuth, however, maintains that the Vatican had a network of informants, beginning with the Polish government in exile (*S* 95, 361–62, 387–98). Subsequent scholarship has confirmed that the Vatican had many sources of information. Cardinal Innitzer of Vienna wrote to the Pope about the threatened deportation of Viennese Jews in January 1941. The nuncio in Bratislava reported in October 1941 that Jews were being systematically murdered. In January 1942 the military chaplain Pirro Scavizzi informed the Pope in person that on the Eastern front 'it is the government of occupation's intention to eliminate as many Jews as possible' by machine-gunning them en masse.[38] That March, the nuncio in Bratislava told him that Josef Tiso, the Catholic priest who was president of Slovakia, had ordered all the Jews in his domains to be deported, even without pressure from the Nazis.[39] The US representative at the Holy See told him about extermination camps in September 1942. Gerstein's report on the mass gassing of Jews at Belzec, which Orsenigo in Berlin refused to listen to, was sent to the Vatican, which has never denied receiving it.[40] And very recently it has been revealed that in December 1942 Father Leiber himself received a letter from a German Jesuit, Lothar König, giving details of the transportation of Jews and Poles

---

35   Hochhuth borrows the word 'umfassender' from Father Leiber's defence of the Pope's conduct (*S* 409).
36   Quoted in Cornwell, *Hitler's Pope*, p. 311.
37   Zuccotti, *Under his Very Windows*, p. 93. On the Vatican's allegedly scanty sources of information, see Chadwick, *Britain and the Vatican*, pp. 201–02.
38   Kertzer, *The Pope at War*, p. 225.
39   Ibid., pp. 225–26.
40   Zuccotti, *Under his Very Windows*, pp. 98, 99, 104, 108.

at Rawa Ruska (then in Poland, now in Ukraine) and their murder in the nearby death camp Belzec.[41] The defence of ignorance will not stand.

A charge made by Hochhuth which has been thought particularly offensive is that the Pope was too concerned about the Vatican's finances. On his first appearance, he says to his lay adviser, Count Fontana, whom an earlier stage direction has described as a level-headed financier (*S* 118):

> Lieber Fontana! Wir freuen uns, Sie zu empfangen, um Ihren Rat und auch den Unseres ehrwürdigen Bruders zu hören — von brennender Sorge um Unsere Fabriken erfüllt. Auch Kraftwerke, Bahnhöfe, Talsperren, *jeder Betrieb* fordern gebieterisch Schutz. (*S* 240)
>
> > My good Fontana! We are delighted to receive you,
> > to hear your advice and also that of our honourable brother —
> > filled, as we are, with burning concern
> > for our factories. Power stations,
> > railway stations, dams,
> > *every undertaking* demands supervision and protection. (*R* 177)[42]

Hochhuth's irony here is broad. The Pope's phrasing quotes the title of his predecessor's encyclical, 'With Burning Concern'. In saying his undertakings demand protection, he inadvertently reminds us that the Jews of Rome need protection and are not receiving it. It is not inappropriate, however, that the Pope should talk about the Vatican's finances. He is speaking to Count Fontana, described in a stage direction as 'Finanzmann' and 'Manager' (*S* 117–18), a lay adviser with special responsibility for finance, and Pacelli had himself been Camerlengo, administrator of the Vatican's revenues and property, from 1935 to 1939. The Vatican is described, both in the play and in Hochhuth's epilogue, as the world's largest shareholder (*S* 132, 445). The Pope asks Fontana to sell the Vatican's shares in Hungarian railways to a purchaser in Switzerland, without identifying the seller, in case the Red Army invades Hungary (*S* 265). Fontana hands the Pope two cheques, one of them from the Jesuits, who have profited from their investment in the US aircraft industry (*S* 241–42) and also sell mercury to Russia from the mines they own in Tuscany (*S* 242–43). Thus the Vatican profits materially from the war. That the Pope personally received cheques is attested by his biographer Cardinal Domenico Tardini.[43] There is irony here, but no defamation.

The question of 'Staatsräson' arises over the Pope's attitude to Germany and the Jews. The word does not occur in the available sources, but Osborne came close to it when he commented on the Vatican's policy as outlined in a Swiss newspaper article:

> [I]t is stated that the exercise of the right to take a moral stand will be subordinated to political exigencies. ... We have here the admission that the moral leadership of the Papacy is conditioned by considerations of opportunism and

---

41   Antonio Cariati, 'Pio XII sapeva della Shoah: la prova in una lettera 1942 da un gesuita tedesco', *Corriere della Sera*, 16 September 2023. I thank Graham Nelson for this reference.
42   The 'honourable brother' is the unnamed Cardinal who is prominent in this scene.
43   Domenico Tardini, *Pio XII* (Rome: Tipografia Poliglotta Vaticana, 1960), p. 95; *S* 444 (citing the German translation).

expedience. This means, for instance, that the Pope does not condemn Nazi religious persecution because, if he did so, the lot of the Catholics concerned might be worsened ... (This is a favourite argument at the Vatican.)[44]

In a similar spirit, Fontana senior insists in conversation with his son that the Pope's silence is merely tactical and that he will come out against Hitler when the latter is no longer a threat to the Church:

> Er weiß, warum er schweigen *muß*.
> Er wird nicht immer schweigen.
> Hitlers Kriegsglück wendet sich. Die Zeit
> arbeitet für Großbritannien. Wenn erst
> die Staatsräson dem Papst erlaubt,
> sich gegen Hitler zu erheben, ohne
> die Kirche zu gefährden, so wird ... (*S* 127)

> He knows the reasons why he *must* be silent;
> he will not be silent for *ever*.
> Hitler's fortune is on the turn. Time
> is on England's side. The moment
> raison d'état allows the Pope
> to protest against Hitler, without endangering the Church ... (*R* 83)

Later in this scene (set on 2 February 1943) news comes of the German defeat at Stalingrad. To the Vatican's representatives this is not unequivocally welcome. For an outright Russian victory, with Western Europe occupied by the Soviets and the Churches facing eradication by a regime of militant atheists, would be the ultimate disaster. Hitler can at least form a bulwark protecting Europe from such a fate (*S* 131).[45] Hence the Pope later wishes that the Allies, instead of demanding 'unconditional surrender', would negotiate with Germany so as to preserve it, with or without Hitler, as a buffer state (*S* 257–58). In the meantime, Hitler's power is uncontested (the Americans will not invade Italy for another six months, and the much-discussed Second Front will not be opened until June 1944). Reason of state, according to the Pope, requires Hitler to be treated as a reputable negotiating partner:

> Wie dem auch sei: die Staatsräson verbietet,
> Herrn Hitler als Banditen anzuprangern,
> er muß verhandlungswürdig bleiben.
> Wir haben keine Wahl. (*S* 254f)

> But come what may: *Raison d'état* forbids
> us to denounce Herr Hitler as a bandit:
> We have no choice. (*R* 188)[46]

---

44   Letter from Osborne to Anthony Eden, quoted from the Foreign Office archives by Kertzer, *The Pope at War*, p. 236 (ellipses in Kertzer). As the article was drawn to his attention by the deputy Secretary of State Giovanni Battista Montini (later Pope Paul VI), Osborne had good reason to interpret it as a statement of the Vatican's policy.

45   See Michael Phayer, 'Pope Pius XII, the Holocaust, and the Cold War', *Holocaust and Genocide Studies*, 12 (1998), 233–56 (p. 236).

46   MacDonald here omits a line, which might be translated: 'He must remain a possible negotiating

For Riccardo, however, who is passionately committed to helping the persecuted Jews, reason of state seems no better than cynicism. He even doubts his father's claim that the Pope longs to help the persecuted and would do so if reason of state did not restrain him:

> Vater? — glaubst du, der Papst —
> bist du ganz *sicher*, daß der Papst
> sich überhaupt in dem Konflikt befindet:
> Staatsräson — Nächstenliebe? (*S* 128)

> Father? — do you think the Pope —
> are you quite *sure* that the Pope
> is involved in this conflict at all?
> Raison d'état? — love thy neighbour? (*R* 84)

After all, he points out, it is many years since Pacelli last performed pastoral duties. He is a diplomat and administrator and temperamentally averse to contact with other people. He has never witnessed the distress of the persecuted, and therefore cannot really feel what they are going through. Perhaps he does not even care?

This discreditable suspicion — suggested only by one character, who meets with much opposition — is underlined by the dramatic presentation of Pius XII in Act IV. It accords with his biographers' portrayal of him as sensitive, studious, even saintly, but also practical and realistic, and in conversation even caustic.[47] He was devoted to the sacred mysteries of the Church. Riccardo is astonished to find him preoccupied with formulating a dogmatic statement to the effect that the Virgin Mary was received into heaven at the moment of her death (*S* 78).[48] He was temperamentally disinclined to take decisive steps or issue clear statements on contemporary issues. A sympathetic historian, Owen Chadwick, says:

> His thought was subtle. But he clothed it in an envelope of old-fashioned if not obsolete rhetoric, which had the effect of making every point that he made sound weaker. He grew up in a nineteenth-century tradition of Vatican circumlocution, fitted it naturally, and carried it to the ultimate.[49]

This corresponds to the figure Hochhuth shows us.

One of Pius XII's traits was an extreme love of cleanliness. This gives Hochhuth an authentic basis for an unmistakable symbolic moment. After dictating his proclamation, the Pope is about to sign it when he notices that Riccardo has pinned a yellow star to his own cassock. The Pope is so shocked by this violation of clerical garb that he loses his grip on his pen and stains his fingers with ink. He holds out his ink-stained hand reproachfully, 'like a wound' (s.d., *S* 269).[50] The implication is that the sanctity of the Church must not be stained by involvement in the sinful

partner.'
47   *S* 278, based on Father Leiber's recollections. See the description of his character, drawing on diverse and sometimes conflicting accounts, in Zuccotti, *Under his Very Windows*, pp. 59–62.
48   Pius XII officially proclaimed this dogma as *Munificentissimus Deus* in 1951.
49   Chadwick, *Britain and the Vatican*, p. 50.
50   Hochhuth found the Pope's compulsive hand-washing attested by biographers (*S* 446). Cf. Chadwick, *Britain and the Vatican*, p. 52.

world. When he washes his hands, the parallel with Pontius Pilate does not need to be made explicit (S 271). Nor do the further implications of maintaining a spotless external appearance when charged with moral failure.

Although I have so far discussed *Der Stellvertreter* only as a political drama, it is also a theological drama. The title refers not only the Pope as Vicar of Christ, but to Fontana's voluntary martyrdom in going to Auschwitz as representative of the Pope, who, it is suggested, ought to have been at the side of the sufferers. Accordingly, the text of the play is preceded by the commemoration of two martyrs: Father Maximilian Kolbe (1894–1941), who was sent to Auschwitz and voluntarily took the place of a young man sentenced to death by starvation, and Father Bernhard Lichtenberg (1875–1943), who opted to accompany Jewish prisoners to the East and was sent by the Nazis to a concentration camp. These heroic acts of witnessing to faith ('witness' being the original meaning of 'martyr') demand admiration, but, at least to readers at a remove from Christianity, it must be a question how far they can be considered exemplary.

At the opposite extreme, the addition of the Doctor, based on Mengele, seems a mistake, both dramatically and intellectually. Dramatically, because some at least of his supposedly evil actions, such as singing an obscene song to the carousing Nazis in Act I, feel bathetic. Intellectually, because it is not clear how such a person as Mengele was qualitatively worse than Eichmann (a character in the play) who enthusiastically plotted the murder of millions.[51] Is there a point where extreme wickedness tips over into metaphysical evil? If so, are we to think that an Eichmann is not quite so bad after all? Or that the intervention of a demonic force goes some way to exonerate individuals from the guilt of Nazi crimes? Egon Schwarz, who raises this objection, concludes that the Doctor is 'derived from a completely different realm of the imagination and ought to have no place in a sociologico-historical drama'.[52]

Act V, in which the Doctor holds a metaphysical dialogue with Riccardo Fontana, is set in Auschwitz. This too feels like a mistake, even though Hochhuth denies that he aimed to represent Auschwitz realistically (S 277).[53] Granted, the logic of the action takes Fontana there, and the intention is presumably to confront us with the reality that the Church authorities have tried to ignore. This confrontation takes two forms. First, Act V begins with monologues uttered by anonymous deportees in cattle-trucks. Their anonymity may evoke the millions of faceless victims. But this technique, the affectless and factual recitation of sufferings, is very different from Hochhuth's earlier practice of showing us relatable individuals like the Luccanis being bullied, robbed and deported by individual Nazis. It risks erasing

51 Hochhuth seems to accept Hannah Arendt's view of Eichmann as a mindless bureaucrat illustrating the banality of evil. We now know, however, that this was a mask that Eichmann assumed at his trial, and that in reality he was a fanatical Jew-hater who is on record as boasting of his responsibility for 6 million deaths and wishing it had been 10 million. See Bettina Stangneth, *Eichmann before Jerusalem: The Unknown Life of a Mass Murderer*, trans. by Ruth Martin (London: Bodley Head, 2014), pp. 297, 304.

52 Schwarz, 'Hochhuth's *The Representative*', p. 225.

53 See Margaret Ward, *Rolf Hochhuth* (Boston: Twayne, 1977), pp. 40–41.

the humanity of the victims and making them into statistics. Second, it is debatable whether Auschwitz can be represented at all. It is not just another location. When I visited Auschwitz in the mid-1990s, our whole tour group was struck dumb for two hours, except when people burst into tears outside the glass cases displaying suitcases, shoes, and (most pathetically) jars of face cream. That feeling of almost palpable horror cannot be conveyed on stage. And even if it could be, it would be trivialized by being turned into a merely aesthetic experience.

To treat *Der Stellvertreter* as primarily a political drama is therefore, in my view, to acknowledge its considerable strengths. Some serious arguments can be advanced to defend the Pope's silence. His position between the dictatorships was truly horrible. He did not like Hitler or Nazism, but at least, despite Hitler's contempt for the Concordat and the many restrictions imposed on the Churches, they were permitted to exist. After Stalingrad, when an Allied victory seemed increasingly likely, he feared that Russian communism would overwhelm Western Europe, in which case Christians could expect much more severe persecution. (He may not have known that Hitler himself talked of eventually extirpating Christianity.[54]) Hence it was logical for him to hope that Hitler's regime would defeat Russia but be so weakened by its victory that it would be amenable to the Church's influence. He would have preferred a stable and predictable right-wing dictatorship, like Franco's rule in Spain.

Pius XII's priority throughout was the survival of the Catholic Church as an institution.[55] It was consistent with this priority that he did not show concern for Jews as such, only for those who had converted to Catholicism. In the text of *Der Stellvertreter* published in his collected plays, Hochhuth made a highly significant addition. Having declared emphatically that the Nazis' anti-Jewish terror is loathsome, the Pope adds that he nevertheless must not forget:

> Jerusalem hat Jesu Christi
> Einladung und seine Gnade mit jener starren Verblendung
> und jenem hartnäckigen Undank beantwortet,
> die auf den Weg der Schuld bis zum Gottesmord
> geführt hat. (S 259)

Jerusalem responded to the invitation from Jesus Christ and to His grace with that rigid blindness and that obdurate ingratitude which led it on the path of guilt to the murder of God.

At this point Hochhuth inserts a parenthesis giving a source for this utterance, lest it should be thought completely incredible. It comes verbatim from an address by Pius XII to the Curia in 1942, when the campaign to exterminate the Jews was in full swing and the Pope knew it.[56] But it is by no means incredible that the

---

54   See Cornwell, *Hitler's Pope*, p. 261, and the violent threats quoted in Michael Rissmann, *Hitlers Gott: Vorsehungsglaube und Sendungsbewußtsein des deutschen Diktators* (Zurich: Pendo, 2001), pp. 88–89.
55   Kertzer, *The Pope at War*, p. 478.
56   Hochhuth found it quoted in Rudolf Krämer-Badoni, *Judenmord, Frauenmord, Heilige Kirche* (Munich: Knesebeck & Schuler, 1988), pp. 112–13. This book is an unsparing denunciation of the Church for its theological antisemitism, antifeminism, and intellectual falsifications. Like Nietzsche's *Der Antichrist* (1888), it is crude and sometimes inaccurate, but not fundamentally wrong.

Pope should make such a statement. He was repeating the age-old charge that the Jews, by rejecting Jesus's message and demanding that he should be crucified rather than Barabbas, became the murderers of God and are still being punished for their wilful blindness. This charge is commonly supported by the verse from St Matthew's Gospel according to which the crowd said: 'His blood be on us, and on our children' (Matt. 27. 25). This theological condemnation was still standard among orthodox Catholics in the early twentieth century. It was drummed into the young Eugenio Pacelli by the headmaster of his private Catholic school.[57]

In the Vatican, theological anti-Judaism was reinforced by familiar economic antisemitism. In 1943 the Papal delegate to Istanbul, Angelo Roncalli (later Pope John XXIII), transmitted to the Vatican a request from Slovakian Jews that a thousand of their children should be allowed to go to Palestine instead of being sent to Poland (which by that time everyone knew meant extermination). One of Pius XII's administrative staff, Monsignor Giuseppe di Meglio, was asked to compile a report on the policy the Vatican should adopt towards Zionism. In it, di Meglio noted that until recently not many Jews had wanted to emigrate to Palestine. This, he said, was because 'most Jews are mainly dedicated to industry and, for the most part, commerce', which was profitable while they were living among Christians: 'If, on the contrary, *all* and *only* the Jews come together, one has an enormous gathering in of [...] swindlers, while lacking those to be swindled.'[58] The conclusion, endorsed by the Pope, was that the Vatican should continue to discourage Jewish emigration to Palestine; no exception was made for the Slovakian children. This advice was supported by Monsignor Angelo dell'Acqua, whom the Pope considered his expert on Jewish matters, and who expressed antisemitism when dealing with requests for Papal support for persecuted Jews.[59] Clearly di Meglio and dell'Acqua did not expect the Pope to disapprove of their antisemitism.

The silence of Pius XII can therefore be attributed to 'Staatsräson', as Hochhuth charges. But his 'reason of state' may have been in part a rationalization of anti-Jewish prejudice, constantly reinforced by the conservative Catholic circles in which he moved. In any case, reason of state proved in some measure self-defeating. For the Pope's excessive prudence in refusing to denounce the Nazis' extermination campaign, despite being repeatedly urged to do so from many quarters, damaged the moral authority of the Papacy and did indeed make him, in Cornwell's provocative phrase, 'Hitler's Pope'. It was not that Pius XII particularly sympathized with Hitler, but rather that his caution removed a possible hindrance to Hitler's schemes and made him unwillingly complicit in them.

57   Cornwell, *Hitler's Pope*, pp. 16–17. We now have a scholarly, wide-ranging and scrupulous history of these ideas: David Nirenberg, *Anti-Judaism: The Western Tradition* (New York: Norton, 2013).
58   Quoted in Kertzer, *The Pope at War*, p. 275.
59   Kertzer, *The Pope at War*, p. 241.

CONCLUSION

In this book I have not offered a definition of 'tragedy'. Tragedies are plays that are commonly accepted as tragedies. There have been many attempts at normative definition, specifying what criteria a play must fulfil in order to count as a proper tragedy.[1] But they always end by disqualifying some plays that are generally recognized as tragedies. It may be said, for example, that a tragedy, by definition, ends in disaster. But what about Aeschylus's *Oresteia*, which ends well with Orestes' liberation from the Furies and Athena's replacement of blood-vengeance by a legal process? So I have felt free to discuss *Iphigenie auf Tauris* and *Prinz Friedrich von Homburg*, both of which end happily (albeit somewhat ambiguously).

The word 'tragedy' only applies to literature: to drama in the first instance, though there are also many tragic novels such as Goethe's *Die Leiden des jungen Werthers* and Hardy's *Tess of the D'Urbervilles*. Of course we constantly use the words 'tragic' and 'tragedy' of distressing and dreadful events in real life, but it would be futile to try to correct common usage. The philosopher Max Scheler insisted that 'the tragic' occurred in real life, independently of literature, but he undermined his case by taking all his examples, whether positive or negative, from drama (Aeschylus, Shakespeare, Ibsen).[2]

I have focused on political tragedies, plays that turn on a political decision. Modern German literature offers a great wealth of tragic drama, so some of my exclusions may cause surprise. Why not discuss Kleist's great play *Penthesilea*, which is more obviously a tragedy than *Prinz Friedrich von Homburg* or *Die Herrmannsschlacht*? I exclude *Penthesilea* because it is centrally a tragedy of relationships, turning on the disastrous mutual infatuation of Penthesilea and Achilles. It helps to inaugurate modern tragedies of relationships: Grillparzer's *Medea*, Ibsen's *Hedda Gabler*, Strindberg's *The Dance of Death*, and, stepping outside drama, the destructive relationship between Gudrun and Gerald in Lawrence's *Women in Love*. Nor do I consider the great German tradition of domestic tragedy (*bürgerliches Trauerspiel*), founded by Lessing with *Miß Sara Sampson* (1755), and with a remarkable offshoot in Wedekind's *Frühlings Erwachen* (1891), subtitled 'Eine Kindertragödie', 'a children's tragedy'. I regret excluding Grillparzer's historical tragedies *König Ottokars Glück und Ende* and *Ein Bruderzwist in Habsburg*, both of which contain intriguers (Zawisch von Rosenberg, Bishop Klesel) who could fairly be called 'Machiavellian', but they do not centre on decisions that fit the label 'necessary crime'. I did consider adding

---

1   Many of these are entertainingly and convincingly demolished by Terry Eagleton, *Sweet Violence: The Idea of the Tragic* (Oxford: Blackwell, 2003), chs 1 and 2.
2   Max Scheler, 'Zum Phänomen des Tragischen', in his *Vom Umsturz der Werte: Abhandlungen und Aufsätze*, ed. by Maria Scheler (Bern: Francke, 1955), pp. 149–69.

a chapter on Gerhart Hauptmann's *Atriden-Tetralogie* (1941–48), an underappreciated work, in which Agamemnon's reluctant decision to sacrifice his daughter could qualify as a 'necessary crime', but this action does not sustain the entire tetralogy.

When one contemplates, however briefly, this abundance of tragic drama, one wonders if there is anything distinctive that applies to the whole range. I think there is. Modern German tragedy is post-Christian. It presupposes the scepticism about the historical and philosophical foundations of Christianity that stems from the biblical scholarship of the eighteenth century, to which Lessing made a contribution, and which was enormously reinforced by David Strauss's masterpiece *Das Leben Jesu, kritisch bearbeitet* (1835–36). Such scepticism penetrates English literature in the age of Hardy and George Eliot (who translated Strauss), but we find it much earlier in German literature. Even those nineteenth-century writers who were professed Christians wrestle with doubts (the self-torment of Annette von Droste-Hülshoff's poem-cycle *Das geistliche Jahr* (1851), the visions of cosmic emptiness that render precarious the idylls of Adalbert Stifter). Eduard Mörike, a clergyman, in whose poetry Christian feeling sometimes finds simple and beautiful expression, was a sceptic on matters theological and agreed with the criticisms made by his friend Strauss. The Romantic generation certainly were attracted to Catholicism, but its expression may be primarily aesthetic, as with Novalis, or a violent attempt to fight down spiritual despair, as with Clemens Brentano. We do not find in any significant German writer of the nineteenth century the warm sympathy with the spirit of Christianity that is so evident in Dickens.[3]

Its post-Christian location gives modern German tragedy a distinctive character. Earlier tragic drama generally presupposed a cosmic background, whether its imagery was derived from Christianity or classical sources. Ernst Robert Curtius deplored the absence of such a cosmic background in the anthropocentric drama of Racine and Goethe, blaming it on Renaissance humanism, and welcomed the restoration of a cosmic setting in Goethe's *Faust* and in Hofmannsthal's updating of Calderón, *Das Salzburger große Welttheater* (1922).[4] However, as we have seen, the cosmic setting of *Faust* is a set of vivid metaphors for themes of the Enlightenment and its aftermath, while Hofmannsthal's reinvented Christian cosmos is as hard for modern spectators to take seriously as T. S. Eliot's attempt to present the Furies on stage in *The Family Reunion*.

The anthropocentrism of which Curtius complained is not a weakness, but marks a step forward. *Iphigenie*, which he seems to have in mind, represents the gods as the projection of human emotions. It transfers agency from the gods, who in contrast to the original play by Euripides never appear on stage, to human beings, above all to Iphigenie when after much hesitation she tells the truth to Thoas and appeals to his humanity. The Furies who pursue Orest, and who in Goethe's version never appear either, can be understood as a metaphor expressing his state of suicidal depression.

---

3   A case might be made for Jeremias Gotthelf, the pseudonym of the Swiss clergyman Albert Bitzius, but even in his deservedly most famous work, *Die schwarze Spinne* (*The Black Spider*, 1842), his tub-thumping preacher-like style underlines how out of touch he was with contemporary thought.
4   Ernst Robert Curtius, *European Literature and the Latin Middle Ages*, trans. by Willard R. Trask (New York: Pantheon Books, 1953), pp. 142–43.

The antagonists Iphigenie confronts, whether political or psychological, are human and can be overcome by human means — among them the inclusion of a woman as an agent in the plot, not simply, as Pylades would like to see her, an object of manipulation by men.

Since modern tragedy is human-centred, its protagonists confront, not a blind fate, but ultimately contingent political, social and economic circumstances. No ineluctable fate or cosmic necessity is at work. Hegel, in his account of tragedy, deprecates those tragedies in which the fates of the central characters are not shown to be necessary but result from accidental circumstances, as with the lovers' deaths in *Romeo and Juliet*.[5] In most of the tragedies to be discussed here, however, the catastrophe results from ultimately accidental circumstances, that is, from conflicts within human-made institutions. Often such conflicts have no good solution, and when they are resolved by such means as judicial murder, in *Maria Stuart* or *Agnes Bernauer*, the result is a political tragedy, but not a cosmic one. The resolution is no less tragic because it proceeds from a conflict among man-made institutions and human intentions. The words that Brecht, explaining his dramatic innovations, puts into the mouth of a spectator at epic theatre, would apply to most of the plays discussed in this book: 'This person's suffering shocks me, because there might be a way out.'[6] Tragic suffering is poignant precisely because it did not have to happen. The ruler could always have retired from politics, as Machiavelli advises when discussing Philip of Macedon, rather than commit a crime. But for a ruler trying to hold a fragile political body together, such as Schiller's Elisabeth or Hebbel's Duke Ernst, that is only a theoretical possibility. To step aside from their responsibilities when these become agonizingly difficult is not really an option: it would mean betraying their office and their country.

Such a conclusion is grim, but the appeal of tragedies lies partly in their acknowledgement of the reality principle and their rejection of wishful thinking. Hence in the twentieth century the most compelling of Shakespeare's tragedies was often felt to be *King Lear*, which ends with unmitigated disaster and no attempt at reconciliation or redemption.[7] Earlier tragedy sometimes offered a hopeful ending by resorting to theodicy — arguments that in the universe directed by a benevolent God, apparent disasters were ultimately for the best.[8] Thus the Chorus in Milton's *Samson Agonistes* (1671) reassures the audience:

> All is best, though we oft doubt,
> What the unsearchable dispose
> Of highest wisdom brings about,
> And ever best found in the close.[9]

5   *Hegel's Aesthetics*, trans. by T. M. Knox, 2 vols (Oxford: Clarendon Press, 1975), II, 1232.
6   'Theatre for Pleasure or Theatre for Instruction', in *Brecht on Theatre*, ed. by Marc Silberman, Steve Giles, and Tom Kuhn (London: Bloomsbury, 2015), pp. 131–39 (p. 134).
7   See Maynard Mack, *'King Lear' in our Time* (Berkeley: University of California Press, 1965).
8   On the history and shortcomings of theodicy, see Mara van der Lugt, *Dark Matters: Pessimism and the Problem of Suffering* (Princeton: Princeton University Press, 2021).
9   *The Poems of John Milton*, ed. by John Carey and Alastair Fowler (London: Longmans, 1968), p. 401.

In modernity, theodicy has been transformed into a hopeful philosophy of history.[10] Redemption, no longer sought in heaven, is postponed until the end of history, when millennia of conflict will at last come to a resolution. Kant, in perhaps the most convincing attempt at a teleological theory of history, also formulated the obvious objection:

> What remains disconcerting about all this is firstly, that the earlier generations seem to perform their laborious tasks only for the sake of the later ones, so as to prepare for them a further stage from which they can raise still higher the structure intended by nature; and secondly, that only the later generations will in fact have the good fortune to inhabit the building on which a whole series of their forefathers (admittedly, without any conscious intention) had worked without themselves being able to share in the happiness they were preparing.[11]

The last generation which will benefit from all its predecessors' struggles is very far away, while in the present humanity confronts, not a blind fate, but a political, social, and economic edifice which seems immovable but which, after all, has been created by human beings and can be changed by human effort. 'Humankind is changeable and able to change things': that is one of the lessons that Brecht wanted epic theatre to teach.[12] However, as Brecht was less willing to acknowledge, positive change is a painfully slow and difficult incremental process. It requires innumerable small steps with the modest-sounding goal of making the world a better place. Hence modern thinkers often entertain the fantasy that the process can be drastically shortened: that the political edifice towering above them can be blown up, and a new order instituted, by revolution. This implies not just throwing off an oppressive government by violent, or occasionally non-violent, insurrection, as in the North American colonies in their war of independence, or in Eastern Europe in 1989. It means not just the overthrow of the old regime but a complete transformation of human life involving even the creation of a new type of human being, the 'emancipated man' eloquently envisaged by Trotsky in the final pages of *Literature and Revolution*.[13]

Transformative revolution is one of the most powerful, appealing, and consequential myths of modernity. The history of the last two centuries, however, shows repeatedly that when revolution overthrows an old order, it institutes a new order which soon settles back into the same groove and may be even worse than the order it has displaced. In the nineteenth century it seemed that nothing could be more appalling than the Tsarist system of dealing with political offenders by making them walk in chains to Siberia and settling them in squalid, overcrowded penal colonies

---

10   See Alessandro Costazza, 'Der "gräßliche Fatalismus der Geschichte" und die Funktion des Theodizee-Diskurses in Georg Büchners *Dantons Tod*', in *Die Tragödie der Moderne*, ed. by Fulda and Valk, pp. 107–26 (p. 121).

11   'Idea for a Universal History with a Cosmopolitan Purpose', in *Kant: Political Writings*, pp. 41–53 (p. 44).

12   'Theatre for Pleasure or Theatre for Instruction', in *Brecht on Theatre*, p. 133.

13   Leon Trotsky, *Literature and Revolution* [no translator named] (New York: Russell & Russell, 1957), p. 255.

where there was often not even enough work for them to do.[14] The archipelago of labour camps which the subsequent regime set up across the most inhospitable regions of the Soviet Union was even more inhumane and on a much greater scale, as a large body of memoirs and historical studies now abundantly testifies. If one wants to use the word 'tragic', it can be applied to the process whereby a revolutionary programme of emancipation, designed to liberate suffering humanity, imposed even worse sufferings, which dwarf the undoubted achievements of revolutionary communism. In this sense Brecht's *Die Maßnahme* pinpoints the fatal, and arguably tragic, flaw of violent revolution: revolutionaries who become inured to violence are thereby unable to realize the humane ambitions with which they started out.

An alternative viewpoint, the one favoured in this book, would advocate gradual, incremental improvement of social institutions without extravagant or apocalyptic hopes. The term 'liberal' suggests itself, but is better avoided, since 'liberal' has in the past two centuries spanned a wide variety of political creeds from 'liberal socialism', encouraging intervention by governments, to 'laissez-faire' policies which aim to minimize the role of government in social life.[15]

It would be childish, however, to suppose that modern democracy can avoid difficult choices that inflict pain on some people. This is why, even in a modern democracy, Machiavelli's political thinking is still pertinent. It is not only, as Jonathan Powell shows in *The New Machiavelli*, that his writings contain much shrewd advice which can be applied to the day-to-day conduct of democratic politics. Machiavelli also sets out a way of thinking about politics which acknowledges the likelihood that from time to time morally criminal actions will be necessary, or at least unavoidable. Often, of course, claims of political necessity are hypocritical. Milton's Satan, resolving to take revenge on God by ruining Adam and Eve, 'with necessity, | The tyrant's plea, excused his devilish deeds'.[16] It is easy also to fall into the self-flattering delusion that decisive, tough, or even brutal action justifies itself by proving one's determination. The political concepts whose history has been recounted in this book — Machiavellianism, reason of state, *Realpolitik* — have lent themselves to such delusions. But if you reject them outright, you may be merely be signalling your own virtue. And you will be implying that there is a way of doing politics with minimal loss and pain. Yet the plays discussed here explore, from varying viewpoints and with diverse emphases, Machiavelli's assumption that politics is about power, hence about conflict, and that success in ruling means success in managing conflict. In the resolution of conflict, somebody must always lose out: even in Goethe's *Iphigenie*, that great Enlightenment play of reconciliation, Thoas, in his reluctant magnanimity, has to relinquish his hope of marrying Iphigenie.

14   Daniel Beer, *The House of the Dead: Siberian Exile under the Tsars* (London: Allen Lane, 2016).
15   See Helena Rosenblatt, *The Lost History of Liberalism: from Ancient Rome to the Twenty-First Century* (Princeton: Princeton University Press, 2018).
16   *Paradise Lost*, IV. 393–94.

Machiavelli anticipated what is now known in political theory as the problem of 'dirty hands'.[17] In recent discussions, it concerns the relation between morality and political action, and the question whether it is justified to transgress morality, either to achieve a desirable political end, or to ward off a looming political catastrophe (such as the invasion of one's country and the destruction of one's society). Machiavelli himself set the bar much lower. A prince should 'not deviate from right conduct if possible, but be capable of entering upon the path of wrongdoing when this becomes necessary' (P xviii, 62). In the early twentieth century Max Weber developed this idea in his concept of *Verantwortungsethik* or 'ethics of responsibility'. We saw earlier, in Chapter 20, how this concept is contrasted with *Gesinnungsethik*, the 'ethics of principled convictions'. As the supreme example of *Gesinnungsethik* Weber takes the Sermon on the Mount with its injunction not to resist evil (Matt. 5. 39). But, he maintains, 'while it is a consequence of the unworldly ethic of love to say, "resist not evil with force," the politician is governed by the contrary maxim, namely, "You *shall* resist evil with force, for if you do not, you are *responsible* for the spread of evil".'[18]

For both Machiavelli and Weber, therefore, politicians must sometimes get their hands dirty by doing what they know to be morally wrong. To maintain otherwise, and to demand unstained ethical purity in politics, is, as Weber makes abundantly clear, a kind of virtue-signalling which is incompatible with responsibility. And it must be underlined that the ethic of responsibility is entirely different from the view, often called political realism and identified with *Realpolitik*, that morality has no place in politics.

The politician, in Weber's view, needs passion, understood as passionate devotion to a cause. Hence a politician is different from a civil servant or other bureaucratic functionary. Responsibility to that cause must guide all the politician's actions. 'This requires (and this is the decisive psychological quality of the politician) *judgement*, the ability to maintain one's inner composure and calm while being receptive to realities, in other words *distance* from things and people.'[19]

Passionate involvement, combined with critical distance: this is also the appropriate stance for the spectator or reader of drama. Hence the plays discussed in this book may be understood as exercises in politics. They invite involvement, but not partisanship. The spectator can see both sides of a conflict and recognize it, as in Hegel's reading of *Antigone*, as in some measure a conflict of right with right. Even when the dramatist clearly favours one side, as Hebbel favours Duke Ernst, the honesty inseparable from great literature obliges him to display not only the innocence of his victim Agnes but the shabbiness implied in Ernst's delegating the task of execution to subordinates. And even when the dramatist is effectively

---

17   See C. A. J. Coady, 'The Problem of Dirty Hands', in *Stanford Encyclopedia of Philosophy* (updated August 2023), <https://plato.stanford.edu/entries/dirty-hands> [accessed 1 November 2023]. The last few decades' discussion was prompted by Michael Walzer, 'Political Action: The Problem of Dirty Hands', *Philosophy and Public Affairs*, 2.2 (1973), 160–80, who engages with both Machiavelli and Weber. I thank Michael Rosen for drawing my attention to this discussion.

18   *Weber: Political Writings*, p. 358.

19   Ibid., p. 353.

making the case for the prosecution, as Hochhuth does in *Der Stellvertreter*, he nevertheless sets out the issues and allows the defendant — in this instance, Pius XII — to put forward arguments, however specious, on his own behalf.

The dramatist's distance is also an aesthetic distance which removes the obligation to indicate what the characters *should* have done. A tragic dilemma is not a problem to be solved. In setting out the dilemma, the dramatist is entirely different from, say, a civil servant composing a position paper. The dramatist is able to focus on the human cost of tragedy. Hence Büchner in *Danton's Tod*, for example, insists on the ineluctable reality of suffering. Among the prisoners who try to distract themselves with philosophical arguments, one puts forward a pessimistic thesis:

> Man kann das Böse leugnen, aber nicht den Schmerz; nur der Verstand kann Gott beweisen, das Gefühl empört sich dagegen. Merke dir es, Anaxagoras, warum leide ich? Das ist der Fels des Atheismus. Das leiseste Zucken des Schmerzes und rege es sich nur in einem Atom, macht einen Riß in der Schöpfung von oben bis unten.

> Evil you can deny, but not pain. Only the intellect can prove the notion of God, all the emotions rebel against it. Mark this, Anaxagoras: why do I suffer? That is the rock of atheism. The tiniest spasm of pain, be it in a single atom, and creation is utterly torn asunder.[20]

If the undeniable experience of pain disproves the existence of a benevolent God, it must also challenge attempts to find hope in history. The prospect of a future utopia, or at least of a vastly improved state of human affairs, cannot, as Kant acknowledges, undo the sufferings of all the previous generations that will have made it possible.

This is where literature, and especially tragedy, makes its contribution. Literature, in contrast to the philosophy of history, draws our attention to the individual and the individual's experience as something unchallengeably real. It gives us moments like that in which the ideological carapace of the agitators in *Die Maßnahme* is briefly pierced by the look on the Young Comrade's face as he prepares for his death. Tragedy does not give us answers; it makes us aware, or deepens our awareness, of the problem.

---

20 Büchner, *Complete Plays*, pp. 45–46.

SELECT BIBLIOGRAPHY

Primary Texts

BACON, FRANCIS, *Collected Works*, ed. by James Spedding, Robert Leslie Ellis and Douglas Denon Heath (1879; repr. London: Routledge/Thoemmes, 1996)

BISMARCK, OTTO VON, *Gedanken und Erinnerungen* (Stuttgart: Cotta, 1972)

BOLLMANN, KARL, *Vertheidigung des Machiavellismus* (Quedlinburg: H. C. Huch, 1858)

BOTERO, GIOVANNI, *The Reason of State*, ed. and trans. by Robert Bireley, Cambridge Texts in the History of Political Thought (Cambridge: Cambridge University Press, 2017)

BRECHT, BERTOLT, *Die Maßnahme*. Kritische Ausgabe mit einer Spielanleitung, ed. by Reiner Steinweg (Frankfurt a.M.: Suhrkamp, 1972)

—— *The Measures Taken*, trans. by Carl R. Mueller (London: Eyre Methuen, 1977)

—— *Die Maßnahme*, in *Große kommentierte Berliner und Frankfurter Ausgabe*, ed. by Werner Hecht and Jan Knopf (Berlin and Weimar: Aufbau; Frankfurt a.M.: Suhrkamp, 1988–2000), vol. iii

BÜCHNER, GEORG, *Complete Plays, 'Lenz' and Other Writings*, trans. by John Reddick (London: Penguin, 1993)

—— *Sämtliche Werke, Briefe und Dokumente*, ed. by Henri Poschmann, 2 vols (Frankfurt a.M.: Deutscher Klassiker Verlag, 1999)

CALDERÓN DE LA BARCA, PEDRO, *Life's a Dream / La vida es sueño*, trans. and ed. by Michael Kidd (Oxford: Aris & Phillips, 2011)

CORNEILLE, PIERRE, *Œuvres complètes*, ed. by Georges Couton, 3 vols, Bibliothèque de la Pléiade (Paris: Gallimard, 1980–87)

DIDEROT, DENIS, and OTHERS, eds, *Encyclopédie ou Dictionnaire raisonné des sciences, des arts et des métiers*, 17 vols (Neuchâtel: Faulche, 1765)

ECKERMANN, JOHANN PETER, *Conversations with Goethe in the Last Years of his Life*, trans. by Allan Blunden, ed. by Ritchie Robertson (London: Penguin, 2022)

ERASMUS, *The Education of a Christian Prince*, trans. by Neil M. Cheshire and Michael J. Heath, ed. by Lisa Jardine, Cambridge Texts in the History of Political Thought (Cambridge: Cambridge University Press, 1997)

FERGUSON, ADAM, *An Essay on the History of Civil Society*, ed. by Duncan Forbes (Edinburgh: Edinburgh University Press, 1966)

FEUERBACH, LUDWIG, *The Essence of Christianity*, trans. by George Eliot (New York: Harper & Row, 1957)

—— *Das Wesen des Christenthums*, in *Sämtliche Werke*, ed. by Wilhelm Bolin and Friedrich Jodl, 10 vols, 2nd edn (Stuttgart: Frommann-Holzboog, 1960), vol. vi.

FICHTE, JOHANN GOTTLIEB, 'Ueber Machiavell, als Schriftsteller, und Stellen aus seinen Schriften', in *Gesamtausgabe*, ed. by Reinhard Lauth and others (Stuttgart and Bad Cannstatt: Frommann-Holzboog, 1962–2012), IX: *Werke 1806–1807*, ed. by Reinhard Lauth and Hans Gliwitzky (1995), pp. 223–75

—— *Reden an die deutsche Nation*, ed. by Reinhard Lauth, Philosophische Bibliothek 204 (Hamburg: Meiner, 1978)

——Fichte, Addresses to the German Nation, trans. by Gregory Moore, Cambridge Texts in the History of Political Thought (Cambridge: Cambridge University Press, 2008)

Five German Tragedies, trans. by F. J. Lamport (Harmondsworth: Penguin, 1969)

FONTANE, THEODOR, Der Stechlin, in his Sämtliche Romane, Erzählungen, Gedichte, Nachgelassenes, 2nd edn, ed. by Walter Keitel and Helmut Nürnberger, 7 vols (Munich: Hanser, 1970–84)

[FREDERICK THE GREAT] L'Anti-Machiavel, par Frédéric II, roi de Prusse, édition critique avec les remaniements de Voltaire par les deux versions, ed. by Charles Fleischauer (= SVEC, vol. 5; Geneva: Institut et Musée Voltaire, 1958)

Frederick the Great's Political Writings, ed. by Avi Lifschitz, trans. by Angela Scholar (Princeton: Princeton University Press, 2021)

GENTILLET, INNOCENT, A discourse vpon the meanes of vvel governing and maintaining in good peace, a kingdome, or other principalitie. Divided into three parts, namely the counsell, the religion, and the policie, vvhich a prince ought to hold and follow. Against Nicholas Machiavell the Florentine. Translated into English by Simon Patericke (London: Adam Islip, 1602)

GERVINUS, G. G., Geschichte der florentinischen Historiographie bis zum sechzehnten Jahrhundert, nebst einer Charakteristik des Machiavell (Frankfurt a.M.: Franz Varrentrapp, 1833)

GIBBON, EDWARD, The History of the Decline and Fall of the Roman Empire, ed. by David Womersley, 3 vols (London: Penguin, 1994)

GOETHE, JOHANN WOLFGANG, Sämtliche Werke: Briefe, Tagebücher und Gespräche, ed. by Friedmar Apel and others, 40 vols (Frankfurt a.M.: Deutscher Klassiker Verlag, 1986–2000)

——Faust Part One, trans. by David Luke, Oxford World's Classics (Oxford: Oxford University Press, 1987)

——Faust Part Two, trans. by David Luke, Oxford World's Classics (Oxford: Oxford University Press, 1994)

——The Natural Daughter (with Schiller, The Bride of Messina), trans. by F. J. Lamport (Cambridge: Modern Humanities Research Association, 2018)

GRYPHIUS, ANDREAS, Dramen, ed. by Eberhard Mannack (Frankfurt a.M.: Deutscher Klassiker Verlag, 1991)

GUICCIARDINI, FRANCESCO, The History of Italy, in his History of Italy and History of Florence (excerpts), ed. by J. R. Hale, trans. by Cecil Grayson (New York: New English Library, 1966)

HARRINGTON, JAMES, The Commonwealth of Oceana and A System of Politics, ed. by J. G. A. Pocock (Cambridge: Cambridge University Press, 1992)

HEBBEL, FRIEDRICH, Werke, ed. by Gerhard Fricke, Werner Keller and Karl Pörnbacher, 5 vols (Munich: Hanser, 1963)

HEGEL, G. W. F., The Philosophy of History, trans. by J. Sibree (New York: Dover, 1956)

——Hegel's Political Writings, trans. by T. M. Knox with an introduction by Z. A. Pelczynski (Oxford: Clarendon Press, 1964)

——Lectures on the Philosophy of World History: Introduction, trans. by H. B. Nisbet (Cambridge: Cambridge University Press, 1975)

——Werke, ed. by Eva Moldenhauer and Karl Markus Michel, 20 vols (Frankfurt a.M.: Suhrkamp, 1986)

HERDER, JOHANN GOTTFRIED, Ideen zur Philosophie der Geschichte der Menschheit (1784–91), in his Werke, ed. by Günter Arnold and others, 10 vols (Frankfurt a.M.: Deutscher Klassiker Verlag, 1985–2000)

HOBBES, THOMAS, Leviathan, ed. by J. C. A. Gaskin, Oxford World's Classics (Oxford: Oxford University Press, 1996)

HOCHHUTH, ROLF, Der Stellvertreter: Schauspiel (Reinbek bei Hamburg: Rowohlt, 1963)

—— *The Representative*, trans. by Robert David MacDonald (London: Methuen, 1963)

—— *Der Stellvertreter: Eine christliche Tragödie* (Reinbek bei Hamburg: Rowohlt, 1967)

—— *Der Stellvertreter* in Hochhuth, *Alle Dramen*, 2 vols (Reinbek bei Hamburg: Rowohlt, 1991), I, 9–448

HOFMANNSTHAL, HUGO VON, *Sämtliche Werke*, ed. by Rudolf Hirsch and others, 37 vols (Frankfurt a.M.: Fischer, 1975–)

HUME, DAVID, *Essays Moral, Political and Literary*, ed. by Eugene F. Miller (Indianapolis: Liberty Fund, 1987)

KANT, IMMANUEL, *Werke*, ed. by Wilhelm Weischedel, 6 vols (Darmstadt: Wissenschaftliche Buchgesellschaft, 1956–64)

—— *Kant: Political Writings*, ed. by Hans Reiss, trans. by by H. B. Nisbet, Cambridge Texts in the History of Political Thought, 2nd edn (Cambridge: Cambridge University Press, 1991)

KLEIST, HEINRICH VON, *Sämtliche Werke und Briefe*, ed. by Ilse-Maria Barth and others, 4 vols (Frankfurt a.M.: Deutscher Klassiker Verlag, 1989)

LEE, NATHANIEL, *The Works*, ed. by Thomas B. Stroup and Arthur L. Cooke, 2 vols (New Brunswick, NJ: The Scarecrow Press, 1954–55)

LEITZMANN, ALBERT, ed., *Die Hauptquellen zu Schillers Wallenstein* (Halle: Niemeyer, 1915)

LESSING, GOTTHOLD EPHRAIM, *Werke und Briefe*, ed. by Wilfried Barner and others, 12 vols (Frankfurt a.M.: Deutscher Klassiker Verlag, 1987–98)

LOEN, JOHANN MICHAEL VON, 'Von der Staats-Kunst des Machiavels', in *Des Herrn von Loen gesammelte kleine Schriften*, 4 vols (Frankfurt a.M. and Leipzig: Philipp Heinrich Hutter, 1750), IV, 270–81

LOHENSTEIN, DANIEL CASPER VON, *Sämtliche Werke*, ed. by Lothar Mundt, Wolfgang Neuber, and Thomas Rahn (Berlin: De Gruyter, 2005–). Abteilung II: Dramen, vol. I: *Ibrahim Bassa, Cleopatra*, ed. by Lothar Mundt (2008); vol. II: *Agrippina, Epicharis*, ed. by Lothar Mundt (2005); vol. III: *Ibrahim Sultan, Sophonisbe*, ed. by Lothar Mundt (2013)

MACHIAVELLI, NICCOLÒ, *Florentine Histories*, trans. by Laura F. Banfield and Harvey C. Mansfield, Jr (Princeton: Princeton University Press, 1988)

—— *The Prince*, ed. by Quentin Skinner and Russell Price, trans. by Russell Price, Cambridge Texts in the History of Political Thought (Cambridge: Cambridge University Press, 1988)

—— *Discourses on Livy*, trans. by Julia Conaway Bondanella and Peter Bondanella, Oxford World's Classics (Oxford: Oxford University Press, 1997)

MONTESQUIEU, *The Spirit of the Laws*, ed. and trans. by Anne M. Cohler, Basia C. Miller, and Harold S. Stone, Cambridge Texts in the History of Political Thought (Cambridge: Cambridge University Press, 1989)

MÜLLER, ADAM, *Die Elemente der Staatskunst*, 2 vols (Berlin: Sander, 1809)

NIETZSCHE, FRIEDRICH, *Beyond Good and Evil*, trans. by R. J. Hollingdale (Harmondsworth: Penguin, 1973)

—— *Kritische Studienausgabe*, ed. Giorgio Colli and Mazzino Montinari, 15 vols (Munich: dtv; Berlin: De Gruyter, 1988)

—— *On the Genealogy of Morals*, trans. by Douglas Smith, Oxford World's Classics (Oxford: Oxford University Press, 1996)

—— *The Birth of Tragedy*, trans. by Douglas Smith, Oxford World's Classics (Oxford: Oxford University Press, 2000)

—— *Twilight of the Idols and The Anti-Christ*, trans. by R. J. Hollingdale (London: Penguin, 2003)

NOVALIS, *Schriften*, ed. by Paul Kluckhohn and Richard Samuel, 5 vols (Stuttgart: Kohlhammer, 1960–88)

ROBERTSON, WILLIAM, *History of Scotland during the Reigns of Queen Mary and of James VI*, 2 vols (1759; 1794 edition reprinted, London: Routledge/Thoemmes Press, 1996)

[ROCHAU, AUGUST LUDWIG VON], *Grundsätze der Realpolitik, angewendet auf die staatlichen Zustände Deutschlands*, 2nd edn (Stuttgart: Göpel, 1859)

ROUSSEAU, JEAN-JACQUES, *The Social Contract and the Discourses*, trans. by G. D. H. Cole, rev. by J. H. Brumfitt and John C. Hall, Everyman's Library (London: David Campbell, 1973)

SAINT-RÉAL, ABBÉ DE, *Don Carlos: Nouvelle historique, 1672, par Saint-Réal*, ed. by André Lebois (Avignon: Edouard Aubanel, 1964)

SCHILLER, FRIEDRICH, *Werke: Nationalausgabe*, ed. by Julius Petersen and others, 42 vols (Weimar: Hermann Böhlaus Nachfolger, 1943–2010)

—— *On the Aesthetic Education of Man in a Series of Letters*, ed. and trans. by Elizabeth M. Wilkinson and L. A. Willoughby (Oxford: Clarendon Press, 1967)

—— *The Robbers and Wallenstein*, trans. by F. J. Lamport (Harmondsworth: Penguin, 1979)

—— *Werke und Briefe*, Bibliothek deutscher Klassiker, ed. by Klaus Harro Hilzinger, later by Otto Dann and others, 12 vols (Frankfurt a.M.: Deutscher Klassiker Verlag, 1992–2005)

—— *Don Carlos* and *Mary Stuart*, trans. by Hilary Collier Sy-quia and Peter Oswald, Oxford World's Classics (Oxford: Oxford University Press, 1996)

—— *Wilhelm Tell*, trans. by Francis Lamport (London: Libris, 2005)

SCHMITT, CARL, *Political Theology: Four Chapters on the Concept of Sovereignty*, trans. by George Schwab, 2nd edn (Chicago: University of Chicago Press, 1985)

SHAKESPEARE, WILLIAM, *The Complete Works*, ed. by Peter Alexander (London and Glasgow: Collins, 1951)

STRADA, FAMIANUS, *De bello Belgico. The history of the Low-Countrey warres*, written in Latine by Famianus Strada; in English by Sr. Rob. Stapylton (London: Humphrey Modseley, 1650)

TACITUS, *The Histories*, Books IV–V, trans. by Clifford H. Moore; *The Annals*, Books I–III, trans. by John Jackson (Cambridge, MA: Harvard University Press, 1959)

—— *The Annals of Imperial Rome*, trans. by Michael Grant, rev. edn (London: Penguin, 1996)

THIERS, ADOLPHE, *Histoire de la Révolution française*, 13th edn, 10 vols (Paris: Furne, 1847–65)

VOLTAIRE, *Œuvres complètes de Voltaire / The Complete Works of Voltaire*, ed. by Nicholas Cronk and others, 205 vols (Geneva: Institut et Musée Voltaire; Toronto: University of Toronto Press; later Oxford: Voltaire Foundation, 1968–2022)

WAGNER, RICHARD, *Sämtliche Schriften und Dichtungen*, Volks-Ausgabe, 12 vols (Leipzig: Breitkopf & Härtel, n.d.)

—— *Skizzen und Entwürfe zur Ring-Dichtung, mit der Dichtung 'Der junge Siegfried'*, ed. by Otto Strobel (Munich: Bruckmann, 1930)

—— *Mein Leben* (Munich: List, 1963)

—— *Sämtliche Briefe*, ed. by various editors, 27 vols to date (orig. Leipzig: VEB Deutscher Verlag für Musik, now Breitkopf & Härtel, 1967–)

—— *Wagner's 'Ring of the Nibelung: A Companion*, text trans. by Stewart Spencer, with commentaries by Barry Millington and others (London: Thames & Hudson, 1993)

WEBER, MAX, 'The Profession and Vocation of Politics', in *Weber: Political Writings*, ed. by Peter Lassman and Ronald Speirs, Cambridge Texts in the History of Political Thought (Cambridge: Cambridge University Press, 1994), pp. 309–69

WEISE, CHRISTIAN, *Bäurischer Machiavellus*, ed. by Werner Schubert (Berlin: De Gruyter, 1966)

WIELAND, CHRISTOPH MARTIN, *Der goldne Spiegel* (1772), in *Wielands Gesammelte Schriften*, ed. by the Deutsche Kommission der Königlich Preußischen Akademie der Wissenschaften. I. Abteilung: Werke, 23 vols (Berlin: Weidmannsche Buchhandlung, later Berlin: Akademie-Verlag, 1909–69), IX: *Der goldne Spiegel, Singspiele und kleine Dichtungen 1772–1775*, ed. by Wilhelm Kurrelmeyer (1931)

Secondary Sources

AIKIN, JUDITH POPOVICH, *The Mission of Rome in the Dramas of Daniel Casper von Lohenstein: Historical Tragedy as Prophecy and Polemic* (Stuttgart: Heinz, 1976)

ALT, PETER-ANDRÉ, *Schiller: Leben — Werk — Zeit*, 2 vols (Munich: Beck, 2000)

ANGLO, SYDNEY, *Machiavelli: The First Century* (Oxford: Oxford University Press, 2005)

AURNHAMMER, ACHIM, KLAUS MANGER, and FRIEDRICH STRACK, eds, *Schiller und die höfische Welt* (Tübingen: Niemeyer, 1990)

BÉHAR, PIERRE, *Silesia Tragica: Épanouissement et fin de l'école dramatique silésienne dans l'œuvre tragique de Daniel Casper von Lohenstein (1635–1683)* (Wiesbaden: Harrassowitz, 1988)

BEISER, FREDERICK, *Schiller as Philosopher: A Re-examination* (Oxford: Clarendon Press, 2005)

BENJAMIN, WALTER, *Der Ursprung des deutschen Trauerspiels*, in his *Gesammelte Schriften*, ed. by Rolf Tiedemann and Hermann Schweppenhauser, 7 vols (Frankfurt a.M.: Suhrkamp, 1972–89), I/1 (1974)

—— *The Origin of German Tragic Drama*, trans. by John Osborne, with an introduction by George Steiner (London: New Left Books, 1977)

BERLIN, ISAIAH, 'The Originality of Machiavelli', in his *Against the Current: Essays in the History of Ideas*, ed. by Henry Hardy (Oxford: Clarendon Press, 1989), pp. 25–79

BEW, JOHN, *Realpolitik: A History* (New York: Oxford University Press, 2016)

BIRELEY, ROBERT, SJ, *The Counter-Reformation Prince: Anti-Machiavellianism or Catholic Statecraft in Early Modern Europe* (Chapel Hill, NC: University of North Carolina Press, 1990)

BLACK, ROBERT, *Machiavelli* (Abingdon: Routledge, 2013)

BÖDEKER, HANS ERICH, and ULRICH HERRMANN, eds, *Aufklärung als Politisierung — Politisierung der Aufklärung* (Hamburg: Felix Meiner, 1987)

BORCHMEYER, DIETER, *Macht und Melancholie: Schillers 'Wallenstein'* (Frankfurt a.M.: Athenäum, 1988)

BOYLE, NICHOLAS, 'Goethe's Theory of Tragedy', *Modern Language Review*, 105 (2010), 1072–86

BROWN, H. M., *Heinrich von Kleist: The Ambiguity of Art and the Necessity of Form* (Oxford: Clarendon Press, 1998)

BURCKHARDT, JACOB, *The Civilization of the Renaissance in Italy*, trans. by S. C. G. Middlemore (Oxford: Phaidon, 1944)

CAPPONI, NICCOLÒ, *An Unlikely Prince: The Life and Times of Machiavelli* (New York: Capo Press, 2010)

CARON, PIERRE, *Les Massacres de septembre* (Paris: La Maison du livre français, 1935)

CHADWICK, OWEN, *Britain and the Vatican during the Second World War* (Cambridge: Cambridge University Press, 1986)

CLAIRMONT, HEINRICH, 'Die Figur des Machiavell in Goethes *Egmont*', *Poetica*, 15 (1983), 289–313

CLARK, CHRISTOPHER, *Iron Kingdom: The Rise and Downfall of Prussia 1600–1947* (London: Allen Lane, 2006)

COOKE, DERYCK, *I Saw the World End: A Study of Wagner's 'Ring'* (London: Oxford University Press, 1979)

CORNWELL, JOHN, *Hitler's Pope: The Secret History of Pius XII* (London: Viking, 1999)

DANBY, JOHN F., *Shakespeare's Doctrine of Nature: A Study of 'King Lear'* (London: Faber, 1948)

DAVIES, STEFFAN, *The Wallenstein Figure in German Literature and Historiography 1790–1920* (London: Maney, 2010)

—— '"Du wagst es, meine Worte zu *deuten*?": Unreliable Evidence on Schiller's Stage', *Modern Language Review*, 106 (2011), 518–35

DEISSNER, DAVID, *Moral und Motivation im Werk Heinrich von Kleists* (Tübingen: Niemeyer, 2009)

DE POL, ROBERTO, ed., *The First Translations of Machiavelli's 'Prince' from the Sixteenth to the First Half of the Nineteenth Century* (Amsterdam and New York: Rodopi, 2010)

DICKSON, KEITH, *Towards Utopia: A Study of Brecht* (Oxford: Clarendon Press, 1978)

DONALDSON, PETER S., *Machiavelli and Mystery of State* (Cambridge: Cambridge University Press, 1988)

DUINDAM, JEROEN, *Dynasties: A Global History of Power, 1300–1800* (Cambridge: Cambridge University Press, 2016)

ELLIOTT, J. H., *Imperial Spain 1469–1716* (London: Arnold, 1963)

——*Richelieu and Olivares* (Cambridge: Cambridge University Press, 1984)

——, and L. W. B. BROCKLISS, eds, *The World of the Favourite* (New Haven: Yale University Press, 1999)

ELLIS, JOHN M., *Kleist's 'Prinz Friedrich von Homburg': A Critical Study* (Berkeley: University of California Press, 1970)

——'The Vexed Question of Egmont's Political Judgment', in *Tradition and Creation: Essays in Honour of Elizabeth Mary Wilkinson*, ed. by C. P. Magill, Brian A. Rowley, and Christopher J. Smith (Leeds: Maney, 1978), pp. 116–30

ESSEN, GESA VON, *Hermannsschlachten: Germanen- und Römerbilder in der Literatur des 18. und 19. Jahrhunderts* (Göttingen: Wallstein, 1998)

EVANS, RICHARD J., *Rituals of Retribution: Capital Punishment in Germany, 1600–1987* (Oxford: Oxford University Press, 1996)

——*The Third Reich in Power* (London: Allen Lane, 2005)

FELDKAMP, MICHAEL, *Pius XII. und Deutschland* (Göttingen: Vandenhoeck & Ruprecht, 2000)

FULDA, DANIEL, and THORSTEN VALK, eds, *Die Tragödie der Moderne: Gattungsgeschichte — Kulturtheorie — Epochendiagnose* (Berlin: De Gruyter, 2010)

GAJDA, ALEXANDRA, 'Tacitus and Political Thought in Early Modern Europe, c. 1530–c. 1640', in *The Cambridge Companion to Tacitus*, ed. by A. J. Woodman (Cambridge: Cambridge University Press, 2010), pp. 253–68

GILLESPIE, G. E. P., *Daniel Casper von Lohenstein's Historical Tragedies* (Athens, OH: Ohio State University Press, 1965)

GRATHOFF, DIRK, *Kleist: Geschichte, Politik, Sprache* (Opladen: Westdeutscher Verlag, 1999)

GREGOR-DELLIN, MARTIN, *Richard Wagner: Sein Leben, sein Werk, sein Jahrhundert* (Munich: Piper, 1980)

GUÉNÉE, BERNARD, *States and Rulers in Later Medieval Europe*, trans. by Juliet Vale (Oxford: Blackwell, 1985)

GUTHKE, KARL S., *Schillers Dramen: Idealismus und Skepsis* (Tübingen: Francke, 1994)

GUY, JOHN, *My Heart is my Own: The Life of Mary Queen of Scots* (London: HarperCollins, 2004)

HALE, J. R., *Machiavelli and Renaissance Italy* (Harmondsworth: Penguin, 1972)

HANKINS, JAMES, *Virtue Politics: Soulcraft and Statecraft in Renaissance Italy* (Cambridge, MA: Harvard University Press, 2019)

HIGH, JEFFREY L., *Schillers Rebellionskonzept und die Französische Revolution* (Lewiston, ME: Mellen, 2004)

HIGH, JEFFREY L., NICHOLAS MARTIN, and NORBERT OELLERS, eds, *Who is this Schiller Now? Essays on his Reception and Significance* (Rochester, NY: Camden House, 2011)

HILLIARD, K. F., *Freethinkers, Libertines and 'Schwärmer': Heterodoxy in German Literature, 1750–1800* (London: Institute of Germanic and Romance Studies, 2011)

HOBSON, IRMGARD, 'Oranien and Alba: The Two Political Dialogues in Egmont', *Germanic Review*, 50 (1975), 260–74

HOFFMEISTER, REINHART, ed., *Rolf Hochhuth: Dokumente zur politischen Wirkung* (Munich: Kindler, 1980)

HOLT, MACK P., *The French Wars of Religion, 1562–1629*, 2nd edn (Cambridge: Cambridge University Press, 2005)

HÖPFL, HARRO, *Jesuit Political Thought: The Society of Jesus and the State, c. 1540–1630* (Cambridge: Cambridge University Press, 2004)

HOWE, STEVEN, 'Erziehung zur Nation: Die antinapoleonischen Kampfschriften, *Die Herrmannsschlacht* und *Prinz Friedrich von Homburg*', in *Unverhoffte Wirkungen: Erziehung und Gewalt im Werk Heinrich von Kleists*, ed. by Ricarda Schmidt, Seán Allan, and Steven Howe (Würzburg: Königshausen & Neumann, 2014), pp. 129–59

HUGHES, DEREK, *Culture and Sacrifice: Ritual Deaths in Literature and Opera* (Cambridge: Cambridge University Press, 2007)

HULLIUNG, MARK, *Citizen Machiavelli* (Princeton: Princeton University Press, 1983)

ISRAEL, JONATHAN I., *The Dutch Republic: Its Rise, Greatness, and Fall, 1477–1806* (Oxford: Clarendon Press, 1995)

JAMES, DOROTHY, *Georg Büchner's 'Dantons Tod': A Reappraisal* (London: MHRA, 1982)

KELLY, DUNCAN, 'August Ludwig von Rochau and *Realpolitik* as Historical Political Theory', *Global Intellectual History*, 3 (2018), 301–30

KERTZER, DAVID I., *The Pope at War: The Secret History of Pius XII, Mussolini, and Hitler* (Oxford: Oxford University Press, 2022)

KITTLER, WOLF, *Die Geburt des Partisanen aus dem Geist der Poesie: Heinrich von Kleist und die Strategie der Befreiungskriege* (Freiburg: Rombach, 1987)

KREUZER, HELMUT, ed., *Hebbel in neuer Sicht*, 2nd edn (Stuttgart: Kohlhammer, 1969)

LAMPORT, F. J., 'The Silence of Wilhelm Tell', *Modern Language Review*, 76 (1981), 857–68

LEWY, GUENTER, *The Catholic Church and Nazi Germany* (London: Weidenfeld & Nicolson, 1964)

LUKÁCS, GEORG, *German Realists in the Nineteenth Century*, trans. by Jeremy Gaines and Paul Keast (London: Libris, 1993)

LUNDING, ERIK, *Das schlesische Kunstdrama* (Copenhagen: Haase, 1940)

MAGEE, ELIZABETH, *Richard Wagner and the Nibelungs* (Oxford: Clarendon Press, 1990)

MAINLAND, WILLIAM F., *Schiller and the Changing Past* (London: Heinemann, 1957)

MARTINO, ALBERTO, *Daniel Casper von Lohenstein: Storia della sua ricezione*, I (1661–1800) (Pisa: Libreria Editrice Athenaeum, 1975)

MASON, EUDO C., *Goethe's 'Faust': Its Genesis and Purport* (Berkeley: University of California Press, 1967)

McGRATH, WILLIAM J., *German Freedom and the Greek Ideal: The Cultural Legacy from Goethe to Mann* (New York: Palgrave Macmillan, 2013)

MEINECKE, FRIEDRICH, *Die Idee der Staatsräson in der neueren Geschichte*, ed. by Walther Hofer (Munich: Oldenbourg, 1957)

——*Machiavellism: The Doctrine of raison d'état and its Place in Modern History*, trans. by M. Douglas Scott (London: Routledge & Kegan Paul, 1957)

MEYER-KALKUS, REINHART, *Wollust und Grausamkeit: Affektenlehre und Affektdarstellung in Lohensteins Dramatik am Beispiel 'Agrippina'* (Göttingen: Vandenhoeck & Ruprecht, 1986)

MICHELSEN, PETER, 'Egmonts Freiheit', *Euphorion*, 65 (1971), 274–97

MIONSKOWSKI, ALEXANDER, *Souveränität als Mythos: Hugo von Hofmannsthals Poetologie des Politischen und die Inszenierung moderner Herrschaftsformen in seinem Trauerspiel 'Der Turm' (1924/25/26)* (Vienna: Böhlau, 2015)

MISTRY, FRENY, 'Towards Buddhahood: Some Remarks on the Sigismund Figure in Hofmannsthal's *Turm* Plays', *Modern Language Review*, 69 (1974), 337–47

MORTIMER, GEOFF, *Wallenstein: The Enigma of the Thirty Years War* (Basingstoke: Palgrave, 2010)

MÜLLER-SEIDEL, WALTER, *Friedrich Schiller und die Politik* (Munich: Beck, 2009)

NAJEMY, JOHN M., *A History of Florence 1200–1575* (Oxford: Blackwell, 2006)

NAKHIMOVSKY, ISAAC, 'The Enlightened Prince and the Future of Europe: Voltaire and Frederick the Great's Anti-Machiavel of 1740', in *Commerce and Peace in the Enlightenment*, ed. by Béla Kapossy, Isaac Nakhimovsky and Richard Whatmore (Cambridge: Cambridge University Press, 2017), pp. 44–77

NEHRING, WOLFGANG, *Die Tat bei Hofmannsthal* (Stuttgart: Metzler, 1966)

NEWMAN, JANE O., *The Intervention of Philology: Gender, Learning, and Power in Lohenstein's Roman Plays* (Chapel Hill, NC: University of North Carolina Press, 2000)

NICOLAUS, UTE, *Souverän und Märtyrer: Hugo von Hofmannsthals späte Trauerspieldichtung vor dem Hintergrund seiner politischen und ästhetischen Reflexionen* (Würzburg: Königshausen & Neumann, 2004)

NILGES, YVONNE, *Schiller und das Recht* (Göttingen: Wallstein, 2012)

NUTTALL, A. D., *Shakespeare the Thinker* (New Haven and London: Yale University Press, 2007)

PARKER, GEOFFREY, *The Dutch Revolt* (London: Allen Lane, 1977)

—— *Imprudent King: A New Life of Philip II* (New Haven: Yale University Press, 2014)

PARKER, STEPHEN, *Bertolt Brecht: A Literary Life* (London: Bloomsbury, 2014)

PETER, KLAUS, 'Für ein anderes Preußen: Romantik und Politik in Kleists *Prinz Friedrich von Homburg*', *Kleist-Jahrbuch* 1992, pp. 95–125

POWELL, JONATHAN, *The New Machiavelli: How to Wield Power in the Modern World* (London: Bodley Head, 2010)

PRICE, RUSSELL, 'The Theme of *gloria* in Machiavelli', *Renaissance Quarterly*, 30 (1977), 588–631

RAAB, FELIX, *The English Face of Machiavelli: A Changing Interpretation, 1500–1700* (London: Routledge & Kegan Paul, 1964)

RASCH, WOLFDIETRICH, *Goethes 'Iphigenie auf Tauris' als Drama der Autonomie* (Munich: Beck, 1979)

REDDICK, JOHN, *Georg Büchner: The Shattered Whole* (Oxford: Clarendon Press, 1994)

REED, T. J., *Light in Germany: Scenes from an Unknown Enlightenment* (Chicago: University of Chicago Press, 2015)

REEVE, WILLIAM C., *In Pursuit of Power: Heinrich von Kleist's Machiavellian Protagonists* (Toronto: University of Toronto Press, 1987)

RIEDL, PETER PHILIPP, 'Texturen des Terrors: Politische Gewalt im Werk Heinrich von Kleists', *Publications of the English Goethe Society*, 78 (2009), 32–46

RITTER, GERHARD, *Machtstaat und Utopie: Vom Streit um die Dämonie der Macht seit Machiavelli und Morus* (Munich and Berlin: Oldenbourg, 1943)

RITZER, MONIKA, *Friedrich Hebbel: Der Individualist und seine Epoche. Eine Biographie* (Göttingen: Wallstein, 2018)

ROBERTSON, RITCHIE, *Enlightenment and Religion in German and Austrian Literature* (Cambridge: Legenda, 2017)

RUPP, STEPHEN, *Allegories of Kingship: Calderón and the Anti-Machiavellian Tradition* (University Park, PA: Pennsylvania State University Press, 1996)

SAMMONS, JEFFREY L., 'Rethinking Kleist's *Hermannsschlacht*', in *Heinrich von Kleist Studien*, ed. by Alexej Ugrinsky (Berlin: Erich Schmidt, 1980), pp. 33–40

SAMUEL, RICHARD, 'Kleists *Hermannsschlacht* und der Freiherr vom Stein', in *Heinrich von Kleist: Aufsätze und Essays*, ed. by Walter Müller-Seidel (Darmstadt: Wissenschaftliche Buchgesellschaft, 1973), pp. 312–58

SCHAMA, SIMON, *Citizens: A Chronicle of the French Revolution* (New York: Viking, 1989)

SCHMITT, AXEL, '"Auctoritas", "Veritas" oder "Divinitas"? Zur Legitimierung der Gewalt in Hebbels *Agnes Bernauer*', in *'Alles Leben ist Raub': Aspekte der Gewalt bei Friedrich Hebbel*, ed. by Günter Häntzschel (Munich: iudicium, 1992), pp. 165–82

SCHULZ, GERHARD, *Kleist: Eine Biographie* (Munich: Beck, 2007)

SCHWARZ, EGON, 'Rolf Hochhuth's *The Representative*', *Germanic Review*, 39 (1964), 211–30

SENGLE, FRIEDRICH, *Biedermeierzeit*, 3 vols (Stuttgart: Metzler, 1971–80)

SERVICE, ROBERT, *Lenin: A Biography* (London: Macmillan, 2000)

SHAW, G. B., *The Perfect Wagnerite* (first published 1898), in his *Major Critical Essays* (London: Constable, 1932)

SHEEHAN, JAMES J., *German History 1770–1866* (Oxford: Oxford University Press, 1989)

SKINNER, QUENTIN, *The Foundations of Modern Political Thought*, 2 vols (Cambridge: Cambridge University Press, 1978)

——*Machiavelli* (Oxford: Oxford University Press, 1981)

SLANEY, HELEN, *The Senecan Aesthetic: A Performance History* (Oxford: Oxford University Press, 2016)

STACHEL, PAUL, *Seneca und das deutsche Renaissancedrama* (Berlin: Mayer & Müller, 1907)

STEPHENS, ANTHONY, *Heinrich von Kleist: The Dramas and Stories* (Oxford: Berg, 1994)

TACKETT, TIMOTHY, *The Coming of the Terror in the French Revolution* (Cambridge, MA: Harvard University Press, 2015)

THOMSEN, FRANK, HANS-HARALD MÜLLER, and TOM KINDT, *Ungeheuer Brecht: Eine Biographie seines Werks* (Göttingen: Vandenhoeck & Ruprecht, 2006)

THUAU, ÉTIENNE, *Raison d'état et pensée politique à l'époque de Richelieu* (Paris: Armand Colin, 1966)

TROCINI, FEDERICO, 'Machiavellismus, Realpolitik und Machtpolitik', in *Machiavellismus in Deutschland*, ed. by Cornel Zwierlein and Annette Meyer, Beiheft zu *Historische Zeitschrift*, 51 (2010), 215–32

TWELLMANN, MARCUS, *Das Drama der Souveränität: Hugo von Hofmannsthal und Carl Schmitt* (Munich: Fink, 2004)

VOSSKAMP, WILHELM, *Untersuchungen zur Zeit- und Geschichtsauffassung im 17. Jahrhundert bei Gryphius und Lohenstein* (Bonn: Bouvier, 1967)

WATANABE-O'KELLY, HELEN, *Beauty or Beast? The Woman Warrior in the German Imagination from the Renaissance to the Present* (Oxford: Oxford University Press, 2010)

WEINZIERL, ULRICH, *Hofmannsthal: Skizzen zu seinem Bild* (Vienna: Zsolnay, 2005)

WHITFIELD, J. H., *Discourses on Machiavelli* (Cambridge: Heffer, 1969)

WILSON, W. DANIEL, 'Hunger/Artist: Goethe's Revolutionary Agitators in *Götz*, *Satyros*, *Egmont* and *Der Bürgergeneral*', *Monatshefte*, 86 (1994), 80–94

WINDELL, GEORGE G., 'Hegel, Feuerbach, and Wagner's *Ring*', *Central European History*, 9 (1976), 27–57

WOLFF, HANS M., *Heinrich von Kleist als politischer Dichter* (Berkeley and Los Angeles: University of California Press, 1947)

WOOTTON, DAVID, *Power, Pleasure and Profit: Insatiable Appetites from Machiavelli to Madison* (Cambridge, MA: Harvard University Press, 2018)

ZUCCOTTI, SUSAN, *Under his very Windows: The Vatican and the Holocaust in Italy* (New Haven and London: Yale University Press, 2000)

INDEX

This index includes many historical figures who also appear as characters in the plays discussed. Entries refer only to the historical figures. For their dramatic counterparts, see the references to the plays concerned.

Milton Keynes UK
Ingram Content Group UK Ltd.
UKHW010621171124
451117UK00002B/11